CODEX
IURIS CANONICI

AUCTORITATE
IOANNIS PAULI PP. II
PROMULGATUS

TYPIS POLYGLOTTIS VATICANIS
M·DCCCC·LXXXIII

CODE
OF
CANON LAW
LATIN–ENGLISH EDITION

Translation prepared under the auspices of the
Canon Law Society of America

Canon Law Society of America
Washington, D.C. 20064

TABLE OF CONTENTS

FOREWORD TO THE TRANSLATION

Arduum sane munus, a difficult task indeed, was the way that Pope Pius X described the work of reordering the law of the Church back in 1904. Those who labored over this translation of the 1983 Code of Canon Law might use the same words to tell of their experience. The following explanation of the process and of the principles which guided the work is presented to aid the user in understanding this arduous effort.

The process and the people. The decision to translate the revised Code into English was taken by those who had been named by the Canon Law Society of America to direct the writing of a commentary on the Code. The process began early in 1980. The preparation of an English version of the canons seemed to be an obvious first step toward composing a commentary. The editorial board of the commentary consisted in James Coriden, Thomas Green and Donald Heintschel. They selected Martin Lavin, a member of the Canon Law faculty at The Catholic University of America, to undertake the task of translation. He courageously consented and began the awesome effort by working on the latest Latin *schemata* of the canons available at that time. When the "final draft" of the entire Code was circulated by the Commission for the Revision of the Code in late 1980, Dr. Lavin shifted his attention to that modified version. He gradually accomplished the initial translation of roughly two-thirds of those canons. Eight other canonists completed the translation of the remaining third, working separately on disparate sections: Thomas Green, Richard Hill, S.J., James McEnerney, S.J., Frederick McManus, John Myers, James O'Connor, S.J., Ellen O'Hara, C.S.J., and Gennaro Sesto, S.D.B.

The work of this first stage of translation was finished by the late spring of 1982. The resulting "working translation" was sent to those canonists who were composing the commentary on the various parts of the Code; it was also used for a series of workshops in which more than five hundred diocesan personnel took part during the summer of 1982. Both the commentators and the workshop participants were asked to offer criticism. Many provided valuable comments on the working translation which helped to improve the work.

vii

The final and official Latin text of the Code became available in February, 1983; then began the task of correcting and polishing the working translation. Four persons went over the text of the translation, checking for changes made in the final Latin version, striving for accuracy and consistency of usage, and searching for more felicitous expression. Thomas Green did his work first; then James McEnerney, S.J., with the benefit of Dr. Green's revisions, systematically examined the translation. Finally, James Coriden and Barbara Anne Cusack, S.H.C.J., reviewed the entire text, edited it, and entered it into the C.L.S.A. word processor. All of this was completed by the end of June. The whole translation project up to this point was under the direction of the editorial board of the Canon Law Society's commentary on the Code.

The Vatican Secretariat of State issued Norms on January 28, 1983 requiring that all vernacular translations of the Code receive the approval of the local episcopal conference. For this reason the C.L.S.A. translation was submitted to the Canonical Affairs Committee of the National Conference of Catholic Bishops in early July. Bishop Anthony Bevilacqua, who chairs the committee, distributed copies of the translation to the other members: Cardinal Joseph Bernardin, Bishop James Hoffman, Bishop John Kinney, and Archbishop Edmund Szoka. Each of these committee members commissioned a person or group to scrutinize the translation, and each submitted a set of recommendations. Bishop Bevilacqua forwarded these extensive suggestions to the C.L.S.A. and, consequently, a number of improvements were made in the translation. The improved translation was again reviewed by Bishop Bevilacqua and representatives of the committee members: John Alesandro, John Dolciamore, Clarence Klausing, and Robert Sable. They proposed some further modifications. After these were agreed upon, approval was given to the translation by the N.C.C.B. Executive Committee at the end of October.

Principles and policies. Certain policies were adopted by the C.L.S.A. commentary board which guided the work of translation. They are reflected in this work in the following manner.

1. The Latin text is and will remain the only official version of the Code. This was affirmed by the Vatican Secretariat of State in January, 1983. The English translation does not replace or replicate the Latin. Indeed, the Latin must be consulted for clarification of meaning and complete accuracy.

2. The English ought to be as accurate and faithful to the Latin original as reasonably possible. Although to translate is in some sense to interpret, the meaning of the Latin has been conveyed carefully, making every effort to avoid distortions.

3. Terms have been used with consistency throughout the Code unless there are good canonical reasons to vary the translation in different contexts.

For example, *munus* is used for several meanings in Latin and consequently must be rendered by "function," "office," "duty" or "responsibility" depending on the context. *Procurator* means "proxy" in the law on marriage but is rendered "procurator" in procedural law.

4. The canons should be intelligible to educated readers. The English, therefore, must be readable. An imitation of the style and structure of Latin impedes intelligibility in English. All terms, even technical ones, are either translated or, if left in Latin, are listed in the Glossary where they are clearly defined in understandable English. Some terms have been adopted because of their familiar usage in church practice; others are selected as understandable from their secular usage.

5. The language in the translation is sexually inclusive wherever that is consonant with the law being expressed. Exclusive masculine or feminine word forms are not used unless absolutely required by the text. In some instances it has been necessary to render in the plural what appears in Latin in the singular, or to change to the passive voice, but this has been done only where it does not affect the meaning of the canon.

6. Subjunctive verb forms are normally rendered by straightforward imperative or obligatory language rather than by shades of exhortation or recommendation (e.g., "is to appoint" rather than "should appoint"), unless another meaning is clear from the context.

7. Rather than following the Latin style for capitalization of nouns, capitalization has been minimized in keeping with current American usage and retained only in reference to God, Christ, Eucharist, Roman Pontiff, the Church universal, Catholic Church, etc.

Those several persons named above, and others unnamed, who labored generously over this translation harbor the hope that the text will contribute in some modest way to good order and enhanced freedom among God's people, so that our common task on earth might be carried out more effectively. *Arduum sane munus!*

APOSTOLIC CONSTITUTION
SACRAE DISCIPLINAE LEGES

To our venerable brothers, cardinals, archbishops,
bishops, priests, deacons
and to the other members of the people of God,
John Paul, bishop,
servant of the servants of God
as a perpetual record.

During the course of the centuries the Catholic Church has been accustomed to reform and renew the laws of canonical discipline so that in constant fidelity to its divine founder, they may be better adapted to the saving mission entrusted to it. Prompted by this same purpose and fulfilling at last the expectations of the whole Catholic world, I order today, January 25, 1983, the promulgation of the revised Code of Canon Law. In so doing, my thoughts go back to the same day of the year 1959 when my predecessor of happy memory, John XXIII, announced for the first time his decision to reform the existing *corpus* of canonical legislation which had been promulgated on the feast of Pentecost in the year 1917.

Such a decision to reform the Code was taken together with two other decisions of which the Pontiff spoke on that same day: the intention to hold a synod of the Diocese of Rome and to convoke an ecumenical council. Of these two events, the first was not closely connected with the reform of the Code; but the second, the council, is of supreme importance in regard to the present matter and is closely connected with it.

If we ask why John XXIII considered it necessary to reform the existing Code, the answer can perhaps be found in the Code itself which was promulgated in the year 1917. But there exists also another answer and it is the decisive one: namely, that the reform of the Code of Canon Law appeared to be definitely desired and requested by the same council which devoted such great attention to the Church.

As is obvious, when the revision of the Code was first announced the council was an event of the future. Moreover, the acts of its magisterium and especially its doctrine on the Church would be decided in the years 1962-1965; however, it is clear to everyone that John XXIII's intuition was very true, and with good reason it must be said that his decision was for the long-term good of the Church.

Therefore the new Code which is promulgated today necessarily required the previous work of the council. Although it was announced together with the ecumenical council, nevertheless it follows it chronologically because the work undertaken in its preparation, which had to be based upon the council, could not begin until after the latter's completion.

Turning our minds today to the beginning of this long journey, to that January 25, 1959 and to John XXIII himself who initiated the revision of the Code, I must recognize that this Code derives from one and the same intention, the renewal of Christian living. From such an intention, in fact, the entire work of the council drew its norms and its direction.

If we now pass on to consider the nature of the work which preceded the promulgation of the Code and also the manner in which it was carried out, especially during the pontificates of Paul VI and John Paul I, and from then until the present day, it must be clearly pointed out that this work was brought to completion in an outstandingly *collegial* spirit. This applies not only in regard to the material drafting of the work, but also to the very substance of the laws enacted.

This note of collegiality eminently characterizes and distinguishes the process of developing the present Code; it corresponds perfectly with the teaching and the character of the Second Vatican Council. Therefore not only because of its content but also because of its very origin, the Code manifests the spirit of this council in whose documents the Church, the universal "sacrament of salvation" (dogmatic constitution on the Church *Lumen gentium*, nn. 1, 9, 48), is presented as the people of God and its hierarchical constitution appears based on the college of bishops united with its head.

For this reason, therefore, the bishops individually and as episcopates were invited to collaborate in the preparation of the new Code so that by means of such a long process, by as collegial a method as possible, juridical formulae would gradually mature which would later serve for the use of the entire Church. *Experts* chosen from all over the world also took part in all these phases of the work, specialists in theology, history and especially canon law.

To one and all of them I wish to express today my sentiments of deep gratitude.

In the first place there come before my eyes the figures of the deceased cardinals who presided over the preparatory commission: Cardinal Pietro Ciriaci who began the work, and Cardinal Pericle Felici who, for many years, guided the course of the work almost to its end. I think then of the secretaries of the same commission: Monsignor Giacomo Violardo, later cardinal, and Father Raimondo Bidagor, S.J., both of whom in carrying out this task poured out the treasures of their doctrine and wisdom. Together with them I recall the cardinals, archbishops, bishops and all those who were members of that commission, as well as the consultors of the individual study groups engaged during these years in such a difficult work, and whom God in the meantime has called to their eternal reward. I pray to God for all of them.

I am pleased to remember also the living, beginning with the present pro-president of the commission, our venerable brother Archbishop Rosalio Castillo Lara. For a very long time he has done excellent work in a task of such great responsibility. I pass then to our beloved son, Monsignor William Onclin, whose devotion and diligence have greatly contributed to the happy outcome of the work. I finally mention all the others in the commission itself, whether as cardinal members or as officials, consultors and collaborators in the various study groups, or in other offices who have given their appreciated contribution to the drafting and the completion of such a weighty and complex work.

Therefore, in promulgating the Code today, I am fully aware that this act is an expression of pontifical authority and therefore is invested with a *primatial character*. But I am also aware that this Code in its objective content reflects the *collegial sollicitude* of all my brothers in the episcopate for the Church. Indeed, by a certain analogy with the council, it should be considered as the fruit of a *collegial collaboration* because of the united efforts on the part of specialized persons and institutions throughout the whole Church.

A second question arises concerning the very nature of the Code of Canon Law. To reply adequately to this question one must mentally recall the distant patrimony of law contained in the books of the Old and New Testament from which is derived the whole juridical-legislative tradition of the Church, as from its first source.

Christ the Lord, indeed, did not in the least wish to destroy the very rich heritage of the law and the prophets which was gradually formed from the history and experience of the people of God in the Old Testament, but he brought it to completion (cf. Mt. 5:17) such that in a new and higher way it became part of the heritage of the New Testament. Therefore, although in expounding the paschal mystery St. Paul teaches that justification is not

obtained by the works of the law but by means of faith (cf. Rom. 3:28; Gal. 2:16), he does not thereby exclude the binding force of the Decalogue (cf. Rom. 13:28; Gal. 5:13-25, 6:2), nor does he deny the importance of discipline in the Church of God (cf. I Cor. 5 and 6). Thus the writings of the New Testament enable us to undersand even better the importance of discipline and make us see better how it is more closely connected with the saving character of the evangelical message itself.

This being so, it appears sufficiently clear that the Code is in no way intended as a substitute for faith, grace, charisms, and especially charity in the life of the Church and of the faithful. On the contrary, its purpose is rather to create such an order in the ecclesial society that, while assigning the primacy to love, grace and charisms, it at the same time renders their organic development easier in the life of both the ecclesial society and the individual persons who belong to it.

As the Church's principal legislative document founded on the juridical-legislative heritage of revelation and tradition, the Code is to be regarded as an indispensable instrument to ensure order both in individual and social life, and also in the Church's own activity. Therefore, besides containing the fundamental elements of the hierarchical and organic structure of the Church as willed by her divine founder or as based upon apostolic, or in any case most ancient, tradition, and besides the fundamental principles which govern the exercise of the threefold office entrusted to the Church itself, the Code must also lay down certain rules and norms of behavior.

The instrument which the Code is, fully corresponds to the nature of the Church, especially as it is proposed by the teaching of the Second Vatican Council in general and in a particular way by its ecclesiological teaching. Indeed, in a certain sense this new Code could be understood as a great effort to translate this same conciliar doctrine and ecclesiology into *canonical* language. If, however, it is impossible to translate perfectly into *canonical* language the conciliar image of the Church, nevertheless the Code must always be referred to this image as the primary pattern whose outline the Code ought to express insofar as it can by its very nature.

From this, certain fundamental criteria are derived which should govern the entire new Code within the limits of its specific matter and of the language appropriate to that material.

It could indeed be said that from this there is derived that note of complementarity which the Code presents in relation to the teaching of the Second Vatican Council, in particular with reference to the two constitutions, the dogmatic constitution *Lumen gentium* and the pastoral constitution *Gaudium et spes*.

Hence it follows that what constitutes the substantial *newness* of the Second Vatican Council, in line with the legislative tradition of the Church, especially in regard to ecclesiology, constitutes likewise the *newness* of the new Code.

Among the elements which characterize the true and genuine image of the Church we should emphasize especially the following: the doctrine in which the Church is presented as the people of God (cf. dogmatic constitution *Lumen gentium*, chapter 2) and hierarchical authority as service (cf. ibid., chapter 3); the doctrine in which the Church is seen as a *communion* and which therefore determines the relations which are to exist between the particular churches and the universal Church, and between collegiality and the primacy; likewise the doctrine according to which all the members of the people of God, in the way suited to each of them, participate in the threefold priestly, prophetic and kingly office of Christ, to which doctrine is also linked that which concerns the duties and rights of the faithful and particularly of the laity; and finally, the Church's commitment to ecumenism.

If, therefore, the Second Vatican Council has drawn both new and old from the treasury of tradition, and the new consists precisely in the elements which I have enumerated, then it is clear that the Code should also reflect the same note of fidelity in newness and of newness in fidelity, and conform itself to this in its own subject matter and in its own particular manner of expression.

The new Code of Canon Law appears at a moment when the bishops of the whole Church not only are asking for its promulgation, but are crying out for it insistently and almost with impatience.

As a matter of fact, the Code of Canon Law is extremely necessary for the Church. Since the Church is organized as a social and visible structure, it must also have norms: in order that its hierarchical and organic structure be visible; in order that the exercise of the functions divinely entrusted to it, especially that of sacred power and of the administration of the sacraments, may be adequately organized; in order that the mutual relations of the faithful may be regulated according to justice based upon charity, with the rights of individuals guaranteed and well-defined; in order, finally, that common initiatives undertaken to live a Christian life ever more perfectly may be sustained, strengthened and fostered by canonical norms.

Finally, by their very nature canonical laws are to be observed. The greatest care has therefore been taken to ensure that in the lengthy preparation of the Code the wording of the norms should be accurate, and that they should be based on a solid juridical, canonical and theological foundation.

After all these considerations it is naturally to be hoped that the new canonical legislation will prove to be an efficacious means in order that the

Church may progress in conformity with the spirit of the Second Vatican Council and may every day be ever more suited to carry out its office of salvation in this world.

With a confident spirit I am pleased to entrust these considerations of mine to all as I promulgate this fundamental body of ecclesiastical laws for the Latin Church.

May God grant that joy and peace with justice and obedience obtain favor for this Code, and that what has been ordered by the head be observed by the body.

Trusting therefore in the help of divine grace, sustained by the authority of the blessed apostles Peter and Paul, with certain knowledge, in response to the wishes of the bishops of the whole world who have collaborated with me in a collegial spirit, and with the supreme authority with which I am vested, by means of this Constitution, to be valid forever in the future, I promulgate the present Code as it has been set in order and revised. I command that for the future it is to have the force of law for the whole Latin Church, and I entrust it to the watchful care of all those concerned in order that it may be observed. So that all may more easily be informed and have a thorough knowledge of these norms before they have juridical binding force, I declare and order that they will have the force of law beginning from the first day of Advent of this year 1983, and this notwithstanding any contrary ordinances, constitutions, privileges (even worthy of special or individual mention), or customs.

I therefore exhort all the faithful to observe the proposed legislation with a sincere spirit and good will in the hope that there may flower again in the Church a renewed discipline and that consequently the salvation of souls may be rendered ever more easy under the protection of the Blessed Virgin Mary, Mother of the Church.

Given at Rome, January 25, 1983, from the Vatican Palace, the fifth year of my pontificate.

IOANNES PAULUS PP. II

PREFACE TO THE LATIN EDITION

From the time of the primitive Church it has been customary to collect the sacred canons into one book to facilitate a knowledge of them as well as their use and observance especially by sacred ministers, since "no priest is permitted to be ignorant of the sacred canons" as Pope Celestine warned in a letter to the bishops of Apulia and Calabria (July 21, 429: cf. Jaffe,[2] n. 371; Mansi IV, col. 469). His words are echoed by the Fourth Council of Toledo (633), which prescribed the following after the restoration of ecclesiastical discipline in the kingdom of the Visigoths once the Church had been freed from Arianism: "Priests are to know the sacred scripture and the canons" because "ignorance, the mother of all errors, is especially to be avoided by priests of God" (can. 25: Mansi X, col. 627).

In fact during the first ten centuries nearly everywhere there flourished countless collections of ecclesiastical laws. These private collections contained norms issued especially by the councils and the Roman Pontiffs as well as other norms taken from lesser sources. In the middle of the twelfth century, this mass of collections and norms, not infrequently contradicting one another, was put in order again through the private initiative of the monk Gratian. This concordance of laws and collections, later called the *Decretum Gratiani*, constituted the first part of that significant collection of laws of the Church which, in imitation of the *Corpus Iuris Civilis* of the Emperor Justinian, was called the *Corpus Iuris Canonici* and contained the laws which had been passed during two centuries by the supreme authority of the Roman pontiffs with the assistance of experts in canon law called glossators. Besides the Decree of Gratian, in which the earlier norms were contained, the *Corpus* consists of the *Liber Extra* of Gregory IX, the *Liber Sextus* of Boniface VIII, the *Clementinae*, i.e. the collection of Clement V promulgated by John XXII, to which are added the *Extravagantes* of this pope and the *Extravagantes communes*, decretals of various Roman pontiffs never gathered in an authentic collection. The ecclesiastical law which this *Corpus* embraces constitutes the classical law of the Catholic Church and is commonly called by this name.

To this corpus of law of the Latin Church corresponds to some extent the *Syntagma canonum* or oriental corpus of canons of the Greek Church.

Subsequent laws, especially those enacted by the Council of Trent during the time of the Catholic Reformation and those issued later by various dicasteries of the Roman Curia, were never digested into one collection. This was the reason why during the course of time legislation outside the *Corpus Iuris Canonici* constituted "an immense pile of laws piled on top of other laws." The lack of a systematic arrangement of the laws and the lack of legal certainty along with the obsolescence of and *lacunae* in many laws led to a situation where church discipline was increasingly imperiled and jeopardized.

Therefore during the preparatory period prior to the First Vatican Council, many bishops asked that a new and sole collection laws be prepared to expedite the pastoral care of the people of God in a more certain and secure fashion. Although this task could not be implemented through conciliar action, the Apostolic See subsequently addressed certain more urgent disciplinary issues through a new organization of laws. Finally, Pope Pius X, at the very beginning of his pontificate, undertook this task when he proposed to collect and reform all ecclesiastical laws and determined that the enterprise be carried out under the leadership of Cardinal Pietro Gasparri.

The first issue to be resolved in such a significant and difficult undertaking was the internal and external form of the new collection. It was decided to forego the method of compilations of laws whereby individual laws would have been expressed in the extensiveness of the original text; rather the modern method of codification was chosen. Hence texts containing and proposing a precept were expressed in a new and briefer form. However, all of the material was organized in five books which substantially imitated the system of Roman law institutes on persons, things and actions. The work took twelve years with the collaboration of experts, consultors and bishops throughout the Church. The character of the new Code was clearly enunciated in the beginning of canon 6: "The Code generally retains the existing discipline although it introduces appropriate changes." Therefore it was not a case of enacting a new law but rather a matter of arranging in a new fashion the operative legislation at that time. After the death of Pius X, this universal, exclusive, and authentic collection was promulgated on May 27, 1917 by his successor Benedict XV; it took effect on May 19, 1918.

Everyone hailed the universal law of this Pio-Benedictine Code, which made a significant contribution to the effective promotion of pastoral ministry throughout the Church, which in the meantime was experiencing new growth. Nevertheless, both the external situation of the Church in a world which had experienced sweeping changes and significant shifts in customs within a few decades as well as progressive internal factors within the ecclesiastical community necessarily brought it about that a new reform of canon

law was increasingly more imperative and was requested. The Supreme Pontiff John XXIII clearly recognized the signs of the times, for when he first announced the Roman Synod and the Second Vatican Council, he also announced that these events would be a necessary preparation for undertaking the desired renewal of the Code.

Shortly after the Ecumenical Council had begun, the Commission for the Revision of the Code of Canon Law was established on March 28, 1963 with Cardinal Pietro Ciriaci as president and Monsignor Giacomo Violardo as secretary. However, the cardinal members of the Commission in a meeting with the president on November 12 of that same year agreed that the true and proper efforts of the Commission should be deferred and should commence only at the conclusion of the Council. The reform was to be carried out according to the decisions and principles to be determined by that same Council. Meanwhile on April 17, 1964 Paul VI added seventy consultors to the Commission established by his predecessor John XXIII; he subsequently named other cardinal members and consultors from all over the world to participate in the expediting of the project. On February 24, 1965 the Supreme Pontiff named Rev. Raimondo Bidagor, S.J. the new secretary of the Commission since Monsignor Violardo had been promoted to the office of secretary of the Congregation for the Discipline of the Sacraments; on November 17 of the same year the pope appointed Monsignor Willy Onclin as adjunct secretary of the Commission. After the death of Cardinal Ciriaci, Archbishop Pericle Felici, former general secretary of Vatican Council II, was named pro-president on February 21, 1967. On June 26 of that same year he became a member of the Sacred College of Cardinals and subsequently assumed the office of president of the Commission. Since Father Bidagor ceased functioning as secretary of the Commission on November 1, 1973 on the occasion of his eightieth birthday, Most Reverend Rosalio Castillo Lara, S.D.B., titular bishop of Praecausa and coadjutor bishop of Trujillo, Venezuela, was named the new secretary of the Commission. On May 17, 1982 he was appointed pro-president of the Commission upon the premature death of Cardinal Felici.

On November 20, 1965, just before the closing of the Second Vatican Council, there was a solemn session of the Commission in the presence of the Supreme Pontiff Paul VI, at which were present the cardinal members of the Commission, the secretaries, consultors and officials of the Secretariat appointed in the meantime. This session publicly inaugurated the work of the Code Commission. The allocution of the Supreme Pontiff laid the foundations of the whole enterprise to a certain extent. It was recalled that canon law flows from the nature of the Church, that it is rooted in the power of jurisdiction entrusted to the Church by Christ, and that its purpose is to be viewed in terms of the care of souls in view of external salvation. Furthermore, the character of church law was illustrated; its necessity was vindi-

cated against the more common objections; the history of the progress of law and its collections was alluded to; and especially there was highlighted the urgent need of a new reform of the law to respond to the ongoing need of appropriately adapting church discipline to changing circumstances.

The Supreme Pontiff further indicated to the Commission two elements which should underly the whole revision effort. First of all it was not simply a matter of a new organization of the laws as had occurred at the time of the Pio-Benedictine Code; but rather it was also and especially a matter of reforming the norms to accommodate them to a new mentality and new needs even if the old law was to supply the foundation for the work of revision. Careful attention was to be paid to all the decrees and acts of the Second Vatican Council since they contain the main lines of legislative renewal either because norms were issued which directly affected new institutes and ecclesiastical discipline, or because it was necessary that the doctrinal riches of the Council, which contributed so much to pastoral life, have their consequences and necessary impact on canonical legislation.

Repeatedly in allocutions, precepts and decisions during the following years, the two above mentioned elements were recalled to the minds of the Commission members by the Supreme Pontiff, who continued to oversee the whole enterprise from on high and assiduously pursue it.

If the subcommissions or study groups were to carry on their work in a methodical fashion, it was necessary above all that there be identified and approved certain principles which would serve as guidelines during the process of revising the whole Code. The central committee of consultors prepared the text of a document, which, at the request of the Supreme Pontiff, was submitted to the examination of a general session of the synod of bishops in October 1967. The following principles were approved nearly unanimously.

1. In renewing the law the juridic character of the new Code, which the social nature of the Church requires, is to be retained. Therefore the Code is to furnish norms so that the members of the Christian faithful in living the Christian life may share in the goods offered by the Church to lead them to eternal salvation. Hence, in view of this end, the Code must define and protect the rights and obligations of each person towards others and towards the ecclesiastical society to the extent that these rights and obligations pertain to divine worship and the salvation of souls.

2. There is to be a coordination between the external forum and the internal forum, which is proper to the Church and has been operative for centuries, so as to preclude any conflict between the two.

3. To foster the pastoral care of souls as much as possible, the new law, besides the virtue of justice, is to take cognizance of charity,

temperance, humaneness and moderation, whereby equity is to be pursued not only in the application of the laws by pastors of souls but also in the legislation itself. Hence unduly rigid norms are to be set aside and rather recourse is to be taken to exhortations and persuasions where there is no need of a strict observance of the law on account of the public good and general ecclesiastical discipline.

4. In order that the Supreme Legislator and the bishops may collaborate in the care of souls and may exercise the pastoral office in a more positive fashion, those faculties to dispense from general laws which until now have been extraordinary are to become ordinary with reservations to the supreme power of the universal Church or other higher authorities only in those areas which require an exception on account of the common good.

5. Careful attention is to be given to the greater application of the so-called principle of subsidiarity within the Church. It is a principle which is rooted in a higher one because the office of bishops with its attached powers is a reality of divine law. In virtue of this principle one may defend the appropriateness and even the necessity of providing for the welfare especially of individual institutes through particular laws and the recognition of a healthy autonomy for particular executive power while legislative unity and universal and general law are observed. On the basis of the same principle, the new Code entrusts either to particular laws or to executive power whatever is not necessary for the unity of the discipline of the universal Church so that appropriate provision is made for a healthy "decentralization" while avoiding the danger of division into or the establishment of national churches.

6. On account of the fundamental equality of all members of the Christian faithful and the diversity of offices and functions rooted in the hierarchical order of the Church, it is expedient that the rights of persons be appropriately defined and safeguarded. This brings it about that the exercise of authority appears more clearly as service, that its use is more clearly reinforced, and that abuses are removed.

7. In order that such objectives may be appropriately implemented, it is necessary that particular attention be given to the organization of a procedure which envisions the protection of subjective rights. Therefore in renewing the law attention should be paid to those elements which are most especially lacking in this area, i.e. administrative recourses and the administration of justice. To achieve this it is necessary that the various functions of ecclesiastical power be clearly distinguished, i.e. the legislative, administrative, and judicial functions.

What individual functions are to be exercised by which governmental organs is also to be defined.

8. The principle of territoriality in the exercise of ecclesiastical government is to be revised somewhat, for contemporary apostolic factors seem to recommend personal jurisdictional units. Therefore the new Code is to affirm the following principle: generally speaking the portions of the people of God to be governed are to be determined territorially; however, if it is advantageous, other factors can be admitted as criteria for determining a community of the faithful, at least along with territoriality.

9. As an external, visible and independent society, the Church cannot renounce penal law. However, penalties are generally to be *ferendae sententiae* and are to be inflicted and remitted only in the external forum. *Latae sententiae* penalties are to be reduced to a few cases and are to be inflicted only for the most serious offenses.

10. Finally, as is admitted by all, the new systematic arrangement of the Code required by the revision process can only be sketched at the outset but cannot be defined and determined precisely. Therefore the new organization of the Code will have to be pursued only after a sufficient revision of its individual parts, in fact only after nearly the whole work has been completed.

From these principles which ought to guide the process of revising the Code, it is quite clear that there is a need to apply everywhere the doctrine of the Church expressed by the Second Vatican Council, especially its determination that attention is to be paid not only to the external social dimensions of the Mystical Body of Christ but also and especially to its internal life.

And in point of fact the consultors were guided by these principles in drafting the new text of the Code.

Meanwhile a January 15, 1966 letter of the cardinal president of the Commission to the presidents of the conferences of bishops asked the bishops of the whole Catholic world to express their concerns and advice regarding the law to be drafted and the best way of structuring relationships between the conferences of bishops and the Commission so as to maximize their cooperation for the good of the Church. Furthermore, the bishops were also asked to send to the Secretariat of the Commission the names of canonical experts in their respective regions who in the judgment of the bishops were the most distinguished in terms of canonical expertise; the special competence of these experts was also to be indicated. The consultors and their collaborators could be selected and named from these individuals. Actually, at the very beginning and throughout the working of the Commission, besides its cardinal members the following collaborated in the drafting of the new Code of Canon Law: bishops, priests, religious, laity, experts in canon law,

theology, pastoral practice, and civil law from all over the Catholic world. During the whole revision process 105 cardinals, 77 archbishops and bishops, 73 secular presbyters, 47 religious presbyters, 3 religious women and 12 lay persons from 5 continents and 31 countries served as members, consultors and other types of collaborators with the Commission.

Even before the last session of the Second Vatican Council, the consultors of the Commission were gathered in a private session on May 6, 1965, in which, with the consent of the Holy Father, the Commission president submitted three fundamental questions for their study. It was asked first whether one or two codes, i.e. Latin and Oriental, were to be drafted; it was also asked what methodology was to be followed in the drafting process or how the Commission and its organs were to proceed; finally, it was asked what would be an appropriate division of labor among the various subcommissions, which would be functioning simultaneously. Reports prepared by three groups established to deal with these questions were forwarded to all the Commission members.

The cardinal members of the Commission met for the second time on November 25, 1965 to discuss these same questions and respond to certain proposals (*dubia*) formulated concerning them.

A principle regarding the systematic organization of the new Code to be proposed to the synod of bishops was drawn up from a *votum* of the central committee of consultors, which had met on April 3-7, 1967. After the meeting of the synod, it was deemed appropriate to establish in November, 1967 a special committee of consultors to study the systematic organization of the Code. At a meeting of this committee at the beginning of April, 1968, all agreed on not incorporating in the Code properly liturgical laws, norms on beatification and canonization processes, and norms on the external relations of the Church. All agreed as well that in the part on the people of God there would be placed norms on the juridic status of all members of the Christian faithful and a distinct treatment of the powers and faculties which pertain to the exercise of the different functions and offices. Finally all agreed that the structure of the books of the Pio-Benedictine Code could not be maintained in its integrity.

During the third meeting of the cardinal members of the Commission on May 28, 1968, they substantially approved a temporary arrangement according to which the study groups already established were organized in a new way: "the systematic organization of the Code," "general norms," "the sacred hierarchy," "institutes of perfection," "laity," "physical and moral persons in general," "marriage," "sacraments other than marriage," "the ecclesiastical magisterium," "the patrimonial law of the Church," "processes," "penal law."

The issues dealt with by the study group on "physical and juridic persons" (it was subsequently called this) were later incorporated in the book on

"general norms." Furthermore it was deemed appropriate to establish a study group on "sacred places and times and divine worship." In view of their broader competence, the names of some other study groups were changed: the group on "the laity" was later called the group on "the rights and associations of the faithful and the laity"; the group on "religious" was later called the group on "institutes of perfection" and finally the group on "institutes of life consecrated through the profession of the evangelical counsels."

The principal features of the method followed during the more than sixteen year revision process are to be briefly recalled. The consultors of the individual groups fulfilled their significant duties with the greatest dedication, considering only the good of the Church either in preparing written observations on the parts of their own schemata, or in discussing various issues at meetings in Rome at determined times, or in examining the animadversions, observations and opinions on their schemata which were forwarded to the Commission. The procedure was as follows. To each of the consultors, who numbered from eight to fourteen on the individual study groups, was assigned a certain issue which was to be studied in view of the revision process, with the present Code as the point of departure. After an examination of the questions, each consultor was to transmit a written opinion to the Secretariat of the Commission as well as a copy to the *relator* and, if time permitted, to all the members of the study group. The consultors of the study group met in Rome according to a predetermined schedule. With the *relator* leading the discussions, all the questions and opinions were considered until a text of canons was approved, at times after a process of voting on individual parts, and drafted in schema form. During the session the *relator* was aided by an official who functioned as an actuary.

The number of meetings for each study group was greater or lesser depending on the concrete issues, and the work was carried on for years.

Especially during the latter stages of the process, certain mixed study groups were established so that consultors from different groups could meet and discuss issues which directly pertained to several groups and had to be resolved through common counsel.

After the drafting of some schemata was completed by the study groups, the Supreme Legislator was asked to give some concrete indications of the subsequent steps to be taken in continuing the work. According to the norms handed down at the time, those steps were as follows.

The schemata together with an explanatory report were sent to the Supreme Pontiff, who determined whether they were to be forwarded for consultation purposes. After this permission was obtained, the printed schemata were submitted to the examination of the universal episcopate and other consultative organs (namely, the dicasteries of the Roman Curia, ecclesiastical uni-

versities and faculties, and the Union of Superiors General) in order that they might express their opinion within a prudently determined time frame— not less than six months. At the same time, the schemata were also forwarded to the cardinal members of the Commission so as to enable them to make their general or particular observations at this stage of the process.

The order in which the schemata were sent is as follows:

1972 — the schema on administrative procedure;

1973 — the schema on sanctions in the Church;

1975 — the schema on the sacraments;

1976 — the schema on the procedure for the protection of rights or processes;

1977 — the schema on institutes of life consecrated by the profession of the evangelical counsels, the schema on general norms, the schema on the people of God, the schema on the Church's teaching office, the schema on sacred times and places and divine worship, and the schema on the patrimonial law of the Church.

Undoubtedly the revised Code could not have been appropriately prepared without the inestimable and continuous cooperation afforded the Commission by numerous very valid animadversions especially of a pastoral character offered by bishops and conferences of bishops. The bishops submitted very many written animadversions, either general ones on the schemata considered as a whole or particular ones on individual canons.

Of great benefit also were those general and particular animadversions submitted by the sacred congregations, tribunals and other institutes of the Roman Curia, based on their experience in the central government of the Church. This was also true for the scientific and technical proposals and suggestions offered by ecclesiastical universities and faculties reflecting different schools and ways of thinking.

The study, examination and collegial discussion of all the animadversions, general and particular, which were forwarded to the Commission constituted a weighty and veritably immense burden which lasted seven years. The Secretariat of the Commission took pains carefully to organize and synthesize all the animadversions, proposals and suggestions which, after they had been forwarded to the consultors and carefully examined by them, were subsequently collegially discussed in working sessions conducted by the ten study groups.

Every animadversion was considered with the utmost care and diligence. This was true even in the case of animadversions contradicting one another (which frequently happened). Due consideration was given not only to their sociological importance (namely, the number of consultative organs and

persons who proposed them), but especially to their doctrinal and pastoral value, their coherence with the doctrine and implementing norms of the Second Vatican Council, the pontifical magisterium, and their necessary coherence with the juridic canonical system when examined from a specifically technical and scientific standpoint. In fact, as often as it was a case of a doubtful matter or when questions of special importance were debated, the opinion of the cardinal members of the Commission was sought during one of their plenary sessions. In other cases in view of the specific matter under discussion, the Congregation for the Doctrine of the Faith and other dicasteries of the Roman Curia were consulted. Finally, many corrections and changes were incorporated in the canons of the early schemata at the request or suggestion of the bishops and other consultative organs, so that some schemata were entirely renewed or changed.

After all the schemata had been reworked, the Secretariat of the Commission and the consultors undertook a further weighty task. It was a matter of seeing to an internal coordination of all the schemata, of ensuring a uniform terminology throughout especially from a technical-juridic standpoint, of drafting canons in brief and elegant formulations, and finally of definitively determining a systematic organization so that all of the schemata, prepared by distinct study groups, could be integrated into one completely harmonious Code.

The new systematic organization which, as it were, spontaneously emerged slowly during the revision process, is based on two principles, one of which is fidelity to the more general principles already determined by the central committee, the other of which is its practical usefulness so that the new Code can be easily understood and used not only by experts but also by pastors and indeed by all members of the Christian faithful.

The new Code therefore consists of seven books which are entitled: General Norms, The People of God, The Church's Teaching Office, The Church's Sanctifying Office, Temporal Goods of the Church, Sanctions in the Church, and Processes. Even if the different rubrics which precede the individual books of the old and new Code appear to indicate sufficiently the differences between the two systems, nonetheless the systematic innovations of the new Code are much more evident in light of its parts, sections, titles and rubrics. But it is certain that the new organization not only corresponds better to the proper matter and character of canon law than the old organization, but also, and what is of greater importance, the new is more in keeping with the ecclesiology of the Second Vatical Council and those principles flowing from it which were proposed at the very outset of the revision process.

On June 29, 1980, the solemnity of the blessed Apostles Peter and Paul, the printed schema of the whole Code was presented to the Supreme Pontiff, who decided it was to be forwarded to the cardinal members of the Commis-

sion for their definitive examination and judgment. In order to highlight even more the participation of the whole Church in the last phase of the revision process, the Supreme Pontiff determined that other members be added to the Commission, cardinals and even bishops selected from the whole Church, conferences of bishops or councils or groups of conferences of bishops proposing candidates. Thus the expanded Commission numbered seventy-four members. At the beginning of 1981 they forwarded many animadversions which subsequently were subjected to a careful examination, diligent study and collegial discussion by the Secretariat of the Commission, with the help of consultors endowed with special expertise in the individual issues being discussed. A synthesis of all the animadversions together with the responses given by the Secretariat and the consultors was forwarded to the members of the Commission in August, 1981.

A plenary session was convoked by order of the Supreme Pontiff to deliberate on the entire text of the new Code and to cast a definitive vote on it. The session took place October 20-28, 1981 in the aula of the synod of bishops. There was a discussion of six questions of particular weight and importance as well as of other questions proposed at the request of at least ten Fathers. At the end of the plenary session, the Fathers unanimously responded *placet* (affirmatively) to the following question: whether it pleased the Fathers that, after the examination during the plenary session of the schema of the Code and the emendations already introduced, the same schema along with the changes which had received a majority vote during the plenary session was worthy of being presented as soon as possible to the Supreme Pontiff, who would issue the Code at a time and in a way which seemed best. Consideration was also to be given to other animadversions which had been presented as well as to a certain polishing of the text regarding its style and Latinity (which tasks were entrusted to the president and the Secretariat).

The entire text of the Code thereby reworked and approved was enlarged by the addition of canons from the schema on the Fundamental Law of the Church which had to be inserted in the Code in light of the material with which they dealt. After the Latin style of the text was further polished, it was printed and given to the Supreme Pontiff on April 22, 1982 with a view toward promulgation.

The Supreme Pontiff, however, personally reviewed this latest schema with the help of certain experts and in consultation with the pro-president of the Pontifical Commission for the Revision of the Code of Canon Law. After mature consideration the Supreme Pontiff decreed that the new Code was to be promulgated on January 25, 1983, i.e., the anniversary of the first announcement by Pope John XXIII of the undertaking of the Code's revision.

Since after nearly twenty years the pontifical Commission established for

this purpose has felicitously completed the difficult task entrusted to it, there is now available to pastors and other members of the Christian faithful the most recent law of the Church, which is characterized by simplicity, precision, elegance and true legal science. Furthermore, since it is fully pervaded by charity, equity, humanity and a true Christian spirit, it attempts to correspond to the divinely given external and internal characteristics of the Church. It also seeks to take cognizance of the conditions and needs of the contemporary world. But if on account of the excessively swift changes in contemporary human society certain elements of the new law become less perfect and require a new review, the Church is endowed with such a wealth of resources that, not unlike prior centuries, it will be able to undertake the task of renewing the laws of its life.

Now, however, the law can no longer be unknown. Pastors have at their disposal secure norms by which they may correctly direct the exercise of the sacred ministry. To each person is given a source of knowing his or her own proper rights and duties. Arbitrariness in acting can be precluded. Abuses which perhaps have crept into ecclesiastical discipline because of a lack of legislation can be more easily rooted out and prevented. Finally, all the works, institutes and initiatives of the apostolate may progress expeditiously and may be promoted since a healthy juridic organization is quite necessary for the ecclesiastical community to live, grow and flourish. May our most gracious God grant this through the intercession of the Blessed Virgin Mary, the Mother of the Church, her spouse St. Joseph, Patron of the Church, and Saints Peter and Paul.

OUTLINE OF THE CODE BY CANONS

BOOK II
THE PEOPLE OF GOD

PART I
THE CHRISTIAN FAITHFUL

BOOK IV
THE OFFICE OF SANCTIFYING
IN THE CHURCH

PART I
THE SACRAMENTS

PART II
THE CONTENTIOUS TRIAL 1501-1670

Section I
THE ORDINARY CONTENTIOUS TRIAL 1501-1655

CANONS OF THE CODE
IN LATIN AND ENGLISH

LIBER I
DE NORMIS GENERALIBUS

Can. 1 – Canones huius Codicis unam Ecclesiam latinam respiciunt.

Can. 2 – Codex plerumque non definit ritus, qui in actionibus liturgicis celebrandis sunt servandi; quare leges liturgicae hucusque vigentes vim suam retinent, nisi earum aliqua Codicis canonibus sit contraria.

Can. 3 – Codicis canones initas ab Apostolica Sede cum nationibus aliisve societatibus politicis conventiones non abrogant neque iis derogant; eaedem idcirco perinde ac in praesens vigere pergent, contrariis huius Codicis praescriptis minime obstantibus.

Can. 4 – Iura quaesita, itemque privilegia quae, ab Apostolica Sede ad haec usque tempora personis sive physicis sive iuridicis concessa, in usu sunt nec revocata, integra manent, nisi huius Codicis canonibus expresse revocentur.

Can. 5 – § 1. Vigentes in praesens contra horum praescripta canonum consuetudines sive universales sive particulares, quae ipsis canonibus huius Codicis reprobantur, prorsus suppressae sunt, nec in posterum reviviscere sinantur; ceterae quoque suppressae habeantur, nisi expresse Codice aliud caveatur, aut centenariae sint vel immemorabiles, quae quidem, si de iudicio Ordinarii pro locorum ac personarum adiunctis submoveri nequeant, tolerari possunt.

§ 2. Consuetudines praeter ius hucusque vigentes, sive universales sive particulares, servantur.

Can. 6 – § 1. Hoc Codice vim obtinente, abrogantur:

1° Codex Iuris Canonici anno 1917 promulgatus;

2° aliae quoque leges, sive universales sive particulares, praescriptis huius Codicis contrariae, nisi de particularibus aliud expresse caveatur;

BOOK I
GENERAL NORMS

Can. 1 — The canons of this Code affect only the Latin Church.

Can. 2 — For the most part the Code does not define the rites which are to be observed in celebrating liturgical actions. For this reason current liturgical norms retain their force unless a given liturgical norm is contrary to the canons of the Code.

Can. 3 — The canons of the Code neither abrogate nor derogate from the pacts entered upon by the Apostolic See with nations or other political societies. They therefore continue in force as presently, notwithstanding any prescriptions of this Code to the contrary.

Can. 4 — Acquired rights as well as privileges granted up to this time by the Apostolic See to physical or juridic persons remain unimpaired provided they are presently in use and have not been revoked, unless they are expressly revoked by the canons of this Code.

Can. 5 — §1. Presently existing universal or particular customs contrary to the prescriptions of these canons which are reprobated by the very canons of this Code are entirely suppressed, nor are they permitted to revive in the future. Other customs are also considered suppressed unless the Code expressly provides otherwise or unless they are centenary or immemorial, in which case they can be tolerated if in the judgment of the ordinary they cannot be removed due to circumstances of place and persons.

§2. Presently existing universal or particular customs which are apart from the law (*praeter ius*) are preserved.

Can. 6 — §1. When this Code goes into effect, the following are abrogated:

1° the Code of Canon Law promulgated in 1917;

2° other universal or particular laws contrary to the prescriptions of this Code, unless particular laws are otherwise expressly provided for;

3° leges poenales quaelibet, sive universales sive particulares a Sede Apostolica latae, nisi in ipso hoc Codice recipiantur;

4° ceterae quoque leges disciplinares universales materiam respicientes, quae hoc Codice ex integro ordinatur.

§ 2. Canones huius Codicis, quatenus ius vetus referunt, aestimandi sunt ratione etiam canonicae traditionis habita.

TITULUS I

DE LEGIBUS ECCLESIASTICIS

Can. 7 – Lex instituitur cum promulgatur.

Can. 8 – § 1. Leges ecclesiasticae universales promulgantur per editionem in *Actorum Apostolicae Sedis commentario officiali,* nisi in casibus particularibus alius promulgandi modus fuerit praescriptus, et vim suam exserunt tantum expletis tribus mensibus a die qui *Actorum* numero appositus est, nisi ex natura rei illico ligent aut in ipsa lege brevior aut longior vacatio specialiter et expresse fuerit statuta.

§ 2. Leges particulares promulgantur modo a legislatore determinato et obligare incipiunt post mensem a die promulgationis, nisi alius terminus in ipsa lege statuatur.

Can. 9 – Leges respiciunt futura, non praeterita, nisi nominatim in eis de praeteritis caveatur.

Can. 10 – Irritantes aut inhabilitantes eae tantum leges habendae sunt, quibus actum esse nullum aut inhabilem esse personam expresse statuitur.

Can. 11 – Legibus mere ecclesiasticis tenentur baptizati in Ecclesia catholica vel in eandem recepti, quique sufficienti rationis usu gaudent et, nisi aliud iure expresse caveatur, septimum aetatis annum expleverunt.

Can. 12 – § 1. Legibus universalibus tenentur ubique terrarum omnes pro quibus latae sunt.

§ 2. A legibus autem universalibus, quae in certo territorio non vigent, eximuntur omnes qui in eo territorio actu versantur.

§ 3. Legibus conditis pro peculiari territorio ii subiciuntur pro quibus latae sunt, quique ibidem domicilium vel quasi-domicilium habent et simul actu commorantur, firmo praescripto can. 13.

3° any universal or particular penal laws whatsoever issued by the Apostolic See, unless they are contained in this Code;

4° other universal disciplinary laws dealing with a matter which is regulated *ex integro* by this Code.

§2. The canons of this Code insofar as they refer to the old law are to be assessed also in accord with canonical tradition.

TITLE I
ECCLESIASTICAL LAWS

Can. 7 — A law comes into existence when it is promulgated.

Can. 8 — §1. Universal ecclesiastical laws are promulgated by being published in the official commentary *Acta Apostolicae Sedis* unless another form of promulgation is prescribed for individual cases. These laws become effective only after three months have elapsed from the date of that issue of the *Acta*, unless they have binding force immediately from the very nature of the matter they treat or unless the law itself specifically and expressly suspends its force for a shorter or longer period.

§2. Particular laws are promulgated in a manner determined by the legislator, and they begin to bind one month from the date of promulgation, unless another time period is determined in the law itself.

Can. 9 — Laws deal with the future and not the past, unless specific provision be made in the laws concerning the past.

Can. 10 — Only those laws which expressly state that an act is null or that a person is incapable of acting are to be considered to be invalidating or incapacitating.

Can. 11 — Merely ecclesiastical laws bind those baptized in the Catholic Church or received into it and who enjoy the sufficient use of reason and, unless the law expressly provides otherwise, have completed seven years of age.

Can. 12 — §1. All persons for whom universal laws were passed are bound by them everywhere.

§2. However, all persons who are actually present in a certain territory are exempted from the universal laws which do not have force in that territory.

§3. With due regard for the prescription of can. 13, laws established for a particular territory bind those for whom they were passed when these persons have a domicile or a quasi-domicile there and are likewise actually present in the territory.

Can. 13 – § 1. Leges particulares non praesumuntur personales, sed territoriales, nisi aliud constet.

§ 2. Peregrini non adstringuntur :

1° legibus particularibus sui territorii quamdiu ab eo absunt, nisi aut earum transgressio in proprio territorio noceat, aut leges sint personales ;

2° neque legibus territorii in quo versantur, iis exceptis quae ordini publico consulunt, aut actuum sollemnia determinant, aut res immobiles in territorio sitas respiciunt.

§ 3. Vagi obligantur legibus tam universalibus quam particularibus quae vigent in loco in quo versantur.

Can. 14 – Leges, etiam irritantes et inhabilitantes, in dubio iuris non urgent; in dubio autem facti Ordinarii ab eis dispensare possunt, dummodo, si agatur de dispensatione reservata, concedi soleat ab auctoritate cui reservatur.

Can. 15 – § 1. Ignorantia vel error circa leges irritantes vel inhabilitantes earundem effectum non impediunt, nisi aliud expresse statuatur.

§ 2. Ignorantia vel error circa legem aut poenam aut circa factum proprium aut circa factum alienum notorium non praesumitur; circa factum alienum non notorium praesumitur, donec contrarium probetur.

Can. 16 – § 1. Leges authentice interpretatur legislator et is cui potestas authentice interpretandi fuerit ab eodem commissa.

§ 2. Interpretatio authentica per modum legis exhibita eandem vim habet ac lex ipsa et promulgari debet; si verba legis in se certa declaret tantum, valet retrorsum ; si legem coarctet vel extendat aut dubiam explicet, non retrotrahitur.

§ 3. Interpretatio autem per modum sententiae iudicialis aut actus administrativi in re peculiari, vim legis non habet et ligat tantum personas atque afficit res pro quibus data est.

Can. 17 – Leges ecclesiasticae intellegendae sunt secundum propriam verborum significationem in textu et contextu consideratam ; quae si dubia et obscura manserit, ad locos parallelos, si qui sint, ad legis finem ac circumstantias et ad mentem legislatoris est recurrendum.

Can. 18 – Leges quae poenam statuunt aut liberum iurium exercitium coarctant aut exceptionem a lege continent, strictae subsunt interpretationi.

Can. 13 — §1. Particular laws are not presumed to be personal but territorial, unless it is otherwise evident.

§2. Travelers:

1° are not bound by the particular laws of their own territory as long as they are absent from it unless their violation would cause harm in their own territory or unless the laws are personal ones;

2° are not bound by the laws of the territory in which they are present with the exception of those laws which provide for public order, which determine the formalities of legal actions, or which deal with immovable goods situated in that territory.

§3. Transients (*vagi*) are bound by both universal laws and the particular laws which are in force in the place where they are present.

Can. 14 — When there is a doubt of law, laws do not bind even if they be nullifying and disqualifying ones. When there is a doubt of fact, however, ordinaries can dispense from them. In the latter case, if it is a question of a reserved dispensation, the ordinaries can dispense so long as the dispensation is usually granted by the authority to whom it is reserved.

Can. 15 — §1. Ignorance or error concerning invalidating or incapacitating laws does not hinder their effectiveness unless it is expressly determined otherwise.

§2. Ignorance or error about a law, a penalty, a fact concerning oneself, or a notorious fact concerning another is not presumed; it is presumed about a fact concerning another which is not notorious until the contrary is proven.

Can. 16 — §1. Laws are authentically interpreted by the legislator and by the one to whom the legislator has granted the power to interpret them authentically.

§2. An authentic interpretation communicated in the form of a law has the same force as the law itself and must be promulgated. Furthermore, if such an interpretation merely declares what was certain in the words of the law in themselves, it has retroactive force; if it restricts or extends the law or if it explains a doubtful law, it is not retroactive.

§3. However, an interpretation contained in a judicial decision or an administrative act in a particular matter does not have the force of law and binds only the persons and affects only those matters for which it was given.

Can. 17 — Ecclesiastical laws are to be understood in accord with the proper meaning of the words considered in their text and context. If the meaning remains doubtful and obscure, recourse is to be taken to parallel passages, if such exist, to the purpose and the circumstances of the law, and to the mind of the legislator.

Can. 18 — Laws which establish a penalty or restrict the free exercise of rights or which contain an exception to the law are subject to a strict interpretation.

Can. 19 – Si certa de re desit expressum legis sive universalis sive particularis praescriptum aut consuetudo, causa, nisi sit poenalis, dirimenda est attentis legibus latis in similibus, generalibus iuris principiis cum aequitate canonica servatis, iurisprudentia et praxi Curiae Romanae, communi constantique doctorum sententia.

Can. 20 – Lex posterior abrogat priorem aut eidem derogat, si id expresse edicat aut illi sit directe contraria, aut totam de integro ordinet legis prioris materiam; sed lex universalis minime derogat iuri particulari aut speciali, nisi aliud in iure expresse caveatur.

Can. 21 – In dubio revocatio legis praeexsistentis non praesumitur, sed leges posteriores ad priores trahendae sunt et his, quantum fieri potest, conciliandae.

Can. 22 – Leges civiles ad quas ius Ecclesiae remittit, in iure canonico iisdem cum effectibus serventur, quatenus iuri divino non sint contrariae et nisi aliud iure canonico caveatur.

TITULUS II
DE CONSUETUDINE

Can. 23 – Ea tantum consuetudo a communitate fidelium introducta vim legis habet, quae a legislatore approbata fuerit, ad normam canonum qui sequuntur.

Can. 24 – § 1. Nulla consuetudo vim legis obtinere potest, quae sit iuri divino contraria.

§ 2. Nec vim legis obtinere potest consuetudo contra aut praeter ius canonicum, nisi sit rationabilis; consuetudo autem quae in iure expresse reprobatur, non est rationabilis.

Can. 25 – Nulla consuetudo vim legis obtinet, nisi a communitate legis saltem recipiendae capaci cum animo iuris inducendi servata fuerit.

Can. 26 – Nisi a competenti legislatore specialiter fuerit probata, consuetudo vigenti iuri canonico contraria aut quae est praeter legem canonicam, vim legis obtinet tantum, si legitime per annos triginta continuos et completos servata fuerit; contra legem vero canonicam, quae clausulam contineat futuras consuetudines prohibentem, sola praevalere potest consuetudo centenaria aut immemorabilis.

Can. 27 – Consuetudo est optima legum interpres.

Can. 19 — Unless it is a penal matter, if an express prescription of universal or particular law or a custom is lacking in some particular matter, the case is to be decided in light of laws passed in similar circumstances, the general principles of law observed with canonical equity, the jurisprudence and praxis of the Roman Curia, and the common and constant opinion of learned persons.

Can. 20 — A later law abrogates a former law or derogates from it if it expressly states so, if it is directly contrary to it, or if it entirely re-orders the subject matter of the former law; but a universal law in no way derogates from a particular or special law unless the law itself expressly provides otherwise.

Can. 21 — In a case of doubt the revocation of a pre-existent law is not presumed, but later laws are to be related to earlier ones and, insofar as it is possible, harmonized with them.

Can. 22 — Civil laws to which the law of the Church defers should be observed in canon law with the same effects, insofar as they are not contrary to divine law and unless it is provided otherwise in canon law.

TITLE II
CUSTOM

Can. 23 — Only that custom introduced by the community of the faithful and approved by the legislator has the force of law, according to the following canons.

Can. 24 — §1. No custom which is contrary to divine law can obtain the force of law.

§2. Unless it be a reasonable one, no custom which is contrary to or apart from (*praeter ius*) canon law can obtain the force of law; however, a custom which is expressly reprobated in law is not a reasonable one.

Can. 25 — No custom obtains the force of law unless it has been observed with the intention of introducing a law by a community capable at least of receiving law.

Can. 26 — Unless it has been specifically approved by the competent legislator, a custom contrary to the current canon law or one which is apart from (*praeter ius*) canon law obtains the force of law only when it has been legitimately observed for thirty continuous and complete years; only a centenary or immemorial custom can prevail over a canon which contains a clause forbidding future customs.

Can. 27 — Custom is the best interpreter of laws.

Can. 28 – Firmo praescripto can. 5, consuetudo, sive contra sive praeter legem, per contrariam consuetudinem aut legem revocatur; sed, nisi expressam de iis mentionem faciat, lex non revocat consuetudines centenarias aut immemorabiles, nec lex universalis consuetudines particulares.

TITULUS III
DE DECRETIS GENERALIBUS ET DE INSTRUCTIONIBUS

Can. 29 – Decreta generalia, quibus a legislatore competenti pro communitate legis recipiendae capaci communia feruntur praescripta, proprie sunt leges et reguntur praescriptis canonum de legibus.

Can. 30 – Qui potestate exsecutiva tantum gaudet, decretum generale, de quo in can. 29, ferre non valet, nisi in casibus particularibus ad normam iuris id ipsi a legislatore competenti expresse fuerit concessum et servatis condicionibus in actu concessionis statutis.

Can. 31 – § 1. Decreta generalia exsecutoria, quibus nempe pressius determinantur modi in lege applicanda servandi aut legum observantia urgetur, ferre valent, intra fines suae competentiae, qui potestate gaudent exsecutiva.

§ 2. Ad decretorum promulgationem et vacationem quod attinet, de quibus in § 1, serventur praescripta can. 8.

Can. 32 – Decreta generalia exsecutoria eos obligant qui tenentur legibus, quarum eadem decreta modos applicationis determinant aut observantiam urgent.

Can. 33 – § 1. Decreta generalia exsecutoria, etiamsi edantur in directoriis aliusve nominis documentis, non derogant legibus, et eorum praescripta quae legibus sint contraria omni vi carent.

§ 2. Eadem vim habere desinunt revocatione explicita aut implicita ab auctoritate competenti facta, necnon cessante lege ad cuius exsecutionem data sunt; non autem cessant resoluto iure statuentis, nisi contrarium expresse caveatur.

Can. 34 – § 1. Instructiones, quae nempe legum praescripta declarant atque rationes in iisdem exsequendis servandas evolvunt et determinant, ad usum eorum dantur quorum est curare ut leges exsecutioni

Can. 28 — With due regard for the prescription of can. 5, a custom, whether it is contrary to or apart from the law (*praeter legem*), is revoked by a contrary custom or law; however, unless it makes express mention of centenary or immemorial customs, a law does not revoke them, nor does a universal law revoke particular customs.

TITLE III
GENERAL DECREES AND INSTRUCTIONS

Can. 29 — General decrees, by which common prescriptions are issued by a competent legislator for a community capable of receiving a law, are laws properly speaking and are governed by the prescriptions of the canons on laws.

Can. 30 — Persons who possess only executive power are not able to issue the general decree mentioned in can. 29, unless in particular cases such power has expressly been granted to them by a competent legislator in accord with the norm of law and the conditions stated in the act of the grant have been observed.

Can. 31 — §1. General executory decrees determine more precisely the methods to be observed in applying the law or themselves urge the observance of laws. Persons who possess executive power are able to issue such decrees within the limits of their competency.

§2. The prescriptions of can. 8 should be observed concerning the promulgation of the decrees mentioned in §1 and concerning the period of time to elapse before they become effective.

Can. 32 — General executory decrees oblige those who are bound by the laws whose methods of application such decrees determine or whose observance they urge.

Can. 33 — §1. General executory decrees, even if they are published in directories or in documents having some other title, do not derogate from laws, and the prescriptions of such decrees which are contrary to laws lack all force.

§2. Such decrees cease to have force through explicit or implicit revocation by competent authority as well as through cessation of the law for whose execution they were given, but they do not cease to have force with the termination of the authority of the one issuing them unless the contrary has been expressly provided.

Can. 34 — §1. Instructions which clarify the prescriptions of laws and elaborate on and determine an approach to be followed in implementing them, are given for the use of those persons whose concern it is to see that the

mandentur, eosque in legum exsecutione obligant; eas legitime edunt, intra fines suae competentiae, qui potestate exsecutiva gaudent.

§ 2. Instructionum ordinationes legibus non derogant, et si quae cum legum praescriptis componi nequeant, omni vi carent.

§ 3. Vim habere desinunt instructiones non tantum revocatione explicita aut implicita auctoritatis competentis, quae eas edidit, eiusve superioris, sed etiam cessante lege ad quam declarandam vel exsecutioni mandandam datae sunt.

TITULUS IV
DE ACTIBUS ADMINISTRATIVIS SINGULARIBUS

CAPUT I
NORMAE COMMUNES

Can. 35 – Actus administrativus singularis, sive est decretum aut praeceptum sive est rescriptum, elici potest, intra fines suae competentiae, ab eo qui potestate exsecutiva gaudet, firmo praescripto can. 76, § 1.

Can. 36 – § 1. Actus administrativus intellegendus est secundum propriam verborum significationem et communem loquendi usum; in dubio, qui ad lites referuntur aut ad poenas comminandas infligendasve attinent aut personae iura coarctant aut iura aliis quaesita laedunt aut adversantur legi in commodum privatorum, strictae subsunt interpretationi; ceteri omnes, latae.

§ 2. Actus administrativus non debet ad alios casus praeter expressos extendi.

Can. 37 – Actus administrativus, qui forum externum respicit, scripto est consignandus; item, si fit in forma commissoria, actus huius exsecutionis.

Can. 38 – Actus administrativus, etiam si agatur de rescripto *Motu proprio* dato, effectu caret quatenus ius alteri quaesitum laedit aut legi consuetudinive probatae contrarius est, nisi auctoritas competens expresse clausulam derogatoriam addiderit.

Can. 39 – Condiciones in actu administrativo tunc tantum ad validitatem censentur adiectae, cum per particulas *si, nisi, dummodo* exprimuntur.

laws are implemented and oblige such persons in the execution of the laws. Persons who possess executive power legitimately issue such instructions within the limits of their competency.

§2. Regulations found in instructions do not derogate from laws, and if any of them cannot be reconciled with the prescriptions of laws, they lack all force.

§3. Instructions cease to have force not only through their explicit or implicit revocation by the competent authority who issued them or by the same authority's superior but also through the cessation of the law for whose clarification or implementation they were given.

TITLE IV
INDIVIDUAL ADMINISTRATIVE ACTS

CHAPTER I
COMMON NORMS

Can. 35 — With due regard for can. 76, §1, an individual administrative act, be it a decree, a precept or a rescript, can be issued by one who possesses executive power within the limits of that person's competency.

Can. 36 — §1. An administrative act is to be understood in accord with the proper meaning of the words and the common usage of speech. In a doubtful situation administrative acts are subject to a broad interpretation except for the following administrative acts which are subject to a strict interpretation: those dealing with lawsuits, those threatening or inflicting penalties, those which restrict the rights of a person, those which injure the acquired rights of others, or those which benefit private individuals and are contrary to the law.

§2. An administrative act must not be extended to cases other than those actually expressed in it.

Can. 37 — An administrative act which deals with the external forum is to be set forth in writing; likewise, if the administrative act is issued in commissorial form, its act of execution is to be in writing.

Can. 38 — Even in the case of a rescript given at the initiative of its issuer (*motu proprio*), an administrative act lacks effect insofar as it injures the acquired right of another or is contrary to a law or an approved custom, unless the competent authority expressly adds to it a derogating clause.

Can. 39 — Conditions attached to an administrative act are considered to affect its validity only when they are expressed by the particles *if* (*si*), *unless* (*nisi*), or *provided that* (*dummodo*).

Can. 40 – Exsecutor alicuius actus administrativi invalide suo munere fungitur, antequam litteras receperit earumque authenticitatem et integritatem recognoverit, nisi praevia earundem notitia ad ipsum auctoritate eundem actum edentis transmissa fuerit.

Can. 41 – Exsecutor actus administrativi cui committitur merum exsecutionis ministerium, exsecutionem huius actus denegare non potest, nisi manifesto appareat eundem actum esse nullum aut alia ex gravi causa sustineri non posse aut condiciones in ipso actu administrativo appositas non esse adimpletas; si tamen actus administrativi exsecutio adiunctorum personae aut loci ratione videatur inopportuna, exsecutor exsecutionem intermittat; quibus in casibus statim certiorem faciat auctoritatem quae actum edidit.

Can. 42 – Exsecutor actus administrativi procedere debet ad mandati normam; si autem condiciones essentiales in litteris appositas non impleverit ac substantialem procedendi formam non servaverit, irrita est exsecutio.

Can. 43 – Actus administrativi exsecutor potest alium pro suo prudenti arbitrio sibi substituere, nisi substitutio prohibita fuerit, aut electa industria personae, aut substituti persona praefinita; hisce autem in casibus exsecutori licet alteri committere actus praeparatorios.

Can. 44 – Actus administrativus exsecutioni mandari potest etiam ab exsecutoris successore in officio, nisi fuerit electa industria personae.

Can. 45 – Exsecutori fas est, si quoquo modo in actus administrativi exsecutione erraverit, eundem actum iterum exsecutioni mandare.

Can. 46 – Actus administrativus non cessat resoluto iure statuentis, nisi aliud iure expresse caveatur.

Can. 47 – Revocatio actus administrativi per alium actum administrativum auctoritatis competentis effectum tantummodo obtinet a momento, quo legitime notificatur personae pro qua datus est.

Caput II
DE DECRETIS ET PRAECEPTIS SINGULARIBUS

Can. 48 – Decretum singulare intellegitur actus administrativus a competenti auctoritate exsecutiva editus, quo secundum iuris normas pro casu particulari datur decisio aut fit provisio, quae natura sua petitionem ab aliquo factam non supponunt.

Can. 40 — The executor of an administrative act who executes it before receiving the letter and verifying its authenticity and accuracy functions invalidly, unless previous notice of the letter had been given to the executor by the authority who issued the act.

Can. 41 — The executor of an administrative act whose competency is limited to executing it cannot refuse to execute it unless it is manifestly apparent that the act is null, that it cannot be upheld due to another serious cause, or that the conditions attached to the administrative act itself have not been fulfilled. Nevertheless, if the execution of the administrative act appears inopportune due to circumstances of person or place, the executor should delay its execution; in all these cases the executor should immediately inform the authority who issued the act.

Can. 42 — The executor of an administrative act must proceed in accord with the norm of the mandate; the execution is invalid unless the essential conditions attached in the letter have been fulfilled and unless the executor has substantially observed the procedural formalities.

Can. 43 — The executor of an administrative act can with prudent judgment substitute another as executor unless such substitution has been forbidden or the executor has been chosen for personal qualifications, or the person of the substitute has been predetermined; however, in these cases the executor may entrust preparatory acts to another.

Can. 44 — Unless the executor was chosen on account of personal qualifications, an administrative act can also be implemented by the executor's successor in office.

Can. 45 — If in some way the executor erred in the execution of an administrative act, the executor may implement the same act again.

Can. 46 — Unless it is expressly provided otherwise in law, an administrative act does not cease with the termination of the authority of the one issuing it.

Can. 47 — The revocation of an administrative act by means of another administrative act of a competent authority takes effect only from the moment at which the latter act has legitimately been made known to the person for whom it has been given.

Chapter II
INDIVIDUAL DECREES AND PRECEPTS

Can. 48 — An individual decree is an administrative act issued by a competent executive authority in which a decision is given or a provision is made in a particular case in accord with the norms of law; such decisions or provisions of their nature do not presuppose that a petition has been made by someone.

Can. 49 – Praeceptum singulare est decretum quo personae aut personis determinatis aliquid faciendum aut omittendum directe et legitime imponitur, praesertim ad legis observantiam urgendam.

Can. 50 – Antequam decretum singulare ferat, auctoritas necessarias notitias et probationes exquirat, atque, quantum fieri potest, eos audiat quorum iura laedi possint.

Can. 51 – Decretum scripto feratur expressis, saltem summarie, si agatur de decisione, motivis.

Can. 52 – Decretum singulare vim habet tantum quoad res de quibus decernit et pro personis quibus datum est; eas vero ubique obligat, nisi aliud constet.

Can. 53 – Si decreta inter se sint contraria, peculiare, in iis quae peculiariter exprimuntur, praevalet generali; si aeque sint peculiaria aut generalia, posterius tempore obrogat priori, quatenus ei contrarium est.

Can. 54 – § 1. Decretum singulare, cuius applicatio committitur exsecutori, effectum habet a momento exsecutionis; secus a momento quo personae auctoritate ipsius decernentis intimatur.

§ 2. Decretum singulare, ut urgeri possit, legitimo documento ad normam iuris intimandum est.

Can. 55 – Firmo praescripto cann. 37 et 51, cum gravissima ratio obstet ne scripti decreti textus tradatur, decretum intimatum habetur si ei, cui destinatur, coram notario vel duobus testibus legatur, actis redactis, ab omnibus praesentibus subscribendis.

Can. 56 – Decretum pro intimato habetur, si is cui destinatur, rite vocatus ad decretum accipiendum vel audiendum, sine iusta causa non comparuerit vel subscribere recusaverit.

Can. 57 – § 1. Quoties lex iubeat decretum ferri vel ab eo, cuius interest, petitio vel recursus ad decretum obtinendum legitime proponatur, auctoritas competens intra tres menses a recepta petitione vel recursu provideat, nisi alius terminus lege praescribatur.

§ 2. Hoc termino transacto, si decretum nondum datum fuerit, responsum praesumitur negativum, ad propositionem ulterioris recursus quod attinet.

§ 3. Responsum negativum praesumptum non eximit competentem auctoritatem ab obligatione decretum ferendi, immo et damnum forte illatum, ad normam can. 128, reparandi.

Can. 49 — An individual precept is a decree directly and legitimately enjoining a determined person or persons to do or to omit something, especially concerning the urging of the observance of a law.

Can. 50 — Before issuing an individual decree an authority should seek out the necessary information and proofs, and also hear those whose rights can be injured, insofar as this is possible.

Can. 51 — A decree should be issued in writing, giving, in the case of a decision, the reasons which prompted it, at least in a summary fashion.

Can. 52 — An individual decree has force only in respect to the matters it decides and only on behalf of the persons for whom it was given; it obliges these persons everywhere, unless it is otherwise evident.

Can. 53 — If decrees are contrary to one another, a special decree prevails over a general decree in those matters which are specifically expressed; if they are equally special or general, the later decree modifies the prior one to the extent that the later is contrary to the prior.

Can. 54 — §1. An individual decree whose application is entrusted to an executor takes effect from the moment of its execution; otherwise, from the moment it is made known to the person through the authority of its issuer.

§2. For an individual decree to be enforced it must be communicated by means of a legitimate d ocument in accord with the norm of law.

Can. 55 — With due regard for the prescription of cann. 37 and 51, when a most serious reason prevents the handing over of the written text of a decree, the decree is considered to have been communicated if it is read before a notary or two witnesses to the person for whom it is destined and all present sign an instrument stating this was done.

Can. 56 — A decree is considered to have been communicated when the person for whom it was destined was properly summoned to receive or hear it, even if the person without a just cause, did not appear or refused to sign it.

Can. 57 — §1. As often as the law requires a decree to be issued or if an interested party legitimately presents either a petition or a recourse to obtain a decree, the competent authority should provide for the matter within three months from the receipt of the petition or recourse unless another time period is prescribed by law.

§2. When this period of time has passed, if the decree has not yet been given, the response is presumed to be negative regarding the presentation of a further recourse.

§3. A presumed negative response does not exempt the competent authority from the obligation of issuing the decree and even making reparation for damages possibly incurred in accord with the norm of can. 128.

Can. 58 – § 1. Decretum singulare vim habere desinit legitima revocatione ab auctoritate competenti facta necnon cessante lege ad cuius exsecutionem datum est.

§ 2. Praeceptum singulare, legitimo documento non impositum, cessat resoluto iure praecipientis.

CAPUT III

DE RESCRIPTIS

Can. 59 – § 1. Rescriptum intellegitur actus administrativus a competenti auctoritate exsecutiva in scriptis elicitus, quo suapte natura, ad petitionem alicuius, conceditur privilegium, dispensatio aliave gratia.

§ 2. Quae de rescriptis statuuntur praescripta, etiam de licentiae concessione necnon de concessionibus gratiarum vivae vocis oraculo valent, nisi aliud constet.

Can. 60 – Rescriptum quodlibet impetrari potest ab omnibus qui expresse non prohibentur.

Can. 61 – Nisi aliud constet, rescriptum impetrari potest pro alio, etiam praeter eius assensum, et valet ante eiusdem acceptationem, salvis clausulis contrariis.

Can. 62 – Rescriptum in quo nullus datur exsecutor, effectum habet a momento quo datae sunt litterae; cetera, a momento exsecutionis.

Can. 63 – § 1. Validitati rescripti obstat subreptio seu reticentia veri, si in precibus expressa non fuerint quae secundum legem, stilum et praxim canonicam ad validitatem sunt exprimenda, nisi agatur de rescripto gratiae, quod *Motu proprio* datum sit.

§ 2. Item validitati rescripti obstat obreptio seu expositio falsi, si ne una quidem causa motiva proposita sit vera.

§ 3. Causa motiva in rescriptis quorum nullus est exsecutor, vera sit oportet tempore quo rescriptum datum est; in ceteris, tempore exsecutionis.

Can. 64 – Salvo iure Paenitentiariae pro foro interno, gratia a quovis dicasterio Romanae Curiae denegata, valide ab alio eiusdem Curiae dicasterio aliave competenti auctoritate infra Romanum Pontificem concedi nequit, sine assensu dicasterii quocum agi coeptum est.

Can. 65 – § 1. Salvis praescriptis §§ 2 et 3, nemo gratiam a proprio

Can. 58 — §1. An individual decree ceases to have force through its legitimate revocation by competent authority and also through the cessation of the law for whose execution it has been given.

§2. An individual precept which has not been imposed through a legitimate document ceases with the termination of the authority of the one issuing it.

Chapter III
RESCRIPTS

Can. 59 — §1. A rescript is an administrative act issued in writing by competent executive authority by which through its very nature a privilege, dispensation, or other favor is granted in response to someone's request.

§2. The prescriptions established for rescripts also apply to the verbal granting of a permission or of favors, unless it is otherwise evident.

Can. 60 — Any rescript whatsoever can be requested by all who are not expressly forbidden to do so.

Can. 61 — Unless it is otherwise evident, a rescript can be requested on behalf of another person, even without that person's consent, and it takes effect before the person's acceptance, with due regard for contrary clauses.

Can. 62 — A rescript for which no executor is given takes effect from the moment when the letter is issued; other rescripts take effect from the moment of execution.

Can. 63 — §1. Subreption, or the concealment of the truth, invalidates a rescript if those things which must be expressed in the request for validity according to the law, style, and canonical practice were not expressed; this does not apply to a rescript of favor which was given *motu proprio*.

§2. Obreption, or statements of falsehood, likewise invalidates a rescript if not even one proposed motivating reason is true.

§3. For rescripts which have no executor the motivating reason must be true at the time when the rescript is issued; for other rescripts, at the time of execution.

Can. 64 — With due regard for the authority of the Sacred Penitentiary in the internal forum, a favor which has been denied by one dicastery of the Roman Curia cannot be validly granted by another dicastery or by another competent authority below the Roman Pontiff without the consent of the dicastery before which the matter was initiated.

Can. 65 — §1. With due regard for the prescriptions of §§2 and 3, no one

Ordinario denegatam ab alio Ordinario petat, nisi facta denegationis mentione; facta autem mentione, Ordinarius gratiam ne concedat, nisi habitis a priore Ordinario denegationis rationibus.

§ 2. Gratia a Vicario generali vel a Vicario episcopali denegata, ab alio Vicario eiusdem Episcopi, etiam habitis a Vicario denegante denegationis rationibus, valide concedi nequit.

§ 3. Gratia a Vicario generali vel a Vicario episcopali denegata et postea, nulla facta huius denegationis mentione, ab Episcopo dioecesano impetrata, invalida est; gratia autem ab Episcopo dioecesano denegata nequit valide, etiam facta denegationis mentione, ab eius Vicario generali vel Vicario episcopali, non consentiente Episcopo, impetrari.

Can. 66 – Rescriptum non fit irritum ob errorem in nomine personae cui datur vel a qua editur, aut loci in quo ipsa residet, aut rei de qua agitur, dummodo iudicio Ordinarii nulla sit de ipsa persona vel de re dubitatio.

Can. 67 – § 1. Si contingat ut de una eademque re duo rescripta inter se contraria impetrentur, peculiare, in iis quae peculiariter exprimuntur, praevalet generali.

§ 2. Si sint aeque peculiaria aut generalia, prius tempore praevalet posteriori, nisi in altero fiat mentio expressa de priore, aut nisi prior impetrator dolo vel notabili neglegentia sua rescripto usus non fuerit.

§ 3. In dubio num rescriptum irritum sit necne, recurratur ad rescribentem.

Can. 68 – Rescriptum Sedis Apostolicae in quo nullus datur exsecutor, tunc tantum debet Ordinario impetrantis praesentari, cum id in iisdem litteris praecipitur, aut de rebus agitur publicis, aut comprobari condiciones oportet.

Can. 69 – Rescriptum, cuius praesentationi nullum est definitum tempus, potest exsecutori exhiberi quovis tempore, modo absit fraus et dolus.

Can. 70 – Si in rescripto ipsa concessio exsecutori committatur,

should petition for a favor from another ordinary which has been denied by one's own ordinary unless mention of the denial has been made. Even after such mention has been made, the second ordinary should not grant the favor unless he has obtained the reasons for the denial from the prior ordinary.

§2. A favor which has been denied by a vicar general or by an episcopal vicar cannot be granted validly by another vicar of the same bishop even if the reasons for the denial have been obtained from the vicar who denied it.

§3. A favor which has been denied by a vicar general or by an episcopal vicar and later procured from the diocesan bishop without mentioning this denial is invalid. But a favor which has been denied by the diocesan bishop cannot be procured validly from his vicar general or episcopal vicar without the consent of the bishop, even if mention of the denial has been made.

Can. 66 — A rescript does not become invalid due to an error in the name of the person to whom it is given or from whom it is issued or an error in the name of the place where the person is staying or the matter being treated provided that there is no doubt concerning the identity of the person or the matter in question in the judgment of the ordinary.

Can. 67 — §1. If it happens that two contradictory rescripts are procured concerning one and the same thing the special rescript prevails over the general one in those matters which are specifically expressed.

§2. If they are equally special or general in character, the first one issued prevails over the one issued later, unless express mention of the prior one is made in the second one or unless the person who had procured the prior rescript had not used it out of deceit or notable negligence.

§3. When there is doubt about whether a rescript is valid or not, recourse should be had to the one issuing it.

Can. 68 — A rescript of the Apostolic See in which no executor is given must be presented to the ordinary of the person who obtained it only when such action is ordered by the rescript itself, or when it deals with public affairs, or when it is necessary to prove that the attached conditions have been satisfied.

Can. 69 — When no definite time is set for its presentation, a rescript can be presented to its executor at any time whatsoever, provided fraud and deceit are absent.

Can. 70 — If the granting of a rescript is entrusted to an executor, the

ipsius est pro suo prudenti arbitrio et conscientia gratiam concedere vel denegare.

Can. 71 – Nemo uti tenetur rescripto in sui dumtaxat favorem concesso, nisi aliunde obligatione canonica ad hoc teneatur.

Can. 72 – Rescripta ab Apostolica Sede concessa, quae exspiraverint, ab Episcopo dioecesano iusta de causa semel prorogari possunt, non tamen ultra tres menses.

Can. 73 – Per legem contrariam nulla rescripta revocantur, nisi aliud in ipsa lege caveatur.

Can. 74 – Quamvis gratia oretenus sibi concessa quis in foro interno uti possit, tenetur illam pro foro externo probare, quoties id legitime ab eo petatur.

Can. 75 – Si rescriptum contineat privilegium vel dispensationem, serventur insuper praescripta canonum qui sequuntur.

CAPUT IV

DE PRIVILEGIIS

Can. 76 – § 1. Privilegium, seu gratia in favorem certarum personarum sive physicarum sive iuridicarum per peculiarem actum facta, concedi potest a legislatore necnon ab auctoritate exsecutiva cui legislator hanc potestatem concesserit.

§ 2. Possessio centenaria vel immemorabilis praesumptionem inducit concessi privilegii.

Can. 77 – Privilegium interpretandum est ad normam can. 36, § 1; sed ea semper adhibenda est interpretatio, qua privilegio aucti aliquam revera gratiam consequantur.

Can. 78 – § 1. Privilegium praesumitur perpetuum, nisi contrarium probetur.

§ 2. Privilegium personale, quod scilicet personam sequitur, cum ipsa extinguitur.

§ 3. Privilegium reale cessat per absolutum rei vel loci interitum; privilegium vero locale, si locus intra quinquaginta annos restituatur, reviviscit.

Can. 79 – Privilegium cessat per revocationem competentis auctoritatis ad normam can. 47, firmo praescripto can. 46.

favor can be granted or denied in accord with the executor's prudent judgment and conscience.

Can. 71 — No one is bound to use a rescript granted for one's own advantage alone, unless one is otherwise bound to do so by a canonical obligation.

Can. 72 — Rescripts granted by the Apostolic See which have expired can be extended once by a diocesan bishop for a just reason, but not beyond three months.

Can. 73 — No rescripts are revoked by a contrary law unless it is provided otherwise in the law itself.

Can. 74 — Although a person can use in the internal forum a favor granted only orally, the person is bound to prove it for the external forum whenever this is legitimately requested.

Can. 75 — If a rescript contains a privilege or a dispensation, the prescriptions of the following canons are likewise to be observed.

CHAPTER IV
PRIVILEGES

Can. 76 — §1. A privilege or a favor granted to certain persons, whether physical or juridical, by means of a special act can be granted by the legislator as well as by an executive authority to whom the legislator has granted this power.

§2. Centenary or immemorial possession induces a presumption that a privilege has been granted.

Can. 77 — A privilege is to be interpreted in accord with the norm of can. 36, §1, but that interpretation is always to be used so that the beneficiaries of a privilege actually obtain some favor.

Can. 78 — §1. A privilege is presumed to be perpetual unless the contrary is proved.

§2. A personal privilege, namely one which follows the person, ceases with the person's death.

§3. A real privilege ceases with the complete destruction of the thing or place; but a local privilege revives if the place is restored within fifty years.

Can. 79 — A privilege ceases through its revocation by competent authority in accord with the norm of can. 47, with due regard for the prescription of can. 46.

Can. 80 – § 1. Nullum privilegium per renuntiationem cessat, nisi haec a competenti auctoritate fuerit acceptata.

§ 2. Privilegio in sui dumtaxat favorem concesso quaevis persona physica renuntiare potest.

§ 3. Privilegio concesso alicui personae iuridicae, aut ratione dignitatis loci vel rei, singulae personae renuntiare nequeunt; nec ipsi personae iuridicae integrum est privilegio sibi concesso renuntiare, si renuntiatio cedat in Ecclesiae aliorumve praeiudicium.

Can. 81 – Resoluto iure concedentis, privilegium non extinguitur, nisi datum fuerit cum clausula *ad beneplacitum nostrum* vel alia aequipollenti.

Can. 82 – Per non usum vel per usum contrarium privilegium aliis haud onerosum non cessat; quod vero in aliorum gravamen cedit, amittitur, si accedat legitima praescriptio.

Can. 83 – § 1. Cessat privilegium elapso tempore vel expleto numero casuum pro quibus concessum fuit, firmo praescripto can. 142, § 2.

§ 2. Cessat quoque, si temporis progressu rerum adiuncta ita iudicio auctoritatis competentis immutata sint, ut noxium evaserit aut eius usus illicitus fiat.

Can. 84 – Qui abutitur potestate sibi ex privilegio data, privilegio ipso privari meretur; quare, Ordinarius, frustra monito privilegiario, graviter abutentem privet privilegio quod ipse concessit; quod si privilegium concessum fuerit ab Apostolica Sede, eandem Ordinarius certiorem facere tenetur.

CAPUT V

DE DISPENSATIONIBUS

Can. 85 – Dispensatio, seu legis mere ecclesiasticae in casu particulari relaxatio, concedi potest ab iis qui potestate gaudent exsecutiva intra limites suae competentiae, necnon ab illis quibus potestas dispensandi explicite vel implicite competit sive ipso iure sive vi legitimae delegationis.

Can. 86 – Dispensationi obnoxiae non sunt leges quatenus ea definiunt, quae institutorum aut actuum iuridicorum essentialiter sunt constitutiva.

Can. 87 – § 1. Episcopus dioecesanus fideles, quoties id ad eorundem spirituale bonum conferre iudicet, dispensare valet in legibus disciplinaribus tam universalibus quam particularibus pro suo territo-

Can. 80 — §1. No privilege ceases through renunciation unless the renunciation has been accepted by the competent authority.

§2. Any physical person can renounce a privilege granted on behalf of that person alone.

§3. Individual persons cannot renounce a privilege which has been granted to some juridic person or has been granted by reason of the dignity of a place or thing; nor is a juridic person competent to renounce a privilege granted to it if its renunciation prejudices the Church or others.

Can. 81 — A privilege is not terminated with the termination of the authority of the one issuing it unless it has been granted with the provision *ad beneplacitum nostrum* or some equivalent terminology.

Can. 82 — A privilege which is not a burden on others does not cease through non-usage or through contrary usage; but if it is to the disadvantage of others, it is lost through legitimate prescription.

Can. 83 — §1. A privilege ceases through the lapse of the period of time or after the completion of the number of cases for which it was granted, with due regard for the provision of can. 142, §2.

§2. A privilege also ceases if in the course of time circumstances change to such a degree that the privilege becomes harmful or its use illicit in the judgment of the competent authority.

Can. 84 — Whoever abuses the power given by privilege deserves to be deprived of it; therefore, the ordinary, after having admonished the grantee in vain, may deprive the one who seriously abuses it of a privilege which he himself had granted; if, however, the privilege was granted by the Apostolic See, the ordinary is bound to notify the Apostolic See.

CHAPTER V

DISPENSATIONS

Can. 85 — A dispensation, or the relaxation of a merely ecclesiastical law in a particular case, can be granted by those who enjoy executive power, within the limits of their competence, as well as by those to whom the power of dispensing has been given explicitly or implicitly either by the law itself or by lawful delegation.

Can. 86 — Laws, to the extent that they define that which essentially constitutes juridical institutes or acts, are not subject to dispensation.

Can. 87 — §1. As often as he judges that a dispensation will contribute to the spiritual good of the faithful, the diocesan bishop can dispense from both universal and particular disciplinary laws established for his territory or for

rio vel suis subditis a suprema Ecclesiae auctoritate latis, non tamen in legibus processualibus aut poenalibus, nec in iis quarum dispensatio Apostolicae Sedi aliive auctoritati specialiter reservatur.

§ 2. Si difficilis sit recursus ad Sanctam Sedem et simul in mora sit periculum gravis damni, Ordinarius quicumque dispensare valet in iisdem legibus, etiam si dispensatio reservatur Sanctae Sedi, dummodo agatur de dispensatione quam ipsa in iisdem adiunctis concedere solet, firmo praescripto can. 291.

Can. 88 – Ordinarius loci in legibus dioecesanis atque, quoties id ad fidelium bonum conferre iudicet, in legibus a Concilio plenario vel provinciali aut ab Episcoporum conferentia latis dispensare valet.

Can. 89 – Parochus aliique presbyteri aut diaconi a lege universali et particulari dispensare non valent, nisi haec potestas ipsis expresse concessa sit.

Can. 90 – § 1. A lege ecclesiastica ne dispensetur sine iusta et rationabili causa, habita ratione adiunctorum casus et gravitatis legis a qua dispensatur; alias dispensatio illicita est et, nisi ab ipso legislatore eiusve superiore data sit, etiam invalida.

§ 2. Dispensatio in dubio de sufficientia causae valide et licite conceditur.

Can. 91 – Qui gaudet potestate dispensandi eam exercere valet, etiam extra territorium exsistens, in subditos, licet e territorio absentes, atque, nisi contrarium expresse statuatur, in peregrinos quoque in territorio actu degentes, necnon erga seipsum.

Can. 92 – Strictae subest interpretationi non solum dispensatio ad normam can. 36, § 1, sed ipsamet potestas dispensandi ad certum casum concessa.

Can. 93 – Dispensatio quae tractum habet successivum cessat iisdem modis quibus privilegium, necnon certa ac totali cessatione causae motivae.

TITULUS V
DE STATUTIS ET ORDINIBUS

Can. 94 – § 1. Statuta, sensu proprio, sunt ordinationes quae in universitatibus sive personarum sive rerum ad normam iuris conduntur, et quibus definiuntur earundem finis, constitutio, regimen atque agendi rationes.

his subjects by the supreme authority of the Church. He cannot dispense, however, from procedural or penal laws or from those laws whose dispensation is especially reserved to the Apostolic See or to another authority.

§2. If recourse to the Holy See is difficult and, at the same time, there is danger of grave harm in delay, any ordinary can dispense from the above-mentioned disciplinary laws, even if the dispensation is reserved to the Holy See, provided that the matter concerns a dispensation which the Holy See is wont to grant under the same circumstances with due regard for the prescription of can. 291.

Can. 88 — The local ordinary can dispense from diocesan laws and, as often as he judges that a dispensation will contribute to the good of the faithful, from laws passed by a plenary or provincial council or by the conference of bishops.

Can. 89 — The pastor and other presbyters or deacons cannot dispense from a universal or particular law unless this power has been expressly granted to them.

Can. 90 — §1. A dispensation from an ecclesiastical law may not be granted without a just and reasonable cause and without taking into consideration the circumstances of the case and the gravity of the law from which the dispensation is to be given; otherwise the dispensation is illicit and, unless it is given by the legislator himself or his superior, it is also invalid.

§2. When there is a doubt about the sufficiency of the cause, a dispensation is granted validly and licitly.

Can. 91 — One who possesses the power of dispensing can exercise it, even though he is outside his own territory, for his subjects, though they are absent from his territory, and also, unless the contrary is expressly established, for travelers actually present in his territory, as well as on his own behalf.

Can. 92 — A strict interpretation must be given not only to a dispensation according to can. 36, §1, but also to the very power of dispensing granted for a particular case.

Can. 93 — A dispensation which has successive applications ceases in the same ways as a privilege and also because of the certain and complete cessation of the motivating cause.

TITLE V

STATUTES AND RULES OF ORDER

Can. 94 — §1. Statutes in the proper sense are ordinances which are established in aggregates of persons or of things according to the norm of law and by which their purpose, constitution, government and operation are defined.

§ 2. Statutis universitatis personarum obligantur solae personae quae legitime eiusdem membra sunt; statutis rerum universitatis, ii qui eiusdem moderamen curant.

§ 3. Quae statutorum praescripta vi potestatis legislativae condita et promulgata sunt, reguntur praescriptis canonum de legibus.

Can. 95 – § 1. Ordines sunt regulae seu normae quae servari debent in personarum conventibus, sive ab auctoritate ecclesiastica indictis sive a christifidelibus libere convocatis, necnon aliis in celebrationibus, et quibus definiuntur quae ad constitutionem, moderamen et rerum agendarum rationes pertinent.

§ 2. In conventibus celebrationibusve, ii regulis ordinis tenentur, qui in iisdem partem habent.

TITULUS VI
DE PERSONIS PHYSICIS ET IURIDICIS

CAPUT I
DE PERSONARUM PHYSICARUM CONDICIONE CANONICA

Can. 96 – Baptismo homo Ecclesiae Christi incorporatur et in eadem constituitur persona, cum officiis et iuribus quae christianis, attenta quidem eorum condicione, sunt propria, quatenus in ecclesiastica sunt communione et nisi obstet lata legitime sanctio.

Can. 97 – § 1. Persona quae duodevigesimum aetatis annum explevit, maior est; infra hanc aetatem, minor.

§ 2. Minor, ante plenum septennium, dicitur infans et censetur non sui compos, expleto autem septennio, usum rationis habere praesumitur.

Can. 98 – § 1. Persona maior plenum habet suorum iurium exercitium.

§ 2. Persona minor in exercitio suorum iurium potestati obnoxia manet parentum vel tutorum, iis exceptis in quibus minores lege divina aut iure canonico ab eorum potestate exempti sunt; ad constitutionem tutorum eorumque potestatem quod attinet, serventur praescripta iuris civilis, nisi iure canonico aliud caveatur, aut Episcopus dioecesanus in certis casibus iusta de causa per nominationem alius tutoris providendum aestimaverit.

Can. 99 – Quicumque usu rationis habitu caret, censetur non sui compos et infantibus assimilatur.

§2. The statutes of an aggregate of persons bind only its legitimate members; the statutes of an aggregate of things bind only those who govern it.

§3. Those prescriptions of statutes which were issued and promulgated in virtue of legislative power are governed by the prescriptions of the canons on laws.

Can. 95 — §1. Rules of order (*ordines*) are rules or norms to be observed in assemblies of persons, whether the assemblies were convoked by ecclesiastical authority or called together freely by the Christian faithful or are other kinds of celebrations. These rules define the constitution, government and procedures of the assembly.

§2. In assemblies or celebrations the rules of order oblige all those who participate.

TITLE VI
PHYSICAL AND JURIDIC PERSONS

CHAPTER I
THE CANONICAL CONDITION OF PHYSICAL PERSONS

Can. 96 — By baptism one is incorporated into the Church of Christ and is constituted a person in it with duties and rights which are proper to Christians, in keeping with their condition, to the extent that they are in ecclesiastical communion and unless a legitimately issued sanction stands in the way.

Can. 97 — §1. A person who has completed the eighteenth year of age is an adult, below this age, a person is a minor.

§2. Before the completion of the seventh year a minor is called to be an infant and is held to be incompetent (*non sui compos*); with the completion of the seventh year one is presumed to have the use of reason.

Can. 98 — §1. An adult person enjoys the full use of his or her rights.

§2. A minor person remains subject to the authority of parents or guardians in the exercise of his or her rights, with the exception of those areas in which minors by divine law or canon law are exempt from their power; with reference to the designation of guardians and their authority, the prescriptions of the civil law are to be followed unless canon law determines otherwise or unless the diocesan bishop in certain cases for a just cause has decided to provide otherwise through the designation of some other guardian.

Can. 99 — Whoever habitually lacks the use of reason is held to be incompetent (*non sui compos*) and is equated with infants.

Can. 100 – Persona dicitur : *incola,* in loco ubi est eius domicilium ; *advena,* in loco ubi quasi-domicilium habet; *peregrinus,* si versetur extra domicilium et quasi-domicilium quod adhuc retinet; *vagus,* si nullibi domicilium habeat vel quasi-domicilium.

Can. 101 – § 1. Locus originis filii, etiam neophyti, est ille in quo cum filius natus est, domicilium, aut, eo deficiente, quasi-domicilium habuerunt parentes vel, si parentes non habuerint idem domicilium vel quasi-domicilium, mater.

§ 2. Si agatur de filio vagorum, locus originis est ipsemet nativitatis locus ; si de exposito, est locus in quo inventus est.

Can. 102 – § 1. Domicilium acquiritur ea in territorio alicuius paroeciae aut saltem dioecesis commoratione, quae aut coniuncta sit cum animo ibi perpetuo manendi si nihil inde avocet, aut ad quinquennium completum sit protracta.

§ 2. Quasi-domicilium acquiritur ea commoratione in territorio alicuius paroeciae aut saltem dioecesis, quae aut coniuncta sit cum animo ibi manendi saltem per tres menses si nihil inde avocet, aut ad tres menses reapse sit protracta.

§ 3. Domicilium vel quasi-domicilium in territorio paroeciae dicitur paroeciale ; in territorio dioecesis, etsi non in paroecia, dioecesanum.

Can. 103 – Sodales institutorum religiosorum et societatum vitae apostolicae domicilium acquirunt in loco ubi sita est domus cui adscribuntur ; quasi-domicilium in domo ubi, ad normam can. 102, § 2, commorantur.

Can. 104 – Coniuges commune habeant domicilium vel quasi-domicilium ; legitimae separationis ratione vel alia iusta de causa, uterque habere potest proprium domicilium vel quasi-domicilium.

Can. 105 – § 1. Minor necessario retinet domicilium et quasi-domicilium illius, cuius potestati subicitur. Infantia egressus potest etiam quasi-domicilium proprium acquirere ; atque legitime ad normam iuris civilis emancipatus, etiam proprium domicilium.

§ 2. Quicumque alia ratione quam minoritate, in tutelam vel curatelam legitime traditus est alterius, domicilium et quasi-domicilium habet tutoris vel curatoris.

Can. 106 – Domicilium et quasi-domicilium amittitur discessione a loco cum animo non revertendi, salvo praescripto can. 105.

Can. 100 — A person is called a resident (*incola*) in the place where one has a domicile; a temporary resident (*advena*) in the place where one has a quasi-domicile; a traveler (*peregrinus*) when outside the place of domicile or quasi-domicile which is still retained; and a transient (*vagus*) if one has neither domicile nor quasi-domicile anywhere.

Can. 101 — §1. The place of origin of a child, even of a neophyte, is that in which the parents had a domicile, or in its absence a quasi-domicile, at the time the child was born or, if the parents did not have the same domicile or quasi-domicile, that of the mother.

§2. In the case of a child of transients, the place of origin is the place of birth; in the case of an abandoned child, it is the place in which the child was found.

Can. 102 — §1. Domicile is acquired by residence within the territory of a certain parish or at least of a diocese, which either is joined with the intention of remaining there permanently unless called away, or has been protracted for five complete years.

§2. Quasi-domicile is acquired by residence within the territory of a certain parish or at least of a diocese which either is joined with the intention of remaining there at least three months, unless called away, or has in fact been protracted for three months.

§3. A domicile or quasi-domicile within the territory of a parish is called parochial; in the territory of a diocese, even though not in a particular parish, it is called diocesan.

Can. 103 — Members of religious institutes and societies of apostolic life acquire a domicile in the place of the house to which they are attached; they acquire a quasi-domicile in the house where they are living according to the norm of can. 102, §2.

Can. 104 — Spouses may have a common domicile or quasi-domicile; either can have a proper domicile or quasi-domicile by reason of a legitimate separation or some other just cause.

Can. 105 — §1. A minor necessarily keeps the domicile or quasi-domicile of the one to whose power he or she is subject. After passing beyond infancy one can also acquire a quasi-domicile of one's own; and one who has been legally emancipated according to the norm of civil law can also acquire a domicile of his or her own.

§2. Whoever has been legally placed under the guardianship or care of another, for some reason other than minority, has the domicile or quasi-domicile of the guardian or curator.

Can. 106 — Domicile and quasi-domicile are lost by departure from the place with the intention of not returning, with due regard for the prescription of can. 105.

Can. 107 – § 1. Tum per domicilium tum per quasi-domicilium suum quisque parochum et Ordinarium sortitur.

§ 2. Proprius vagi parochus vel Ordinarius est parochus vel Ordinarius loci in quo vagus actu commoratur.

§ 3. Illius quoque qui non habet nisi domicilium vel quasi-domicilium dioecesanum, parochus proprius est parochus loci in quo actu commoratur.

Can. 108 – § 1. Consanguinitas computatur per lineas et gradus.

§ 2. In linea recta tot sunt gradus quot generationes, seu quot personae, stipite dempto.

§ 3. In linea obliqua tot sunt gradus quot personae in utraque simul linea, stipite dempto.

Can. 109 – § 1. Affinitas oritur ex matrimonio valido, etsi non consummato, atque viget inter virum et mulieris consanguineos, itemque mulierem inter et viri consanguineos.

§ 2. Ita computatur ut qui sunt consanguinei viri, iidem in eadem linea et gradu sint affines mulieris, et vice versa.

Can. 110 – Filii, qui ad normam legis civilis adoptati sint, habentur ut filii eius vel eorum qui eos adoptaverint.

Can. 111 – § 1. Ecclesiae latinae per receptum baptismum adscribitur filius parentum, qui ad eam pertineant vel, si alteruter ad eam non pertineat, ambo concordi voluntate optaverint ut proles in Ecclesia latina baptizaretur; quodsi concors voluntas desit, Ecclesiae rituali ad quam pater pertinet adscribitur.

§ 2. Quilibet baptizandus qui quartum decimum aetatis annum expleverit, libere potest eligere ut in Ecclesia latina vel in alia Ecclesia rituali sui iuris baptizetur; quo in casu, ipse ad eam Ecclesiam pertinet quam elegerit.

Can. 112 – § 1. Post receptum baptismum, alii Ecclesiae rituali sui iuris adscribuntur:

1° qui licentiam ab Apostolica Sede obtinuerit;

2° coniux qui, in matrimonio ineundo vel eo durante, ad Ecclesiam ritualem sui iuris alterius coniugis se transire declaraverit; matrimonio autem soluto, libere potest ad latinam Ecclesiam redire;

3° filii eorum, de quibus in nn. 1 et 2, ante decimum quartum aetatis annum completum itemque, in matrimonio mixto, filii partis catholicae quae ad aliam Ecclesiam ritualem legitime transierit; adepta vero hac aetate, iidem possunt ad latinam Ecclesiam redire.

Can. 107 — §1. Each person acquires a proper pastor and ordinary through both domicile and quasi-domicile.

§2. The proper pastor or ordinary of a transient is the pastor or ordinary of the place in which the transient is actually staying.

§3. The proper pastor of one who has only a diocesan domicile or quasi-domicile is the pastor of the place in which such a person is actually staying.

Can. 108 — §1. Consanguinity is calculated through lines and degrees.

§2. In the direct line, there are as many degrees as there are generations or persons, not counting the common ancestor.

§3. In the collateral line, there are as many degrees as there are persons in both lines together, not counting the common ancestor.

Can. 109 — §1. Affinity arises from a valid marriage, even if not consummated, and exists between a man and the blood relatives of the woman and between the woman and blood relatives of the man.

§2. It is so calculated that those who are blood relatives of the man are related in the same line and degree by affinity to the woman, and vice versa.

Can. 110 — Children who have been adopted according to the norm of civil law are considered as being the children of the person or persons who have adopted them.

Can. 111 — §1. A child of parents who belong to the Latin Church is ascribed to it by reception of baptism, or, if one or the other parent does not belong to the Latin Church and both parents agree in choosing that the child be baptized in the Latin Church, the child is ascribed to it by reception of baptism; but, if the agreement is lacking, the child is ascribed to the Ritual Church to which the father belongs.

§2. Anyone to be baptized who has completed the fourteenth year of age can freely choose to be baptized in the Latin Church or in another Ritual Church *sui iuris*, and in this case the person belongs to that Church which is chosen.

Can. 112 — §1. After the reception of baptism, the following are enrolled in another Ritual Church *sui iuris*:

1° one who has obtained permission from the Apostolic See;

2° a spouse who declares at the time of marriage or during marriage that he or she is transferring to the Ritual Church *sui iuris* of the other spouse; but when the marriage has ended, that person can freely return to the Latin Church;

3° children of those in nn. 1 and 2 under fourteen complete years of age; and similarly children of a Catholic party in a mixed marriage who legitimately transferred to another Ritual Church. But, when such persons reach fourteen complete years of age, they may return to the Latin Church.

§ 2. Mos, quamvis diuturnus, sacramenta secundum ritum alicuius Ecclesiae ritualis sui iuris recipiendi, non secumfert adscriptionem eidem Ecclesiae.

Caput II

DE PERSONIS IURIDICIS

Can. 113 – § 1. Catholica Ecclesia et Apostolica Sedes, moralis personae rationem habent ex ipsa ordinatione divina.

§ 2. Sunt etiam in Ecclesia, praeter personas physicas, personae iuridicae, subiecta scilicet in iure canonico obligationum et iurium quae ipsarum indoli congruunt.

Can. 114 – § 1. Personae iuridicae constituuntur aut ex ipso iuris praescripto aut ex speciali competentis auctoritatis concessione per decretum data, universitates sive personarum sive rerum in finem missioni Ecclesiae congruentem, qui singulorum finem transcendit, ordinatae.

§ 2. Fines, de quibus in § 1, intelleguntur qui ad opera pietatis, apostolatus vel caritatis sive spiritualis sive temporalis attinent.

§ 3. Auctoritas Ecclesiae competens personalitatem iuridicam ne conferat nisi iis personarum aut rerum universitatibus, quae finem persequuntur reapse utilem atque, omnibus perpensis, mediis gaudent quae sufficere posse praevidentur ad finem praestitutum assequendum.

Can. 115 – § 1. Personae iuridicae in Ecclesia sunt aut universitates personarum aut universitates rerum.

§ 2. Universitas personarum, quae quidem nonnisi ex tribus saltem personis constitui potest, est collegialis, si eius actionem determinant membra, in decisionibus ferendis concurrentia, sive aequali iure sive non, ad normam iuris et statutorum; secus est non collegialis.

§ 3. Universitas rerum seu fundatio autonoma constat bonis seu rebus, sive spiritualibus sive materialibus, eamque, ad normam iuris et statutorum, moderantur sive una vel plures personae physicae sive collegium.

Can. 116 – § 1. Personae iuridicae publicae sunt universitates personarum aut rerum, quae ab ecclesiastica auctoritate competenti constituuntur ut intra fines sibi praestitutos nomine Ecclesiae, ad normam praescriptorum iuris, munus proprium intuitu boni publici ipsis commissum expleant; ceterae personae iuridicae sunt privatae.

§ 2. Personae iuridicae publicae hac personalitate donantur sive ipso iure sive speciali competentis auctoritatis decreto eandem expresse

§2. The custom, however prolonged, of receiving the sacraments according to the rite of another Ritual Church *sui iuris*, does not carry with it enrollment in that Church.

CHAPTER II
JURIDIC PERSONS

Can. 113 — §1. The Catholic Church and the Apostolic See have the nature of a moral person by divine law itself.

§2. Besides physical persons, there are also in the Church juridic persons, that is, subjects in canon law of obligations and rights which correspond to their nature.

Can. 114 — §1. Juridic persons are constituted either by prescription of law or by special concession of the competent authority given through a decree; they are aggregates of persons or of things ordered towards a purpose congruent with the mission of the Church and which transcends the purpose of the individuals that make them up.

§2. The purposes spoken of in §1 are understood as those which pertain to works of piety, of the apostolate or of charity, whether spiritual or temporal.

§3. The competent ecclesiastical authority is not to confer juridic personality except upon those aggregates of persons or things which pursue a truly useful purpose and, all things considered, have resources which are foreseen to be sufficient to achieve their designated end.

Can. 115 — §1. Juridic persons within the Church are aggregates either of persons or of things.

§2. An aggregate of persons, which cannot be constituted unless it consists of at least three persons, is collegial if its members determine its action through participation in making its decisions, whether by equal right or not, according to the norm of law and its own statutes; otherwise it is non-collegial.

§3. An aggregate of things or an autonomous foundation consists of goods or things, whether spiritual or material, and is directed by one or several physical persons or a college according to the norm of law and its statutes.

Can. 116 — §1. Public juridic persons are aggregates of persons or things which are so constituted by the competent ecclesiastical authority that, within the limits set for them in the name of the Church, they fulfill a proper function entrusted to them in view of the common good, in accord with the prescripts of law; other juridic persons are private.

§2. Public juridic persons are given this personality either through the law itself or by a special decree of the competent authority expressly granting it;

concedenti; personae iuridicae privatae hac personalitate donantur tantum per speciale competentis auctoritatis decretum eandem personalitatem expresse concedens.

Can. 117 – Nulla personarum vel rerum universitas personalitatem iuridicam obtinere intendens, eandem consequi valet nisi ipsius statuta a competenti auctoritate sint probata.

Can. 118 – Personam iuridicam publicam repraesentant, eius nomine agentes, ii quibus iure universali vel particulari aut propriis statutis haec competentia agnoscitur; personam iuridicam privatam, ii quibus eadem competentia per statuta tribuitur.

Can. 119 – Ad actus collegiales quod attinet, nisi iure vel statutis aliud caveatur:

1° si agatur de electionibus, id vim habet iuris, quod, praesente quidem maiore parte eorum qui convocari debent, placuerit parti absolute maiori eorum qui sunt praesentes; post duo inefficacia scrutinia, suffragatio fiat super duobus candidatis qui maiorem suffragiorum partem obtinuerint, vel, si sunt plures, super duobus aetate senioribus; post tertium scrutinium, si paritas maneat, ille electus habeatur qui senior sit aetate;

2° si agatur de aliis negotiis, id vim habet iuris, quod, praesente quidem maiore parte eorum qui convocari debent, placuerit parti absolute maiori eorum qui sunt praesentes; quod si post duo scrutinia suffragia aequalia fuerint, praeses suo voto paritatem dirimere potest;

3° quod autem omnes uti singulos tangit, ab omnibus approbari debet.

Can. 120 – § 1. Persona iuridica natura sua perpetua est; extinguitur tamen si a competenti auctoritate legitime supprimatur aut per centum annorum spatium agere desierit; persona iuridica privata insuper extinguitur, si ipsa consociatio ad normam statutorum dissolvatur, aut si, de iudicio auctoritatis competentis, ipsa fundatio ad normam statutorum esse desierit.

§ 2. Si vel unum ex personae iuridicae collegialis membris supersit, et personarum universitas secundum statuta esse non desierit, exercitium omnium iurium universitatis illi membro competit.

Can. 121 – Si universitates sive personarum sive rerum, quae sunt personae iuridicae publicae, ita coniungantur ut ex iisdem una constituatur universitas personalitate iuridica et ipsa pollens, nova haec persona iuridica bona iuraque patrimonialia prioribus propria obtinet atque onera suscipit, quibus eaedem gravabantur; ad destinationem autem praesertim bonorum et ad onerum adimpletionem quod attinet,

private juridic persons are given this personality only through a special decree of the competent authority expressly granting this personality.

Can. 117 — No aggregate of persons or things, intending to obtain juridic personality, can achieve it unless its statutes have been approved by the competent authority.

Can. 118 — They alone represent a public juridic person and act in its name who are acknowledged to have this competence either by universal or particular law or by its own statutes; they represent a private juridic person who have been given this competency by statute.

Can. 119 — With regard to collegial acts, unless provision is made otherwise by law or statutes:

1° if it is a question of elections, that action has the force of law which, when a majority of those who must be convoked are present, receives the approval of an absolute majority of those who are present; after two indecisive ballots, the choice is between the two candidates who have obtained the greater number of the votes, or, if there are several (with the same numbers), upon the two who are senior in age; after a third ballot, if the tie remains, the one who is the senior in age is considered elected;

2° if it is a question of other matters, that action will have the force of law which, when a majority of those who must be convoked are present, receives the approval of an absolute majority of those who are present; if after two ballots it is a tie vote, the presiding officer can break the tie by his or her vote;

3° what touches all as individuals must be approved by all.

Can. 120 — §1. A juridic person is of its nature perpetual; nevertheless it is extinguished if it is legitimately suppressed by a competent authority or has ceased activity for a hundred years; a private juridic person is furthermore extinguished if the association is dissolved according to the norm of its statutes, or if, in the judgment of the competent authority, the foundation itself has ceased to exist according to the norm of its statutes.

§2. If even one member of a collegial juridic person survives, and the aggregate of persons has not ceased to exist according to its statutes, the exercise of all of the rights of the aggregate devolves upon that one member.

Can. 121 — If aggregates, whether of persons or of things, which are public juridic persons, are so joined that out of all of them one aggregate is constituted, itself enjoying juridic personality, this new juridic person obtains the goods and patrimonial rights proper to the prior ones, and it also takes upon itself the obligations with which they have been burdened; however, the intention of the founders and donors and acquired rights must be respected,

fundatorum oblatorumque voluntas atque iura quaesita salva esse debent.

Can. 122 – Si universitas, quae gaudet personalitate iuridica publica, ita dividatur ut aut illius pars alii personae iuridicae uniatur aut ex parte dismembrata distincta persona iuridica publica erigatur, auctoritas ecclesiastica, cui divisio competat, curare debet per se vel per exsecutorem, servatis quidem in primis tum fundatorum ac oblatorum voluntate tum iuribus quaesitis tum probatis statutis :

1° ut communia, quae dividi possunt, bona atque iura patrimonialia necnon aes alienum aliaque onera dividantur inter personas iuridicas, de quibus agitur, debita cum proportione ex aequo et bono, ratione habita omnium adiunctorum et necessitatum utriusque ;

2° ut usus et ususfructus communium bonorum, quae divisioni obnoxia non sunt, utrique personae iuridicae cedant, oneraque iisdem propria utrique imponantur, servata item debita proportione ex aequo et bono definienda.

Can. 123 – Extincta persona iuridica publica, destinatio eiusdem bonorum iuriumque patrimonialium itemque onerum regitur iure et statutis, quae, si sileant, obveniunt personae iuridicae immediate superiori, salvis semper fundatorum vel oblatorum voluntate necnon iuribus quaesitis ; extincta persona iuridica privata, eiusdem bonorum et onerum destinatio propriis statutis regitur.

TITULUS VII
DE ACTIBUS IURIDICIS

Can. 124 – § 1. Ad validitatem actus iuridici requiritur ut a persona habili sit positus, atque in eodem adsint quae actum ipsum essentialiter constituunt, necnon sollemnia et requisita iure ad validitatem actus imposita.

§ 2. Actus iuridicus quoad sua elementa externa rite positus praesumitur validus.

Can. 125 – § 1. Actus positus ex vi ab extrinseco personae illata, cui ipsa nequaquam resistere potuit, pro infecto habetur.

§ 2. Actus positus ex metu gravi, iniuste incusso, aut ex dolo, valet, nisi aliud iure caveatur ; sed potest per sententiam iudicis rescindi, sive ad instantiam partis laesae eiusve in iure successorum sive ex officio.

particularly as regards the allocation of goods and the fulfillment of obligations.

Can. 122 — If an aggregate which has public juridic personality is so to be divided so that a part of it is united to another public juridic person, or that a distinct public juridic person is established from the separated part, it is the obligation of the ecclesiastical authority which is competent to make the division, having observed before all else the intention of founders and donors, acquired rights, and approved statutes, to see to it personally or through an executor:

1° that things held in common which are capable of division, both goods and patrimonial rights as well as the debts and other obligations, are divided among the juridic persons concerned with due proportion based on equity and justice, taking into account all the circumstances and the needs of each;

2° that the use and usufruct of those common goods which are not susceptible to division accrue to each juridic person, and that the obligations proper to them fall upon each, to be determined in like manner with proper regard for due proportion based on equity and justice.

Can. 123 — Upon the extinction of a public juridic person, the allocation of its goods, patrimonial rights and obligations, is ruled by law and by statutes; if these give no indication, they go to the juridic person immediately superior, with due regard for the will of the founders or donors and for acquired rights; upon the extinction of a private juridic person the allocation of its goods and obligations is regulated by its own statutes.

TITLE VII
JURIDIC ACTS

Can. 124 — §1. For the validity of a juridic act it is required that it be placed by a person capable of placing it, and that it include those elements which essentially constitute it as well as the formalities and requisites imposed by law for the validity of the act.

§2. A juridic act correctly placed with respect to its external elements is presumed to be valid.

Can. 125 — §1. An act placed because of extrinsic force brought to bear upon a person, which the person was not in any way able to resist, is considered not to have been placed.

§2. An act placed because of grave fear, which has been unjustly inflicted, or because of fraud is valid unless the law makes some other provision; but such an act can be rescinded by the decision of a judge, either at the instance of an injured party, or that party's successors in law, or ex officio.

Can. 126 – Actus positus ex ignorantia aut ex errore, qui versetur circa id quod eius substantiam constituit, aut qui recidit in condicionem *sine qua non,* irritus est; secus valet, nisi aliud iure caveatur, sed actus ex ignorantia aut ex errore initus locum dare potest actioni rescissoriae ad normam iuris.

Can. 127 – § 1. Cum iure statuatur ad actus ponendos Superiorem indigere consensu aut consilio alicuius collegii vel personarum coetus, convocari debet collegium vel coetus ad normam can. 166, nisi, cum agatur de consilio tantum exquirendo, aliter iure particulari aut proprio cautum sit; ut autem actus valeant requiritur ut obtineatur consensus partis absolute maioris eorum qui sunt praesentes aut omnium exquiratur consilium.

§ 2. Cum iure statuatur ad actus ponendos Superiorem indigere consensu aut consilio aliquarum personarum, uti singularum :

1° si consensus exigatur, invalidus est actus Superioris consensum earum personarum non exquirentis aut contra earum vel alicuius votum agentis ;

2° si consilium exigatur, invalidus est actus Superioris easdem personas non audientis ; Superior, licet nulla obligatione teneatur accedendi, ad earundem votum, etsi concors, tamen sine praevalenti ratione, suo iudicio aestimanda, ab earundem voto, praesertim concordi, ne discedat.

§ 3. Omnes quorum consensus aut consilium requiritur, obligatione tenentur sententiam suam sincere proferendi atque, si negotiorum gravitas id postulat, secretum sedulo servandi; quae quidem obligatio a Superiore urgeri potest.

Can. 128 – Quicumque illegitime actu iuridico, immo quovis alio actu dolo vel culpa posito, alteri damnum infert, obligatione tenetur damnum illatum reparandi.

TITULUS VIII
DE POTESTATE REGIMINIS

Can. 129 – § 1. Potestatis regiminis, quae quidem ex divina institutione est in Ecclesia et etiam potestas iurisdictionis vocatur, ad normam praescriptorum iuris, habiles sunt qui ordine sacro sunt insigniti.

§ 2. In exercitio eiusdem potestatis, christifideles laici ad normam iuris cooperari possunt.

Can. 130 – Potestas regiminis de se exercetur pro foro externo,

Can. 126 — An act placed because of ignorance or error concerning an element which constitutes its substance or which amounts to a condition *sine qua non* is invalid; otherwise it is valid, unless the law makes some other provision. However, an act placed out of ignorance or error can be the occasion for a recissory action in accord with the norm of law.

Can. 127 — §1. When the law determines that in order to place certain acts a superior requires the consent or counsel of a college or group of persons, the college or group must be convoked according to the norm of can. 166, unless particular or proper law provides otherwise when counsel only is to be sought; however, for such acts to be valid it is required that the consent of an absolute majority of those present be obtained or that the counsel of all who are present be sought.

§2. When the law determines that a superior in order to place certain acts requires the consent or the counsel of certain persons as individuals:

1° if consent is required, the action of the superior is invalid if the superior does not seek the consent of those persons or acts contrary to the opinion of the persons or person;

2° if counsel is required, the action of the superior is invalid if the superior does not listen to those persons; although in no way obliged to accede to their recommendation, even if it be unanimous, nevertheless the superior should not act contrary to it, especially when there is a consensus, unless there be a reason which, in the superior's judgment, is overriding.

§3. All whose consent or counsel is required are obliged to offer their opinion sincerely and, if the seriousness of the matter requires it, to observe secrecy sedulously, and this obligation can be insisted upon by the superior.

Can. 128 — Anyone who unlawfully inflicts damage upon someone by a juridic act, or indeed by any other act placed with malice or culpability, is obliged to compensate for the damage inflicted.

TITLE VIII
THE POWER OF GOVERNANCE

Can. 129 — §1. In accord with the prescriptions of law, those who have received sacred orders are capable of the power of governance, which exists in the Church by divine institution and is also called the power of jurisdiction.

§2. Lay members of the Christian faithful can cooperate in the exercise of this power in accord with the norm of law.

Can. 130 — The power of governance is normally exercised in the exter-

quandoque tamen pro solo foro interno, ita quidem ut effectus quos eius exercitium natum est habere pro foro externo, in hoc foro non recognoscantur, nisi quatenus id determinatis pro casibus iure statuatur.

Can. 131 – § 1. Potestas regiminis ordinaria ea est, quae ipso iure alicui officio adnectitur; delegata, quae ipsi personae non mediante officio conceditur.

§ 2. Potestas regiminis ordinaria potest esse sive propria sive vicaria.

§ 3. Ei qui delegatum se asserit, onus probandae delegationis incumbit.

Can. 132 – § 1. Facultates habituales reguntur praescriptis de potestate delegata.

§ 2. Attamen nisi in eius concessione aliud expresse caveatur aut electa sit industria personae, facultas habitualis Ordinario concessa non perimitur resoluto iure Ordinarii cui concessa est, etiamsi ipse eam exsequi coeperit, sed transit ad quemvis Ordinarium qui ipsi in regimine succedit.

Can. 133 – § 1. Delegatus qui sive circa res sive circa personas mandati sui fines excedit, nihil agit.

§ 2. Fines sui mandati excedere non intellegitur delegatus qui alio modo ac in mandato determinatur, ea peragit ad quae delegatus est, nisi modus ab ipso delegante ad validitatem fuerit praescriptus.

Can. 134 – § 1. Nomine Ordinarii in iure intelleguntur, praeter Romanum Pontificem, Episcopi dioecesani aliique qui, etsi ad interim tantum, praepositi sunt alicui Ecclesiae particulari vel communitati eidem aequiparatae ad normam can. 368, necnon qui in iisdem generali gaudent potestate exsecutiva ordinaria, nempe Vicarii generales et episcopales; itemque, pro suis sodalibus, Superiores maiores clericalium institutorum religiosorum iuris pontificii et clericalium societatum vitae apostolicae iuris pontificii, qui ordinaria saltem potestate exsecutiva pollent.

§ 2. Nomine Ordinarii loci intelleguntur omnes qui in § 1 recensentur, exceptis Superioribus institutorum religiosorum et societatum vitae apostolicae.

§ 3. Quae in canonibus nominatim Episcopo dioecesano, in ambitu potestatis exsecutivae tribuuntur, intelleguntur competere dumtaxat Episcopo dioecesano aliisque ipsi in can. 381, § 2 aequiparatis, exclusis Vicario generali et episcopali, nisi de speciali mandato.

Can. 135 – § 1. Potestas regiminis distinguitur in legislativam, ex-

nal forum, but sometimes it is exercised in the internal forum only, but in such a way that the effects which its exercise normally has in the external forum are not acknowledged in this forum except as is established by law in certain instances.

Can. 131 — §1. The ordinary power of governance is that which is joined to a certain office by the law itself; delegated power is that which is granted to a person, but not by means of an office.

§2. The ordinary power of governance can be either proper or vicarious.

§3. The burden of proving delegation rests with the person who claims to have been delegated.

Can. 132 — §1. Habitual faculties are governed by the prescriptions for delegated power.

§2. However, unless otherwise expressly provided in the grant of faculties or unless an ordinary was chosen for his personal qualifications, a habitual faculty granted to an ordinary is not withdrawn when that ordinary's authority ceases, even though he has started to execute the faculty, but it transfers to any ordinary who succeeds him in governance.

Can. 133 — §1. A delegate who exceeds the limits of the mandate with respect to matters or to persons acts invalidly.

§2. A delegate who acts in delegated matters in a manner other than that determined in the mandate is not considered to have exceeded the limits of the mandate unless the manner of acting was prescribed for validity by the one delegating.

Can. 134 — §1. By the title of ordinary in the law are understood, in addition to the Roman Pontiff, diocesan bishops and others who, even if only on an interim basis, have been placed over a particular church or over a community which is equivalent to it according to the norm of can. 368, as well as those who possess ordinary general executive power in said churches and communities, namely vicars general and episcopal vicars; and likewise for their own members the major superiors of clerical religious institutes of pontifical right and of clerical societies of apostolic life of pontifical right, who possess at least ordinary executive power.

§2. By the title of local ordinary are understood all those mentioned in §1, except superiors of religious institutes and societies of apostolic life.

§3. Whatever things in the canons in the realm of executive power which are attributed by name to the diocesan bishop are understood to pertain only to the diocesan bishop and to others equivalent to him in can. 381, §2, excluding the vicar general and the episcopal vicar unless they have received a special mandate.

Can. 135 — §1. The power of governance is distinguished as legislative,

secutivam et iudicialem.

§ 2. Potestas legislativa exercenda est modo iure praescripto, et ea qua in Ecclesia gaudet legislator infra auctoritatem supremam, valide delegari nequit, nisi aliud iure explicite caveatur; a legislatore inferiore lex iuri superiori contraria valide ferri nequit.

§ 3. Potestas iudicialis, qua gaudent iudices aut collegia iudicialia, exercenda est modo iure praescripto, et delegari nequit, nisi ad actus cuivis decreto aut sententiae praeparatorios perficiendos.

§ 4. Ad potestatis exsecutivae exercitium quod attinet, serventur praescripta canonum qui sequuntur.

Can. 136 – Potestatem exsecutivam aliquis, licet extra territorium exsistens, exercere valet in subditos, etiam a territorio absentes, nisi aliud ex rei natura aut ex iuris praescripto constet; in peregrinos in territorio actu degentes, si agatur de favoribus concedendis aut de exsecutioni mandandis sive legibus universalibus sive legibus particularibus, quibus ipsi ad normam can. 13, § 2, n. 2 tenentur.

Can. 137 – § 1. Potestas exsecutiva ordinaria delegari potest tum ad actum tum ad universitatem casuum, nisi aliud iure expresse caveatur.

§ 2. Potestas exsecutiva ab Apostolica Sede delegata subdelegari potest sive ad actum sive ad universitatem casuum, nisi electa fuerit industria personae aut subdelegatio fuerit expresse prohibita.

§ 3. Potestas exsecutiva delegata ab alia auctoritate potestatem ordinariam habente, si ad universitatem casuum delegata sit, in singulis tantum casibus subdelegari potest; si vero ad actum aut ad actus determinatos delegata sit, subdelegari nequit, nisi de expressa delegantis concessione.

§ 4. Nulla potestas subdelegata iterum subdelegari potest, nisi id expresse a delegante concessum fuerit.

Can. 138 – Potestas exsecutiva ordinaria necnon potestas ad universitatem casuum delegata, late interpretanda est, alia vero quaelibet stricte; cui tamen delegata potestas est, ea quoque intelleguntur concessa sine quibus eadem potestas exerceri nequit.

Can. 139 – § 1. Nisi aliud iure statuatur, eo quod quis aliquam auctoritatem, etiam superiorem, competentem adeat, non suspenditur alius auctoritatis competentis exsecutiva potestas, sive haec ordinaria est sive delegata.

§ 2. Causae tamen ad superiorem auctoritatem delatae ne se immisceat inferior, nisi ex gravi urgentique causa; quo in casu statim superiorem de re moneat.

executive and judicial.

§2. Legislative power is to be exercised in the manner prescribed by law, and that legislative power in the Church possessed by a legislator below the highest authority cannot be validly delegated, unless otherwise explicitly provided for in the law; a law which is contrary to a higher law cannot be validly enacted by a lower level legislator.

§3. Judicial power, which is possessed by judges or judicial colleges, is to be exercised in the manner prescribed by law and cannot be delegated, except to carry out acts which are preparatory to a decree or a decision.

§4. In regard to the exercise of executive power, the prescriptions of the following canons are to be observed.

Can. 136 — A person can exercise executive power over his subjects, even though he himself is outside his own territory and even when they are outside his territory, unless the contrary is certain from the nature of the case or from the prescription of the law; he can also exercise this power over travelers actually present in his territory, provided it is a matter of granting favors or of enforcing either universal laws or particular laws by which they are bound according to the norm of can. 13, §2, n. 2.

Can. 137 — §1. Ordinary executive power can be delegated both for a single act and for all cases, unless the law expressly provides otherwise.

§2. Executive power delegated by the Apostolic See can be subdelegated, whether for a single act or for all cases, unless the delegation was granted in view of the special qualifications of the delegate or unless subdelegation was expressly prohibited.

§3. If executive power delegated by another authority having ordinary power was delegated for all cases, it can be subdelegated only for individual cases; if, however, it was delegated for a single act or for determined acts it cannot be subdelegated except by the expressed grant of the one delegating.

§4. No subdelegated power can be again subdelegated, unless this has been expressly granted by the one delegating.

Can. 138 — Ordinary executive power as well as power delegated for all cases is to be broadly interpreted; any other is to be strictly interpreted; however, a person who has received delegated power is understood to have also been granted whatever is necessary to exercise that power.

Can. 139 — §1. Unless other provision is made in the law, the fact that a person approaches a competent authority, even one which is higher, does not suspend the executive power of another competent authority, whether this be ordinary or delegated.

§2. Nevertheless, a lower authority should not become involved in cases which have been submitted to a higher authority, except for a grave and urgent reason, in which case the lower authority should immediately notify the higher concerning the matter.

Can. 140 – § 1. Pluribus in solidum ad idem negotium agendum delegatis, qui prius negotium tractare inchoaverit alios ab eodem agendo excludit, nisi postea impeditus fuerit aut in negotio peragendo ulterius procedere noluerit.

§ 2. Pluribus collegialiter ad negotium agendum delegatis, omnes procedere debent ad normam can. 119, nisi in mandato aliud cautum sit.

§ 3. Potestas exsecutiva pluribus delegata, praesumitur iisdem delegata in solidum.

Can. 141 – Pluribus successive delegatis, ille negotium expediat, cuius mandatum anterius est, nec postea revocatum fuit.

Can. 142 – § 1. Potestas delegata extinguitur : expleto mandato ; elapso tempore vel exhausto numero casuum pro quibus concessa fuit ; cessante causa finali delegationis ; revocatione delegantis delegato directe intimata necnon renuntiatione delegati deleganti significata et ab eo accepta ; non autem resoluto iure delegantis, nisi id ex appositis clausulis appareat.

§ 2. Actus tamen ex potestate delegata, quae exercetur pro solo foro interno, per inadvertentiam positus, elapso concessionis tempore, validus est.

Can. 143 – § 1. Potestas ordinaria extinguitur amisso officio cui adnectitur.

§ 2. Nisi aliud iure caveatur, suspenditur potestas ordinaria, si contra privationem vel amotionem ab officio legitime appellatur vel recursus interponitur.

Can. 144 – § 1. In errore communi de facto aut de iure, itemque in dubio positivo et probabili sive iuris sive facti, supplet Ecclesia, pro foro tam externo quam interno, potestatem regiminis exsecutivam.

§ 2. Eadem norma applicatur facultatibus de quibus in cann. 883, 966, et 1111, § 1.

TITULUS IX
DE OFFICIIS ECCLESIASTICIS

Can. 145 – § 1. Officium ecclesiasticum est quodlibet munus ordinatione sive divina sive ecclesiastica stabiliter constitutum in finem spiritualem exercendum.

Can. 140 — §1. When several persons have been delegated *in solidum* to transact the same business, the one who first undertakes to deal with it excludes the others from acting, unless thereafter that person is impeded or does not wish to proceed further in treating the matter.

§2. When several persons have been delegated to transact some business collegially, all must proceed according to the norm of can. 119, unless in their mandate some other provision has been made.

§3. Executive power delegated to several persons is presumed to have been delegated to them *in solidum*.

Can. 141 — If several persons have been successively delegated, that person should transact the business whose mandate is prior to the others and has not later been revoked.

Can. 142 — §1. Delegated power ceases by fulfillment of the mandate, by the lapse of the time or by the completion of the number of cases for which it was granted, by cessation of the final cause of the delegation, by the revocation of the one delegating directly communicated to the delegate, as well as by the resignation of the delegate made known to and accepted by the one delegating; it does not cease, however, by the expiration of the authority of the one delegating, unless this is clear from clauses appended to the grant.

§2. An act of delegated power, however, which is exercised only for the internal forum and which is placed inadvertently after the lapse of the time of the grant, is valid.

Can. 143 — §1. Ordinary power ceases by the loss of the office to which it is connected.

§2. Unless the law provides otherwise, ordinary power is suspended in the event that a privation of or removal from office is legitimately appealed or recourse taken.

Can. 144 — §1. In common error about fact or about law, and also in positive and probable doubt about law or about fact, the Church supplies executive power of governance both for the external and for the internal forum.

§2. This same norm applies to the faculties mentioned in cann. 883, 966 and 1111, §1.

TITLE IX
ECCLESIASTICAL OFFICES

Can. 145 — §1. An ecclesiastical office is any function constituted in a stable manner by divine or ecclesiastical law to be exercised for a spiritual purpose.

§ 2. Obligationes et iura singulis officiis ecclesiasticis propria definiuntur sive ipso iure quo officium constituitur, sive decreto auctoritatis
competentis quo constituitur simul et confertur.

Caput I

DE PROVISIONE OFFICII ECCLESIASTICI

Can. 146 – Officium ecclesiasticum sine provisione canonica valide
obtineri nequit.

Can. 147 – Provisio officii ecclesiastici fit : per liberam collationem
ab auctoritate ecclesiastica competenti ; per institutionem ab eadem
datam, si praecesserit praesentatio ; per confirmationem vel admissionem ab eadem factam, si praecesserit electio vel postulatio ; tandem
per simplicem electionem et electi acceptationem, si electio non egeat
confirmatione.

Can. 148 – Auctoritati, cuius est officia erigere, innovare et supprimere, eorundem provisio quoque competit, nisi aliud iure statuatur.

Can. 149 – § 1. Ut ad officium ecclesiasticum quis promoveatur,
debet esse in Ecclesiae communione necnon idoneus, scilicet iis qualitatibus praeditus, quae iure universali vel particulari aut lege fundationis ad idem officium requiruntur.

§ 2. Provisio officii ecclesiastici facta illi qui caret qualitatibus
requisitis, irrita tantum est, si qualitates iure universali vel particulari
aut lege fundationis ad validitatem provisionis expresse exigantur ;
secus valida est, sed rescindi potest per decretum auctoritatis competentis aut per sententiam tribunalis administrativi.

§ 3. Provisio officii simoniace facta ipso iure irrita est.

Can. 150 – Officium secumferens plenam animarum curam, ad quam
adimplendam ordinis sacerdotalis exercitium requiritur, ei qui sacerdotio nondum auctus est valide conferri nequit.

Can. 151 – Provisio officii animarum curam secumferentis, sine
gravi causa ne differatur.

Can. 152 – Nemini conferantur duo vel plura officia incompatibilia,
videlicet quae una simul ab eodem adimpleri nequeunt.

Can. 153 – § 1. Provisio officii de iure non vacantis est ipso facto
irrita, nec subsequenti vacatione convalescit.

§2. The obligations and the rights proper to individual ecclesiastical offices are defined either in the law by which the office is constituted or in the decree of a competent authority by which it is at the same time constituted and conferred.

CHAPTER I

PROVISION OF ECCLESIASTICAL OFFICES

Can. 146 — An ecclesiastical office cannot be validly acquired without canonical provision.

Can. 147 — Provision of an ecclesiastical office occurs by the free conferral of a competent ecclesiastical authority, or by installation by the same authority if presentation preceded it, or by confirmation or admission granted by the same authority if election or postulation preceded it, or, finally, by simple election and acceptance by the one elected if the election does not require confirmation.

Can. 148 — That authority which is competent to establish, modify and suppress offices is also competent to make provision for them unless the law establishes otherwise.

Can. 149 — §1. In order to be promoted to an ecclesiastical office, a person must be in the communion of the Church as well as suitable, namely endowed with those qualities which are required for the office in question by universal or particular law or by the law of the foundation.

§2. Provision of an ecclesiastical office made in favor of a person who lacks the required qualities is invalid only if the qualities are expressly required for the validity of the provision by universal or particular law or the law of the foundation; otherwise the provision is valid, but it can be rescinded by the decree of the competent authority or by the sentence of an administrative tribunal.

§3. Simoniacal provision of an office is invalid by the law itself.

Can. 150 — An office entailing the full care of souls, for whose fulfillment the exercise of the priestly order is required, cannot be validly conferred upon someone who has not yet received priestly ordination.

Can. 151 — The provision of an office entailing the care of souls is not to be deferred without serious cause.

Can. 152 — Two or more incompatible offices, that is, offices which cannot be fulfilled at the same time by the same person may not be conferred upon one person.

Can. 153 — §1. The provision of an office which is by law not vacant is by that very fact invalid, and a subsequent vacancy does not validate the provision.

§ 2. Si tamen agatur de officio quod de iure ad tempus determinatum confertur, provisio intra sex menses ante expletum hoc tempus fieri potest, et effectum habet a die officii vacationis.

§ 3. Promissio alicuius officii, a quocumque est facta, nullum parit iuridicum effectum.

Can. 154 – Officium de iure vacans, quod forte adhuc ab aliquo illegitime possidetur, conferri potest, dummodo rite declaratum fuerit eam possessionem non esse legitimam, et de hac declaratione mentio fiat in litteris collationis.

Can. 155 – Qui, vicem alterius negligentis vel impediti supplens, officium confert, nullam inde potestatem acquirit in personam cui collatum est, sed huius condicio iuridica perinde constituitur, ac si provisio ad ordinariam iuris normam peracta fuisset.

Can. 156 – Cuiuslibet officii provisio scripto consignetur.

Art. 1

DE LIBERA COLLATIONE

Can. 157 – Nisi aliud explicite iure statuatur, Episcopi dioecesani est libera collatione providere officiis ecclesiasticis in propria Ecclesia particulari.

Art. 2

DE PRAESENTATIONE

Can. 158 – § 1. Praesentatio ad officium ecclesiasticum ab eo, cui ius praesentandi competit, fieri debet auctoritati cuius est ad officium de quo agitur institutionem dare, et quidem, nisi aliud legitime cautum sit, intra tres menses ab habita vacationis officii notitia.

§ 2. Si ius praesentationis cuidam collegio aut coetui personarum competat, praesentandus designetur servatis cann. 165-179 praescriptis.

Can. 159 – Nemo invitus praesentetur; quare qui praesentandus proponitur, mentem suam rogatus, nisi intra octiduum utile recuset, praesentari potest.

§2. But if it is a question of an office which by law is conferred for a determined period of time the provision can be made within six months before the expiration of this time, and it takes effect on the day of the vacancy of the office.

§3. A promise of an office, no matter by whom it is made, has no juridic effect.

Can. 154 — An office which is vacant by law but perhaps held by someone illegitimately can be conferred provided that it is duly declared that the possession is illegitimate and provided that this declaration is mentioned in the document of conferral.

Can. 155 — A person who confers an office, while supplying for someone who is negligent or impeded, thereby acquires no power over the person upon whom the office was conferred, and the juridic situation of that person is determined just as though the provision had been made according to the ordinary norm of law.

Can. 156 — The provision of any office whatsoever is to be made in writing.

Art. 1

FREE CONFERRAL

Can. 157 — Unless otherwise explicitly determined by law, it is within the competence of the diocesan bishop to provide for ecclesiastical offices in his own particular church by free conferral.

Art. 2

PRESENTATION

Can. 158 — §1. Presentation for an ecclesiastical office must be made by the person who has the right of presentation to the authority whose right it is to install someone in the office in question, and furthermore this presentation must be made within three months from the receipt of notice of the vacancy of the office, unless something else has been legitimately established.

§2. If the right of presentation belongs to a certain college or group of persons, the person to be presented is to be designated according to the prescriptions of cann. 165–179.

Can. 159 — No one may be presented who is unwilling; hence a person proposed for presentation who has been asked about his or her willingness can be presented unless the person has declined it within eight days of available time.

Can. 160 – § 1. Qui iure praesentationis gaudet, unum aut etiam plures, et quidem tum una simul tum successive, praesentare potest.

§ 2. Nemo potest seipsum praesentare; potest autem collegium aut coetus personarum aliquem suum sodalem praesentare.

Can. 161 – § 1. Nisi aliud iure statuatur, potest qui aliquem praesentaverit non idoneum repertum, altera tantum vice, intra mensem, alium candidatum praesentare.

§ 2. Si praesentatus ante institutionem factam renuntiaverit aut de vita decesserit, potest qui iure praesentandi pollet, intra mensem ab habita renuntiationis aut mortis notitia, ius suum rursus exercere.

Can. 162 – Qui intra tempus utile, ad normam can. 158, § 1 et can. 161, praesentationem non fecerit, itemque qui bis praesentaverit non idoneum repertum, pro eo casu ius praesentationis amittit, atque auctoritati, cuius est institutionem dare, competit libere providere officio vacanti, assentiente tamen proprio provisi Ordinario.

Can. 163 – Auctoritas, cui ad normam iuris competit praesentatum instituere, instituat legitime praesentatum quem idoneum reppererit et qui acceptaverit; quod si plures legitime praesentati idonei reperti sint, eorundem unum instituere debet.

Art. 3

De electione

Can. 164 – Nisi aliud iure provisum fuerit, in electionibus canonicis serventur praescripta canonum qui sequuntur.

Can. 165 – Nisi aliud iure aut legitimis collegii vel coetus statutis cautum sit, si cui collegio aut coetui personarum sit ius eligendi ad officium, electio ne differatur ultra trimestre utile computandum ab habita notitia vacationis officii; quo termino inutiliter elapso, auctoritas ecclesiastica, cui ius confirmandae electionis vel ius providendi successive competit, officio vacanti libere provideat.

Can. 166 – § 1. Collegii aut coetus praeses convocet omnes ad collegium aut ad coetum pertinentes; convocatio autem, quando personalis esse debet, valet, si fiat in loco domiciiii vel quasi-domicilii aut in loco commorationis.

§ 2. Si quis ex vocandis neglectus et ideo absens fuerit, electio valet; attamen ad eiusdem instantiam, probata quidem praeteritione et absentia, electio, etiam si confirmata fuerit, a competenti auctoritate rescindi debet, dummodo iuridice constet recursum saltem intra

Can. 160 — §1. A person who enjoys the right of presentation can present one or even several candidates either at one time or successively.

§2. No one can present himself or herself; a college or group of persons, however, can present one of its own members.

Can. 161 — §1. Unless otherwise determined by law, a person who has presented someone found to be unsuitable can present someone else only once more and within a month.

§2. If the person presented declines or dies before the installation, the person having the right of presentation can again exercise such right within a month of the receipt of notice of the refusal or death.

Can. 162 — A person who has not made a presentation within the available time according to the norm of cann. 158, §1 and 161 or who has twice presented someone who has been found unsuitable loses the right of presentation for that instance; and the authority whose right it is to install is competent to provide freely for the vacant office, with the consent, however, of the candidate's own ordinary.

Can. 163 — The authority which is competent according to law to install someone who has been presented is to install the person who has been legitimately presented, whom he or she found suitable and who accepted the office; but if several have been legitimately presented who are found to be suitable, the authority must install one of them.

Art. 3

ELECTION

Can. 164 — Unless the law has provided otherwise, the prescriptions of the following canons are to be observed in canonical elections.

Can. 165 — Unless the law or the legitimate statutes of a college or group provide otherwise, if a college or group of persons has the right of election to office the election is not to be deferred beyond three months of available time from receipt of the notice of vacancy of the office; if this period of time has elapsed without action, the ecclesiastical authority having the right to confirm the election or provide for the office successively is to make provision freely for the vacant office.

Can. 166 — §1. The presiding officer of the college or group shall convoke all the members of the college or group; and the notice of convocation, when it must be communicated to each member personally, is valid if it is directed to the place of domicile or quasi-domicile or actual residence.

§2. If one of those to be convoked is overlooked and is therefore absent, the election is valid; however, upon the instance of such a one and after proof of the oversight and absence, the election, even if it has been confirmed, must

triduum ab habita notitia electionis fuisse transmissum.

§ 3. Quod si plures quam tertia pars electorum neglecti fuerint, electio est ipso iure nulla, nisi omnes neglecti reapse interfuerint.

Can. 167 – § 1. Convocatione legitime facta, suffragium ferendi ius habent praesentes die et loco in eadem convocatione determinatis, exclusa, nisi aliud statutis legitime caveatur, facultate ferendi suffragia sive per epistolam sive per procuratorem.

§ 2. Si quis ex electoribus praesens in ea domo sit, in qua fit electio, sed electioni ob infirmam valetudinem interesse nequeat, suffragium eius scriptum a scrutatoribus exquiratur.

Can. 168 – Etsi quis plures ob titulos ius habeat ferendi nomine proprio suffragii, non potest nisi unicum suffragium ferre.

Can. 169 – Ut valida sit electio, nemo ad suffragium admitti potest, qui ad collegium vel coetum non pertineat.

Can. 170 – Electio, cuius libertas quoquo modo reapse impedita fuerit, ipso iure invalida est.

Can. 171 – § 1. Inhabiles sunt ad suffragium ferendum :
1° incapax actus humani ;
2° carens voce activa ;
3° poena excommunicationis innodatus sive per sententiam iudicialem sive per decretum quo poena irrogatur vel declaratur :
4° qui ab Ecclesiae communione notorie defecit.

§ 2. Si quis ex praedictis admittatur, eius suffragium est nullum, sed electio valet, nisi constet, eo dempto, electum non rettulisse requisitum suffragiorum numerum.

Can. 172 – § 1. Suffragium, ut validum sit, esse debet :
1° liberum ; ideoque invalidum est suffragium eius, qui metu gravi aut dolo, directe vel indirecte, adactus fuerit ad eligendam certam personam aut diversas personas disiunctive ;
2° secretum, certum, absolutum, determinatum.

§ 2. Condiciones ante electionem suffragio appositae tamquam non adiectae habeantur.

Can. 173 – § 1. Antequam incipiat electio, deputentur e gremio collegii aut coetus duo saltem scrutatores.

§ 2. Scrutatores suffragia colligant et coram praeside electionis inspiciant an schedularum numerus respondeat numero electorum, suffragia ipsa scrutentur palamque faciant quot quisque rettulerit.

be rescinded by the competent authority, provided that it has been juridically established that recourse was made within at least three days of receipt of the notice of the election.

§3. But if more than one-third of the electors were overlooked, the election is invalid by the law itself, unless all those overlooked were in fact present.

Can. 167 — §1. Once the convocation has been legitimately made, those present on the day and in the place designated in the convocation have the right to vote; the faculty of voting by mail or by proxy is excluded, unless the statutes legitimately provide otherwise.

§2. If one of the electors is present in the house in which the election takes place but cannot be present for the election because of ill health, his or her written ballot is to be obtained by the tellers.

Can. 168 — Even if a person has the right to vote in his or her own name by more than one title, such a person can cast only one ballot.

Can. 169 — In order that the election be valid, no one can be permitted to vote who is not a member of the college or group.

Can. 170 — An election whose freedom was in fact impaired in any way whatever is invalid by the law itself.

Can. 171 — §1. Those persons are ineligible to vote:

1° who are incapable of placing a human act;

2° who lack active voice;

3° who have been excommunicated either by a judicial sentence or by a decree in virtue of which the penalty has been inflicted or declared;

4° who have notoriously defected from the communion of the Church.

§2. If one of the above has been admitted, the vote is null but the election is valid, unless it is clear that by subtracting the vote the person elected did not receive the required number of votes.

Can. 172 — §1. For a vote to be valid it must be:

1° free; therefore, a vote is invalid if one has been coerced directly or indirectly by grave fear or by fraud to vote for a certain person or different persons disjunctively;

2° secret, certain, absolute, determinate.

§2. Conditions appended to a vote prior to the election are to be considered as not having been appended.

Can. 173 — §1. Before the election begins at least two tellers are to be designated from the membership of the college or group.

§2. The tellers are to gather the ballots, determine in the presence of the presiding officer that the number of ballots is the same as the number of electors, read the ballots themselves and announce clearly how many votes

§ 3. Si numerus suffragiorum superet numerum eligentium, nihil est actum.

§ 4. Omnia electionis acta ab eo qui actuarii munere fungitur accurate describantur, et saltem ab eodem actuario, praeside ac scrutatoribus subscripta, in collegii tabulario diligenter asserventur.

Can. 174 – § 1. Electio, nisi aliud iure aut statutis caveatur, fieri etiam potest per compromissum, dummodo nempe electores, unanimi et scripto consensu, in unum vel plures idoneos sive de gremio sive extraneos ius eligendi pro ea vice transferant, qui nomine omnium ex recepta facultate eligant.

§ 2. Si agatur de collegio aut coetu ex solis clericis constanti, compromissarii in sacris debent esse constituti; secus electio est invalida.

§ 3. Compromissarii debent iuris praescripta de electione servare atque, ad validitatem electionis, condiciones compromisso appositas, iuri non contrarias, observare; condiciones autem iuri contrariae pro non appositae habeantur.

Can. 175 – Cessat compromissum et ius suffragium ferendi redit ad compromittentes:

1° revocatione a collegio aut coetu facta, re integra;
2° non impleta aliqua condicione compromisso apposita;
3° electione absoluta, si fuerit nulla.

Can. 176 – Nisi aliud iure aut statutis caveatur, is electus habeatur et a collegii aut coetus praeside proclametur, qui requisitum suffragiorum numerum rettulerit, ad normam can. 119, n. 1.

Can. 177 – § 1. Electio illico intimanda est electo, qui debet intra octiduum utile a recepta intimatione significare collegii aut coetus praesidi utrum electionem acceptet necne; secus electio effectum non habet.

§ 2. Si electus non acceptaverit, omne ius ex electione amittit nec subsequenti acceptatione convalescit, sed rursus eligi potest; collegium autem aut coetus intra mensem a cognita non-acceptatione ad novam electionem procedere debet.

Can. 178 – Electus, acceptata electione, quae confirmatione non egeat, officium pleno iure statim obtinet; secus non acquirit nisi ius ad rem.

each person has received.

§3. If the number of ballots exceeds the number of electors the vote is invalid.

§4. The secretary is to record accurately all the acts of the election and carefully preserve them in the file of the college, after signing them along with at least the presiding officer and the tellers.

Can. 174 — §1. Unless the law or the statutes provide otherwise, an election can also be effected by compromise, provided that the electors unanimously and in writing consent to transfer to a qualified individual or to several qualified individuals, from within the membership or from outside it, the right to elect for that instance; such person or persons elect in the name of all in virtue of the faculty they have received.

§2. In the case of a college or group composed only of clerics, the persons commissioned must themselves be ordained; otherwise the election is invalid.

§3. The persons commissioned must observe the prescriptions of law concerning elections and, for the validity of the election, they must fulfill whatever conditions have been attached to the compromise agreement which are not contrary to law; conditions contrary to the law, however, are to be considered as not having been attached.

Can. 175 — The compromise is terminated and the right to elect reverts to the electors authorizing the compromise:

1° by revocation by the college or group, before the persons commissioned have begun to act;

2° if a condition attached to the compromise agreement has not been fulfilled;

3° if the election has been completed but is invalid.

Can. 176 — Unless the law or the statutes provide otherwise, the person who has received the required number of votes according to the norm of can. 119, n.1 is to be considered elected, and this is to be announced by the presiding officer of the college or the group.

Can. 177 — §1. The election is to be communicated forthwith to the person elected, who must, within eight days of available time after having been notified, inform the college or the presiding officer of the group whether or not he or she accepts the election; otherwise the election has no effect.

§2. A person elected who does not accept loses any right deriving from the election and does not regain any such right by a subsequent acceptance; such a person however, can be elected again; the college or group must proceed to a new election within a month of notification of the non-acceptance.

Can. 178 — The person elected who has accepted the election immediately acquires the office in full right if the election does not require confirmation; otherwise the person acquires only the right to the office.

Can. 179 – § 1. Electus, si electio confirmatione indigeat, intra octiduum utile a die acceptatae electionis confirmationem ab auctoritate competenti petere per se vel per alium debet; secus omni iure privatur, nisi probaverit se a petenda confirmatione iusto impedimento detentum fuisse.

§ 2. Competens auctoritas, si electum reppererit idoneum ad normam can. 149, § 1, et electio ad normam iuris fuerit peracta, confirmationem denegare nequit.

§ 3. Confirmatio in scriptis dari debet.

§ 4. Ante intimatam confirmationem, electo non licet sese immiscere administrationi officii sive in spiritualibus sive in temporalibus, et actus ab eo forte positi nulli sunt.

§ 5. Intimata confirmatione, electus pleno iure officium obtinet, nisi aliud iure caveatur.

Art. 4

DE POSTULATIONE

Can. 180 – § 1. Si electioni illius quem electores aptiorem putent ac praeferant, impedimentum canonicum obstet, super quo dispensatio concedi possit ac soleat, suis ipsi suffragiis eum possunt, nisi aliud iure caveatur, a competenti auctoritate postulare.

§ 2. Compromissarii postulare nequeunt, nisi id in compromisso fuerit expressum.

Can. 181 – § 1. Ut postulatio vim habeat, requiruntur saltem duae tertiae partes suffragiorum.

§ 2. Suffragium pro postulatione exprimi debet per verbum : *postulo,* aut aequivalens; formula : *eligo vel postulo,* aut aequipollens, valet pro electione, si impedimentum non exsistat, secus pro postulatione.

Can. 182 – § 1. Postulatio a praeside intra octiduum utile mitti debet ad auctoritatem competentem ad quam pertinet electionem confirmare, cuius est dispensationem de impedimento concedere, aut, si hanc potestatem non habeat, eandem ab auctoritate superiore petere ; si non requiritur confirmatio, postulatio mitti debet ad auctoritatem competentem ut dispensatio concedatur.

§ 2. Si intra praescriptum tempus postulatio missa non fuerit, ipso facto nulla est, et collegium vel coetus pro ea vice privatur iure eligendi aut postulandi, nisi probetur praesidem a mittenda postulatione iusto fuisse detentum impedimento aut dolo vel neglegentia ab

Can. 179 — §1. If the election requires confirmation the person elected must personally or through someone else request confirmation by the competent authority within eight days of available time from the day of acceptance of the election; otherwise the person elected is deprived of any right unless it is proved that the person has been constrained from petitioning confirmation by a just impediment.

§2. The competent authority cannot deny confirmation if the person elected is qualified according to the norm of can. 149, §1 and the election was conducted in accord with the law.

§3. The confirmation must be given in writing.

§4. Before being informed of confirmation the person may not become involved in the administration of the office, whether this be in matters spiritual or temporal, and any acts placed by such a person are invalid.

§5. Once notified of confirmation the person elected acquires the office in full right, unless the law provides otherwise.

Art. 4

POSTULATION

Can. 180 — §1. If a canonical impediment, which can be and usually is dispensed, prevents the election of the person whom the electors believe to be more qualified and whom they prefer, they can vote to postulate such a person from the competent authority, unless something else is provided by the law.

§2. Those commissioned to elect in virtue of a compromise cannot postulate anyone unless this was expressed in their document of compromise.

Can. 181 — §1. At least two-thirds of the votes are required for postulation to have any effect.

§2. A vote for postulation must be expressed by the words, "I postulate," or the equivalent; the formula, "I elect or I postulate," or the equivalent, is valid for an election if an impediment does not exist, otherwise for a postulation.

Can. 182 — §1. A postulation must be sent within eight days of available time by the presiding officer to the competent authority to whom confirmation of the election belongs, who is authorized to grant the dispensation from the impediment, or, lacking the faculty to do so, to request the dispensation from a higher authority; if confirmation is not required, the postulation must be sent to the competent authority so that the dispensation may be granted.

§2. If the postulation has not been sent within the prescribed time, it is by that very fact invalid and the college or group is deprived for that instance of the right to elect or postulate, unless it is demonstrated that the presiding officer had been constrained from forwarding the postulation by a just im-

eadem tempore opportuno mittenda abstinuisse.

§ 3. Postulato nullum ius acquiritur ex postulatione; eam admittendi auctoritas competens obligatione non tenetur.

§ 4. Factam auctoritati competenti postulationem electores revocare non possunt, nisi auctoritate consentiente.

Can. 183 – § 1. Non admissa ab auctoritate competenti postulatione, ius eligendi ad collegium vel coetum redit.

§ 2. Quod si postulatio admissa fuerit, id significetur postulato, qui respondere debet ad normam can. 177, § 1.

§ 3. Qui admissam postulationem acceptat, pleno iure statim officium obtinet.

Caput II
DE AMISSIONE OFFICII ECCLESIASTICI

Can. 184 – § 1. Amittitur officium ecclesiasticum lapsu temporis praefiniti, expleta aetate iure definita, renuntiatione, translatione, amotione necnon privatione.

§ 2. Resoluto quovis modo iure auctoritatis a qua fuit collatum, officium ecclesiasticum non amittitur, nisi aliud iure caveatur.

§ 3. Officii amissio, quae effectum sortita est, quam primum omnibus nota fiat, quibus aliquod ius in officii provisionem competit.

Can. 185 – Ei, qui ob impletam aetatem aut renuntiationem acceptatam officium amittit, titulus emeriti conferri potest.

Can. 186 – Lapsu temporis praefiniti vel adimpleta aetate, amissio officii effectum habet tantum a momento, quo a competenti auctoritate scripto intimatur.

Art. 1
DE RENUNTIATIONE

Can. 187 – Quisquis sui compos potest officio ecclesiastico iusta de causa renuntiare.

Can. 188 – Renuntiatio ex metu gravi, iniuste incusso, dolo vel errore substantiali aut simoniace facta, ipso iure irrita est.

Can. 189 – § 1. Renuntiatio, ut valeat, sive acceptatione eget sive non, auctoritati fieri debet cui provisio ad officium de quo agitur per-

pediment, or had failed to send it at the opportune time out of fraud or negligence.

§3. The one postulated acquires no right from the postulation; the competent authority is not obliged to admit it.

§4. The electors cannot revoke a postulation already sent to a competent authority unless this authority consents to it.

Can. 183 — §1. If the postulation has not been admitted by the competent authority the right of electing reverts to the college or group.

§2. But if the postulation has been admitted, this is to be made known to the one postulated, who is obliged to respond according to the norm of can. 177, §1.

§3. The person who accepts the postulation which has been admitted immediately acquires the office in full right.

CHAPTER II
LOSS OF ECCLESIASTICAL OFFICE

Can. 184 — §1. Ecclesiastical office is lost by the lapse of a predetermined time, by reaching the age determined by the law, by resignation, by transfer, by removal and by privation.

§2. An ecclesiastical office is not lost by the expiration in any way of the authority of the one who conferred it, unless the law provides otherwise.

§3. The loss of an office once it has taken effect, is to be made known as soon as possible to all who enjoy any right with respect to the provision of the office.

Can. 185 — The title of emeritus can be conferred upon the person who loses an office by reason of age or by a resignation which has been accepted.

Can. 186 — Loss of office by lapse of the determined time or by reaching a certain age takes effect only from the moment when it has been communicated in writing by the competent authority.

Art. 1
RESIGNATION

Can. 187 — Any person of sound mind can resign an ecclesiastical office for a just cause.

Can. 188 — A resignation submitted out of grave fear, which has been unjustly inflicted, or because of fraud, substantial error or simony is invalid by the law itself.

Can. 189 — §1. To be valid a resignation, whether it requires acceptance or not, must be submitted to the authority who is responsible for the provi-

tinet, et quidem scripto vel oretenus coram duobus testibus.

§ 2. Auctoritas renuntiationem iusta et proportionata causa non innixam ne acceptet.

§ 3. Renuntiatio quae acceptatione indiget, nisi intra tres menses acceptetur, omni vi caret; quae acceptatione non indiget effectum sortitur communicatione renuntiantis ad normam iuris facta.

§ 4. Renuntiatio, quamdiu effectum sortita non fuerit, a renuntiante revocari potest; effectu secuto revocari nequit, sed qui renuntiavit, officium alio ex titulo consequi potest.

Art. 2

DE TRANSLATIONE

Can. 190 – § 1. Translatio ab eo tantum fieri potest, qui ius habet providendi officio quod amittitur et simul officio quod committitur.

§ 2. Si translatio fiat invito officii titulari, gravis requiritur causa et, firmo semper iure rationes contrarias exponendi, servetur modus procedendi iure praescriptus.

§ 3. Translatio, ut effectum sortiatur, scripto intimanda est.

Can. 191 – § 1. In translatione, prius officium vacat per possessionem alterius officii canonice habitam, nisi aliud iure cautum aut a competenti auctoritate praescriptum fuerit.

§ 2. Remunerationem cum priore officio conexam translatus percipit, donec alterius possessionem canonice obtinuerit.

Art. 3

DE AMOTIONE

Can. 192 – Ab officio quis amovetur sive decreto ab auctoritate competenti legitime edito, servatis quidem iuribus forte ex contractu quaesitis, sive ipso iure ad normam can. 194.

Can. 193 – § 1. Ab officio quod alicui confertur ad tempus indefinitum, non potest quis amoveri nisi ob graves causas atque servato procedendi modo iure definito.

sion of the office, and this is to be done in writing or orally in the presence of two witnesses.

§2. The authority is not to accept a resignation which is not based on a just and proportionate cause.

§3. A resignation which requires acceptance lacks all effect if it is not accepted within three months; one which does not require acceptance takes effect when it has been communicated by the one resigning in accord with the norm of law.

§4. A resignation can be withdrawn by the one resigning as long as it has not yet become effective; once it has become effective it cannot be withdrawn, but a person who has resigned can obtain the office by some other title.

Art. 2
TRANSFER

Can. 190 — §1. Transfer can be effected only by one who has the right of providing for the office which is being lost as well as for the office which is being conferred.

§2. If a transfer is to be made when the officeholder is unwilling, a grave cause is required and the procedure prescribed by law is to be observed, with due regard for the right to bring forward arguments against the transfer.

§3. To take effect a transfer must be communicated in writing.

Can. 191 — §1. In the event of a transfer, the prior office becomes vacant through canonical possession of the other office unless the law provides otherwise or something else has been prescribed by the competent authority.

§2. The person transferred continues to receive the compensation assigned to the prior office until taking canonical possession of the other office.

Art. 3
REMOVAL

Can. 192 — A person is removed from office either by a decree legitimately issued by a competent authority, with due regard for rights which may have been acquired by contract, or by the law itself according to the norm of can. 194.

Can. 193 — §1. A person cannot be removed from an office conferred for an indefinite period of time except for grave reasons and according to the procedure determined by law.

§ 2. Idem valet, ut quis ab officio, quod alicui ad tempus determinatum confertur, ante hoc tempus elapsum amoveri possit, firmo praescripto can. 624, § 3.

§ 3. Ab officio quod, secundum iuris praescripta, alicui confertur ad prudentem discretionem auctoritatis competentis, potest quis iusta ex causa, de iudicio eiusdem auctoritatis, amoveri.

§ 4. Decretum amotionis, ut effectum sortiatur, scripto intimandum est.

Can. 194 – § 1. Ipso iure ab officio ecclesiastico amovetur :

1° qui statum clericalem amiserit ;

2° qui a fide catholica aut a communione Ecclesiae publice defecerit ;

3° clericus qui matrimonium etiam civile tantum attentaverit.

§ 2. Amotio, de qua in nn. 2 et 3, urgeri tantum potest, si de eadem auctoritatis competentis declaratione constet.

Can. 195 – Si quis, non quidem ipso iure, sed per decretum auctoritatis competentis ab officio amoveatur quo eiusdem subsistentiae providetur, eadem auctoritas curet ut ipsius subsistentiae per congruum tempus prospiciatur, nisi aliter provisum sit.

Art. 4

DE PRIVATIONE

Can. 196 – § 1. Privatio ab officio, in poenam scilicet delicti, ad normam iuris tantummodo fieri potest.

§ 2. Privatio effectum sortitur secundum praescripta canonum de iure poenali.

TITULUS X

DE PRAESCRIPTIONE

Can. 197 – Praescriptionem, tamquam modum iuris subiectivi acquirendi vel amittendi necnon ab obligationibus sese liberandi, Ecclesia recipit prout est in legislatione civili respectivae nationis, salvis exceptionibus quae in canonibus huius Codicis statuuntur.

Can. 198 – Nulla valet praescriptio, nisi bona fide nitatur, non solum initio, sed toto decursu temporis ad praescriptionem requisiti, salvo praescripto can. 1362.

§2. The same holds for the removal of someone from an office conferred for a specified period of time before the term has expired, with due regard for the prescription of can. 624, §3.

§3. When, in accord with the prescriptions of law, an office has been conferred on someone at the prudent discretion of a competent authority, that person can be removed from office for a cause which is, in the judgment of the same authority, considered just.

§4. In order to be effective the decree of removal must be communicated in writing.

Can. 194 — §1. One is removed from an ecclesiastical office by the law itself:

1° who has lost the clerical state;

2° who has publicly defected from the Catholic faith or from the communion of the Church;

3° a cleric who has attempted marriage even if only civilly.

§2. The removal from office referred to in nn. 2 and 3 can be enforced only if it is established by the declaration of a competent authority.

Can. 195 — If a person is removed from an office which is the source of financial support, not by the law itself, but by a decree of the competent authority, this same authority is to take care such support is seen to for a suitable time, unless it is provided otherwise.

Art. 4

PRIVATION

Can. 196 — §1. Privation of office, namely removal as a penalty for an offense can be effected only according to the norm of law.

§2. Privation takes effect in accord with the prescriptions of the canons on penal law.

TITLE X

PRESCRIPTION

Can. 197 — The Church accepts prescription as it exists in the civil legislation of the respective nations, as a means of acquiring or losing a subjective right and of freeing oneself from obligations, the exceptions which are determined in the canons of this Code remaining intact.

Can. 198 — No prescription has any effect which is not grounded in good faith, not only at the beginning but through the entire course of the time required for prescription with due regard for the prescription of can. 1362.

Can. 199 – Praescriptioni obnoxia non sunt:

1° iura et obligationes quae sunt legis divinae naturalis aut positivae;

2° iura quae obtineri possunt ex solo privilegio apostolico;

3° iura et obligationes quae spiritualem christifidelium vitam directe respiciunt;

4° fines certi et indubii circumscriptionum ecclesiasticarum;

5° stipes et onera Missarum;

6° provisio officii ecclesiastici quod ad normam iuris exercitium ordinis sacri requirit;

7° ius visitationis et obligatio obœdientiae, ita ut christifideles a nulla auctoritate ecclesiastica visitari possint et nulli auctoritati iam subsint.

TITULUS XI

DE TEMPORIS SUPPUTATIONE

Can. 200 – Nisi aliud expresse iure caveatur, tempus supputetur ad normam canonum qui sequuntur.

Can. 201 – § 1. Tempus continuum intellegitur quod nullam patitur interruptionem.

§ 2. Tempus utile intellegitur quod ita ius suum exercenti aut persequenti competit, ut ignoranti aut agere non valenti non currat.

Can. 202 – § 1. In iure, dies intellegitur spatium constans 24 horis continuo supputandis, et incipit a media nocte, nisi aliud expresse caveatur; hebdomada spatium 7 dierum; mensis spatium 30 et annus spatium 365 dierum, nisi mensis et annus dicantur sumendi prout sunt in calendario.

§ 2. Prout sunt in calendario semper sumendi sunt mensis et annus, si tempus est continuum.

Can. 203 – § 1. Dies *a quo* non computatur in termino, nisi huius initium coincidat cum initio diei aut aliud expresse in iure caveatur.

§ 2. Nisi contrarium statuatur, dies *ad quem* computatur in termino, qui, si tempus constet uno vel pluribus mensibus aut annis, una vel pluribus hebdomadis, finitur expleto ultimo die eiusdem numeri aut, si mensis die eiusdem numeri careat, expleto ultimo die mensis.

Can. 199 — Not subject to prescription are:

1° rights and obligations which are of the divine natural or positive law;

2° rights which can be acquired only from an apostolic privilege;

3° rights and obligations which directly affect the spiritual life of the Christian faithful;

4° the certain and unchallenged boundaries of ecclesiastical territories;

5° Mass stipends and obligations;

6° the provision of an ecclesiastical office which requires the exercise of a sacred order, according to the norm of law;

7° the right of visitation and the obligation of obedience if it should result that the Christian faithful can be visited by no ecclesiastical authority and are no longer subject to any ecclesiastical authority.

TITLE XI
COMPUTATION OF TIME

Can. 200 — Time is computed according to the norms of the following canons unless otherwise expressly provided by law.

Can. 201 — §1. Continuous time is understood as that which is subject to no interruption.

§2. Available time is understood as that which a person has to exercise or pursue a right but which does not run if the person is unaware or unable to act.

Can. 202 — §1. In the law, a day is understood as a period of time consisting of 24 continuous hours, and it begins at midnight, unless otherwise expressly provided; a week is a period of 7 days; a month is a period of 30 days and a year one of 365 days, unless the month and the year are said to be taken as they appear in the calendar.

§2. If the time is continuous, a month and a year are always to be taken as they appear in the calendar.

Can. 203 — §1. The day from which the computation is to be made is not counted in the total, unless the beginning of the reckoning coincides with the beginning of the day or unless the law expressly provides otherwise.

§2. Unless the contrary is determined the final day is counted in the total, in such a way that, if the total consists of one or more months or years, of one or more weeks, the terminus is reached at the end of the last day of the same number or, if the month lacks a day of the same number, at the end of the last day of the month.

LIBER II
DE POPULO DEI

PARS I
DE CHRISTIFIDELIBUS

Can. 204 – § 1. Christifideles sunt qui, utpote per baptismum Christo incorporati, in populum Dei sunt constituti, atque hac ratione muneris Christi sacerdotalis, prophetici et regalis suo modo participes facti, secundum propriam cuiusque condicionem, ad missionem exercendam vocantur, quam Deus Ecclesiae in mundo adimplendam concredidit.

§ 2. Haec Ecclesia, in hoc mundo ut societas constituta et ordinata, subsistit in Ecclesia catholica, a successore Petri et Episcopis in eius communione gubernata.

Can. 205 – Plene in communione Ecclesiae catholicae his in terris sunt illi baptizati, qui in eius compage visibili cum Christo iunguntur, vinculis nempe professionis fidei, sacramentorum et ecclesiastici regiminis.

Can. 206 – § 1. Speciali ratione cum Ecclesia conectuntur catechumeni, qui nempe, Spiritu Sancto movente, explicita voluntate ut eidem incorporentur expetunt, ideoque hoc ipso voto, sicut et vita fidei, spei et caritatis quam agunt, coniunguntur cum Ecclesia, quae eos iam ut suos fovet.

§ 2. Catechumenorum specialem curam habet Ecclesia quae, dum eos ad vitam ducendam evangelicam invitat eosque ad sacros ritus celebrandos introducit, eisdem varias iam largitur praerogativas, quae christianorum sunt propriae.

Can. 207 – § 1. Ex divina institutione, inter christifideles sunt in Ecclesia ministri sacri, qui in iure et clerici vocantur; ceteri autem et laici nuncupantur.

§ 2. Ex utraque hac parte habentur christifideles, qui professione

BOOK II
THE PEOPLE OF GOD

PART I
THE CHRISTIAN FAITHFUL

Can. 204 — §1. The Christian faithful are those who, inasmuch as they have been incorporated in Christ through baptism, have been constituted as the people of God; for this reason, since they have become sharers in Christ's priestly, prophetic and royal office in their own manner, they are called to exercise the mission which God has entrusted to the Church to fulfill in the world, in accord with the condition proper to each one.

§2. This Church, constituted and organized as a society in this world, subsists in the Catholic Church, governed by the successor of Peter and the bishops in communion with him.

Can. 205 — Those baptized are fully in communion with the Catholic Church on this earth who are joined with Christ in its visible structure by the bonds of profession of faith, of the sacraments and of ecclesiastical governance.

Can. 206 — §1. Catechumens are in union with the Church in a special manner, that is, under the influence of the Holy Spirit, they ask to be incorporated into the Church by explicit choice and are therefore united with the Church by that choice just as by a life of faith, hope and charity which they lead; the Church already cherishes them as its own.

§2. The Church has special care for catechumens; the Church invites them to lead the evangelical life and introduces them to the celebration of sacred rites, and grants them various prerogatives which are proper to Christians.

Can. 207 — §1. Among the Christian faithful by divine institution there exist in the Church sacred ministers, who are also called clerics in law, and other Christian faithful, who are also called laity.

§2. From both groups there exist Christian faithful who are consecrated

consiliorum evangelicorum per vota aut alia sacra ligamina, ab Ecclesia agnita et sancita, suo peculiari modo Deo consecrantur et Ecclesiae missioni salvificae prosunt; quorum status, licet ad hierarchicam Ecclesiae structuram non spectet, ad eius tamen vitam et sanctitatem pertinet.

TITULUS I

DE OMNIUM CHRISTIFIDELIUM OBLIGATIONIBUS ET IURIBUS

Can. 208 – Inter christifideles omnes, ex eorum quidem in Christo regeneratione, vera viget quoad dignitatem et actionem aequalitas, qua cuncti, secundum propriam cuiusque condicionem et munus, ad aedificationem Corporis Christi cooperantur.

Can. 209 – § 1. Christifideles obligatione adstringuntur, sua quoque ipsorum agendi ratione, ad communionem semper servandam cum Ecclesia.

§ 2. Magna cum diligentia officia adimpleant, quibus tenentur erga Ecclesiam tum universam, tum particularem ad quam, secundum iuris praescripta, pertinent.

Can. 210 – Omnes christifideles, secundum propriam condicionem, ad sanctam vitam ducendam atque ad Ecclesiae incrementum eiusque iugem sanctificationem promovendam vires suas conferre debent.

Can. 211 – Omnes christifideles officium habent et ius adlaborandi ut divinum salutis nuntium ad universos homines omnium temporum ac totius orbis magis magisque perveniat.

Can. 212 – § 1. Quae sacri Pastores, utpote Christum repraesentantes, tamquam fidei magistri declarant aut tamquam Ecclesiae rectores statuunt, christifideles, propriae responsabilitatis conscii, christiana oboedientia prosequi tenentur.

§ 2. Christifidelibus integrum est, ut necessitates suas, praesertim spirituales, suaque optata Ecclesiae Pastoribus patefaciant.

§ 3. Pro scientia, competentia et praestantia quibus pollent, ipsis ius est, immo et aliquando officium, ut sententiam suam de his quae ad bonum Ecclesiae pertinent sacris Pastoribus manifestent eamque, salva fidei morumque integritate ac reverentia erga Pastores, attentisque communi utilitate et personarum dignitate, ceteris christifidelibus notam faciant.

Can. 213 – Ius est christifidelibus ut ex spiritualibus Ecclesiae bo-

to God in their own special manner and serve the salvific mission of the Church through the profession of the evangelical counsels by means of vows or other sacred bonds recognized and sanctioned by the Church. Such persons also are of service to the saving mission of the Church; although their state does not belong to the hierarchical structure of the Church, they nevertheless do belong to its life and holiness.

TITLE I
THE OBLIGATIONS AND RIGHTS OF ALL THE CHRISTIAN FAITHFUL

Can. 208 — In virtue of their rebirth in Christ there exists among all the Christian faithful a true equality with regard to dignity and the activity whereby all cooperate in the building up of the Body of Christ in accord with each one's own condition and function.

Can. 209 — §1. The Christian faithful are bound by an obligation, even in their own patterns of activity, always to maintain communion with the Church.

§2. They are to fulfill with great diligence the duties which they owe to the universal Church and to the particular church to which they belong according to the prescriptions of law.

Can. 210 — All the Christian faithful must make an effort, in accord with their own condition, to live a holy life and to promote the growth of the Church and its continual sanctification.

Can. 211 — All the Christian faithful have the duty and the right to work so that the divine message of salvation may increasingly reach the whole of humankind in every age and in every land.

Can. 212 — §1. The Christian faithful, conscious of their own responsibility, are bound by Christian obedience to follow what the sacred pastors, as representatives of Christ, declare as teachers of the faith or determine as leaders of the Church.

§2. The Christian faithful are free to make known their needs, especially spiritual ones, and their desires to the pastors of the Church.

§3. In accord with the knowledge, competence and preeminence which they possess, they have the right and even at times a duty to manifest to the sacred pastors their opinion on matters which pertain to the good of the Church, and they have a right to make their opinion known to the other Christian faithful, with due regard for the integrity of faith and morals and reverence toward their pastors, and with consideration for the common good and the dignity of persons.

Can. 213 — The Christian faithful have the right to receive assistance

nis, praesertim ex verbo Dei et sacramentis, adiumenta a sacris Pastoribus accipiant.

Can. 214 – Ius est christifidelibus, ut cultum Deo persolvant iuxta praescripta proprii ritus a legitimis Ecclesiae Pastoribus approbati, utque propriam vitae spiritualis formam sequantur, doctrinae quidem Ecclesiae consentaneam.

Can. 215 – Integrum est christifidelibus, ut libere condant atque moderentur consociationes ad fines caritatis vel pietatis, aut ad vocationem christianam in mundo fovendam, utque conventus habeant ad eosdem fines in communi persequendos.

Can. 216 – Christifideles cuncti, quippe qui Ecclesiae missionem participent, ius habent ut propriis quoque inceptis, secundum suum quisque statum et condicionem, apostolicam actionem promoveant vel sustineant; nullum tamen inceptum nomen catholicum sibi vindicet, nisi consensus accesserit competentis auctoritatis ecclesiasticae.

Can. 217 – Christifideles, quippe qui baptismo ad vitam doctrinae evangelicae congruentem ducendam vocentur, ius habent ad educationem christianam, qua ad maturitatem humanae personae prosequendam atque simul ad mysterium salutis cognoscendum et vivendum rite instruantur.

Can. 218 – Qui disciplinis sacris incumbunt iusta libertate fruuntur inquirendi necnon mentem suam prudenter in iis aperiendi, in quibus peritia gaudent, servato debito erga Ecclesiae magisterium obsequio.

Can. 219 – Christifideles omnes iure gaudent ut a quacumque coactione sint immunes in statu vitae eligendo.

Can. 220 – Nemini licet bonam famam, qua quis gaudet, illegitime laedere, nec ius cuiusque personae ad propriam intimitatem tuendam violare.

Can. 221 – § 1. Christifidelibus competit ut iura, quibus in Ecclesia gaudent, legitime vindicent atque defendant in foro competenti ecclesiastico ad normam iuris.

§ 2. Christifidelibus ius quoque est ut, si ad iudicium ab auctoritate competenti vocentur, iudicentur servatis iuris praescriptis, cum aequitate applicandis.

§ 3. Christifidelibus ius est, ne poenis canonicis nisi ad normam legis plectantur.

from the sacred pastors out of the spiritual goods of the Church, especially the word of God and the sacraments.

Can. 214 — The Christian faithful have the right to worship God according to the prescriptions of their own rite approved by the legitimate pastors of the Church, and to follow their own form of spiritual life consonant with the teaching of the Church.

Can. 215 — The Christian faithful are at liberty freely to found and to govern associations for charitable and religious purposes or for the promotion of the Christian vocation in the world; they are free to hold meetings to pursue these purposes in common.

Can. 216 — All the Christian faithful, since they participate in the mission of the Church, have the right to promote or to sustain apostolic action by their own undertakings in accord with each one's state and condition; however, no undertaking shall assume the name Catholic unless the consent of competent ecclesiastical authority is given.

Can. 217 — The Christian faithful since they are called by baptism to lead a life in conformity with the teaching of the gospel, have the right to a Christian education by which they will be properly instructed so as to develop the maturity of a human person and at the same time come to know and live the mystery of salvation.

Can. 218 — Those who are engaged in the sacred disciplines enjoy a lawful freedom of inquiry and of prudently expressing their opinions on matters in which they have expertise, while observing a due respect for the magisterium of the Church.

Can. 219 — All the Christian faithful have the right to be free from any kind of coercion in choosing a state in life.

Can. 220 — No one is permitted to damage unlawfully the good reputation which another person enjoys nor to violate the right of another person to protect his or her own privacy.

Can. 221 — §1. The Christian faithful can legitimately vindicate and defend the rights which they enjoy in the Church before a competent ecclesiastical court in accord with the norm of law.

§2. The Christian faithful also have the right, if they are summoned to judgment by competent authority, that they be judged in accord with the prescriptions of the law to be applied with equity.

§3. The Christian faithful have the right not to be punished with canonical penalties except in accord with the norm of law.

Can. 222 – § 1. Christifideles obligatione tenentur necessitatibus subveniendi Ecclesiae, ut eidem praesto sint quae ad cultum divinum, ad opera apostolica et caritatis atque ad honestam ministrorum sustentationem necessaria sunt.

§ 2. Obligatione quoque tenentur iustitiam socialem promovendi necnon, praecepti Domini memores, ex propriis reditibus pauperibus subveniendi.

Can. 223 – § 1. In iuribus suis exercendis christifideles tum singuli tum in consociationibus adunati rationem habere debent boni communis Ecclesiae necnon iurium aliorum atque suorum erga alios officiorum.

§ 2. Ecclesiasticae auctoritati competit, intuitu boni communis, exercitium iurium, quae christifidelibus sunt propria, moderari.

TITULUS II
DE OBLIGATIONIBUS
ET IURIBUS CHRISTIFIDELIUM LAICORUM

Can. 224 – Christifideles laici, praeter eas obligationes et iura, quae cunctis christifidelibus sunt communia et ea quae in aliis canonibus statuuntur, obligationibus tenentur et iuribus gaudent quae in canonibus huius tituli recensentur.

Can. 225 – § 1. Laici, quippe qui uti omnes christifideles ad apostolatum a Deo per baptismum et confirmationem deputentur, generali obligatione tenentur et iure gaudent, sive singuli sive in consociationibus coniuncti, allaborandi ut divinum salutis nuntium ab universis hominibus ubique terrarum cognoscatur et accipiatur; quae obligatio eo vel magis urget iis in adiunctis, in quibus nonnisi per ipsos Evangelium audire et Christum cognoscere homines possunt.

§ 2. Hoc etiam peculiari adstringuntur officio, unusquisque quidem secundum propriam condicionem, ut rerum temporalium ordinem spiritu evangelico imbuant atque perficiant, et ita specialiter in iisdem rebus gerendis atque in muneribus saecularibus exercendis Christi testimonium reddant.

Can. 226 – § 1. Qui in statu coniugali vivunt, iuxta propriam vocationem, peculiari officio tenentur per matrimonium et familiam ad aedificationem populi Dei allaborandi.

§ 2. Parentes, cum vitam filiis contulerint, gravissima obligatione tenentur et iure gaudent eos educandi; ideo parentum christianorum imprimis est christianam filiorum educationem secundum doctrinam ab Ecclesia traditam curare.

Can. 227 – Ius est christifidelibus laicis, ut ipsis agnoscatur ea in

Can. 222 — §1. The Christian faithful are obliged to assist with the needs of the Church so that the Church has what is necessary for divine worship, for apostolic works and works of charity and for the decent sustenance of ministers.

§2. They are also obliged to promote social justice and, mindful of the precept of the Lord, to assist the poor from their own resources.

Can. 223 — §1. In exercising their rights the Christian faithful, both as individuals and when gathered in associations, must take account of the common good of the Church and of the rights of others as well as their own duties toward others.

§2. In the interest of the common good, ecclesiastical authority has competence to regulate the exercise of the rights which belong to the Christian faithful.

TITLE II

THE OBLIGATIONS AND RIGHTS OF
THE LAY CHRISTIAN FAITHFUL

Can. 224 — In addition to those obligations and rights which are common to all the Christian faithful and those which are determined in other canons, the lay Christian faithful are bound by the obligations and possess the rights which are enumerated in the canons of this title.

Can. 225 — §1. Since the laity like all the Christian faithful, are deputed by God to the apostolate through their baptism and confirmation, they are therefore bound by the general obligations and enjoy the general right to work as individuals or in associations so that the divine message of salvation becomes known and accepted by all persons throughout the world; this obligation has a greater impelling force in those circumstances in which people can hear the gospel and know Christ only through lay persons.

§2. Each lay person in accord with his or her condition is bound by a special duty to imbue and perfect the order of temporal affairs with the spirit of the gospel; they thus give witness to Christ in a special way in carrying out those affairs and in exercising secular duties.

Can. 226 — §1. Lay persons who live in the married state in accord with their own vocation are bound by a special duty to work for the upbuilding of the people of God through their marriage and their family.

§2. Because they have given life to their children, parents have a most serious obligation and enjoy the right to educate them; therefore Christian parents are especially to care for the Christian education of their children according to the teaching handed on by the Church.

Can. 227 — Lay Christian faithful have the right to have recognized that

rebus civitatis terrenae libertas, quae omnibus civibus competit; eadem tamen libertate utentes, curent ut suae actiones spiritu evangelico imbuantur, et ad doctrinam attendant ab Ecclesiae magisterio propositam, caventes tamen ne in quaestionibus opinabilibus propriam sententiam uti doctrinam Ecclesiae proponant.

Can. 228 – § 1. Laici qui idonei reperiantur, sunt habiles ut a sacris Pastoribus ad illa officia ecclesiastica et munera assumantur, quibus ipsi secundum iuris praescripta fungi valent.

§ 2. Laici debita scientia, prudentia et honestate praestantes, habiles sunt tamquam periti aut consiliarii, etiam in consiliis ad normam iuris, ad Ecclesiae Pastoribus adiutorium praebendum.

Can. 229 – § 1. Laici, ut secundum doctrinam christianam vivere valeant, eandemque et ipsi enuntiare atque, si opus sit, defendere possint, utque in apostolatu exercendo partem suam habere queant, obligatione tenentur et iure gaudent acquirendi eiusdem doctrinae cognitionem, propriae uniuscuiusque capacitati et condicioni aptatam.

§ 2. Iure quoque gaudent pleniorem illam in scientiis sacris acquirendi cognitionem, quae in ecclesiasticis universitatibus facultatibusve aut in institutis scientiarum religiosarum traduntur, ibidem lectiones frequentando et gradus academicos consequendo.

§ 3. Item, servatis praescriptis quoad idoneitatem requisitam statutis, habiles sunt ad mandatum docendi scientias sacras a legitima auctoritate ecclesiastica recipiendum.

Can. 230 – § 1. Viri laici, qui aetate dotibusque pollent Episcoporum conferentiae decreto statutis, per ritum liturgicum praescriptum ad ministeria lectoris et acolythi stabiliter assumi possunt; quae tamen ministeriorum collatio eisdem ius non confert ad sustentationem remunerationemve ab Ecclesia praestandam.

§ 2. Laici ex temporanea deputatione in actionibus liturgicis munus lectoris implere possunt; item omnes laici muneribus commentatoris, cantoris aliisve ad normam iuris fungi possunt.

§ 3. Ubi Ecclesiae necessitas id suadeat, deficientibus ministris, possunt etiam laici, etsi non sint lectores vel acolythi, quaedam eorundem officia supplere, videlicet ministerium verbi exercere, precibus liturgicis praeesse, baptismum conferre atque sacram Communionem distribuere, iuxta iuris praescripta.

Can. 231 – § 1. Laici, qui permanenter aut ad tempus speciali Ecclesiae servitio addicuntur, obligatione tenentur ut aptam acquirant

freedom in the affairs of the earthly city which belongs to all citizens; when they exercise such freedom, however, they are to take care that their actions are imbued with the spirit of the gospel and take into account the doctrine set forth by the magisterium of the Church; but they are to avoid proposing their own opinion as the teaching of the Church in questions which are open to various opinions.

Can. 228 — §1. Qualified lay persons are capable of assuming from their sacred pastors those ecclesiastical offices and functions which they are able to exercise in accord with the prescriptions of law.

§2. Lay persons who excel in the necessary knowledge, prudence, and uprightness are capable of assisting the pastors of the Church as experts or advisors; they can do so even in councils, in accord with the norm of law.

Can. 229 — §1. Lay persons are bound by the obligation and possess the right to acquire a knowledge of Christian doctrine adapted to their capacity and condition so that they can live in accord with that doctrine, announce it, defend it when necessary, and be enabled to assume their role in exercising the apostolate.

§2. Lay persons also possess the right to acquire that deeper knowledge of the sacred sciences which are taught in ecclesiastical universities or faculties or in institutes of religious sciences by attending classes and obtaining academic degrees.

§3. Likewise, the prescriptions as to the required suitability having been observed, lay persons are capable of receiving from legitimate ecclesiastical authority a mandate to teach the sacred sciences

Can. 230 — §1. Lay men who possess the age and qualifications determined by decree of the conference of bishops can be installed on a stable basis in the ministries of lector and acolyte in accord with the prescribed liturgical rite; the conferral of these ministries, however, does not confer on these lay men a right to obtain support or remuneration from the Church.

§2. Lay persons can fulfill the function of lector during liturgical actions by temporary deputation; likewise all lay persons can fulfill the functions of commentator or cantor or other functions, in accord with the norm of law.

§3. When the necessity of the Church warrants it and when ministers are lacking, lay persons, even if they are not lectors or acolytes, can also supply for certain of their offices, namely, to exercise the ministry of the word, to preside over liturgical prayers, to confer baptism, and to distribute Holy Communion in accord with the prescriptions of law.

Can. 231 — §1. Lay persons who devote themselves permanently or temporarily to some special service of the Church are obliged to acquire the

formationem ad munus suum debite implendum requisitam, utque hoc munus conscie, impense et diligenter adimpleant.

§ 2. Firmo praescripto can. 230, § 1, ius habent ad honestam remunerationem suae condicioni aptatam, qua decenter, servatis quoque iuris civilis praescriptis, necessitatibus propriis ac familiae providere valeant; itemque iis ius competit ut ipsorum praevidentiae et securitati sociali et assistentiae sanitariae, quam dicunt, debite prospiciatur.

TITULUS III
DE MINISTRIS SACRIS SEU DE CLERICIS

Caput I
DE CLERICORUM INSTITUTIONE

Can. 232 – Ecclesiae officium est atque ius proprium et exclusivum eos instituendi, qui ad ministeria sacra deputantur.

Can. 233 – § 1. Universae communitati christianae officium incumbit fovendarum vocationum, ut necessitatibus ministerii sacri in tota Ecclesia sufficienter provideatur; speciatim hoc officio tenentur familiae christianae, educatores atque peculiari ratione sacerdotes, praesertim parochi. Episcopi dioecesani, quorum maxime est de vocationibus provehendis curam habere, populum sibi commissum de momento ministerii sacri deque ministrorum in Ecclesia necessitate edoceant, atque incepta ad vocationes fovendas, operibus praesertim ad hoc institutis, suscitent ac sustentent.

§ 2. Solliciti sint insuper sacerdotes, praesertim vero Episcopi dioecesani, ut qui maturioris aetatis viri ad ministeria sacra sese vocatos aestiment, prudenter verbo opereque adiuventur ac debite praeparentur.

Can. 234 – § 1. Serventur, ubi exsistunt, atque foveantur seminaria minora aliave instituta id genus, in quibus nempe, vocationum fovendarum gratia, provideatur ut peculiaris formatio religiosa una cum institutione humanistica et scientifica tradatur; immo, ubi id expedire iudicaverit Episcopus dioecesanus, seminarii minoris similisve instituti erectioni prospiciat.

§ 2. Nisi certis in casibus adiuncta aliud suadeant, iuvenes quibus animus est ad sacerdotium ascendere, ea ornentur humanistica et scientifica formatione, qua iuvenes in sua quisque regione ad studia superiora peragenda praeparantur.

appropriate formation which is required to fulfill their function properly and to carry it out conscientiously, zealously, and diligently.

§2. With due regard for can. 230, §1, they have a right to a decent remuneration suited to their condition; by such remuneration they should be able to provide decently for their own needs and for those of their family with due regard for the prescriptions of civil law; they likewise have a right that their pension, social security and health benefits be duly provided.

TITLE III
SACRED MINISTERS OR CLERICS

CHAPTER I
THE FORMATION OF CLERICS

Can. 232 — The Church has the duty and the proper and exclusive right to form those who are commissioned for the sacred ministries.

Can. 233 — §1. A duty rests upon the entire Christian community to foster vocations so that sufficient provision is made for the needs of the sacred ministry throughout the entire Church; Christian families, educators and in a special way priests, especially pastors, are particularly bound by this duty. Since it is principally the concern of diocesan bishops to promote vocations, they should instruct the people entrusted to them concerning the importance of the sacred ministry and the necessity of ministers in the Church; therefore they are to encourage and support endeavors to foster vocations by means of projects especially established for that purpose.

§2. Moreover priests, and especially diocesan bishops, are also to be solicitous that men of a more mature age who consider themselves called to the sacred ministries are prudently assisted in word and in deed and duly prepared.

Can. 234 — §1. Wherever minor seminaries or other such institutions exist they are to be maintained and supported; such institutions are those in which, for the sake of fostering vocations, special religious formation along with instruction in the humanities and sciences is provided; whenever the diocesan bishop judges it expedient he should provide for the erection of a minor seminary or a similar institution.

§2. Unless in certain cases circumstances indicate otherwise, young men who intend to be advanced to the priesthood are to be equipped with that training in the humanities and sciences by which young people in their own region are prepared to pursue higher studies.

Can. 235 – § 1. Iuvenes, qui ad sacerdotium accedere intendunt, ad formationem spiritualem convenientem et ad officia propria instituantur in seminario maiore per totum formationis tempus, aut, si adiuncta de iudicio Episcopi dioecesani id postulent, per quattuor saltem annos.

§ 2. Qui extra seminarium legitime morantur, ab Episcopo dioecesano commendentur pio et idoneo sacerdoti, qui invigilet ut ad vitam spiritualem et ad disciplinam sedulo efformentur.

Can. 236 – Aspirantes ad diaconatum permanentem secundum Episcoporum conferentiae praescripta ad vitam spiritualem alendam informentur atque ad officia eidem ordini propria rite adimplenda instruantur :

1º iuvenes per tres saltem annos in aliqua domo peculiari degentes, nisi graves ob rationes Episcopus dioecesanus aliter statuerit ;

2º maturioris aetatis viri, sive coelibes sive coniugati, ratione ad tres annos protracta et ab eadem Episcoporum conferentia definita.

Can. 237 – § 1. In singulis dioecesibus sit seminarium maius, ubi id fieri possit atque expediat ; secus concredantur alumni, qui ad sacra ministeria sese praeparent, alieno seminario aut erigatur seminarium interdioecesanum.

§ 2. Seminarium interdioecesanum ne erigatur nisi prius approbatio Apostolicae Sedis, tum ipsius seminarii erectionis tum eiusdem statutorum, obtenta fuerit, et quidem ab Episcoporum conferentia, si agatur de seminario pro universo eius territorio, secus ab Episcopis quorum interest.

Can. 238 – § 1. Seminaria legitime erecta ipso iure personalitate iuridica in Ecclesia gaudent.

§ 2. In omnibus negotiis pertractandis personam seminarii gerit eius rector, nisi de certis negotiis auctoritas competens aliud statuerit.

Can. 239 – § 1. In quolibet seminario habeantur rector, qui ei praesit, et si casus ferat vice-rector, oeconomus, atque si alumni in ipso seminario studiis se dedant, etiam magistri, qui varias disciplinas tradant apta ratione inter se compositas.

§ 2. In quolibet seminario unus saltem adsit spiritus director, relicta libertate alumnis adeundi alios sacerdotes, qui ad hoc munus ab Episcopo deputati sint.

§ 3. Seminarii statutis provideantur rationes, quibus curam rectoris, in disciplina praesertim servanda, participent ceteri moderatores, magistri, immo et ipsi alumni.

Can. 235 — §1. Young men who intend to enter the priesthood are to be given a suitable spiritual formation and trained for the duties of the priesthood in a major seminary throughout the entire time of formation, or, if circumstances demand it in the judgment of the diocesan bishop, at least for four years.

§2. Those who legitimately live outside a seminary are to be entrusted by the diocesan bishop to a devout and suitable priest, who is to see to it that they are carefully formed in the spiritual life and in discipline.

Can. 236 — According to the prescriptions of the conference of bishops, aspirants to the permanent diaconate are to be formed to nourish a spiritual life and instructed in the correct fulfillment of the duties proper to this order in the following manner:

1° young men are to live for at least three years in some special house unless the diocesan bishop decides otherwise for serious reasons;

2° men of a more mature age, whether celibate or married, are to spend three years in a program determined by the conference of bishops.

Can. 237 — §1. Wherever it is possible and expedient, there is to be a major seminary in every diocese; otherwise the students who are preparing themselves for the sacred ministries are to be entrusted to another seminary, or an interdiocesan seminary is to be erected.

§2. An interdiocesan seminary is not to be erected unless the approval of the Apostolic See has first been obtained for both its erection and its statutes; the approval will be obtained by the conference of bishops if it involves the entire territory, otherwise by the bishops involved.

Can. 238 — §1. By the law itself seminaries legitimately erected possess juridic personality in the Church.

§2. The rector of the seminary represents it in the handling of all matters unless the competent authority has determined otherwise concerning certain matters.

Can. 239 — §1. Every seminary is to have a rector who presides over it, a vice-rector if necessary, and a finance officer; moreover, if the students pursue their studies within the seminary itself it is also to have teachers who give instruction in the several disciplines in an appropriately coordinated curriculum.

§2. Every seminary is to have at least one spiritual director; the students, however, are free to approach other priests who have been appointed for this function by the bishop.

§3. The statutes of the seminary are to provide for ways in which the other moderators, professors, and even the students themselves share in the concerns of the rector especially regarding the observance of discipline.

Can. 240 – § 1. Praeter confessarios ordinarios, alii regulariter ad seminarium accedant confessarii, atque, salva quidem seminarii disciplina, integrum semper sit alumnis quemlibet confessarium sive in seminario sive extra illud adire.

§ 2. In decisionibus ferendis. de alumnis ad ordines admittendis aut e seminario dimittendis, numquam directoris spiritus et confessariorum votum exquiri potest.

Can. 241 – § 1. Ad seminarium maius ab Episcopo dioecesano admittantur tantummodo ii qui, attentis eorum dotibus humanis et moralibus, spiritualibus et intellectualibus, eorum valetudine physica et psychica necnon recta voluntate, habiles aestimantur qui ministeriis sacris perpetuo sese dedicent.

§ 2. Antequam recipiantur, documenta exhibere debent de susceptis baptismo et confirmatione aliaque quae, secundum praescripta institutionis sacerdotalis Rationis requiruntur.

§ 3. Si agatur de iis admittendis, qui ex alieno seminario vel instituto religioso dimissi fuerint, requiritur insuper testimonium respectivi superioris praesertim de causa eorum dimissionis vel discessus.

Can. 242 – § 1. In singulis nationibus habeatur institutionis sacerdotalis Ratio, ab Episcoporum conferentia, attentis quidem normis a suprema Ecclesiae auctoritate latis, statuenda et a Sancta Sede approbanda, novis quoque adiunctis, approbante item Sancta Sede, accommodanda, qua institutionis in seminario tradendae definiantur summa principia atque normae generales necessitatibus pastoralibus uniuscuiusque regionis vel provinciae, aptatae.

§ 2. Normae Rationis, de qua in § 1, serventur in omnibus seminariis, tum dioecesanis tum interdioecesanis.

Can. 243 – Habeat insuper unumquodque seminarium ordinationem propriam, ab Episcopo dioecesano aut, si de seminario interdioecesano agatur, ab Episcopis quorum interest, probatam, qua normae institutionis sacerdotalis Rationis adiunctis particularibus accommodentur, ac pressius determinentur praesertim disciplinae capita quae ad alumnorum cotidianam vitam et totius seminarii ordinem spectant.

Can. 244 – Alumnorum in seminario formatio spiritualis et institutio doctrinalis harmonice componantur, atque ad id ordinentur, ut iidem iuxta uniuscuiusque indolem una cum debita maturitate humana spiritum Evangelii et arctam cum Christo necessitudinem acquirant.

Can. 245 – § 1. Per formationem spiritualem alumni idonei fiant ad ministerium pastorale fructuose exercendum et ad spiritum missionalem efformentur, discentes ministerium expletum semper in fide viva et in

Can. 240 — §1. In addition to the ordinary confessors, other confessors are to come regularly to the seminary; moreover, with due regard for the discipline of the seminary, a student is always at liberty to go to any confessor in the seminary or outside of it.

§2. In making decisions concerning the admission of students to orders or their dismissal from the seminary, the opinion of the spiritual director and the confessors can never be sought.

Can. 241 — §1. The diocesan bishop is to admit to the major seminary only those who are judged capable of dedicating themselves permanently to the sacred ministries in light of their human, moral, spiritual and intellectual characteristics, their physical and psychological health and their proper motivation.

§2. Before they are accepted, they must submit documents certifying that baptism and confirmation have been received and other documents which are required in accord with the prescriptions of the program for priestly formation.

§3. When persons seek admission after they have been dismissed from another seminary or from a religious institute, further testimony is required from their respective superior, especially regarding the cause of their dismissal or their leaving.

Can. 242 — §1. Each nation should have a program for priestly formation which is to be determined by the conference of bishops in light of the norms issued by the supreme authority of the Church and which is also to be approved by the Holy See; when new circumstances require it the program is to be updated with the similar approval of the Holy See; this program is to define the main principles for imparting formation in the seminary as well as general norms which have been adapted to the pastoral needs of each region or province.

§2. The norms of the program mentioned in §1 are to be observed in all seminaries, both diocesan and interdiocesan.

Can. 243 — Furthermore, each seminary is to have its own rule, approved by the diocesan bishop or, in the case of an interdiocesan seminary, by the bishops involved; in the seminary rule the norms of the program for priestly formation should be adapted to particular circumstances, and those areas of discipline which affect the daily life of the students and the order of the entire seminary are to be determined more precisely.

Can. 244 — The spiritual formation of the students in the seminary and their doctrinal instruction are to be harmonized and arranged so that in accord with the unique character of each student, they acquire the spirit of the gospel and a close relationship with Christ along with appropriate human maturity.

Can. 245 — §1. Through their spiritual formation the students are to be-

caritate ad propriam sanctificationem conferre; itemque illas exco-
lere discant virtutes quae in hominum consortione pluris fiunt, ita
quidem ut ad aptam conciliationem inter bona humana et supernatu-
ralia pervenire valeant.

§ 2. Ita formentur alumni ut, amore Ecclesiae Christi imbuti, Pontifici Romano Petri successori humili et filiali caritate devinciantur,
proprio Episcopo tamquam fidi cooperatores adhaereant et sociam cum
fratribus operam praestent; per vitam in seminario communem atque
per amicitiae coniunctionisque necessitudinem cum aliis excultam praeparentur ad fraternam unionem cum dioecesano presbyterio, cuius in
Ecclesiae servitio erunt consortes.

Can. 246 – § 1. Celebratio Eucharistica centrum sit totius vitae
seminarii, ita ut cotidie alumni, ipsam Christi caritatem participantes, animi robur pro apostolico labore et pro vita sua spirituali praesertim ex hoc ditissimo fonte hauriant.

§ 2. Efformentur ad celebrationem liturgiae horarum, qua Dei ministri, nomine Ecclesiae pro toto populo sibi commisso, immo pro
universo mundo, Deum deprecantur.

§ 3. Foveantur cultus Beatae Mariae Virginis etiam per mariale
rosarium, oratio mentalis aliaque pietatis exercitia, quibus alumni spiritum orationis acquirant atque vocationis suae robur consequantur.

§ 4. Ad sacramentum paenitentiae frequenter accedere assuescant
alumni, et commendatur ut unusquisque habeat moderatorem suae
vitae spiritualis libere quidem electum, cui confidenter conscientiam
aperire possit.

§ 5. Singulis annis alumni exercitiis spiritualibus vacent.

Can. 247 – § 1. Ad servandum statum coelibatus congrua educatione praeparentur, eumque ut peculiare Dei donum in honore habere
discant.

§ 2. De officiis et oneribus quae ministris sacris Ecclesiae propria
sunt, alumni debite reddantur certiores, nulla vitae sacerdotalis difficultate reticita.

Can. 248 – Institutio doctrinalis tradenda eo spectat, ut alumni,
una cum cultura generali necessitatibus loci ac temporis consentanea,
amplam atque solidam acquirant in disciplinis sacris doctrinam, ita
ut, propria fide ibi fundata et inde nutrita, Evangelii doctrinam hominibus sui temporis apte, ratione eorundem ingenio accommodata, nun-
tiare valeant.

come equipped to exercise fruitfully the pastoral ministry and they are to be formed in a missionary spirit; in the course of their formation they are to learn that a ministry which is always carried out in living faith and in charity fosters their own sanctity; they are to learn to cultivate those virtues which are highly valued in human relations so that they can achieve an appropriate integration of human and supernatural qualities.

§2. The students are to be so formed that, imbued with the love for the Church of Christ, they are devoted with a humble and filial love to the Roman Pontiff, the successor of Peter, are attached to their own bishop as his trustworthy co-workers, and work as companions with their brothers; through the common life in the seminary and through cultivating relationships of friendship and association with others they are to be prepared for fraternal union with the diocesan presbyterate, with whose members they will share in the service of the Church.

Can. 246 — §1. The celebration of the Most Holy Eucharist is to be the center of the entire life of the seminary, so that daily the students, sharing in the very love of Christ, may draw especially from this richest of all sources the strength of spirit needed for their apostolic work and their spiritual life.

§2. They are to be formed to celebrate the liturgy of the hours by which the ministers of God pray to God in the name of the Church on behalf of all the people committed to them, indeed on behalf of the entire world.

§3. Devotion to the Blessed Virgin Mary, including the rosary, mental prayer and other devotional exercises are to be fostered so that the students acquire a spirit of prayer and gain strength in their vocation.

§4. The students are to become accustomed to approach the sacrament of penance frequently, and it is also recommended that each one have a director for his spiritual life who has been freely chosen and to whom he can open his conscience with confidence.

§5. Each year the students are to make a retreat.

Can. 247 — §1. The students are to be prepared through suitable education to observe the state of celibacy, and they are also to learn to honor it as a special gift of God.

§2. They are to be duly informed of the duties and burdens of sacred ministers of the Church; no difficulty of the priestly life is to be kept back from them.

Can. 248 — The doctrinal instruction which is to be given has as its goal that the students acquire, along with a general culture which is in accord with the needs of time and place, extensive and solid learning in the sacred disciplines; after they have thereby been grounded and nourished in their own faith, they should be able to announce the teaching of the gospel in a suitable fashion to the people of their times and in a manner which is adapted to their understanding.

Can. 249 – Institutionis sacerdotalis Ratione provideatur ut alumni non tantum accurate linguam patriam edoceantur, sed etiam linguam latinam bene calleant necnon congruam habeant cognitionem alienarum linguarum, quarum scientia ad eorum formationem aut ad ministerium pastorale exercendum necessaria aut utilis videatur.

Can. 250 – Quae in ipso seminario philosophica et theologica studia ordinantur, aut successive aut coniuncte peragi possunt, iuxta institutionis sacerdotalis Rationem ; eadem completum saltem sexennium complectantur, ita quidem ut tempus philosophicis disciplinis dedicandum integrum biennium, studiis vero theologicis integrum quadriennium adaequet.

Can. 251 – Philosophica institutio, quae innixa sit oportet patrimonio philosophico perenniter valido, et rationem etiam habeat philosophicae investigationis progredientis aetatis, ita tradatur, ut alumnorum formationem humanam perficiat, mentis aciem provehat, eosque ad studia theologica peragenda aptiores reddat.

Can. 252 – § 1. Institutio theologica, in lumine fidei, sub Magisterii ductu, ita impertiatur, ut alumni integram doctrinam catholicam, divina Revelatione innixam, cognoscant, propriae vitae spiritualis reddant alimentum eamque, in ministerio exercendo, rite annuntiare ac tueri valeant.

§ 2. In sacra Scriptura peculiari diligentia erudiantur alumni, ita ut totius sacrae Scripturae conspectum acquirant.

§ 3. Lectiones habeantur theologiae dogmaticae, verbo Dei scripto una cum sacra Traditione semper innixae, quarum ope alumni mysteria salutis, s. Thoma praesertim magistro, intimius penetrare addiscant, itemque lectiones theologiae moralis et pastoralis, iuris canonici, liturgiae, historiae ecclesiasticae, necnon aliarum disciplinarum, auxiliarium atque specialium, ad normam praescriptorum institutionis sacerdotalis Rationis.

Can. 253 – § 1. Ad magistri munus in disciplinis philosophicis, theologicis et iuridicis, ab Episcopo aut ab Episcopis, quorum interest, ii tantum nominentur qui, virtutibus praestantes, laurea doctorali aut licentia potiti sunt in universitate studiorum aut facultate a Sancta Sede recognita.

§ 2. Curetur ut distincti totidem nominentur magistri qui doceant sacram Scripturam, theologiam dogmaticam, theologiam moralem, liturgiam, philosophiam, ius canonicum, historiam ecclesiasticam, aliasque, quae propria methodo tradendae sunt, disciplinas.

§ 3. Magister qui a munere suo graviter deficiat, ab auctoritate, de qua in § 1, amoveatur.

Can. 249 — The program for priestly formation is to make provision that the students are not only carefully taught their native language but also that they are well skilled in the Latin language; they are also to have a suitable familiarity with those foreign languages which seem necessary or useful for their own formation or for the exercise of pastoral ministry.

Can. 250 — Philosophical and theological studies which are conducted in the seminary itself can be pursued successively or conjointly in accord with the program of priestly formation; these studies are to encompass a period of at least six full years in such a way that two full years are devoted to the philosophical disciplines and four full years to theological studies.

Can. 251 — Philosophical training ought to be based upon that heritage of philosophy which is perennially valid, and it also is to take into account contemporary philosophical investigation; it is to be so imparted that it perfects the human development of the students, sharpens their minds, and renders them more suitable for pursuing theological studies.

Can. 252 — §1. Theological training is to be so imparted in the light of faith and under the guidance of the magisterium that the students have a thorough understanding of Catholic doctrine in its integrity based on divine revelation, that they gather nourishment from it for their own spiritual lives, and that they can properly announce and safeguard it in the exercise of their ministry.

§2. The students are to be taught Sacred Scripture with special diligence so that they acquire a perception of the whole of Sacred Scripture.

§3. There are to be classes in dogmatic theology which are always to be based upon the written word of God along with sacred tradition, in which the students may learn to penetrate ever more profoundly the mysteries of salvation, with St. Thomas as their teacher in a special way; there are likewise to be classes in moral and pastoral theology, in canon law, liturgy, church history, and other auxiliary and special disciplines; all these classes should be in accord with the prescriptions of the program for priestly formation.

Can. 253 — §1. Only those persons are to be appointed by the appropriate bishop or bishops to teach the philosophical, theological and juridical disciplines in a seminary who, being outstanding in virtue, have obtained a doctorate or licentiate from a university or faculty recognized by the Holy See.

§2. Care is to be taken that distinct and individual teachers are appointed to teach Sacred Scripture, dogmatic theology, moral theology, liturgy, philosophy, canon law, church history, and other disciplines all of which are to be taught in accord with their own proper methodology.

§3. A teacher who is seriously deficient in his or her duty, is to be removed by the authority mentioned in §1.

Can. 254 – § 1. Magistri in disciplinis tradendis de intima universae doctrinae fidei unitate et harmonia iugiter solliciti sint, ut unam
scientiam alumni se discere experiantur; quo aptius id obtineatur,
adsit in seminario qui integram studiorum ordinationem moderetur.

§ 2. Ita alumni edoceantur, ut et ipsi habiles fiant ad quaestiones
aptis investigationibus propriis scientifica methodo examinandas; habeantur igitur exercitationes, in quibus, sub moderamine magistrorum,
alumni proprio labore studia quaedam persolvere discant.

Can. 255 – Licet universa alumnorum in seminario formatio pastoralem finem persequatur, institutio stricte pastoralis in eodem ordinetur, qua alumni principia et artes addiscant quae, attentis quoque
loci ac temporis necessitatibus, ad ministerium Dei populum docendi,
sanctificandi et regendi exercendum pertineant.

Can. 256 – § 1. Diligenter instruantur alumni in iis quae peculiari
ratione ad sacrum ministerium spectant, praesertim in arte catechetica
et homiletica exercenda, in cultu divino peculiarique modo in sacramentis celebrandis, in commercio cum hominibus, etiam non catholicis
vel non credentibus, habendo, in paroecia administranda atque in
ceteris muneribus adimplendis.

§ 2. Edoceantur alumni de universae Ecclesiae necessitatibus, ita
ut sollicitudinem habeant de vocationibus promovendis, de quaestionibus missionalibus, oecumenicis necnon de aliis, socialibus quoque,
urgentioribus.

Can. 257 – § 1. Alumnorum institutioni ita provideatur, ut non
tantum Ecclesiae particularis in cuius servitio incardinentur, sed universae quoque Ecclesiae sollicitudinem habeant, atque paratos se exhibeant Ecclesiis particularibus, quarum gravis urget necessitas, sese
devovere.

§ 2. Curet Episcopus dioecesanus ut clerici, a propria Ecclesia
particulari ad Ecclesiam particularem alterius regionis transmigrare
intendentes, apte praeparentur ad ibidem sacrum ministerium exercendum, ut scilicet et linguam regionis addiscant, et eiusdem institutorum, condicionum socialium, usuum et consuetudinum intellegen-
tiam habeant.

Can. 258 – Ut apostolatus exercendi artem in opere ipso etiam
addiscant, alumni, studiorum curriculo decurrente, praesertim vero
feriarum tempore, praxi pastorali initientur per opportunas, sub moderamine semper sacerdotis periti, exercitationes, alumnorum aetati
et locorum condicioni aptatas, de iudicio Ordinarii determinandas.

Can. 254 — §1. In imparting their disciplines, teachers are to be constantly concerned for the close unity and harmony of the entire doctrine of the faith so that their students experience that they are learning one science; in order for this objective to be more suitably realized, there is to be someone in the seminary who moderates the whole curriculum of studies.

§2. The students are to be instructed so that they become capable of examining questions in a scientific method through their own qualified research; therefore projects are to be conducted under the supervision of the teachers by which the students learn to pursue certain studies through their own efforts.

Can. 255 — Although the entire formation of the students in the seminary is for a pastoral purpose, strictly pastoral training is also to be arranged by which the students are taught the principles and skills which pertain to the ministry of teaching, sanctifying and ruling the people of God in light of the needs of the place and time.

Can. 256 — §1. The students are to be instructed diligently in those matters which have a special relationship to sacred ministry, especially catechetics and homiletics, the celebration of divine worship, particularly that of the sacraments, the conducting of relationships with people, even non-Catholics or non-believers, the administration of a parish, and the fulfillment of all other duties.

§2. The students are to be instructed in the needs of the universal Church so that they have a concern for the promotion of vocations, for missionary questions, for ecumenical concerns and other more urgent issues including those of a social nature.

Can. 257 — §1. The formation of students is to prepare them so that they are concerned not only for the particular church into whose service they are incardinated but also for the universal Church; hence they are to show that they are ready to devote themselves to particular churches which are in serious need.

§2. The diocesan bishop is to take care that the clergy who intend to transfer from their own particular church to a particular church in another region are suitably prepared to exercise the sacred ministry there, namely, that they learn the language of that region and understand the region's institutions, social conditions, usages, and customs.

Can. 258 — In order that they may also learn through practice the art of exercising the apostolate, during the course of their studies and especially during holiday times the students are to be initiated into pastoral practice; this is to be accomplished by means of suitable activities, determined by the judgment of the ordinary and adapted to the age of the students and to local conditions and always under the supervision of a skilled priest.

Can. 259 – § 1. Episcopo dioecesano aut, si de seminario interdioecesano agatur, Episcopis quorum interest, competit quae ad seminarii superius regimen et administrationem spectant, decernere.

§ 2. Episcopus dioecesanus aut, si de seminario interdioecesano agatur, Episcopi quorum interest, frequenter seminarium ipsi visitent, in formationem suorum alumnorum necnon in institutionem, quae in eodem tradatur, philosophicam et theologicam invigilent, et de alumnorum vocatione, indole, pietate ac profectu cognitionem sibi comparent, maxime intuitu sacrarum ordinationum conferendarum.

Can. 260 – Rectori, cuius est cotidianum moderamen curare seminarii, ad normam quidem institutionis sacerdotalis Rationis ac seminarii ordinationis, omnes in propriis muneribus adimplendis obtemperare debent.

Can. 261 – § 1. Seminarii rector itemque, sub eiusdem auctoritate, moderatores et magistri pro parte sua curent ut alumni normas Ratione institutionis sacerdotalis necnon seminarii ordinatione praescriptas adamussim servent.

§ 2. Sedulo provideant seminarii rector atque studiorum moderator ut magistri suo munere rite fungantur, secundum praescripta Rationis institutionis sacerdotalis ac seminarii ordinationis.

Can. 262 – Exemptum a regimine paroeciali seminarium esto : et pro omnibus qui in seminario sunt, parochi officium, excepta materia matrimoniali et firmo praescripto can. 985, obeat seminarii rector eiusve delegatus.

Can. 263 – Episcopus dioecesanus vel, si de seminario interdioecesano agatur, Episcopi quorum interest, pro parte ab eis communi consilio determinata, curare debent ut provideatur seminarii constitutioni et conservationi, alumnorum sustentationi necnon magistrorum remunerationi aliisque seminarii necessitatibus.

Can. 264 – § 1. Ut seminarii necessitatibus provideatur, praeter stipem de qua in can. 1266, potest Episcopus in dioecesi tributum imponere.

§ 2. Tributo pro seminario obnoxiae sunt cunctae personae iuridicae ecclesiasticae, etiam privatae quae sedem in dioecesi habeant, nisi solis eleemosynis sustententur aut in eis collegium discentium vel docentium ad commune Ecclesiae bonum promovendum actu habeatur ; huiusmodi tributum debet esse generale, reditibus eorum qui eidem obnoxii sunt proportionatum, atque iuxta necessitates seminarii determinatum.

Can. 259 — §1. The diocesan bishop or, if it is a question of an interdiocesan seminary, the bishops involved, are competent to make decisions concerning the above-mentioned governance and administration of the seminary.

§2. The diocesan bishop or if it is a question of an interdiocesan seminary, the bishops involved, are to visit the seminary frequently in person; they are to watch over the formation of the students and the philosophical and theological instruction given them in the seminary; they are also to keep themselves informed concerning their students' vocation, character, piety and progress, especially in view of the conferral of sacred ordination.

Can. 260 — In carrying out their duties all are to obey the rector who has the responsibility to see to the daily administration of the seminary in accord with the norms of the program for priestly formation and the rule of the seminary.

Can. 261 — §1. The rector of the seminary and, under his authority, the moderators and teachers for their part are to see to it that the students exactly observe the norms of the program for priestly formation and the prescriptions of the rule of the seminary.

§2. The rector of the seminary and the director of studies are carefully to see to it that the teachers duly perform their function in accord with the prescriptions of the program for priestly formation and the rule of the seminary.

Can. 262 — The seminary is to be exempt from parochial governance; the rector of the seminary or his delegate is to fulfill the office of pastor for all who are in the seminary, with the exception of matrimonial matters and with due regard for the prescription of can. 985.

Can. 263 — The diocesan bishop must see to it that provision is made for the establishment and maintenance of the seminary, the support of the students, the remuneration of the teachers, and other needs of the seminary; if the seminary is interdiocesan the bishops involved must make such provisions based upon a mutual agreement worked out by them.

Can. 264 — §1. In addition to the collection mentioned in can. 1266 the bishop can impose a tax within the diocese to provide for the needs of the seminary.

§2. All ecclesiastical juridic persons, even private ones, which have a foundation in the diocese are subject to this tax for the seminary, unless they are maintained through alms alone or they contain a college of students or teachers to promote the common good of the Church; a tax of this type must be general, proportioned to the revenues of those who are subject to it, and determined in accord with the needs of the seminary.

Caput II

DE CLERICORUM ADSCRIPTIONE SEU INCARDINATIONE

Can. 265 – Quemlibet clericum oportet esse incardinatum aut alicui Ecclesiae particulari vel Praelaturae personali, aut alicui instituto vitae consecratae vel societati hac facultate praeditis, ita ut clerici acephali seu vagi minime admittantur.

Can. 266 – § 1. Per receptum diaconatum aliquis fit clericus et incardinatur Ecclesiae particulari vel Praelaturae personali pro cuius servitio promotus est.

§ 2. Sodalis in instituto religioso votis perpetuis professus aut societati clericali vitae apostolicae definitive incorporatus, per receptum diaconatum incardinatur tamquam clericus eidem instituto aut societati, nisi ad societates quod attinet aliter ferant constitutiones.

§ 3. Sodalis instituti saecularis per receptum diaconatum incardinatur Ecclesiae particulari pro cuius servitio promotus est, nisi vi concessionis Sedis Apostolicae ipsi instituto incardinetur.

Can. 267 – § 1. Ut clericus iam incardinatus alii Ecclesiae particulari valide incardinetur, ab Episcopo dioecesano obtinere debet litteras ab eodem subscriptas excardinationis; et pariter ab Episcopo dioecesano Ecclesiae particularis cui se incardinari desiderat, litteras ab eodem subscriptas incardinationis.

§ 2. Excardinatio ita concessa effectum non sortitur nisi incardinatione obtenta in alia Ecclesia particulari.

Can. 268 – § 1. Clericus qui a propria Ecclesia particulari in aliam legitime transmigraverit, huic Ecclesiae particulari, transacto quinquennio, ipso iure incardinatur, si talem voluntatem in scriptis manifestaverit tum Episcopo dioecesano Ecclesiae hospitis tum Episcopo dioecesano proprio, neque horum alteruter ipsi contrariam scripto mentem intra quattuor menses a receptis litteris significaverit.

§ 2. Per admissionem perpetuam aut definitivam in institutum vitae consecratae aut in societatem vitae apostolicae, clericus qui, ad normam can. 266, eidem instituto aut societati incardinatur, a propria Ecclesia particulari excardinatur.

Can. 269 – Ad incardinationem clerici Episcopus dioecesanus ne deveniat nisi:

1° necessitas aut utilitas suae Ecclesiae particularis id exigat, et salvis iuris praescriptis honestam sustentationem clericorum respicientibus;

2° ex legitimo documento sibi constiterit de concessa excardina-

CHAPTER II
INSCRIPTION OR INCARDINATION OF CLERICS

Can. 265 — Every cleric must be incardinated into some particular church or personal prelature or into an institute of consecrated life or society endowed with this faculty, so that unattached or transient clerics are not allowed at all.

Can. 266 — §1. A person becomes a cleric through the reception of diaconate and is incardinated into the particular church or personal prelature for whose service he has been advanced.

§2. A professed member of a religious institute in perpetual vows or a definitively incorporated member of a clerical society of apostolic life is incardinated as a cleric to the institute or society through the reception of diaconate unless in the case of societies their constitutions establish otherwise.

§3. A member of a secular institute is incardinated into a particular church for whose service he has been advanced through the reception of diaconate unless he is incardinated into the institute itself by virtue of a grant of the Apostolic See.

Can. 267 — §1. In order for a cleric already incardinated to be incardinated validly into another particular church, he must obtain from the diocesan bishop a letter of excardination signed by the bishop; he must likewise obtain from the diocesan bishop of the particular church into which he desires to be incardinated a letter of incardination signed by that bishop.

§2. Excardination thus granted does not take effect unless incardination into another particular church has been obtained.

Can. 268 — §1. A cleric who has legitimately moved from his own particular church into another one is incardinated into this other particular church by the law itself after five years if he made such a desire known in writing both to the diocesan bishop of the host church and to his own diocesan bishop and provided neither of them informed the cleric of his opposition in writing within four months of the reception of his letter.

§2. Through perpetual or definitive admission to an institute of consecrated life or to a society of apostolic life a cleric who is incardinated into that institute or society in accord with the norm of can. 266 is excardinated from his own particular church.

Can. 269 — A diocesan bishop is not to allow the incardination of a cleric unless:

1° the necessity or advantage of his own particular church demands it, with due regard for the prescriptions of the law concerning the decent support of clerics;

2° he is certain from a legitimate document that excardination has been

tione, et habuerit praeterea ab Episcopo dioecesano excardinanti, sub secreto si opus sit, de clerici vita, moribus ac studiis opportuna testimonia;

3° clericus eidem Episcopo dioecesano scripto declaraverit se novae Ecclesiae particularis servitio velle addici ad normam iuris.

Can. 270 – Excardinatio licite concedi potest iustis tantum de causis, quales sunt Ecclesiae utilitas aut bonum ipsius clerici; denegari autem non potest nisi exstantibus gravibus causis; licet tamen clerico, qui se gravatum censuerit et Episcopum receptorem invenerit, contra decisionem recurrere.

Can. 271 – § 1. Extra casum verae necessitatis Ecclesiae particularis propriae, Episcopus dioecesanus ne deneget licentiam transmigrandi clericis, quos paratos sciat atque aptos aestimet qui regiones petant gravi cleri inopia laborantes, ibidem sacrum ministerium peracturi; prospiciat vero ut per conventionem scriptam cum Episcopo dioecesano loci, quem petunt, iura et officia eorundem clericorum stabiliantur.

§ 2. Episcopus dioecesanus licentiam ad aliam Ecclesiam particularem transmigrandi concedere potest suis clericis ad tempus praefinitum, etiam pluries renovandum, ita tamen ut iidem clerici propriae Ecclesiae particulari incardinati maneant, atque in eandem redeuntes omnibus gaudeant iuribus, quae haberent si in ea sacro ministerio addicti fuissent.

§ 3. Clericus qui legitime in aliam Ecclesiam particularem transierit propriae Ecclesiae manens incardinatus, a proprio Episcopo dioecesano iusta de causa revocari potest, dummodo serventur conventiones cum altero Episcopo initae atque naturalis aequitas; pariter, iisdem condicionibus servatis, Episcopus dioecesanus alterius Ecclesiae particularis iusta de causa poterit eidem clerico licentiam ulterioris commorationis in suo territorio denegare.

Can. 272 – Excardinationem et incardinationem, itemque licentiam ad aliam Ecclesiam particularem transmigrandi concedere nequit Administrator dioecesanus, nisi post annum a vacatione sedis episcopalis, et cum consensu collegii consultorum.

Caput III
DE CLERICORUM OBLIGATIONIBUS ET IURIBUS

Can. 273 – Clerici speciali obligatione tenentur Summo Pontifici et suo quisque Ordinario reverentiam et oboedientiam exhibendi.

Can. 274 – § 1. Soli clerici obtinere possunt officia ad quorum exer-

granted, and he also has in addition appropriate testimonials from the excardinating diocesan bishop, in secrecy if necessary, concerning the cleric's life, morals, and studies;

3° the cleric has declared in writing to the same diocesan bishop that he wishes to be dedicated to the service of the new particular church in accord with the norm of law.

Can. 270 — Excardination can be granted licitly for just causes only, such as the benefit of the Church or the good of the cleric himself; however, it cannot be denied except for serious reasons; a cleric, however, who thinks that he has been wronged and who has found a bishop to accept him may have recourse against the decision.

Can. 271 — §1. Outside the case of the true necessity of his own particular church, the diocesan bishop is not to deny clerics permission to move to regions which suffer from a serious dearth of clergy and to exercise the sacred ministry there when he knows that such clerics are prepared and when he judges them fit to do so; he is also to make provision that the rights and duties of these clerics are established through a written agreement with the diocesan bishop of the place where they are going.

§2. A diocesan bishop can grant his clerics permission to move to another particular church for a predetermined period of time which can be renewed several times; such clerics remain incardinated in their own particular church and, when they return to it, they possess all the rights which they would have had if they had exercised the sacred ministry there.

§3. A cleric who has legitimately moved to another particular church while remaining incardinated in his own church can for a just cause be recalled by his own diocesan bishop provided the agreements made with the other bishop and natural equity are observed; under the same conditions the diocesan bishop of the other particular church can likewise for a just cause deny the same cleric permission for a longer stay in his territory.

Can. 272 — A diocesan administrator cannot grant excardination, incardination or permission to move to another particular church unless the episcopal see has been vacant for a year and unless he has the consent of the college of consultors.

CHAPTER III

THE OBLIGATIONS AND RIGHTS OF CLERICS

Can. 273 — Clerics are bound by a special obligation to show reverence and obedience to the Supreme Pontiff and to their own ordinary.

Can. 274 — §1. Only clerics can obtain those offices for whose exercise

citium requiritur potestas ordinis aut potestas regiminis ecclesiastici.

§ 2. Clerici, nisi legitimo impedimento excusentur, munus, quod ipsis a suo Ordinario commissum fuerit, suscipere ac fideliter adimplere tenentur.

Can. 275 – § 1. Clerici, quippe qui omnes ad unum conspirent opus, ad aedificationem nempe Corporis Christi, vinculo fraternitatis et orationis inter se uniti sint, et cooperationem inter se prosequantur, iuxta iuris particularis praescripta.

§ 2. Clerici missionem agnoscant et promoveant, quam pro sua quisque parte laici in Ecclesia et in mundo exercent.

Can. 276 – § 1. In vita sua ducenda ad sanctitatem persequendam peculiari ratione tenentur clerici, quippe qui, Deo in ordinis receptione novo titulo consecrati, dispensatores sint mysteriorum Dei in servitium Eius populi.

§ 2. Ut hanc perfectionem persequi valeant:

1° imprimis ministerii pastoralis officia fideliter et indefesse adimpleant;

2° duplici mensa sacrae Scripturae et Eucharistiae vitam suam spiritualem nutriant; enixe igitur sacerdotes invitantur ut cotidie Sacrificium eucharisticum offerant, diaconi vero ut eiusdem oblationem cotidie participent;

3° obligatione tenentur sacerdotes necnon diaconi ad presbyteratum aspirantes cotidie liturgiam horarum persolvendi secundum proprios et probatos liturgicos libros; diaconi autem permanentes eandem persolvant pro parte ab Episcoporum conferentia definita;

4° pariter tenentur ad vacandum recessibus spiritualibus, iuxta iuris particularis praescripta;

5° sollicitantur ut orationi mentali regulariter incumbant, frequenter ad paenitentiae sacramentum accedant, Deiparam Virginem peculiari veneratione colant, aliisque mediis sanctificationis utantur communibus et particularibus.

Can. 277 – § 1. Clerici obligatione tenentur servandi perfectam perpetuamque propter Regnum coelorum continentiam, ideoque ad coelibatum adstringuntur, quod est peculiare Dei donum, quo quidem sacri ministri indiviso corde Christo facilius adhaerere possunt atque Dei hominumque servitio liberius sese dedicare valent.

§ 2. Debita cum prudentia clerici se gerant cum personis, quarum frequentatio ipsorum obligationem ad continentiam servandam in discrimen vocare aut in fidelium scandalum vertere possit.

there is required the power of orders or the power of ecclesiastical governance.

§2. Unless they are excused by a legitimate impediment, clerics are bound to undertake and faithfully fulfill a duty which has been entrusted to them by their ordinary.

Can. 275 — §1. Since they all work toward one end, the building up of the Body of Christ, clerics are to be united among themselves by the bond of brotherhood and of prayer; they are to strive for cooperation among themselves in accord with the prescriptions of particular law.

§2. Clerics are to acknowledge and promote that mission which lay persons exercise in their own way in the Church and in the world.

Can. 276 — §1. In leading their lives clerics are especially bound to pursue holiness because they are consecrated to God by a new title in the reception of orders as dispensers of God's mysteries in the service of His people.

§2. In order for them to pursue this perfection:

1° first of all they are faithfully and untiringly to fulfill the duties of pastoral ministry;

2° they are to nourish their spiritual life from the two-fold table of Sacred Scripture and the Eucharist; priests are therefore earnestly invited to offer the sacrifice of the Eucharist daily and deacons are earnestly invited to participate daily in offering it;

3° priests as well as deacons aspiring to the priesthood are obliged to fulfill the liturgy of the hours daily in accordance with the proper and approved liturgical books; permanent deacons, however, are to do the same to the extent it is determined by the conference of bishops;

4° they are also bound to make a retreat according to the prescriptions of particular law;

5° they are to be conscientious in devoting time regularly to mental prayer, in approaching the sacrament of penance frequently, in cultivating special devotion to the Virgin Mother of God, and in using other common and particular means for their sanctification.

Can. 277 — §1. Clerics are obliged to observe perfect and perpetual continence for the sake of the kingdom of heaven and therefore are obliged to observe celibacy, which is a special gift of God, by which sacred ministers can adhere more easily to Christ with an undivided heart and can more freely dedicate themselves to the service of God and humankind.

§2. Clerics are to conduct themselves with due prudence in associating with persons whose company could endanger their obligation to observe continence or could cause scandal for the faithful.

§ 3. Competit Episcopo dioecesano ut hac de re normas statuat magis determinatas utque de huius obligationis observantia in casibus particularibus iudicium ferat.

Can. 278 – § 1. Ius est clericis saecularibus sese consociandi cum aliis ad fines statui clericali congruentes prosequendos.

§ 2. Magni habeant clerici saeculares praesertim illas consociationes quae, statutis a competenti auctoritate recognitis, per aptam et convenienter approbatam vitae ordinationem et fraternum iuvamen, sanctitatem suam in ministerii exercitio fovent, quaeque clericorum inter se et cum proprio Episcopo unioni favent.

§ 3. Clerici abstineant a constituendis aut participandis consociationibus, quarum finis aut actio cum obligationibus statui clericali propriis componi nequeunt vel diligentem muneris ipsis ab auctoritate ecclesiastica competenti commissi adimpletionem praepedire possunt.

Can. 279 – § 1. Clerici studia sacra, recepto etiam sacerdotio, prosequantur, et solidam illam doctrinam, sacra Scriptura fundatam, a maioribus traditam et communiter ab Ecclesia receptam sectentur, uti documentis praesertim Conciliorum ac Romanorum Pontificum determinatur, devitantes profanas vocum novitates et falsi nominis scientiam.

§ 2. Sacerdotes, iuxta iuris particularis praescripta, praelectiones pastorales post ordinationem sacerdotalem instituendas frequentent atque, statutis eodem iure temporibus, aliis quoque intersint praelectionibus, conventibus theologicis aut conferentiis, quibus ipsis praebeatur occasio pleniorem scientiarum sacrarum et methodorum pastoralium cognitionem acquirendi.

§ 3. Aliarum quoque scientiarum, earum praesertim quae cum sacris conectuntur, cognitionem prosequantur, quatenus praecipue ad ministerium pastorale exercendum confert.

Can. 280 – Clericis valde commendatur quaedam vitae communis consuetudo ; quae quidem, ubi viget, quantum fieri potest, servanda est.

Can. 281 – § 1. Clerici, cum ministerio ecclesiastico se dedicant, remunerationem merentur quae suae condicioni congruat, ratione habita tum ipsius muneris naturae, tum locorum temporumque condicionum, quaque ipsi possint necessitatibus vitae suae necnon aequae retributioni eorum, quorum servitio egent, providere.

§ 2. Item providendum est ut gaudeant illa sociali adsistentia, qua eorum necessitatibus, si infirmitate, invaliditate vel senectute laborent, apte prospiciatur.

§3. The diocesan bishop has the competence to issue more specific norms concerning this matter and to pass judgment in particular cases concerning the observance of this obligation.

Can. 278 — §1. Secular clerics have the right to associate with others for the purpose of pursuing ends which befit the clerical state.

§2. Secular clerics are to place great value upon those associations in particular which, having statutes recognized by competent authority, foster holiness in the exercise of the ministry by means of a suitable and properly approved style of life and by means of fraternal assistance, and which promote the unity of the clergy among themselves and with their own bishop.

§3. Clerics are to refrain from establishing or participating in associations whose ends or activity cannot be reconciled with the obligations proper to the clerical state or which could hinder the diligent fulfillment of the duty entrusted to them by competent ecclesiastical authority.

Can. 279 — §1. Even after their ordination to the priesthood clerics are to continue to pursue sacred studies; they are to strive after that solid doctrine which is based upon Sacred Scripture, handed down by their predecessors and commonly accepted by the Church and which is contained especially in the documents of the councils and of the Roman Pontiffs; they are to avoid profane novelties and pseudo-science.

§2. In accord with the prescriptions of particular law, priests are to attend pastoral lectures which are to be held after priestly ordination; at times determined by the same particular law they are also to attend lectures and theological meetings or conferences which afford them opportunities to acquire a fuller knowledge of the sacred sciences and of pastoral methods.

§3. They are likewise to pursue a knowledge of the other sciences, especially those which are connected with the sacred sciences, particularly insofar as such knowledge contributes to the exercise of the pastoral ministry.

Can. 280 — Some community of life is highly recommended to clerics; wherever such a practice exists, it is to be preserved to the extent possible.

Can. 281 — §1. When clerics dedicate themselves to the ecclesiastical ministry they deserve a remuneration which is consistent with their condition in accord with the nature of their responsibilities and with the conditions of time and place; this remuneration should enable them to provide for the needs of their own life and for the equitable payment of those whose services they need.

§2. Provision is likewise to be made so that they possess that social assistance by which their needs are suitably provided for if they suffer from illness, incapacity or old age.

§ 3. Diaconi uxorati, qui plene ministerio ecclesiastico sese devovent, remunerationem merentur qua sui suaeque familiae sustentationi providere valeant; qui vero ratione professionis civilis, quam exercent aut exercuerunt, remunerationem obtineant, ex perceptis inde reditibus sibi suaeque familiae necessitatibus consulant.

Can. 282 – § 1. Clerici vitae simplicitatem colant et ab omnibus quae vanitatem sapiunt se abstineant.

§ 2. Bona, quae occasione exercitii ecclesiastici officii ipsis obveniunt, quaeque supersunt, provisa ex eis honesta sustentatione et omnium officiorum proprii status adimpletione, ad bonum Ecclesiae operaque caritatis impendere velint.

Can. 283 – § 1. Clerici, licet officium residentiale non habeant, a sua tamen dioecesi per notabile tempus, iure particulari determinandum, sine licentia saltem praesumpta Ordinarii proprii, ne discedant.

§ 2. Ipsis autem competit ut debito et sufficienti quotannis gaudeant feriarum tempore, iure universali vel particulari determinato.

Can. 284 – Clerici decentem habitum ecclesiasticum, iuxta normas ab Episcoporum conferentia editas atque legitimas locorum consuetudines, deferant.

. **Can. 285** – § 1. Clerici ab iis omnibus, quae statum suum dedecent, prorsus abstineant, iuxta iuris particularis praescripta.

§ 2. Ea quae, licet non indecora, a clericali tamen statu aliena sunt, clerici vitent.

§ 3. Officia publica, quae participationem in exercitio civilis potestatis secumferunt, clerici assumere vetantur.

§ 4. Sine licentia sui Ordinarii, ne ineant gestiones bonorum ad laicos pertinentium aut officia saecularia, quae secumferunt onus reddendarum rationum; a fideiubendo, etiam de bonis propriis, inconsulto proprio Ordinario, prohibentur; item a subscribendis syngraphis, quibus nempe obligatio solvendae pecuniae, nulla definita causa, suscipitur, abstineant.

Can. 286 – Prohibentur clerici per se vel per alios, sive in propriam sive in aliorum utilitatem, negotiationem aut mercaturam exercere, nisi de licentia legitimae auctoritatis ecclesiasticae.

Can. 287 – § 1. Clerici pacem et concordiam iustitia innixam inter homines servandam quam maxime semper foveant.

§3. Married deacons who dedicate themselves completely to the ecclesiastical ministry deserve a remuneration by which they can provide for their own support and that of their families; married deacons, however, who receive remuneration by reason of a civil profession which they exercise or have exercised are to take care of their own and their family's needs from the incomes derived from their profession.

Can. 282 — §1. Clerics are to cultivate a simple style of life and are to avoid whatever has a semblance of vanity.

§2. After they have provided for their own decent support and for the fulfillment of all the duties of their state of life from the goods which they receive on the occasion of exercising an ecclesiastical office, clerics should want to use any superfluous goods for the good of the Church and for works of charity.

Can. 283 — §1. Even if they do not have a residential office, clerics nevertheless are not to leave their diocese for a notable period of time, to be determined by particular law, without at least the presumed permission of their proper ordinary.

§2. Clerics are entitled to a due and sufficient period of vacation each year, to be determined by universal or particular law.

Can. 284 — Clerics are to wear suitable ecclesiastical garb in accord with the norms issued by the conference of bishops and in accord with legitimate local custom.

Can. 285 — §1. In accord with the prescriptions of particular law, clerics are to refrain completely from all those things which are unbecoming to their state.

§2. Clerics are to avoid those things which, although not unbecoming, are nevertheless alien to the clerical state.

§3. Clerics are forbidden to assume public offices which entail a participation in the exercise of civil power.

§4. Without the permission of their ordinary clerics are neither to become agents for goods belonging to laypersons nor assume secular offices which entail an obligation to render accounts; they are forbidden to act as surety, even on behalf of their own goods [with their personal property], without consultation with their proper ordinary; they are likewise to refrain from signing promissory notes whereby they undertake the obligation to pay an amount of money without any determined reason.

Can. 286 — Clerics are forbidden personally or through others to conduct business or trade either for their own benefit or that of others without the permission of legitimate ecclesiastical authority.

Can. 287 — §1. Most especially, clerics are always to foster that peace and harmony based on justice which is to be observed among all persons.

§ 2. In factionibus politicis atque in regendis consociationibus syndicalibus activam partem ne habeant, nisi iudicio competentis auctoritatis ecclesiasticae, Ecclesiae iura tuenda aut bonum commune promovendum id requirant.

Can. 288 – Diaconi permanentes praescriptis canonum 284, 285, §§ 3 et 4, 286, 287, § 2 non tenentur, nisi ius particulare aliud statuat.

Can. 289 – § 1. Cum servitium militare statui clericali minus congruat, clerici itemque candidati ad sacros ordines militiam ne capessant voluntarii, nisi de sui Ordinarii licentia.

§ 2. Clerici utantur exemptionibus, quas ab exercendis muneribus et publicis civilibus officiis a statu clericali alienis, in eorum favorem eaedem leges aut conventiones vel consuetudines concedunt, nisi in casibus particularibus aliter Ordinarius proprius decreverit.

Caput IV
DE AMISSIONE STATUS CLERICALIS

Can. 290 – Sacra ordinatio, semel valide recepta, numquam irrita fit. Clericus tamen statum clericalem amittit:

1° sententia iudiciali aut decreto administrativo, quo invaliditas sacrae ordinationis declaratur;

2° poena dimissionis legitime irrogata;

3° rescripto Apostolicae Sedis; quod vero rescriptum diaconis ob graves tantum causas, presbyteris ob gravissimas causas ab Apostolica Sede conceditur.

Can. 291 – Praeter casus de quibus in can. 290, n. 1, amissio status clericalis non secumfert dispensationem ab obligatione coelibatus, quae ab uno tantum Romano Pontifice conceditur.

Can. 292 – Clericus qui statum clericalem ad normam iuris amittit, cum eo amittit iura statui clericali propria, nec ullis iam adstringitur obligationibus status clericalis, firmo praescripto can. 291; potestatem ordinis exercere prohibetur, salvo praescripto can. 976; eo ipso privatur omnibus officiis, muneribus et potestate qualibet delegata.

Can. 293 – Clericus qui statum clericalem amisit, nequit denuo inter clericos adscribi, nisi per Apostolicae Sedis rescriptum.

§2. Clerics are not to have an active role in political parties and in the direction of labor unions unless the need to protect the rights of the Church or to promote the common good requires it in the judgment of the competent ecclesiastical authority.

Can. 288 — Permanent deacons are not bound by the prescriptions of cann. 284, 285, §§3 and 4, 286, 287, §2, unless particular law determines otherwise.

Can. 289 — §1. Since military service is hardly consistent with the clerical state, clerics and candidates for sacred orders are not to volunteer for military service without the permission of their own ordinary.

§2. Clerics are to make use of those exemptions from exercising duties and public civil offices alien to the clerical state which laws, agreements or customs grant in their favor, unless in particular cases their own proper ordinary has decided otherwise.

CHAPTER IV

LOSS OF THE CLERICAL STATE

Can. 290 — After it has been validly received, sacred ordination never becomes invalid. A cleric, however, loses the clerical state:

1° by a judicial decision or administrative decree which declares the invalidity of sacred ordination;

2° by the legitimate infliction of the penalty of dismissal;

3° by a rescript of the Apostolic See which is granted by the Apostolic See to deacons only for serious reasons and to presbyters only for the most serious reasons.

Can. 291 — Besides the case mentioned in can. 290, n.1, loss of the clerical state does not entail a dispensation from the obligation of celibacy, which is granted by the Roman Pontiff alone.

Can. 292 — A cleric who loses the clerical state in accord with the norm of law also loses with it the rights which pertain to the clerical state; nor is he bound by any of the obligations of the clerical state, with due regard for the prescription of can. 291; he is prohibited from exercising the power of orders with due regard for the prescription of can. 976; and by the very fact he is deprived of all offices, functions and any delegated power.

Can. 293 — A cleric who has lost the clerical state cannot become a member of the clergy again without a rescript of the Apostolic See.

TITULUS IV
DE PRAELATURIS PERSONALIBUS

Can. 294 – Ad aptam presbyterorum distributionem promovendam aut ad peculiaria opera pastoralia vel missionalia pro variis regionibus aut diversis coetibus socialibus perficienda, praelaturae personales quae presbyteris et diaconis cleri saecularis constent, ab Apostolica Sede, auditis quarum interest Episcoporum conferentiis, erigi possunt.

Can. 295 – § 1. Praelatura personalis regitur statutis ab Apostolica Sede conditis, eique praeficitur Praelatus ut Ordinarius proprius, cui ius est nationale vel internationale seminarium erigere necnon alumnos incardinare, eosque titulo servitii praelaturae ad ordines promovere.

§ 2. Praelatus prospicere debet sive spirituali institutioni illorum, quos titulo praedicto promoverat, sive eorundem decorae sustentationi.

Can. 296 – Conventionibus cum praelatura initis, laici operibus apostolicis praelaturae personalis sese dedicare possunt; modus vero huius organicae cooperationis atque praecipua officia et iura cum illa coniuncta in statutis apte determinentur.

Can. 297 – Statuta pariter definiant rationes praelaturae personalis cum Ordinariis locorum, in quorum Ecclesiis particularibus ipsa praelatura sua opera pastoralia vel missionalia, praevio consensu Episcopi dioecesani, exercet vel exercere desiderat.

TITULUS V
DE CHRISTIFIDELIUM CONSOCIATIONIBUS

CAPUT I
NORMAE COMMUNES

Can. 298 – § 1. In Ecclesia habentur consociationes distinctae ab institutis vitae consecratae et societatibus vitae apostolicae, in quibus christifideles, sive clerici sive laici sive clerici et laici simul, communi opera contendunt ad perfectiorem vitam fovendam, aut ad cultum publicum vel doctrinam christianam promovendam, aut ad alia apostolatus opera, scilicet ad evangelizationis incepta, ad pietatis vel caritatis opera exercenda et ad ordinem temporalem christiano spiritu animandum.

§ 2. Christifideles sua nomina dent iis praesertim consociationibus, quae a competenti auctoritate ecclesiastica aut erectae aut laudatae vel commendatae sint.

TITLE IV
PERSONAL PRELATURES

Can. 294 — Personal prelatures which consist of presbyters and deacons of the secular clergy can be erected by the Apostolic See, after consulting the conferences of bishops involved, in order to promote an appropriate distribution of presbyters or to perform particular pastoral or missionary works for various regions or different social groups.

Can. 295 — §1. A personal prelature is governed by the statutes established by the Apostolic See, and it is presided over by a prelate as its proper ordinary, who has the right to erect a national or international seminary, to incardinate the students, and to promote them to orders under the title of service to the prelature.

§2. The prelate must see to the spiritual formation and to the decent support of those whom he has promoted by the above-mentioned title.

Can. 296 — Lay persons can dedicate themselves to the apostolic works of a personal prelature by agreements entered with the prelature; the mode of this organic cooperation and the principal duties and rights connected with it shall be appropriately determined in the statutes.

Can. 297 — The statutes shall likewise define the relations of the personal prelature with the local ordinaries in whose particular churches the prelature itself exercises or desires to exercise its pastoral or missionary works, with the prior consent of the diocesan bishop.

TITLE V
ASSOCIATIONS OF THE CHRISTIAN FAITHFUL

CHAPTER I
COMMON NORMS

Can. 298 — §1. In the Church there are associations distinct from institutes of consecrated life and societies of apostolic life, in which the Christian faithful, either clergy or laity, or clergy and laity together, strive by common effort to promote a more perfect life or to foster public worship or Christian doctrine or to exercise other apostolic works, namely to engage in efforts of evangelization, to exercise works of piety or charity and to animate the temporal order with the Christian spirit.

§2. The Christian faithful should enroll especially in associations which are erected or praised or recommended by competent ecclesiastical authority.

Can. 299 – § 1. Integrum est christifidelibus, privata inter se con-ventione inita, consociationes constituere ad fines de quibus in can. 298, § 1 persequendos, firmo praescripto can. 301, § 1.

§ 2. Huiusmodi consociationes, etiamsi ab auctoritate ecclesiastica laudentur vel commendentur, consociationes privatae vocantur.

§ 3. Nulla christifidelium consociatio privata in Ecclesia agnosci-tur, nisi eius statuta ab auctoritate competenti recognoscantur.

Can. 300 – Nulla consociatio nomen « catholica » sibi assumat, nisi de consensu competentis auctoritatis ecclesiasticae, ad normam can. 312.

Can. 301 – § 1. Unius auctoritatis ecclesiasticae competentis est erigere christifidelium consociationes, quae sibi proponant doctrinam christianam nomine Ecclesiae tradere aut cultum publicum promo-vere, vel quae alios intendant fines, quorum prosecutio natura sua eidem auctoritati ecclesiasticae reservatur.

§ 2. Auctoritas ecclesiastica competens, si id expedire iudicaverit, christifidelium consociationes quoque erigere potest ad alios fines spi-rituales directe vel indirecte prosequendos, quorum consecutioni per privatorum incepta non satis provisum sit.

§ 3. Christifidelium consociationes quae a competenti auctoritate ecclesiastica eriguntur, consociationes publicae vocantur.

Can. 302 – Christifidelium consociationes clericales, eae dicuntur, quae sub moderamine sunt clericorum, exercitium ordinis sacri assu-munt atque uti tales a competenti auctoritate agnoscuntur.

Can. 303 – Consociationes, quarum sodales, in saeculo spiritum alicuius instituti religiosi participantes, sub altiore eiusdem instituti moderamine, vitam apostolicam ducunt et ad perfectionem christianam contendunt, tertii ordines dicuntur aliove congruenti nomine vocantur.

Can. 304 – § 1. Omnes christifidelium consociationes, sive publicae sive privatae, quocumque titulo seu nomine vocantur, sua habeant statuta, quibus definiantur consociationis finis seu obiectum sociale, sedes, regimen et condiciones ad partem in iisdem habendam requi-sitae, quibusque determinentur agendi rationes, attentis quidem tem-poris et loci necessitate vel utilitate.

§ 2. Titulum seu nomen sibi eligant, temporis et loci usibus accom-modatum, maxime ab ipso fine, quem intendunt, selectum.

Can. 305 – § 1. Omnes christifidelium consociationes subsunt vigi-lantiae auctoritatis ecclesiasticae competentis, cuius est curare ut in

Can. 299 — §1. The Christian faithful are free, by means of a private agreement made among themselves, to establish associations to attain the aims mentioned in can. 298, §1, with due regard for the prescriptions of can. 301, §1.

§2. Such associations are called private associations even though they are praised or recommended by ecclesiastical authority.

§3. No private association of the Christian faithful in the Church is recognized unless its statutes are reviewed by competent authority.

Can. 300 — No association shall assume the name "Catholic" without the consent of competent ecclesiastical authority, in accord with the norm of can. 312.

Can. 301 — §1. Competent ecclesiastical authority alone has the right to erect associations of the Christian faithful which set out to teach Christian doctrine in the name of the Church or to promote public worship or which aim at other ends whose pursuit by their nature is reserved to the same ecclesiastical authority.

§2. Competent ecclesiastical authority, if it judges it expedient, can also erect associations of the Christian faithful in order to attain directly or indirectly other spiritual ends whose accomplishment has not been sufficiently provided for by the efforts of private persons.

§3. Associations of the Christian faithful which are erected by competent ecclesiastical authority are called public associations.

Can. 302 — Associations of the Christian faithful are called clerical associations when they are under the direction of the clergy, when they presume the exercise of sacred orders, and when they are recognized as such by competent authority.

Can. 303 — Associations whose members lead an apostolic life and strive for Christian perfection while living in the world and who share the spirit of some religious institute under the higher direction of that same institute are called third orders or some other appropriate name.

Can. 304 — §1. All associations of the Christian faithful, whether public or private, by whatever title or name they are called, are to have their own statutes which define the end of the association or its social objective, its headquarters, its government, the conditions of membership and by whom its policies are to be determined, according to the need or utility of time and place.

§2. They are to choose a title or name for themselves which is adapted to the usage of their time and place, selected especially in view of their intended purpose.

Can. 305 — §1. All associations of the Christian faithful are subject to the vigilance of competent ecclesiastical authority, whose duty it is to take care

iisdem integritas fidei ac morum servetur, et invigilare ne in disciplinam ecclesiasticam abusus irrepant, cui itaque officium et ius competunt ad normam iuris et statutorum easdem invisendi; subsunt etiam eiusdem auctoritatis regimini secundum praescripta canonum, qui sequuntur.

§ 2. Vigilantiae Sanctae Sedis subsunt consociationes cuiuslibet generis; vigilantiae Ordinarii loci subsunt consociationes dioecesanae necnon aliae consociationes, quatenus in dioecesi operam exercent.

Can. 306 – Ut quis consociationis iuribus atque privilegiis, indulgentiis aliisque gratiis spiritualibus eidem consociationi concessis fruatur, necesse est et sufficit ut secundum iuris praescripta et propria consociationis statuta, in eandem valide receptus sit et ab eadem non sit legitime dimissus.

Can. 307 – § 1. Membrorum receptio fiat ad normam iuris ac statutorum uniuscuiusque consociationis.

§ 2. Eadem persona adscribi potest pluribus consociationibus.

§ 3. Sodales institutorum religiosorum possunt consociationibus, ad normam iuris proprii, de consensu sui Superioris nomen dare.

Can. 308 – Nemo legitime adscriptus a consociatione dimittatur, nisi iusta de causa ad normam iuris et statutorum.

Can. 309 – Consociationibus legitime constitutis ius est, ad normam iuris et statutorum, edendi peculiares normas ipsam consociationem respicientes, celebrandi comitia, designandi moderatores, officiales, ministros atque bonorum administratores.

Can. 310 – Consociatio privata quae persona iuridica non fuerit constituta, qua talis subiectum esse non potest obligationum et iurium; christifideles tamen in ea consociati coniunctim obligationes contrahere atque uti condomini et compossessores iura et bona acquirere et possidere possunt; quae iura et obligationes per mandatarium seu procuratorem exercere valent.

Can. 311 – Sodales institutorum vitae consecratae qui consociationibus suo instituto aliquo modo unitis praesunt aut assistunt, curent ut eaedem consociationes operibus apostolatus in dioecesi exsistentibus adiutorium praebeant, cooperantes praesertim, sub directione Ordinarii loci, cum consociationibus quae ad apostolatum in dioecesi exercendum ordinantur.

that integrity of faith and morals is preserved in them and to watch lest abuse creep into ecclesiastical discipline; therefore that authority has the right and duty to visit them in accord with the norm of law and the statutes; such associations are also subject to the governance of the same authority according to the prescriptions of the following canons.

§2. Associations of any kind whatever are subject to the vigilance of the Holy See; diocesan associations and also other associations to the extent that they work in the diocese are subject to the vigilance of the local ordinary.

Can. 306 — In order for a person to enjoy the rights and privileges, indulgences and other spiritual favors granted to the association, it is necessary and suffices that the person has been validly received into it and not legitimately dismissed from it, in accord with the prescriptions of the law and the proper statutes of the association.

Can. 307 — §1. The reception of members is to be done in accord with the norm of law and the statutes of each association.

§2. The same person can be enrolled in several associations.

§3. Members of religious institutes can enroll in associations in accord with their own law with the consent of their superior.

Can. 308 — No one who has been legitimately enrolled may be dismissed from an association except for a just cause in accord with the norm of law and the statutes.

Can. 309 — Legitimately constituted associations have the right, in accord with the law and the statutes, to issue particular norms respecting the association itself, to hold meetings, to designate moderators, officials, other officers and administrators of goods.

Can. 310 — A private association which has not been constituted a juridic person cannot as such be a subject of obligations and rights; however, the Christian faithful associated together in it can jointly contract obligations and acquire rights and possess goods as co-owners and co-possessors; they can exercise their rights and obligations through an agent or proxy.

Can. 311 — Members of institutes of consecrated life who preside over or assist associations in some way united to their institute are to see to it that these associations give assistance to the works of the apostolate in a diocese, especially cooperating, under the direction of the local ordinary, with associations which are ordered to the exercise of the apostolate in the diocese.

Caput II

DE CHRISTIFIDELIUM CONSOCIATIONIBUS PUBLICIS

Can. 312 – § 1. Ad erigendas consociationes publicas auctoritas competens est :

1° pro consociationibus universalibus atque internationalibus, Sancta Sedes ;

2° pro consociationibus nationalibus, quae scilicet ex ipsa erectione destinantur ad actionem in tota natione exercendam, Episcoporum conferentia in suo territorio ;

3° pro consociationibus dioecesanis, Episcopus dioecesanus in suo cuiusque territorio, non vero Administrator dioecesanus, iis tamen consociationibus exceptis quarum erigendarum ius ex apostolico privilegio aliis reservatum est.

§ 2. Ad validam erectionem consociationis aut sectionis consociationis in dioecesi, etiamsi id vi privilegii apostolici fiat, requiritur consensus Episcopi dioecesani scripto datus ; consensus tamen ab Episcopo dioecesano praestitus pro erectione domus instituti religiosi valet etiam ad erigendam in eadem domo vel ecclesia ei adnexa consociationem quae illius instituti sit propria.

Can. 313 – Consociatio publica itemque consociationum publicarum confoederatio, ipso decreto quo ab auctoritate ecclesiastica ad normam can. 312 competenti erigitur, persona iuridica constituitur et missionem recipit, quatenus requiritur, ad fines quos ipsa sibi nomine Ecclesiae persequendos proponit.

Can. 314 – Cuiuslibet consociationis publicae statuta, eorumque recognitio vel mutatio, approbatione indigent auctoritatis ecclesiasticae cui competit consociationis erectio ad normam can. 312, § 1.

Can. 315 – Consociationes publicae incepta propriae indoli congrua sua sponte suscipere valent, eaedemque reguntur ad normam statutorum, sub altiore tamen directione auctoritatis ecclesiasticae, de qua in can. 312, § 1.

Can. 316 – § 1. Qui publice fidem catholicam abiecerit vel a communione ecclesiastica defecerit vel excommunicatione irrogata aut declarata irretitus sit, valide in consociationes publicas recipi nequit.

§ 2. Qui legitime adscripti in casum inciderint de quo in § 1, praemissa monitione, a consociatione dimittantur, servatis eius statutis et salvo iure recursus ad auctoritatem ecclesiasticam, de qua in can. 312, § 1.

CHAPTER II

PUBLIC ASSOCIATIONS OF THE CHRISTIAN FAITHFUL

Can. 312 — §1. The authority competent to erect public associations is:

1° the Holy See for universal and international associations;

2° the conference of bishops in its own territory for national associations, that is, those which are directed by their founding purpose toward action in the whole nation;

3° the diocesan bishop in his own territory for diocesan associations, but not the diocesan administrator; however, those associations are excepted for whose erection the right has been reserved to others by apostolic privilege.

§2. The written consent of the diocesan bishop is required for the valid erection of an association or a branch of an association in a diocese, even if this is done in virtue of an apostolic privilege; however, the consent given by a diocesan bishop for the erection of a house of a religious institute also allows for the erection in the same house or church attached to it, of an association proper to the institute.

Can. 313 — A public association as well as a confederation of public associations is constituted a juridic person by the decree by which it is erected by competent ecclesiastical authority in accord with the norm of can. 312; it also thereby receives a mission to pursue the ends which it proposes for itself in the name of the Church, to the extent that such a mission is required.

Can. 314 — The statutes of any public association as well as their revision or change require the approval of the ecclesiastical authority which is competent to erect the association in accord with the norm of can. 312, §1.

Can. 315 — Public associations on their own initiative can begin undertakings in keeping with their character, and they can direct them in accord with their statutes, but under the further direction of the ecclesiastical authority mentioned in can. 312, §1.

Can. 316 — §1. One who has publicly rejected the Catholic faith or abandoned ecclesiastical communion or been punished with an imposed or declared excommunication cannot be validly received into public associations.

§2. Those legitimately enrolled who fall into the situations mentioned in §1, are, after a warning, to be dismissed from the association, observing the association's statutes and reserving the right of recourse to the ecclesiastical authority mentioned in can. 312, §1.

Can. 317 – § 1. Nisi aliud in statutis praevideatur, auctoritatis ecclesiasticae, de qua in can. 312, § 1, est consociationis publicae moderatorem ab ipsa consociatione publica electum confirmare aut praesentatum instituere aut iure proprio nominare; cappellanum vero seu assistentem ecclesiasticum, auditis ubi id expediat consociationis officialibus maioribus, nominat eadem auctoritas ecclesiastica.

§ 2. Norma in § 1 statuta valet etiam pro consociationibus a sodalibus institutorum religiosorum vi apostolici privilegii extra proprias ecclesias vel domos erectis; in consociationibus vero a sodalibus institutorum religiosorum in propria ecclesia vel domo erectis, nominatio aut confirmatio moderatoris et cappellani pertinet ad Superiorem instituti, ad normam statutorum.

§ 3. In consociationibus quae non sunt clericales, laici exercere valent munus moderatoris; cappellanus seu adsistens ecclesiasticus ad illud munus ne assumatur, nisi aliud in statutis caveatur.

§ 4. In publicis christifidelium consociationibus quae directe ad apostolatum exercendum ordinantur, moderatores ne ii sint, qui in factionibus politicis officium directionis adimplent.

Can. 318 – § 1. In specialibus adiunctis, ubi graves rationes id requirant, potest ecclesiastica auctoritas, de qua in can. 312, § 1, designare commissarium, qui eius nomine consociationem ad tempus moderetur.

§ 2. Moderatorem consociationis publicae iusta de causa removere potest qui eum nominavit aut confirmavit, auditis tamen tum ipso moderatore tum consociationis officialibus maioribus ad normam statutorum; cappellanum vero removere potest, ad normam cann. 192-195, qui eum nominavit.

Can. 319 – § 1. Consociatio publica legitime erecta, nisi aliud cautum sit, bona quae possidet ad normam statutorum administrat sub superiore directione auctoritatis ecclesiasticae de qua in can. 312, § 1, cui quotannis administrationis rationem reddere debet.

§ 2. Oblationum quoque et eleemosynarum, quas collegerit, eidem auctoritati fidelem erogationis rationem reddere debet.

Can. 320 – § 1. Consociationes a Sancta Sede erectae nonnisi ab eadem supprimi possunt.

§ 2. Ob graves causas ab Episcoporum conferentia supprimi possunt consociationes ab eadem erectae; ab Episcopo dioecesano consociationes a se erectae, et etiam consociationes ex apostolico indulto a sodalibus institutorum religiosorum de consensu Episcopi dioecesani erectae.

Can. 317 — §1. Unless otherwise provided in the statutes, the ecclesiastical authority mentioned in can. 312, §1, has the right to confirm as moderator of a public association the person elected by the association or to install the one presented or to name the person by his own right; the same ecclesiastical authority also names the chaplain or ecclesiastical assistant, having heard the major officials of the association where this is expedient.

§2. The norm stated in §1 is also valid for associations erected outside their own churches or houses by members of religious institutes in virtue of apostolic privilege; however, in associations erected by members of religious institutes in their own church or house, the nomination or confirmation of the moderator and chaplain belongs to the superior of the institute, in accord with the statutes.

§3. In associations which are not clerical, lay persons can exercise the office of moderator; the chaplain or ecclesiastical assistant shall not assume that role unless the statutes provide otherwise.

§4. Those who exercise leadership in political parties are not to be moderators in public associations of the Christian faithful which are directly ordered to the exercise of the apostolate.

Can. 318 — §1. In special circumstances where grave reasons require it the ecclesiastical authority mentioned in can. 312, §1, can designate a trustee who is to direct the association temporarily in the name of the authority.

§2. The one who named or confirmed the moderator of a public association can remove the moderator for a just cause, having heard both the moderator and the major officials of the association in accord with the norm of the statutes; however, the one who named the chaplain can remove him in accord with the norm of cann. 192–195.

Can. 319 — §1. Unless other provision has been made, a legitimately erected public association administers the goods which it possesses in accord with the norm of its statutes under the higher direction of the ecclesiastical authority mentioned in can. 312, §1, to whom the association must render an account of the administration each year.

§2. The association must also render to the same ecclesiastical authority a faithful account of the disposition of offerings and alms which it collects.

Can. 320 — §1. Associations erected by the Holy See can be suppressed only by the Holy See.

§2. Associations erected by a conference of bishops can be suppressed by the same conference for grave reasons; associations erected by a diocesan bishop can be suppressed by him, and also associations erected through an apostolic indult by members of religious institutes with the consent of the diocesan bishop.

§ 3. Consociatio publica ab auctoritate competenti ne supprimatur, nisi auditis eius moderatore aliisque officialibus maioribus.

Caput III

DE CHRISTIFIDELIUM CONSOCIATIONIBUS PRIVATIS

Can. 321 – Consociationes privatas christifideles secundum statutorum praescripta dirigunt et moderantur.

Can. 322 – § 1. Consociatio christifidelium privata personalitatem iuridicam acquirere potest per decretum formale auctoritatis ecclesiasticae competentis, de qua in can. 312.

§ 2. Nulla christifidelium consociatio privata personalitatem iuridicam acquirere potest, nisi eius statuta ab auctoritate ecclesiastica, de qua in can. 312, § 1, sint probata; statutorum vero probatio consociationis naturam privatam non immutat.

Can. 323 – § 1. Licet christifidelium consociationes privatae autonomia gaudeant ad normam can. 321, subsunt vigilantiae auctoritatis ecclesiasticae ad normam can. 305, itemque eiusdem auctoritatis regimini.

§ 2. Ad auctoritatem ecclesiasticam etiam spectat, servata quidem autonomia consociationibus privatis propria, invigilare et curare ut virium dispersio vitetur, earumque apostolatus exercitium ad bonum commune ordinetur.

Can. 324 – § 1. Christifidelium consociatio privata libere sibi moderatorem et officiales designat, ad normam statutorum.

§ 2. Christifidelium consociatio privata consiliarium spiritualem, si quemdam exoptet, libere sibi eligere potest inter sacerdotes ministerium legitime in dioecesi exercentes; qui tamen indiget confirmatione Ordinarii loci.

Can. 325 – § 1. Christifidelium consociatio privata ea bona quae possidet libere administrat, iuxta statutorum praescripta, salvo iure auctoritatis ecclesiasticae competentis vigilandi ut bona in fines associationis adhibeantur.

§ 2. Eadem subest loci Ordinarii auctoritati ad normam can. 1301 quod attinet ad administrationem erogationemque bonorum, quae ipsi ad pias causas donata aut relicta sint.

Can. 326 – § 1. Extinguitur christifidelium consociatio privata ad

§3. A public association is not to be suppressed by competent authority without having heard its moderator and other major officials.

CHAPTER III
PRIVATE ASSOCIATIONS OF THE CHRISTIAN FAITHFUL

Can. 321 — The Christian faithful guide and direct private associations according to the prescripts of their statutes.

Can. 322 — §1. A private association of the Christian faithful can acquire juridic personality by means of a formal decree of the competent ecclesiastical authority mentioned in can. 312.

§2. No private association of the Christian faithful can acquire juridic personality unless its statutes have been approved by the ecclesiastical authority mentioned in can. 312, §1; however, the approval of the statutes does not change the private nature of the association.

Can. 323 — §1. Although private associations of the Christian faithful enjoy autonomy in accord with the norm of can. 321, they are subject to the vigilance of ecclesiastical authority in accord with the norm of can. 305, and are subject to the governance of the same authority.

§2. It is also the responsibility of ecclesiastical authority, while observing the autonomy proper to private associations, to be watchful and take care that their energies are not dissipated and that their exercise of their apostolate is ordered toward the common good.

Can. 324 — §1. A private association of the Christian faithful freely selects its own moderator and officials in accord with the norm of its statutes.

§2. A private association of the Christian faithful can freely choose a spiritual advisor, if it desires one, from among the priests legitimately exercising ministry in the diocese; however, he needs the confirmation of the local ordinary.

Can. 325 — §1. A private association of the Christian faithful freely administers the goods which it possesses according to the prescriptions of its statutes, with due regard for the right of competent ecclesiastical authority to be watchful that the goods are used for the purposes of the association.

§2. An association is subject to the authority of the local ordinary in accord with the norm of can. 1301 concerning administration and disposition of funds which have been donated to it or left to it for pious causes.

Can. 326 — §1. A private association of the Christian faithful ceases to

normam statutorum; supprimi etiam potest a competenti auctoritate,
si eius actio in grave damnum cedit doctrinae vel disciplinae ecclesiasticae, aut scandalo est fidelium.

§ 2. Destinatio bonorum consociationis extinctae ad normam statutorum determinanda est, salvis iuribus quaesitis atque oblatorum
voluntate.

CAPUT IV

NORMAE SPECIALES DE LAICORUM CONSOCIATIONIBUS

Can. 327 – Christifideles laici magni faciant consociationes ad spirituales fines, de quibus in can. 298, constitutas, eas speciatim quae
rerum temporalium ordinem spiritu christiano animare sibi proponunt
atque hoc modo intimam inter fidem et vitam magnopere fovent unionem.

Can. 328 – Qui praesunt consociationibus laicorum, iis etiam quae
vi privilegii apostolici erectae sunt, curent ut suae cum aliis christifidelium consociationibus, ubi id expediat, cooperentur, utque variis
operibus christianis, praesertim in eodem territorio exsistentibus, libenter auxilio sint.

Can. 329 – Moderatores consociationum laicorum curent, ut sodales consociationis ad apostolatum laicis proprium exercendum debite efformentur.

PARS II

DE ECCLESIAE
CONSTITUTIONE HIERARCHICA

SECTIO I

DE SUPREMA ECCLESIAE AUCTORITATE

CAPUT I

DE ROMANO PONTIFICE DEQUE COLLEGIO EPISCOPORUM

Can. 330 – Sicut, statuente Domino, sanctus Petrus et ceteri Apo-
stoli unum Collegium constituunt, pari ratione Romanus Pontifex, successor Petri, et Episcopi, successores Apostolorum, inter se coniunguntur.

exist in accord with the norm of its statutes; it can also be suppressed by competent authority if its activity causes serious harm to ecclesiastical doctrine or discipline or is a scandal to the faithful.

§2. The allocation of the goods of an extinct association is to be determined in accord with the norm of its statutes, with due regard for acquired rights and the will of the donors.

CHAPTER IV
SPECIAL NORMS FOR ASSOCIATIONS OF THE LAITY

Can. 327 — Lay members of the Christian faithful are to esteem greatly associations established for the spiritual purposes mentioned in can. 298, and especially those which propose to animate the temporal order with the Christian spirit and in this way greatly foster an intimate union between faith and life.

Can. 328 — Those who preside over associations of the laity, even those associations erected in virtue of an apostolic privilege, are to see to it that they cooperate with other associations of the Christian faithful, where it is expedient, and willingly assist the various Christian works especially those in the same territory.

Can. 329 — Moderators of associations of the laity are to see to it that the members of the association are duly formed for the exercise of the apostolate which is proper to the laity.

PART II
THE HIERARCHICAL CONSTITUTION OF THE CHURCH

SECTION I
SUPREME CHURCH AUTHORITY

CHAPTER I
THE ROMAN PONTIFF AND THE COLLEGE OF BISHOPS

Can. 330 — Just as, by the Lord's decision, Saint Peter and the other Apostles constitute one college, so in a similar way the Roman Pontiff, successor of Peter, and the bishops, successors of the Apostles, are joined together.

Art. 1

DE ROMANO PONTIFICE

Can. 331 – Ecclesiae Romanae Episcopus, in quo permanet munus a Domino singulariter Petro, primo Apostolorum, concessum et successoribus eius transmittendum, Collegii Episcoporum est caput, Vicarius Christi atque universae Ecclesiae his in terris Pastor; qui ideo vi muneris sui suprema, plena, immediata et universali in Ecclesia gaudet ordinaria potestate, quam semper libere exercere valet.

Can. 332 – § 1. Plenam et supremam in Ecclesia potestatem Romanus Pontifex obtinet legitima electione ab ipso acceptata una cum episcopali consecratione. Quare, eandem potestatem obtinet a momento acceptationis electus ad summum pontificatum, qui episcopali charactere insignitus est. Quod si charactere episcopali electus careat, statim ordinetur Episcopus.

§ 2. Si contingat ut Romanus Pontifex muneri suo renuntiet, ad validitatem requiritur ut renuntiatio libere fiat et rite manifestetur, non vero ut a quopiam acceptetur.

Can. 333 – § 1. Romanus Pontifex, vi sui muneris, non modo in universam Ecclesiam potestate gaudet, sed et super omnes Ecclesias particulares earumque coetus ordinariae potestatis obtinet principatum, quo quidem insimul roboratur atque vindicatur potestas propria, ordinaria et immediata, qua in Ecclesias particulares suae curae commissas Episcopi pollent.

§ 2. Romanus Pontifex in munere supremi Ecclesiae Pastoris explendo, communione cum ceteris Episcopis immo et universa Ecclesia semper est coniunctus; ipsi ius tamen est, iuxta Ecclesiae necessitates, determinare modum, sive personalem sive collegialem, huius muneris exercendi.

§ 3. Contra sententiam vel decretum Romani Pontificis non datur appellatio neque recursus.

Can. 334 – In eius munere exercendo, Romano Pontifici praesto sunt Episcopi, qui eidem cooperatricem operam navare valent variis rationibus, inter quas est synodus Episcoporum. Auxilio praeterea ei sunt Patres Cardinales, necnon aliae personae itemque varia secundum temporum necessitates instituta; quae personae omnes et instituta, nomine et auctoritate ipsius, munus sibi commisum explent, in bonum omnium Ecclesiarum, iuxta normas iure definitas.

Can. 335 – Sede romana vacante aut prorsus impedita, nihil inno-

Art. I

THE ROMAN PONTIFF

Can. 331 — The bishop of the Church of Rome, in whom resides the office given in a special way by the Lord to Peter, first of the Apostles and to be transmitted to his successors, is head of the college of bishops, the Vicar of Christ and Pastor of the universal Church on earth; therefore, in virtue of his office he enjoys supreme, full, immediate and universal ordinary power in the Church, which he can always freely exercise.

Can. 332 — §1. The Roman Pontiff obtains full and supreme power in the Church by means of legitimate election accepted by him together with episcopal consecration; therefore, one who is already a bishop obtains this same power from the moment he accepts his election to the pontificate, but if the one elected lacks the episcopal character, he is to be ordained a bishop immediately.

§2. If it should happen that the Roman Pontiff resigns his office, it is required for validity that he makes the resignation freely and that it be duly manifested, but not that it be accepted by anyone.

Can. 333 — §1. The Roman Pontiff, by virtue of his office, not only has power in the universal Church but also possesses a primacy of ordinary power over all particular churches and groupings of churches by which the proper, ordinary and immediate power which bishops possess in the particular churches entrusted to their care is both strengthened and safeguarded.

§2. The Roman Pontiff, in fulfilling the office of the supreme pastor of the Church is always united in communion with the other bishops and with the universal Church; however, he has the right, according to the needs of the Church, to determine the manner, either personal or collegial, of exercising this function.

§3. There is neither appeal nor recourse against a decision or decree of the Roman Pontiff.

Can. 334 — In exercising his office the Roman Pontiff is assisted by the bishops who aid him in various ways and among these is the synod of bishops; moreover the cardinals assist him as do other persons and other institutes according to the needs of the times; all these persons and institutes, in his name and by his authority, carry out the task committed to them for the good of all the churches, according to the norms defined by law.

Can. 335 — When the Roman See is vacant or entirely impeded nothing is

vetur in Ecclesiae universae regimine : serventur autem leges speciales
pro iisdem adiunctis latae.

Art. 2

DE COLLEGIO EPISCOPORUM

Can. 336 – Collegium Episcoporum, cuius caput est Summus Pontifex cuiusque membra sunt Episcopi vi sacramentalis consecrationis et
hierarchica communione cum Collegii capite et membris, et in quo
corpus apostolicum continuo perseverat, una cum capite suo, et numquam sine hoc capite, subiectum quoque supremae et plenae potestatis
in universam Ecclesiam exsistit.

Can. 337 – § 1. Potestatem in universam Ecclesiam Collegium Episcoporum sollemni modo exercet in Concilio Oecumenico.

§ 2. Eandem potestatem exercet per unitam Episcoporum in mundo
dispersorum actionem, quae uti talis a Romano Pontifice sit indicta
aut libere recepta, ita ut verus actus collegialis efficiatur.

§ 3. Romani Pontificis est secundum necessitates Ecclesiae seligere
et promovere modos, quibus Episcoporum Collegium munus suum quoad
universam Ecclesiam collegialiter exerceat.

Can. 338 – § 1. Unius Romani Pontificis est Concilium Oecumenicum convocare, eidem per se vel per alios praesidere, item Concilium
transferre, suspendere vel dissolvere, eiusque decreta approbare.

§ 2. Eiusdem Romani Pontificis est res in Concilio tractandas
determinare atque ordinem in Concilio servandum constituere; pro-
positis a Romano Pontifice quaestionibus Patres Concilii alias addere
possunt, ab eodem Romano Pontifice probandas.

Can. 339 – § 1. Ius est et officium omnibus et solis Episcopis qui
membra sint Collegii Episcoporum, ut Concilio Oecumenico cum suffragio deliberativo intersint.

§ 2. Ad Concilium Oecumenicum insuper alii aliqui, qui episcopali
dignitate non sint insigniti, vocari possunt a suprema Ecclesiae auctoritate, cuius est eorum partes in Concilio determinare.

Can. 340 – Si contingat Apostolicam Sedem durante Concilii celebratione vacare, ipso iure hoc intermittitur, donec novus Summus
Pontifex illud continuari iusserit aut dissolverit.

Can. 341 – § 1. Concilii Oecumenici decreta vim obligandi non habent nisi una cum Concilii Patribus a Romano Pontifice approbata,

to be innovated in the governance of the universal Church; however, special laws enacted for these circumstances are to be observed.

Art. 2

THE COLLEGE OF BISHOPS

Can. 336 — The college of bishops, whose head is the Supreme Pontiff and whose members are the bishops by virtue of sacramental consecration and hierarchical communion with the head and members of the college, and in which the apostolic body endures, together with its head, and never without its head, is also the subject of supreme and full power over the universal Church.

Can. 337 — §1. The college of bishops exercises power over the universal Church in a solemn manner in an ecumenical council.

§2. The college exercises the same power through the united action of the bishops dispersed in the world, which action as such has been inaugurated or has been freely accepted by the Roman Pontiff so that a truly collegial act results.

§3. It is for the Roman Pontiff, in keeping with the needs of the Church, to select and promote the ways by which the college of bishops is to exercise collegially its function regarding the universal Church.

Can. 338 — §1. It is for the Roman Pontiff alone to convoke an ecumenical council, to preside over it personally or through others, to transfer, suspend or dissolve it, and to approve its decrees.

§2. It is for the same Roman Pontiff to determine matters to be treated in a council and to establish the order to be followed in a council; to the questions proposed by the Roman Pontiff the fathers of a council can add other questions, to be approved by the same Roman Pontiff.

Can. 339 — §1. It is the right and duty of all and only the bishops who are members of the college of bishops to take part in an ecumenical council with a deliberative vote.

§2. The supreme authority of the Church can call others who are not bishops to an ecumenical council and determine the degree of their participation in it.

Can. 340 — If the Apostolic See becomes vacant during the celebration of a council, it is interrupted by the law itself until a new Supreme Pontiff orders it to be continued or dissolves it.

Can. 341 — §1. Decrees of an ecumenical council do not have obligatory force unless they are approved by the Roman Pontiff together with the

ab eodem fuerint confirmata et eius iussu promulgata.

§ 2. Eadem confirmatione et promulgatione, vim obligandi ut habeant, egent decreta quae ferat Collegium Episcoporum, cum actionem proprie collegialem ponit iuxta alium a Romano Pontifice inductum vel libere receptum modum.

CAPUT II

DE SYNODO EPISCOPORUM

Can. 342 – Synodus Episcoporum coetus est Episcoporum qui, ex diversis orbis regionibus selecti, statutis temporibus una conveniunt ut arctam coniunctionem inter Romanum Pontificem et Episcopos foveant, utque eidem Romano Pontifici ad incolumitatem incrementumque fidei et morum, ad disciplinam ecclesiasticam servandam et firmandam consiliis adiutricem operam praestent, necnon quaestiones ad actionem Ecclesiae in mundo spectantes perpendant.

Can. 343 – Synodi Episcoporum est de quaestionibus pertractandis disceptare atque expromere optata, non vero easdem dirimere de iisque ferre decreta, nisi certis in casibus potestate deliberativa eandem instruxerit Romanus Pontifex, cuius est in hoc casu decisiones synodi ratas habere.

Can. 344 – Synodus Episcoporum directe subest auctoritati Romani Pontificis, cuius quidem est:

1° synodum convocare, quotiescumque id ipsi opportunum videatur, locumque designare ubi coetus habendi sint;

2° sodalium, qui ad normam iuris peculiaris eligendi sunt, electionem ratam habere aliosque sodales designare et nominare;

3° argumenta quaestionum pertractandarum statuere opportuno tempore ad normam iuris peculiaris ante synodi celebrationem;

4° rerum agendarum ordinem definire;

5° synodo per se aut per alios praeesse;

6° synodum ipsam concludere, transferre, suspendere et dissolvere.

Can. 345 – Synodus Episcoporum congregari potest aut in coetum generalem, in quo scilicet res tractantur ad bonum Ecclesiae universae directe spectantes, qui quidem coetus est sive ordinarius sive extraordinarius, aut etiam in coetum specialem, in quo nempe aguntur negotia quae directe ad determinatam determinatasve regiones attinent.

Can. 346 – § 1. Synodus Episcoporum quae in coetum generalem

fathers of the council and are confirmed by the Roman Pontiff and promulgated at his order.

§2. For decrees which the college of bishops issues to have obligatory force this same confirmation and promulgation is needed, when the college takes collegial action in another manner, initiated or freely accepted by the Roman Pontiff.

CHAPTER II
THE SYNOD OF BISHOPS

Can. 342 — The synod of bishops is that group of bishops who have been chosen from different regions of the world and who meet at stated times to foster a closer unity between the Roman Pontiff and the bishops, to assist the Roman Pontiff with their counsel in safeguarding and increasing faith and morals and in preserving and strengthening ecclesiastical discipline, and to consider questions concerning the Church's activity in the world.

Can. 343 — It is the role of the synod of bishops to discuss the questions on their agenda and to express their desires about them but not to resolve them or to issue decrees about them, unless the Roman Pontiff in certain cases has endowed the synod with deliberative power, and, in this event, it is his role to ratify its decisions.

Can. 344 — A synod of bishops is directly under the authority of the Roman Pontiff whose role it is to:

1° convoke a synod as often as he deems it opportune and to designate the place where its sessions are to be held;

2° ratify the election of those members who are to be elected in accord with the norm of special law and to designate and name its other members;

3° determine topics for discussion at a suitable time before the celebration of the synod in accord with the norm of special law;

4° determine the agenda;

5° preside over the synod in person or through others;

6° conclude, transfer, suspend and dissolve the synod.

Can. 345 — A synod of bishops can meet in a general session, which deals with matters which directly concern the good of the entire Church; such a session is either ordinary or extraordinary; a synod of bishops can also meet in a special session, which deals with matters which directly concern a definite region or regions.

Can. 346 — §1. The membership of a synod of bishops gathered in ordi-

ordinarium congregatur, constat sodalibus quorum plerique sunt Episcopi, electi pro singulis coetibus ab Episcoporum conferentiis secundum rationem iure peculiari synodi determinatam; alii vi eiusdem iuris deputantur; alii a Romano Pontifice directe nominantur; quibus accedunt aliqui sodales institutorum religiosorum clericalium, qui ad normam eiusdem iuris peculiaris eliguntur.

§ 2. Synodus Episcoporum in coetum generalem extraordinarium congregata ad negotia tractanda quae expeditam requirant definitionem, constat sodalibus quorum plerique, Episcopi, a iure peculiari synodi deputantur ratione officii quod adimplent, alii vero a Romano Pontifice directe nominantur; quibus accedunt aliqui sodales institutorum religiosorum clericalium ad normam eiusdem iuris electi.

§ 3. Synodus Episcoporum, quae in coetum specialem congregatur, constat sodalibus delectis praecipue ex iis regionibus pro quibus convocata est, ad normam iuris peculiaris, quo synodus regitur.

Can. 347 – § 1. Cum synodi Episcoporum coetus a Romano Pontifice concluditur, explicit munus in eadem Episcopis aliisque sodalibus commissum.

§ 2. Sede Apostolica post convocatam synodum aut inter eius celebrationem vacante, ipso iure suspenditur synodi coetus, itemque munus sodalibus in eodem commissum, donec novus Pontifex coetum aut dissolvendum aut continuandum decreverit.

Can. 348 – § 1. Synodi Episcoporum habetur secretaria generalis permanens, cui praeest Secretarius generalis, a Romano Pontifice nominatus, cuique praesto est consilium secretariae, constans Episcopis, quorum alii, ad normam iuris peculiaris, ab ipsa synodo Episcoporum eliguntur, alii a Romano Pontifice nominantur, quorum vero omnium munus explicit, ineunte novo coetu generali.

§ 2. Pro quolibet synodi Episcoporum coetu praeterea unus aut plures secretarii speciales constituuntur qui a Romano Pontifice nominantur, atque in officio ipsis commisso permanent solum usque ad expletum synodi coetum.

CAPUT III

DE SANCTAE ROMANAE ECCLESIAE CARDINALIBUS

Can. 349 – S. R. E. Cardinales peculiare Collegium constituunt, cui competit ut electioni Romani Pontificis provideat ad normam iuris peculiaris; Cardinales item Romano Pontifici adsunt sive collegialiter agendo, cum ad quaestiones maioris momenti tractandas in unum con-

nary general session consists of the following: for the most part, bishops elected to represent their individual groups by the conferences of bishops in accord with the special law of the synod; other bishops designated in virtue of this law itself; other bishops directly named by the Roman Pontiff. To this membership are added some members of clerical religious institutes elected in accord with the norm of the same special law.

§2. A synod of bishops is gathered in extraordinary general session to deal with matters which require a speedy solution; its membership consists of the following: most of them are bishops designated by the special law of the synod in virtue of the office which they hold; others are bishops directly named by the Roman Pontiff. To this membership are added some members of clerical religious institutes elected in accord with the same law.

§3. The membership of a synod of bishops gathered in special session consists of those who have been especially selected from the regions for which the synod has been convoked, in accord with the norm of the special law which governs such a synod.

Can. 347 — §1. When a session of a synod of bishops is concluded by the Roman Pontiff, the responsibility entrusted to the bishops and other members in the synod ceases.

§2. If the Apostolic See becomes vacant after a synod has been called or during its celebration the meeting of the synod is suspended by the law itself as is the responsibility which had been entrusted to its members in connection with it; such a suspension continues until a new Pontiff decrees either that the session be dissolved or continued.

Can. 348 — §1. The synod of bishops has a permanent general secretariat presided over by a general secretary who is appointed by the Roman Pontiff; he is assisted by the council of the secretariat; this council consists of bishops, some of whom are elected in accord with the norm of its special law by the synod of bishops itself while others are appointed by the Roman Pontiff; the responsibility of all these members ceases when a new general session begins.

§2. Furthermore one or several special secretaries are established who are named by the Roman Pontiff for each session of a synod of bishops, but they remain in the role entrusted to them only until the session of the synod has been completed.

Chapter III

THE CARDINALS OF THE HOLY ROMAN CHURCH

Can. 349 — The cardinals of the Holy Roman Church constitute a special college whose responsibility is to provide for the election of the Roman Pontiff in accord with the norm of special law; the cardinals assist the Roman Pontiff collegially when they are called together to deal with questions of

vocantur, sive ut singuli, scilicet variis officiis, quibus funguntur, eidem Romano Pontifici operam praestando in cura praesertim cotidiana universae Ecclesiae.

Can. 350 – § 1. Cardinalium Collegium in tres ordines distribuitur: episcopalem, ad quem pertinent Cardinales quibus a Romano Pontifice titulus assignatur Ecclesiae suburbicariae, necnon Patriarchae orientales qui in Cardinalium Collegium relati sunt; presbyteralem et diaconalem.

§ 2. Cardinalibus ordinis presbyteralis ac diaconalis suus cuique titulus aut diaconia in Urbe assignatur a Romano Pontifice.

§ 3. Patriarchae orientales in Cardinalium Collegium assumpti in titulum habent suam patriarchalem sedem.

§ 4. Cardinalis Decanus in titulum habet dioecesim Ostiensem, una cum alia Ecclesia quam in titulum iam habebat.

§ 5. Per optionem in Consistorio factam et a Summo Pontifice approbatam, possunt, servata prioritate ordinis et promotionis, Cardinales ex ordine presbyterali transire ad alium titulum et Cardinales ex ordine diaconali ad aliam diaconiam et, si per integrum decennium in ordine diaconali permanserint, etiam ad ordinem presbyteralem.

§ 6. Cardinalis ex ordine diaconali transiens per optionem ad ordinem presbyteralem, locum obtinet ante omnes illos Cardinales presbyteros, qui post ipsum ad Cardinalatum assumpti sunt.

Can. 351 – § 1. Qui Cardinales promoveantur, libere a Romano Pontifice seliguntur viri, saltem in ordine presbyteratus constituti, doctrina, moribus, pietate necnon rerum agendarum prudentia egregie praestantes; qui nondum sunt Episcopi, consecrationem episcopalem recipere debent.

§ 2. Cardinales creantur Romani Pontificis decreto, quod quidem coram Cardinalium Collegio publicatur; inde a publicatione facta officiis tenentur atque iuribus gaudent lege definitis.

§ 3. Promotus ad cardinalitiam dignitatem, cuius creationem Romanus Pontifex annuntiaverit, nomen autem in pectore sibi reservans, nullis interim tenetur Cardinalium officiis nullisque eorum gaudet iuribus; postquam autem a Romano Pontifice eius nomen publicatum fuerit, iisdem tenetur officiis fruiturque iuribus, sed iure praecedentiae gaudet a die reservationis in pectore.

Can. 352 – § 1. Cardinalium Collegio praeest Decanus, eiusque impediti vices sustinet Subdecanus; Decanus, vel Subdecanus, nulla in ceteros Cardinales gaudet potestate regiminis, sed ut primus inter

major importance; they do so individually when they assist the Roman Pontiff especially in the daily care of the universal Church by means of the different offices which they perform.

Can. 350 — §1. The college of cardinals is divided into three ranks: the episcopal rank which consists of both the cardinals to whom the Roman Pontiff assigns the title of a suburbicarian church and the oriental patriarchs who have become members of the college of cardinals; the presbyteral rank; and the diaconal rank.

§2. The Roman Pontiff assigns to each of the cardinals of presbyteral or diaconal rank his own title or *diaconia* in the city of Rome.

§3. The oriental patriarchs who have become members of the college of cardinals have as their title their own patriarchal see.

§4. The cardinal dean holds as his title the diocese of Ostia along with the other titular church which he already holds.

§5. With due regard for priority in rank and in promotion, through an option made during a consistory and approved by the Roman Pontiff, cardinals from the presbyteral rank can transfer to another title, and cardinals from the diaconal rank can transfer to another *diaconia*, and if they have remained in the diaconal rank for a period of ten full years they can transfer also to the presbyteral rank.

§6. A cardinal from the diaconal rank who transfers through option to the presbyteral rank precedes all those cardinal presbyters who became cardinals after him.

Can. 351 — §1. Those promoted as cardinals are men freely selected by the Roman Pontiff, who are at least in the order of the presbyterate and are especially outstanding for their doctrine, morals, piety and prudence in action; those, however, who are not yet bishops must receive episcopal consecration.

§2. Cardinals are created by a decree of the Roman Pontiff, which is published in the presence of the college of cardinals; from the time of this publication they are bound by the duties and possess the rights defined in law.

§3. When a person has been promoted to the dignity of cardinal and his creation has been announced by the Roman Pontiff who, however, reserves the person's name *in pectore*, he is not bound by any of the duties of cardinals nor does he possess any of their rights in the meantime; however, after his name has been made public by the Roman Pontiff he is bound by those duties and possesses those rights; but he enjoys his right of precedence from the day on which his name was reserved *in pectore*.

Can. 352 — §1. The dean presides over the college of cardinals; if he is impeded from doing so, the assistant dean takes his place; the dean or assistant dean does not possess any power of governance over the other

pares habetur.

§ 2. Officio Decani vacante, Cardinales titulo Ecclesiae suburbicariae decorati, iique soli, praesidente Subdecano si adsit, aut antiquiore ex ipsis, e coetus sui gremio unum eligant qui Decanum Collegii agat; eius nomen ad Romanum Pontificem deferant, cui competit electum probare.

§ 3. Eadem ratione de qua in § 2, praesidente ipso Decano, eligitur Subdecanus; Subdecani quoque electionem probare Romano Pontifici competit.

§ 4. Decanus et Subdecanus, si in Urbe domicilium non habeant, illud ibidem acquirant.

Can. 353 – § 1. Cardinales collegiali actione supremo Ecclesiae Pastori praecipue auxilio sunt in Consistoriis, in quibus iussu Romani Pontificis eoque praesidente congregantur; Consistoria habentur ordinaria aut extraordinaria.

§ 2. In Consistorium ordinarium, convocantur omnes Cardinales, saltem in Urbe versantes, ad consultationem de quibusdam negotiis gravibus, communius tamen contingentibus, aut ad actus quosdam maxime sollemnes peragendos.

§ 3. In Consistorium extraordinarium, quod celebratur cum peculiares Ecclesiae necessitates vel graviora negotia tractanda id suadeant, convocantur omnes Cardinales.

§ 4. Solum Consistorium ordinarium, in quo aliquae sollemnitates celebrantur, potest esse publicum, cum scilicet praeter Cardinales admittuntur Praelati, legati societatum civilium aliive ad illud invitati.

Can. 354 – Patres Cardinales dicasteriis aliisve institutis permanentibus Romanae Curiae et Civitatis Vaticanae praepositi, qui septuagesimum quintum aetatis annum expleverint, rogantur ut renuntiationem ab officio exhibeant Romano Pontifici qui, omnibus perpensis, providebit.

Can. 355 – § 1. Cardinali Decano competit electum Romanum Pontificem in Episcopum ordinare, si electus ordinatione indigeat; impedito Decano, idem ius competit Subdecano, eoque impedito, antiquiori Cardinali ex ordine episcopali.

§ 2. Cardinalis Proto-diaconus nomen novi electi Summi Pontificis populo annuntiat; item pallia Metropolitis imponit eorumve procuratoribus tradit, vice Romani Pontificis.

Can. 356 – Cardinales obligatione tenentur cum Romano Pontifice

cardinals but is considered to be first among equals.

§2. When the office of dean becomes vacant, the cardinals who possess a title to a suburbicarian church and they alone elect someone from their own number to act as dean of the college; this election is to be presided over by the assistant dean if he is available or by the oldest elector; they are to take the name of the person elected to the Roman Pontiff who is competent to approve the one elected.

§3. The assistant dean is elected in the same manner described in §2, with the dean himself presiding over the election; the Roman Pontiff is also competent to approve the election of the assistant dean.

§4. The dean and the assistant dean are to acquire a domicile in the city of Rome if they do not already have it there.

Can. 353 — §1. The cardinals are of special assistance to the Supreme Pastor of the Church through their collegial activity in consistories to which they are called by order of the Roman Pontiff who also presides over them; consistories are ordinary or extraordinary.

§2. All the cardinals, at least all those present in the city of Rome, are called together for an ordinary consistory to be consulted on certain serious matters which nevertheless occur rather frequently, or to carry out certain very solemn acts.

§3. All the cardinals are called together for an extraordinary consistory which is celebrated when the special needs of the Church or the conducting of more serious affairs suggests that it should be held.

§4. Only the ordinary consistory in which some solemnities are celebrated can be public, that is, a consistory to which, in addition to the cardinals, there are admitted prelates, legates of civil societies, or others who are invited to it.

Can. 354 — Cardinals who preside over the dicasteries and other permanent institutions of the Roman Curia and Vatican City and who have completed their seventy-fifth year of age are requested to tender their resignation from office to the Roman Pontiff, who will decide on the matter after he has weighed all the circumstances.

Can. 355 — §1. The cardinal dean is competent to ordain to the episcopate the person elected to be Roman Pontiff if that person requires ordination; if the dean is hindered from doing so the assistant dean has the same right; if the assistant dean is likewise hindered from doing so then the oldest cardinal from the episcopal rank has this right.

§2. The first cardinal deacon announces to the people the name of the newly elected Supreme Pontiff; he likewise invests metropolitans with the pallium or hands it over to their proxies in place of the Roman Pontiff.

Can. 356 — Cardinals are obliged to cooperate assiduously with the

sedulo cooperandi ; Cardinales itaque quovis officio in Curia fungentes, qui non sint Episcopi dioecesani, obligatione tenentur residendi in Urbe ; Cardinales qui alicuius dioecesis curam habent ut Episcopi dioecesani, Urbem petant quoties a Romano Pontifice convocentur.

Can. 357 – § 1. Cardinales, quibus Ecclesia suburbicaria aut ecclesia in Urbe in titulum est assignata, postquam in eiusdem venerunt possessionem, earundem dioecesium et ecclesiarum bonum consilio et patrocinio promoveant, nulla tamen in easdem potestate regiminis pollentes, ac nulla ratione sese in iis interponentes, quae ad earum bonorum administrationem, ad disciplinam aut ecclesiarum servitium spectant.

§ 2. Cardinales extra Urbem et extra propriam dioecesim degentes, in iis quae ad sui personam pertinent exempti sunt a potestate regiminis Episcopi dioecesis in qua commorantur.

Can. 358 – Cardinali, cui a Romano Pontifice hoc munus committitur ut in aliqua sollemni celebratione vel personarum coetu eius personam sustineat, uti *Legatus a latere,* scilicet tamquam eius alter ego, sicuti et illi cui adimplendum concreditur tamquam ipsius *misso speciali* certum munus pastorale, ea tantum competunt quae ab ipso Romano Pontifice eidem demandantur.

Can. 359 – Sede Apostolica vacante, Cardinalium Collegium ea tantum in Ecclesia gaudet potestate, quae in peculiari lege eidem tribuitur.

Caput IV

DE CURIA ROMANA

Can. 360 – Curia Romana, qua negotia Ecclesiae universae Summus Pontifex expedire solet et quae nomine et auctoritate ipsius munus explet in bonum et in servitium Ecclesiarum, constat Secretaria Status seu Papali, Consilio pro publicis Ecclesiae negotiis, Congregationibus, Tribunalibus, aliisque Institutis, quorum omnium constitutio et competentia lege peculiari definiuntur.

Can. 361 – Nomine Sedis Apostolicae vel Sanctae Sedis in hoc Codice veniunt non solum Romanus Pontifex, sed etiam, nisi ex rei natura vel sermonis contextu aliud appareat, Secretaria Status, Consilium pro publicis Ecclesiae negotiis, aliaque Romanae Curiae Instituta.

Roman Pontiff; therefore cardinals who exercise any office in the Curia and who are not diocesan bishops are obliged to reside in Rome; the cardinals who care for a diocese as diocesan bishops are to come to Rome whenever they are called there by the Roman Pontiff.

Can. 357 — §1. The cardinals who have been assigned title to a suburbicarian church or to a church in Rome are to promote the good of these dioceses and churches by their counsel and patronage after they have taken possession of them; they do not, however, possess any power of governance over them; nor are they to intervene in any way in matters which concern the administration of their goods, their discipline or the service of the churches.

§2. The cardinals who are staying outside Rome and outside their own diocese are exempt from the power of governance of the bishop of the diocese in which they are staying in those matters which concern their own person.

Can. 358 — At times the Roman Pontiff commissions a cardinal to represent him in some solemn celebration or in some group of persons as his *legatus a latere*, that is, as his alter ego; likewise at times the Roman Pontiff commissions a cardinal to fulfill a certain pastoral duty as his special envoy (*missus specialis*); such cardinals possess competence only over those matters entrusted to them by the Roman Pontiff.

Can. 359 — When the Apostolic See becomes vacant the college of cardinals possesses only that power in the Church which is given to it in special law.

CHAPTER IV

THE ROMAN CURIA

Can. 360 — The Supreme Pontiff usually conducts the business of the universal Church by means of the Roman Curia, which fulfills its duty in his name and by his authority for the good and the service of the churches; it consists of the Secretariat of State or the Papal Secretariat, the Council for the Public Affairs of the Church, congregations, tribunals and other institutions, whose structure and competency are defined in special law.

Can. 361 — In this Code the term "Apostolic See" or "Holy See" applies not only to the Roman Pontiff but also to the Secretariat of State, the Council for the Public Affairs of the Church and other institutions of the Roman Curia, unless the nature of the matter or the context of the words makes the contrary evident.

Caput V

DE ROMANI PONTIFICIS LEGATIS

Can. 362 – Romano Pontifici ius est nativum et independens Legatos suos nominandi ac mittendi sive ad Ecclesias particulares in variis nationibus vel regionibus, sive simul ad Civitates et ad publicas Auctoritates, itemque eos transferendi et revocandi, servatis quidem normis iuris internationalis, quod attinet ad missionem et revocationem Legatorum apud Res Publicas constitutorum.

Can. 363 – § 1. Legatis Romani Pontificis officium committitur ipsius Romani Pontificis stabili modo gerendi personam apud Ecclesias particulares aut etiam apud Civitates et publicas Auctoritates, ad quas missi sunt.

§ 2. Personam gerunt Apostolicae Sedis ii quoque, qui in pontificiam Missionem ut Delegati aut Observatores deputantur apud Consilia internationalia aut apud Conferentias et Conventus.

Can. 364 – Praecipuum munus Legati pontificii est ut firmiora et efficaciora in dies reddantur unitatis vincula, quae inter Apostolicam Sedem et Ecclesias particulares intercedunt. Ad pontificium ergo Legatum pertinet pro sua dicione :

1° ad Apostolicam Sedem notitias mittere de condicionibus in quibus versantur Ecclesiae particulares, deque omnibus quae ipsam vitam Ecclesiae et bonum animarum attingant ;

2° Episcopis actione et consilio adesse, integro quidem manente eorundem legitimae potestatis exercitio ;

3° crebras fovere relationes cum Episcoporum conferentia, eidem omnimodam operam praebendo ;

4° ad nominationem Episcoporum quod attinet, nomina candidatorum Apostolicae Sedi transmittere vel proponere necnon processum informativum de promovendis instruere, secundum normas ab Apostolica Sede datas ;

5° anniti ut promoveantur res quae ad pacem, ad progressum et consociatam populorum operam spectant ;

6° operam conferre cum Episcopis, ut opportuna foveantur commercia inter Ecclesiam catholicam et alias Ecclesias vel communitates ecclesiales, immo et religiones non christianas ;

7° ea quae pertinent ad Ecclesiae et Apostolicae Sedis missionem, consociata cum Episcopis actione, apud moderatores Civitatis tueri ;

8° exercere praeterea facultates et cetera explere mandata quae ipsi ab Apostolica Sede committantur.

CHAPTER V

THE LEGATES OF THE ROMAN PONTIFF

Can. 362 — The Roman Pontiff possesses the innate and independent right to nominate, send, transfer and recall his own legates to particular churches in various nations or regions, to states and to public authorities; the norms of international law are to be observed concerning the sending and the recalling of legates appointed to states.

Can. 363 — §1. To legates of the Roman Pontiff is entrusted the responsibility of representing him in a stable manner to particular churches and also to states and public authorities to which they are sent.

§2. They also represent the Apostolic See who are appointed to a pontifical mission as delegates or observers at International Councils or at conferences and meetings.

Can. 364 — The principal duty of a pontifical legate is to work so that day by day the bonds of unity which exist between the Apostolic See and the particular churches become stronger and more efficacious. Therefore, it belongs to the pontifical legate for his area:

1° to send information to the Apostolic See on the conditions of the particular churches and all that touches the life of the Church and the good of souls;

2° to assist the bishops by action and counsel, while leaving intact the exercise of the bishops' legitimate power;

3° to foster close relations with the conference of bishops by offering it assistance in every way;

4° to transmit or propose the names of candidates to the Apostolic See in reference to the naming of bishops and to instruct the informative process concerning those to be promoted in accord with the norms given by the Apostolic See;

5° to strive for the promotion of matters which concern peace, progress and the cooperative efforts of peoples;

6° to cooperate with the bishops in fostering suitable relationships between the Catholic Church and other churches or ecclesial communities and non-Christian religions also;

7° in concerted action with the bishops to protect what pertains to the mission of the Church and the Apostolic See in relations with the leaders of the state;

8° to exercise the faculties and fulfill the other mandates committed to him by the Apostolic See.

Can. 365 – § 1. Legati pontificii, qui simul legationem apud Civitates iuxta iuris internationalis normas exercet, munus quoque peculiare est:

1° promovere et fovere necessitudines inter Apostolicam Sedem et Auctoritates Rei Publicae;

2° quaestiones pertractare quae ad relationes inter Ecclesiam et Civitatem pertinent; et peculiari modo agere de concordatis aliisque huiusmodi conventionibus conficiendis et ad effectum deducendis.

§ 2. In negotiis, de quibus in § 1, expediendis, prout adiuncta suadeant, Legatus pontificius sententiam et consilium Episcoporum dicionis ecclesiasticae exquirere ne omittat, eosque de negotiorum cursu certiores faciat.

Can. 366 – Attenta peculiari Legati muneris indole:

1° sedes Legationis pontificiae a potestate regiminis Ordinarii loci exempta est, nisi agatur de matrimoniis celebrandis;

2° Legato pontificio fas est, praemonitis, quantum fieri potest, locorum Ordinariis, in omnibus ecclesiis suae legationis liturgicas celebrationes, etiam in pontificalibus, peragere.

Can. 367 – Pontificii Legati munus non exspirat vacante Sede Apostolica, nisi aliud in Litteris pontificiis statuatur; cessat autem expleto mandato, revocatione eidem intimata, renuntiatione a Romano Pontifice acceptata.

SECTIO II

DE ECCLESIIS PARTICULARIBUS
DEQUE EARUNDEM COETIBUS

TITULUS I

DE ECCLESIIS PARTICULARIBUS
ET DE AUCTORITATE IN IISDEM CONSTITUTA

Caput I

DE ECCLESIIS PARTICULARIBUS

Can. 368 – Ecclesiae particulares, in quibus et ex quibus una et unica Ecclesia catholica exsistit, sunt imprimis dioeceses, quibus, nisi aliud constet, assimilantur praelatura territorialis et abbatia territorialis, vicariatus apostolicus et praefectura apostolica necnon administratio apostolica stabiliter erecta.

Can. 365 — §1. It is the special responsibility of a pontifical legate who also exercises a legation to states in accord with the norms of international law:

1° to promote and foster relations between the Apostolic See and the authorities of the state;

2° to deal with questions concerning the relations between the Church and the state; and in a special manner to deal with the drafting and implementation of concordats and other agreements of this type.

§2. In conducting the negotiations mentioned in §1, as circumstances suggest, the pontifical legate is to seek out the opinion and counsel of the bishops of the ecclesiastical jurisdiction and also inform them on the progress of these negotiations.

Can. 366 — In view of the special character of a legate's role:

1° the headquarters of a pontifical legation is exempt from the power of governance of the local ordinary unless it is a question of celebrating marriages;

2° after he has previously advised the local ordinaries insofar as this is possible, a pontifical legate is allowed to perform liturgical celebrations, even in pontificals, in all the churches within his legation.

Can. 367 — The function of pontifical legate does not cease when the Apostolic See becomes vacant unless the contrary is determined in the pontifical letters; it does cease, however, when his mandate has been fulfilled, when he has been informed of his recall, or when his resignation has been accepted by the Roman Pontiff.

SECTION II
PARTICULAR CHURCHES AND THEIR GROUPINGS

TITLE I
PARTICULAR CHURCHES AND THE AUTHORITY ESTABLISHED IN THEM

CHAPTER I
PARTICULAR CHURCHES

Can. 368 — Particular churches in which and from which exists the one and unique Catholic Church are first of all dioceses; to which unless otherwise evident are likened a territorial prelature, a territorial abbacy, an apostolic vicariate, an apostolic prefecture, and an apostolic administration which has been erected on a stable basis.

Can. 369 – Dioecesis est populi Dei portio, quae Episcopo cum cooperatione presbyterii pascenda concreditur, ita ut, pastori suo adhaerens ab eoque per Evangelium et Eucharistiam in Spiritu Sancto congregata, Ecclesiam particularem constituat, in qua vere inest et operatur una sancta catholica et apostolica Christi Ecclesia.

Can. 370 – Praelatura territorialis aut abbatia territorialis est certa populi Dei portio, territorialiter quidem circumscripta, cuius cura, specialia ob adiuncta, committitur alicui Praelato aut Abbati, qui eam, ad instar Episcopi dioecesani, tamquam proprius eius pastor regat.

Can. 371 – § 1. Vicariatus apostolicus vel praefectura apostolica est certa populi Dei portio quae, ob peculiaria adiuncta, in dioecesim nondum est constituta, quaeque pascenda committitur Vicario apostolico aut Praefecto apostolico, qui eam nomine Summi Pontificis regant.

§ 2. Administratio apostolica est certa populi Dei portio, quae ob speciales et graves omnino rationes a Summo Pontifice in dioecesim non erigitur, et cuius cura pastoralis committitur Administratori apostolico, qui eam nomine Summi Pontificis regat.

Can. 372 – § 1. Pro regula habeatur ut portio populi Dei quae Dioecesim aliamve Ecclesiam particularem constituat, certo territorio circumscribatur, ita ut omnes comprehendat fideles in territorio habitantes.

§ 2. Attamen, ubi de iudicio supremae Ecclesiae auctoritatis, auditis Episcoporum conferentiis quarum interest, utilitas id suadeat, in eodem territorio erigi possunt Ecclesiae particulares ritu fidelium aliave simili ratione distinctae.

Can. 373 – Unius supremae auctoritatis est Ecclesias particulares erigere; quae legitime erectae, ipso iure personalitate iuridica gaudent.

Can. 374 – § 1. Quaelibet dioecesis aliave Ecclesia particularis dividatur in distinctas partes seu paroecias.

§ 2. Ad curam pastoralem per communem actionem fovendam plures paroeciae viciniores coniungi possunt in peculiares coetus, uti sunt vicariatus foranei.

Can. 369 — A diocese is a portion of the people of God which is entrusted for pastoral care to a bishop with the cooperation of the presbyterate so that, adhering to its pastor and gathered by him in the Holy Spirit through the gospel and the Eucharist, it constitutes a particular church in which the one, holy, catholic and apostolic Church of Christ is truly present and operative.

Can. 370 — A territorial prelature or territorial abbacy is a certain portion of the people of God which is established within certain territorial boundaries and whose care, due to special circumstances, is entrusted to some prelate or abbot who governs it as its proper pastor, like a diocesan bishop.

Can. 371 — §1. An apostolic vicariate or an apostolic prefecture is a certain portion of the people of God which is not yet erected into a diocese, due to particular circumstances, and whose pastoral care is entrusted to an apostolic vicar or to an apostolic prefect who governs it in the name of the Supreme Pontiff.

§2. An apostolic administration is a certain portion of the people of God which is not erected into a diocese by the Supreme Pontiff due to particular and very serious reasons and whose pastoral care is entrusted to an apostolic administrator who governs it in the name of the Supreme Pontiff.

Can. 372 — §1. As a rule that portion of the people of God which constitutes a diocese or some other particular church is limited to a definite territory so that it comprises all the faithful who inhabit that territory.

§2. Nevertheless, there can be erected within the same territory particular churches which are distinct by reason of the rite of the faithful or some similar reason when such is deemed advantageous in the judgment of the supreme authority of the Church after it has listened to the conferences of bishops concerned.

Can. 373 — It is within the sole competence of the supreme authority of the Church to erect particular churches; once they have been legitimately erected these churches enjoy juridic personality by reason of the law itself.

Can. 374 — §1. Each and every diocese or other paricular church is to be divided into distinct parts or parishes.

§2. In order to foster pastoral care through common action several neighboring parishes can be joined together into special groups such as vicariates forane.

Caput II

DE EPISCOPIS

Art. 1

De Episcopis in genere

Can. 375 − § 1. Episcopi, qui ex divina institutione in Apostolorum locum succedunt per Spiritum Sanctum qui datus est eis, in Ecclesia Pastores constituuntur, ut sint et ipsi doctrinae magistri, sacri cultus sacerdotes et gubernationis ministri.

§ 2. Episcopi ipsa consecratione episcopali recipiunt cum munere sanctificandi munera quoque docendi et regendi, quae tamen natura sua nonnisi in hierarchica communione cum Collegii capite et membris exercere possunt.

Can. 376 − Episcopi vocantur *dioecesani,* quibus scilicet alicuius dioecesis cura commissa est; ceteri *titulares* appellantur.

Can. 377 − § 1. Episcopos libere Summus Pontifex nominat, aut legitime electos confirmat.

§ 2. Singulis saltem trienniis Episcopi provinciae ecclesiasticae vel, ubi adiuncta id suadeant, Episcoporum conferentiae, communi consilio et secreto elenchum componant presbyterorum etiam sodalium institutorum vitae consecratae, ad episcopatum aptiorum, eumque Apostolicae Sedi transmittant, firmo manente iure uniuscuiusque Episcopi Apostolicae Sedi nomina presbyterorum, quos episcopali munere dignos et idoneos putet, seorsim patefaciendi.

§ 3. Nisi aliter legitime statutum fuerit, quoties nominandus est Episcopus dioecesanus aut Episcopus coadiutor, ad ternos, qui dicuntur, Apostolicae Sedi proponendos, pontificii Legati est singillatim requirere et cum ipsa Apostolica Sede communicare, una cum suo voto, quid suggerant Metropolita et Suffraganei provinciae, ad quam providenda dioecesis pertinet vel quacum in coetum convenit, necnon conferentiae Episcoporum praeses; pontificius Legatus, insuper, quosdam e collegio consultorum et capitulo cathedrali audiat et, si id expedire iudicaverit, sententiam quoque aliorum ex utroque clero necnon laicorum sapientia praestantium singillatim et secreto exquirat.

§ 4. Nisi aliter legitime provisum fuerit, Episcopus dioecesanus, qui auxiliarem suae dioecesi dandum aestimet, elenchum trium saltem presbyterorum ad hoc officium aptiorum Apostolicae Sedi proponat.

CHAPTER II
BISHOPS

Art. 1
BISHOPS IN GENERAL

Can. 375 — §1. Through the Holy Spirit who has been given to them, bishops are the successors of the apostles by divine institution; they are constituted pastors within the Church so that they are teachers of doctrine, priests of sacred worship and ministers of governance.

§2. By the fact of their episcopal consecration bishops receive along with the function of sanctifying also the functions of teaching and of ruling, which by their very nature, however, can be exercised only when they are in hierarchical communion with the head of the college and its members.

Can. 376 — Bishops are called *diocesan* when the care of a diocese has been entrusted to them; all others are called *titular.*

Can. 377 — §1. The Supreme Pontiff freely appoints bishops or confirms those who have been legitimately elected.

§2. At least every three years the bishops of an ecclesiastical province or, if circumstances suggest this, the bishops of a conference of bishops are to compose in common counsel and in secret a list of presbyters, including members of institutes of consecrated life, who are suitable for the episcopacy and send it to the Apostolic See; each bishop retains the right to make known to the Apostolic See on his own the names of presbyters whom he thinks worthy and suitable for the episcopal office.

§3. Unless other provisions have legitimately been made, whenever a diocesan bishop or a coadjutor bishop is to be named, in regard to the *ternus*, as it is called, to be proposed to the Apostolic See it is the responsibility of the pontifical legate to seek out individually the suggestions of the metropolitan and the suffragans of the province to which the diocese to be provided for belongs or with which it is joined and of the president of the conference of bishops and to communicate them to the Apostolic See together his own preference; moreover, the pontifical legate is to hear some members of the college of consultors and of the cathedral chapter, and if he judges it expedient, he shall also obtain, individually and in secret, the opinion of other members of the secular and religious clergy as well as of the laity who are outstanding for their wisdom.

§4. Unless other provisions have been legitimately made, a diocesan bishop who judges that an auxiliary bishop ought to be given to his diocese is to propose to the Apostolic See a list of at least three priests who are quite suitable for this office.

§ 5. Nulla in posterum iura et privilegia electionis, nominationis, praesentationis vel designationis Episcoporum civilibus auctoritatibus conceduntur.

Can. 378 – § 1. Ad idoneitatem candidatorum Episcopatus requiritur ut quis sit :

1° firma fide, bonis moribus, pietate, animarum zelo, sapientia, prudentia et virtutibus humanis excellens, ceterisque dotibus praeditus quae ipsum aptum efficiant ad officium de quo agitur explendum ;

2° bona exsistimatione gaudens ;

3° annos natus saltem triginta quinque ;

4° a quinquennio saltem in presbyteratus ordine constitutus ;

5° laurea doctoris vel saltem licentia in sacra Scriptura, theologia aut iure canonico potitus in instituto studiorum superiorum a Sede Apostolica probato, vel saltem in iisdem disciplinis vere peritus.

§ 2. Iudicium definitivum de promovendi idoneitate ad Apostolicam Sedem pertinet.

Can. 379 – Nisi legitimo detineatur impedimento, quicumque ad Episcopatum promotus debet intra tres menses ab acceptis apostolicis litteris consecrationem episcopalem recipere, et quidem antequam officii sui possessionem capiat.

Can. 380 – Antequam canonicam possessionem sui officii capiat, promotus fidei professionem emittat atque iusiurandum fidelitatis erga Apostolicam Sedem praestet secundum formulam ab eadem Apostolica Sede probatam.

Art. 2

De Episcopis dioecesanis

Can. 381 – § 1. Episcopo dioecesano in dioecesi ipsi commissa omnis competit potestas ordinaria, propria et immediata, quae ad exercitium eius muneris pastoralis requiritur, exceptis causis quae iure aut Summi Pontificis decreto supremae aut alii auctoritati ecclesiasticae reserventur.

§ 2. Qui praesunt aliis communitatibus fidelium, de quibus in can. 368, Episcopo dioecesano in iure aequiparantur, nisi ex rei natura aut iuris praescripto aliud appareat.

Can. 382 – § 1. Episcopus promotus in exercitium officii sibi commissi sese ingerere nequit, ante captam dioecesis canonicam possessionem ; exercere tamen valet officia, quae in eadem dioecesi tempore promotionis iam retinebat, firmo praescripto can. 409, § 2.

§ 2. Nisi legitimo detineatur impedimento, promotus ad officium

§5. No rights and privileges of election, nomination, presentation, or designation of bishops are hereafter granted to civil authorities.

Can. 378 — §1. In order for a person to be a suitable candidate for the episcopacy it is required that he be:

1° outstanding for his solid faith, good morals, piety, zeal for souls, wisdom, prudence and human virtues and endowed with the other talents which make him fit to fulfill the office in question;

2° in possession of a good reputation;

3° at least thirty-five years of age;

4° ordained a priest for at least five years;

5° in possession of a doctorate or at least a licentiate in sacred scripture, theology, or canon law from an institute of higher studies approved by the Apostolic See or at least truly expert in these same disciplines.

§2. The definitive judgment concerning the suitability of the person to be promoted belongs to the Apostolic See.

Can. 379 — Unless he is held back by a legitimate impediment, whoever is promoted to the episcopacy must receive episcopal consecration within three months from the reception of the apostolic letter and before he takes possession of his office.

Can. 380 — Before he takes canonical possession of his office, the person promoted is to make a profession of faith and take an oath of fidelity to the Apostolic See in accord with a formula approved by the same Apostolic See.

Art. 2

DIOCESAN BISHOPS

Can. 381 — §1. A diocesan bishop in the diocese committed to him possesses all the ordinary, proper and immediate power which is required for the exercise of his pastoral office except for those cases which the law or a decree of the Supreme Pontiff reserves to the supreme authority of the Church or to some other ecclesiastical authority.

§2. Unless it appears otherwise from the nature of the matter or from a prescription of the law, persons who head the other communities of the faithful mentioned in can. 368 are equivalent in law to a diocesan bishop.

Can. 382 — §1. A bishop promoted to a diocese cannot exercise the office entrusted to him unless he has first taken canonical possession of the diocese, but he can exercise the offices which he already had in the same diocese at the time of promotion, with due regard for the prescription of can. 409, §2.

§2. Unless he is held back by a legitimate impediment, a person promoted

Episcopi dioecesani debet canonicam suae dioecesis possessionem capere, si iam non sit consecratus Episcopus, intra quattuor menses a
receptis apostolicis litteris; si iam sit consecratus, intra duos menses
ab iisdem receptis.

§ 3. Canonicam dioecesis possessionem capit Episcopus simul ac
in ipsa dioecesi, per se vel per procuratorem, apostolicas litteras collegio consultorum ostenderit, praesente curiae cancellario, qui rem
in acta referat, aut, in dioecesibus noviter erectis, simul ac clero
populoque in ecclesia cathedrali praesenti earundem litterarum com-
municationem procuraverit, presbytero inter praesentes seniore in acta
referente.

§ 4. Valde commendatur ut captio canonicae possessionis cum
actu liturgico in ecclesia cathedrali fiat, praesente clero et populo.

Can. 383 – § 1. In exercendo munere pastoris, Episcopus dioecesanus sollicitum se praebeat erga omnes christifideles qui suae curae
committuntur, cuiusvis sint aetatis, condicionis vel nationis, tum in
territorio habitantes tum in eodem ad tempus versantes, animum
intendens apostolicum ad eos etiam qui ob vitae suae condicionem
ordinaria cura pastorali non satis frui valeant necnon ad eos qui a religionis praxi defecerint.

§ 2. Fideles diversi ritus in sua dioecesi si habeat, eorum spiritualibus necessitatibus provideat sive per sacerdotes aut paroecias eiusdem ritus, sive per Vicarium episcopalem.

§ 3. Erga fratres, qui in plena communione cum Ecclesia catholica non sint, cum humanitate et caritate se gerat, oecumenismum
quoque fovens prout ab Eclesia intellegitur.

§ 4. Commendatos sibi in Domino habeat non baptizatos, ut et
ipsis caritas eluceat Christi, cuius testis coram omnibus Episcopus
esse debet.

Can. 384 – Episcopus dioecesanus peculiari sollicitudine prosequatur presbyteros, quos tamquam adiutores et consiliarios audiat, eorum
iura tutetur et curet ut ipsi obligationes suo statui proprias rite adimpleant iisdemque praesto sint media et institutiones, quibus ad vitam
spiritualem et intellectualem fovendam egeant; item curet ut eorum
honestae sustentationi atque adsistentiae sociali, ad normam iuris,
prospiciatur.

Can. 385 – Episcopus dioecesanus vocationes ad diversa ministeria
et ad vitam consecratam quam maxime foveat, speciali cura vocationum sacerdotalium et missionalium adhibita.

to the office of diocesan bishop must take canonical possession of his diocese within four months from the reception of the apostolic letter if he has not yet been consecrated a bishop or within two months if he has already been consecrated.

§3. A bishop takes canonical possession of a diocese as soon as he personally or through a proxy has presented within the diocese the apostolic letter to the college of consultors, in the presence of the chancellor of the curia who officially records the event; in newly erected dioceses, however, he takes canonical possession as soon as he has seen to the communication of the apostolic letter to the clergy and the people present in the cathedral church, with the senior presbyter among those present officially recording the event.

§4. It is strongly recommended that the act of taking canonical possession occur within a liturgical act in the cathedral church and in the presence of the clergy and the people.

Can. 383 — §1. In the exercise of his pastoral office a diocesan bishop is to show that he is concerned with all the Christian faithful who are committed to his care regardless of age, condition or nationality, both those who live within his territory and those who are staying in it temporarily; he is to extend his apostolic spirit to those who cannot sufficiently make use of ordinary pastoral care due to their condition in life and to those who no longer practice their religion.

§2. If he has faithful of a different rite within his diocese, he is to provide for their spiritual needs either by means of priests or parishes of that rite or by means of an episcopal vicar.

§3. He is to act with kindness and charity toward those who are not in full communion with the Catholic Church, fostering ecumenism as it is understood by the Church.

§4. He is to consider non-baptized as being committed to him in the Lord so that there may shine upon them the charity of Christ for whom the bishop must be a witness before all.

Can. 384 — The diocesan bishop is to attend to presbyters with special concern and listen to them as his assistants and advisers; he is to protect their rights and see to it that they correctly fulfill the obligations proper to their state and that means and institutions which they need are available to them to foster their spiritual and intellectual life; he is also to make provision for their decent support and social assistance, in accord with the norm of law.

Can. 385 — As much as is possible the diocesan bishop is to foster vocations to the different ministries and to the consecrated life, with special care shown for priestly and missionary vocations.

Can. 386 – § 1. Veritates fidei credendas et moribus applicandas Episcopus dioecesanus fidelibus proponere et illustrare tenetur, per se ipse frequenter praedicans; curet etiam ut praescripta canonum de ministerio verbi, de homilia praesertim et catechetica institutione sedulo serventur, ita ut universa doctrina christiana omnibus tradatur.

§ 2. Integritatem et unitatem fidei credendae mediis, quae aptiora videantur, firmiter tueatur, iustam tamen libertatem agnoscens in veritatibus ulterius perscrutandis.

Can. 387 – Episcopus dioecesanus, cum memor sit se obligatione teneri exemplum sanctitatis praebendi in caritate, humilitate et vitae simplicitate, omni ope promovere studeat sanctitatem christifidelium secundum uniuscuiusque propriam vocationem atque, cum sit praecipuus mysteriorum Dei dispensator, iugiter annitatur ut christifideles suae curae commissi sacramentorum celebratione in gratia crescant utque paschale mysterium cognoscant et vivant.

Can. 388 – § 1. Episcopus dioecesanus, post captam dioecesis possessionem, debet singulis diebus dominicis aliisque diebus festis de praecepto in sua regione Missam pro populo sibi commisso applicare.

§ 2. Episcopus Missam pro populo diebus, de quibus in § 1, per se ipse celebrare et applicare debet; si vero ab hac celebratione legitime impediatur, iisdem diebus per alium, vel aliis diebus per se ipse applicet.

§ 3. Episcopus cui praeter propriam dioecesim aliae, titulo etiam administrationis, sunt commissae, obligationi satisfacit unam Missam pro universo populo sibi commisso applicando.

§ 4. Episcopus qui obligationi, de qua in §§ 1-3, non satisfecerit, quam primum pro populo tot Missas applicet quot omiserit.

Can. 389 – Frequenter praesit in ecclesia cathedrali aliave ecclesia suae dioecesis sanctissimae Eucharistiae celebrationi, in festis praesertim de praecepto aliisque sollemnitatibus.

Can. 390 – Episcopus dioecesanus in universa sua dioecesi pontificalia exercere potest; non vero extra propriam dioecesim sine expresso vel saltem rationabiliter praesumpto Ordinarii loci consensu.

Can. 391 – § 1. Episcopi dioecesani est Ecclesiam particularem sibi commissam cum potestate legislativa, exsecutiva et iudiciali regere, ad normam iuris.

Can. 386 — §1. The diocesan bishop is bound to present and explain to the faithful the truths of the faith which are to be believed and applied to moral issues, frequently preaching in person; he is also to see to the careful observance of the prescriptions of the canons concerning the ministry of the word, especially those concerning the homily and catechetical formation, so that the whole of Christian doctrine is imparted to all.

§2. Through suitable means he is strongly to safeguard the integrity and unity of the faith to be believed while nevertheless acknowledging a rightful freedom in the further investigation of its truths.

Can. 387 — Since the diocesan bishop is mindful that he is obliged to set a personal example of holiness, in charity, humility and simplicity of life, he is to make every effort to promote the holiness of the Christian faithful according to each one's own vocation; since he is the foremost dispenser of the mysteries of God, he is constantly to endeavor to have the Christian faithful entrusted to his care grow in grace through the celebration of the sacraments and both understand and live the paschal mystery.

Can. 388 — §1. After he has taken possession of his diocese the diocesan bishop must apply a Mass for the people committed to him on Sundays and the other holy days of obligation within his region.

§2. The bishop himself must personally celebrate and apply Mass for the people on the days mentioned in §1; but if he is legitimately hindered from such celebration, he is to apply Mass on these days through another priest or personally do so on other days.

§3. A bishop satisfies this obligation by applying one Mass for all the people entrusted to him if, besides his own diocese, other dioceses are entrusted to him, even under the title of administration.

§4. A bishop who has not satisfied the obligation mentioned in §§1-3 is to apply as many Masses for the people as he has missed as soon as possible.

Can. 389 — He is to preside frequently over the celebration of the Eucharist in the cathedral church or in another church of his diocese, especially on holy days of obligation and other solemnities.

Can. 390 — A diocesan bishop can conduct pontifical functions throughout his entire diocese; he cannot do so, however, outside his own diocese without the express or at least reasonably presumed consent of the local ordinary.

Can. 391 — §1. The diocesan bishop is to rule the particular church committed to him with legislative, executive and judicial power in accord with the norm of law.

§ 2. Potestatem legislativam exercet ipse Episcopus; potestatem exsecutivam exercet sive per se sive per Vicarios generales aut episcopales ad normam iuris; potestatem iudicialem sive per se sive per Vicarium iudicialem et iudices ad normam iuris.

Can. 392 – § 1. Ecclesiae universae unitatem cum tueri debeat, Episcopus disciplinam cunctae Ecclesiae communem promovere et ideo observantiam omnium legum ecclesiasticarum urgere tenetur.

§ 2. Advigilet ne abusus in ecclesiasticam disciplinam irrepant, praesertim circa ministerium verbi, celebrationem sacramentorum et sacramentalium, cultum Dei et sanctorum, necnon bonorum administrationem.

Can. 393 – In omnibus negotiis iuridicis dioecesis, Episcopus dioecesanus eiusdem personam gerit.

Can. 394 – § 1. Varias apostolatus rationes in dioecesi foveat Episcopus, atque curet ut in universa dioecesi, vel in eiusdem particularibus districtibus, omnia apostolatus opera, servata uniuscuiusque propria indole, sub suo moderamine coordinentur.

§ 2. Urgeat officium, quo tenentur fideles ad apostolatum pro sua cuiusque condicione et aptitudine exercendum, atque ipsos adhortetur ut varia opera apostolatus, secundum necessitates loci et temporis, participent et iuvent.

Can. 395 – § 1. Episcopus dioecesanus, etiamsi coadiutorem aut auxiliarem habeat, tenetur lege personalis in dioecesi residentiae.

§ 2. Praeterquam causa visitationis Sacrorum Liminum, vel Conciliorum, Episcoporum synodi, Episcoporum conferentiae, quibus interesse debet, aliusve officii sibi legitime commissi, a dioecesi aequa de causa abesse potest non ultra mensem, sive continuum sive intermissum, dummodo cautum sit ne ex eius absentia dioecesis quidquam detrimenti capiat.

§ 3. A dioecesi ne absit diebus Nativitatis, Hebdomadae Sanctae et Resurrectionis Domini, Pentecostes et Corporis Christi, nisi ex gravi urgentique causa.

§ 4. Si ultra sex menses Episcopus a dioecesi illegitime abfuerit, de eius absentia Metropolita Sedem Apostolicam certiorem faciat; quod si agatur de Metropolita, idem faciat antiquior suffraganeus.

Can. 396 – § 1. Tenetur Episcopus obligatione dioecesis vel ex toto vel ex parte quotannis visitandae, ita ut singulis saltem quinquenniis

§2. The bishop personally exercises legislative power; he exercises executive power either personally or through vicars general or episcopal vicars in accord with the norm of law; he exercises judicial power either personally or through a judicial vicar and judges in accord with the norm of law.

Can. 392 — §1. Since he must protect the unity of the universal Church, the bishop is bound to promote the common discipline of the whole Church and therefore to urge the observance of all ecclesiastical laws.

§2. He is to be watchful lest abuses creep into ecclesiastical discipline, especially concerning the ministry of the word, the celebration of the sacraments and sacramentals, the worship of God and devotion to the saints, and also the administration of property.

Can. 393 — The diocesan bishop represents his diocese in all its juridic affairs.

Can. 394 — §1. The bishop is to foster the various aspects of the apostolate within his diocese and see to it that within the entire diocese or within its individual districts all the works of the apostolate are coordinated under his direction, with due regard for their distinctive character.

§2. He is to urge the faithful to exercise the apostolate in proportion to each one's condition and ability, since it is a duty to which they are bound; he is also to recommend to them that they participate and assist in the various works of the apostolate in accord with the needs of place and time.

Can. 395 — §1. Even if he has a coadjutor or an auxiliary bishop, a diocesan bishop is bound by the law of personal residence within his diocese.

§2. Provided provision is made that the diocese not suffer any disadvantage through his absence from it, he can be absent from his diocese for a just cause but not for more than one month, whether continuous or interrupted; this period does not include the time spent on his *ad limina* visit, or at councils, at a synod of bishops or at a conference of bishops, whenever he must be present, or the time spent on another office which has been legitimately entrusted to him.

§3. Except for a serious and urgent reason he is not to be absent from his diocese on Christmas, during Holy Week, on Easter, Pentecost, or Corpus Christi.

§4. If the bishop has been absent illegally from his diocese beyond six months, the metropolitan is to inform the Apostolic See; the senior suffragan is to do so if the metropolitan is illegally absent.

Can. 396 — §1. The bishop is obliged to visit his diocese annually, either in its entirety or in part, in such a way that the entire diocese is visited at least

universam dioecesim, ipse per se vel, si legitime fuerit impeditus, per Episcopum coadiutorem, aut per auxiliarem, aut per Vicarium generalem vel episcopalem, aut per alium presbyterum visitet.

§ 2. Fas est Episcopo sibi eligere quos maluerit clericos in visitatione comites atque adiutores, reprobato quocumque contrario privilegio vel consuetudine.

Can. 397 – § 1. Ordinariae episcopali visitationi obnoxiae sunt personae, instituta catholica, res et loca sacra, quae intra dioecesis ambitum continentur.

§ 2. Sodales institutorum religiosorum iuris pontificii eorumque domos Episcopus visitare potest in casibus tantum iure expressis.

Can. 398 – Studeat Episcopus debita cum diligentia pastoralem visitationem absolvere; caveat ne superfluis sumptibus cuiquam gravis onerosusve sit.

Can. 399 – § 1. Episcopus dioecesanus tenetur singulis quinquenniis relationem Summo Pontifici exhibere super statu dioecesis sibi commissae, secundum formam et tempus ab Apostolica Sede definita.

§ 2. Si annus pro exhibenda relatione determinatus ex toto vel ex parte inciderit in primum biennium ab inito dioecesis regimine, Episcopus pro ea vice a conficienda et exhibenda relatione abstinere potest.

Can. 400 – § 1. Episcopus dioecesanus, eo anno quo relationem Summo Pontifici exhibere tenetur, nisi aliter ab Apostolica Sede statutum fuerit, ad Urbem, Beatorum Apostolorum Petri et Pauli sepulcra veneraturus, accedat et Romano Pontifici se sistat.

§ 2. Episcopus praedictae obligationi per se ipse satisfaciat, nisi legitime sit impeditus; quo in casu eidem satisfaciat per coadiutorem, si quem habeat, vel auxiliarem, aut per idoneum sacerdotem sui presbyterii, qui in sua dioecesi resideat.

§ 3. Vicarius apostolicus huic obligationi satisfacere potest per procuratorem etiam in Urbe degentem; Praefectus apostolicus hac obligatione non tenetur.

Can. 401 – § 1. Episcopus dioecesanus, qui septuagesimum quintum aetatis annum expleverit, rogatur ut renuntiationem ab officio exhibeat Summo Pontifici, qui omnibus inspectis adiunctis providebit.

§ 2. Enixe rogatur Episcopus dioecesanus, qui ob infirmam valetudinem aliamve gravem causam officio suo adimplendo minus aptus evaserit, ut renuntiationem ab officio exhibeat.

every five years; he may make this visitation personally or if he is legitimately hindered from doing so personally, he may do so through the coadjutor or auxiliary bishop, through a vicar general or episcopal vicar, or through another presbyter.

§2. The bishop has the right to choose for himself those clerics he prefers to be his companions and assistants on the visitation; any other contrary privilege or custom whatsoever is reprobated.

Can. 397 — §1. Persons, Catholic institutions, and sacred things and places are subject to the ordinary episcopal visitation if they are located within the area of the diocese.

§2. The bishop can visit members of religious institutes of pontifical right and their houses only in those cases expressly mentioned in law.

Can. 398 — The bishop is to strive to complete his pastoral visitation with due diligence, and he is to take care lest anyone be imposed upon or burdened by unnecessary expenses.

Can. 399 — §1. The diocesan bishop is bound to present a report to the Supreme Pontiff every five years concerning the state of the diocese committed to him, according to a form and at a time determined by the Apostolic See.

§2. If the year set for the presentation of this report falls entirely or in part within the first two-year period of his governance of the diocese, the bishop can omit the composition and presentation of the report on this one occasion.

Can. 400 — §1. During the year in which he is bound to present his report to the Supreme Pontiff and unless other provisions have been made by the Apostolic See, the diocesan bishop is to come to Rome to venerate the tombs of the blessed apostles Peter and Paul and is to appear before the Roman Pontiff.

§2. Unless he is legitimately hindered from doing so, the bishop is to satisfy this aforementioned obligation personally; if he is so hindered, he is to satisfy this obligation through his coadjutor, if he has one, through an auxiliary bishop, or through a suitable priest of his presbyterate who resides in his diocese.

§3. An apostolic vicar can satisfy this obligation through an agent, even through one living in Rome; an apostolic prefect is not bound by this obligation.

Can. 401 — §1. A diocesan bishop who has completed his seventy-fifth year of age is requested to present his resignation from office to the Supreme Pontiff who will make provisions after he has examined all the circumstances.

§2. A diocesan bishop is earnestly requested to present his resignation from office when he has become less able to fulfill his office due to ill health or another serious reason.

Can. 402 – § 1. Episcopus, cuius renuntiatio ab officio acceptata fuerit, titulum emeriti suae dioecesis retinet, atque habitationis sedem, si id exoptet, in ipsa dioecesi servare potest, nisi certis in casibus ob specialia adiuncta ab Apostolica Sede aliter provideatur.

§ 2. Episcoporum conferentia curare debet ut congruae et dignae Episcopi renuntiantis sustentationi provideatur, attenta quidem primaria obligatione, qua tenetur dioecesis cui ipse inservivit.

Art. 3

De Episcopis coadiutoribus et auxiliaribus

Can. 403 – § 1. Cum pastorales dioecesis necessitates id suadeant, unus vel plures Episcopi auxiliares, petente Episcopo dioecesano, constituantur; Episcopus auxiliaris iure successionis non gaudet.

§ 2. Gravioribus in adiunctis, etiam indolis personalis, Episcopo dioecesano dari potest Episcopus auxiliaris specialibus instructus facultatibus.

§ 3. Sancta Sedes, si magis opportunum id ipsi videatur, ex officio constituere potest Episcopum coadiutorem, qui et ipse specialibus instruitur facultatibus; Episcopus coadiutor iure successionis gaudet.

Can. 404 – § 1. Episcopus coadiutor officii sui possessionem capit, cum litteras apostolicas nominationis, per se vel per procuratorem, ostenderit Episcopo dioecesano atque collegio consultorum, praesente curiae cancellario, qui rem in acta referat.

§ 2. Episcopus auxiliaris officii sui possessionem capit, cum litteras apostolicas nominationis ostenderit Episcopo dioecesano, praesente curiae cancellario, qui rem in acta referat.

§ 3. Quod si Episcopus dioecesanus plene sit impeditus, sufficit ut tum Episcopus coadiutor, tum Episcopus auxiliaris litteras apostolicas nominationis ostendant collegio consultorum, praesente curiae cancellario.

Can. 405 – § 1. Episcopus coadiutor, itemque Episcopus auxiliaris, obligationes et iura habent quae determinantur praescriptis canonum qui sequuntur, atque in litteris suae nominationis definiuntur.

§ 2. Episcopus coadiutor et Episcopus auxiliaris, de quo in can. 403, § 2, Episcopo dioecesano in universo dioecesis regimine adstant atque eiusdem absentis vel impediti vices supplent.

Can. 406 – § 1. Episcopus coadiutor, itemque Episcopus auxiliaris, de quo in can. 403, § 2, ab Episcopo dioecesano Vicarius generalis

Can. 402 — §1. A bishop whose resignation from office has been accepted retains the title of bishop emeritus of his diocese and can retain a place of residence in his diocese if he so desires, unless other provisions have been made by the Apostolic See in certain cases due to special circumstances.

§2. The conference of bishops must see to it that suitable and decent support is provided for a resigned bishop, with due regard for the primary obligation which rests upon the diocese which he has served.

Art. 3

Coadjutor and Auxiliary Bishops

Can. 403 — §1. When the pastoral needs of the diocese warrant it one or several auxiliary bishops are to be appointed at the request of the diocesan bishop; an auxiliary bishop does not possess the right of succession.

§2. An auxiliary bishop equipped with special faculties can be given to a diocesan bishop in more serious circumstances even of a personal character.

§3. If it appears more opportune to the Holy See, it can ex officio appoint a coadjutor bishop who is also equipped with special faculties; a coadjutor bishop does possess the right of succession.

Can. 404 — §1. A coadjutor bishop takes possession of his office when he personally or through his proxy has presented the apostolic letter of appointment to the diocesan bishop and the college of consultors in the presence of the chancellor of the curia who officially records the event.

§2. An auxiliary bishop takes possession of his office when he has presented the apostolic letter of appointment to the diocesan bishop in the presence of the chancellor of the curia who officially records the event.

§3. If, however, the diocesan bishop is completely hindered, it is sufficient for both a coadjutor bishop and an auxiliary bishop to present the apostolic letter of appointment to the college of consultors in the presence of the chancellor of the curia.

Can. 405 — §1. A coadjutor bishop and an auxiliary bishop have the obligations and rights which are determined in the prescriptions of the following canons as well as those which are defined in the letter of their appointment.

§2. A coadjutor bishop and the auxiliary bishop mentioned in can. 403, §2, aid the diocesan bishop in the entire governance of the diocese and take his place if he is absent or impeded.

Can. 406 — §1. A coadjutor bishop as well as the auxiliary bishop mentioned in can. 403, §2, is to be appointed a vicar general by the diocesan

constituatur; insuper ipsi prae ceteris Episcopus dioecesanus committat quae ex iure mandatum speciale requirant.

§ 2. Nisi in litteris apostolicis aliud provisum fuerit et firmo praescripto § 1, Episcopus dioecesanus auxiliarem vel auxiliares suos constituat Vicarios generales vel saltem Vicarios episcopales, ab auctoritate sua, aut Episcopi coadiutoris vel Episcopi auxiliaris de quo in can. 403, § 2, dumtaxat dependentes.

Can. 407 – § 1. Ut quam maxime praesenti et futuro dioecesis bono faveatur, Episcopus dioecesanus, coadiutor atque Episcopus auxiliaris de quo in can. 403, § 2, in rebus maioris momenti sese invicem consulant.

§ 2. Episcopus dioecesanus in perpendendis causis maioris momenti, praesertim indolis pastoralis, Episcopos auxiliares prae ceteris consulere velit.

§ 3. Episcopus coadiutor et Episcopus auxiliaris, quippe qui in partem sollicitudinis Episcopi dioecesani vocati sint, munia sua ita exerceant, ut concordi cum ipso opera et animo procedant.

Can. 408 – § 1. Episcopus coadiutor et Episcopus auxiliaris, iusto impedimento non detenti, obligantur ut, quoties Episcopus dioecesanus id requirat, pontificalia et alias functiones obeant, ad quas Episcopus dioecesanus tenetur.

§ 2. Quae episcopalia iura et functiones Episcopus coadiutor aut auxiliaris potest exercere, Episcopus dioecesanus habitualiter alii ne committat.

Can. 409 – § 1. Vacante sede episcopali, Episcopus coadiutor statim fit Episcopus dioecesis pro qua fuerat constitutus, dummodo possessionem legitime ceperit.

§ 2. Vacante sede episcopali, nisi aliud a competenti auctoritate statutum fuerit, Episcopus auxiliaris, donec novus Episcopus possessionem sedis ceperit, omnes et solas servat potestates et facultates quibus sede plena, tamquam Vicarius generalis vel tamquam Vicarius episcopalis, gaudebat; quod si ad munus Administratoris dioecesani non fuerit designatus, eandem suam potestatem, a iure quidem collatam, exerceat sub auctoritate Administratoris dioecesani, qui regimini dioecesis praeest.

Can. 410 – Episcopus coadiutor et Episcopus auxiliaris obligatione tenentur, sicut et ipse Episcopus dioecesanus, residendi in dioecesi; a qua, praeterquam ratione alicuius officii extra dioecesim implendi aut feriarum causa, quae ultra mensem ne protrahantur, nonnisi ad breve tempus discedant.

bishop; moreover the diocesan bishop is to commit to such a bishop rather than to others those matters which by law require a special mandate.

§2. Unless another provision has been made in the apostolic letter and with due regard for the prescription of §1, the diocesan bishop should appoint his auxiliary or auxiliaries as vicars general or at least episcopal vicars, dependent upon his authority alone, or that of a coadjutor bishop or the auxiliary bishop mentioned in can. 403, §2.

Can. 407 — §1. In order to foster the present and future good of the diocese as much as possible, the diocesan bishop, the coadjutor and the auxiliary bishop mentioned in can. 403, §2, are to consult with one another on matters of major importance.

§2. In considering matters of major importance, especially of a pastoral character, the diocesan bishop is to consult his auxiliary bishops before others.

§3. Because they have been called upon to share part of the concerns of the diocesan bishop, a coadjutor bishop and an auxiliary bishop are so to fulfill their duties that they proceed in harmony with him in their efforts and intentions.

Can. 408 — §1. Unless they are prevented from doing so by reason of a just impediment, a coadjutor bishop and an auxiliary bishop are obliged to perform the pontifical and other functions to which the diocesan bishop is bound whenever he requests them to.

§2. The diocesan bishop is not to entrust habitually to another those episcopal rights and functions which the coadjutor or auxiliary bishop can exercise.

Can. 409 — §1. Upon the vacancy of the episcopal see the coadjutor bishop immediately becomes the bishop of the diocese for which he had been appointed provided he has legitimately taken possession of it.

§2. Unless other provisions have been made by the competent authority, upon the vacancy of the episcopal see an auxiliary bishop retains all and only those powers and faculties which he possessed as vicar general or as episcopal vicar while the see was filled until a new bishop takes possession of the see; if, however, he has not been designated diocesan administrator, he may exercise this same power, conferred by law, under the authority of the diocesan administrator who presides over the governance of the diocese.

Can. 410 — A coadjutor bishop and an auxiliary bishop are obliged to reside within the diocese like the diocesan bishop and they are not to leave the diocese except for a short time, unless they are fulfilling some other office outside the diocese or they are on vacation, which is not to exceed one month.

Can. 411 – Episcopo coadiutori et auxiliari, ad renuntiationem ab officio quod attinet, applicantur praescripta cann. 401 et 402, § 2.

Caput III
DE SEDE IMPEDITA ET DE SEDE VACANTE

Art. 1
De sede impedita

Can. 412 – Sedes episcopalis impedita intellegitur, si captivitate, relegatione, exsilio aut inhabilitate Episcopus dioecesanus plane a munere pastorali in dioecesi procurando praepediatur, ne per litteras quidem valens cum dioecesanis communicare.

Can. 413 – § 1. Sede impedita, regimen dioecesis, nisi aliter Sancta Sedes providerit, competit Episcopo coadiutori, si adsit ; eo deficiente aut impedito, alicui Episcopo auxiliari aut Vicario generali vel episcopali aliive sacerdoti, servato personarum ordine statuto in elencho ab Episcopo dioecesano quam primum a capta dioecesis possessione componendo ; qui elenchus cum Metropolita communicandus singulis saltem trienniis renovetur atque a cancellario sub secreto servetur.

§ 2. Si deficiat aut impediatur Episcopus coadiutor atque elenchus, de quo in § 1, non suppetat, collegii consultorum est sacerdotem eligere, qui dioecesim regat.

§ 3. Qui dioecesis regimen, ad normam §§ 1 vel 2, susceperit, quam primum Sanctam Sedem moneat de sede impedita ac de suscepto munere.

Can. 414 – Quilibet ad normam can. 413 vocatus ut ad interim dioecesis curam pastoralem gerat pro tempore quo sedes impeditur tantum, in cura pastorali dioecesis exercenda tenetur obligationibus atque potestate gaudet, quae iure Administratori dioecesano competunt.

Can. 415 – Si Episcopus dioecesanus poena ecclesiastica a munere exercendo prohibeatur, Metropolita aut, si is deficiat vel de eodem agatur, suffraganeus antiquior promotione ad Sanctam Sedem statim recurrat, ut ipsa provideat.

Can. 411 — The prescriptions of cann. 401 and 402, §2 on resignation from office are applicable to a coadjutor and an auxiliary bishop.

CHAPTER III
THE IMPEDED SEE AND THE VACANT SEE

Art. 1
THE IMPEDED SEE

Can. 412 — An episcopal see is understood to be impeded if by reason of captivity, banishment, exile or incapacity, the diocesan bishop is wholly prevented from fulfilling his pastoral function in the diocese, and cannot communicate with the people of his diocese even by letter.

Can. 413 — §1. When the see is impeded the governance of the diocese, unless the Holy See provides otherwise, belongs to the coadjutor bishop if there is one; if there is none or if he is impeded, it belongs to an auxiliary bishop or the vicar general or the episcopal vicar or to another priest, following the order of persons determined in a list to be composed by the diocesan bishop immediately upon taking possession of the diocese, which list is to be communicated to the metropolitan and renewed at least every three years; it is to be preserved in secret by the chancellor.

§2. If there is no coadjutor bishop or he is impeded, and the list mentioned in §1 is also lacking, the college of consultors is to select a priest who is to govern the diocese.

§3. Whoever assumes the governance of the diocese according to the norms of §1 or §2 shall immediately advise the Holy See of the see's being impeded and of his assuming the function.

Can. 414 — Whoever is called to exercise temporarily the pastoral care of a diocese according to the norm of can. 413 is bound by the obligations and enjoys the power which belong by law to a diocesan administrator only for the time during which the see is impeded.

Can. 415 — If the diocesan bishop is prohibited from exercising his function by an ecclesiastical penalty, the metropolitan is to make recourse immediately to the Holy See in order that it may provide; if there is no metropolitan or if he himself is the penalized bishop, the senior suffragan in terms of promotion is to make such recourse.

Art. 2

DE SEDE VACANTE

Can. 416 – Sedes episcopalis vacat Episcopi dioecesani morte, renuntiatione a Romano Pontifice acceptata, translatione ac privatione Episcopo intimata.

Can. 417 – Vim habent omnia quae gesta sunt a Vicario generali aut Vicario episcopali, donec certam de obitu Episcopi dioecesani notitiam iidem acceperint, itemque quae ab Episcopo dioecesano aut a Vicario generali vel episcopali gesta sunt, donec certam de memoratis actibus pontificiis notitiam receperint.

Can. 418 – § 1. A certa translationis notitia, Episcopus intra duos menses debet dioecesim *ad quam* petere eiusque canonicam possessionem capere; die autem captae possessionis dioecesis novae, dioecesis *a qua* vacat.

§ 2. A certa translationis notitia usque ad canonicam novae dioecesis possessionem, Episcopus translatus in dioecesi *a qua*:

1° Administratoris dioecesani potestatem obtinet eiusdemque obligationibus tenetur, cessante qualibet Vicarii generalis et Vicarii episcopalis potestate, salvo tamen can. 409, § 2;

2° integram percipit remunerationem officio propriam.

Can. 419 – Sede vacante, regimen dioecesis, usque ad constitutionem Administratoris dioecesani, ad Episcopum auxiliarem, et si plures sint, ad eum qui promotione sit antiquior devolvitur; deficiente autem Episcopo auxiliari, ad collegium consultorum, nisi a Sancta Sede aliter provisum fuerit. Qui ita regimen dioecesis assumit, sine mora convocet collegium competens ad deputandum Administratorem dioecesanum.

Can. 420 – In vicariatu vel praefectura apostolica, sede vacante, regimen assumit Pro-Vicarius vel Pro-Praefectus ad hunc tantum effectum a Vicario vel a Praefecto immediate post captam possessionem nominatus, nisi aliter a Sancta Sede statutum fuerit.

Can. 421 – § 1. Intra octo dies ab accepta vacationis sedis episcopalis notitia, Administrator dioecesanus, qui nempe dioecesim ad interim regat, eligendus est a collegio consultorum, firmo praescripto can. 502, § 3.

§ 2. Si intra praescriptum tempus Administrator dioecesanus, quavis de causa, non fuerit legitime electus, eiusdem deputatio devolvitur ad Metropolitam, et si vacans sit ipsa Ecclesia metropolitana aut metropolitana simul et suffraganea, ad Episcopum suffraganeum promotione antiquiorem.

Art. 2

THE VACANT SEE

Can. 416 — An episcopal see is vacant upon the death of the diocesan bishop, upon his resignation accepted by the Roman Pontiff, and upon transferral or deprivation of office made known to the bishop.

Can. 417 — All those things done by the vicar general or episcopal vicar have full force until they have received certain notice of the death of the diocesan bishop; likewise, those things done by the diocesan bishop or the vicar general or episcopal vicar have full force until they have received certain notice of the above-mentioned pontifical actions.

Can. 418 — §1. Upon certain notice of transferral the bishop must go to the new diocese within two months and take canonical possession of it; and from the day he takes possession of the new diocese his former diocese is vacant.

§2. From the reception of certain notice of transferral until taking canonical possession of the new diocese, the transferred bishop in his former diocese:

1° obtains the power of a diocesan administrator and is bound by those obligations; all authority of the vicar general and episcopal vicars ceases, with due regard for can. 409, §2;

2° continues to receive the entire salary proper to this office.

Can. 419 — When the see is vacant, until the establishment of a diocesan administrator, the governance of the diocese devolves upon the auxiliary bishop or if there are several, upon the senior auxiliary bishop in terms of promotion, or if there is no auxiliary bishop upon the college of consultors, unless the Holy See has provided otherwise; whoever assumes the governance of the diocese in this fashion is to convoke without delay the college which is competent to designate the diocesan administrator.

Can. 420 — Unless the Holy See has determined otherwise, when the see is vacant in an apostolic vicariate or prefecture, its governance is assumed by a pro-vicar or pro-prefect named for this purpose by the vicar or prefect immediately after taking possession.

Can. 421 — §1. Within eight days of receiving the notice of the vacancy of the episcopal see, the diocesan administrator, that is, he who governs the diocese in the interim, must be elected by the college of consultors, with due regard for the prescription of can. 502, §3.

§2. If within the prescribed time the diocesan administrator for any reason at all has not been legitimately elected, the choosing of the same devolves upon the metropolitan, and if the vacant see is itself the metropolitan church or the metropolitan church is vacant as well as the suffragan, it devolves upon the senior suffragan bishop in terms of promotion.

Can. 422 – Episcopus auxiliaris et, si is deficiat, collegium consultorum quantocius de morte Episcopi, itemque electus in Administratorem dioecesanum de sua electione Sedem Apostolicam certiorem faciant.

Can. 423 – § 1. Unus deputetur Administrator dioecesanus, reprobata contraria consuetudine; secus electio irrita est.

§ 2. Administrator dioecesanus ne simul sit oeconomus; quare si oeconomus dioecesis in Administratorem electus fuerit, alium pro tempore oeconomum eligat consilium a rebus oeconomicis.

Can. 424 – Administrator dioecesanus eligatur ad normam cann. 165-178.

Can. 425 – § 1. Valide ad munus Administratoris dioecesani deputari tantum potest sacerdos qui trigesimum quintum aetatis annum expleverit et ad eandem vacantem sedem non fuerit iam electus, nominatus vel praesentatus.

§ 2. In Administratorem dioecesanum eligatur sacerdos, qui sit doctrina et prudentia praestans.

§ 3. Si praescriptae in § 1 condiciones posthabitae fuerint, Metropolita aut, si ipsa Ecclesia metropolitana vacans fuerit, Episcopus suffraganeus promotione antiquior, agnita rei veritate, Administratorem pro ea vice deputet; actus autem illius qui contra praescripta § 1 sit electus, sunt ipso iure nulli.

Can. 426 – Qui, sede vacante, ante deputationem Administratoris dioecesani, dioecesim regat, potestate gaudet quam ius Vicario generali agnoscit.

Can. 427 – § 1. Administrator dioecesanus tenetur obligationibus et gaudet potestate Episcopi dioecesani, iis exclusis quae ex rei natura aut ipso iure excipiuntur.

§ 2. Administrator dioecesanus, acceptata electione, potestatem obtinet, quin requiratur ullius confirmatio, firma obligatione de qua in can. 833, n. 4.

Can. 428 – § 1. Sede vacante nihil innovetur.

§ 2. Illi qui ad interim dioecesis regimen curant, vetantur quidpiam agere quod vel dioecesi vel episcopalibus iuribus praeiudicium aliquod afferre possit; speciatim prohibentur ipsi, ac proinde alii quicumque, quominus sive per se sive per alium curiae dioecesanae documenta quaelibet subtrahant vel destruant, aut in iis quidquam immutent.

Can. 429 – Administrator dioecesanus obligatione tenetur residendi in dioecesi et applicandi Missam pro populo ad normam can. 388.

Can. 422 — The auxiliary bishop, or if there is none, the college of consultors, is to inform the Holy See immediately of the death of the bishop; the one elected diocesan administrator is to do the same concerning his own election.

Can. 423 — §1. One person is to be chosen diocesan administrator, and all contrary customs are revoked; otherwise the election is invalid.

§2. The diocesan administrator is not to be the finance officer at the same time; accordingly if the finance officer of the diocese has been elected administrator another temporary finance officer is to be chosen by the finance council.

Can. 424 — The diocesan administrator is to be elected according to the norms of cann. 165-178.

Can. 425 — §1. To be validly chosen diocesan administrator one must be a priest of at least thirty-five years of age who has not been elected, nominated or presented for the same vacant see.

§2. A priest who is outstanding in doctrine and prudence is to be elected diocesan administrator.

§3. If the conditions previously mentioned in §1 have been neglected, the metropolitan, or if the metropolitan church itself is vacant, the senior suffragan bishop in terms of promotion, having ascertained the truth of the matter, is to appoint an administrator in his stead; the acts of the one who was elected contrary to the prescriptions of §1 are invalid by law.

Can. 426 — Whoever governs the diocese while the see is vacant and before an administrator is designated enjoys the power which the law grants to the vicar general.

Can. 427 — §1. The diocesan administrator is bound by the obligations and enjoys the power of the diocesan bishop, excluding those things which are excepted by their very nature or by the law itself.

§2. Once the diocesan administrator has accepted the election he obtains power; no further confirmation is required, but the obligation of can. 833, §4, remains.

Can. 428 — §1. When the see is vacant there are to be no innovations.

§2. Those who temporarily govern the diocese are prohibited from doing anything which could in any way be prejudicial to the diocese or episcopal rights; they themselves and any other persons are specifically prohibited from removing, destroying or altering any documents of the diocesan curia, whether personally or through another.

Can. 429 — The diocesan administrator is obliged to reside in the diocese and to apply Mass for the people according to the norm of can. 388.

Can. 430 – § 1. Munus Administratoris dioecesani cessat per captam a novo Episcopo dioecesis possessionem.

§ 2. Administratoris dioecesani remotio Sanctae Sedi reservatur; renuntiatio quae forte ab ipso fiat, authentica forma exhibenda est collegio ad electionem competenti, neque acceptatione eget; remoto aut renuntiante Administratore dioecesano, aut eodem defuncto, alius eligatur Administrator dioecesanus ad normam can. 421.

TITULUS II
DE ECCLESIARUM PARTICULARIUM COETIBUS

Caput I
DE PROVINCIIS ECCLESIASTICIS
ET DE REGIONIBUS ECCLESIASTICIS

Can. 431 – § 1. Ut communis diversarum dioecesium vicinarum, iuxta personarum et locorum adiuncta, actio pastoralis promoveatur, utque Episcoporum dioecesanorum inter se relationes aptius foveantur, Ecclesiae particulares viciniores componantur in provincias ecclesiasticas certo territorio circumscriptas.

§ 2. Dioeceses exemptae deinceps pro regula ne habeantur; itaque singulae dioeceses aliaeque Ecclesiae particulares intra territorium alicuius provinciae ecclesiasticae exsistentes huic provinciae ecclesiasticae adscribi debent.

§ 3. Unius supremae Ecclesiae auctoritatis est, auditis quorum interest Episcopis, provincias ecclesiasticas constituere, supprimere aut innovare.

Can. 432 – § 1. In provincia ecclesiastica auctoritate, ad normam iuris, gaudent concilium provinciale atque Metropolita.

§ 2. Provincia ecclesiastica ipso iure personalitate iuridica gaudet.

Can. 433 – § 1. Si utilitas id suadeat, praesertim in nationibus ubi numerosiores adsunt Ecclesiae particulares, provinciae ecclesiasticae viciniores, proponente Episcoporum conferentia, a Sancta Sede in regiones ecclesiasticas coniungi possunt.

§ 2. Regio ecclesiastica in personam iuridicam erigi potest.

Can. 434 – Ad conventum Episcoporum regionis ecclesiasticae pertinet cooperationem et actionem pastoralem communem in regione fovere; quae tamen in canonibus huius Codicis conferentiae Episcoporum tribuuntur potestates eidem conventui non competunt, nisi quaedam specialiter a Sancta Sede ei concessa fuerint.

Can. 430 — §1. The responsibilities of the diocesan administrator cease with the taking possession of the diocese by the new bishop.

§2. The removal of the diocesan administrator is reserved to the Holy See; any resignation must be presented in authentic form to the college which is competent to elect but it does not have to be accepted by this body; if the diocesan administrator has been removed or resigned or dies another administrator is to be elected according to the norm of can. 421.

TITLE II
GROUPINGS OF PARTICULAR CHURCHES

Chapter I
ECCLESIASTICAL PROVINCES AND ECCLESIASTICAL REGIONS

Can. 431 — §1. Neighboring particular churches are to be brought together into ecclesiastical provinces limited to a certain territory in order that the common pastoral activity of the various neighboring dioceses may be promoted in accord with the circumstances of persons and places and in order that the relationships of the diocesan bishops among themselves may be more suitably fostered.

§2. As a rule exempt dioceses are no longer to exist; individual dioceses, therefore, and the other particular churches which exist within the territory of an ecclesiastical province must belong to this ecclesiastical province.

§3. The supreme authority of the Church alone is competent to establish, suppress or change ecclesiastical provinces, after hearing the bishops involved.

Can. 432 — §1. In accord with the norm of law the provincial council and the metropolitan possess authority within the ecclesiastical province.

§2. An ecclesiastical province enjoys juridic personality by the law itself.

Can. 433 — §1. If it appears useful, especially in nations where particular churches are more numerous, neighboring ecclesiastical provinces can be united into ecclesiastical regions by the Holy See at the proposal of the conference of bishops.

§2. An ecclesiastical region can be erected into a juridic person.

Can. 434 — The gathering of the bishops of an ecclesiastical region is to foster cooperation and common pastoral action in the region; however, the powers which are given in the canons of this code to the conference of bishops do not belong to such a gathering, unless some of them shall have been specially granted to it by the Holy See.

Caput II

DE METROPOLITIS

Can. 435 – Provinciae ecclesiasticae praeest Metropolita, qui est Archiepiscopus dioecesis cui praeficitur; quod officium cum sede episcopali, a Romano Pontifice determinata aut probata, coniunctum est.

Can. 436 – § 1. In dioecesibus suffraganeis Metropolitae competit:

1° vigilare ut fides et disciplina ecclesiastica accurate serventur, et de abusibus, si qui habeantur, Romanum Pontificem certiorem facere;

2° canonicam visitationem peragere, causa prius ab Apostolica Sede probata, si eam suffraganeus neglexerit;

3° deputare Administratorem dioecesanum, ad normam cann. 421, § 2 et 425, § 3.

§ 2. Ubi adiuncta id postulent, Metropolita ab Apostolica Sede instrui potest peculiaribus muneribus et potestate in iure particulari determinandis.

§ 3. Nulla alia in dioecesibus suffraganeis competit Metropolitis potestas regiminis; potest vero in omnibus ecclesiis, Episcopo dioecesano praemonito, si ecclesia sit cathedralis, sacras exercere functiones, uti Episcopus in propria dioecesi.

Can. 437 – § 1. Metropolita obligatione tenetur, intra tres menses a recepta consecratione episcopali, aut, si iam consecratus fuerit, a provisione canonica, per se aut per procuratorem a Romano Pontifice petendi pallium, quo quidem significatur potestas qua, in communione cum Ecclesia Romana, Metropolita in propria provincia iure instruitur.

§ 2. Metropolita, ad normam legum liturgicarum, pallio uti potest intra quamlibet ecclesiam provinciae ecclesiasticae cui praeest, minime vero extra eandem, ne accedente quidem Episcopi dioecesani assensu.

§ 3. Metropolita, si ad aliam sedem metropolitanam transferatur, novo indiget pallio.

Can. 438 – Patriarchae et Primatis titulus, praeter praerogativam honoris, nullam in Ecclesia latina secumfert regiminis potestatem, nisi de aliquibus ex privilegio apostolico aut probata consuetudine aliud constet.

CHAPTER II
METROPOLITANS

Can. 435 — The metropolitan, who is the archbishop of the diocese which he heads, presides over an ecclesiastical province; this office is connected with an episcopal see which has been determined or approved by the Roman Pontiff.

Can. 436 — §1. Within the suffragan dioceses the metropolitan is competent:

1° to be vigilant that the faith and ecclesiastical discipline are carefully preserved and to inform the Roman Pontiff of abuses if there are any;

2° to perform the canonical visitation if the suffragan bishop has neglected it, after the reason for doing so has first been approved by the Apostolic See;

3° to appoint a diocesan administrator in accord with the norm of cann. 421, §2 and 425, §3.

§2. Where circumstances demand it a metropolitan can be invested by the Apostolic See with special duties and power to be determined in particular law.

§3. The metropolitan possesses no other power of governance within the suffragan dioceses; he can, however, perform sacred functions in all the churches as if he were a bishop in his own diocese, but he is to inform the diocesan bishop if it is the cathedral church.

Can. 437 — §1. Within three months from the reception of episcopal consecration or from the time of canonical provision if he has already been consecrated a bishop, a metropolitan is obliged personally or through his proxy to request the pallium of the Roman Pontiff; the pallium signifies the power with which the metropolitan is invested by law within his own province in communion with the Roman Church.

§2. In accord with the norm of liturgical laws a metropolitan can use the pallium in any church whatsoever within the ecclesiastical province over which he presides, but not outside it, even if the diocesan bishop gives his assent.

§3. A metropolitan requires a new pallium if he is transferred to another metropolitan see.

Can. 438 — The title of patriarch or primate besides being a prerogative of honor, carries with it no power of governance in the Latin Church unless the contrary is clear in some instances in virtue of apostolic privilege or approved custom.

Caput III
DE CONCILIIS PARTICULARIBUS

Can. 439 – § 1. Concilium plenarium, pro omnibus scilicet Ecclesiis particularibus eiusdem conferentiae Episcoporum, celebretur quoties id ipsi Episcoporum conferentiae, approbante Apostolica Sede, necessarium aut utile videatur.

§ 2. Norma in § 1 statuta valet etiam de concilio provinciali celebrando in provincia ecclesiastica, cuius termini cum territorio nationis coincidunt.

Can. 440 – § 1. Concilium provinciale, pro diversis Ecclesiis particularibus eiusdem provinciae ecclesiasticae, celebretur quoties id, de iudicio maioris partis Episcoporum dioecesanorum provinciae, opportunum videatur, salvo can. 439, § 2.

§ 2. Sede metropolitana vacante, concilium provinciale ne convocetur.

Can. 441 – Episcoporum conferentiae est :

1° convocare concilium plenarium ;

2° locum ad celebrandum concilium intra territorium conferentiae Episcoporum eligere ;

3° inter Episcopos dioecesanos concilii plenarii eligere praesidem, ab Apostolica Sede approbandum ;

4° ordinem agendi et quaestiones tractandas determinare, concilii plenarii initium ac periodum indicere, illud transferre, prorogare et absolvere.

Can. 442 – § 1. Metropolitae, de consensu maioris partis Episcoporum suffraganeorum, est :

1° convocare concilium provinciale ;

2° locum ad celebrandum concilium provinciale intra provinciae territorium eligere ;

3° ordinem agendi et quaestiones tractandas determinare, concilii provincialis initium et periodum indicere, illud transferre, prorogare et absolvere.

§ 2. Metropolitae, eoque legitime impedito, Episcopi suffraganei ab aliis Episcopis suffraganeis electi est concilio provinciali praeesse.

Can. 443 – § 1. Ad concilia particularia convocandi sunt atque in eisdem ius habent suffragii deliberativi :

1° Episcopi dioecesani ;

2° Episcopi coadiutores et auxiliares ;

CHAPTER III
PARTICULAR COUNCILS

Can. 439 — §1. A plenary council, that is, one which is held for all the particular churches belonging to the same conference of bishops, is to be celebrated as often as it seems necessary or advantageous to the conference of bishops, with the approval of the Apostolic See.

§2. The norm established in §1 is also valid for the celebration of a provincial council in an ecclesiastical province whose boundaries coincide with the territory of a nation.

Can. 440 — §1. With due regard for can. 439, §2, a provincial council for the various particular churches of the same ecclesiastical province is to be celebrated as often as it seems opportune in the judgment of the majority of the diocesan bishops of the province.

§2. When the metropolitan see is vacant a provincial council is not to be convoked.

Can. 441 — It is the role of the conference of bishops:

1° to convoke a plenary council;

2° to select the place in which to celebrate a council within the territory of the conference of bishops;

3° to select the president of the plenary council from among the diocesan bishops, but he is to be approved by the Apostolic See;

4° to determine its agenda and the questions to be treated; to establish the date for the opening and closing of the plenary council; to transfer, prolong and dissolve it.

Can. 442 — §1. With the consent of the majority of the suffragan bishops, it is the role of the metropolitan to:

1° convoke a provincial council;

2° to select the place in which to celebrate a provincial council within the territory of the province;

3° to determine its agenda and the questions to be treated; to establish the date for the opening and closing of the provincial council; to transfer, prolong and dissolve it.

§2. It is the role of the metropolitan to preside over a provincial council; if he is legitimately hindered from doing so this role devolves upon the suffragan bishop elected by the other suffragans.

Can. 443 — §1. The following are to be called to particular councils and have the right of a deliberative vote in them:

1° diocesan bishops;

2° coadjutor and auxiliary bishops;

3° alii Episcopi titulares qui peculiari munere sibi ab Apostolica Sede aut ab Episcoporum conferentia demandato in territorio funguntur.

§ 2. Ad concilia particularia vocari possunt alii Episcopi titulares etiam emeriti in territorio degentes; qui quidem ius habent suffragii deliberativi.

§ 3. Ad concilia particularia vocandi sunt cum suffragio tantum consultivo:

1° Vicarii generales et Vicarii episcopales omnium in territorio Ecclesiarum particularium;

2° Superiores maiores institutorum religiosorum et societatum vitae apostolicae numero tum pro viris tum pro mulieribus ab Episcoporum conferentia aut a provinciae Episcopis determinando, respective electi ab omnibus Superioribus maioribus institutorum et societatum, quae in territorio sedem habent;

3° Rectores universitatum ecclesiasticarum et catholicarum atque decani facultatum theologiae et iuris canonici, quae in territorio sedem habent;

4° Rectores aliqui seminariorum maiorum, numero ut in n. 2 determinando, electi a rectoribus seminariorum quae in territorio sita sunt.

§ 4. Ad concilia particularia vocari etiam possunt, cum suffragio tantum consultivo, presbyteri aliique christifideles, ita tamen ut eorum numerus non excedat dimidiam partem eorum de quibus in §§ 1-3.

§ 5. Ad concilia provincialia praeterea invitentur capitula cathedralia, itemque consilium presbyterale et consilium pastorale uniuscuiusque Ecclesiae particularis, ita quidem ut eorum singula duos ex suis membris mittant, collegialiter ab iisdem designatos; qui tamen votum habent tantum consultivum.

§ 6. Ad concilia particularia, si id iudicio Episcoporum conferentiae pro concilio plenario aut Metropolitae una cum Episcopis suffraganeis pro concilio provinciali expediat, etiam alii ut hospites invitari poterunt.

Can. 444 – § 1. Omnes qui ad concilia particularia convocantur, eisdem interesse debent, nisi iusto detineantur impedimento, de quo concilii praesidem certiorem facere tenentur.

§ 2. Qui ad concilia particularia convocantur et in eis suffragium habent deliberativum, si iusto detineantur impedimento, procuratorem mittere possunt; qui procurator votum habet tantum consultivum.

Can. 445 – Concilium particulare pro suo territorio curat ut necessitatibus pastoralibus populi Dei provideatur atque potestate gaudet

3° other titular bishops who fulfill within the territory a special function committed to them by the Apostolic See or by the conference of bishops.

§2. Other titular bishops who are living in the territory, even if they be emeriti, can be called to particular councils and they have the right of a deliberative vote.

§3. The following are to be called to particular councils but they have only a consultative vote:

1° the vicars general and the episcopal vicars of all the particular churches in the territory;

2° the major superiors of religious institutes and societies of apostolic life; the number of men and women, however, is to be determined by the conference of bishops or by the bishops of the province; and the superiors are in turn to be elected by all the major superiors of the institutes and societies which have their headquarters within the territory;

3° rectors of ecclesiastical and Catholic universities and the deans of faculties of theology and of canon law which are located within the territory;

4° some rectors of major seminaries; their number is to be determined in accord with n. 2 above; and they are elected by the rectors of the seminaries which are located within the territory.

§4. Presbyters and other members of the Christian faithful can also be called to particular councils with only a consultative vote; their number is not to exceed half of the number of those mentioned in §§ 1-3.

§5. The cathedral chapters, the presbyteral council and the pastoral council of each of the particular churches are likewise to be invited to provincial councils in such a way that each sends two of its members as representatives; these should be selected in a collegial manner by each of these bodies; they possess only a consultative vote.

§6. Others also can be invited to particular councils as guests if it seems advantageous in the judgment of the conference of bishops in regard to a plenary council or in the judgment of the metropolitan along with his suffragan bishops in regard to a provincial council.

Can. 444 — §1. All who are invited to attend particular councils must attend them unless they are detained by a just impediment about which they are bound to inform the president of the council.

§2. Those who are invited to attend particular councils and who have a deliberative vote in them can send a proxy if they are detained by a just impediment; however, the proxy has only a consultative vote.

Can. 445 — A particular council sees to it that provision is made for the pastoral needs of the people of God in its own territory, and it possesses the

regiminis, praesertim legislativa, ita ut, salvo semper iure universali Ecclesiae, decernere valeat quae ad fidei incrementum, ad actionem pastoralem communem ordinandam et ad moderandos mores et disciplinam ecclesiasticam communem servandam, inducendam aut tuendam opportuna videantur.

Can. 446 – Absoluto concilio particulari, praeses curet ut omnia acta concilii ad Apostolicam Sedem transmittantur; decreta a concilio edicta ne promulgentur, nisi postquam ab Apostolica Sede recognita fuerint; ipsius concilii est definire modum promulgationis decretorum et tempus quo decreta promulgata obligare incipiant.

Caput IV
DE EPISCOPORUM CONFERENTIIS

Can. 447 – Episcoporum conferentia, institutum quidem permanens, est coetus Episcoporum alicuius nationis vel certi territorii, munera quaedam pastoralia coniunctim pro christifidelibus eius territorii exercentium, ad maius bonum provehendum, quod hominibus praebet Ecclesia, praesertim per apostolatus formas et rationes temporis et loci adiunctis apte accommodatas, ad normam iuris.

Can. 448 – § 1. Episcoporum conferentia regula generali comprehendit praesules omnium Ecclesiarum particularium eiusdem nationis, ad normam can. 450.

§ 2. Si vero, de iudicio Apostolicae Sedis, auditis quorum interest Episcopis dioecesanis, personarum aut rerum adiuncta id suadeant, Episcoporum conferentia erigi potest pro territorio minoris aut maioris amplitudinis, ita ut vel tantum comprehendat Episcopos aliquarum Ecclesiarum particularium in certo territorio constitutarum vel praesules Ecclesiarum particularium in diversis nationibus exstantium; eiusdem Apostolicae Sedis est pro earundem singulis peculiares normas statuere.

Can. 449 – § 1. Unius supremae Ecclesiae auctoritatis est, auditis quorum interest Episcopis, Episcoporum conferentias erigere, supprimere aut innovare.

§ 2. Episcoporum conferentia legitime erecta ipso iure personalitate iuridica gaudet.

Can. 450 – § 1. Ad Episcoporum conferentiam ipso iure pertinent omnes in territorio Episcopi dioecesani eisque iure aequiparati, itemque Episcopi coadiutores, Episcopi auxiliares atque ceteri Episcopi titulares peculiari munere, sibi ab Apostolica Sede vel ab Episcoporum conferentia demandato, in eodem territorio fungentes; invitari quoque

power of governance, especially legislative power, so that with due regard always for the universal law of the Church it can decree what seems appropriate for increasing faith, organizing common pastoral activity, directing morals and preserving, promoting or protecting common ecclesiastical discipline.

Can. 446 — At the conclusion of a particular council the president is to see to it that all the acts of the council are sent to the Apostolic See; decrees issued by the council are not to be promulgated until after they have been reviewed by the Apostolic See; it is the role of the council itself to define the manner of the promulgation of its decrees and the time at which the promulgated decrees begin to oblige.

Chapter IV
CONFERENCES OF BISHOPS

Can. 447 — The conference of bishops, a permanent institution, is a grouping of bishops of a given nation or territory whereby, according to the norm of law, they jointly exercise certain pastoral functions on behalf of the Christian faithful of their territory in view of promoting that greater good which the Church offers humankind, especially through forms and programs of the apostolate which are fittingly adapted to the circumstances of the time and place.

Can. 448 — §1. Generally the conference of bishops encompasses all who preside over particular churches of the same nation according to can. 450.

§2. If, however, in the judgment of the Apostolic See, having consulted the diocesan bishops who are involved, circumstances of persons or things suggest it, a conference of bishops may be erected for a smaller or larger territory so that it takes in either the bishops of some particular churches constituted in a given territory or those presiding over particular churches in different nations; it is for the same Apostolic See to determine special norms for individual conferences.

Can. 449 — §1. After hearing the bishops involved, it pertains to the supreme church authority alone to erect, suppress or change the conferences of bishops.

§2. The conference of bishops once legitimately erected enjoys a juridic personality by the law itself.

Can. 450 — §1. The members of the episcopal conference are, by law, all diocesan bishops and those equivalent to them in law, also coadjutor bishops, auxiliary bishops and other titular bishops who fulfill within the same territory a particular function for which they are mandated by the Apostolic See or by the conference of bishops; ordinaries of another rite may also be

possunt Ordinarii alterius ritus, ita tamen ut votum tantum consultivum habeant, nisi Episcoporum conferentiae statuta aliud decernant.

§ 2. Ceteri Episcopi titulares necnon Legatus Romani Pontificis
non sunt de iure membra Episcoporum conferentiae.

Can. 451 – Quaelibet Episcoporum conferentia sua conficiat statuta, ab Apostolica Sede recognoscenda, in quibus, praeter alia, ordinentur conferentiae conventus plenarii habendi, et provideantur consilium Episcoporum permanens et secretaria generalis conferentiae,
atque alia etiam officia et commissiones quae iudicio conferentiae fini
consequendo efficacius consulant.

Can. 452 – § 1. Quaelibet Episcoporum conferentia sibi eligat praesidem, determinet quisnam, praeside legitime impedito, munere pro-
praesidis fungatur, atque secretarium generalem designet, ad normam
statutorum.

§ 2. Praeses conferentiae, atque eo legitime impedito pro-praeses,
non tantum Episcoporum conferentiae conventibus generalibus, sed
etiam consilio permanenti praeest.

Can. 453 – Conventus plenarii Episcoporum conferentiae habeantur semel saltem singulis annis, et praeterea quoties id postulent peculiaria adiuncta, secundum statutorum praescripta.

Can. 454 – § 1. Suffragium deliberativum in conventibus plenariis
Episcoporum conferentiae ipso iure competit Episcopis dioecesanis
eisque qui iure ipsis aequiparantur, necnon Episcopis coadiutoribus.

§ 2. Episcopis auxiliaribus ceterisque Episcopis titularibus qui ad
Episcoporum conferentiam pertinent, suffragium competit deliberativum aut consultivum, iuxta statutorum conferentiae praescripta ; firmum
tamen sit eis solis, de quibus in § 1, competere suffragium deliberativum, cum agitur de statutis conficiendis aut immutandis.

Can. 455 – § 1. Episcoporum conferentia decreta generalia ferre
tantummodo potest in causis, in quibus ius universale id praescripserit
aut peculiare Apostolicae Sedis mandatum sive motu proprio sive ad
petitionem ipsius conferentiae id statuerit.

§ 2. Decreta de quibus in § 1, ut valide ferantur in plenario conventu, per duas saltem ex tribus partibus suffragiorum Praesulum, qui
voto deliberativo fruentes ad conferentiam pertinent, proferri debent,
atque vim obligandi non obtinent, nisi ab Apostolica Sede recognita,
legitime promulgata fuerint.

§ 3. Modus promulgationis et tempus a quo decreta vim suam

invited, however in such manner that they enjoy only consultative vote, unless the statutes of the conference of bishops determine otherwise.

§2. The other titular bishops and the legates of the Roman Pontiff are not by law members of the conference of bishops.

Can. 451 — Each conference of bishops is to prepare its own statutes, which must be reviewed by the Holy See, and which among other things are to provide for the holding of plenary meetings of the conference as well as a permanent council of bishops, a general secretary of the conference, and other offices and commissions, which in the judgment of the conference will help it fulfill its purpose more effectively.

Can. 452 — §1. Each conference of bishops is to elect a president for itself; it is also to determine who is to serve in the role of pro-president when the president is legitimately impeded; and it is also to appoint a general secretary of the conference, according to the norm of the statutes.

§2. The president of the conference, and the pro-president when the former is legitimately impeded, preside not only at the general meetings of the conference of bishops but also over its permanent council.

Can. 453 — The plenary sessions of the episcopal conference are to be held at least annually, and in addition, as often as special circumstances require, according to the prescriptions of the statutes.

Can. 454 — §1. Diocesan bishops, those equivalent to them in law and also coadjutor bishops have a deliberative vote in plenary sessions of the conference of bishops by the law itself.

§2. Auxiliary bishops and other titular bishops who are members of the episcopal conference enjoy either a deliberative or consultative vote according to the prescriptions of the statutes of the conference; however, only those mentioned in §1 enjoy a deliberative vote when it is a question of drawing up or modifying the statutes.

Can. 455 — §1. The conference of bishops can issue general decrees only in those cases in which the common [universal] law prescribes it, or a special mandate of the Apostolic See, given either *motu proprio* or at the request of the conference, determines it.

§2. The general decrees mentioned in §1 can be validly passed in a plenary session only if two-thirds of the members of the conference having a deliberative vote approve them; such decrees do not have binding force, unless they have been legitimately promulgated, after having been reviewed by the Apostolic See.

§3. The manner of promulgation and the time from which the decrees take

exserunt, ab ipsa Episcoporum conferentia determinantur.

§ 4. In casibus in quibus nec ius universale nec peculiare Apostolicae Sedis mandatum potestatem, de qua in § 1, Episcoporum conferentiae concessit, singuli Episcopi dioecesani competentia integra manet, nec conferentia eiusve praeses nomine omnium Episcoporum agere
valet, nisi omnes et singuli Episcopi consensum dederint.

Can. 456 – Absoluto conventu plenario Episcoporum conferentiae,
relatio de actis conferentiae necnon eius decreta a praeside ad Apostolicam Sedem transmittantur, tum ut in eiusdem notitiam acta per-
ferantur, tum ut decreta, si quae sint, ab eadem recognosci possint.

Can. 457 – Consilii Episcoporum permanentis est curare, ut res in
plenario conventu conferentiae agendae praeparentur et decisiones in
conventu plenario statutae debite exsecutioni mandentur; eiusdem
etiam est alia negotia peragere, quae ipsi ad normam statutorum committuntur.

Can. 458 – Secretariae generalis est :

1° relationem componere actorum et decretorum conventus plenarii conferentiae necnon actorum consilii Episcoporum permanentis,
et eadem cum omnibus conferentiae membris communicare, alia etiam
acta conscribere, quae ipsi a conferentiae praeside aut a consilio permanenti componenda committuntur;

2° communicare cum Episcoporum conferentiis finitimis acta et
documenta quae a conferentia in plenario conventu aut a consilio
Episcoporum permanenti ipsis transmitti statuuntur.

Can. 459 – § 1. Foveantur relationes inter Episcoporum conferentias, praesertim viciniores, ad maius bonum promovendum ac tuendum.

§ 2. Quoties vero actiones aut rationes a conferentiis ineuntur
formam internationalem praeseferentes, Apostolica Sedes audiatur
oportet.

TITULUS III

DE INTERNA ORDINATIONE
ECCLESIARUM PARTICULARIUM

CAPUT I

DE SYNODO DIOECESANA

Can. 460 – Synodus dioecesana est coetus delectorum sacerdotum
aliorumque christifidelium Ecclesiae particularis, qui in bonum totius

effect are to be determined by the conference of bishops itself.

§4. In the cases where neither the universal law nor a special mandate of the Apostolic See has granted the conference of bishops the power mentioned above in §1, the competence of individual diocesan bishops remains intact; and neither the conference nor its president may act in the name of all the bishops unless each and every bishop has given his consent.

Can. 456 — When the plenary session of the conference of bishops has been completed, a report of the acts of the conference and its decrees are to be sent to the Apostolic See by the president, so that these acts may be brought to its attention and it may review the decrees, if there be any.

Can. 457 — The permanent council of bishops is to prepare the agenda for the plenary meeting of the conference and see to it that the decisions made during the plenary sessions are properly implemented; it is also to care for other matters which are entrusted to it according to the norm of the statutes.

Can. 458 — It is the responsibility of the general secretary:

1° to prepare a report of the acts and decrees of the plenary meeting of the conference, and also the acts of the permanent council of bishops and to communicate the same to all the members of the conference; he is also to draw up the other acts which are entrusted to him by the president of the conference or by the permanent council;

2° to communicate to neighboring conferences of bishops those acts and documents which the conference in plenary session or the permanent council of bishops decided to send to them.

Can. 459 — §1. Mutual relationships are to be fostered between the conferences of bishops of different regions, especially those who are neighbors, for the promotion and protection of the greater good.

§2. Whenever the actions or programs entered into by the conferences take on an international aspect it is necessary to consult the Apostolic See.

TITLE III

THE INTERNAL ORDERING OF PARTICULAR CHURCHES

CHAPTER I

THE DIOCESAN SYNOD

Can. 460 — A diocesan synod is a group of selected priests and other Christian faithful of a particular church which offers assistance to the dioce-

communitatis dioecesanae Episcopo dioecesano adiutricem operam praestant, ad normam canonum qui sequuntur.

Can. 461 – § 1. Synodus dioecesana in singulis Ecclesiis particularibus celebretur cum, iudicio Episcopi dioecesani et audito consilio presbyterali, adiuncta id suadeant.

§ 2. Si Episcopus plurium dioecesium curam habet, aut unius curam
habet uti Episcopus proprius alterius vero uti Administrator, unam
synodum dioecesanam ex omnibus dioecesibus sibi commissis convocare
potest.

Can. 462 – § 1. Synodum dioecesanam convocat solus Episcopus
dioecesanus, non autem qui ad interim dioecesi praeest.

§ 2. Synodo dioecesanae praeest Episcopus dioecesanus, qui tamen
Vicarium generalem aut Vicarium episcopalem pro singulis sessionibus
synodi ad hoc officium implendum delegare potest.

Can. 463 – § 1. Ad synodum dioecesanam vocandi sunt uti synodi
sodales eamque participandi obligatione tenentur :

1º Episcopus coadiutor atque Episcopi auxiliares ;

2º Vicarii generales et Vicarii episcopales, necnon Vicarius
iudicialis ;

3º canonici ecclesiae cathedralis ;

4º membra consilii presbyteralis ;

5º christifideles laici, etiam sodales institutorum vitae consecratae, a consilio pastorali eligendi, modo et numero ab Episcopo dioecesano determinandis, aut, ubi hoc consilium non exstet, ratione ab
Episcopo dioecesano determinata ;

6º rector seminarii dioecesani maioris ;

7º vicarii foranei ;

8º unus saltem presbyter ex unoquoque vicariatu foraneo eligendus ab omnibus qui curam animarum inibi habeant ; item eligendus
est alius presbyter qui, eodem impedito, in eius locum substituatur ;

9º aliqui Superiores institutorum religiosorum et societatum vitae
apostolicae, quae in dioecesi domum habent, eligendi numero et modo
ab Episcopo dioecesano determinatis.

§ 2. Ad synodum dioecesanam ab Episcopo dioecesano vocari uti
synodi sodales possunt alii quoque, sive clerici, sive institutorum vitae
consecratae sodales, sive christifideles laici.

§ 3. Ad synodum dioecesanam Episcopus dioecesanus, si id opportunum duxerit, invitare potest uti observatores aliquos ministros aut
sodales Ecclesiarum vel communitatum ecclesialium, quae non sunt
in plena cum Ecclesia catholica communione.

Can. 464 – Synodi sodalis, si legitimo detineatur impedimento, non

san bishop for the good of the entire diocesan community according to the norm of the following canons.

Can. 461 — §1. A diocesan synod is to be celebrated in each of the particular churches when circumstances warrant it in the judgment of the diocesan bishop, after he has consulted the presbyteral council.

§2. If a bishop has the care of several dioceses or if he has the care of one as its proper bishop and of another as its administrator, he can convoke one diocesan synod for all the dioceses entrusted to him.

Can. 462 — §1. Only the diocesan bishop convokes the diocesan synod, not however one who presides over a diocese *ad interim*.

§2. The diocesan bishop presides over the diocesan synod; he can, however, delegate the vicar general or an episcopal vicar to fulfill this office for individual sessions of the synod.

Can. 463 — §1. The following persons are to be called to the diocesan synod as its members and are obliged to participate in it:

1° the coadjutor bishop and the auxiliary bishops;

2° the vicars general, the episcopal vicars and the judicial vicar;

3° the canons of the cathedral church;

4° the members of the presbyteral council;

5° lay members of the Christian faithful and members of institutes of consecrated life, to be selected by the pastoral council in a manner and number to be determined by the diocesan bishop or, where such a council does not exist, in a manner determined by the diocesan bishop;

6° the rector of the diocesan major seminary;

7° the vicars forane;

8° at least one presbyter to be selected from each vicariate forane by all who have the care of souls there; also to be selected is another presbyter who would take the place of the first one selected if he were impeded;

9° some superiors of the religious institutes and societies of apostolic life which have a house in the diocese, to be selected in a manner and number determined by the diocesan bishop.

§2. Others can be called as members to the diocean synod by the diocesan bishop; these can be clerics, members of institutes of consecrated life, or lay members of the Christian faithful.

§3. If he should judge it opportune, the diocesan bishop can invite as observers to the diocesan synod some ministers or members of churches or ecclesial communities which are not in full communion with the Catholic Church.

Can. 464 — A member of the synod who is hindered by a legitimate

potest mittere procuratorem qui ipsius nomine eidem intersit; Episcopum vero dioecesanum de hoc impedimento certiorem faciat.

Can. 465 – Propositae quaestiones omnes liberae sodalium discep-
tationi in synodi sessionibus subiciantur.

Can. 466 – Unus in synodo dioecesana legislator est Episcopus
dioecesanus, aliis synodi sodalibus voto tantummodo consultivo gau-
dentibus; unus ipse synodalibus declarationibus et decretis subscribit,
quae eius auctoritate tantum publici iuris fieri possunt.

Can. 467 – Episcopus dioecesanus textus declarationum ac decretorum synodalium communicet cum Metropolita necnon cum Episcoporum conferentia.

Can. 468 – § 1. Episcopo dioecesano competit pro suo prudenti iudicio synodum dioecesanam suspendere necnon dissolvere.

§ 2. Vacante vel impedita sede episcopali, synodus dioecesana ipso
iure intermittitur, donec Episcopus dioecesanus, qui succedit, ipsam
continuari decreverit aut eandem extinctam declaraverit.

Caput II

DE CURIA DIOECESANA

Can. 469 – Curia dioecesana constat illis institutis et personis, quae
Episcopo operam praestant in regimine universae dioecesis, praesertim in
actione pastorali dirigenda, in administratione dioecesis curanda, necnon in potestate iudiciali exercenda.

Can. 470 – Nominatio eorum, qui officia in curia dioecesana exercent, spectat ad Episcopum dioecesanum.

Can. 471 – Omnes qui ad officia in curia admittuntur debent:

1° promissionem emittere de munere fideliter adimplendo, secundum rationem iure vel ab Episcopo determinatam;

2° secretum servare intra fines et secundum modum iure aut ab
Episcopo determinatos.

Can. 472 – Circa causas atque personas quae in curia ad exercitium
potestatis iudicialis pertinent, serventur praescripta Libri VII *De processibus;* de iis autem quae ad administrationem dioecesis spectant,
serventur praescripta canonum qui sequuntur.

Can. 473 – § 1. Episcopus dioecesanus curare debet ut omnia negotia
quae ad universae dioecesis administrationem pertinent, debite coordinentur et ad bonum portionis populi Dei sibi commissae aptius pro-
curandum ordinentur.

impediment cannot send a proxy to attend in his or her name; such a member is to inform the diocesan bishop of this impediment.

Can. 465 — All the proposed questions are to be subject to the free discussion of the members during the sessions of the synod.

Can. 466 — The diocesan bishop is the sole legislator at a diocesan synod while the remaining members of the synod possess only a consultative vote; he alone signs the synodal declarations and decrees which can be published only through his authority.

Can. 467 — The diocesan bishop is to communicate the texts of the synodal declarations and decrees to the metropolitan and to the conference of bishops.

Can. 468 — §1. It is within the competence of the diocesan bishop to suspend or dissolve a diocesan synod in accord with his own prudent judgment.

§2. If the episcopal see should become vacant or impeded, a diocesan synod is interrupted by the law itself until the succeeding diocesan bishop has decreed that it is to continue or that it is terminated.

CHAPTER II
THE DIOCESAN CURIA

Can. 469 — The diocesan curia consists of those institutions and persons which furnish assistance to the bishop in the governance of the entire diocese, especially in directing pastoral activity, in providing for the administration of the diocese and in exercising judicial power.

Can. 470 — The diocesan bishop appoints those who exercise offices within the diocesan curia.

Can. 471 — All persons who are admitted to offices within the curia must:

1° promise to fulfill their function faithfully according to the manner determined by law or by the bishop;

2° observe secrecy within the limits and according to the manner determined by law or by the bishop.

Can. 472 — The prescriptions of Book VII: *Processes* are to be observed concerning cases and persons which refer to the exercise of judicial power in the curia; the prescriptions of the following canons are to be observed concerning those matters which involve the administration of the diocese.

Can. 473 — §1. The diocesan bishop must see to it that all matters which concern the administration of the entire diocese are duly coordinated and arranged in such a manner that the good of the portion of God's people entrusted to him is more suitably attained.

§ 2. Ipsius Episcopi dioecesani est coordinare actionem pastoralem Vicariorum sive generalium sive episcopalium; ubi id expediat, nominari potest Moderator curiae, qui sacerdos sit oportet, cuius est sub Episcopi auctoritate ea coordinare quae ad negotia administrativa tractanda attinent, itemque curare ut ceteri curiae addicti officium sibi commissum rite adimpleant.

§ 3. Nisi locorum adiuncta iudicio Episcopi aliud suadeant, Moderator curiae nominetur Vicarius generalis aut, si plures sint, unus ex Vicariis generalibus.

§ 4. Ubi id expedire iudicaverit, Episcopus, ad actionem pastoralem aptius fovendam, constituere potest consilium episcopale, constans scilicet Vicariis generalibus et Vicariis episcopalibus.

Can. 474 – Acta curiae quae effectum iuridicum habere nata sunt, subscribi debent ab Ordinario a quo emanant, et quidem ad validitatem, ac simul a curiae cancellario vel notario; cancellarius vero Moderatorem curiae de actis certiorem facere tenetur.

Art. 1
DE VICARIIS GENERALIBUS ET EPISCOPALIBUS

Can. 475 – § 1. In unaquaque dioecesi constituendus est ab Episcopo dioecesano Vicarius generalis, qui potestate ordinaria ad normam canonum qui sequuntur instructus, ipsum in universae dioecesis regimine adiuvet.

§ 2. Pro regula generali habeatur ut unus constituatur Vicarius generalis, nisi dioecesis amplitudo vel incolarum numerus aut aliae rationes pastorales aliud suadeant.

Can. 476 – Quoties rectum dioecesis regimen id requirat, constitui etiam possunt ab Episcopo dioecesano unus vel plures Vicarii episcopales, qui nempe aut in determinata dioecesis parte aut in certo negotiorum genere aut quoad fideles determinati ritus vel certi personarum coetus, eadem gaudent potestate ordinaria, quae iure universali Vicario generali competit, ad normam canonum qui sequuntur.

Can. 477 – § 1. Vicarius generalis et episcopalis libere ab Episcopo dioecesano nominantur et ab ipso libere removeri possunt, firmo praescripto can. 406; Vicarius episcopalis, qui non sit Episcopus auxiliaris, nominetur tantum ad tempus, in ipso constitutionis actu determinandum.

§ 2. Vicario generali absente vel legitime impedito, Episcopus dioecesanus alium nominare potest, qui eius vices suppleat; eadem norma applicatur pro Vicario episcopali.

§2. It is the responsibility of the diocesan bishop himself to coordinate the pastoral activity of the vicars general or episcopal vicars; whenever it is expedient he can appoint a moderator of the curia, who ought to be a priest, and whose task it is, under the authority of the bishop, to coordinate the exercise of administrative responsibilities and to see to it that the other members of the curia duly fulfill the office entrusted to them.

§3. Unless in the judgment of the bishop local circumstances warrant otherwise, the vicar general or, if there are several, one of the vicars general is to be appointed moderator of the curia.

§4. If he judges it expedient in fostering more suitable pastoral activity, the bishop can establish an episcopal council consisting of the vicars general and the episcopal vicars.

Can. 474 — Those curial acts which are to have a juridic effect must, for their validity, be signed by the ordinary from whom they emanate; likewise they are to be signed by the chancellor or the notary of the curia; the chancellor is bound to inform the moderator of the curia concerning such acts.

Art. 1

VICARS GENERAL AND EPISCOPAL VICARS

Can. 475 — §1. A vicar general is to be appointed in each diocese by the diocesan bishop; he is to assist the diocesan bishop in the governance of the entire diocese and is endowed with ordinary power according to the following canons.

§2. As a general rule only one vicar general is to be appointed unless the size of the diocese, the number of its inhabitants or other pastoral reasons warrant otherwise.

Can. 476 — As often as the correct goverance of the diocese requires it the diocesan bishop can also appoint one or several episcopal vicars, who possess the same ordinary power which the universal law gives to the vicar general according to the following canons either in a determined section of the diocese or in a certain type of business or over the faithful of a determined rite or over certain groups of persons.

Can. 477 — §1. With due regard for the prescription of can. 406, the diocesan bishop freely appoints and freely removes a vicar general and an episcopal vicar; an episcopal vicar who is not an auxiliary bishop is to be appointed only for a time to be determined in the act of appointment.

§2. When a vicar general is absent or legitimately impeded the diocesan bishop can appoint another to take his place; the same norm applies to an episcopal vicar.

Can. 478 – § 1. Vicarius generalis et episcopalis sint sacerdotes annos nati non minus triginta, in iure canonico aut theologia doctores vel licentiati vel saltem in iisdem disciplinis vere periti, sana doctrina, probitate, prudentia ac rerum gerendarum experientia commendati.

§ 2. Vicarii generalis et episcopalis munus componi non potest cum munere canonici paenitentiarii, neque committi consanguineis Episcopi usque ad quartum gradum.

Can. 479 – § 1. Vicario generali, vi officii, in universa dioecesi competit potestas exsecutiva quae ad Episcopum dioecesanum iure pertinet, ad ponendos scilicet omnes actus administrativos, iis tamen exceptis quos Episcopus sibi reservaverit vel qui ex iure requirant speciale Episcopi mandatum.

§ 2. Vicario episcopali ipso iure eadem competit potestas de qua in § 1, sed quoad determinatam territorii partem aut negotiorum genus aut fideles determinati ritus vel coetus tantum pro quibus constitutus est, iis causis exceptis quas Episcopus sibi aut Vicario generali reservaverit, aut quae ex iure requirunt speciale Episcopi mandatum.

§ 3. Ad Vicarium generalem atque ad Vicarium episcopalem, intra ambitum eorum competentiae, pertinent etiam facultates habituales ab Apostolica Sede Episcopo concessae, necnon rescriptorum exsecutio, nisi aliud expresse cautum fuerit aut electa fuerit industria personae Episcopi dioecesani.

Can. 480 – Vicarius generalis et Vicarius episcopalis de praecipuis negotiis et gerendis et gestis Episcopo dioecesano referre debent, nec umquam contra voluntatem et mentem Episcopi dioecesani agant.

Can. 481 – § 1. Expirat potestas Vicarii generalis et Vicarii episcopalis expleto tempore mandati, renuntiatione, itemque, salvis cann. 406 et 409, remotione eisdem ab Episcopo dioecesano intimata, atque sedis episcopalis vacatione.

§ 2. Suspenso munere Episcopi dioecesani, suspenditur potestas Vicarii generalis et Vicarii episcopalis, nisi episcopali dignitate aucti sint.

Art. 2

DE CANCELLARIO ALIISQUE NOTARIIS ET DE ARCHIVIS

Can. 482 – § 1. In qualibet curia constituatur cancellarius, cuius praecipuum munus, nisi aliter iure particulari statuatur, est curare

Can. 478 — §1. A vicar general and an episcopal vicar are to be priests, not less than thirty years of age, holding a doctorate or licentiate in canon law or in theology or at least being truly expert in these disciplines, as well as being recommended by reason of their sound doctrine, integrity, prudence, and experience in handling matters.

§2. The role of vicar general and episcopal vicar cannot be assumed by the same person who functions as canon penitentiary; nor is this office to be entrusted to persons who are related by blood to the bishop up to the fourth degree.

Can. 479 — §1. In virtue of his office the vicar general possesses that executive power in the entire diocese which belongs to the diocesan bishop in law, that is, he possesses the power to place all administrative acts with the exception of those which the bishop has reserved to himself or which in law require the special mandate of the bishop.

§2. The episcopal vicar possesses by the law itself the same power mentioned in §1 but only over that determined section of territory, that type of business, or those faithful of a determined rite or group for which he was appointed, with the exception of those cases which the bishop has reserved to himself or to the vicar general or which in law require the special mandate of the bishop.

§3. Within the limits of their competency the vicar general and episcopal vicar also possess the habitual faculties granted to the bishop by the Apostolic See as well as the power to execute rescripts, unless other provisions have been expressly made or unless the diocesan bishop has been chosen to act because of some personal qualification.

Can. 480 — The vicar general and the episcopal vicar must report to the diocesan bishop on the principal matters which are to be treated and which have been treated, and they are never to act contrary to his will and mind.

Can. 481 — §1. The power of a vicar general or of an episcopal vicar ceases when the time of their mandate has expired, when they resign and with due regard for cann. 406 and 409, when they are informed of their removal by the diocesan bishop and when the episcopal see is vacant.

§2. Unless they possess the episcopal dignity the power of the vicar general and of the episcopal vicar is suspended with the suspension from office of the diocesan bishop.

Art. 2

The Chancellor, Other Notaries and the Archives

Can. 482 — §1. In every curia, a chancellor is to be appointed whose principal task is, unless particular law determines otherwise, to see to it that

ut acta curiae redigantur et expediantur, atque eadem in curiae archivo custodiantur.

§ 2. Si necesse videatur, cancellario dari potest adiutor, cui nomen sit vice-cancellarii.

§ 3. Cancellarius necnon vice-cancellarius sunt eo ipso notarii et secretarii curiae.

Can. 483 – § 1. Praeter cancellarium, constitui possunt alii notarii, quorum quidem scriptura seu subscriptio publicam fidem facit, et quidem sive ad quaelibet acta, sive ad acta iudicialia dumtaxat, sive ad acta certae causae aut negotii tantum.

§ 2. Cancellarius et notarii debent esse integrae famae et omni suspicione maiores; in causis quibus fama sacerdotis in discrimen vocari possit, notarius debet esse sacerdos.

Can. 484 – Officium notariorum est:

1° conscribere acta et instrumenta circa decreta, dispositiones, obligationes vel alia quae eorum operam requirunt;

2° in scriptis fideliter redigere quae geruntur, eaque cum significatione loci, diei, mensis et anni subsignare;

3° acta vel instrumenta legitime petenti ex regesto, servatis servandis, exhibere et eorum exempla cum autographo conformia declarare.

Can. 485 – Cancellarius aliique notarii libere ab officio removeri possunt ab Episcopo dioecesano, non autem ab Administratore dioecesano, nisi de consensu collegii consultorum.

Can. 486 – § 1. Documenta omnia, quae dioecesim vel paroecias respiciunt, maxima cura custodiri debent.

§ 2. In unaquaque curia erigatur, in loco tuto, archivum seu tabularium dioecesanum, in quo instrumenta et scripturae quae ad negotia dioecesana tum spiritualia tum temporalia spectant, certo ordine disposita et diligenter clausa custodiantur.

§ 3. Documentorum, quae in archivo continentur, conficiatur inventarium seu catalogus, cum brevi singularum scripturarum synopsi.

Can. 487 – § 1. Archivum clausum sit oportet eiusque clavem habeant solum Episcopus et cancellarius; nemini licet illud ingredi nisi de Episcopi aut Moderatoris curiae simul et cancellarii licentia.

§ 2. Ius est iis quorum interest, documentorum, quae natura sua sunt publica quaeque ad statum suae personae pertinent, documentum authenticum scriptum vel photostaticum per se vel per procuratorem recipere.

the acts of the curia are gathered, arranged and safeguarded in the archive of the curia.

§2. If it seems necessary the chancellor can be given an assistant, whose title is vice-chancellor.

§3. The chancellor and vice-chancellor are automatically notaries and secretaries of the curia.

Can. 483 — §1. Besides the chancellor other notaries can be appointed, whose writing or signature establishes the authenticity of any acts what-soever, of judicial acts only or of the acts of a certain case or transaction only.

§2. The chancellor and the notaries must be of good character and above reproach; a priest must be the notary in cases in which the reputation of a priest can be called into question.

Can. 484 — The duties of notaries are:

1° to write the acts and instruments relating to decrees, dispositions, obligations and other tasks required of them;

2° to record faithfully in writing what has taken place and sign the record with a notation of the place, day, month and year;

3° with due consideration of all requirements, to furnish acts or instruments to one legitimately requesting them from the files and to declare copies of them to be in conformity with the original.

Can. 485 — Chancellors and notaries can be freely removed from office by the diocesan bishop, but not by the diocesan administrator except with the consent of the college of consultors.

Can. 486 — §1. All diocesan and parochial documents must be protected with the greatest care.

§2. In every curia, there is to be established in a safe place a diocesan archive or store-room in which the instruments and writings which refer to both the spiritual and temporal affairs of the diocese, properly arranged and diligently secured, are to be safeguarded.

§3. There is to be an inventory or catalog of the documents contained in the archive, with a brief synopsis of the contents of each one.

Can. 487 — §1. It is necessary that the archive be locked and that only the bishop and the chancellor have a key to it; no one may licitly enter it without the permission either of the bishop or of both the moderator of the curia and the chancellor.

§2. It is a right of interested parties to obtain personally or through their proxy an authentic written copy or a photocopy of documents which are public by their nature and which pertain to the status of such persons.

Can. 488 – Ex archivo non licet efferre documenta, nisi ad breve tempus tantum atque de Episcopi aut insimul Moderatoris curiae et cancellarii consensu.

Can. 489 – § 1. Sit in curia dioecesana archivum quoque secretum, aut saltem in communi archivo armarium seu scrinium, omnino clausum et obseratum, quod de loco amoveri nequeat, in quo scilicet documenta secreto servanda cautissime custodiantur.

§ 2. Singulis annis destruantur documenta causarum criminalium in materia morum, quarum rei vita cesserunt aut quae a decennio sententia condemnatoria absolutae sunt, retento facti brevi summario cum textu sententiae definitivae.

Can. 490 – § 1. Archivi secreti clavem habeat tantummodo Episcopus.

§ 2. Sede vacante, archivum vel armarium secretum ne aperiatur, nisi in casu verae necessitatis, ab ipso Administratore dioecesano.

§ 3. Ex archivo vel armario secreto documenta ne efferantur.

Can. 491 – § 1. Curet Episcopus dioecesanus ut acta et documenta archivorum quoque ecclesiarum cathedralium, collegiatarum, paroecialium, aliarumque in suo territorio exstantium diligenter serventur, atque inventaria seu catalogi conficiantur duobus exemplaribus, quorum alterum in proprio archivo, alterum in archivo dioecesano serventur.

§ 2. Curet etiam Episcopus dioecesanus ut in dioecesi habeatur archivum historicum atque documenta valorem historicum habentia in eodem diligenter custodiantur et systematice ordinentur.

§ 3. Acta et documenta de quibus in §§ 1 et 2, ut inspiciantur aut efferantur, serventur normae ab Episcopo dioecesano statutae.

Art. 3

DE CONSILIO A REBUS OECONOMICIS ET DE OECONOMO

Can. 492 – § 1. In singulis dioecesibus constituatur consilium a rebus oeconomicis, cui praesidet ipse Episcopus dioecesanus eiusve delegatus, et quod constat tribus saltem christifidelibus, in re oeconomica necnon in iure civili vere peritis et integritate praestantibus, ab Episcopo nominatis.

§ 2. Membra consilii a rebus oeconomicis ad quinquennium nominentur, sed expleto hoc tempore ad alia quinquennia assumi possunt.

§ 3. A consilio a rebus oeconomicis excluduntur personae quae cum Episcopo usque ad quartum gradum consanguinitatis vel affinitatis coniunctae sunt.

Can. 488 — It is not permitted to remove documents from the archives, except for a brief time only and with the consent either of the bishop or of both the moderator of the curia and the chancellor.

Can. 489 — §1. There is also to be a secret archive in the diocesan curia or at least a safe or file in the ordinary archive, completely closed and locked which cannot be removed from the place, and in which documents to be kept secret are to be protected most securely.

§2. Every year documents of criminal cases are to be destroyed in matters of morals in which the criminal has died or in which ten years have passed since the condemnatory sentence; but a brief summary of the case with the text of the definitive sentence is to be retained.

Can. 490 — §1. Only the bishop may have the key to the secret archive.

§2. When the see is vacant the secret archive or safe is not to be opened, except in a case of true necessity by the diocesan administrator himself.

§3. Documents are not to be removed from the secret archive or safe.

Can. 491 — §1. The diocesan bishop is to see to it that the acts and documents of the archives of cathedral, collegiate, parochial and other churches in his territory also are diligently preserved; also, inventories or catalogs are to be made in duplicate, one of which is to be kept in the church's own archive and the other in the diocesan archive.

§2. The diocesan bishop is also to see to it that there is an historical archive in the diocese in which documents having an historical value are diligently preserved and systematically arranged.

§3. In order to inspect or remove the acts and documents spoken of in §§1 and 2 above, the norms established by the diocesan bishop are to be observed.

Art. 3

THE FINANCE COUNCIL AND THE FINANCE OFFICER

Can. 492 — §1. In each diocese a finance council is to be established by the bishop, over which he himself or his delegate presides, and which is to be composed of at least three members of the Christian faithful truly skilled in financial affairs as well as in civil law, of outstanding integrity and appointed by the bishop.

§2. Members of the finance council are to be named for a five year term; but having completed this term they may be named to other five year terms.

§3. Those persons are excluded from the finance council who are related to the bishop up to the fourth degree of consanguinity or affinity.

Can. 493 – Praeter munera ipsi commissa in Libro V *De bonis Ecclesiae temporalibus,* consilii a rebus oeconomicis est quotannis, iuxta Episcopi dioecesani indicationes, rationem apparare quaestuum et erogationum quae pro universo dioecesis regimine anno venturo praevidentur, necnon, anno exeunte, rationem accepti et expensi probare.

Can. 494 – § 1. In singulis dioecesibus ab Episcopo, auditis collegio consultorum atque consilio a rebus oeconomicis, nominetur oeconomus, qui sit in re oeconomica vere peritus et probitate prorsus praestans.

§ 2. Oeconomus nominetur ad quinquennium, sed expleto hoc tempore ad alia quinquennia nominari potest; durante munere, ne amoveatur nisi ob gravem causam ab Episcopo aestimandam, auditis collegio consultorum atque consilio a rebus oeconomicis.

§ 3. Oeconomi est, secundum rationem a consilio a rebus oeconomicis definitam, bona dioecesis sub auctoritate Episcopi administrare atque ex quaestu dioecesis constituto expensas facere, quas Episcopus aliive ab ipso deputati legitime ordinaverint.

§ 4. Anno vertente, oeconomus consilio a rebus oeconomicis rationem accepti et expensi reddere debet.

Caput III
DE CONSILIO PRESBYTERALI
ET DE COLLEGIO CONSULTORUM

Can. 495 – § 1. In unaquaque dioecesi constituatur consilium presbyterale, coetus scilicet sacerdotum, qui tamquam senatus sit Episcopi, presbyterium repraesentans, cuius est Episcopum in regimine dioecesis ad normam iuris adiuvare, ut bonum pastorale portionis populi Dei ipsi commissae quam maxime provehatur.

§ 2. In vicariatibus et praefecturis apostolicis Vicarius vel Praefectus constituant consilium ex tribus saltem presbyteris missionariis, quorum sententiam, etiam per epistolam, audiant in gravioribus negotiis.

Can. 496 – Consilium presbyterale habeat propria statuta ab Episcopo dioecesano approbata, attentis normis ab Episcoporum conferentia prolatis.

Can. 497 – Ad designationem quod attinet sodalium consilii presbyteralis :

1° dimidia circiter pars libere eligatur a sacerdotibus ipsis, ad

Can. 493 — In addition to the duties committed to it in Book V: *The Temporal Goods of the Church*, the finance council is to prepare each year according to the directions of the diocesan bishop a budget of the income and expenditures foreseen for the governance of the entire diocese in the coming year; moreover at the close of the year it is to examine a report of receipts and expenditures.

Can. 494 — §1. In each diocese, after listening to the college of consultors and also the finance council, the bishop is to name a finance officer who is to be truly skilled in financial affairs and absolutely distinguished for honesty.

§2. The finance officer is to be appointed for a five year term but, having completed this term, may be reappointed for other five year terms; during the term of office the finance officer may not be removed except for a grave cause, to be assessed by the bishop after listening to the college of consultors and the finance council.

§3. It is the role of the finance officer to administer the goods of the diocese under the authority of the bishop in accordance with the budget determined by the finance council; from the income of the diocese the finance officer is to meet the expenditures which the bishop or others deputized by him have legitimately authorized.

§4. At the end of the year the finance officer must give to the finance council a report of receipts and expenditures.

CHAPTER III

THE PRESBYTERAL COUNCIL AND THE COLLEGE OF CONSULTORS

Can. 495 — §1. A presbyteral council is to be established in each diocese, that is, a body of priests who are to be like a senate of the bishop, representing the presbyterate; this council is to aid the bishop in the governance of the diocese according to the norm of law, in order that the pastoral welfare of the portion of the people of God entrusted to him may be promoted as effectively as possible.

§2. In apostolic vicariates and prefectures the vicar or the prefect is to establish a council of at least three missionary presbyters whose opinion is to be heard in more serious matters, even by letter.

Can. 496 — The presbyteral council is to have its own statutes approved by the diocesan bishop, in light of the norms issued by the conference of bishops.

Can. 497 — With regard to the designation of the members of the presbyteral council:

1° about half the members are to be freely elected by the priests them-

normam canonum qui sequuntur, necnon statutorum;

2° aliqui sacerdotes, ad normam statutorum, esse debent membra nata, qui scilicet ratione officii ipsis demandati ad consilium pertineant;

3° Episcopo dioecesano integrum est aliquos libere nominare.

Can. 498 – § 1. Ius electionis tum activum tum passivum ad consilium presbyterale constituendum habent:

1° omnes sacerdotes saeculares in dioecesi incardinati;

2° sacerdotes saeculares in dioecesi non incardinati, necnon sacerdotes sodales alicuius instituti religiosi aut societatis vitae apostolicae, qui in dioecesi commorantes, in eiusdem bonum aliquod officium exercent.

§ 2. Quatenus statuta id provideant, idem ius electionis conferri potest aliis sacerdotibus, qui domicilium aut quasi-domicilium in dioecesi habent.

Can. 499 – Modus eligendi membra consilii presbyteralis statutis determinandus est, ita quidem ut, quatenus id fieri possit, sacerdotes presbyterii repraesententur, ratione habita maxime diversorum ministeriorum variarumque dioecesis regionum.

Can. 500 – § 1. Episcopi dioecesani est consilium presbyterale convocare, eidem praesidere atque quaestiones in eodem tractandas determinare aut a membris propositas recipere.

§ 2. Consilium presbyterale gaudet voto tantum consultivo; Episcopus dioecesanus illud audiat in negotiis maioris momenti, eius autem consensu eget solummodo in casibus iure expresse definitis.

§ 3. Consilium presbyterale numquam agere valet sine Episcopo dioecesano, ad quem solum etiam cura spectat ea divulgandi quae ad normam § 2 statuta sunt.

Can. 501 – § 1. Membra consilii presbyteralis designentur ad tempus, in statutis determinatum, ita tamen ut integrum consilium vel aliqua eius pars intra quinquennium renovetur.

§ 2. Vacante sede, consilium presbyterale cessat eiusque munera implentur a collegio consultorum; intra annum a capta possessione Episcopus debet consilium presbyterale noviter constituere.

§ 3. Si consilium presbyterale munus sibi in bonum dioecesis commissum non adimpleat aut eodem graviter abutatur, Episcopus dioecesanus, facta consultatione cum Metropolita, aut si de ipsa sede metropolitana agatur cum Episcopo suffraganeo promotione antiquiore, illud dissolvere potest, sed intra annum debet noviter constituere.

Can. 502 – § 1. Inter membra consilii presbyteralis ab Episcopo

selves according to the norm of the following canons as well as the council's statutes;

2° some priests, according to the council's statutes, ought to be ex-officio members, that is, members of the council in virtue of their office;

3° the diocesan bishop is free to name some others.

Can. 498 — §1. The following have the right to both active and passive vote in constituting the presbyteral council:

1° all secular priests incardinated in the diocese;

2° secular priests not incardinated in the diocese, and priests who are members of an institute of consecrated life or a society of apostolic life, who live in the diocese and exercise some office for the good of the diocese.

§2. To the extent the statutes provide for it, the same right of election can be extended to other priests who have a domicile or quasi-domicile in the diocese.

Can. 499 — The manner of electing members of the presbyteral council is to be determined in the statutes in such a way that, insofar as it is possible, the priests of the presbyterate are represented, taking into account especially the diversity of ministries and various regions of the diocese.

Can. 500 — §1. It pertains to the diocesan bishop to convoke the presbyteral council, to preside over it, and to determine the questions to be treated by it or to receive proposals from its members.

§2. The presbyteral council enjoys only a consultative vote; the bishop is to listen to it in matters of greater moment, but he needs its consent only in cases expressly defined by law.

§3. The presbyteral council is never able to act without the diocesan bishop who alone can divulge what was determined in keeping with §2.

Can. 501 — §1. Members of the presbyteral council are to be designated for a term determined in the statutes in such a way that the full council or some part of it is renewed within a five year period.

§2. When the see is vacant the presbyteral council ceases and its functions are fulfilled by the college of consultors; within a year of taking possession of the diocese the bishop must establish the presbyteral council anew.

§3. If the presbyteral council is no longer fulfilling the function committed to it for the good of the diocese or is gravely abusing it, the diocesan bishop can dissolve it after consulting with the metropolitan or, if it is a question of the metropolitan see itself, with the suffragan senior by promotion, but the bishop must establish it anew within a year.

Can. 502 — §1. Some priests are to be freely selected by the diocesan

dioecesano libere nominantur aliqui sacerdotes, numero non minore quam sex nec maiore quam duodecim, qui collegium consultorum ad quinquennium constituant, cui competunt munera iure determinata; expleto tamen quinquennio munera sua propria exercere pergit usque-dum novum collegium constituatur.

§ 2. Collegio consultorum praeest Episcopus dioecesanus; sede autem impedita aut vacante, is qui ad interim Episcopi locum tenet aut, si constitutus nondum fuerit, sacerdos ordinatione antiquior in collegio consultorum.

§ 3. Episcoporum conferentia statuere potest ut munera collegii consultorum capitulo cathedrali committantur.

§ 4. In vicariatu et praefectura apostolica munera collegii consultorum competunt consilio missionis, de quo in can. 495, § 2, nisi aliud iure statuatur.

Caput IV

DE CANONICORUM CAPITULIS

Can. 503 – Capitulum canonicorum, sive cathedrale sive collegiale, est sacerdotum collegium, cuius est functiones liturgicas sollemniores in ecclesia cathedrali aut collegiali persolvere; capituli cathedralis praeterea est munera adimplere, quae iure aut ab Episcopo dioecesano ei committuntur.

Can. 504 – Capituli cathedralis erectio, innovatio aut suppressio Sedi Apostolicae reservantur.

Can. 505 – Unumquodque capitulum, sive cathedrale sive collegiale, sua habeat statuta, per legitimum actum capitularem condita atque ab Episcopo dioecesano probata; quae statuta ne immutentur neve abro-gentur, nisi approbante eodem Episcopo dioecesano.

Can. 506 – § 1. Statuta capituli, salvis semper fundationis legibus, ipsam capituli constitutionem et numerum canonicorum determinent; definiant quaenam a capitulo et a singulis canonicis ad cultum divi-num necnon ad ministerium persolvendum sint peragenda; decernant conventus in quibus capituli negotia agantur atque, salvis quidem iuris universalis praescriptis, condiciones statuant ad validitatem liceita-temque negotiorum requisitas.

§ 2. In statutis etiam definiantur emolumenta, tum stabilia tum occa-sione perfuncti muneris solvenda necnon, attentis normis a Sancta Sede latis, quaenam sint canonicorum insignia.

Can. 507 – § 1. Inter canonicos habeatur qui capitulo praesit, atque

bishop from among the members of the presbyteral council to constitute a college of consultors; their number is to be not less than six nor more than twelve; the college is established for a five year term, and is responsible for the functions determined in the law; when the five year term is over, the college continues to exercise its proper functions until a new college is established.

§2. The diocesan bishop presides over the college of consultors; if the see is impeded or vacant, the one who takes the place of the bishop in the interim presides, or, if such a person has not yet been established, the priest who is oldest in ordination in the college of consultors.

§3. The conference of bishops can determine that the functions of the college of consultors be committed to the cathedral chapter.

§4. In apostolic vicariates and prefectures the functions of the college of consultors belong to the mission council mentioned in can. 495, §2, unless the law determines otherwise.

Chapter IV

CHAPTERS OF CANONS

Can. 503 — The chapter of canons, whether cathedral or collegial, is a college of priests whose responsibility it is to perform the more solemn liturgical functions in the cathedral or collegial church; moreover, the cathedral chapter is to fulfill the duties which have been committed to it by the law itself or by the diocesan bishop.

Can. 504 — The erection, change or suppression of a cathedral chapter is reserved to the Apostolic See.

Can. 505 — Each and every chapter, whether cathedral or collegial, is to have its own statutes, drawn up by a legitimate capitular act and approved by the diocesan bishop; these statutes are not to be changed or abrogated without the approval of the same diocesan bishop.

Can. 506 — §1. With due regard always for the laws of its foundation, the statutes of the chapter are to determine the constitution of the chapter and the number of canons, define which things must be done by the chapter and which by the individual canons in the performance of divine worship and the ministry, schedule the meetings in which the business of the chapter is taken care of, and, with due regard for the prescriptions of universal law, determine the conditions required for valid and legitimate transactions.

§2. The statutes are also to define, having observed the norms laid down by the Holy See, the proper insignia of the canons and their financial compensation, whether stable or to be given on the occasion of the performance of duty.

Can. 507 — §1. One of the canons is to preside over the chapter, and

alia etiam constituantur officia ad normam statutorum, ratione quoque habita usus in regione vigentis.

§ 2. Clericis ad capitulum non pertinentibus, committi possunt alia officia, quibus ipsi, ad normam statutorum, canonicis auxilium praebent.

Can. 508 – § 1. Paenitentiarius canonicus tum ecclesiae cathedralis tum ecclesiae collegialis vi officii habet facultatem ordinariam, quam tamen aliis delegare non potest, absolvendi in foro sacramentali a censuris latae sententiae non declaratis, Apostolicae Sedi non reservatis, in dioecesi extraneos quoque, dioecesanos autem etiam extra territorium dioecesis.

§ 2. Ubi deficit capitulum, Episcopus dioecesanus sacerdotem constituat ad idem munus implendum.

Can. 509 – § 1. Episcopi dioecesani, audito capitulo, non autem Administratoris dioecesani, est omnes et singulos conferre canonicatus, tum in ecclesia cathedrali tum in ecclesia collegiali, revocato quolibet contrario privilegio; eiusdem Episcopi est confirmare electum ab ipso capitulo, qui eidem praesit.

§ 2. Canonicatus Episcopus dioecesanus conferat tantum sacerdotibus doctrina vitaeque integritate praestantibus, qui laudabiliter ministerium exercuerunt.

Can. 510 – § 1. Capitulo canonicorum ne amplius uniantur paroeciae; quae unitae alicui capitulo exstent, ab Episcopo dioecesano a capitulo separentur.

§ 2. In ecclesia, quae simul sit paroecialis et capitularis, designetur parochus, sive inter capitulares delectus, sive non; qui parochus omnibus obstringitur officiis atque gaudet iuribus et facultatibus quae ad normam iuris propria sunt parochi.

§ 3. Episcopi dioecesani est certas statuere normas, quibus officia pastoralia parochi atque munera capitulo propria debite componantur, cavendo ne parochus capitularibus nec capitulum paroecialibus functionibus impedimento sit; conflictus, si quidam habeantur, dirimat Episcopus dioecesanus, qui imprimis curet ut fidelium necessitatibus pastoralibus apte prospiciatur.

§ 4. Quae ecclesiae, paroeciali simul et capitulari, conferantur eleemosynae, praesumuntur datae paroeciae, nisi aliud constet.

other offices are also to be established according to the norm of the statutes, taking cognizance as well of the usages prevailing in the region.

§2. Other offices which may aid the canons can be entrusted to clerics who do not belong to the chapter, according to the norms of the statutes.

Can. 508 — §1. The canon penitentiary, both of a cathedral church and of a collegial church, in virtue of his office has the ordinary faculty, which nevertheless he cannot delegate to another, of absolving in the sacramental forum from undeclared *latae sententiae* censures not reserved to the Apostolic See, even outsiders within the diocese and members of the diocese outside it.

§2. Where there is no chapter the diocesan bishop is to appoint a diocesan priest to fulfill this same function.

Can. 509 — §1. It is for the diocesan bishop, having listened to the chapter, but not for the diocesan administrator, to confer each and every individual canonry whether in the cathedral church or in the collegial church, every contrary privilege being revoked; it is for the same bishop to confirm the election by the chapter of the one who shall preside over it.

§2. The diocesan bishop is to confer the canonry only upon priests outstanding in doctrine and integrity of life who have exercised the ministry in a praiseworthy manner.

Can. 510 — §1. Parishes are no longer to be joined to a chapter of canons; those which are united to some chapter are to be separated from the chapter by the diocesan bishop.

§2. In a church which is at the same time parochial and capitular, a pastor is to be designated, whether chosen from among the members of the chapter or not; this pastor is bound by all the duties and enjoys all the rights and faculties which are proper to a pastor according to the norm of law.

§3. It is for the diocesan bishop to establish definite norms by which the pastoral duties of the pastor and the responsibilities proper to the chapter are to be fittingly integrated; these norms are to preclude the pastor's impeding capitular functions or the chapter's impeding parochial functions; the diocesan bishop is to resolve conflicts, should any arise; his first concern will be seeing to it that the pastoral necessities of the faithful are fittingly provided for.

§4. Any alms which are given to a church which is at the same time parochial and capitular are presumed to be given to the parish unless otherwise evident.

Caput V

DE CONSILIO PASTORALI

Can. 511 – In singulis dioecesibus, quatenus pastoralia adiuncta id suadeant, constituatur consilium pastorale, cuius est sub auctoritate Episcopi ea quae opera pastoralia in dioecesi spectant investigare, perpendere atque de eis conclusiones practicas proponere.

Can. 512 – § 1. Consilium pastorale constat christifidelibus qui in plena communione sint cum Ecclesia catholica, tum clericis, tum membris institutorum vitae consecratae, tum praesertim laicis, quique designantur modo ab Episcopo dioecesano determinato.

§ 2. Christifideles, qui deputantur ad consilium pastorale, ita seligantur ut per eos universa populi Dei portio, quae dioecesim constituat, revera configuretur, ratione habita diversarum dioecesis regionum, condicionum socialium et professionum, necnon partis quam sive singuli sive cum aliis coniuncti in apostolatu habent.

§ 3. Ad consilium pastorale ne deputentur nisi christifideles certa fide, bonis moribus et prudentia praestantes.

Can. 513 – § 1. Consilium pastorale constituitur ad tempus, iuxta praescripta statutorum, quae ab Episcopo dantur.

§ 2. Sede vacante, consilium pastorale cessat.

Can. 514 – § 1. Consilium pastorale, quod voto gaudet tantum consultivo, iuxta necessitates apostolatus convocare eique praeesse ad solum Episcopum dioecesanum pertinet; ad quem etiam unice spectat, quae in consilio pertractata sunt publici iuris facere.

§ 2. Saltem semel in anno convocetur.

Caput VI

DE PAROECIIS,
DE PAROCHIS ET DE VICARIIS PAROECIALIBUS

Can. 515 – § 1. Paroecia est certa communitas christifidelium in Ecclesia particulari stabiliter constituta, cuius cura pastoralis, sub auctoritate Episcopi dioecesani, committitur parocho, qua proprio eiusdem pastori.

§ 2. Paroecias erigere, supprimere aut eas innovare unius est Episcopi dioecesani, qui paroecias ne erigat aut supprimat, neve eas notabiliter innovet, nisi audito consilio presbyterali.

§ 3. Paroecia legitime erecta personalitate iuridica ipso iure gaudet.

CHAPTER V

THE PASTORAL COUNCIL

Can. 511 — In each diocese, to the extent that pastoral circumstances recommend it, a pastoral council is to be established whose responsibility it is to investigate under the authority of the bishop all those things which pertain to pastoral works, to ponder them and to propose practical conclusions about them.

Can. 512 — §1. The pastoral council consists of Christian faithful who are in full communion with the Catholic Church, clerics, members of institutes of consecrated life and especially lay persons, who are designated in a manner determined by the diocesan bishop.

§2. The Christian faithful who are appointed to the pastoral council are to be so selected that the entire portion of the people of God which constitutes the diocese is truly reflected, with due regard for the diverse regions, social conditions and professions of the diocese as well as the role which they have in the apostolate, either as individuals or in conjunction with others.

§3. No one except Christians of proven faith, good morals and outstanding prudence are to be appointed to the pastoral council.

Can. 513 — §1. The pastoral council is to be established for a period of time according to the prescriptions of the statutes which are issued by the bishop.

§2. When the see is vacant the pastoral council ceases to exist.

Can. 514 — §1. It pertains exclusively to the diocesan bishop to convoke the pastoral council according to the necessities of the apostolate and to preside over it; the pastoral council enjoys only a consultative vote; it is for the bishop alone to make public what has been done in the council.

§2. The pastoral council is to be convoked at least once a year.

CHAPTER VI

PARISHES, PASTORS AND PAROCHIAL VICARS

Can. 515 — §1. A parish is a definite community of the Christian faithful established on a stable basis within a particular church; the pastoral care of the parish is entrusted to a pastor as its own shepherd under the authority of the diocesan bishop.

§2. The diocesan bishop alone is competent to erect, suppress or alter parishes; he is not to erect, suppress or notably alter them without hearing the presbyteral council.

§3. A legitimately erected parish has juridic personality by the law itself.

Can. 516 – § 1. Nisi aliud iure caveatur, paroeciae aequiparatur quasi-paroecia, quae est certa in Ecclesia particulari communitas christifidelium, sacerdoti uti pastori proprio commissa, ob peculiaria adiuncta in paroeciam nondum erecta.

§ 2. Ubi quaedam communitates in paroeciam vel quasi-paróeciam erigi non possint, Episcopus dioecesanus alio modo earundem pastorali curae prospiciat.

Can. 517 – § 1. Ubi adiuncta id requirant, paroeciae aut diversarum simul paroeciarum cura pastoralis committi potest pluribus in solidum sacerdotibus, ea tamen lege, ut eorundem unus curae pastoralis exercendae sit moderator, qui nempe actionem coniunctam dirigat atque de eadem coram Episcopo respondeat.

§ 2. Si ob sacerdotum penuriam Episcopus dioecesanus aestimaverit participationem in exercitio curae pastoralis paroeciae concredendam esse diacono aliive personae sacerdotali charactere non insignitae aut personarum communitati, sacerdotem constituat aliquem qui, potestatibus et facultatibus parochi instructus, curam pastoralem moderetur.

Can. 518 – Paroecia regula generali sit territorialis, quae scilicet omnes complectatur christifideles certi territorii; ubi vero id expediat, constituantur paroeciae personales, ratione ritus, linguae, nationis christifidelium alicuius territorii atque alia etiam ratione determinatae.

Can. 519 – Parochus est pastor proprius paroeciae sibi commissae, cura pastorali communitatis sibi concreditae fungens sub auctoritate Episcopi dioecesani, cuius in partem ministerii Christi vocatus est, ut pro eadem communitate munera exsequatur docendi, sanctificandi et regendi, cooperantibus etiam aliis presbyteris vel diaconis atque operam conferentibus christifidelibus laicis, ad normam iuris.

Can. 520 – § 1. Persona iuridica ne sit parochus; Episcopus autem dioecesanus, non vero Administrator dioecesanus, de consensu competentis Superioris, potest paroeciam committere instituto religioso clericali vel societati clericali vitae apostolicae, eam erigendo etiam in ecclesia instituti aut societatis, hac tamen lege ut unus presbyter sit paroeciae parochus, aut, si cura pastoralis pluribus in solidum committatur, moderator, de quo in can. 517, § 1.

§ 2. Paroeciae commissio, de qua in § 1, fieri potest sive in perpetuum sive ad certum praefinitum tempus; in utroque casu fiat mediante conventione scripta inter Episcopum dioecesanum et competentem Superiorem instituti vel societatis inita, qua inter alia expresse et accurate definiantur, quae ad opus explendum, ad personas eidem

Can. 516 — §1. Unless the law provides otherwise, a quasi-parish is equivalent to a parish; a quasi-parish is a definite community of the Christian faithful within a particular church which has been entrusted to a priest as its proper pastor but due to particular circumstances has not yet been erected as a parish.

§2. When certain communities cannot be erected as a parish or quasi-parish, the diocesan bishop is to provide for their pastoral care in another manner.

Can. 517 — §1. When circumstances require it, the pastoral care of a parish or of several parishes together can be entrusted to a team of several priests *in solidum* with the requirement, however, that one of them should be the moderator in exercising pastoral care, that is, he should direct their combined activity and answer for it to the bishop.

§2. If the diocesan bishop should decide that due to a dearth of priests a participation in the exercise of the pastoral care of a parish is to be entrusted to a deacon or to some other person who is not a priest or to a community of persons, he is to appoint some priest endowed with the powers and faculties of a pastor to supervise the pastoral care.

Can. 518 — As a general rule a parish is to be territorial, that is it embraces all the Christian faithful within a certain territory; whenever it is judged useful, however, personal parishes are to be established based upon rite, language, the nationality of the Christian faithful within some territory or even upon some other determining factor.

Can. 519 — The pastor is the proper shepherd of the parish entrusted to him, exercising pastoral care in the community entrusted to him under the authority of the diocesan bishop in whose ministry of Christ he has been called to share; in accord with the norm of law he carries out for his community the duties of teaching, sanctifying and governing, with the cooperation of other presbyters or deacons and the assistance of lay members of the Christian faithful.

Can. 520 — §1. A juridic person is not to be a pastor; however, the diocesan bishop, but not the diocesan administrator, with the consent of the competent superior, can entrust a parish to a clerical religious institute or to a clerical society of apostolic life, even erecting the parish in a church of the institute or society, with the requirement, however, that one presbyter should be the pastor of the parish or one presbyter should act as the moderator mentioned in can. 517, §1, if its pastoral care is entrusted to a team.

§2. The assignment of the parish mentioned in §1 can be permanent or for a definite predetermined period of time; in either case the assignment should be made by means of a written agreement between the diocesan bishop and the competent superior of the institute or society; among other matters this agreement is expressly and carefully to determine the work to be done, the

addicendas et ad res oeconomicas spectent.

Can. 521 – § 1. Ut quis valide in parochum assumatur, oportet sit in sacro presbyteratus ordine constitutus.

§ 2. Sit praeterea sana doctrina et morum probitate praestans, animarum zelo aliisque virtutibus praeditus, atque insuper qualitatibus gaudeat quae ad paroeciam, de qua agitur, curandam iure sive universali sive particulari requiruntur.

§ 3. Ad officium parochi alicui conferendum, oportet de eius idoneitate, modo ab Episcopo dioecesano determinato, etiam per examen, certo constet.

Can. 522 – Parochus stabilitate gaudeat oportet ideoque ad tempus indefinitum nominetur; ad certum tempus tantum ab Episcopo dioecesano nominari potest, si id ab Episcoporum conferentia, per decretum admissum fuerit.

Can. 523 – Firmo praescripto can. 682, parochi officii provisio Episcopo dioecesano competit et quidem libera collatione, nisi cuidam sit ius praesentationis aut electionis.

Can. 524 – Vacantem paroeciam Episcopus dioecesanus conferat illi quem, omnibus perpensis adiunctis, aestimet idoneum ad paroecialem curam in eadem implendam, omni personarum acceptione remota; ut iudicium de idoneitate ferat, audiat vicarium foraneum aptasque investigationes peragat, auditis, si casus ferat, certis presbyteris necnon christifidelibus laicis.

Can. 525 – Sede vacante aut impedita, ad Administratorem dioecesanum aliumve dioecesim ad interim regentem pertinet:

1° institutionem vel confirmationem concedere presbyteris, qui ad paroeciam legitime praesentati aut electi fuerint;

2° parochos nominare, si sedes ab anno vacaverit aut impedita sit.

Can. 526 – § 1. Parochus unius paroeciae tantum curam paroecialem habeat; ob penuriam tamen sacerdotum aut alia adiuncta, plurium vicinarum paroeciarum cura eidem parocho concredi potest.

§ 2. In eadem paroecia unus tantum habeatur parochus aut moderator ad normam can. 517, § 1, reprobata contraria consuetudine et revocato quolibet contrario privilegio.

Can. 527 – § 1. Qui ad curam pastoralem paroeciae gerendam promotus est, eandem obtinet et exercere tenetur a momento captae possessionis.

persons to be attached to the parish and the financial arrangements.

Can. 521 — §1. To assume the office of pastor validly one must be in the sacred order of the presbyterate.

§2. He should also be distinguished for his sound doctrine and integrity of morals and endowed with a zeal for souls and other virtues; he should also possess those qualities which are required by universal and particular law to care for the parish in question.

§3. For the office of pastor to be conferred on someone, it is necessary that his suitability be clearly evident by means of some method determined by the diocesan bishop, even by means of an examination.

Can. 522 — The pastor ought to possess stability in office and therefore he is to be named for an indefinite period of time; the diocesan bishop can name him for a certain period of time only if a decree of the conference of bishops has permitted this.

Can. 523 — With due regard for the prescription of can. 682, the diocesan bishop is the person competent to provide for the office of pastor by means of free conferral unless someone possesses the right of presentation or of election.

Can. 524 — After he has weighed all the circumstances, the diocesan bishop is to confer a vacant parish on the person whom he judges suited to fulfill its parochial care without any partiality; in order to make a judgment concerning a person's suitability he is to listen to the vicar forane, conduct appropriate investigations and, if it is warranted, listen to certain presbyters and lay members of the Christian faithful.

Can. 525 — When a see is vacant or impeded the diocesan administrator or another person who is ruling the diocese in the meantime is competent:

1° to install or confirm presbyters who have been legitimately presented or elected for a parish;

2° to appoint pastors if the see has been vacant or impeded for a year.

Can. 526 — §1. A pastor is to have the parochial care of only one parish; however the care of several neighboring parishes can be entrusted to the same pastor due to a dearth of priests or in other circumstances.

§2. In the same parish there is to be only one pastor or one moderator in accord with can. 517, §1; any custom contrary to this is reprobated and any privilege contrary to this is revoked.

Can. 527 — §1. The person who has been promoted to carry out the pastoral care of a parish acquires that care and is bound to exercise it from the moment he takes possession of the parish.

§ 2. Parochum in possessionem mittit loci Ordinarius aut sacerdos ab eodem delegatus, servato modo lege particulari aut legitima consuetudine recepto; iusta tamen de causa potest idem Ordinarius ab eo modo dispensare; quo in casu dispensatio paroeciae communicata locum tenet captae possessionis.

§ 3. Loci Ordinarius praefiniat tempus intra quod paroeciae possessio capi debeat; quo inutiliter praeterlapso, nisi iustum obstiterit impedimentum, paroeciam vacare declarare potest.

Can. 528 – § 1. Parochus obligatione tenetur providendi ut Dei verbum integre in paroecia degentibus annuntietur; quare curet ut christifideles laici in fidei veritatibus edoceantur, praesertim homilia diebus dominicis et festis de praecepto habenda necnon catechetica institutione tradenda, atque foveat opera quibus spiritus evangelicus, etiam ad iustitiam socialem quod attinet, promoveatur; peculiarem curam habeat de puerorum iuvenumque educatione catholica; omni ope satagat, associata etiam sibi christifidelium opera, ut nuntius evangelicus ad eos quoque perveniat, qui a religione colenda recesserint aut veram fidem non profiteantur.

§ 2. Consulat parochus ut sanctissima Eucharistia centrum sit congregationis fidelium paroecialis; allaboret ut christifideles, per devotam sacramentorum celebrationem, pascantur, peculiarique modo ut frequenter ad sanctissimae Eucharistiae et paenitentiae sacramenta accedant; annitatur item ut iidem ad orationem etiam in familiis peragendam ducantur atque conscie et actuose partem habeant in sacra liturgia, quam quidem, sub auctoritate Episcopi dioecesani, parochus in sua paroecia moderari debet et, ne abusus irrepant, invigilare tenetur.

Can. 529 – § 1. Officium pastoris sedulo ut adimpleat, parochus fideles suae curae commissos cognoscere satagat; ideo familias visitet, fidelium sollicitudines, angores et luctus praesertim, participans eosque in Domino confortans necnon, si in quibusdam defecerint, prudenter corrigens; aegrotos, praesertim morti proximos, effusa caritate adiuvet, eos sollicite sacramentis reficiendo eorumque animas Deo commendando; peculiari diligentia prosequatur pauperes, afflictos, solitarios, e patria exsules itemque peculiaribus difficultatibus gravatos; allaboret etiam ut coniuges et parentes ad officia propria implenda sustineantur et in familia vitae christianae incrementum foveat.

§ 2. Partem quam christifideles laici in missione Ecclesiae propriam habent, parochus agnoscat et promoveat, consociationes eorundem ad fines religionis fovendo. Cum proprio Episcopo et cum dioecesis

§2. While observing the method accepted by particular law or legitimate custom, the local ordinary or a priest delegated by him places the pastor in possession of the parish; for a just cause, however, the same ordinary can dispense from such a method of installation; in such a situation the dispensation communicated to the parish replaces the formal taking of possession.

§3. The local ordinary is to define a period of time within which the parish is to be taken possession of; if the time lapses needlessly and there be no legitimate impediment, he can declare the parish vacant.

Can. 528 — §1. The pastor is obliged to see to it that the word of God in its entirety is announced to those living in the parish; for this reason he is to see to it that the lay Christian faithful are instructed in the truths of the faith, especially through the homily which is to be given on Sundays and holy days of obligation and through the catechetical formation which he is to give; he is to foster works by which the spirit of the gospel, including issues involving social justice, is promoted; he is to take special care for the Catholic education of children and of young adults; he is to make every effort with the aid of the Christian faithful, to bring the gospel message also to those who have ceased practicing their religion or who do not profess the true faith.

§2. The pastor is to see to it that the Most Holy Eucharist is the center of the parish assembly of the faithful; he is to work to see to it that the Christian faithful are nourished through a devout celebration of the sacraments and especially that they frequently approach the sacrament of the Most Holy Eucharist and the sacrament of penance; he is likewise to endeavor that they are brought to the practice of family prayer as well as to a knowing and active participation in the sacred liturgy, which the pastor must supervise in his parish under the authority of the diocesan bishop, being vigilant lest any abuses creep in.

Can. 529 — §1. In order to fulfill his office in earnest the pastor should strive to come to know the faithful who have been entrusted to his care; therefore he is to visit families, sharing the cares, worries, and especially the griefs of the faithful, strengthening them in the Lord, and correcting them prudently if they are wanting in certain areas; with a generous love he is to help the sick, particularly those close to death, refreshing them solicitously with the sacraments and commending their souls to God; he is to make a special effort to seek out the poor, the afflicted, the lonely, those exiled from their own land, and similarly those weighed down with special difficulties; he is also to labor diligently so that spouses and parents are supported in fulfilling their proper duties, and he is to foster growth in the Christian life within the family.

§2. The pastor is to acknowledge and promote the proper role which the lay members of the Christian faithful have in the Church's mission by fostering their associations for religious purposes; he is to cooperate with his own

presbyterio cooperetur, allaborans etiam ut fideles communionis paroecialis curam habeant, iidemque tum dioecesis tum Ecclesiae universae
membra se sentiant operaque ad eandem communionem promovendam
participent vel sustineant.

Can. 530 – Functiones specialiter parocho commissae sunt quae
sequuntur :

1° administratio baptismi ;

2° administratio sacramenti confirmationis iis qui in periculo
mortis versantur, ad normam can. 883, n. 3 ;

3° administratio Viatici necnon unctionis infirmorum, firmo praescripto can. 1003, §§ 2 et 3, atque apostolicae benedictionis impertitio ;

4° assistentia matrimoniis et benedictio nuptiarum ;

5° persolutio funerum ;

6° fontis baptismalis tempore paschali benedictio, ductus pro-
cessionum extra ecclesiam, necnon benedictiones extra ecclesiam sollemnes ;

7° celebratio eucharistica sollemnior diebus dominicis et festis de
praecepto.

Can. 531 – Licet paroeciale quoddam munus alius expleverit, oblationes quas hac occasione a christifidelibus recipit ad massam paroecialem deferat, nisi de contraria offerentis voluntate constet quoad
oblationes voluntarias ; Episcopo dioecesano, audito consilio presbyterali, competit statuere praescripta, quibus destinationi harum oblationum necnon remunerationi clericorum idem munus implentium provideatur.

Can. 532 – In omnibus negotiis iuridicis parochus personam gerit
paroeciae, ad normam iuris ; curet ut bona paroeciae administrentur
ad normam cann. 1281-1288.

Can. 533 – § 1. Parochus obligatione tenetur residendi in domo
paroeciali prope ecclesiam ; in casibus tamen particularibus, si iusta
adsit causa, loci Ordinarius permittere potest ut alibi commoretur,
praesertim in domo pluribus presbyteris communi, dummodo paroecialium perfunctioni munerum rite apteque sit provisum.

§ 2. Nisi gravis obstet ratio, parocho, feriarum gratia, licet quotannis a paroecia abesse ad summum per unum mensem continuum aut
intermissum ; quo in feriarum tempore dies non computantur, quibus
semel in anno parochus spirituali recessui vacat ; parochus autem, ut
ultra hebdomadam a paroecia absit, tenetur de hoc loci Ordinarium
monere.

§ 3. Episcopi dioecesani est normas statuere quibus prospiciatur
ut, parochi absentia durante, curae provideatur paroeciae per sacer-

bishop and with the presbyterate of the diocese in working hard so that the faithful be concerned for parochial communion and that they realize that they are members both of the diocese and of the universal Church and participate in and support efforts to promote such communion.

Can. 530 — The following functions are especially entrusted to the pastor:

1° the administration of baptism;

2° the administration of the sacrament of confirmation to those who are in danger of death, according to the norm of can. 883, 3°;

3° the administration of Viaticum and the anointing of the sick with due regard for the prescription of can. 1003, §§2 and 3, as well as the imparting of the apostolic blessing;

4° the assistance at marriages and the imparting of the nuptial blessing;

5° the performing of funerals;

6° the blessing of the baptismal font during the Easter season, the leading of processions outside the church and the imparting of solemn blessings outside the church;

7° the more solemn celebration of the Eucharist on Sundays and holy days of obligation.

Can. 531 — Although another person may have performed some parochial function, that person is to put the offerings received from the Christian faithful on that occasion into the parish account, unless it is obvious that such would be contrary to the will of the donor in the case of voluntary offerings; after he has listened to the presbyteral council, the diocesan bishop is competent to issue regulations which provide for the allocation of these offerings and the remuneration of clerics who fulfill the same function.

Can. 532 — The pastor represents the parish in all juridic affairs in accord with the norm of law; he is to see to it that the goods of the parish are administered in accord with the norms of cann. 1281-1288.

Can. 533 — §1. The pastor is obliged to reside in a parish house close to the church; in particular cases, however, the local ordinary can permit him to live elsewhere, especially in a house shared by several presbyters, provided there is a just cause and suitable and due provision is made for the performance of parochial functions.

§2. Unless there is a serious reason to the contrary, the pastor may be absent each year from the parish on vacation for at most one continuous or interrupted month; the days which the pastor spends once a year in spiritual retreat are not counted in his vacation days; if the pastor is to be absent from the parish beyond a week he is bound to inform the local ordinary of this.

§3. The diocesan bishop is to issue norms which provide for the care of a parish by a priest possessing the needed faculties during the absence of the pastor.

dotem debitis facultatibus instructum.

Can. 534 – § 1. Parochus, post captam paroeciae possessionem, obligatione tenetur singulis diebus dominicis atque festis in sua dioecesi de praecepto Missam pro populo sibi commisso applicandi; qui vero ab hac celebratione legitime impediatur, iisdem diebus per alium aut aliis diebus per se ipse applicet.

§ 2. Parochus, qui plurium paroeciarum curam habet, diebus de quibus in § 1, unam tantum Missam pro universo sibi commisso populo applicare tenetur.

§ 3. Parochus qui obligationi de qua in §§ 1 et 2 non satisfecerit, quam primum pro populo tot Missas applicet, quot omiserit.

Can. 535 – § 1. In unaquaque paroecia habeantur libri paroeciales, liber scilicet baptizatorum, matrimoniorum, defunctorum, aliique secundum Episcoporum conferentiae aut Episcopi dioecesani praescripta; prospiciat parochus ut iidem libri accurate conscribantur atque diligenter asserventur.

§ 2. In libro baptizatorum adnotentur quoque confirmatio, necnon quae pertinent ad statum canonicum christifidelium, ratione matrimonii, salvo quidem praescripto can. 1133, ratione adoptionis, itemque ratione suscepti ordinis sacri, professionis perpetuae in instituto religioso emissae necnon mutati ritus; eaeque adnotationes in documento accepti baptismi semper referantur.

§ 3. Unicuique paroeciae sit proprium sigillum; testimonia quae de statu canonico christifidelium dantur, sicut et acta omnia quae momentum iuridicum habere possunt, ab ipso parocho eiusve delegato subscribantur et sigillo paroeciali muniantur.

§ 4. In unaquaque paroecia habeatur tabularium seu archivum, in quo libri paroeciales custodiantur, una cum Episcoporum epistulis aliisque documentis, necessitatis utilitatisve causa servandis; quae omnia, ab Episcopo dioecesano eiusve delegato, visitationis vel alio opportuno tempore inspicienda, parochus caveat ne ad extraneorum manus perveniant.

§ 5. Libri paroeciales antiquiores quoque diligenter custodiantur, secundum praescripta iuris particularis.

Can. 536 – § 1. Si, de iudicio Episcopi dioecesani, audito consilio presbyterali, opportunum sit, in unaquaque paroecia constituatur consilium pastorale, cui parochus praeest et in quo christifideles una cum illis qui curam pastoralem vi officii sui in paroecia participant, ad actionem pastoralem fovendam suum adiutorium praestent.

Can. 534 — §1. After he has taken possession of his parish the pastor is obliged to apply Mass for the people entrusted to him each Sunday and holy day of obligation within the diocese; if he is legitimately prevented from this celebration, he is to apply Mass on these same days through another priest or he himself is to apply it on other days.

§2. A pastor who has the care of several parishes is obliged to apply only one Mass for all the people entrusted to him on those days mentioned in §1.

§3. A pastor who has not satisfied the obligation mentioned in §§1 and 2 is to apply as many Masses for his people as he has missed as soon as possible.

Can. 535 — §1. Each parish is to possess a set of parish books including baptismal, marriage and death registers as well as other registers prescribed by the conference of bishops or the diocesan bishop; the pastor is to see to it that these registers are accurately inscribed and carefully preserved.

§2. In the baptismal register are also to be noted the person's confirmation and whatever affects the canonical status of the Christian faithful by reason of marriage, with due regard for the prescription of can. 1133, adoption, reception of sacred orders, perpetual profession in a religious institute, and change of rite; these notations are always to be noted on a document which certifies the reception of baptism.

§3. Each parish is to possess its own seal; documents which are issued to certify the canonical status of the Christian faithful as well as all acts which can have juridic importance are to be signed by the pastor or his delegate and sealed with the parish seal.

§4. Each parish is to have a registry or archive in which the parish books are kept along with episcopal letters and other documents which ought to be preserved due to necessity or usefulness; all these are to be inspected by the diocesan bishop or his delegate during his visitation or at another suitable time; the pastor is to take care that they do not come into the hands of outsiders.

§5. The older parish books are also to be carefully preserved in accord with the prescriptions of particular law.

Can. 536 — §1. After the diocesan bishop has listened to the presbyteral council and if he judges it opportune, a pastoral council is to be established in each parish; the pastor presides over it, and through it the Christian faithful along with those who share in the pastoral care of the parish in virtue of their office give their help in fostering pastoral activity.

§ 2. Consilium pastorale voto gaudet tantum consultivo et regitur normis ab Episcopo dioecesano statutis.

Can. 537 – In unaquaque paroecia habeatur consilium a rebus oeconomicis, quod praeterquam iure universali, regitur normis ab Episcopo dioecesano latis .et in quo christifideles, secundum easdem normas selecti, parocho in administratione bonorum paroeciae adiutorio sint, firmo praescripto can. 532.

Can. 538 – § 1. Parochus ab officio cessat amotione aut translatione ab Episcopo dioecesano ad normam iuris peracta, renuntiatione iusta de causa ab ipso parocho facta et, ut valeat, ab eodem Episcopo acceptata, necnon lapsu temporis si, iuxta iuris particularis de quo in can. 522 praescripta, ad tempus determinatum constitutus fuerit.

§ 2. Parochus, qui est sodalis instituti religiosi aut in societate vitae apostolicae incardinatus, ad normam can. 682, § 2 amovetur.

§ 3. Parochus, expleto septuagesimo quinto aetatis anno, rogatur ut renuntiationem ab officio exhibeat Episcopo dioecesano, qui, omnibus personae et loci inspectis adiunctis, de eadem acceptanda aut differenda decernat; renuntiantis congruae sustentationi et habitationi ab Episcopo dioecesano providendum est, attentis normis ab Episcoporum conferentia statutis.

Can. 539 – Cum vacat paroecia aut cum parochus ratione captivitatis, exsilii vel relegationis, inhabilitatis vel infirmae valetudinis aliusve causae a munere pastorali in paroecia exercendo praepeditur, ab Episcopo dioecesano quam primum deputetur administrator paroecialis, sacerdos scilicet qui parochi vicem suppleat ad normam can. 540.

Can. 540 – § 1. Administrator paroecialis iisdem adstringitur officiis iisdemque gaudet iuribus ac parochus, nisi ab Episcopo dioecesano aliter statuatur.

§ 2. Administratori paroeciali nihil agere licet, quod praeiudicium afferat iuribus parochi aut damno esse possit bonis paroecialibus.

§ 3. Administrator paroecialis post expletum munus, parocho rationem reddat.

Can. 541 – § 1. Vacante paroecia itemque parocho a munere pastorali exercendo impedito, ante administratoris paroecialis constitutionem, paroeciae regimen interim assumat vicarius paroecialis; si plures sint, is qui sit nominatione antiquior, et si vicarii desint, parochus iure particulari definitus.

§ 2. Qui paroeciae regimen ad normam § 1 assumpserit, loci Ordinarium de paroeciae vacatione statim certiorem faciat.

§2. This pastoral council possesses a consultative vote only and is governed by norms determined by the diocesan bishop.

Can. 537 — Each parish is to have a finance council which is regulated by universal law as well as by norms issued by the diocesan bishop; in this council the Christian faithful, selected according to the same norms, aid the pastor in the administration of parish goods with due regard for the prescription of can. 532.

Can. 538 — §1. A pastor ceases from office by means of removal or transfer by the diocesan bishop which has been done in accord with the norm of law, by resignation of the pastor submitted for a just cause and accepted by the same diocesan bishop for validity and by lapse of time if the pastor has been appointed for a definite period of time in accord with the prescriptions of particular law mentioned in can. 522.

§2. A pastor who is a member of a religious institute or a society of apostolic life is removed in accord with the norm of can. 682, §2.

§3. When a pastor has completed his seventy-fifth year of age he is asked to submit his resignation from office to the diocesan bishop, who, after considering all the circumstances of person and place, is to decide whether to accept or defer the resignation; the diocesan bishop, taking into account the norms determined by the conference of bishops, is to provide for the suitable support and housing of the resigned pastor.

Can. 539 — When a parish becomes vacant or when the pastor is prevented from exercising his pastoral office in the parish due to captivity, exile, banishment, incapacity, ill health or some other cause, the diocesan bishop is to appoint as soon as possible a parochial administrator, that is, a priest who substitutes for the pastor in accord with the norm of can. 540.

Can. 540 — §1. A parochial administrator is bound by the same duties and enjoys the same rights as a pastor unless the diocesan bishop determines otherwise.

§2. A parochial administrator is not permitted to do anything which can prejudice the rights of the pastor or harm parish goods.

§3. After he has fulfilled his function the parochial administrator is to render an account to the pastor.

Can. 541 — §1. When a parish becomes vacant or when the pastor is hindered from exercising his pastoral duty the parochial vicar is to assume the governance of the parish in the meantime until a parochial administrator is appointed; if there are several parochial vicars, the senior vicar in terms of appointment assumes the governance; if there are no parochial vicars, then a pastor specified by particular law assumes the governance.

§2. The person who has assumed the governance of a parish in accord with the norm of §1 is to inform the local ordinary immediately that the parish is vacant.

Can. 542 – Sacerdotes quibus in solidum, ad normam can. 516, § 1, alicuius paroeciae aut diversarum simul paroeciarum cura pastoralis committitur :

1° praediti sint oportet qualitatibus, de quibus in can. 521;

2° nominentur vel instituantur ad normam praescriptorum cann. 522 et 524;

3° curam pastoralem obtinent tantum a momento captae possessionis; eorundem moderator in possessionem mittitur ad normam praescriptorum can. 527, § 2; pro ceteris vero sacerdotibus fidei professio legitime facta locum tenet captae possessiónis.

Can. 543 – § 1. Si sacerdotibus in solidum cura pastoralis alicuius paroeciae aut diversarum simul paroeciarum committatur, singuli eorum, iuxta ordinationem ab iisdem statutam. obligatione tenentur munera et functiones parochi persolvendi de quibus in cann. 528, 529 et 530; facultas matrimoniis assistendi, sicuti et potestates omnes dispensandi ipso iure parocho concessae. omnibus competunt, exercendae tamen sunt sub directione moderatoris.

§ 2. Sacerdotes omnes qui ad coetum pertinent :

1° obligatione tenentur residentiae ;

2° communi consilio ordinationem statuant, qua eorum unus Missam pro populo celebret, ad normam can. 534 ;

3° solus moderator in negotiis iuridicis personam gerit paroeciae aut paroeciarum coetui commissarum.

Can. 544 – Cum cesset ab officio aliquis sacerdos e coetu, de quo in can. 517, § 1, vel coetus moderator, itemque cum eorundem aliquis inhabilis fiat ad munus pastorale exercendum, non vacat paroecia vel paroeciae, quarum cura coetui committitur; Episcopi autem dioecesani est alium nominare moderatorem; antequam vero ab Episcopo alius nominetur, hoc munus adimpleat sacerdos eiusdem coetus nominatione antiquior.

Can. 545 – § 1. Quoties ad pastoralem paroeciae curam debite adimplendam necesse aut opportunum sit, parocho adiungi possunt unus aut plures vicarii paroeciales, qui, tamquam parochi cooperatores eiusque sollicitudinis participes, communi cum parocho consilio et studio, atque sub eiusdem auctoritate operam in ministerio pastorali praestent.

§ 2. Vicarius paroecialis constitui potest sive ut opem ferat in universo ministerio pastorali explendo, et quidem aut pro tota paroecia aut pro determinata paroeciae parte aut pro certo paroeciae christifidelium coetu, sive etiam ut operam impendat in certum ministerium in diversis simul paroeciis persolvendum.

Can. 542 — The priests who as a team have been entrusted with the pastoral care of some parish or group of different parishes in accord with the norm of can. 516, §1*:

1° are to be endowed with the qualities mentioned in can. 521;

2° are to be appointed or installed in accord with the prescriptions of cann. 522 and 524;

3° are responsible for pastoral care only from the moment of taking possession; their moderator is to be placed in possession of the parish in accord with the prescriptions of can. 527, §2; for the other priests a legitimately made profession of faith substitutes for taking possession.

Can. 543 — §1. Each of the priests who as a team have been entrusted with the pastoral care of some parish or group of different parishes is obliged to perform the duties and functions of the pastor which are mentioned in cann. 528, 529 and 530 in accord with an arrangement determined by themselves; all these priests possess the faculty to assist at marriages as well as all the faculties to dispense which are granted to the pastor by the law itself, to be exercised, however, under the direction of the moderator.

§2. All the priests of the team:

1° are bound by the obligation of residence;

2° through common counsel are to establish an arrangement by which one of them celebrates Mass for the people in accord with the norm of can. 534;

3°** in juridic affairs only the moderator represents the parish or parishes entrusted to the team.

Can. 544 — When one of the priests in the team mentioned in can. 517, §1 or its moderator ceases from office or when one of them becomes incapable of exercising pastoral duties the parish or parishes entrusted to the care of the team do not become vacant; however, the diocesan bishop is to name another moderator; the senior priest on the team in terms of assignment is to fulfill the office of moderator until another is appointed by the diocesan bishop.

Can. 545 — §1. A parochial vicar or several of them can be associated with the pastor whenever it is necessary or suitable for duly implementing the pastoral care of the parish; parochial vicars are priests who render their services in pastoral ministry as co-workers with the pastor in common counsel and endeavor with him and also under his authority.

§2. A parochial vicar can be assigned to assist in fulfilling the entire pastoral ministry on behalf of an entire parish, a definite part of the parish, or a certain group of the Christian faithful of the parish; he can also be

*Apparently should read 517, §1.—Trans.   **Apparently should read §3.—Trans.

Can. 546 – Ut quis valide vicarius paroecialis nominetur, oportet sit in sacro presbyteratus ordine constitutus.

Can. 547 – Vicarium paroècialem libere nominat Episcopus dioecesanus, auditis, si opportunum id iudicaverit, parocho aut parochis paroeciarum pro quibus constituitur, necnon vicario foraneo, firmo praescripto can. 682, § 1.

Can. 548 – § 1. Vicarii paroecialis obligationes et iura, praeterquam canonibus huius capitis, statutis dioecesanis necnon litteris Episcopi dioecesani definiuntur, specialius autem mandato parochi determinantur.

§ 2. Nisi aliud expresse litteris Episcopi dioecesani caveatur, vicarius paroecialis ratione officii obligatione tenetur parochum in universo paroeciali ministerio adiuvandi, excepta quidem applicatione Missae pro populo, itemque, si res ferat ad normam iuris, parochi vicem supplendi.

§ 3. Vicarius paroecialis regulariter de inceptis pastoralibus prospectis et susceptis ad parochum referat, ita ut parochus et vicarius aut vicarii, coniunctis viribus, pastorali curae providere valeant paroeciae, cuius simul sunt sponsores.

Can. 549 – Absente parocho, nisi aliter Episcopus dioecesanus providerit ad normam can. 533, § 3, et nisi Administrator paroecialis constitutus fuerit, serventur praescripta can. 541, § 1; vicarius hoc in casu omnibus etiam obligationibus tenetur parochi, excepta obligatione applicandi Missam pro populo.

Can. 550 – § 1. Vicarius paroecialis obligatione tenetur residendi in paroecia aut, si pro diversis simul paroeciis constitutus est, in earum aliqua; loci tamen Ordinarius, iusta de causa, permittere potest ut alibi resideat, praesertim in domo pluribus presbyteris communi, dummodo pastoralium perfunctio munerum nullum exinde detrimentum capiat.

§ 2. Curet loci Ordinarius ut inter parochum et vicarios aliqua vitae communis consuetudo in domo paroeciali, ubi id fieri possit, provehatur.

§ 3. Ad tempus feriarum quod attinet, vicarius paroecialis eodem gaudet iure ac parochus.

Can. 551 – Ad oblationes quod attinet, quas occasione perfuncti ministerii pastoralis christifideles vicario faciunt, serventur praescripta can. 531.

assigned to assist in fulfilling a certain type of ministry in different parishes concurrently.

Can. 546 — To be validly named parochial vicar one must be constituted in the sacred order of the presbyterate.

Can. 547 — The diocesan bishop freely names a parochial vicar, having heard, if he judges it opportune, the pastor or pastors of the parishes for which he is appointed and the vicar forane, with due regard for the prescription of can. 682, §1.

Can. 548 — §1. The obligations and rights of the parochial vicar are defined in the canons of this chapter, in the diocesan statutes, in the letter of the diocesan bishop and more specifically in the mandate given him by the pastor.

§2. Unless the letter of the diocesan bishop expressly states otherwise the parochial vicar is obliged by reason of his office to assist the pastor in fulfilling the total parochial ministry, except for the obligation to apply Mass for the people, and if circumstances warrant it, to substitute for the pastor in accord with the norm of law.

§3. The parochial vicar is regularly to consult with the pastor on planned or existing programs so that the pastor and the parochial vicar or vicars can provide through their combined efforts for the pastoral care of the parish for which they are responsible together.

Can. 549 — Unless the diocesan bishop has provided otherwise in accord with the norm of can. 533, §3, and unless a parochial administrator has been appointed, the prescriptions of can. 541, §1, should be observed during the absence of the pastor; in this case the parochial vicar is bound by all the obligations of the pastor with the exception of the obligation to apply Mass for the people.

Can. 550 — §1. The parochial vicar is obliged to reside within the parish, or, if he has been appointed to different parishes concurrently, he is obliged to live in one of them; however, the local ordinary can permit him to reside elsewhere, especially in a house shared by several priests provided there is a just cause and such an arrangement does not hinder the discharge of his pastoral duties.

§2. The local ordinary is to see to it that some community of life is fostered between the pastor and the parochial vicars within the rectory whenever this can be done.

§3. The parochial vicar possesses the same rights as the pastor in the matter of vacation time.

Can. 551 — The prescriptions of can. 531 are to be observed concerning the offerings which the Christian faithful give to the parochial vicar on the occasion of his performing his pastoral ministry.

Can. 552 – Vicarius paroecialis ab Episcopo dioecesano aut ab Administratore dioecesano amoveri potest, iusta de causa, firmo praescripto can. 682, § 2.

Caput VII
DE VICARIIS FORANEIS

Can. 553 – § 1. Vicarius foraneus, qui etiam decanus vel archipresbyter vel alio nomine vocatur, est sacerdos qui vicariatui foraneo praeficitur.

§ 2. Nisi aliud iure particulari statuatur, vicarius foraneus nominatur ab Episcopo dioecesano, auditis pro suo prudenti iudicio sacerdotibus qui in vicariatu de quo agitur ministerium exercent.

Can. 554 – § 1. Ad officium vicarii foranei, quod cum officio parochi certae paroeciae non ligatur, Episcopus seligat sacerdotem quem, inspectis loci ac temporis adiunctis, idoneum iudicaverit.

§ 2. Vicarius foraneus nominetur ad certum tempus, iure particulari determinatum.

§ 3. Vicarium foraneum iusta de causa, pro suo prudenti arbitrio, Episcopus dioecesanus ab officio libere amovere potest.

Can. 555 – § 1. Vicario foraneo, praeter facultates iure particulari ei legitime tributas, officium et ius est :

1° actionem pastoralem in vicariatu communem promovendi et coordinandi ;

2° prospiciendi ut clerici sui districtus vitam ducant proprio statui congruam atque officiis suis diligenter satisfaciant ;

3° providendi ut religiosae functiones secundum sacrae liturgiae praescripta celebrentur, ut decor et nitor ecclesiarum sacraeque supellectilis, maxime in celebratione eucharistica et custodia sanctissimi Sacramenti, accurate serventur, ut recte conscribantur et debite custodiantur libri paroeciales, ut bona ecclesiastica sedulo administrentur ; denique ut domus paroecialis debita diligentia curetur.

§ 2. In vicariatu sibi concredito vicarius foraneus :

1° operam det ut clerici, iuxta iuris particularis praescripta, statutis temporibus intersint praelectionibus, conventibus theologicis aut conferentiis, ad normam can. 272, § 2 ;

2° curet ut presbyteris sui districtus subsidia spiritualia praesto sint, itemque maxime sollicitus sit de iis, qui in difficilioribus versantur circumstantiis aut problematibus anguntur.

Can. 552 — With due regard for the prescription of can. 682, §2, the parochial vicar can be removed by the diocesan bishop or by the diocesan administrator for a just cause.

CHAPTER VII
VICARS FORANE

Can. 553 — §1. A vicar forane, who is also called a dean or an archpriest or some other name, is a priest who is placed over a vicariate forane.

§2. Unless particular law determines otherwise the vicar forane is named by the diocesan bishop after, in accord with his own prudent judgment, he has consulted the priests who exercise ministry within the vicariate in question.

Can. 554 — §1. For the office of vicar forane, which is not linked to the office of pastor of a certain parish, the bishop is to select a priest whom he has judged suitable after he has considered the circumstances of place and time.

§2. A vicar forane is to be appointed for a certain period of time determined in particular law.

§3. The diocesan bishop can freely remove a vicar forane from office for a just cause in accord with his own prudent judgment.

Can. 555 — §1. In addition to the faculties legitimately granted him in particular law, a vicar forane has the duty and right:

1° to promote and coordinate the common pastoral activity within the vicariate;

2° to see to it that the clerics of his district lead a life which is in harmony with their state of life and diligently perform their duties;

3° to see to it that religious functions are celebrated in accord with the prescriptions of the sacred liturgy, that the good appearance and condition of the churches and of sacred furnishings are carefully maintained especially in the celebration of the Eucharist and the custody of the Blessed Sacrament, that the parish books are correctly inscribed and duly cared for, that ecclesiastical goods are carefully administered, and finally that the rectory is maintained with proper care.

§2. Within the vicariate entrusted to him the vicar forane:

1° is to see to it that clerics, in accord with the prescriptions of particular law and at the times stated in such law, attend theological lectures, meetings or conferences in accord with the norm of can. 272, §2*;

2° is to take care that the presbyters of his district have ready access to spiritual helps and is to be particularly concerned about those priests who find themselves in rather difficult circumstances or who are beset with problems.

*Apparently should read 279, §2.—Trans.

§ 3. Curet vicarius foraneus ut parochi sui districtus, quos graviter aegrotantes noverit, spiritualibus ac materialibus auxiliis ne careant, utque eorum qui decesserint, funera digne celebrentur; provideat quoque ne, occasione aegrotationis vel mortis, libri, documenta, sacra supellex aliaque, quae ad Ecclesiam pertinent, depereant aut asportentur.

§ 4. Vicarius foraneus obligatione tenetur secundum determinationem ab Episcopo dioecesano factam, sui districtus paroecias visitare.

Caput VIII
DE ECCLESIARUM RECTORIBUS ET DE CAPPELLANIS

Art. 1
De ecclesiarum rectoribus

Can. 556 – Ecclesiarum rectores hic intelleguntur sacerdotes, quibus cura demandatur alicuius ecclesiae, quae nec sit paroecialis nec capitularis, nec adnexa domui communitatis religiosae aut societatis vitae apostolicae, quae in eadem officia celebret.

Can. 557 – § 1. Ecclesiae rector libere nominatur ab Episcopo dioecesano, salvo iure eligendi aut praesentandi, si cui legitime competat; quo in casu Episcopi dioecesani est rectorem confirmare vel instituere.

§ 2. Etiam si ecclesia pertineat ad aliquod clericale institutum religiosum iuris pontificii, Episcopo dioecesano competit rectorem a Superiore praesentatum instituere.

§ 3. Rector ecclesiae, quae coniuncta sit cum seminario aliove collegio quod a clericis regitur, est rector seminarii vel collegii, nisi aliter Episcopus dioecesanus constituerit.

Can. 558 – Salvo can. 262, rectori non licet functiones paroeciales de quibus in can. 530, nn. 1-6, in ecclesia sibi commissa peragere, nisi consentiente aut, si res ferat, delegante parocho.

Can. 559 – Potest rector in ecclesia sibi commissa liturgicas celebrationes etiam sollemnes peragere, salvis legitimis fundationis legibus, atque dummodo de iudicio loci Ordinarii nullo modo ministerio paroeciali noceant.

Can. 560 – Loci Ordinarius, ubi id opportunum censeat, potest rectori praecipere ut determinatas in ecclesia sua pro populo celebret functiones etiam paroeciales, necnon ut ecclesia pateat certis christifidelium coetibus ibidem liturgicas celebrationes peracturis.

§3. The vicar forane is to take care that the pastors of his district whom he knows to be seriously ill do not lack spiritual and material aids, while seeing to it that the funerals of those who die are celebrated with dignity; he is likewise to make provision that when they are sick or dying, the books, documents, sacred furnishings or other things which belong to the Church are not lost or transported elsewhere.

§4. The vicar forane is obliged to visit the parishes of his district in accord with the regulations made by the diocesan bishop.

Chapter VIII
RECTORS OF CHURCHES AND CHAPLAINS

Art. 1
Rectors of Churches

Can. 556 — Rectors of churches are understood to be priests to whom is given the care of some church which is neither parochial nor capitular nor connected with a house of a religious community or of a society of apostolic life which celebrates services in such a church.

Can. 557 — §1. The diocesan bishop freely names the rector of a church, with due regard for the right of election or of presentation if someone legitimately possesses it; in this case the diocesan bishop is competent to confirm or to install the rector.

§2. Even if the church belongs to some clerical religious institute of pontifical right the diocesan bishop is competent to install the rector presented by the superior.

§3. Unless the diocesan bishop has determined otherwise, the rector of a church which is connected with a seminary or other college which is governed by clerics is the rector of that seminary or college.

Can. 558 — With due regard for can. 262, a rector is not allowed to perform the parochial functions mentioned in can. 530, nn. 1-6, in the church committed to him unless the pastor consents or delegates the rector if the matter warrants it.

Can. 559 — A rector can perform liturgical celebrations, even solemn ones, in the church committed to him with due regard for the legitimate laws of the foundation and as long as they do not harm the parochial ministry in the judgment of the local ordinary.

Can. 560 — Where he thinks it advisable, the local ordinary can order the rector to celebrate within the church particular functions, even parochial ones, for the people and to make the church available to certain groups of the Christian faithful for the conducting of liturgical celebrations.

Can. 561 – Sine rectoris aliusve legitimi superioris licentia, nemini licet in ecclesia Eucharistiam celebrare, sacramenta administrare aliasve sacras functiones peragere; quae licentia danda aut deneganda est ad normam iuris.

Can. 562 – Ecclesiae rector, sub auctoritate loci Ordinarii servatisque legitimis statutis et iuribus quaesitis, obligatione tenetur prospiciendi ut sacrae functiones secundum normas liturgicas et canonum praescripta digne in ecclesia celebrentur, onera fideliter adimpleantur, bona diligenter administrentur, sacrae supellectilis atque aedium sacrarum conservationi et decori provideatur, neve quidpiam fiat quod sanctitati loci ac reverentiae domui Dei debitae quoquo modo non congruat.

Can. 563 – Rectorem ecclesiae, etsi ab aliis electum aut praesentatum, loci Ordinarius ex iusta causa, pro suo prudenti arbitrio ab officio amovere potest, firmo praescripto can. 682, § 2.

Art. 2

De cappellanis

Can. 564 – Cappellanus est sacerdos, cui stabili modo committitur cura pastoralis, saltem ex parte, alicuius communitatis aut peculiaris coetus christifidelium, ad normam iuris universalis et particularis exercenda.

Can. 565 – Nisi iure aliud caveatur aut cuidam specialia iura legitime competant, cappellanus nominatur ab Ordinario loci, cui etiam pertinet praesentatum instituere aut electum confirmare.

Can. 566 – § 1. Cappellanus omnibus facultatibus instructus sit oportet quas recta cura pastoralis requirit. Praeter eas quae iure particulari aut speciali delegatione conceduntur, cappellanus vi officii facultate gaudet audiendi confessiones fidelium suae curae commissorum, verbi Dei eis praedicandi, Viaticum et unctionem infirmorum administrandi necnon sacramentum confirmationis eis conferendi, qui in periculo mortis versentur.

§ 2. In valetudinariis, carceribus et itineribus maritimis, cappellanus praeterea facultatem habet, his tantum in locis exercendam, a censuris latae sententiae non reservatis neque declaratis absolvendi, firmo tamen praescripto can. 976.

Can. 567 – § 1. Ad nominationem cappellani domus instituti religiosi laicalis, Ordinarius loci ne procedat, nisi consulto Superiore, cui ius est, audita communitate, quemdam sacerdotem proponere.

Can. 561 — Without the permission of the rector or of another legitimate superior no one is allowed to celebrate the Eucharist, administer the sacraments or perform other sacred functions in the church; this permission is to be granted or denied in accord with the norm of law.

Can. 562 — Under the authority of the local ordinary with due regard for legitimate statutes and vested rights, the rector of a church is obliged to see to it that the sacred functions are celebrated with dignity in the church in accord with the liturgical norms and the prescriptions of the canons, that obligations are faithfully fulfilled, that its goods are carefully administered, that the maintenance and the good appearance of sacred furnishings and buildings are provided for and that nothing whatever is done which is in any way out of harmony with the sanctity of the place and the reverence due to a house of God.

Can. 563 — For a just cause and in accord with his own judgment the local ordinary can remove from office a rector of a church, even if he had been elected or presented by others, with due regard for the prescription of can. 682, §2.

Art. 2

CHAPLAINS

Can. 564 — A chaplain is a priest to whom is entrusted in a stable manner the pastoral care, at least in part, of some community or particular group of the Christian faithful, to be exercised in accord with universal and particular law.

Can. 565 — Unless the law provides otherwise or special rights belong legitimately to someone, a chaplain is appointed by the local ordinary, who is also competent to install one who is presented or to confirm one who is elected.

Can. 566 — §1. A chaplain ought to be given all the faculties which proper pastoral care requires. Besides those which are granted by particular law or special delegation, a chaplain in virtue of his office enjoys the faculty to hear the confessions of the faithful entrusted to his care, to preach the word of God to them, to administer Viaticum and the anointing of the sick, and to confer the sacrament of confirmation on those who are in danger of death.

§2. In hospitals, prisons and on sea journeys a chaplain, moreover, has the faculty, to be exercised only in those places, to absolve from censures *latae sententiae* which are not reserved nor declared, with due regard for the prescription of can. 976.

Can. 567 — §1. The local ordinary is not to proceed to the appointment of a chaplain for the house of a lay religious institute without consulting the superior who has the right to propose a priest after hearing the community.

§ 2. Cappellani est liturgicas functiones celebrare aut moderari; ipsi tamen non licet in regimine interno instituti sese immiscere.

Can. 568 – Pro iis qui ob vitae condicionem ordinaria parochorum cura frui non valent, uti sunt migrantes, exsules, profugi, nomades, navigantes, constituantur, quatenus fieri possit, cappellani.

Can. 569 – Cappellani militum legibus specialibus reguntur.

Can. 570 – Si communitatis aut coetus sedi adnexa est ecclesia non paroecialis, cappellanus sit rector ipsius ecclesiae, nisi cura communitatis aut ecclesiae aliud exigat.

Can. 571 – In exercitio sui pastoralis muneris, cappellanus debitam cum parocho servet coniunctionem.

Can. 572 – Quod attinet ad amotionem cappellani, servetur praescriptum can. 563.

PARS III
DE INSTITUTIS VITAE CONSECRATAE ET DE SOCIETATIBUS VITAE APOSTOLICAE

SECTIO I
DE INSTITUTIS VITAE CONSECRATAE

TITULUS I
NORMAE COMMUNES OMNIBUS INSTITUTIS VITAE CONSECRATAE

Can. 573 – § 1. Vita consecrata per consiliorum evangelicorum professionem est stabilis vivendi forma qua fideles, Christum sub actione Spiritus Sancti pressius sequentes, Deo summe dilecto totaliter dedicantur, ut, in Eius honorem atque Ecclesiae aedificationem mundique salutem novo et peculiari titulo dediti, caritatis perfectionem in servitio Regni Dei consequantur et, praeclarum in Ecclesia signum effecti, caelestem gloriam praenuntient.

§ 2. Quam vivendi formam in institutis vitae consecratae, a competenti Ecclesiae auctoritate canonice erectis, libere assumunt christifideles, qui per vota aut alia sacra ligamina iuxta proprias institutorum leges, consilia evangelica castitatis, paupertatis et oboedientiae profitentur et per caritatem, ad quam ducunt, Ecclesiae eiusque mysterio speciali modo coniunguntur.

§2. It is the chaplain who celebrates or moderates liturgical functions; but he is not allowed to involve himself in the internal governance of the institute.

Can. 568 — To the extent it is possible, chaplains are to be appointed for those who cannot avail themselves of the ordinary care of a pastor because of the condition of their life, such as migrants, exiles, refugees, nomads, sailors.

Can. 569 — Military chaplains are governed by special laws.

Can. 570 — If the headquarters of a community or group is attached to a non-parochial church the chaplain is to be the rector of that church, unless the care of the community or church requires otherwise.

Can. 571 — In exercising his pastoral office a chaplain is to maintain an appropriately close relationship with the pastor.

Can. 572 — In regard to the removal of a chaplain the prescription of can. 563 shall be observed.

PART III

INSTITUTES OF CONSECRATED LIFE AND SOCIETIES OF APOSTOLIC LIFE

SECTION I
INSTITUTES OF CONSECRATED LIFE

TITLE I
NORMS COMMON TO ALL INSTITUTES OF CONSECRATED LIFE

Can. 573 — §1. Life consecrated by the profession of the evangelical counsels is a stable form of living by which faithful, following Christ more closely under the action of the Holy Spirit, are totally dedicated to God who is loved most of all, so that, having dedicated themselves to His honor, the upbuilding of the Church and the salvation of the world by a new and special title, they strive for the perfection of charity in service to the Kingdom of God and, having become an outstanding sign in the Church, they may foretell the heavenly glory.

§2. Christian faithful who profess the evangelical counsels of chastity, poverty and obedience by vows or other sacred bonds according to the proper laws of institutes freely assume this form of living in institutes of consecrated life canonically erected by competent church authority and through the charity to which these counsels lead they are joined to the Church and its mystery in a special way.

Can. 574 – § 1. Status eorum, qui in huiusmodi institutis consilia evangelica profitentur, ad vitam et sanctitatem Ecclesiae pertinet, et ideo ab omnibus in Ecclesia fovendus et promovendus est.

§ 2. Ad hunc statum quidam christifideles specialiter a Deo vocantur, ·ut in vita Ecclesiae peculiari dono fruantur et, secundum finem et spiritum instituti, eiusdem missioni salvificae prosint.

Can. 575 – Consilia evangelica in Christi Magistri doctrina et exemplis fundata, donum sunt divinum, quod Ecclesia a Domino accepit Eiusque gratia semper conservat.

Can. 576 – Competentis Ecclesiae auctoritatis est consilia evangelica interpretari, eorundem praxim legibus moderari atque stabiles inde vivendi formas canonica approbatione constituere itemque, pro parte sua, curare ut instituta secundum spiritum fundatorum et sanas traditiones crescant et floreant.

Can. 577 – Permulta in Ecclesia sunt instituta vitae consecratae, quae donationes habent differentes secundum gratiam quae data est eis : Christum, enim, pressius sequuntur sive orantem, sive Regnum Dei annuntiantem, sive hominibus benefacientem, sive cum eis in saeculo conversantem, semper autem voluntatem Patris facientem.

Can. 578 – Fundatorum mens atque proposita a competenti auctoritate ecclesiastica sancita circa naturam, finem, spiritum et indolem instituti, necnon eius sanae traditiones, quae omnia patrimonium eiusdem instituti constituunt, ab omnibus fideliter servanda sunt.

Can. 579 – Episcopi dioecesani, in suo quisque territorio, instituta vitae consecratae formali decreto erigere possunt, dummodo Sedes Apostolica consulta fuerit.

Can. 580 – Aggregatio alicuius instituti vitae consecratae ad aliud reservatur competenti auctoritati instituti aggregantis, salva semper canonica autonomia instituti aggregati.

Can. 581 – Dividere institutum in partes, quocumque nomine veniant, novas erigere, erectas coniungere vel aliter circumscribere ad competentem instituti auctoritatem pertinet, ad normam constitutionum.

Can. 582 – Fusiones et uniones institutorum vitae consecratae uni Sedi Apostolicae reservantur; eidem quoque reservantur confoederationes et foederationes.

Can. 574 — §1. The state of those who profess the evangelical counsels in institutes of this kind pertains to the life and sanctity of the Church and for this reason is to be fostered and promoted by all in the Church.

§2. Certain Christian faithful are specially called to this state by God so that they may enjoy a special gift in the life of the Church and contribute to its salvific mission according to the purpose and spirit of the institute.

Can. 575 — The evangelical counsels, based on the teaching and examples of Christ the Teacher, are a divine gift which the Church has received from the Lord and always preserves through His grace.

Can. 576 — It belongs to the competent authority of the Church to interpret the evangelical counsels, to regulate their practice by laws, to constitute therefrom stable forms of living by canonical approbation, and, for its part, to take care that the institutes grow and flourish according to the spirit of the founders and wholesome traditions.

Can. 577 — In the Church there are very many institutes of consecrated life which have different gifts according to the grace which has been given them: they follow Christ more closely as He prays, announces the Kingdom of God, performs good works for people, shares His life with them in the world, and yet always does the will of the Father.

Can. 578 — The intention of the founders and their determination concerning the nature, purpose, spirit and character of the institute which have been ratified by competent ecclesiastical authority as well as its wholesome traditions, all of which constitute the patrimony of the institute itself, are to be observed faithfully by all.

Can. 579 — Diocesan bishops each in his own territory can erect institutes of consecrated life by a formal decree, provided that the Apostolic See has been consulted.

Can. 580 — The aggregation of one institute of consecrated life to another is reserved to the competent authority of the aggregating institute, always safeguarding the canonical autonomy of the aggregated institute.

Can. 581 — Dividing an institute into parts, whatever the parts are called, erecting new ones, joining previously erected parts or defining them in another way pertains to the competent authority of the institute, in accord with the norm of the constitutions.

Can. 582 — Mergers and unions of institutes of consecrated life are reserved to the Apostolic See alone; confederations and federations are also reserved to it.

Can. 583 – Immutationes in institutis vitae consecratae ea afficientes, quae a Sede Apostolica approbata fuerunt, absque eiusdem licentia fieri nequeunt.

Can. 584 – § 1. Institutum supprimere ad unam Sedem Apostolicam spectat, cui etiam reservatur de eius bonis temporalibus statuere.

Can. 585 – Instituti partes supprimere ad auctoritatem competentem eiusdem instituti pertinet.

Can. 586 – § 1. Singulis institutis iusta autonomia vitae, praesertim regiminis, agnoscitur, qua gaudeant in Ecclesia propria disciplina atque integrum servare valeant suum patrimonium, de quo in can. 578.

§ 2. Ordinariorum locorum est hanc autonomiam servare ac tueri.

Can. 587 – § 1. Ad propriam singulorum institutorum vocationem et identitatem fidelius tuendam, in cuiusvis instituti codice fundamentali seu constitutionibus contineri debent, praeter ea quae in can. 578 servanda statuuntur, normae fundamentales circa instituti regimen et sodalium disciplinam, membrorum incorporationem atque institutionem, necnon proprium sacrorum ligaminum obiectum.

§ 2. Codex huiusmodi a competenti auctoritate Ecclesiae approbatur et tantummodo cum eiusdem consensu mutari potest.

§ 3. In hoc codice elementa spiritualia et iuridica apte componantur; normae tamen absque necessitate ne multiplicentur.

§ 4. Ceterae normae a competenti instituti auctoritate statutae apte in aliis codicibus colligantur, quae tamen iuxta exigentias locorum et temporum congrue recognosci et aptari possunt.

Can. 588 – § 1. Status vitae consecratae, suapte natura, non est nec clericalis nec laicalis.

§ 2. Institutum clericale illud dicitur quod, ratione finis seu propositi a fundatore intenti vel vi legitimae traditionis, sub moderamine est clericorum, exercitium ordinis sacri assumit, et qua tale ab Ecclesiae auctoritate agnoscitur.

§ 3. Institutum vero laicale illud appellatur quod, ab Ecclesiae auctoritate qua tale agnitum, vi eius naturae, indolis et finis munus habet proprium, a fundatore vel legitima traditione definitum, exercitium ordinis sacri non includens.

Can. 589 – Institutum vitae consecratae dicitur iuris pontificii, si a Sede Apostolica erectum aut per eiusdem formale decretum approbatum est; iuris vero dioecesani, si ab Episcopo dioecesano erectum, ap-

Can. 583 — Changes in institutes of consecrated life which affect matters which have been approved by the Apostolic See cannot be made without its permission.

Can. 584— §1.* Suppressing an institute pertains to the Apostolic See alone, to whom also it is reserved to determine what is to be done with the temporal goods of the institute.

Can. 585 — Suppressing parts of an institute pertains to the competent authority of the institute itself.

Can. 586 — §1. For individual institutes there is acknowledged a rightful autonomy of life, especially of governance, by which they enjoy their own discipline in the Church and have the power to preserve their own patrimony intact as mentioned in can. 578.

§2. It belongs to local ordinaries to safeguard and protect this autonomy.

Can. 587 — §1. In order to protect more faithfully the particular vocation and identity of each institute, its fundamental code or constitutions must contain, besides what must be observed according to can. 578, fundamental norms about the governance of the institute and the discipline of members, the incorporation and formation of members, and the proper object of sacred bonds.

§2. A code of this kind is approved by the competent authority of the Church and can be changed only with its consent.

§3. In this code spiritual and juridical elements are to be suitably joined together; however norms are not to be multiplied unless it is necessary.

§4. Other norms established by the competent authority of the institute are to be suitably collected in other codes, which can moreover be fittingly reviewed and adapted according to the needs of places and times.

Can. 588 — §1. The state of consecrated life by its very nature is neither clerical nor lay.

§2. An institute is said to be clerical if, by reason of the purpose or design intended by its founder or in virtue of legitimate tradition, it is under the supervision of clerics, it assumes the exercise of sacred orders, and it is recognized as such by church authority.

§3. An institute is called lay if recognized as such by church authority, by virtue of its nature, character and purpose it has a proper function defined by the founder or by legitimate tradition which does not include the exercise of sacred orders.

Can. 589 — An institute of consecrated life is said to be of pontifical right if it has been erected by the Apostolic See or approved by a formal decree of the Apostolic See; on the other hand an institute is said to be of diocesan

---

*There is no §2.—Trans.

probationis decretum a Sede Apostolica non est consecutum.

Can. 590 – § 1. Instituta vitae consecratae, utpote ad Dei totiusque Ecclesiae servitium speciali modo dicata, supremae eiusdem auctoritati peculiari ratione subduntur.

§ 2. Singuli sodales Summo Pontifici, tamquam supremo eorum Superiori, etiam ratione sacri vinculi oboedientiae parere tenentur.

Can. 591 – Quo melius institutorum bono atque apostolatus necessitatibus provideatur, Summus Pontifex, ratione sui in universam Ecclesiam primatus, intuitu utilitatis communis, instituta vitae consecratae ab Ordinariorum loci regimine eximere potest sibique soli vel alii ecclesiasticae auctoritati subicere.

Can. 592 – § 1. Quo melius institutorum communio cum Sede Apostolica foveatur, modo et tempore ab eadem statutis, quilibet supremus Moderator brevem conspectum status et vitae instituti eidem Apostolicae Sedi mittat.

§ 2. Cuiuslibet instituti Moderatores promoveant notitiam documentorum Sanctae Sedis, quae sodales sibi concreditos respiciunt, eorumque observantiam curent.

Can. 593 – Firmo praescripto can. 586, instituta iuris pontificii quoad regimen internum et disciplinam immediate et exclusive potestati Sedis Apostolicae subiciuntur.

Can. 594 – Institutum iuris dioecesani, firmo can. 586, permanet sub speciali cura Episcopi dioecesani.

Can. 595 – § 1. Episcopi sedis principis est constitutiones approbare et immutationes in eas legitime introductas confirmare, salvis iis in quibus Apostolica Sedes manus apposuerit, necnon negotia maiora totum institutum respicientia tractare, quae potestatem internae auctoritatis superent, consultis tamen ceteris Episcopis dioecesanis, si institutum ad plures dioeceses propagatum fuerit.

§ 2. Episcopus dioecesanus potest dispensationes a constitutionibus concedere in casibus particularibus.

Can. 596 – § 1. Institutorum Superiores et capitula in sodales ea gaudent potestate, quae iure universali et constitutionibus definitur.

§ 2. In institutis autem religiosis clericalibus iuris pontificii pollent insuper potestate ecclesiastica regiminis pro foro tam externo quam interno.

§ 3. Potestati de qua in § 1 applicantur praescripta cann. 131, 133 et 137-144.

right if, after having been erected by a diocesan bishop, it has not obtained a decree of approval from the Apostolic See.

Can. 590 — §1. Institutes of consecrated life, inasmuch as they are dedicated in a special way to the service of God and of the entire Church, are subject to the supreme authority of this same Church in a special manner.

§2. Individual members are also bound to obey the Supreme Pontiff as their highest superior by reason of the sacred bond of obedience.

Can. 591 — In order to provide better for the good of institutes and the needs of the apostolate, the Supreme Pontiff, by reason of his primacy over the universal Church and considering the common good, can exempt institutes of consecrated life from the governance of local ordinaries and subject them either to himself alone or to another ecclesiastical authority.

Can. 592 — §1. In order that the communion of institutes with the Apostolic See be better fostered each supreme moderator is to send a brief report on the status and life of the institute to the Apostolic See in a manner and at a time determined by the latter.

§2. The moderators of every institute are to promote knowledge of the documents of the Holy See which affect members entrusted to them and be concerned about their observance of them.

Can. 593 — With due regard for the prescription of can. 586, institutes of pontifical right are immediately and exclusively subject to the power of the Apostolic See in internal governance and discipline.

Can. 594 — With due regard for can. 586, an institute of diocesan right remains under the special care of the diocesan bishop.

Can. 595 — §1. It belongs to the bishop of the principal seat of the institute to approve the constitutions and confirm any changes legitimately introduced into them, except in those matters in which the Apostolic See has intervened; it also belongs to him to deal with business of greater importance which affects the whole institute and which are beyond the power of its internal authority; he does so after consulting other diocesan bishops if the institute has spread to several dioceses.

§2. The diocesan bishop can grant dispensations from the constitutions in particular cases.

Can. 596 — §1. Superiors and chapters of institutes enjoy that power over members which is defined in universal law and the constitutions.

§2. Moreover, in clerical religious institutes of pontifical right they also possess ecclesiastical power of governance for both the external and the internal forum.

§3. The prescriptions of cann. 131, 133 and 137-144 are applicable to the power referred to in §1.

Can. 597 – § 1. In vitae consecratae institutum admitti potest quilibet catholicus, recta intentione praeditus, qui qualitates habeat iure universali et proprio requisitas nulloque detineatur impedimento.

§ 2. Nemo admitti potest sine congrua praeparatione.

Can. 598 – § 1. Unumquodque institutum, attentis indole et finibus propriis, in suis constitutionibus definiat modum quo consilia evangelica castitatis, paupertatis et oboedientiae, pro sua vivendi ratione, servanda sunt.

§ 2. Sodales vero omnes debent non solum consilia evangelica fideliter integreque servare, sed etiam secundum ius proprium instituti vitam componere atque ita ad perfectionem sui status contendere.

Can. 599 – Evangelicum castitatis consilium propter Regnum coelorum assumptum, quod signum est mundi futuri et fons uberioris fecunditatis in indiviso corde, obligationem secumfert continentiae perfectae in coelibatu.

Can. 600 – Evangelicum consilium paupertatis ad imitationem Christi, qui propter nos egenus factus est cum esset dives, praeter vitam re et spiritu pauperem, operose in sobrietate ducendam et a terrenis divitiis alienam, secumfert dependentiam et limitationem in usu et dispositione bonorum ad normam iuris proprii singulorum institutorum.

Can. 601 – Evangelicum oboedientiae consilium, spiritu fidei et amoris in sequela Christi usque ad mortem oboedientis susceptum, obligat ad submissionem voluntatis erga legitimos Superiores, vices Dei gerentes, cum secundum proprias constitutiones praecipiunt.

Can. 602 – Vita fraterna, unicuique instituto propria, qua sodales omnes in peculiarem veluti familiam in Christo coadunantur, ita definiatur ut cunctis mutuo adiutorio evadat ad suam cuiusque vocationem adimplendam. Fraterna autem communione, in caritate radicata et fundata, sodales exemplo sint universalis in Christo reconciliationis.

Can. 603 – § 1. Praeter vitae consecratae instituta, Ecclesia agnoscit vitam eremiticam seu anachoreticam, qua christifideles arctiore a mundo secessu, solitudinis silentio, assidua prece et paenitentia, suam in laudem Dei et mundi salutem vitam devovent.

§ 2. Eremita, uti Deo deditus in vita consecrata, iure agnoscitur si tria evangelica consilia, voto vel alio sacro ligamine firmata, publice profiteatur in manu Episcopi dioecesani et propriam vivendi rationem sub ductu eiusdem servet.

Can. 597 — §1. Any Catholic, endowed with a right intention, who has the qualities required by universal and proper law and who is not prevented by any impediment can be admitted to an institute of consecrated life.

§2. No one can be admitted without suitable preparation.

Can. 598 — §1. Each institute, keeping in mind its own character and purposes is to define in its constitutions the manner in which the evangelical counsels of chastity, poverty and obedience are to be observed for its way of living.

§2. All members must not only observe the evangelical counsels faithfully and fully, but also organize their life according to the proper law of the institute and thereby strive for the perfection of their state.

Can. 599 — The evangelical counsel of chastity assumed for the sake of the kingdom of heaven, as a sign of the future world and a source of more abundant fruitfulness in an undivided heart, entails the obligation of perfect continence in celibacy.

Can. 600 — The evangelical counsel of poverty in imitation of Christ who, although He was rich became poor for us, entails, besides a life which is poor in fact and in spirit, a life of labor lived in moderation and foreign to earthly riches, a dependence and a limitation in the use and disposition of goods according to the norm of the proper law of each institute.

Can. 601 — The evangelical counsel of obedience, undertaken in a spirit of faith and love in the following of Christ who was obedient even unto death requires a submission of the will to legitimate superiors, who stand in the place of God when they command according to the proper constitutions.

Can. 602 — The life of brothers or sisters proper to each institute, by which all members are united together like a special family in Christ, is to be determined in such a way that it becomes a mutual support for all in fulfilling the vocation of each member. Moreover by their communion as brothers or sisters, rooted in and built on love, the members are to be an example of universal reconciliation in Christ.

Can. 603 — §1. Besides institutes of consecrated life, the Church recognizes the eremitic or anchoritic life by which the Christian faithful devote their life to the praise of God and salvation of the world through a stricter separation from the world, the silence of solitude and assiduous prayer and penance.

§2. A hermit is recognized in the law as one dedicated to God in a consecrated life if he or she publicly professes the three evangelical counsels, confirmed by a vow or other sacred bond, in the hands of the diocesan bishop and observes his or her own plan of life under his direction.

Can. 604 – § 1. Hisce vitae consecratae formis accedit ordo virginum quae, sanctum propositum emittentes Christum pressius sequendi, ab Episcopo dioecesano iuxta probatum ritum liturgicum Deo consecrantur, Christo Dei Filio mystice desponsantur et Ecclesiae servitio dedicantur.

§ 2. Ad suum propositum fidelius servandum et ad servitium Ecclesiae, proprio statui consonum, mutuo adiutorio perficiendum, virgines consociari possunt.

Can. 605 – Novas formas vitae consecratae approbare uni Sedi Apostolicae reservatur. Episcopi dioecesani autem nova vitae consecratae dona a Spiritu Sancto Ecclesiae concredita discernere satagant iidemque adiuvent promotores ut proposita meliore quo fieri potest modo exprimant aptisque statutis protegant, adhibitis praesertim generalibus normis in hac parte contentis.

Can. 606 – Quae de institutis vitae consecratae eorumque sodalibus statuuntur, pari iure de utroque sexu valent, nisi ex contextu sermonis vel ex rei natura aliud constet.

TITULUS II
DE INSTITUTIS RELIGIOSIS

Can. 607 – § 1. Vita religiosa, utpote totius personae consecratio, mirabile in Ecclesia manifestat conubium a Deo conditum, futuri saeculi signum. Ita religiosus plenam suam consummat donationem veluti sacrificium Deo oblatum, quo tota ipsius exsistentia fit continuus Dei cultus in caritate.

§ 2. Institutum religiosum est societas in qua sodales secundum ius proprium vota publica perpetua vel temporaria, elapso tamen tempore renovanda, nuncupant atque vitam fraternam in communi ducunt.

§ 3. Testimonium publicum a religiosis Christo et Ecclesiae reddendum illam secumfert a mundo separationem, quae indoli et fini uniuscuiusque instituti est propria.

Caput I
DE DOMIBUS RELIGIOSIS
EARUMQUE ERECTIONE ET SUPPRESSIONE

Can. 608 – Communitas religiosa habitare debet in domo legitime constituta sub auctoritate Superioris ad normam iuris designati; singulae domus habeant saltem oratorium, in quo Eucharistia celebretur et asservetur ut vere sit centrum communitatis.

Can. 604 — §1. Similar to these forms of consecrated life is the order of virgins, who, committed to the holy plan of following Christ more closely, are consecrated to God by the diocesan bishop according to the approved liturgical rite, are betrothed mystically to Christ, the Son of God, and are dedicated to the service of the Church.

§2. In order to observe their commitment more faithfully and to perform by mutual support service to the Church which is in harmony with their state these virgins can form themselves into associations.

Can. 605 — Approving new forms of consecrated life is reserved to the Apostolic See alone. Diocesan bishops, however, should strive to discern new gifts of consecrated life granted to the Church by the Holy Spirit and they should aid their promoters so that they can express their proposals as well as possible and protect them with suitable statutes, utilizing especially the general norms contained in this section.

Can. 606 — Whatever is determined about institutes of consecrated life and their members applies equally to either sex, unless the contrary is apparent from the context of the wording or nature of the matter.

TITLE II
RELIGIOUS INSTITUTES

Can. 607 — §1. Religious life, as a consecration of the whole person, manifests in the Church a wonderful marriage brought about by God, a sign of the future age. Thus religious bring to perfection their full gift as a sacrifice offered to God by which their whole existence becomes a continuous worship of God in love.

§2. A religious institute is a society in which members, according to proper law, pronounce public vows either perpetual or temporary, which are to be renewed when they have lapsed, and live a life in common as brothers or sisters.

§3. The public witness to be rendered by religious to Christ and to the Church entails a separation from the world proper to the character and purpose of each institute.

Chapter I
RELIGIOUS HOUSES AND THEIR ERECTION AND SUPPRESSION

Can. 608 — A religious community must live in a house legitimately constituted under the authority of the superior designated according to the norm of law; each house is to have at least an oratory in which the Eucharist is celebrated and reserved so that it truly is the center of the community.

Can. 609 – § 1. Instituti religiosi domum eriguntur ab auctoritate competenti iuxta constitutiones, praevio Episcopi dioecesani consensu in scriptis dato.

§ 2. Ad erigendum monasterium monialium requiritur insuper licentia Apostolicae Sedis.

Can. 610 – § 1. Domorum erectio fit prae oculis habita utilitate Ecclesiae et instituti atque in tuto positis iis quae ad vitam religiosam sodalium rite agendam requiruntur, iuxta proprios instituti fines et spiritum.

§ 2. Nulla domus erigatur nisi iudicari prudenter possit fore ut congrue sodalium necessitatibus provideatur.

Can. 611 – Consensus Episcopi dioecesani ad erigendam domum religiosam alicuius instituti secumfert ius :

1° vitam ducendi secundum indolem et fines proprios instituti ;

2° opera instituto propria exercendi ad normam iuris, salvis condicionibus in consensu appositis ;

3° pro institutis clericalibus habendi ecclesiam, salvo praescripto can. 1215, § 3, et sacra ministeria peragendi, servatis de iure servandis.

Can. 612 – Ut domus religiosa ad opera apostolica destinetur diversa ab illis pro quibus constituta est, requiritur consensus Episcopi dioecesani ; non vero, si agatur de conversione, quae, salvis fundationis legibus, ad internum regimen et disciplinam dumtaxat referatur.

Can. 613 – § 1. Domus religiosa canonicorum regularium et monachorum sub proprii Moderatoris regimine et cura sui iuris est, nisi constitutiones aliter ferant.

§ 2. Moderator domus sui iuris est de iure Superior maior.

Can. 614 – Monasteria monialium cuidam virorum instituto consociata propriam vitae rationem et regimen iuxta constitutiones obtinent. Mutua iura et obligationes ita definiantur ut ex consociatione spirituale bonum proficere possit.

Can. 615 – Monasterium sui iuris, quod praeter proprium Moderatorem alium Superiorem maiorem non habet, neque alicui religiosorum instituto ita consociatum est ut eiusdem Superior vera potestate constitutionibus determinata in tale monasterium gaudeat, ad normam iuris peculiari vigilantiae Episcopi dioecesani committitur.

Can. 616 – § 1. Domus religiosa legitime erecta supprimi potest a supremo Moderatore ad normam constitutionum, consulto Episcopo dioecesano. De bonis domus suppressae provideat ius proprium insti-

Can. 609 — §1. Houses of a religious institute are erected by the competent authority according to the constitutions with the previous written consent of the diocesan bishop.

§2. In order to erect a monastery of nuns the permission of the Apostolic See is also required.

Can. 610 — §1. The erection of houses takes place with due regard for their usefulness for the Church and the institute and safeguarding those things which are required for the correct living out of the religious life of the members according to the specific purposes and spirit of the institute.

§2. No house is to be erected unless it can be prudently judged that the needs of the members will be suitably provided for.

Can. 611 — The consent of the diocesan bishop to erect a religious house of any institute brings with it the right:

1° to lead a life according to its own character and the purposes of the institute;

2° to exercise the works proper to the institute according to the norm of law, with due regard for any conditions attached to the consent;

3° for clerical institutes to have a church, with due regard for the prescription of can. 1215, §3, and to perform sacred ministries, observing what is by law to be observed.

Can. 612 — In order that a religious house be converted to apostolic works different from those for which it was established the consent of the diocesan bishop is required; but this is not so if it is a matter of a change which refers only to internal government and discipline, with due regard for the laws of the foundation.

Can. 613 — §1. A religious house of canons regular and monks under the governance and care of its own moderator is autonomous unless the constitutions state otherwise.

§2. A moderator of an autonomous house is by law a major superior.

Can. 614 — Monasteries of nuns which are associated with an institute of men maintain their own order of life and governance according to the constitutions. Mutual rights and obligations are to be so defined that the association is spiritually enriching.

Can. 615 — An autonomous monastery which has no other major superior beyond its own moderator and is not associated with any other institute of religious in such a way that the superior of the latter enjoys true power over such a monastery determined by the constitutions is committed to the special vigilance of the diocesan bishop according to the norm of law.

Can. 616 — §1. A legitimately erected religious house can be suppressed by the supreme moderator according to the norm of the constitutions after having consulted the diocesan bishop. The proper law of the institute is to

tuti, salvis fundatorum vel offerentium voluntatibus et iuribus legitime quaesitis.

§ 2. Suppressio unicae domus instituti ad Sanctam Sedem pertinet, cui etiam reservatur de bonis in casu statuere.

§ 3. Supprimere domum sui iuris, de qua in can. 613, est capituli generalis, nisi constitutiones aliter ferant.

§ 4. Monialium monasterium sui iuris supprimere ad Sedem Apostolicam pertinet, servatis ad bona quod attinet praescriptis constitutionum.

Caput II
DE INSTITUTORUM REGIMINE

Art. 1
De Superioribus et consiliis

Can. 617 – Superiores suum munus adimpleant suamque potestatem exerceant ad normam iuris universalis et proprii.

Can. 618 – Superiores in spiritu servitii suam potestatem a Deo per ministerium Ecclesiae receptam exerceant. Voluntati igitur Dei in munere explendo dociles, ipsi subditos regant uti filios Dei, ac promoventes cum reverentia personae humanae illorum voluntariam oboedientiam, libenter eos audiant necnon eorum conspirationem in bonum instituti et Ecclesiae foveant, firma tamen ipsorum auctoritate decernendi et praecipiendi quae agenda sunt.

Can. 619 – Superiores suo officio sedulo incumbant et una cum sodalibus sibi commissis studeant aedificare fraternam in Christo communitatem, in qua Deus ante omnia quaeratur et diligatur. Ipsi igitur nutriant sodales frequenti verbi Dei pabulo eosque adducant ad sacrae liturgiae celebrationem. Eis exemplo sint in virtutibus colendis et in observantia legum et traditionum proprii instituti ; eorum necessitatibus personalibus convenienter subveniant, infirmos sollicite curent ac visitent, corripiant inquietos, consolentur pusillanimes, patientes sint erga omnes.

Can. 620 – Superiores maiores sunt, qui totum regunt institutum, vel eius provinciam, vel partem eidem aequiparatam, vel domum sui iuris, itemque eorum vicarii. His accedunt Abbas Primas et Superior

provide for the goods of the suppressed house, with due regard for the wills of the founders and donors or for legitimately acquired rights.

§2. The suppression of the only house of an institute pertains to the Holy See, to which is also reserved the right to determine what is to be done in that case with its goods.

§3. The suppression of an autonomous house, such as that described in can. 613, belongs to the general chapter, unless the constitutions state otherwise.

§4. The suppression of an autonomous monastery of nuns pertains to the Apostolic See, with due regard for the prescriptions of the constitutions with regard to its goods.

CHAPTER II
THE GOVERNANCE OF INSTITUTES

Art. 1
SUPERIORS AND COUNCILS

Can. 617 — Superiors are to fulfill their duty and exercise their power according to the norm of universal and proper law.

Can. 618 — Superiors are to exercise their power, received from God through the ministry of the Church, in a spirit of service. Therefore, docile to the will of God in carrying out their duty, they are to govern their subjects as children of God and, promoting their voluntary obedience with reverence for the human person, they are to listen to them willingly and foster their working together for the good of the institute and of the Church, but with the superiors' authority to decide and prescribe what must be done remaining intact.

Can. 619 — Superiors are to devote themselves to their office assiduously and, together with the members entrusted to them, they should be eager to build a community of brothers or sisters in Christ in which God is sought after and loved before all else. Therefore, they are to nourish the members frequently with the food of the word of God and lead them to the celebration of the sacred liturgy. They are to be an example to the members in cultivating virtues and in the observance of the laws and traditions of the particular institute; they are to meet the personal needs of the members in an appropriate fashion, look after solicitously and visit the sick, admonish the restless, console the faint of heart, and be patient toward all.

Can. 620 — Major superiors are those who govern a whole institute, a province of an institute, some part equivalent to a province, or an autonomous house, as well as their vicars. Comparable to these are the abbot

congregationis monasticae, qui tamen non habent omnem potestatem, quam ius universale Superioribus maioribus tribuit.

Can. 621 – Plurium domorum coniunctio quae sub eodem Superiore partem immediatam eiusdem instituti constituat, et ab auctoritate legitima canonice erecta sit, nomine venit provinciae.

Can. 622 – Supremus Moderator potestatem obtinet in omnes instituti provincias, domos et sodales, exercendam secundum ius proprium; ceteri Superiores ea gaudent intra fines sui muneris.

Can. 623 – Ut sodales ad munus Superioris valide nominentur aut eligantur, requiritur congruum tempus post professionem perpetuam vel definitivam, a iure proprio vel, si agatur de Superioribus maioribus, a constitutionibus determinandum.

Can. 624 – § 1. Superiores ad certum et conveniens temporis spatium iuxta naturam et necessitatem instituti constituantur, nisi pro supremo Moderatore et pro Superioribus domus sui iuris constitutiones aliter ferant.

§ 2. Ius proprium aptis normis provideat, ne Superiores, ad tempus definitum constituti, diutius sine intermissione in regiminis officiis versentur.

§ 3. Possunt tamen durante munere ab officio amoveri vel in aliud transferri ob causas iure proprio statutas.

Can. 625 – § 1. Supremus instituti Moderator electione canonica designetur ad normam constitutionum.

§ 2. Electionibus Superioris monasterii sui iuris, de quo in can. 615, et supremi Moderatoris instituti iuris dioecesani praeest Episcopus sedis principis.

§ 3. Ceteri Superiores ad normam constitutionum constituantur; ita tamen ut, si eligantur, confirmatione Superioris maioris competentis indigeant; si vero a Superiore nominentur, apta consultatio praecedat.

Can. 626 – Superiores in collatione officiorum et sodales in electionibus normas iuris universalis et proprii servent, abstineant a quovis abusu et acceptione personarum, et, nihil praeter Deum et bonum instituti prae oculis habentes, nominent aut eligant quos in Domino vere dignos et aptos sciant. Caveant praeterea in electionibus a suffragiorum procuratione sive directe sive indirecte, tam pro seipsis quam pro aliis.

Can. 627 – § 1. Ad normam constitutionum, Superiores proprium habeant consilium, cuius opera in munere exercendo utantur oportet.

primate and superior of a monastic congregation, who nonetheless do not have all the power which universal law grants major superiors.

Can. 621 — The grouping of several houses under the same superior which constitutes an immediate part of the institute and which has been canonically erected by the legitimate authority is called a province.

Can. 622 — The supreme moderator holds power over all provinces, houses and members of the institute, which is to be exercised according to proper law; other superiors enjoy power within the limits of their office.

Can. 623 — In order that members be validly appointed or elected to the office of superior, a suitable time is required after perpetual or definitive profession, to be determined by proper law, or if it is a question of major superiors, by the constitutions.

Can. 624 — §1. Superiors are to be constituted for a certain and appropriate amount of time according to the nature and needs of the institute, unless the constitutions state otherwise for the supreme moderator and for superiors of autonomous houses.

§2. Proper law is to provide in suitable norms that superiors constituted for a definite time do not remain too long in offices of governance without an interruption.

§3. Nevertheless they can be removed from office during their term or transferred to another office for reasons determined in proper law.

Can. 625 — §1. The supreme moderator of an institute is to be designated by canonical election according to the norm of the constitutions.

§2. The bishop of the principal seat presides at elections of the superior of an autonomous monastery, mentioned in can. 615, and of the supreme moderator of an institute of diocesan right.

§3. Other superiors are to be constituted according to the norm of the constitutions, but in such a way that if they are elected they need the confirmation of the competent major superior; if they are appointed by the superior, a suitable consultation is to precede.

Can. 626 — Superiors in the conferral of offices and members in elections are to observe the norms of universal and proper law, abstain from any abuse or partiality and name or elect those whom they know in the Lord to be truly worthy and suitable having nothing in mind but God and the good of the institute. Moreover, in elections they are to avoid any procurement of votes either directly or indirectly for themselves or for others.

Can. 627 — §1. According to the norm of the constitutions, superiors are to have their own council, whose assistance they are to use in carrying out their office.

§ 2. Praeter casus in iure universali praescriptis, ius proprium determinet casus in quibus consensus vel consilium ad valide agendum requiratur ad normam can. 127 exquirendum.

Can. 628 – § 1. Superiores qui iure proprio instituti ad hoc munus designantur, statis temporibus domos et sodales sibi commissos iuxta normas eiusdem iuris proprii visitent.

§ 2. Episcopi dioecesani ius et officium est visitare etiam quoad disciplinam religiosam :

1° monasteria sui iuris de quibus in can. 615 ;

2° singulas domos instituti iuris dioecesani in proprio territorio sitas.

§ 3. Sodales fiducialiter agant cum visitatore, cui legitime interroganti respondere tenentur secuñdum veritatem in caritate ; nemini vero fas est quoquo modo sodales ab hac obligatione avertere, aut visitationis scopum aliter impedire.

Can. 629 – In sua quisque domo Superiores commorentur, nec ab eadem discedant, nisi ad normam iuris proprii.

Can. 630 – § 1. Superiores sodalibus debitam agnoscant libertatem circa paenitentiae sacramentum et conscientiae moderamen, salva tamen instituti disciplina.

§ 2. Solliciti sint Superiores ad normam iuris proprii, ut sodalibus idonei confessarii praesto sint, apud quos frequenter confiteri possint.

§ 3. In monasteriis monialium, in domibus formationis et in communitatibus numerosioribus laicalibus habeantur confessarii ordinarii ab Ordinario loci probati, collatis consiliis cum communitate, nulla tamen facta obligatione ad illos accedendi.

§ 4. Subditorum confessiones Superiores ne audiant, nisi sponte sua sodales id petant.

§ 5. Sodales cum fiducia Superiores adeant, quibus animum suum libere ac sponte aperire possunt. Vetantur autem Superiores eos quoquo modo inducere ad conscientiae manifestationem sibi peragendam.

Art. 2

DE CAPITULIS

Can. 631 – § 1. Capitulum generale, quod supremam auctoritatem ad normam constitutionum in instituto obtinet, ita efformetur ut totum institutum repraesentans, verum signum eiusdem unitatis in caritate evadat. Eius praecipue est : patrimonium instituti, de quo in can. 578,

§2. Besides the cases prescribed in universal law, proper law is to determine cases in which consent or counsel is required in order to act validly, which must be obtained in accord with the norm of can. 127.

Can. 628 — §1. Superiors who are designated for this function by the proper law of the institute are to visit the houses and members entrusted to them at the times designated by the norms of this same proper law.

§2. It is the right and the duty of the diocesan bishop to visit even with respect to religious discipline:

1° autonomous monasteries mentioned in can. 615;

2° individual houses of an institute of diocesan right situated in his territory.

§3. Members are to deal in a trusting manner with a visitator, whose legitimate questions they are obliged to answer according to truth in love; moreover no one is permitted in any way to divert members from this obligation or otherwise to impede the scope of the visitation.

Can. 629 — All superiors are to reside in their respective houses and not absent themselves from it, unless according to the norm of proper law.

Can. 630 — §1. Superiors are to recognize the due freedom of their members concerning the sacrament of penance and the direction of conscience, with due regard however for the discipline of the institute.

§2. According to the norm of proper law superiors are to be solicitous that suitable confessors to whom they can confess frequently be available to members.

§3. In monasteries of nuns, in houses of formation and in more numerous lay communities there are to be ordinary confessors approved by the local ordinary after consultation with the community; members nevertheless have no obligation to approach them.

§4. Superiors are not to hear the confessions of their subjects unless the latter request it of their own initiative.

§5. Members are to approach superiors with trust, to whom they can express their minds freely and willingly. However, superiors are forbidden to induce their subjects in any way whatever to make a manifestation of conscience to them.

Art. 2

CHAPTERS

Can. 631 — §1. The general chapter, which holds supreme authority in the institute according to the norm of the constitutions, is to be so formed that, representing the entire institute, it should be a true sign of its unity in love. Its foremost duty is this: to protect the patrimony of the institute

tueri et accommodatam renovationem iuxta ipsum promovere, Moderatorem supremum eligere, maiora negotia tractare, necnon normas edicere, quibus omnes parere tenentur.

§ 2. Compositio et ambitus potestatis capituli definiantur in constitutionibus; ius proprium ulterius determinet ordinem servandum in celebratione capituli, praesertim quod ad electiones et rerum agendarum rationes attinet.

§ 3. Iuxta normas in iure proprio determinatas, non modo provinciae et communitates locales, sed etiam quilibet sodalis optata sua et suggestiones capitulo generali libere mittere potest.

Can. 632 – Ius proprium accurate determinet quae pertineant ad alia instituti capitula et ad alias similes coadunationes, nempe ad eorum naturam, auctoritatem, compositionem, modum procedendi et tempus celebrationis.

Can. 633 – § 1. Organa participationis vel consultationis munus sibi commissum fideliter expleant ad normam iuris universalis et proprii, eademque suo modo curam et participationem omnium sodalium pro bono totius instituti vel communitatis exprimant.

§ 2. In his mediis participationis et consultationis instituendis et adhibendis sapiens servetur discretio, atque modus eorum agendi indoli et fini instituti sit conformis.

Art. 3

De bonis temporalibus eorumque administratione

Can. 634 – § 1. Instituta, provinciae et domus, utpote personae iuridicae ipso iure, capaces sunt acquirendi, possidendi, administrandi et alienandi bona temporalia, nisi haec capacitas in constitutionibus excludatur vel coarctetur.

§ 2. Vitent tamen quamlibet speciem luxus, immoderati lucri et bonorum cumulationis.

Can. 635 – § 1. Bona temporalia institutorum religiosorum, utpote ecclesiastica, reguntur praescriptis Libri V *De bonis Ecclesiae temporalibus,* nisi aliud expresse caveatur.

§ 2. Quodlibet tamen institutum aptas normas statuat de usu et administratione bonorum, quibus paupertas sibi propria foveatur, defendatur et exprimatur.

Can. 636 – § 1. In quolibet instituto et similiter in qualibet provincia quae a Superiore maiore regitur, habeatur oeconomus, a Superiore maiore distinctus et ad normam iuris proprii constitutus, qui

mentioned in can. 578, and promote suitable renewal in accord with this patrimony, to elect the supreme moderator, to treat major business matters and to publish norms which all are bound to obey.

§2. The composition and the extent of the power of the chapter is to be defined in the constitutions; proper law is to determine further the order to be observed in the celebration of the chapter, especially regarding elections and procedures for handling various matters.

§3. According to norms determined in proper law, not only provinces and local communities but also any member at all can freely send his or her wishes and suggestions to the general chapter.

Can. 632 — Proper law is to determine clearly what pertains to other chapters of the institute and other similar gatherings, namely, regarding their nature, authority, composition, mode of procedure and time of celebration.

Can. 633 — §1. Organs of participation or consultation are to carry out faithfully the duty entrusted to them according to the norm of universal and proper law and to express in their own way the concern and participation of all members for the good of the entire institute or community.

§2. Wise discretion is to be used in establishing and using these means of participation and consultation, and their procedures are to conform to the character and purpose of the institute.

Art. 3

TEMPORAL GOODS AND THEIR ADMINISTRATION

Can. 634 — §1. Institutes, provinces and houses, insofar as they are juridic persons by the law itself, are capable of acquiring, possessing, administering and alienating temporal goods, unless this capacity has been excluded or restricted in the constitutions.

§2. Nevertheless, they are to avoid all appearance of luxury, immoderate wealth and amassing of goods.

Can. 635 — §1. The temporal goods of religious institutes, since they are ecclesiastical goods, are regulated by the prescriptions of Book V, *The Temporal Goods of the Church*, unless it is expressly stated otherwise.

§2. Nevertheless, each institute is to determine appropriate norms for the use and administration of goods so that the poverty appropriate to the institute is fostered, protected and expressed.

Can. 636 — §1. In each institute and likewise in each province which is governed by a major superior there is to be a finance officer, distinct from the major superior and constituted according to the norm of proper law, who

administrationem bonorum gerat sub directione respectivi Superioris. Etiam in communitatibus localibus instituatur, quantum fieri potest, oeconomus a Superiore locali distinctus.

§ 2. Tempore et modo iure proprio statutis, oeconomi et alii administratores auctoritati competenti peractae administrationis rationem reddant.

Can. 637 – Monasteria sui iuris, de quibus in can. 615, Ordinario loci rationem administrationis reddere debent semel in anno ; loci Ordinario insuper ius esto cognoscendi de rationibus oeconomicis domus religiosae iuris dioecesani.

Can. 638 – § 1. Ad ius proprium pertinet, intra ambitum iuris universalis, determinare actus qui finem et modum ordinariae administrationis excedant, atque ea statuere quae ad valide ponendum actum extraordinariae administrationis necessaria sunt.

§ 2. Expensas et actus iuridicos ordinariae administrationis valide, praeter Superiores, faciunt, intra fines sui muneris, officiales quoque, qui in iure proprio ad hoc designantur.

§ 3. Ad validitatem alienationis et cuiuslibet negotii in quo condicio patrimonialis personae iuridicae peior fieri potest, requiritur licentia in scripto data Superioris competentis cum consensu sui consilii. Si tamen agatur de negotio quod summam a Sancta Sede pro cuiusque regione definitam superet, itemque de rebus ex voto Ecclesiae donatis aut de rebus pretiosis artis vel historiae causa, requiritur insuper ipsius Sanctae Sedis licentia.

§ 4. Pro monasteriis sui iuris, de quibus in can. 615, et institutis iuris dioecesani accedat necesse est consensus Ordinarii loci in scriptis praestitus.

Can. 639 – § 1. Si persona iuridica debita et obligationes contraxerit etiam cum Superiorum licentia, ipsa tenetur de eisdem respondere.

§ 2. Si sodalis cum licentia Superioris contraxerit de suis bonis, ipse respondere debet, si vero de mandato Superioris negotium instituti gesserit, institutum respondere debet.

§ 3. Si contraxerit religiosus sine ulla Superiorum licentia, ipse respondere debet, non autem persona iuridica.

§ 4. Firmum tamen esto, contra eum, in cuius rem aliquid ex inito contractu versum est, semper posse actionem institui.

§ 5. Caveant Superiores religiosi ne debita contrahenda permittant, nisi certo constet ex consuetis reditibus posse debiti foenus solvi et intra tempus non nimis longum per legitimam amortizationem reddi summam capitalem.

carries out the administration of goods under the direction of the respective superior. Even in local communities there is to be a finance officer distinct from the local superior to the extent that it is possible.

§2. At the time and in the manner determined by proper law finance officers and other administrators are to render an account of their administrative actions to the competent authority.

Can. 637 — Autonomous monasteries mentioned in can. 615 must render an account of their administration once a year to the local ordinary; moreover, the local ordinary has the right to know about the financial reports of religious houses of diocesan right.

Can. 638 — §1. It is for proper law, within the scope of universal law, to determine acts which exceed the limit and manner of ordinary administration and to determine those things which are necessary to place an act of extraordinary administration validly.

§2. Besides superiors, officials who are designated for this purpose in the proper law can validly incur expenses and perform juridic acts of ordinary administration within the limits of their office.

§3. For the validity of alienation and any other business transaction in which the patrimonial condition of a juridic person can be affected adversely, there is required the written permission of the competent superior with the consent of the council. If, moreover, it concerns a business transaction which exceeds the highest amount defined for a given region by the Holy See, or items given to the Church in virtue of a vow, or items of precious art or of historical value, the permission of the Holy See is also required.

§4. For the autonomous monasteries mentioned in can. 615 and for institutes of diocesan right it is additionally necessary to have the written consent of the local ordinary.

Can. 639 — §1. A juridic person which has contracted debts and obligations even with the permission of the superior is bound to answer for them.

§2. If a member with permission of the superior has made a contract concerning personal goods, the member must answer for it, but if the business of the institute was conducted by order of the superior, the institute must answer.

§3. A religious who has made a contract without any permission of superiors must answer for it, but not the juridic person.

§4. It shall be a fixed rule, nevertheless, that an action can always be brought against one who has profited from the contract entered into.

§5. Religious superiors are to be careful that they do not permit debts to be contracted unless it is certain that the interest on the debt can be paid from ordinary income and that the capital sum can be paid off through legitimate amortization within a time that is not excessively long.

Can. 640 – Instituta, ratione habita singulorum locorum, testimonium caritatis et paupertatis quasi collectivum reddere satagant et pro viribus ex propriis bonis aliquid conferant ad Ecclesiae necessitatibus et egenorum sustentationi subveniendum.

Caput III
DE CANDIDATORUM ADMISSIONE ET DE SODALIUM INSTITUTIONE

Art. 1
De admissione in novitiatum

Can. 641 – Ius candidatos admittendi ad novitiatum pertinet ad Superiores maiores ad normam iuris proprii.

Can. 642 – Superiores vigilanti cura eos tantum admittant qui, praeter aetatem requisitam, habeant valetudinem, aptam indolem et sufficientes maturitatis qualitates ad vitam instituti propriam amplectendam; quae valetudo, indoles et maturitas comprobentur adhibitis etiam, si opus fuerit, peritis, firmo praescripto can. 220.

Can. 643 – § 1. Invalide ad novitiatum admittitur :

1° qui decimum septimum aetatis annum nondum compleverit;

2° coniux, durante matrimonio ;

3° qui sacro vinculo cum aliquo instituto vitae consecratae actu obstringitur vel in aliqua societate vitae apostolicae incorporatus est, salvo praescripto can. 684;

4° qui institutum ingreditur vi, metu gravi aut dolo inductus, vel is quem Superior eodem modo inductus recipit;

5° qui celaverit suam incorporationem in aliquo instituto vitae consecratae aut in aliqua societate vitae apostolicae.

§ 2. Ius proprium potest alia impedimenta etiam ad validitatem admissionis constituere vel condiciones apponere.

Can. 644 – Superiores ad novitiatum ne admittant clericos saeculares inconsulto proprio ipsorum Ordinario, nec aere alieno gravatos qui ad solvendum pares non sint.

Can. 645 – § 1. Candidati, antequam ad novitiatum admittantur, testimonium baptismatis et confirmationis necnon status liberi exhibere debent.

§ 2. Si agatur de admittendis clericis iisve qui in aliud institutum vitae consecratae, in societatem vitae apostolicae vel in seminarium admissi fuerint, requiritur insuper testimonium respective Ordinarii loci vel Superioris maioris instituti, vel societatis, vel rectoris seminarii.

Can. 640 — Taking into account local conditions institutes are to strive to give, as it were, collective witness of charity and poverty and are to contribute what they can of their own goods for the needs of the Church and the sustenance of the poor.

CHAPTER III
ADMISSION OF CANDIDATES AND FORMATION OF MEMBERS

Art. 1
ADMISSION TO THE NOVITIATE

Can. 641 — The right of admitting candidates to the novitiate pertains to major superiors according to the norm of proper law.

Can. 642 — Superiors are to be vigilant about admitting only those who, besides the required age, have health, suitable character and sufficient qualities of maturity to embrace the particular life of the institute; this health, character, and maturity are to be attested to, if necessary by using experts, with due regard for the prescription of can. 220.

Can. 643 — §1. One is invalidly admitted to the novitiate:

1° who has not yet completed the seventeenth year of age;

2° who is a spouse, during a marriage;

3° who is presently held by a sacred bond with any institute of consecrated life or who is incorporated in any society of apostolic life, with due regard for the prescription of can. 684;

4° who enters the institute as a result of force, grave fear or fraud, or whom the superior receives induced in the same way;

5° who has concealed his or her incorporation in any institute of consecrated life or society of apostolic life.

§2. Proper law can establish other impediments to admission, even for validity, or can add other conditions.

Can. 644 — Superiors are not to admit to the novitiate secular clerics if their local ordinary has not been consulted or those who, burdened by debts, cannot repay them.

Can. 645 — §1. Before they are admitted to the novitiate, candidates must show proof of baptism, confirmation and free status.

§2. If it is a question of admitting clerics or those who have been admitted to another institute of consecrated life, a society of apostolic life or a seminary, there is further required the testimony of the local ordinary or major superior of the institute or society or of the rector of the seminary respectively.

§ 3. Ius proprium exigere potest alia testimonia de requisita idoneitate candidatorum et de immunitate ab impedimentis.

§ 4. Superiores alias quoque informationes, etiam sub secreto, petere possunt, si ipsis necessarium visum fuerit.

Art. 2

DE NOVITIATU ET NOVITIORUM INSTITUTIONE

Can. 646 – Novitiatus, quo vita in instituto incipitur, ad hoc ordinatur, ut novitii vocationem divinam, et quidem instituti propriam,
melius agnoscant, vivendi modum instituti experiantur eiusque spiritu
mentem et cor informent, atque ipsorum propositum et idoneitas comprobentur.

Can. 647 – § 1. Domus novitiatus erectio, translatio et suppressio
fiant per decretum scripto datum supremi Moderatoris instituti de
consensu sui consilii.

§ 2. Novitiatus, ut validus sit, peragi debet in domo ad hoc rite
designata. In casibus particularibus et ad modum exceptionis, ex concessione Moderatoris supremi de consensu sui consilii, candidatus novitiatum peragere potest in alia instituti domo, sub moderamine alicuius
probati religiosi, qui vices magistri novitiorum gerat.

§ 3. Superior maior permittere potest ut novitiorum coetus, per
certa temporis spatia, in alia instituti domo, a se designata, commoretur.

Can. 648 – § 1. Novitiatus, ut validus sit, duodecim menses in ipsa
novitiatus communitate peragendos complecti debet, firmo praescripto
can. 647, § 3.

§ 2. Ad novitiorum institutionem perficiendam, constitutiones,
praeter tempus de quo in § 1, unum vel plura exercitationis apostolicae tempora extra novitiatus communitatem peragenda statuere
possunt.

§ 3. Novitiatus ultra biennium ne extendatur.

Can. 649 – § 1. Salvis praescriptis can. 647, § 3 et can. 648, § 2,
absentia a domo novitiatus quae tres menses, sive continuos sive inter-
missos, superet, novitiatum invalidum reddit. Absentia quae quindecim dies superet, suppleri debet.

§ 2. De venia competentis Superioris maioris, prima professio anticipari potest, non ultra quindecim dies.

Can. 650 – § 1. Scopus novitiatus exigit ut novitii sub directione

§3. Proper law can demand other testimonies about the requisite suitability of candidates and their freedom from impediments.

§4. If it appears necessary superiors can ask for other information, even with the obligation of secrecy.

Art. 2

THE NOVITIATE AND FORMATION OF NOVICES

Can. 646 — The novitiate, by which life in the institute begins, is ordered to this, that the novices better recognize their divine vocation and one which is, moreover, proper to the institute, that they experience the institute's manner of living, that they be formed in mind and heart by its spirit, and that their intention and suitability be tested.

Can. 647 — §1. The erection, transfer and suppression of a novitiate house are to take place through a written decree of the supreme moderator of the institute with the consent of his or her council.

§2. In order to be valid a novitiate must be made in a house properly designated for this purpose. In particular cases and as an exception, by concession of the supreme moderator with the consent of the council, a candidate can make the novitiate in another house of the institute under the guidance of an approved religious who assumes the role of director of novices.

§3. A major superior can permit a group of novices to live for a stated period of time in another house of the institute, designated by the same superior.

Can. 648 — §1. In order that the novitiate be valid it must include twelve months spent in the community of the novitiate itself, with due regard for the prescription of can. 647, §3.

§2. To complete the formation of the novices, in addition to the time mentioned in §1, the constitutions can determine one or several periods of apostolic exercises to be spent outside the novitiate community.

§3. The novitiate is not to extend beyond two years.

Can. 649 — §1. With due regard for the prescriptions of cann. 647, §3, and 648, §2, absence from the novitiate house which lasts more than three months, either continuous or interrupted, renders the novitiate invalid. An absence of more than fifteen days must be made up.

§2. With the permission of the competent major superior first profession can be anticipated, but not by more than fifteen days.

Can. 650 — §1. The scope of the novitiate demands that the novices be

magistri efformentur iuxta rationem institutionis iure proprio definiendam.

§ 2. Regimen novitiorum, sub auctoritate Superiorum maiorum,
uni magistro reservatur.

Can. 651 – § 1. Novitiorum magister sit sodalis instituti qui vota
perpetua professus sit et legitime designatus.

§ 2. Magistro, si opus fuerit, cooperatores dari possunt, qui ei subsint quoad moderamen novitiatus et institutionis rationem.

§ 3. Novitiorum institutioni praeficiantur sodales sedulo praeparati qui, aliis oneribus non impediti, munus suum fructuose et stabili
modo absolvere possint.

Can. 652 – § 1. Magistri eiusque cooperatorum est novitiorum vocationem discernere et comprobare, eosque gradatim ad vitam perfectionis instituti propriam rite ducendam efformare.

§ 2. Novitii ad virtutes humanas et christianas excolendas addu-
cantur; per orationem et sui abnegationem in pleniorem perfectionis
viam introducantur; ad mysterium salutis contemplandum et sacras
Scripturas legendas et meditandas instruantur; ad Dei cultum in
sacra liturgia excolendum praeparentur; rationem addiscant vitam
ducendi Deo hominibusque in Christo per consilia evangelica consecratam; de instituti indole et spiritu, fine et disciplina, historia et vita edoceantur atque amore erga Ecclesiam eiusque sacros Pastores imbuantur.

§ 3. Novitii, propriae responsabilitatis conscii, ita cum magistro
suo active collaborent ut gratiae divinae vocationis fideliter respondeant.

§ 4. Curent instituti sodales, ut in opere institutionis novitiorum
pro parte sua cooperentur vitae exemplo et oratione.

§ 5. Tempus novitiatus, de quo in .can. 648, § 1, in opus formationis proprie impendatur, ideoque novitii ne occupentur in studiis et
muniis, quae hanc formationem non directe inserviunt.

Can. 653 – § 1. Novitius institutum libere deserere potest; competens autem instituti auctoritas potest eum dimittere.

§ 2. Exacto novitiatu, si idoneus iudicetur, novitius ad professionem temporariam admittatur, secus dimittatur; si dubium supersit de
eius idoneitate, potest probationis tempus a Superiore maiore ad normam iuris proprii, non tamen ultra sex menses prorogari.

formed under the guidance of a director according to the program of training to be defined by the proper law.

§2. The governance of novices is reserved to one director under the authority of the major superiors.

Can. 651 — §1. The director of novices is to be a member of the institute who has professed perpetual vows and is legitimately designated.

§2. If there is a need, assistants can be given to the director to whom they are subject regarding the governance of the novitiate and the program of training.

§3. Members who have been carefully prepared and who, not impeded by other duties, can carry out this duty fruitfully and in a stable manner are to be in charge of the training of novices.

Can. 652 — §1. It is for the director and assistants to discern and test the vocation of the novices and to form them gradually to lead correctly the life of perfection proper to the institute.

§2. The novices are to be led to cultivate human and Christian virtues; they are to be introduced to a fuller way of perfection by prayer and self-denial; they are to be instructed to contemplate the mystery of salvation and to read and meditate on the Sacred Scriptures; they are to be prepared to cultivate the worship of God in the sacred liturgy; they are to be trained in a way of life consecrated by the evangelical counsels to God and humankind in Christ; they are to be educated about the character and spirit, purpose and discipline, history and life of their institute; and they are to be imbued with a love for the Church and its sacred pastors.

§3. Conscious of their own responsibility, the novices are to collaborate actively with their director so that they may faithfully respond to the grace of a divine vocation.

§4. Members of the institute are to take care that on their part they cooperate in the work of training novices by the example of their life and by prayer.

§5. The time of novitiate mentioned in can. 648, §1, is to be employed properly in the work of formation and therefore the novices are not to be occupied with studies and duties which do not directly serve this formation.

Can. 653 — §1. A novice can freely leave an institute; moreover the competent authority of the institute can dismiss a novice.

§2. When the novitiate is completed, a novice, if judged suitable, is to be admitted to temporary profession; otherwise the novice is to be dismissed. If there is a doubt about the novice's suitability, the time of probation can be extended by the major superior according to the norm of proper law, but not more than six months.

Art. 3

DE PROFESSIONE RELIGIOSA

Can. 654 – Professione religiosa sodales tria consilia evangelica observanda voto publico assumunt, Deo per Ecclesiae ministerium consecrantur et instituto incorporantur cum iuribus et officiis iure definitis.

Can. 655 – Professio temporaria ad tempus iure proprio definitum emittatur, quod neque triennio brevius neque sexennio longius sit.

Can. 656 – Ad validitatem professionis temporariae requiritur ut:

1° qui eam emissurus est, decimum saltem octavum aetatis annum compleverit;

2° novitiatus valide peractus sit;

3° habeatur admissio a competenti Superiore cum voto sui consilii ad normam iuris libere facta;

4° sit expressa et absque vi, metu gravi aut dolo emissa;

5° a legitimo Superiore per se vel per alium recipiatur.

Can. 657 – § 1. Expleto tempore ad quod professio emissa fuerit, religiosus, qui sponte petat et idoneus iudicetur, ad renovationem professionis vel ad professionem perpetuam admittatur, secus discedat.

§ 2. Si opportunum vero videatur, periodus professionis temporariae a competenti Superiore, iuxta ius proprium, prorogari potest, ita tamen ut totum tempus, quo sodalis votis temporariis adstringitur, non superet novennium.

§ 3. Professio perpetua anticipari potest ex iusta causa, non tamen ultra trimestrem.

Can. 658 – Praeter condiciones de quibus in can. 656, nn. 3, 4 et 5 aliasque iure proprio appositas, ad validitatem professionis perpetuae requiritur:

1° vigesimus primus saltem aetatis annus completus;

2° praevia professio temporaria saltem per triennium, salvo praescripto can. 657, § 3.

Art. 4

DE RELIGIOSORUM INSTITUTIONE

Can. 659 – § 1. In singulis institutis, post primam professionem

Art 3

RELIGIOUS PROFESSION

Can. 654 — By religious profession members assume by public vow the observance of the three evangelical counsels, are consecrated to God through the ministry of the Church, and are incorporated into the institute with rights and duties defined by law.

Can. 655 — Temporary profession is made for the time defined in proper law, which may not be less than three years and no longer than six.

Can. 656 — For the validity of temporary profession, it is required that:

1° the person who is about to make the profession shall have completed at least the eighteenth year of age;

2° the novitiate has been validly completed;

3° admission has been freely given by the competent superior with the vote of the council in accord with the norm of law;

4° the profession be expressed and made without force, grave fear or fraud;

5° the profession be received by the legitimate superior personally or through another.

Can. 657 — §1. When the time for which the profession has been made has elapsed the religious who freely requests it and is judged suitable is to be admitted to a renewal of profession or to perpetual profession; otherwise the religious is to leave.

§2. If it seems opportune the period of temporary profession can be extended by the competent superior, according to proper law, but in such a way that the entire time in which the member is bound by temporary vows does not exceed nine years.

§3. Perpetual profession can be anticipated for a just cause, but not by more than three months.

Can. 658 — Besides the conditions mentioned in can. 656, 3°, 4° and 5° and others attached by proper law, for the validity of perpetual profession the following are required:

1° the completion of at least the twenty-first year of age;

2° previous temporary profession for at least three years, with due regard for the prescription of can. 657, §3.

Art. 4

THE FORMATION OF RELIGIOUS

Can. 659 — §1. In individual institutes after first profession the forma-

omnium sodalium institutio perficiatur ad vitam instituti propriam plenius ducendam et ad eius missionem aptius prosequendam.

§ 2. Quapropter ius proprium rationem definire debet huius institutionis eiusdemque durationis, attentis Ecclesiae necessitatibus atque hominum temporumque condicionibus, prout a fine et indole instituti exigitur.

§ 3. Institutio sodalium, qui ad sacros ordines suscipiendos praeparantur, iure universali regitur et propria instituti ratione studiorum.

Can. 660 – § 1. Institutio sit systematica, captui sodalium accommodata, spiritualis et apostolica, doctrinalis simul ac practica, titulis etiam congruentibus, tam ecclesiasticis quam civilibus, pro opportunitate obtentis.

§ 2. Perdurante tempore huius institutionis, sodalibus officia et opera ne committantur, quae eam impediant.

Can. 661 – Per totam vitam religiosi formationem suam spiritualem, doctrinalem et practicam sedulo prosequantur; Superiores autem eis adiumenta et tempus ad hoc procurent.

Caput IV
DE INSTITUTORUM EORUMQUE SODALIUM OBLIGATIONIBUS ET IURIBUS

Can. 662 – Religiosi sequelam Christi in Evangelio propositam et in constitutionibus proprii instituti expressam tamquam supremam vitae regulam habeant.

Can. 663 – § 1. Rerum divinarum contemplatio et assidua cum Deo in oratione unio omnium religiosorum primum et praecipuum sit officium.

§ 2. Sodales cotidie pro viribus Sacrificium eucharisticum participent, sanctissimum Corpus Christi recipiant et ipsum Dominum in Sacramento praesentem adorent.

§ 3. Lectioni sacrae Scripturae et orationi mentali vacent, iuxta iuris proprii praescripta liturgiam horarum digne celebrent, firma pro clericis obligatione de qua in can. 276, § 2, n. 3, et alia pietatis exercitia peragant.

§ 4. Speciali cultu Virginem Deiparam, omnis vitae consecratae exemplum et tutamen, etiam per mariale rosarium prosequantur.

§ 5. Annua sacri recessus tempora fideliter servent.

Can. 664 – In animi erga Deum conversionem insistant religiosi,

tion of all members is to be continued so that they may lead more fully the proper life of the institute and carry out its mission more suitably.

§2. Therefore, proper law must define the program of this formation and its duration, keeping in mind the needs of the Church and the circumstances of human persons and times to the extent this is required by the purpose and character of the institute.

§3. The formation of members who are preparing to receive holy orders is regulated by universal law and by the program of studies proper to the institute.

Can. 660 — §1. The formation is to be systematic, adapted to the capacity of the members, spiritual and apostolic, doctrinal and at the same time practical, and when it seems opportune, leading to appropriate degrees both ecclesiastical and civil.

§2. During the time of this formation duties and jobs which would impede the formation are not to be assigned to members.

Can. 661 — Throughout their entire life religious are to continue carefully their own spiritual, doctrinal, and practical formation, and superiors are to provide them with the resources and time to do this.

CHAPTER IV

THE OBLIGATIONS AND RIGHTS OF INSTITUTES AND THEIR MEMBERS

Can. 662 — Religious are to have as their highest rule of life the following of Christ as proposed in the gospel and expressed in the constitutions of their institute.

Can. 663 — §1. Contemplation of divine things and assiduous union with God in prayer is to be the first and foremost duty of all religious.

§2. Members are to participate in the Eucharistic Sacrifice daily if possible, receive the Most Sacred Body of Christ and adore this same Lord present in the Sacrament.

§3. They should apply themselves to the reading of Sacred Scripture and to mental prayer; they are to celebrate the liturgy of the hours worthily according to the prescriptions of proper law, with due regard for the obligation of clerics in can. 276, §2, 3°, and they are to perform other exercises of piety.

§4. They are to cultivate a special devotion to the Virgin Mother of God, model and protector of all consecrated life, including the Marian rosary.

§5. They are faithfully to observe an annual period of spiritual retreat.

Can. 664 — Religious are to apply themselves to conversion of heart to

conscientiam etiam cotidie examinent et paenitentiae sacramentum frequenter accedant.

Can. 665 – § 1. Religiosi in propria domo religiosa habitent vitam communem servantes, nec ab ea discedant nisi de licentia sui Superioris. Si autem agatur de diuturna a domo absentia, Superior maior, de consensu sui consilii atque iusta de causa, sodali concedere potest ut extra domum instituti degere possit, non tamen ultra annum, nisi causa infirmitatis curandae, ratione studiorum aut apostolatus exercendi nomine instituti.

§ 2. Sodalis, qui e domo religiosa illegitime abest cum animo sese subducendi a potestate Superiorum, sollicite ab eisdem quaeratur et adiuvetur ut redeat et in sua vocatione perseveret.

Can. 666 – In usu mediorum communicationis servetur necessaria discretio atque vitentur quae sunt vocationi propriae nociva et castitati personae consecratae periculosa.

Can. 667 – § 1. In omnibus domibus clausura indoli et missioni instituti accommodata servetur secundum determinationes proprii iuris, aliqua parte domus religiosae solis sodalibus semper reservata.

§ 2. Strictior disciplina clausurae in monasteriis ad vitam contemplativam ordinatis servanda est.

§ 3. Monasteria monialium, quae integre ad vitam contemplativam ordinantur, clausuram *papalem,* iuxta normas scilicet ab Apostolica Sede datas, observare debent. Cetera monialium monasteria clausuram propriae indoli accommodatam et in constitutionibus definitam servent.

§ 4. Episcopus dioecesanus facultatem habet ingrediendi, iusta de causa, intra clausuram monasteriorum monialium, quae sita sunt in sua dioecesi, atque permittendi, gravi de causa et assentiente Antistita, ut alii in clausuram admittantur, ac moniales ex ipsa egrediantur ad tempus vere necessarium.

Can. 668 – § 1. Sodales ante primam professionem suorum bonorum administrationem cedant cui maluerint et, nisi constitutiones aliud ferant, de eorum usu et usufructu libere disponant. Testamentum autem, quod etiam in iure civili sit validum, saltem ante professionem perpetuam condant.

§ 2. Ad has dispositiones iusta de causa mutandas et ad quemlibet actum ponendum circa bona temporalia, licentia Superioris competentis ad normam iuris proprii indigent.

§ 3. Quidquid religiosus propria acquirit industria vel ratione instituti, acquirit instituto. Quae ei ratione pensionis, subventionis vel assecurationis quoquo modo obveniunt, instituto acquiruntur, nisi aliud

God, examine their conscience even daily, and frequently approach the sacrament of penance.

Can. 665 — §1. Observing a common life, religious are to live in their own religious house and not be absent from it without the permission of their superior. However, if it is a question of a lengthy absence from the house the major superior for a just cause and with the consent of the council can permit the member to live outside a house of the institute, but not for more than a year, except for the purpose of caring for poor health, for the purpose of studies or of undertaking an apostolate in the name of the institute.

§2. Members unlawfully absent from the religious house with the intention of withdrawing from the power of their superiors are to be solicitously sought after by them and aided to return and persevere in their vocation.

Can. 666 — Necessary discretion is to be observed in the use of media of communication, and whatever is harmful to one's vocation and dangerous to the chastity of a consecrated person is to be avoided.

Can. 667 — §1. In all houses cloister adapted to the character and mission of the institute is to be observed according to the determinations of proper law, with some part of the religious house always being reserved to the members alone.

§2. A stricter discipline of cloister is to be observed in monasteries ordered to the contemplative life.

§3. Monasteries of nuns which are totally ordered to the contemplative life must observe *papal* cloister, namely according to norms given by the Apostolic See. Other monasteries of nuns are to observe cloister adapted to their own character and defined in the constitutions.

§4. For a just cause the diocesan bishop has the faculty of entering the cloister of monasteries of nuns which are in his diocese, and, for a grave cause and with the consent of the superior, of permitting others to enter the cloister and nuns to leave the cloister for a truly necessary period of time.

Can. 668 — §1. Members are to cede the administration of their goods to whomever they prefer before first profession, and unless the constitutions state otherwise, they are freely to make disposition for their use and their revenues. Moreover, they are to draw up a will, which is also valid in civil law, at least before perpetual profession.

§2. In order to change these dispositions for a just cause and to place any act whatsoever in matters of temporal goods they need the permission of the superior who is competent according to the norm of proper law.

§3. Whatever a religious acquires through personal work or by reason of the institute is acquired for the institute. Unless it is otherwise stated in proper law those things which accrue to a religious by way of pension,

iure proprio statuatur.

§ 4. Qui ex instituti natura plene bonis suis renuntiare debet. illam renuntiationem, forma, quantum fieri potest, etiam iure civili valida, ante professionem perpetuam faciat a die emissae professionis valituram. Idem faciat professus a votis perpetuis, qui ad normam iuris proprii bonis suis pro parte vel totaliter de licentia supremi Moderatoris renuntiare velit.

§ 5. Professus, qui ob instituti naturam plene bonis suis renuntiaverit, capacitatem acquirendi et possidendi amittit, ideoque actus voto paupertatis contrarios invalide ponit. Quae autem ei post renuntiationem obveniunt, instituto cedunt ad normam iuris proprii.

Can. 669 – § 1. Religiosi habitum instituti deferant, ad normam iuris proprii confectum, in signum suae consecrationis et in testimonium paupertatis.

§ 2. Religiosi clerici instituti, quod proprium non habet habitum, vestem clericalem ad normam can. 284 assumant.

Can. 670 – Institutum debet sodalibus suppeditare omnia quae ad normam constitutionum necessaria sunt ad suae vocationis finem assequendum.

Can. 671 – Religiosus munera et officia extra proprium institutum ne recipiat absque licentia legitimi Superioris.

Can. 672 – Religiosi adstringuntur praescriptis cann. 277, 285, 286, 287 et 289, et religiosi clerici insuper praescriptis can. 279 § 2; in institutis laicalibus iuris pontificii, licentia de qua in can. 285, § 4, concedi potest a proprio Superiore maiore.

CAPUT V

DE APOSTOLATU INSTITUTORUM

Can. 673 – Omnium religiosorum apostolatus primum in eorum vitae consecratae testimonio consistit, quod oratione et paenitentia fovere tenentur.

Can. 674 – Instituta, quae integre ad contemplationem ordinantur, in Corpore Christi mystico. praeclaram semper partem obtinent: Deo enim eximium laudis sacrificium offerunt, populum Dei uberrimis sanctitatis fructibus collustrant eumque exemplo movent necnon arcana fecunditate apostolica dilatant. Qua de causa, quantumvis actuosi apostolatus urgeat necessitas, sodales horum institutorum advocari nequeunt ut in variis ministeriis pastoralibus operam adiutricem praestent.

subsidy or insurance in any way whatever are acquired for the institute.

§4. Those who must renounce their goods completely because of the nature of the institute are to make a renunciation before perpetual profession in a form which, if possible, is also valid in civil law and takes effect from the day of profession. Religious in perpetual vows who wish to renounce their goods either in part or totally according to the norm of proper law and with permission of the supreme moderator are to do the same thing.

§5. Professed religious who have fully renounced all their goods because of the nature of the institute lose the capacity of acquiring and possessing, and therefore invalidly place acts contrary to the vow of poverty. Moreover, those things which accrue to them after the act of renunciation belong to the institute, according to the norm of proper law.

Can. 669 — §1. Religious are to wear the habit of the institute made according to the norm of proper law as a sign of their consecration and as a testimony of poverty.

§2. Clerical religious of an institute which does not have its own habit are to wear clerical dress according to the norm of can. 284.

Can. 670 — An institute must furnish for its members all those things which are necessary according to the norm of the constitutions for achieving the purpose of their vocation.

Can. 671 — A religious is not to accept duties and offices outside the institute without the permission of the legitimate superior.

Can. 672 — Religious are bound by the prescriptions of cann. 277, 285, 286, 287, and 289, and, moreover, religious clerics are bound by the prescriptions of can. 279, §2; in lay institutes of pontifical right, the permission mentioned in can. 285, §4 can be granted by the proper major superior.

Chapter V

THE APOSTOLATE OF INSTITUTES

Can. 673 — The apostolate of all religious consists first in their witness of a consecrated life which they are bound to foster by prayer and penance.

Can. 674 — Institutes which are wholly ordered to contemplation always retain a distinguished position in the mystical Body of Christ: for they offer an extraordinary sacrifice of praise to God, they illuminate the people of God with the richest fruits of their sanctity, they move it by their example, and extend it through their hidden apostolic fruitfulness. For this reason, however much the needs of the active apostolate demand it, members of these institutes cannot be summoned to aid in various pastoral ministries.

Can. 675 – § 1. In institutis operibus apostolatus deditis, apostolica actio ad ipsam eorundem naturam pertinet. Proinde, tota vita sodalium spiritu apostolico imbuatur, tota vero actio apostolica spiritu religioso informetur.

§ 2. Actio apostolica ex intima cum Deo unione semper procedat eandemque confirmet et foveat.

§ 3. Actio apostolica, nomine et mandato Ecclesiae exercenda, in eius communione peragatur.

Can. 676 – Laicalia instituta, tum virorum tum mulierum, per misericordiae opera spiritualia et corporalia munus pastorale Ecclesiae participant hominibusque diversissima praestant servitia; quare in suae vocationis gratia fideliter permaneant.

Can. 677 – § 1. Superiores et sodales missionem et opera instituti propria fideliter retineant; ea tamen, attentis temporum et locorum necessitatibus, prudenter accommodent, novis etiam et opportunis mediis adhibitis.

§ 2. Instituta autem, si quas habeant associationes christifidelium sibi coniunctas, speciali cura adiuvent, ut genuino spiritu suae familiae imbuantur.

Can. 678 – § 1. Religiosi subsunt potestati Episcoporum, quos devoto obsequio ac reverentia prosequi tenentur, in iis quae curam animarum, exercitium publicum cultus divini et alia apostolatus opera respiciunt.

§ 2. In apostolatu externo exercendo religiosi propriis quoque Superioribus subsunt et disciplinae instituti fideles permanere debent; quam obligationem ipsi Episcopi, si casus ferat, urgere ne omittant.

§ 3. In operibus apostolatus religiosorum ordinandis Episcopi dioecesani et Superiores religiosi collatis consiliis procedant oportet.

Can. 679 – Episcopus dioecesanus, urgente gravissima causa, sodali instituti religiosi prohibere potest quominus in dioecesi commoretur, si eius Superior maior monitus prospicere neglexerit, re tamen ad Sanctam Sedem statim delata.

Can. 680 – Inter varia instituta, et etiam inter eadem et clerum saecularem, ordinata foveatur cooperatio necnon, sub moderamine Episcopi dioecesani, omnium operum et actionum apostolicarum coordinatio, salvis indole, fine singulorum institutorum et legibus fundationis.

Can. 681 – § 1. Opera quae ab Episcopo dioecesano committuntur

Can. 675 — §1. In institutes dedicated to works of the apostolate, apostolic action pertains to their very nature. Hence, the whole life of members is to be imbued with an apostolic spirit, indeed the whole apostolic action is to be informed by a religious spirit.

§2. Apostolic action is always to proceed from an intimate union with God, and it is to confirm and foster that union.

§3. Apostolic action, to be exercised in the name and by the mandate of the Church, is to be carried out in its communion.

Can. 676 — Lay institutes, whether of men or women, share in the pastoral office of the Church through spiritual and corporal works of mercy and offer the most diverse services to men and women; therefore they are to persevere faithfully in the grace of their vocation.

Can. 677 — §1. Superiors and members are faithfully to retain the mission and works proper to the institute; nevertheless they are to accommodate these prudently to the needs of times and places, including the use of new and appropriate means.

§2. Moreover, if they have associations of the Christian faithful related to them, institutes are to assist them with special care so that they are imbued with a genuine spirit of their family.

Can. 678 — §1. Religious are subject to the authority of bishops, whom they are obliged to follow with devoted humility and respect, in those matters which involve the care of souls, the public exercise of divine worship and other works of the apostolate.

§2. In exercising an external apostolate, religious are also subject to their own superiors and must remain faithful to the discipline of the institute, which obligation bishops themselves should not fail to insist upon in cases which warrant it.

§3. In organizing the works of the apostolate of religious, it is necessary that diocesan bishops and religious superiors proceed after consultation with each other.

Can. 679 — When a most serious reason demands it a diocesan bishop can prohibit a member of a religious institute from living in his diocese; if the major superior of that religious has been advised and neglects to act, the matter is to be referred to the Holy See immediately.

Can. 680 — Among the various institutes and also between them and the secular clergy, orderly cooperation as well as a coordination of all apostolic works and activities, under the direction of the diocesan bishop, with due regard for the character and purpose of individual institutes and the laws of the foundation, is to be promoted.

Can. 681 — §1. Works which are entrusted to religious by the diocesan

religiosis, eiusdem Episcopi auctoritati et directioni subsunt, firmo iure Superiorum religiosorum ad normam can. 678, §§ 2 et 3.

§ 2. In his casibus ineatur conventio scripta inter Episcopum dioecesanum et competentem instituti Superiorem, qua, inter alia, expresse et accurate definiantur quae ad opus explendum, ad sodales eidem addicendos et ad res oeconomicas spectent.

Can. 682 – § 1. Si de officio ecclesiastico in dioecesi alicui sodali religioso conferendo agatur, ab Episcopo dioecesano religiosus nominatur, praesentante vel saltem assentiente competenti Superiore.

§ 2. Religiosus ab officio commisso amoveri potest ad nutum sive auctoritatis committentis, monito Superiore religioso, sive Superioris, monito committente, non requisito alterius consensu.

Can. 683 – § 1. Ecclesias et oratoria, quibus christifideles habitualiter accedunt, scholas aliaque opera religionis vel caritatis sive spiritualis sive temporalis religiosis commissa, Episcopus dioecesanus visitare potest, sive per se sive per alium, tempore visitationis pastoralis et etiam in casu necessitatis; non vero scholas, quae exclusive pateant propriis instituti alumnis.

§ 2. Quod si forte abusus deprehenderit, frustra Superiore religioso monito, propria auctoritate ipse per se providere potest.

Caput VI
DE SEPARATIONE SODALIUM AB INSTITUTO

Art. 1
De transitu ad aliud institutum

Can. 684 – § 1. Sodalis a votis perpetuis nequit a proprio ad aliud institutum religiosum transire, nisi ex concessione supremi Moderatoris utriusque instituti et de consensu sui cuiusque consilii.

§ 2. Sodalis, post peractam probationem quae ad tres saltem annos protrahenda est, ad professionem perpetuam in novo instituto admitti potest. Si autem sodalis hanc professionem emittere renuat vel ad eam emittendam a competentibus Superioribus non admittatur, ad pristinum institutum redeat, nisi indultum saecularizationis obtinuerit.

§ 3. Ut religiosus a monasterio sui iuris ad aliud eiusdem instituti vel foederationis aut confoederationis transire possit, requiritur et sufficit consensus Superioris maioris utriusque monasterii et capituli

bishop are subject to the authority and direction of this same bishop, with due regard for the right of religious superiors according to the norm of can. 678, §§2 and 3.

§2. In these cases a written agreement is to be drawn up between the diocesan bishop and the competent superior of the institute, which, among other things, expressly and accurately defines what pertains to the work to be carried out, the members to be devoted to this, and economic matters.

Can. 682 — §1. If there is a question of conferring an ecclesiastical office in the diocese upon a certain religious, the religious is appointed by the diocesan bishop, following presentation by or at least assent of the competent superior.

§2. A religious can be removed from the office entrusted to him or her either at the discretion of the authority who entrusted it, after having notified the religious superior, or at the discretion of the superior, having notified the authority; and neither requires the consent of the other.

Can. 683 — §1. At the time of the pastoral visitation and also in case of necessity the diocesan bishop, either in person or through someone else, can make a visitation of the churches of religious or of their oratories, which the Christian faithful habitually attend, schools and other works of religion or charity, whether temporal or spiritual, entrusted to religious; however he may not visit schools which are open only to students belonging to the institute.

§2. But if by chance he discovers abuses and has advised the religious superior in vain, he himself can provide for it on his own authority.

CHAPTER VI

SEPARATION OF MEMBERS FROM THE INSTITUTE

Art. 1

TRANSFER TO ANOTHER INSTITUTE

Can. 684 — §1. A member in perpetual vows cannot transfer from one religious institute to another without the permission of the supreme moderator of each institute given with the consent of their respective councils.

§2. After completing a probationary period which is to last at least three years, the member can be admitted to perpetual profession in the new institute. However, if the member refuses to make this profession or is not admitted to making it by competent superiors, the member is to return to the former institute, unless an indult of secularization has been obtained.

§3. For a religious to transfer from an autonomous monastery to another of the same institute or federation or confederation, it is required and is sufficient to have the consent of the major superior of both monasteries and

monasterii recipientis, salvis aliis requisitis iure proprio statutis; nova professio non requiritur.

§ 4. Ius proprium determinet tempus et modum probationis, quae professioni sodalis in novo instituto praemittenda est.

§ 5. Ut ad institutum saeculare aut ad societatem vitae apostolicae vel ex illis ad institutum religiosum fiat transitus, requiritur licentia Sanctae Sedis, cuius mandatis standum est.

Can. 685 – § 1. Usque ad emissionem professionis in novo instituto, manentibus votis, iura et obligationes quae sodalis in priore instituto habebat, suspenduntur; ab incepta tamen probatione, ipse ad observantiam iuris proprii novi instituti tenetur.

§ 2. Per professionem in novo instituto sodalis eidem incorporatur, cessantibus votis, iuribus et obligationibus praecedentibus.

Art. 2
De egressu ab instituto

Can. 686 – § 1. Supremus Moderator, de consensu sui consilii, sodali a votis perpetuis professo, gravi de causa concedere potest indultum exclaustrationis, non tamen ultra triennium, praevio consensu Ordinarii loci in quo commorari debet, si agitur de clerico. Indultum prorogare vel illud ultra triennium concedere Sanctae Sedi vel, si de institutis iuris dioecesani agitur, Episcopo dioecesano reservatur.

§ 2. Pro monialibus indultum exclaustrationis concedere unius Apostolicae Sedis est.

§ 3. Petente supremo Moderatore de consensu sui consilii, exclaustratio imponi potest a Sancta Sede pro sodale instituti iuris pontificii vel ab Episcopo dioecesano pro sodale instituti iuris dioecesani, ob graves causas, servata aequitate et caritate.

Can. 687 – Sodalis exclaustratus exoneratus habetur ab obligationibus, quae cum nova suae vitae condicione componi nequeunt, itemque sub dependentia et cura manet suorum Superiorum et etiam Ordinarii loci, praesertim si de clerico agitur. Habitum instituti deferre potest, nisi aliud in indulto statuatur. Voce tamen activa et passiva caret.

Can. 688 – § 1. Qui expleto professionis tempore ab instituto egredi voluerit, illud derelinquere potest.

§ 2. Qui perdurante professione temporaria, gravi de causa, petit ut institutum derelinquat, indultum discedendi consequi potest in instituto iuris pontificii a supremo Moderatore de consensu sui consilii; in institutis autem iuris dioecesani et in monasteriis de quibus in

the chapter of the receiving monastery, with due regard for other requirements determined in proper law; a new profession is not required.

§4. Proper law is to determine the time and mode of probation which is to precede the profession of a member in the new institute.

§5. For one to transfer to a secular institute or a society of apostolic life or from them to a religious institute permission of the Holy See is required, and its mandates are to be observed.

Can. 685 — §1. Until the religious makes profession in the new institute, while the vows remain, the rights and obligations which the member had in the former institute are suspended; however, the religious is obligated to observe the proper law of the new institute from the beginning of the probationary period.

§2. By profession in the new institute the member is incorporated into it, while the preceding vows, rights and obligations cease.

Art. 2

DEPARTURE FROM THE INSTITUTE

Can. 686 — §1. With the consent of the council the supreme moderator for a grave reason can grant an indult of exclaustration to a member professed of perpetual vows, but not for more than three years, and with the prior consent of the local ordinary where he must remain if this concerns a cleric. Extending the indult or granting it for more than three years is reserved to the Holy See or, if there is question of institutes of diocesan right, to the diocesan bishop.

§2. It belongs to the Apostolic See alone to grant an indult of exclaustration for nuns.

§3. If a supreme moderator with the consent of the council petitions, exclaustration can be imposed by the Holy See on a member of an institute of pontifical right or by a diocesan bishop on a member of an institute of diocesan right for grave reasons, with equity and charity being observed.

Can. 687 — Exclaustrated members are free from obligations which are incompatible with their new condition of life and at the same time remain dependent on and subject to the care of their superiors and also the local ordinary, especially if the member is a cleric. The members may wear the habit of the institute unless it is determined otherwise in the indult. However, they lack active and passive voice.

Can. 688 — §1. Whoever wishes to leave an institute when the time of profession has expired can depart from it.

§2. During the time of temporary profession whoever asks to leave the institute for a grave reason can be granted an indult to leave by the supreme moderator in an institute of pontifical right with the consent of the council;

can. 615 indultum, ut valeat, confirmari debet ab Episcopo domus assignationis.

Can. 689 – § 1. Sodalis, expleta professione temporaria, si iustae causae affuerint, a competenti Superiore maiore, audito suo consilio, a subsequenti professione emittenda excludi potest.

§ 2. Infirmitas physica vel psychica, etiam post professionem contracta, quae, de iudicio peritorum, sodalem, de quo in § 1, reddit ineptum ad vitam in instituto ducendam, causam constituit eum non admittendi ad professionem renovandam vel ad perpetuam emittendam, nisi ob neglegentiam instituti vel ob laborem in instituto peractum infirmitas contracta fuerit.

§ 3. Si vero religiosus, perdurantibus votis temporariis, amens evaserit, etsi novam professionem emittere non valeat, ab instituto tamen dimitti non potest.

Can. 690 – § 1. Qui, expleto novitiatu vel post professionem, legitime ab instituto egressus fuerit, a Moderatore supremo de consensu sui consilii rursus admitti potest sine onere repetendi novitiatum; eiusdem autem Moderatoris erit determinare congruam probationem praeviam professioni temporariae et tempus votorum ante professionem perpetuam praemittendum, ad normam cann. 655 et 657.

§ 2. Eadem facultate gaudet Superior monasterii sui iuris cum consensu sui consilii.

Can. 691 – § 1. Professus a votis perpetuis indultum discedendi ab instituto ne petat, nisi ob gravissimas causas coram Domino perpensas; petitionem suam deferat supremo instituti Moderatori, qui eam una cum voto suo suique consilii auctoritati competenti transmittat.

§ 2. Huiusmodi indultum in institutis iuris pontificii Sedi Apostolicae reservatur; in institutis vero iuris dioecesani, id etiam Episcopus dioecesis, in qua domus assignationis sita est, concedere potest.

Can. 692 – Indultum discedendi legitime concessum et sodali notificatum, nisi in actu notificationis ab ipso sodale reiectum fuerit, ipso iure secumfert dispensationem a votis necnon ab omnibus obligationibus ex professione ortis.

Can. 693 – Si sodalis sit clericus, indultum non conceditur priusquam inveniat Episcopum qui eum in dioecesi incardinet vel saltem ad experimentum recipiat. Si ad experimentum recipiatur, transacto quinquennio, ipso iure dioecesi incardinatur, nisi Episcopus eum recusaverit.

in institutes of diocesan right and in monasteries mentioned in can. 615, the indult, in order to be valid, must be confirmed by the bishop of the house of assignment.

Can. 689 — §1. If just causes are present, when temporary profession has expired a member can be excluded from making a subsequent profession by the competent major superior after listening to the council.

§2. Even if it is contracted after profession, physical or psychic illness which in the judgment of experts renders the member mentioned in §1 unsuited to lead the life of the institute, constitutes a reason for not admitting such a person to a renewal of profession or to making perpetual profession, unless the infirmity had been incurred through the institute's negligence or through work performed in the institute.

§3. A religious, however, who becomes insane during temporary vows, even though unable to make a new profession, cannot be dismissed from the institute.

Can. 690 — §1. A religious who after completing the novitiate or after profession has left the institute legitimately, can be readmitted by the supreme moderator with the consent of the council without the burden of repeating the novitiate; it is up to the same moderator to determine a suitable probationary period before temporary profession and a time in such vows prior to perpetual profession according to the norm of cann. 655 and 657.

§2. With the consent of the council, the superior of an autonomous monastery enjoys this same faculty.

Can. 691 — §1. One who is professed in perpetual vows is not to seek an indult to leave the institute without very grave reasons weighed before the Lord; such a petition is to be presented to the supreme moderator of the institute, who is to transmit it to the competent authority with a personal opinion and that of the council.

§2. An indult of this kind in institutes of pontifical right is reserved to the Apostolic See; but in institutes of diocesan right the diocesan bishop of the house of assignment can also grant it.

Can. 692 — Unless it has been rejected by the member in the act of notification, an indult legitimately granted and made known to the member brings with it, by the law itself, a dispensation from vows and from all obligations arising from profession.

Can. 693 — If the member is a cleric, the indult is not granted before he finds a bishop who will incardinate him into a diocese or at least receive him experimentally. If he is received experimentally, he is incardinated into the diocese by the law itself after five years have passed, unless the bishop has refused him.

Art. 3

DE DIMISSIONE SODALIUM

Can. 694 – § 1. Ipso facto dimissus ab instituto habendus est sodalis qui :

1° a fide catholica notorie defecerit ;

2° matrimonium contraxerit vel, etiam civiliter tantum, attentaverit.

§ 2. His in casibus Superior maior cum suo consilio, nulla mora
interposita, collectis probationibus, declarationem facti emittat, ut
iuridice constet de dimissione.

Can. 695 – § 1. Sodalis dimitti debet ob delicta de quibus in
cann. 1397, 1398 et 1395, nisi in delictis, de quibus in can. 1395, § 2,
Superior censeat dimissionem non esse omnino necessariam et emendationi sodalis atque restitutioni iustitiae et reparationi scandali satis
alio modo consuli posse.

§ 2. Hisce in casibus, Superior maior, collectis probationibus circa
facta et imputabilitatem, sodali dimittendo accusationem atque probationes significet, data eidem facultate sese defendendi. Acta omnia
a Superiore maiore et a notario subscripta, una cum responsionibus
sodalis scripto redactis et ab ipso sodale subscriptis, supremo Moderatori transmittantur.

Can. 696 – § 1. Sodalis dimitti etiam potest ob alias causas, dummodo sint graves, externae, imputabiles et iuridice comprobatae, uti
sunt : habitualis neglectus obligationum vitae consecratae ; iteratae
violationes sacrorum vinculorum ; pertinax inoboedientia legitimis praescriptis Superiorum in materia gravi ; grave scandalum ex culpabili
modo agendi sodalis ortum ; pertinax sustentatio vel diffusio doctrina-
rum ab Ecclesiae magisterio damnatarum ; publica adhaesio ideolo-
giis materialismo vel atheismo infectis ; illegitima absentia, de qua in
can. 665, § 2, per semestre protracta ; aliae causae similis gravitatis
iure proprio instituti forte determinatae.

§ 2. Ad dimissionem sodalis a votis temporariis, etiam causae minoris gravitatis in iure proprio statutae sufficiunt.

Can. 697 – In casibus de quibus in can. 696, si Superior maior,
audito suo consilio, censuerit processum dimissionis esse inchoandum :

1° probationes colligat vel compleat ;

2° sodalem scripto vel coram duobus testibus moneat cum explicita comminatione subsecuturae dimissionis nisi resipiscat, clare significata causa dimissionis et data sodali plena facultate sese defendendi ;
quod si monitio incassum cedat, ad alteram monitionem, spatio saltem

Art. 3

Dismissal of Members

Can. 694 — §1. A member is to be held to be ipso facto dismissed from the institute who:

1° has notoriously abandoned the Catholic faith;

2° has contracted marriage or has attempted it, even only civilly.

§2. In these instances the major superior with the council without any delay and after having collected proofs should issue a declaration of the fact so that the dismissal is established juridically.

Can. 695 — §1. A member must be dismissed for the offenses in cann. 1397, 1398 and 1395, unless in the delicts mentioned in can. 1395, §2, the superior judges that dismissal is not entirely necessary and that the correction of the member and restitution of justice and reparation of scandal can be sufficiently assured in some other way.

[handwritten margin note: homicide / kidnap / abortion / concubinage]

§2. In these cases the major superior, having collected proofs about the facts and imputability, is to make known the accusation and the proofs to the member who is about to be dismissed, giving the member the opportunity of self-defense. All the acts, signed by the major superior and a notary, along with the written and signed responses of the member, are to be transmitted to the supreme moderator.

Can. 696 — §1. A member can also be dismissed for other causes, provided that they are grave, external, imputable and juridically proven, such as: habitual neglect of the obligations of consecrated life; repeated violations of the sacred bonds; pertinacious disobedience to lawful prescriptions of superiors in a serious matter; grave scandal arising from the culpable behavior of the member; pertinacious upholding or spreading of doctrines condemned by the magisterium of the Church; public adherence to ideologies infected by materialism or atheism; unlawful absence mentioned in can. 665, §2 lasting six months; other causes of similar seriousness which may be determined by the proper law of the institute.

§2. Even causes of lesser seriousness determined in proper law suffice for the dismissal of a member in temporary vows.

Can. 697 — In the cases mentioned in can. 696, if the major superior, after having heard the council, believes the process of dismissal is to be begun:

1° the major superior is to collect or complete proofs;

2° the major superior is to warn the member in writing or before two witnesses with an explicit threat of subsequent dismissal unless the member reforms, the cause of the dismissal is to be clearly indicated and the member is to be given the full opportunity of self-defense; but if the warning is in vain

quindecim dierum interposito, procedat;

    3° si haec quoque monitio incassum ceciderit et Superior maior cum suo consilio censuerit de incorrigibilitate satis constare et defensiones sodalis insufficientes esse, post quindecim dies ab ultima monitione frustra elapsos, acta omnia ab ipso Superiore maiore et a notario subscripta una cum responsionibus sodalis ab ipso sodale subscriptis supremo Moderatori transmittat.

    Can. 698 – In omnibus casibus, de quibus in cann. 695 et 696, firmum semper manet ius sodalis cum supremo Moderatore communicandi et illi directe suas defensiones exhibendi.

    Can. 699 – § 1. Supremus Moderator cum suo consilio, quod ad validitatem saltem quattuor membris constare debet, collegialiter procedat ad probationes, argumenta et defensiones accurate perpendenda, et si per secretam suffragationem id decisum fuerit, decretum dimissionis ferat, expressis ad validitatem saltem summarie motivis in iure et in facto.

    § 2. In monasteriis sui iuris, de quibus in can. 615, dimissionem decernere pertinet ad Episcopum dioecesanum, cui Superior acta a consilio suo recognita submittat.

    Can. 700 – Decretum dimissionis vim non habet, nisi a Sancta Sede confirmatum fuerit, cui decretum et acta omnia transmittenda sunt; si agatur de instituto iuris dioecesani, confirmatio spectat ad Episcopum dioecesis ubi sita est domus, cui religiosus adscriptus est. Decretum vero, ut valeat, indicare debet ius, quo dimissus gaudet, recurrendi intra decem dies a recepta notificatione ad auctoritatem competentem. Recursus effectum habet suspensivum.

    Can. 701 – Legitima dimissione ipso facto cessant vota necnon iura et obligationes ex professione promanantia. Si tamen sodalis sit clericus, sacros ordines exercere nequit, donec Episcopum inveniat qui eum post congruam probationem in dioecesi, ad normam can. 693, recipiat vel saltem exercitium sacrorum ordinum permittat.

    Can. 702 – § 1. Qui ex instituto religioso legitime egrediantur vel ab eo legitime dimissi fuerint, nihil ab eodem repetere possunt ob quamlibet operam in eo praestitam.

    § 2. Institutum tamen aequitatem et evangelicam caritatem servet erga sodalem, qui ab eo separatur.

    Can. 703 – In casu gravis scandali exterioris vel gravissimi nocumenti instituto imminentis, sodalis statim a Superiore maiore vel, si periculum sit in mora, a Superiore locali cum consensu sui consilii

the superior is to proceed to a second warning, after an intervening time of at least fifteen days;

3° if this warning also has been in vain and the major superior with the council believes that there is sufficient proof of incorrigibility and that the defenses of the member are insufficient, and fifteen days have elapsed since the last warning without any effect, the major superior is to transmit to the supreme moderator all acts, signed by the major superior and a notary, along with the signed response of the member.

Can. 698 — In all cases mentioned in cann. 695 and 696, the right of a member to communicate with and offer a defense directly to the supreme moderator always remains intact.

Can. 699 — §1. With the council, which must have at least four members for validity, the supreme moderator is to proceed collegially to the careful weighing of the proofs, arguments and defenses; if it has been so decided by a secret ballot, the supreme moderator is to issue the decree of dismissal, with the motives in law and in fact expressed at least in summary fashion for validity.

§2. In autonomous monasteries mentioned in can. 615 the decision on dismissal pertains to the diocesan bishop, to whom the superior is to submit the acts examined by the council.

Can. 700 — A decree of dismissal does not take effect unless it has been confirmed by the Holy See to whom the decree and all the acts are to be transmitted; if it is a question of an institute of diocesan right, the confirmation belongs to the bishop of the diocese where the house to which the religious is assigned is situated. The decree, for validity, must indicate the right which the dismissed religious enjoys to have recourse to competent authority within ten days from receiving the notification. The recourse has a suspensive effect.

Can. 701 — Vows, rights and obligations derived from profession cease ipso facto by legitimate dismissal. However, if the member is a cleric, he cannot exercise sacred orders until he finds a bishop who receives him after a suitable probationary period in the diocese according to can. 693 or at least allows him to exercise sacred orders.

Can. 702 — §1. Those who have legitimately left a religious institute or have been legitimately dismissed from one can request nothing from it for any work done in it.

§2. The institute however is to observe equity and evangelical charity toward the member who is separated from it.

Can. 703 — In the case of serious exterior scandal or very grave imminent harm to the institute a member can be immediately expelled from the religious house by the major superior, or, if there is a danger in delay, by the

e domo religiosa eici potest. Superior maior, si opus sit, dimissionis processum ad normam iuris instituendum curet, aut rem Sedi Apostolicae deferat.

Can. 704 – De sodalibus, qui ab instituto sunt quoquo modo separati, fiat mentio in relatione Sedi Apostolicae mittenda, de qua in can. 592, § 1.

Caput VII

DE RELIGIOSIS AD EPISCOPATUM EVECTIS

Can. 705 – Religiosus ad episcopatum evectus instituti sui sodalis remanet, sed vi voti oboedientiae uni Romano Pontifici obnoxius est, et obligationibus non adstringitur, quas ipse prudenter iudicet cum sua condicione componi non posse.

Can. 706 – Religiosus de quo supra :

1° si per professionem dominium bonorum amiserit, bonorum quae ipsi obveniant habet usum, usumfructum et administrationem ; proprietatem vero Episcopus dioecesanus aliique, de quibus in can. 381, § 2, acquirunt Ecclesiae particulari ; ceteri, instituto vel Sanctae Sedi, prout institutum capax est possidendi vel minus ;

2° si per professionem dominium bonorum non amiserit, bonorum, quae habebat, recuperat usum, usumfructum et administrationem ; quae postea ipsi obveniant, sibi plene acquirit ;

3° in utroque autem casu de bonis, quae ipsi obveniant non intuitu personae, disponere debet secundum offerentium voluntatem.

Can. 707 – § 1. Religiosus Episcopus emeritus habitationis sedem sibi eligere potest etiam extra domos sui instituti, nisi aliud a Sede Apostolica provisum fuerit.

§ 2. Quoad eius congruam et dignam sustentationem, si cuidam dioecesi inserviverit, servetur can. 402, § 2, nisi institutum proprium talem sustentationem providere voluerit ; secus Sedes Apostolica aliter provideat.

Caput VIII

DE CONFERENTIIS SUPERIORUM MAIORUM

Can. 708 – Superiores maiores utiliter in conferentiis seu consiliis consociari possunt ut, collatis viribus, allaborent sive ad finem singulorum institutorum plenius assequendum, salvis semper eorum autonomia, indole proprioque spiritu, sive ad communia negotia pertractanda, sive ad congruam coordinationem et cooperationem cum Episcoporum conferentiis et etiam cum singulis Episcopis instaurandam.

local superior with the consent of the council. If it is necessary the major superior should see that the process of dismissal is begun according to the norm of law or refer the matter to the Apostolic See.

Can. 704 — The report to be sent to the Apostolic See referred to in canon 592, §1 is to mention members separated from the institute in any way whatsoever.

CHAPTER VII

RELIGIOUS RAISED TO THE EPISCOPATE

Can. 705 — A religious raised to the episcopate remains a member of his own institute but is subject to the Roman Pontiff alone in virtue of his vow of obedience and is not bound by obligations which he himself prudently judges cannot be reconciled with his position.

Can. 706 — As regards the above-mentioned religious:

1° if through profession he has lost the ownership of goods, he has the use of goods which come to him as well as their revenues and administration; however the diocesan bishop and those mentioned in can. 381, §2 acquire the ownership for the particular church; all others, for the institute or the Holy See depending on whether the institute is capable of ownership or not;

2° if through profession he has not lost the ownership of goods, he regains the use, revenues and administration of the goods which he had; he fully acquires for himself those which come to him afterwards;

3° in either case, however, he must distribute goods coming to him according to the will of the donors when they do not come to him for personal reasons.

Can. 707 — §1. A retired religious bishop may choose a place to live for himself even outside the houses of his institute unless something else has been provided by the Apostolic See.

§2. If he has served a certain diocese, suitable and worthy sustenance is to be his according to can. 402, §2 unless his own institute wishes to provide that sustenance; otherwise the Apostolic See is to provide.

CHAPTER VIII

CONFERENCES OF MAJOR SUPERIORS

Can. 708 — Major superiors can usefully associate in conferences or councils so that joining forces they can work toward the achievement of the purpose of their individual institutes more fully, always with due regard for their autonomy, character and particular spirit, transact common business and foster suitable coordination and cooperation with conferences of bishops and also with individual bishops.

Can. 709 – Conferentiae Superiorum maiorum sua habeant statuta a Sancta Sede approbata, a qua unice, etiam in personam iuridicam, erigi possunt et sub cuius supremo moderamine manent.

TITULUS III
DE INSTITUTIS SAECULARIBUS

Can. 710 – Institutum saeculare est institutum vitae consecratae, in quo christifideles in saeculo viventes ad caritatis perfectionem contendunt atque ad mundi sanctificationem praesertim ab intus conferre student.

Can. 711 – Instituti saecularis sodalis vi suae consecrationis propriam in populo Dei canonicam condicionem, sive laicalem sive clericalem, non mutat, servatis iuris praescriptis quae instituta vitae consecratae respiciunt.

Can. 712 – Firmis praescriptis cann. 598-601, constitutiones statuant vincula sacra, quibus evangelica consilia in instituto assumuntur, et definiant obligationes quas eadem vincula inducunt, servata tamen in vitae ratione semper propria instituti saecularitate.

Can. 713 – § 1. Sodales horum institutorum propriam consecrationem in actuositate apostolica exprimunt et exercent, iidemque, ad instar fermenti, omnia spiritu evangelico imbuere satagunt ad robur et incrementum Corporis Christi.

§ 2. Sodales laici, munus Ecclesiae evangelizandi, in saeculo et ex saeculo, participant sive per testimonium vitae christianae et fidelitatis erga suam consecrationem, sive per adiutricem quam praebent operam ad ordinandas secundum Deum res temporales atque ad mundum virtute Evangelii informandum. Suam etiam cooperationem, iuxta propriam vitae rationem saecularem, in communitatis ecclesialis servitium offerunt.

§ 3. Sodales clerici per vitae consecratae testimonium, praesertim in presbyterio, peculiari caritate apostolica confratribus adiutorio sunt, et in populo Dei mundi sanctificationem suo sacro ministerio perficiunt.

Can. 714 – Sodales vitam in ordinariis mundi condicionibus vel soli, vel in sua quisque familia, vel in vitae fraternae coetu, ad normam constitutionum ducant.

Can. 715 – § 1. Sodales clerici in dioecesi incardinati ab Episcopo dioecesano dependent, salvis iis quae vitam consecratam in proprio instituto respiciunt.

Can. 709 — Conferences of major superiors are to have their own statutes approved by the Holy See, by which alone they can be erected, even as a juridic person, and under whose supreme governance they remain.

TITLE III
SECULAR INSTITUTES

Can. 710 — A secular institute is an institute of consecrated life in which the Christian faithful living in the world strive for the perfection of charity and work for the sanctification of the world especially from within.

Can. 711 — The consecration of a member of a secular institute does not alter the member's proper canonical condition among the people of God, whether lay or clerical, with due regard for the prescriptions of law affecting institutes of consecrated life.

Can. 712 — With due regard for the prescriptions of cann. 598-601, the constitutions are to determine the sacred bonds by which the evangelical counsels are taken in the institute and are to define the obligations flowing from these same bonds, while always preserving, however, in its way of life the distinctive secularity of the institute.

Can. 713 — §1. The members of these institutes express and exercise their own consecration in their apostolic activity and like a leaven they strive to imbue all things with the spirit of the gospel for the strengthening and growth of the Body of Christ.

§2. Lay members share in the Church's evangelizing task in the world and of the world through their witness of a Christian life and fidelity toward their consecration, and through their efforts to order temporal things according to God and inform the world by the power of the gospel. Also, they cooperate in serving the ecclesial community, according to their particular secular way of life.

§3. Clerical members through the witness of their consecrated life, especially in the presbyterate, help their brothers by their special apostolic charity and in their sacred ministry among the people of God they bring about the sanctification of the world.

Can. 714 — Members are to lead their life according to the norm of the constitutions, in the ordinary conditions of the world, either alone or each in their respective families, or in a group of brothers or sisters.

Can. 715 — §1. Clerical members incardinated in a diocese depend on the diocesan bishop, with due regard for those things which pertain to consecrated life in their particular institute.

§ 2. Qui vero ad normam can. 266, § 3 instituto incardinantur, si ad opera instituti propria vel ad regimen instituti destinentur, ad instar religiosorum ab Episcopo dependent.

Can. 716 – § 1. Sodales omnes vitam instituti, secundum ius proprium, actuose participent.

§ 2. Eiusdem instituti sodales communionem inter se servent, sollicite curantes spiritus unitatem et genuinam fraternitatem.

Can. 717 – § 1. Constitutiones proprium regiminis modum praescribant, tempus quo Moderatores suo officio fungantur et modum quo iidem designantur, definiant.

§ 2. Nemo in Moderatorem supremum designetur, qui non sit definitive incorporatus.

§ 3. Qui regimini instituti praepositi sunt, curent ut eiusdem spiritus unitas servetur et actuosa sodalium participatio promoveatur.

Can. 718 – Administratio bonorum instituti, quae paupertatem evangelicam exprimere et fovere debet, regitur normis Libri V *De bonis Ecclesiae temporalibus* necnon iure proprio instituti. Item ius proprium definiat obligationes praesertim oeconomicas instituti erga sodales, qui pro ipso operam impendunt.

Can. 719 – § 1. Sodales, ut vocationi suae fideliter respondeant eorumque actio apostolica ex ipsa unione cum Christo procedat, sedulo orationi vacent, sacrarum Scripturarum lectioni apto modo incumbant, annua recessus tempora servent atque alia spiritualia exercitia iuxta ius proprium peragant.

§ 2. Eucharistiae celebratio, quantum fieri potest cotidiana, sit totius eorum vitae consecratae fons et robur.

§ 3. Libere ad sacramentum paenitentiae accedant, quod frequenter recipiant.

§ 4. Necessarium conscientiae moderamen libere obtineant atque huius generis consilia a suis etiam Moderatoribus, si velint, requirant.

Can. 720 – Ius admittendi in institutum, vel ad probationem vel ad sacra vincula sive temporaria sive perpetua aut definitiva assumenda, ad Moderatores maiores cum suo consilio ad normam constitutionum pertinet.

Can. 721 – § 1. Invalide admittitur ad initialem probationem :

1° qui maiorem aetatem nondum attigerit ;

2° qui sacro vinculo in aliquo instituto vitae consecratae actu obstringitur, aut in societate vitae apostolicae incorporatus est ;

§2. If those who are incardinated in an institute according to the norm of can. 266, §3, are appointed to particular works of the institute or to the governance of the institute, they depend on the bishop in a way comparable to religious.

Can. 716 — §1. All members are to share actively in the life of the institute according to proper law.

§2. Members of the same institute are to maintain communion among themselves, carefully fostering unity of spirit and genuine relationship as brothers or sisters.

Can. 717 — §1. The constitutions are to prescribe a particular manner of governance and define the time during which moderators hold their office and the way in which they are chosen.

§2. No one is to be chosen supreme moderator who is not definitively incorporated.

§3. Those who are put in charge of the governance of the institute are to take care that the unity of its spirit is kept and that active participation of the members is encouraged.

Can. 718 — The administration of the goods of the institute, which should express and foster evangelical poverty, is ruled by the norms of Book V, *The Temporal Goods of the Church*, and by the proper law of the institute. Likewise the proper law is to define especially the financial obligations of the institute toward members who carry on work for it.

Can. 719 — §1. In order that members may respond faithfully to their vocation and that their apostolic action may proceed from their union with Christ they are to be diligent in prayer, concentrate in a fitting manner on the reading of Sacred Scripture, make an annual retreat and carry out other spiritual exercises according to proper law.

§2. The celebration of the Eucharist, daily if possible, is to be the source and strength of the whole of their consecrated life.

§3. They are freely to approach the sacrament of penance, which they should receive frequently.

§4. They are freely to obtain necessary guidance of conscience and should seek counsel of this kind even from their moderators, if they wish.

Can. 720 — The right of admission into the institute, whether for probation or for the assumption of sacred bonds, whether temporary or perpetual or definitive, pertains to the major moderators with their council according to the norm of the constitutions.

Can. 721 — §1. One is invalidly admitted to the initial probation:

1° who has not yet reached the age of majority;

2° who is still bound by a sacred bond in some institute of consecrated life or who is incorporated in a society of apostolic life;

3° coniux durante matrimonio.

§ 2. Constitutiones possunt alia admissionis impedimenta etiam ad validitatem statuere vel condiciones apponere.

§ 3. Praeterea, ut quis recipiatur, habeat oportet maturitatem, quae ad vitam instituti propriam recte ducendam est necessaria.

Can. 722 – § 1. Probatio initialis eo ordinetur, ut candidati suam divinam vocationem et quidem instituti propriam aptius cognoscant iidemque in spiritu et vivendi modo instituti exerceantur.

§ 2. Ad vitam secundum evangelica consilia ducendam candidati rite instituantur atque ad eandem integre in apostolatum convertendam edoceantur, eas adhibentes evangelizationis formas, quae instituti fini, spiritui et indoli magis respondeant.

§ 3. Huius probationis modus et tempus ante sacra vincula in instituto primum suscipienda, biennio non brevius, in constitutionibus definiantur.

Can. 723 – § 1. Elapso probationis initialis tempore, candidatus qui idoneus iudicetur, tria consilia evangelica, sacro vinculo firmata, assumat vel ab instituto discedat.

§ 2. Quae prima incorporatio, quinquennio non brevior, ad normam constitutionum temporaria sit.

§ 3. Huius incorporationis tempore elapso, sodalis, qui idoneus iudicetur, admittatur ad incorporationem perpetuam vel definitivam, vinculis scilicet temporariis semper renovandis.

§ 4. Incorporatio definitiva, quoad certos effectus iuridicos in constitutionibus statuendos, perpetuae aequiparatur.

Can. 724 – § 1. Institutio post vincula sacra primum assumpta iugiter secundum constitutiones est protrahenda.

§ 2. Sodales in .ebus divinis et humanis pari gressu instituantur; de continua vero eorum spirituali formatione seriam habeant curam instituti Moderatores.

Can. 725 – Institutum sibi associare potest, aliquo vinculo in constitutionibus determinato, alios christifideles, qui ad evangelicam perfectionem secundum spiritum instituti contendant eiusdemque missionem participent.

Can. 726 – § 1. Elapso tempore incorporationis temporariae, sodalis institutum libere derelinquere valet vel a sacrorum vinculorum renovatione iusta de causa a Moderatore maiore, audito suo consilio, excludi potest.

§ 2. Sodalis temporariae incorporationis id sponte petens, indul-

3° who is married while the marriage lasts.

§2. The constitutions can establish other impediments, even for the validity of admission, or place certain conditions.

§3. Moreover, for one to be received it is necessary to have the maturity to lead the life proper to the institute.

Can. 722 — §1. The initial probation is to be so arranged that the candidates may understand more fittingly their divine vocation and indeed the vocation proper to the institute and may be trained in the spirit and way of life of the institute.

§2. The candidates are to be properly formed in living according to the evangelical counsels and taught to translate this life completely into the apostolate, using those forms of spreading the gospel which better respond to the purpose, spirit and character of the institute.

§3. The manner and time of this probation before first undertaking sacred bonds in the institute are to be defined in the constitutions; yet it is to be no less than two years.

Can. 723 — §1. After the time of the initial probation has passed, the candidate who is judged worthy is either to take on the three evangelical counsels strengthened by a sacred bond or to depart from the institute.

§2. This first incorporation, no shorter than five years, is to be temporary according to the norm of the constitutions.

§3. When the time of this incorporation has passed, the member who is judged worthy is to be admitted to perpetual or definitive incorporation, that is, with temporary bonds always to be renewed.

§4. Definitive incorporation is equivalent to perpetual incorporation as far as certain juridic effects are concerned, to be determined in the constitutions.

Can. 724 — §1. After the sacred bonds are first taken formation is to be continued according to the constitutions.

§2. Members are to be formed in divine and human matters equally; the moderators of the institute are to take seriously the continuing spiritual formation of members.

Can. 725 — The institute can associate to itself, by some bond determined in the constitutions, other members of the Christian faithful who strive toward evangelical perfection according to the spirit of the institute and share its mission.

Can. 726 — §1. When the time of temporary incorporation has elapsed, the member can leave the institute freely or be excluded from renewal of the sacred bonds for a just cause by the major moderator after hearing the council.

§2. For a serious reason the temporarily incorporated member can freely

tum discedendi a supremo Moderatore de consensu sui consilii gravi de causa obtinere valet.

Can. 727 – § 1. Sodalis perpetue incorporatus, qui institutum derelinquere velit, indultum discedendi, re coram Domino serio perpensa, a Sede Apostolica per Moderatorem supremum petat, si institutum est iuris pontificii; secus etiam ab Episcopo dioecesano, prout in constitutionibus definitur.

§ 2. Si agatur de clerico instituto incardinato, servetur praescriptum can. 693.

Can. 728 – Indulto discedendi legitime concesso, cessant omnia vincula necnon iura et obligationes ab incorporatione promananti.

Can. 729 – Sodalis ab instituto dimittitur ad normam cann. 694 et 695; constitutiones praeterea determinent alias causas dimissionis, dummodo sint proportionate graves, externae, imputabiles et iuridice comprobatae, atque modus procedendi servetur in cann. 697-700 statutus. Dimisso applicatur praescriptum can. 701.

Can. 730 – Ut sodalis instituti saecularis ad aliud institutum saeculare transeat, serventur praescripta cann. 684, §§ 1, 2, 4 et 685; ut vero ad aliud vel ex alio instituto vitae consecratae fiat transitus, licentia requiritur Sedis Apostolicae, cuius mandatis standum est.

SECTIO II
DE SOCIETATIBUS VITAE APOSTOLICAE

Can. 731 – § 1. Institutis vitae consecratae accedunt societates vitae apostolicae, quarum sodales, sine votis religiosis, finem apostolicum societatis proprium prosequuntur et, vitam fraternam in communi ducentes, secundum propriam vitae rationem, per observantiam constitutionum ad perfectionem caritatis tendunt.

§ 2. Inter has sunt societates in quibus sodales, aliquo vinculo constitutionibus definito, consilia evangelica assumunt.

Can. 732 – Quae in cann. 578-597, et 606 statuuntur, societatibus vitae apostolicae applicantur, salva tamen uniuscuiusque societatis natura; societatibus vero, de quibus in can. 731, § 2, etiam cann. 598-602 applicantur.

Can. 733 – § 1. Domus erigitur et communitas localis constituitur a competenti auctoritate societatis, praevio consensu Episcopi dioecesani in scriptis dato, qui etiam consuli debet, cum agitur de eius suppressione.

petition and obtain from the supreme moderator with the consent of the council an indult to leave.

Can. 727 — §1. The perpetually incorporated member who wishes to leave the institute, having thought seriously about this before God, may seek an indult to leave from the Apostolic See through the supreme moderator if it is an institute of pontifical right; otherwise from the diocesan bishop as it is defined in the constitutions.

§2. If it is a question of a cleric incardinated in the institute, the prescription of can. 693 is to be observed.

Can. 728 — When the indult to leave has been legitimately granted, all bonds, rights and obligations emanating from incorporation cease.

Can. 729 — A member is dismissed from the institute according to the norm established in cann. 694 and 695; furthermore, the constitutions may determine other causes of dismissal, provided they are proportionately serious, external, imputable, and juridically proven and the procedure determined in cann. 697-700 shall be observed. The prescription of can. 701 applies to the dismissed member.

Can. 730 — In order that a member of a secular institute may transfer to another secular institute, the prescriptions of cann. 684, §§1, 2, and 4, and 685 are to be observed. In order that a transfer be made to another or from another institute of consecrated life the permission of the Apostolic See is required and its mandates are to be obeyed.

SECTION II
SOCIETIES OF APOSTOLIC LIFE

Can. 731 — §1. Comparable to institutes of consecrated life are societies of apostolic life whose members without religious vows pursue the particular apostolic purpose of the society, and leading a life as brothers or sisters in common according to a particular manner of life, strive for the perfection of charity through the observance of the constitutions.

§2. Among these there are societies in which the members embrace the evangelical counsels by some bond defined in the constitutions.

Can. 732 — Whatever is determined in cann. 578-597 and 606 is applicable to societies of apostolic life, with due regard for the nature of each society; in addition, cann. 598-602 are applicable to the societies mentioned in can. 731, §2.

Can. 733 — §1. A house is erected and a local community is established by the competent authority of the society with the prior written consent of the diocesan bishop, who must also be consulted for its suppression.

§ 2. Consensus ad erigendam domum secumfert ius habendi saltem oratorium, in quo sanctissima Eucharistia celebretur et asservetur.

Can. 734 – Regimen societatis a constitutionibus determinatur, servatis, iuxta naturam uniuscuiusque societatis, cann. 617-633.

Can. 735 – § 1. Sodalium admissio, probatio, incorporatio et institutio determinantur iure proprio cuiusque societatis.

§ 2. Ad admissionem in societatem quod attinet, serventur condiciones in cann. 642-645 statutae.

§ 3. Ius proprium determinare debet rationem probationis et institutionis fini et indoli societatis accommodatam, praesertim doctrinalem, spiritualem et apostolicam, ita ut sodales vocationem divinam agnoscentes ad missionem et vitam societatis apte praeparentur.

Can. 736 – § 1. In societatibus clericalibus clerici ipsi societati incardinantur, nisi aliter ferant constitutiones.

§ 2. In iis quae ad rationem studiorum et ad ordines suscipiendos pertinent, serventur normae clericorum saecularium, firma tamen § 1.

Can. 737 – Incorporatio secumfert ex parte sodalium obligationes et iura in constitutionibus definita, ex parte autem societatis, curam sodales ad finem propriae vocationis perducendi, iuxta constitutiones.

Can. 738 – § 1. Sodales omnes subsunt propriis Moderatoribus ad normam constitutionum in iis quae vitam internam et disciplinam societatis respiciunt.

§ 2. Subsunt quoque Episcopo dioecesano in iis quae cultum publicum, curam animarum aliaque apostolatus opera respiciunt, attentis cann. 679-683.

§ 3. Relationes sodalis dioecesi incardinati cum Episcopo proprio constitutionibus vel particularibus conventionibus definiuntur.

Can. 739 – Sodales, praeter obligationes quibus, uti sodales, obnoxii sunt secundum constitutiones, communibus obligationibus clericorum adstringuntur, nisi ex natura rei vel ex contextu sermonis aliud constet.

Can. 740 – Sodales habitare debent in domo vel in communitate legitime constituta et servare vitam communem, ad normam iuris proprii, quo quidem etiam absentiae a domo vel communitate reguntur.

Can. 741 – § 1. Societates et, nisi aliter ferant constitutiones, earum partes et domus, personae sunt iuridicae et, qua tales, capaces bona temporalia acquirendi, possidendi, administrandi et alienandi, ad normam praescriptorum Libri V *De bonis Ecclesiae temporalibus,* cann. 636,

§2. Consent to erect a house entails the right of having at least an oratory in which the Most Holy Eucharist is celebrated and reserved.

Can. 734 — The governance of a society is determined by the constitutions, with due regard for cann. 617-633, according to the nature of each society.

Can. 735 — §1. The admission, probation, incorporation and training of members are determined by the proper law of each society.

§2. In respect to admission into the society, the conditions established in cann. 642-645 are to be observed.

§3. Proper law must determine especially the doctrinal, spiritual and apostolic method of probation and training suited to the purpose and character of the society, in such a way that the members, recognizing their divine vocation, may be fittingly prepared for the mission and life of the society.

Can. 736 — §1. In clerical societies the clerics are incardinated in the society itself, unless the constitutions provide otherwise.

§2. In those matters which pertain to the course of studies and the reception of orders the norms for secular clerics are to be observed with due regard however for §1.

Can. 737 — Incorporation entails obligations and rights for the members defined in the constitutions as well as a concern on the part of the society to lead the members to the end of their particular vocation, according to the constitutions.

Can. 738 — §1. All the members are subject to their particular moderators according to the norm of the constitutions in those matters which affect the internal life and discipline of the society.

§2. They are subject also to the diocesan bishop in those matters which affect public worship, the care of souls and other works of the apostolate, with due regard for cann. 679-683.

§3. The relations of a member incardinated in a diocese with his proper bishop are defined by the constitutions or particular agreements.

Can. 739 — Besides the obligations which they have as members according to the constitutions the members are bound by the common obligations of clerics, unless something else is evident from the nature of the matter or from the context.

Can. 740 — Members must live in a house or community legitimately established and observe common life according to the norm of proper law, by which absences from a house or community are also governed.

Can. 741 — §1. Societies and, unless the constitutions state otherwise, their parts and houses are juridic persons, and, as such, capable of acquiring, possessing, administering and alienating temporal goods according to the norm of the prescriptions of Book V, *The Temporal Goods of the Church*,

638 et 639, necnon iuris proprii.

§ 2. Sodales capaces quoque sunt, ad normam iuris proprii, bona temporalia acquirendi, possidendi, administrandi de iisque disponendi, sed quidquid ipsis intuitu societatis obveniat, societati acquiritur.

Can. 742 – Egressus et dimissio sodalis nondum definitive incorporati reguntur constitutionibus cuiusque societatis.

Can. 743 – Indultum discedendi a societate, cessantibus iuribus et obligationibus ex incorporatione promanantibus, firmo praescripto can. 693, sodalis definitive incorporatus a supremo Moderatore cum consensu eius consilii obtinere potest, nisi id iuxta constitutiones Sanctae Sedi reservetur.

Can. 744 – § 1. Supremo quoque Moderatori cum consensu sui consilii pariter reservatur licentiam concedere sodali definitive incorporato ad aliam societatem vitae apostolicae transeundi, suspensis interim iuribus et obligationibus propriae societatis, firmo tamen iure redeundi ante definitivam incorporationem in novam societatem.

§ 2. Ut transitus fiat ad institutum vitae consecratae vel ex eo ad societatem vitae apostolicae, licentia requiritur Sanctae Sedis, cuius mandatis standum est.

Can. 745 – Supremus Moderator cum consensu sui consilii sodali definitive incorporato concedere potest indultum vivendi extra societatem, non tamen ultra triennium, suspensis iuribus et obligationibus quae cum ipsius nova condicione componi non possunt; permanet tamen sub cura Moderatorum. Si agitur de clerico, requiritur praeterea consensus Ordinarii loci in quo commorari debet, sub cuius cura et dependentia etiam manet.

Can. 746 – Ad dimissionem sodalis definitive incorporati serventur, congrua congruis referendo, cann. 694-704.

cann. 636, 638 and 639 and the norm of proper law.

§2. According to the norm of proper law the members are also capable of acquiring, possessing, administering and disposing of temporal goods, but whatever comes to them in consideration of the society belongs to the society.

Can. 742 — The departure and dismissal of a member not yet definitively incorporated is governed by the constitutions of each society.

Can. 743 — A member definitively incorporated can obtain an indult of departure from the society from the supreme moderator with the consent of the council, unless it is reserved to the Holy See by the constitutions; the rights and obligations flowing from incorporation cease, with due regard for the prescription of can. 693.

Can. 744 — §1. It is reserved to the supreme moderator also with the consent of the council to grant permission to a member definitively incorporated to transfer to another society of apostolic life; in the meantime the rights and obligations associated with the prior society are suspended, and the member has the right to return before definitive incorporation into the new society.

§2. In order to transfer to an institute of consecrated life or from that to a society of apostolic life, the permission of the Holy See is required and its mandates must be observed.

Can. 745 — The supreme moderator with the consent of the council can grant to a definitively incorporated member an indult of living outside the society, not however beyond three years, with the rights and obligations which are not suitable for the new condition being suspended; the member remains however under the care of the moderators. If it is a question of a cleric there is required in addition the permission of the ordinary of the place in which he must dwell, under whose care and dependency he also remains.

Can. 746 — For the dismissal of a member definitively incorporated, cann. 694-704 are to be observed with due adaptations being made.

LIBER III
DE ECCLESIAE MUNERE DOCENDI

Can. 747 – § 1. Ecclesiae, cui Christus Dominus fidei depositum concredidit ut ipsa, Spiritu Sancto assistente, veritatem revelatam sancte custodiret, intimius perscrutaretur, fideliter annuntiaret atque exponeret, officium est et ius nativum, etiam mediis communicationis socialis sibi propriis adhibitis, a qualibet humana potestate independens, omnibus gentibus Evangelium praedicandi.

§ 2. Ecclesiae competit semper et ubique principia moralia etiam de ordine sociali annuntiare, necnon iudicium ferre de quibuslibet rebus humanis, quatenus personae humanae iura fundamentalia aut animarum salus id exigant.

Can. 748 – § 1. Omnes homines veritatem in iis, quae Deum eiusque Ecclesiam respiciunt, quaerere tenentur eamque cognitam amplectendi ac servandi obligatione vi legis divinae adstringuntur et iure gaudent.

§ 2. Homines ad amplectendam fidem catholicam contra ipsorum conscientiam per coactionem adducere nemini umquam fas est.

Can. 749 – § 1. Infallibilitate in magisterio, vi muneris sui gaudet Summus Pontifex quando ut supremus omnium christifidelium Pastor et Doctor, cuius est fratres suos in fide confirmare, doctrinam de fide vel de moribus tenendam definitivo actu proclamat.

§ 2. Infallibilitate in magisterio pollet quoque Collegium Episcoporum quando magisterium exercent Episcopi in Concilio Oecumenico coadunati cum, ut fidei et morum doctores et iudices, pro universa Ecclesia doctrinam de fide vel de moribus definitive tenendam declarant; aut quando per orbem dispersi, communionis nexum inter se et cum Petri successore servantes, una cum eodem Romano Pontifice authentice res fidei vel morum docentes, in unam sententiam tamquam definitive tenendam conveniunt.

§ 3. Infallibiliter definita nulla intellegitur doctrina nisi id manifeste constiterit.

BOOK III
THE TEACHING OFFICE OF THE CHURCH

Can. 747 — §1. The Church, to whom Christ the Lord entrusted the deposit of faith so that, assisted by the Holy Spirit, it might reverently safeguard revealed truth, more closely examine it and faithfully proclaim and expound it, has the innate duty and right to preach the gospel to all nations, independent of any human power whatever, using the means of social communication proper to it.

§2. To the Church belongs the right always and everywhere to announce moral principles, including those pertaining to the social order, and to make judgments on any human affairs to the extent that they are required by the fundamental rights of the human person or the salvation of souls.

Can. 748 — §1. All persons are bound to seek the truth in matters concerning God and God's Church; by divine law they also are obliged and have the right to embrace and to observe that truth which they have recognized.

§2. Persons cannot ever be forced by anyone to embrace the Catholic faith against their conscience.

Can. 749 — §1. The Supreme Pontiff, in virtue of his office, possesses infallible teaching authority when, as supreme pastor and teacher of all the faithful, whose task is to confirm his fellow believers in the faith, he proclaims with a definitive act that a doctrine of faith or morals is to be held as such.

§2. The college of bishops also possesses infallible teaching authority when the bishops exercise their teaching office gathered together in an ecumenical council when, as teachers and judges of faith and morals, they declare that for the universal Church a doctrine of faith or morals must be definitively held; they also exercise it scattered throughout the world but united in a bond of communion among themselves and with the successor of Peter when together with that same Roman Pontiff in their capacity as authentic teachers of faith and morals they agree on an opinion to be held as definitive.

§3. No doctrine is understood to be infallibly defined unless it is clearly established as such.

Can. 750 – Fide divina et catholica ea omnia credenda sunt quae verbo Dei scripto vel tradito, uno scilicet fidei deposito Ecclesiae commisso, continentur, et insimul ut divinitus revelata proponuntur, sive ab Ecclesiae magisterio sollemni, sive ab eius magisterio ordinario et universali; quod scilicet communi adhaesione christifidelium sub ductu sacri magisterii manifestatur; tenentur igitur omnes quascumque devitare doctrinas iisdem contrarias.

Can. 751 – Dicitur haeresis, pertinax, post receptum baptismum, alicuius veritatis fide divina et catholica credendae denegatio, aut de eadem pertinax dubitatio; apostasia, fidei christianae ex toto repudiatio; schisma, subiectionis Summo Pontifici aut communionis cum Ecclesiae membris eidem subditis detrectatio.

Can. 752 – Non quidem fidei assensus, religiosum tamen intellectus et voluntatis obsequium praestandum est doctrinae, quam sive Summus Pontifex sive Collegium Episcoporum de fide vel de moribus enuntiant, cum magisterium authenticum exercent, etsi definitivo actu eandem proclamare non intendant; christifideles ergo devitare curent quae cum eadem non congruant.

Can. 753 – Episcopi, qui sunt in communione cum Collegii capite et membris, sive singuli sive in conferentiis Episcoporum aut in conciliis particularibus congregati, licet infallibilitate in docendo non polleant, christifidelium suae curae commissorum authentici sunt fidei doctores et magistri; cui authentico magisterio suorum Episcoporum christifideles religioso animi obsequio adhaerere tenentur.

Can. 754 – Omnes christifideles obligatione tenentur servandi constitutiones et decreta, quae ad doctrinam proponendam et erroneas opiniones proscribendas fert legitima Ecclesiae auctoritas, speciali vero ratione, quae edit Romanus Pontifex vel Collegium Episcoporum.

Can. 755 – § 1. Totius Collegii Episcoporum et Sedis Apostolicae imprimis est fovere et dirigere motum oecumenicum apud catholicos, cuius finis est unitatis redintegratio inter universos christianos ad quam promovendam Ecclesia ex voluntate Christi tenetur.

§ 2. Episcoporum item est, et, ad normam iuris, Episcoporum conferentiarum, eandem unitatem promovere atque pro variis adiunctorum necessitatibus vel opportunitatibus, normas practicas impertire, attentis praescriptis a suprema Ecclesiae auctoritate latis.

Can. 750 — All that is contained in the written word of God or in tradition, that is, in the one deposit of faith entrusted to the Church and also proposed as divinely revealed either by the solemn magisterium of the Church or by its ordinary and universal magisterium, must be believed with divine and catholic faith; it is manifested by the common adherence of the Christian faithful under the leadership of the sacred magisterium; therefore, all are bound to avoid any doctrines whatever which are contrary to these truths.

Can. 751 — Heresy is the obstinate post-baptismal denial of some truth which must be believed with divine and catholic faith, or it is likewise an obstinate doubt concerning the same; apostasy is the total repudiation of the Christian faith; schism is the refusal of submission to the Roman Pontiff or of communion with the members of the Church subject to him.

Can. 752 — A religious respect of intellect and will, even if not the assent of faith, is to be paid to the teaching which the Supreme Pontiff or the college of bishops enuntiate on faith or morals when they exercise the authentic magisterium even if they do not intend to proclaim it with a definitive act; therefore the Christian faithful are to take care to avoid whatever is not in harmony with that teaching.

Can. 753 — Although they do not enjoy infallible teaching authority, the bishops in communion with the head and members of the college, whether as individuals or gathered in conferences of bishops or in particular councils, are authentic teachers and instructors of the faith for the faithful entrusted to their care; the faithful must adhere to the authentic teaching of their own bishops with a sense of religious respect.

Can. 754 — All the Christian faithful are obliged to observe the constitutions and decrees which the legitimate authority of the Church issues in order to propose doctrine and proscribe erroneous opinions; this is especially true of the constitutions and decrees issued by the Roman Pontiff or the college of bishops.

Can. 755 — §1. It is within the special competence of the entire college of bishops and of the Apostolic See to promote and direct the participation of Catholics in the ecumenical movement, whose purpose is the restoration of unity among all Christians, which the Church is bound by the will of Christ to promote.

§2. It is likewise within the competence of bishops and, in accord with the norm of law, of conferences of bishops to promote the same unity and to issue practical norms for the needs and opportunities presented by diverse circumstances in light of the prescriptions of the supreme church authority.

TITULUS I
DE DIVINI VERBI MINISTERIO

Can. 756 – § 1. Quoad universam Ecclesiam munus Evangelii annuntiandi praecipue Romano Pontifici et Collegio Episcoporum commissum est.

§ 2. Quoad Ecclesiam particularem sibi concreditam illud munus exercent singuli Episcopi, qui quidem totius ministerii verbi in eadem sunt moderatores; quandoque vero aliqui Episcopi coniunctim illud explent quoad diversas simul Ecclesias, ad normam iuris.

Can. 757 – Presbyterorum, qui quidem Episcoporum cooperatores sunt, proprium est Evangelium Dei annuntiare; praesertim hoc officio tenentur, quoad populum sibi commissum, parochi aliique quibus cura animarum concreditur; diaconorum etiam est in ministerio verbi populo Dei, in communione cum Episcopo eiusque presbyterio, inservire.

Can. 758 – Sodales institutorum vitae consecratae, vi propriae Deo consecrationis, peculiari modo Evangelii testimonium reddunt, iidemque in Evangelio annuntiando ab Episcopo in auxilium convenienter assumuntur.

Can. 759 – Christifideles laici, vi baptismatis et confirmationis, verbo et vitae christianae exemplo evangelici nuntii sunt testes; vocari etiam possunt ut in exercitio ministerii verbi cum Episcopo et presbyteris cooperentur.

Can. 760 – In ministerio verbi, quod sacra Scriptura, Traditione, liturgia, magisterio vitaque Ecclesiae innitatur oportet, Christi mysterium integre ac fideliter proponatur.

Can. 761 – Varia media ad doctrinam christianam annuntiandam adhibeantur quae praesto sunt, imprimis praedicatio atque catechetica institutio, quae quidem semper principem locum tenent, sed et propositio doctrinae in scholis, in academiis, conferentiis et coadunationibus omnis generis, necnon eiusdem diffusio per declarationes publicas a legitima auctoritate occasione quorundam eventuum factas, prelo aliisque instrumentis communicationis socialis.

Caput I
DE VERBI DEI PRAEDICATIONE

Can. 762 – Cum Dei populus primum coadunetur verbo Dei vivi, quod ex ore sacerdotum omnino fas est requirere, munus praedicatio-

TITLE I

THE MINISTRY OF THE DIVINE WORD

Can. 756 — §1. As regards the universal Church the duty of proclaiming the gospel has been especially entrusted to the Roman Pontiff and to the college of bishops.

§2. As regards the particular church entrusted to them the individual bishops exercise this responsibility since within it they are the moderators of the entire ministry of the word; sometimes, several bishops simultaneously fulfill this office jointly for various churches at once in accord with the norm of law.

Can. 757 — It is proper for presbyters who are co-workers with the bishops to proclaim the gospel of God; pastors and others entrusted with the care of souls are especially bound to this office as regards the people entrusted to them; deacons also are to serve the people of God in the ministry of the word in communion with the bishop and his presbyterate.

Can. 758 — In virtue of their consecration to God, members of institutes of consecrated life give testimony to the gospel in a special manner, and they are appropriately enlisted by the bishop to assist in proclaiming the gospel.

Can. 759 — In virtue of their baptism and confirmation lay members of the Christian faithful are witnesses to the gospel message by word and by example of a Christian life; they can also be called upon to cooperate with the bishop and presbyters in the exercise of the ministry of the word.

Can. 760 — The mystery of Christ is to be expounded completely and faithfully in the ministry of the word, which ought to be based upon sacred scripture, tradition, liturgy, the magisterium and the life of the Church.

Can. 761 — The various means which are available are to be employed to proclaim Christian teaching, especially preaching and catechetical formation, which always hold the primary place; other means to be employed, however, are the exposition of doctrine in schools, academies, conferences and meetings of every type, and its spreading by means of public declarations by legitimate authority made on the occasion of certain events, by the press, and by the other instruments of social communication.

CHAPTER I

THE PREACHING OF THE WORD OF GOD

Can. 762 — Since the people of God are first brought together by the word of the living God, which it is altogether proper to require from the

nis magni habeant sacri ministri, cum inter praecipua ipsorum officia sit Evangelium Dei omnibus annuntiare.

Can. 763 – Episcopis ius est ubique, non exclusis ecclesiis et oratoriis institutorum religiosorum iuris pontificii, Dei verbum praedicare, nisi Episcopus loci in casibus particularibus expresse renuerit.

Can. 764 – Salvo praescripto can. 765, facultate ubique praedicandi, de consensu saltem praesumpto rectoris ecclesiae exercenda, gaudent presbyteri et diaconi, nisi ab Ordinario competenti eadem facultas restricta fuerit aut sublata, aut lege particulari licentia expressa requiratur.

Can. 765 – Ad praedicandum religiosis in eorum ecclesiis vel oratoriis licentia requiritur Superioris ad normam constitutionum competentis.

Can. 766 – Ad praedicandum in ecclesia vel oratorio admitti possunt laici, si certis in adiunctis necessitas id requirat aut in casibus particularibus utilitas id suadeat, iuxta Episcoporum conferentiae praescripta, et salvo can. 767, § 1.

Can. 767 – § 1. Inter praedicationis formas eminet homilia, quae est pars ipsius liturgiae et sacerdoti aut diacono reservatur; in eadem per anni liturgici cursum ex textu sacro fidei mysteria et normae vitae christianae exponantur.

§ 2. In. omnibus Missis diebus dominicis et festis de praecepto, quae concursu populi celebrantur, homilia habenda est nec omitti potest nisi gravi de causa.

§ 3. Valde commendatur ut, si sufficiens detur populi concursus, homilia habeatur etiam in Missis quae infra hebdomadam, praesertim tempore adventus et quadragesimae aut occasione alicuius festi vel luctuosi eventus, celebrentur.

§ 4. Parochi aut ecclesiae rectoris est curare ut haec praescripta religiose serventur.

Can. 768 – § 1. Divini verbi praecones christifidelibus imprimis proponant quae ad Dei gloriam hominumque salutem credere et facere oportet.

§ 2. Impertiant quoque fidelibus doctrinam, quam Ecclesiae magisterium proponit de personae humanae dignitate et libertate, de familiae unitate et stabilitate eiusque muniis, de obligationibus quae ad homines in societate coniunctos pertinent, necnon de rebus temporalibus iuxta ordinem a Deo statutum componendis.

mouth of priests, sacred ministers are to value greatly the task of preaching since among their principal duties is the proclaiming of the gospel of God to all.

Can. 763 — It is the right of bishops to preach the word of God everywhere, including the churches and oratories of religious institutes of pontifical right, unless the local bishop has expressly refused this in particular cases.

Can. 764 — With due regard for the prescription of can. 765, presbyters and deacons possess the faculty to preach everywhere, to be exercised with at least the presumed consent of the rector of the church, unless that faculty has been restricted or taken away by the competent ordinary or unless express permission is required by particular law.

Can. 765 — Preaching to religious in their churches or oratories requires the permission of the superior who is competent in accord with the norm of the constitutions.

Can. 766 — Lay persons can be admitted to preach in a church or oratory if it is necessary in certain circumstances or if it is useful in particular cases according to the prescriptions of the conference of bishops and with due regard for can. 767, §1.

Can. 767 — §1. Among the forms of preaching the homily is preeminent; it is a part of the liturgy itself and is reserved to a priest or to a deacon; in the homily the mysteries of faith and the norms of Christian living are to be expounded from the sacred text throughout the course of the liturgical year.

§2. Whenever a congregation is present a homily is to be given at all Sunday Masses and at Masses celebrated on holy days of obligation; it cannot be omitted without a serious reason.

§3. If a sufficient number of people are present it is strongly recommended that a homily also be given at Masses celebrated during the week, especially during Advent or Lent or on the occasion of some feast day or time of mourning.

§4. It is the duty of the pastor or the rector of a church to see to it that these prescriptions are conscientiously observed.

Can. 768 — §1. It is necessary that those who proclaim the word of God to the Christian faithful are first of all to propose those things which one ought to believe and do for the glory of God and for the salvation of humankind.

§2. They are also to impart to the faithful the teaching which the magisterium of the Church proposes concerning the dignity and freedom of the human person, the unity and stability of the family and its duties, the obligations which men and women have from being joined together in society, and the ordering of temporal affairs according to God's plan.

Can. 769 – Doctrina christiana proponatur modo auditorum condicioni accommodato atque ratione temporum necessitatibus aptata.

Can. 770 – Parochi certis temporibus, iuxta Episcopi dioecesani praescripta, illas ordinent praedicationes, quas exercitia spiritualia et sacras missiones vocant, vel alias formas necessitatibus aptatas.

Can. 771 – § 1. Solliciti sint animarum pastores, praesertim Episcopi et parochi, ut Dei verbum iis quoque fidelibus nuntietur, qui ob vitae suae condicionem communi et ordinaria cura pastorali non satis fruantur aut eadem penitus careant.

§ 2. Provideant quoque, ut Evangelii nuntium perveniat ad non credentes in territorio degentes, quippe quos, non secus ac fideles, animarum cura complecti debeat.

Can. 772 – § 1. Ad exercitium praedicationis quod attinet, ab omnibus praeterea serventur normae ab Episcopo dioecesano latae.

§ 2. Ad sermonem de doctrina christiana faciendum via radiophonica aut televisifica, serventur praescripta ab Episcoporum conferentia statuta.

Caput II
DE CATECHETICA INSTITUTIONE

Can. 773 – Proprium et grave officium pastorum praesertim animarum est catechesim populi christiani curare, ut fidelium fides, per doctrinae institutionem et vitae christianae experientiam, viva fiat explicita atque operosa.

Can. 774 – § 1. Sollicitudo catechesis, sub moderamine legitimae ecclesiasticae auctoritatis, ad omnia Ecclesiae membra pro sua cuiusque parte pertinet.

§ 2. Prae ceteris parentes obligatione tenentur verbo et exemplo filios in fide et vitae christianae praxi efformandi; pari obligatione adstringuntur, qui parentum locum tenent atque patrini.

Can. 775 – § 1. Servatis praescriptis ab Apostolica Sede latis, Episcopi dioecesani est normas de re catechetica edicere itemque prospicere ut apta catechesis instrumenta praesto sint, catechismum etiam parando, si opportunum id videatur, necnon incepta catechetica fovere atque coordinare.

§ 2. Episcoporum conferentiae est, si utile videatur, curare ut catechismi pro suo territorio, praevia Sedis Apostolicae approbatione, edantur.

Can. 769 — Christian doctrine is to be proposed in a manner accommodated to the condition of its listeners and adapted to the needs of the times.

Can. 770 — At certain times according to the prescriptions of the diocesan bishop, pastors are to arrange for those types of preaching which are called spiritual exercises or sacred missions or for other types of preaching adapted to their needs.

Can. 771 — §1. Pastors of souls, especially bishops and pastors, are to take care that the word of God is proclaimed also to those members of the faithful who do not enjoy sufficiently or who lack completely common and ordinary pastoral care due to their condition of life.

§2. They are also to make provision for the message of the gospel to come to non-believers who live in their territory, since the care of souls must embrace them as well as the faithful.

Can. 772 — §1. The norms issued by the diocesan bishop concerning the exercise of preaching are to be observed by all.

§2. The prescriptions of the conference of bishops are to be observed in giving radio or television talks on Christian doctrine.

CHAPTER II

CATECHETICAL INSTRUCTION

Can. 773 — There is a proper and serious duty, especially on the part of pastors of souls, to provide for the catechesis of the Christian people so that the faith of the faithful becomes living, explicit and productive through formation in doctrine and the experience of Christian living.

Can. 774 — §1. Under the supervision of legitimate ecclesiastical authority this concern for catechesis pertains to all the members of the Church in proportion to each one's role.

§2. Parents above others are obliged to form their children in the faith and practice of the Christian life by word and example; godparents and those who take the place of parents are bound by an equivalent obligation.

Can. 775 — §1. While observing the prescriptions of the Apostolic See it is the responsibility of the diocesan bishop to issue norms concerning catechetics and to make provision that suitable instruments for catechesis are available, even by preparing a catechism, if such seems appropriate, and by fostering and co-ordinating catechetical endeavors.

§2. It is within the competence of the conference of bishops, with the prior approval of the Apostolic See, to see to it that catechisms are issued for its territory if such seems useful.

§ 3. Apud Episcoporum conferentiam institui potest officium ca-
techeticum, cuius praecipuum munus sit singulis dioecesibus in re catechetica auxilium praebere.

Can. 776 – Parochus, vi sui muneris, catecheticam efformationem
adultorum, iuvenum et puerorum curare tenetur, quem in finem sociam sibi operam adhibeat clericorum paroeciae addictorum, sodalium
institutorum vitae consecratae necnon societatum vitae apostolicae,
habita ratione indolis uniuscuiusque instituti, necnon christifidelium
laicorum, praesertim catechistarum; hi omnes, nisi legitime impediti,
operam suam libenter praestare ne renuant. Munus parentum, in catechesi familiari, de quo in can. 774, § 2, promoveat et foveat.

Can. 777 – Peculiari modo parochus, attentis normis ab Episcopo
dioecesano statutis, curet:
1° ut apta catechesis impertiatur pro sacramentorum celebratione;
2° ut pueri, ope catecheticae institutionis per congruum tempus
impertitae, rite praeparentur ad primam receptionem sacramentorum
paenitentiae et sanctissimae Eucharistiae necnon ad sacramentum confirmationis;
3° ut iidem, prima communione recepta, uberius ac profundius
catechetica efformatione excolantur;
4° ut catechetica institutio iis etiam tradatur, quantum eorum
condicio sinat, qui corpore vel mente sint praepediti;
5° ut iuvenum et adultorum fides, variis formis et inceptis, mu-
niatur, illuminetur atque evolvatur.

Can. 778 – Curent Superiores religiosi et societatum vitae apostolicae ut in suis ecclesiis, scholis aliisve operibus sibi quoquo modo
concreditis, catechetica institutio sedulo impertiatur.

Can. 779 – Institutio catechetica tradatur omnibus adhibitis auxiliis, subsidiis didacticis et communicationis instrumentis, quae efficaciora videantur ut fideles, ratione eorum indoli, facultatibus et aetati
necnon vitae condicionibus aptata, plenius catholicam doctrinam edi-
scere eamque aptius in praxim deducere valeant.

Can. 780 – Curent locorum Ordinarii ut catechistae ad munus suum
rite explendum debite praeparentur, ut nempe continua formatio eisdem
praebeatur, utque Ecclesiae doctrinam apte cognoscant atque normas
disciplinis paedagogicis proprias theoretice ac practice addiscant.

§3. There can be established within the conference of bishops a catechetical office whose principal task would be to furnish assistance to the individual dioceses in catechetical matters.

Can. 776 — In virtue of his office the pastor is bound to provide for the catechetical formation of adults, young people and children, to which end he is to employ the services of the clerics attached to the parish, members of institutes of consecrated life and of societies of apostolic life, with due regard for the character of each institute, and lay members of the Christian faithful, above all catechists; all of these are not to refuse to furnish their services willingly unless they are legitimately impeded. The pastor is to promote and foster the role of parents in the family catechesis mentioned in can. 774, §2.

Can. 777 — In accord with the norms established by the diocesan bishop, the pastor is to make particular provision:

1° that suitable catechesis is given for the celebration of the sacraments;

2° that children are properly prepared for the first reception of the sacraments of penance and Most Holy Eucharist and the sacrament of confirmation by means of a catechetical formation given over an appropriate period of time;

3° that children are more fruitfully and deeply instructed through catechetical formation after the reception of First Communion;

4° that catechetical formation also be given to those handicapped in body or mind insofar as their condition permits;

5° that the faith of young people and adults be fortified, enlightened and developed through various means and endeavors.

Can. 778 — Superiors of religious institutes and of societies of apostolic life are to see to it that catechetical formation is diligently imparted in their churches, schools and in other works entrusted to them in any manner.

Can. 779 — Catechetical formation is to be given by employing all those helps, teaching aids and communications media which appear to be more effective in enabling the faithful in light of their characteristics, talents, age and conditions of life, to learn the Catholic teaching more fully and practice it more suitably.

Can. 780 — Local ordinaries are to see to it that catechists are duly prepared to fulfill their task correctly, namely, that continuing formation is made available to them, that they acquire a proper knowledge of the Church's teaching, and that they learn in theory and in practice the norms proper to the pedagogical disciplines.

TITULUS II
DE ACTIONE ECCLESIAE MISSIONALI

Can. 781 – Cum tota Ecclesia natura sua sit missionaria et opus evangelizationis habendum sit fundamentale officium populi Dei, christifideles omnes, propriae responsabilitatis conscii, partem suam in opere missionali assumant.

Can. 782 – § 1. Suprema directio et coordinatio inceptorum et actionum quae ad opus missionale atque ad cooperationem missionariam pertinent, competit Romano Pontifici et Collegio Episcoporum.

§ 2. Singuli Episcopi, utpote Ecclesiae universae atque omnium Ecclesiarum sponsores, operis missionalis peculiarem sollicitudinem habeant, praesertim incepta missionalia in propria Ecclesia particulari suscitando, fovendo ac sustinendo.

Can. 783 – Sodales institutorum vitae consecratae, cum vi ipsius consecrationis sese servitio Ecclesiae dedicent, obligatione tenentur ad operam, ratione suo instituto propria, speciali modo in actione missionali navandam.

Can. 784 – Missionarii, qui scilicet a competenti auctoritate ecclesiastica ad opus missionale explendum mittuntur, eligi possunt autochthoni vel non, sive clerici saeculares, sive institutorum vitae consecratae vel societatis vitae apostolicae sodales, sive alii christifideles laici.

Can. 785 – § 1. In opere missionali peragendo assumantur catechistae, christifideles nempe laici debite instructi et vita christiana praestantes, qui, sub moderamine missionarii, doctrinae evangelicae proponendae et liturgicis exercitiis caritatisque operibus ordinandis sese impendant.

§ 2. Catechistae efformentur in scholis ad hoc destinatis vel, ubi desint, sub moderamine missionariorum.

Can. 786 – Actio proprie missionalis, qua Ecclesia implantatur in populis vel coetibus ubi nondum radicata est, ab Ecclesia absolvitur praesertim mittendo Evangelii praecones donec novellae Ecclesiae plene constituantur, instructae scilicet propriis viribus et sufficientibus mediis, quibus opus evangelizandi per se ipsae peragere valeant.

TITLE II
MISSIONARY ACTION OF THE CHURCH

Can. 781 — Since the entire Church is missionary by its nature and since the work of evangelization is to be viewed as a fundamental duty of the people of God, all the Christian faithful, conscious of their own responsibility in this area, are to assume their own role in missionary work.

Can. 782 — §1. The supreme direction and coordination of endeavors and activities which deal with missionary work and missionary cooperation belong to the Roman Pontiff and the college of bishops.

§2. Since they are the sponsors for the universal Church and for all the churches, individual bishops are to have a special concern for missionary work especially by initiating, fostering and sustaining missionary endeavors in their own particular church.

Can. 783 — Since members of institutes of consecrated life dedicate themselves through their consecration to the service of the Church they are obliged in a special manner to engage in missionary work in accord with the character of the institute.

Can. 784 — Missionaries are those persons who are sent to engage in missionary work by competent ecclesiastical authority; they can be chosen from among those who are native or non-native to the country; they may be secular clerics, members of institutes of consecrated life or of societies of apostolic life, or other lay members of the Christian faithful.

Can. 785 — §1. Catechists are to be employed in carrying out missionary work; catechists are those lay members of the Christian faithful who have been duly instructed, who stand out by reason of their Christian manner of life, and who devote themselves to expounding the gospel teaching and organizing liturgical functions and works of charity under the supervision of a missionary.

§2. Catechists are to be educated in schools destined for this purpose or, where such schools are lacking, under the supervision of missionaries.

Can. 786 — Missionary activity, properly so-called, by which the Church is implanted among peoples and groups in which it has not yet taken root, is accomplished by the Church especially by sending heralds of the gospel until the young churches are fully established to the point that they are able to perform the work of evangelization on their own with their own resources and sufficient means.

Can. 787 – § 1. Missionarii, vitae ac verbi testimonio, dialogum sincerum cum non credentibus in Christum instituant, ut ipsis, ratione eorundem ingenio et culturae aptata, aperiantur viae quibus ad evangelicum nuntium cognoscendum adduci valeant.

§ 2. Curent ut quos ad evangelicum nuntium recipiendum aestiment paratos, veritates fidei edoceant, ita quidem ut ipsi ad baptismum recipiendum, libere id petentes, admitti possint.

Can. 788 – § 1. Qui voluntatem amplectendi fidem in Christum manifestaverint, expleto tempore praecatechumenatus, liturgicis caerimoniis admittantur ad catechumenatum, atque eorum nomina scribantur in libro ad hoc destinato.

§ 2. Catechumeni, per vitae christianae institutionem et tirocinium, apte initientur mysterio salutis atque introducantur in vitam fidei, liturgiae et caritatis populi Dei atque apostolatus.

§ 3. Conferentiae Episcoporum est statuta edere quibus catechumenatus ordinetur, determinando quaenam a catechumenis sint praestanda, atque definiendo quaenam eis agnoscantur praerogativae.

Can. 789 – Neophyti, apta institutione ad veritatem evangelicam penitius cognoscendam et officia per baptismum suscepta implenda efformentur; sincero amore erga Christum eiusque Ecclesiam imbuantur.

Can. 790 – § 1. Episcopi dioecesani in territoriis missionis est:

1° promovere, moderari et coordinare incepta et opera, quae ad actionem missionalem spectant;

2° curare ut debitae ineantur conventiones cum Moderatoribus institutorum quae operi missionali se dedicant, utque relationes cum iisdem in bonum cedant missionis.

§ 2. Praescriptis ab Episcopo dioecesano de quibus in § 1, n. 1° editis, subsunt omnes missionarii, etiam religiosi eorumque auxiliares in eius dicione degentes.

Can. 791 – In singulis dioecesibus ad cooperationem missionalem fovendam:

1° promoveantur vocationes missionales;

2° sacerdos deputetur ad incepta pro missionibus efficaciter promovenda, praesertim *Pontificia Opera Missionalia*;

3° celebretur dies annualis pro missionibus;

4° solvatur quotannis congrua pro missionibus stips, Sanctae Sedi transmittenda.

Can. 787 — §1. By the witness of their life and words missionaries are to establish a sincere dialogue with those who do not believe in Christ in order that through methods suited to their characteristics and culture avenues may be open to them by which they can be led to an understanding of the gospel message.

§2. Missionaries are to see to it that they teach the truths of faith to those whom they judge to be ready to accept the gospel message so that these persons can be admitted to the reception of baptism when they freely request it.

Can. 788 — §1. After a period of pre-catechumenate has elapsed, persons who have manifested a willingness to embrace faith in Christ are to be admitted to the catechumenate in liturgical ceremonies and their names are to be registered in a book destined for this purpose.

§2. Through instruction and an apprenticeship in the Christian life catechumens are suitably to be initiated into the mystery of salvation and introduced to the life of faith, liturgy, charity of the people of God and the apostolate.

§3. It is the responsibility of the conference of bishops to issue statutes by which the catechumenate is regulated; these statutes are to determine what things are to be expected of catechumens and define what prerogatives are recognized as theirs.

Can. 789 — Through a suitable instruction neophytes are to be formed to a more thorough understanding of the gospel truth and the baptismal duties to be fulfilled; they are to be imbued with a love of Christ and of His Church.

Can. 790 — §1. It is the responsibility of the diocesan bishop in missionary territories:

1° to promote, supervise and coordinate endeavors and works which concern missionary activity;

2° to provide that the necessary contracts are entered into with the moderators of institutes which dedicate themselves to missionary work and that relations with them redound to the good of the mission.

§2. All missionaries living in his jurisdiction, including religious and their assistants, are subject to the prescriptions issued by the diocesan bishop mentioned in §1, n. 1.

Can. 791 — To foster missionary cooperation in the individual dioceses:

1° missionary vocations are to be promoted;

2° a priest is to be appointed to promote effectively endeavors on behalf of the missions, especially the *Pontifical Missionary Works*;

3° an annual missions' day is to be observed;

4° every year a suitable monetary contribution for the missions is to be forwarded to the Holy See.

Can. 792 – Episcoporum conferentiae opera instituant ac promoveant, quibus ii qui e terris missionum laboris aut studii causa ad earundem territorium accedant, fraterne recipiantur et congruenti pastorali cura adiuventur.

TITULUS III
DE EDUCATIONE CATHOLICA

Can. 793 – § 1. Parentes, necnon qui eorum locum tenent, obligatione adstringuntur et iure gaudent prolem educandi; parentes catholici officium quoque et ius habent ea eligendi. media et instituta quibus, iuxta locorum adiuncta, catholicae filiorum educationi aptius prospicere queant.

§ 2. Parentibus ius est etiam iis fruendi auxiliis a societate civili praestandis, quibus in catholica educatione filiorum procuranda indigeant.

Can. 794 – § 1. Singulari ratione officium et ius educandi spectat ad Ecclesiam, cui divinitus missio concredita est homines adiuvandi, ut ad christianae vitae plenitudinem pervenire valeant.

§ 2. Animarum pastoribus officium est omnia disponendi, ut educatione catholica omnes fideles fruantur.

Can. 795 – Cum vera educatio integram persequi debeat personae humanae formationem, spectantem ad finem eius ultimum et simul ad bonum commune societatum, pueri et iuvenes ita excolantur ut suas dotes physicas, morales et intellectuales harmonice evolvere valeant, perfectiorem responsabilitatis sensum libertatisque rectum usum acquirant et ad vitam socialem active participandam conformentur.

CAPUT I
DE SCHOLIS

Can. 796 – § 1. Inter media ad excolendam educationem christifideles magni faciant scholas, quae quidem parentibus, in munere educationis implendo, praecipuo auxilio sunt.

§ 2. Cum magistris scholarum, quibus filios educandos concredant, parentes arcte cooperentur oportet; magistri vero in officio suo persolvendo intime collaborent cum parentibus, qui quidem libenter audiendi sunt eorumque consociationes vel conventus instaurentur atque magni existimentur.

Can. 792 — The conferences of bishops are to establish and promote works through which persons who come to their territory from missionary lands for the sake of work or study may be received like family and assisted with adequate pastoral care.

TITLE III
CATHOLIC EDUCATION

Can. 793 — §1. Parents as well as those who take their place are obliged and enjoy the right to educate their offspring; Catholic parents also have the duty and the right to select those means and institutions through which they can provide more suitably for the Catholic education of the children according to local circumstances.

§2. Parents also have the right to make use of those aids to be furnished by civil society which they need in order to obtain Catholic education for their children.

Can. 794 — §1. The duty and right of educating belongs in a unique way to the Church which has been divinely entrusted with the mission to assist men and women so that they can arrive at the fullness of the Christian life.

§2. Pastors of souls have the duty to arrange all things so that all the faithful may enjoy a Catholic education.

Can. 795 — Since a true education must strive for the integral formation of the human person, a formation which looks toward the person's final end, and at the same time toward the common good of societies, children and young people are to be so reared that they can develop harmoniously their physical, moral and intellectual talents, that they acquire a more perfect sense of responsibility and a correct use of freedom, and that they be educated for active participation in social life.

CHAPTER I
SCHOOLS

Can. 796 — §1. Among educational means the Christian faithful should greatly value schools, which are of principal assistance to parents in fulfilling their educational task.

§2. It is incumbent upon parents to cooperate closely with the school teachers to whom they entrust their children to be educated; in fulfilling their duty teachers are to collaborate closely with parents who are to be willingly heard and for whom associations or meetings are to be inaugurated and held in great esteem.

Can. 797 – Parentes in scholis eligendis vera libertate gaudeant oportet; quare christifideles solliciti esse debent ut societas civilis hanc libertatem parentibus agnoscat atque, servata iustitia distributiva, etiam subsidiis tueatur.

Can. 798 – Parentes filios concredant illis scholis in quibus educationi catholicae provideatur; quod si facere non valeant, obligatione tenentur curandi, ut extra scholas debitae eorundem educationi catholicae prospiciatur.

Can. 799 – Christifideles enitantur ut in societate civili leges quae iuvenum formationem ordinant, educationi eorum religiosae et morali quoque, iuxta parentum conscientiam, in ipsis scholis prospiciant.

Can. 800 – § 1. Ecclesiae ius est scholas cuiusvis disciplinae, generis et gradus condendi ac moderandi.

§ 2. Christifideles scholas catholicas foveant, pro viribus adiutricem operam conferentes ad easdem condendas et sustentandas.

Can. 801 – Instituta religiosa quibus missio educationis propria est, fideliter hanc suam missionem retinentes, satagant educationi catholicae etiam per suas scholas, consentiente Episcopo dioecesano conditas, sese impendere.

Can. 802 – § 1. Si praesto non sint scholae in quibus educatio tradatur christiano spiritu imbuta, Episcopi dioecesani est curare ut condantur.

§ 2. Ubi id expediat, Episcopus dioecesanus provideat ut scholae quoque condantur professionales et technicae necnon aliae quae specialibus necessitatibus requirantur.

Can. 803 – § 1. Schola catholica ea intellegitur quam auctoritas ecclesiastica competens aut persona iuridica ecclesiastica publica moderatur, aut auctoritas ecclesiastica documento scripto uti talem agnoscit.

§ 2. Institutio et educatio in schola catholica principiis doctrinae catholicae nitatur oportet; magistri recta doctrina et vitae probitate praestent.

§ 3. Nulla schola, etsi reapse catholica, nomen *scholae catholicae* gerat, nisi de consensu competentis auctoritatis ecclesiasticae.

Can. 804 – § 1. Ecclesiae auctoritati subicitur institutio et educatio religiosa catholica quae in quibuslibet scholis impertitur aut variis communicationis socialis instrumentis procuratur; Episcoporum conferentiae est de hoc actionis campo normas generales edicere, atque Episcopi dioecesani est eundem ordinare et in eum invigilare.

Can. 797 — It is necessary that parents enjoy true freedom in selecting schools; the Christian faithful must therefore be concerned that civil society acknowledge this freedom for parents and also safeguard it with its resources in accord with distributive justice.

Can. 798 — Parents are to entrust their children to those schools in which Catholic education is provided; but if they are unable to do this, they are bound to provide for their suitable Catholic education outside the schools.

Can. 799 — The Christian faithful are to strive so that in civil society the laws which regulate the formation of youth provide also for their religious and moral education in the schools themselves in accord with the conscience of the parents.

Can. 800 — §1. The Church has the right to establish and supervise schools of any discipline, type and grade whatsoever.

§2. The Christian faithful are to foster Catholic schools by supporting their establishment and their maintenance in proportion to their resources.

Can. 801 — Religious institutes whose proper mission is that of education, while faithfully retaining this mission of theirs, are also to devote themselves to Catholic education through their schools established with the consent of the diocesan bishop.

Can. 802 — §1. If schools imparting an education imbued with the Christian spirit are not available the diocesan bishop is to see to it that they are established.

§2. The diocesan bishop is to provide for the establishment of professional schools, technical schools and other schools required by special needs whenever such would be advantageous.

Can. 803 — §1. That school is considered to be Catholic which ecclesiastical authority or a public ecclesiastical juridic person supervises or which ecclesiastical authority recognizes as such by means of a written document.

§2. It is necessary that the formation and education given in a Catholic school be based upon the principles of Catholic doctrine; teachers are to be outstanding for their correct doctrine and integrity of life.

§3. Even if it really be Catholic, no school may bear the title *Catholic school* without the consent of the competent ecclesiastical authority.

Can. 804 — §1. Catholic religious formation and education which are imparted in any schools whatsoever as well as that acquired through the various media of social communications are subject to the authority of the Church; it is the responsibility of the conference of bishops to issue general norms in this area, and it is the responsibility of the diocesan bishop to regulate such education and be vigilant over it.

§ 2. Loci Ordinarius sollicitus sit ut qui ad religionis institutionem in scholis, etiam non catholicis, deputentur magistri, recta doctrina, vitae christianae testimonio atque arte paedagogica sint praestantes.

Can. 805 – Loci Ordinario pro sua dioecesi, ius est nominandi aut approbandi magistros religionis, itemque, si religionis morumve ratio id requirat, amovendi aut exigendi ut amoveantur.

Can. 806 – § 1. Episcopo dioecesano competit ius invigilandi et invisendi scholas catholicas in suo territorio sitas, eas etiam quae ab institutorum religiosorum sodalibus conditae sint aut dirigantur; eidem item competit praescripta edere quae ad generalem attinent ordinationem scholarum catholicarum : quae praescripta valent de scholis quoque quae ab iisdem sodalibus diriguntur, salva quidem eorundem quoad internum earum scholarum moderamen autonomia.

§ 2. Curent scholarum catholicarum Moderatores, advigilante loci Ordinario, ut institutio quae in iisdem traditur pari saltem gradu ac in aliis scholis regionis, ratione scientifica sit praestans.

CAPUT II

DE CATHOLICIS UNIVERSITATIBUS
ALIISQUE STUDIORUM SUPERIORUM INSTITUTIS

Can. 807 – Ius est Ecclesiae erigendi et moderandi studiorum universitates, quae quidem ad altiorem hominum culturam et pleniorem personae humanae promotionem necnon ad ipsius Ecclesiae munus docendi implendum conferant.

Can. 808 – Nulla studiorum universitas, etsi reapse catholica, titulum seu nomen *universitatis catholicae* gerat, nisi de consensu competentis auctoritatis ecclesiasticae.

Can. 809 – Episcoporum conferentiae curent ut habeantur, si fieri possit et expediat, studiorum universitates aut saltem facultates, in ipsarum territorio apte distributae, in quibus variae disciplinae, servata quidem earum scientifica autonomia, investigentur et tradantur, doctrinae catholicae ratione habita.

Can. 810 – § 1. Auctoritati iuxta statuta competenti officium est providendi ut in universitatibus catholicis nominentur docentes qui, praeterquam idoneitate scientifica et paedagogica, doctrinae integritate et vitae probitate praestent utque, deficientibus his requisitis, servato modo procedendi in statutis definito, a munere removeantur.

§2. The local ordinary is to be concerned that those who are assigned as religion teachers in schools, even in non-Catholic ones, be outstanding for their correct doctrine, their witness of Christian living and their pedagogical skill.

Can. 805 — For his own diocese the local ordinary has the right to name or approve teachers of religion and likewise to remove or to demand that they be removed if it is required for reasons of religion or morals.

Can. 806 — §1. The diocesan bishop has the right of vigilance over and visitation of the Catholic schools located in his territory, even those schools which have been established or are being directed by members of religious institutes; he is likewise competent to issue prescriptions dealing with the general regulation of Catholic schools; such prescriptions are also operative for those schools which are directed by religious, with due regard for their autonomy regarding the internal management of their schools.

§2. The directors of Catholic schools, under the vigilance of the local ordinary, are to see to it that the instruction given in them is at least as academically distinguished as that given in the other schools of the region.

CHAPTER II

CATHOLIC UNIVERSITIES
AND OTHER INSTITUTES OF HIGHER STUDIES

Can. 807 — The Church has the right to erect and to supervise universities which contribute to a higher level of human culture, to a fuller advancement of the human person and also to the fulfillment of the Church's teaching office.

Can. 808 — Even if it really be Catholic, no university may bear the title or name *Catholic university* without the consent of the competent ecclesiastical authority.

Can. 809 — If it is possible and advantageous the conferences of bishops are to see to it that universities or at least faculties are established, suitably distributed throughout their territory, in which the various disciplines are to be investigated and taught with due regard for their academic autonomy, and with due consideration for Catholic doctrine.

Can. 810 — §1. It is the responsibility of the authority who is competent in accord with the statutes to provide for the appointment of teachers to Catholic universities who besides their scientific and pedagogical suitablity are also outstanding in their integrity of doctrine and probity of life; when those requisite qualities are lacking they are to be removed from their positions in accord with the procedure set forth in the statutes.

§ 2. Episcoporum conferentiae et Episcopi dioecesani, quorum interest, officium habent et ius invigilandi, ut in iisdem universitatibus principia doctrinae catholicae fideliter serventur.

Can. 811 – § 1. Curet auctoritas ecclesiastica competens ut in universitatibus catholicis erigatur facultas aut institutum aut saltem cathedra theologiae, in qua lectiones laicis quoque studentibus tradantur.

§ 2. In singulis universitatibus catholicis lectiones habeantur, in quibus eae praecipue tractentur quaestiones theologicae, quae cum disciplinis earundem facultatum sunt conexae.

Can. 812 – Qui in studiorum superiorum institutis quibuslibet disciplinas tradunt theologicas, auctoritatis ecclesiasticae competentis mandatum habeant oportet.

Can. 813 – Episcopus dioecesanus impensam habeat curam pastoralem studentium, etiam per paroeciae erectionem, vel saltem per sacerdotes ad hoc stabiliter deputatos, et provideat ut apud universitates, etiam non catholicas, centra habeantur universitaria catholica, quae iuventuti adiutorio sint, praesertim spirituali.

Can. 814 – Quae de universitatibus statuuntur praescripta, pari ratione applicantur aliis studiorum superiorum institutis.

Caput III
DE UNIVERSITATIBUS ET FACULTATIBUS ECCLESIASTICIS

Can. 815 – Ecclesiae, vi muneris sui veritatem revelatam nuntiandi, propriae sunt universitates vel facultates ecclesiasticae ad disciplinas sacras vel cum sacris conexas pervestigandas, atque studentes in iisdem disciplinis scientifice instituendos.

Can. 816 – § 1. Universitates et facultates ecclesiasticae constitui tantum possunt erectione ab Apostolica Sede facta aut approbatione ab eadem concessa; eidem competit etiam earundem superius moderamen.

§ 2. Singulae universitates et facultates ecclesiasticae sua habere debent statuta et studiorum rationem ab Apostolica Sede approbata.

Can. 817 – Gradus academicos, qui effectus canonicos in Ecclesia habeant, nulla universitas vel facultas conferre valet, quae non sit ab Apostolica Sede erecta vel approbata.

Can. 818 – Quae de universitatibus catholicis in cann. 810, 812 et 813 statuuntur praescripta, de universitatibus facultatibusque ecclesiasticis quoque valent.

§2. The conference of bishops and the diocesan bishops concerned have the duty and right of being vigilant that in these universities the principles of Catholic doctrine are faithfully observed.

Can. 811 — §1. The competent ecclesiastical authority is to provide that at Catholic universities there be erected a faculty of theology, an institute of theology, or at least a chair of theology so that classes may be given for lay students.

§2. In the individual Catholic universities classes should be given which treat in a special way those theological questions which are connected with the disciplines of their faculties.

Can. 812 — It is necessary that those who teach theological disciplines in any institute of higher studies have a mandate from the competent ecclesiastical authority.

Can. 813 — The diocesan bishop is to have serious pastoral concern for students by erecting a parish for them or by assigning priests for this purpose on a stable basis; he is also to provide for Catholic university centers at universities, even non-Catholic ones, to give assistance, especially spiritual to young people.

Can. 814 — The prescriptions established for universities are equally applicable to other institutes of higher studies.

Chapter III
ECCLESIASTICAL UNIVERSITIES AND FACULTIES

Can. 815 — Ecclesiastical universities or faculties are proper to the Church in virtue of its duty to announce revealed truth; they serve to investigate the sacred disciplines or those disciplines related to the sacred, and to instruct students scientifically in those same disciplines.

Can. 816 — §1. Ecclesiastical universities and faculties can be established only through erection by the Holy See or through its approval; the Holy See also has a supervisory role with respect to them.

§2. Individual ecclesiastical universities and faculties must have their statutes and plan of studies approved by the Apostolic See.

Can. 817 — No university or faculty which has not been erected or approved by the Apostolic See can grant academic degrees which have canonical effects in the Church.

Can. 818 — The prescriptions for Catholic universities specified in cann. 810, 812 and 813 are also applicable to ecclesiastical universities and faculties.

Can. 819 – Quatenus dioecesis aut instituti religiosi immo vel ipsius Ecclesiae universae bonum id requirat, debent Episcopi dioecesani aut institutorum Superiores competentes ad universitates vel facultates ecclesiasticas mittere iuvenes et clericos et sodales indole, virtute et ingenio praestantes.

Can. 820 – Curent universitatum et facultatum ecclesiasticarum Moderatores ac professores ut variae universitatis facultates mutuam sibi, prout obiectum siverit, praestent operam, utque inter propriam universitatem vel facultatem et alias universitates et facultates, etiam non ecclesiasticas, mutua habeatur cooperatio, qua nempe eaedem coniuncta opera, conventibus, investigationibus scientificis coordinatis aliisque mediis, ad maius scientiarum incrementum conspirent.

Can. 821 – Provideant Episcoporum conferentia atque Episcopus dioecesanus ut, ubi fieri possit, condantur instituta superiora scientiarum religiosarum, in quibus nempe edoceantur disciplinae theologicae aliaeque quae ad culturam christianam pertineant.

TITULUS IV
DE INSTRUMENTIS COMMUNICATIONIS SOCIALIS ET IN SPECIE DE LIBRIS

Can. 822 – § 1. Ecclesiae pastores, in suo munere explendo iure Ecclesiae proprio utentes, instrumenta communicationis socialis adhibere satagant.

§ 2. Iisdem pastoribus curae sit fideles edocere se officio teneri cooperandi ut instrumentorum communicationis socialis usus humano christianoque spiritu vivificetur.

§ 3. Omnes christifideles, ii praesertim qui quoquo modo in eorundem instrumentorum ordinatione aut usu partem habent, solliciti sint operam adiutricem actioni pastorali praestare, ita ut Ecclesia etiam iisdem instrumentis munus suum efficaciter exerceat.

Can. 823 – § 1. Ut veritatum fidei morumque integritas servetur, officium et ius est Ecclesiae pastoribus invigilandi, ne scriptis aut usu instrumentorum communicationis socialis christifidelium fidei aut moribus detrimentum afferatur; item exigendi, ut quae scripta fidem moresve tangant a christifidelibus edenda suo iudicio subiciantur; necnon reprobandi scripta quae rectae fidei aut bonis moribus noceant.

Can. 819 — Insofar as the good of a diocese, a religious institute or indeed the universal Church itself requires it, diocesan bishops or the competent superiors of institutes must send to ecclesiastical universities or faculties young people, clerics and members who are outstanding for their character, virtue and talent.

Can. 820 — The directors and professors of ecclesiastical universities and faculties are to see to it that the various faculties of such universities mutually assist one another insofar as their objectives permit this; they are also to see to it that mutual cooperation exists between their own university or faculty and other universities and faculties, even non-ecclesiastical ones; through their combined efforts, meetings, coordinated scientific research and other means, they are to work together for the greater advance of the sciences.

Can. 821 — The conference of bishops and the diocesan bishop are to provide, wherever possible, for the establishment of higher institutes for the religious sciences, namely institutes in which the theological disciplines and other disciplines pertaining to Christian culture are taught.

TITLE IV
INSTRUMENTS OF SOCIAL COMMUNICATION
AND SPECIFICALLY BOOKS

Can. 822 — §1. The pastors of the Church, employing a right which belongs to the Church in fulfilling its responsibility, are to endeavor to make use of the instruments of social communication.

§2. These same pastors are to see to it that the faithful are taught that they are bound in duty to cooperate so that the use of the instruments of social communication is animated with a human and Christian spirit.

§3. All the Christian faithful are to be concerned about furnishing assistance in this pastoral activity in such a way that the Church effectively fulfills its responsibility through such instruments; this is especially true for those who in any way have a role in the regulation or use of these instruments.

Can. 823 — §1. In order for the integrity of the truths of the faith and morals to be preserved, the pastors of the Church have the duty and the right to be vigilant lest harm be done to the faith or morals of the Christian faithful through writings or the use of the instruments of social communication; they likewise have the duty and the right to demand that writings to be published by the Christian faithful which touch upon faith or morals be submitted to their judgment; they also have the duty and right to denounce writings which harm correct faith or good morals.

§ 2. Officium et ius, de quibus in § 1, competunt Episcopis, tum singulis tum in conciliis particularibus vel Episcoporum conferentiis adunatis quoad christifideles suae curae commissos, supremae autem Ecclesiae auctoritati quoad universum Dei populum.

Can. 824 – § 1. Nisi aliud statuatur, loci Ordinarius, cuius licentia aut approbatio ad libros edendos iuxta canones huius tituli est petenda, est loci Ordinarius proprius auctoris aut Ordinarius loci in quo libri publici iuris fient.

§ 2. Quae in canonibus huius tituli statuuntur de libris, quibuslibet scriptis divulgationi publicae destinatis applicanda sunt, nisi aliud constet.

Can. 825 – § 1. Libri sacrarum Scripturarum edi non possunt nisi ab Apostolica Sede aut ab Episcoporum conferentia approbati sint; itemque ut eorundem versiones in linguam vernaculam edi possint, requiritur ut ab eadem auctoritate sint approbatae atque insimul necessariis et sufficientibus explicationibus sint instructae.

§ 2. Versiones sacrarum Scripturarum convenientibus explicationibus instructas, communi etiam cum fratribus seiunctis opera, parare atque edere possunt christifideles catholici, de licentia Episcoporum conferentiae.

Can. 826 – § 1. Ad libros liturgicos quod attinet, serventur praescripta can. 838.

§ 2. Ut iterum edantur libri liturgici necnon eorum versiones in linguam vernaculam eorumve partes, constare debet de concordantia cum editione approbata ex attestatione Ordinarii loci in quo publici iuris fiunt.

§ 3. Libri precum pro publico vel privato fidelium usu ne edantur nisi de licentia loci Ordinarii.

Can. 827 – § 1. Catechismi necnon alia scripta ad institutionem catecheticam pertinentia eorumve versiones, ut edantur, approbatione egent loci Ordinarii, firmo praescripto can. 775, § 2.

§ 2. Nisi cum approbatione competentis auctoritatis ecclesiasticae editi sint aut ab ea postea approbati, in scholis, sive elementariis sive mediis sive superioribus, uti textus, quibus institutio nititur, adhiberi non possunt libri qui quaestiones respiciunt ad sacram Scripturam, ad theologiam, ius canonicum, historiam ecclesiasticam, et ad religiosas aut morales disciplinas pertinentes.

§ 3. Commendatur ut libri materias de quibus in § 2 tractantes, licet non adhibeantur uti textus in institutione tradenda, itemque scripta in quibus aliquid habetur quod religionis aut morum honestatis peculiariter intersit, iudicio subiciantur loci Ordinarii.

§2. The bishops as individuals or gathered in particular councils or conferences of bishops have the duty and the right mentioned in §1 with regard to the Christian faithful committed to their care; the supreme authority of the Church has this duty and right in regard to the whole people of God.

Can. 824 — §1. Unless otherwise established, the local ordinary whose permission or approval to publish books is to be sought according to the canons of this title is the proper local ordinary of the author or the ordinary of the place in which the books are published.

§2. Unless otherwise evident, the prescriptions of the canons of this title concerning books are to be applied to any writings whatsoever which are destined for public distribution.

Can. 825 — §1. Books of the Sacred Scriptures cannot be published unless they have been approved either by the Apostolic See or by the conference of bishops; for their vernacular translations to be published it is required that they likewise be approved by the same authority and also annotated with necessary and sufficient explanations.

§2. With the permission of the conference of bishops Catholic members of the Christian faithful can collaborate with separated brothers and sisters in preparing and publishing translations of the Sacred Scriptures annotated with appropriate explanations.

Can. 826 — §1. The prescriptions of can. 838 are to be observed concerning liturgical books.

§2. For the reprinting in whole or in part of liturgical books as well as their vernacular translation, the ordinary of the place in which they are published must attest that they correspond with the approved edition.

§3. Prayer books for the public or private use of the faithful may not be published without the permission of the local ordinary.

Can. 827 — §1. With due regard for the prescription of can. 775, §2, catechisms and other writings dealing with catechetical formation or their translations need the approval of the local ordinary for their publication.

§2. Books which treat questions of sacred scripture, theology, canon law, church history or which deal with religious or moral disciplines cannot be employed as the textbooks on which instruction is based in elementary, middle or higher schools unless they were published with the approval of the competent ecclesiastical authority or subsequently approved by it.

§3. It is recommended that books which deal with the matters mentioned in §2 be submitted to the judgment of the local ordinary even if they are not employed as textbooks for teaching; the same is true for writings in which something is found to be of special concern to religion or to good moral behavior.

§ 4. In ecclesiis oratoriisve exponi, vendi aut dari non possunt libri vel alia scripta de quaestionibus religionis aut morum tractantia, nisi cum licentia competentis auctoritatis ecclesiasticae edita sint aut ab ea postea approbata.

Can. 828 – Collectiones decretorum aut actorum ab aliqua auctoritate ecclesiastica editas, iterum edere non licet, nisi impetrata prius eiusdem auctoritatis licentia et servatis condicionibus ab eadem praescriptis.

Can. 829 – Approbatio vel licentia alicuius operis edendi pro textu originali valet, non vero pro eiusdem novis editionibus vel translationibus.

Can. 830 – § 1. Integro manente iure uniuscuiusque loci Ordinarii committendi personis sibi probatis iudicium de libris, ab Episcoporum conferentia confici potest elenchus censorum, scientia, recta doctrina et prudentia praestantium, qui curiis dioecesanis praesto sint, aut constitui etiam potest commissio censorum, quam loci Ordinarii consulere possint.

§ 2. Censor, in suo obeundo officio, omni personarum acceptione seposita, prae oculis tantummodo habeat Ecclesiae de fide et moribus doctrinam, uti a magisterio ecclesiastico proponitur.

§ 3. Censor sententiam suam scripto dare debet; quae si faverit, Ordinarius pro suo prudenti iudicio licentiam concedat ut editio fiat, expresso suo nomine necnon tempore ac loco concessae licentiae; quod si eam non concedat, rationes denegationis cum operis scriptore Ordinarius communicet.

Can. 831 – § 1. In diariis, libellis aut foliis periodicis quae religionem catholicam aut bonos mores manifesto impetere solent, ne quidpiam conscribant christifideles, nisi iusta et rationabili de causa : clerici autem et institutorum religiosorum sodales, tantummodo de licentia loci Ordinarii.

§ 2. Episcoporum conferentiae est normas statuere de requisitis ut clericis atque sodalibus institutorum religiosorum partem habere liceat in tractandis via radiophonica aut televisifica quaestionibus, quae ad doctrinam catholicam aut mores attineant.

Can. 832 – Institutorum religiosorum sodales ut scripta quaestiones religionis morumve tractantia edere possint, licentia quoque egent sui Superioris maioris ad normam constitutionum.

§4. Books and other writings which treat of questions of religion or morals cannot be exhibited, sold, or distributed in churches or oratories unless they were published with the permission of the competent ecclesiastical authority or they were subsequently approved by it.

Can. 828 — It is unlawful to reprint collections of decrees or acts issued by some ecclesiastical authority unless prior permission of this same authority has been obtained and its conditions observed.

Can. 829 — The approval or permission to publish some work applies to its original text, but not to new editions or translations of it.

Can. 830 — §1. The conference of bishops can compile a list of censors known for their knowledge, correct doctrine and prudence who could aid diocesan curias, or it can establish a commission of censors which local ordinaries can consult; however, the right of each local ordinary to entrust the judging of books to persons approved by him still remains intact.

§2. In undertaking the office, the censor, laying aside any respect for persons, is to consider only the teaching of the Church concerning faith and morals as it is proposed by the ecclesiastical magisterium.

§3. The censor's opinion must be given in writing; if it is favorable, the ordinary, in his own prudent judgment, is to grant the permission to publish, giving his own name and the time and place of the granting of the permission; if, however, he does not grant the permission, the ordinary is to communicate the reasons for his refusal to the author of the work.

Can. 831 — §1. Without a just and reasonable cause the Christian faithful are not to write anything for newspapers, magazines or periodicals which are accustomed to attack openly the Catholic religion or good morals; clerics and members of religious institutes are to do so only with the permission of the local ordinary.

§2. It is the responsibility of the conference of bishops to establish norms concerning the requirements for clerics and members of religious institutes to take part in radio or television programs which deal with questions concerning Catholic teaching or morals.

Can. 832 — In order for members of religious institutes to publish writings dealing with questions of religion or morals they also need the permission of their major superior in accord with the norm of their constitutions.

TITULUS V
DE FIDEI PROFESSIONE

Can. 833 – Obligatione emittendi personaliter professionem fidei, secundum formulam a Sede Apostolica probatam, tenentur :

1° coram praeside eiusve delegato, omnes qui Concilio Oecumenico vel particulari, synodo Episcoporum atque synodo dioecesanae intersunt cum voto sive deliberativo sive consultivo ; praeses autem coram Concilio aut synodo ;

2° promoti ad cardinalitiam dignitatem iuxta sacri Collegii statuta ;

3° coram delegato ab Apostolica Sede, omnes promoti ad episcopatum, itemque qui Episcopo dioecesano aequiparantur ;

4° coram collegio consultorum, Administrator dioecesanus ;

5° coram Episcopo dioecesano eiusve delegato, Vicarii generales et Vicarii episcopales necnon Vicarii iudiciales ;

6° coram loci Ordinario eiusve delegato, parochi, rector, magistri theologiae et philosophiae in seminariis, initio suscepti muneris ; promovendi ad ordinem diaconatus ;

7° coram Magno Cancellario eoque deficiente coram Ordinario loci eorumve delegatis, rector universitatis ecclesiasticae vel catholicae, initio suscepti muneris ; coram rectore, si sit sacerdos, vel coram loci Ordinario eorumve delegatis, docentes qui disciplinas ad fidem vel mores pertinentes in quibusvis universitatibus tradunt, initio suscepti muneris ;

8° Superiores in institutis religiosis et societatibus vitae apostolicae clericalibus, ad normam constitutionum.

TITLE V

THE PROFESSION OF FAITH

Can. 833 — The following persons are obliged to make a profession of faith personally in accord with a formula approved by the Apostolic See:

1° in the presence of its president or his delegate, all persons who take part with either a deliberative or consultative vote in an ecumenical or particular council, in a synod of bishops, or in a diocesan synod; the president takes it in the presence of the council or synod;

2° those promoted to the cardinalatial dignity, in accord with the statutes of the sacred college;

3° in the presence of one delegated by the Apostolic See, all persons promoted to the episcopacy and those who are equivalent to a diocesan bishop;

4° in the presence of the college of consultors, a diocesan administrator;

5° in the presence of the diocesan bishop or his delegate, vicars general, episcopal vicars and vicars judicial;

6° in the presence of the local ordinary or his delegate and at the beginning of their term of office, pastors, the rector of a seminary, and the professors of theology and philosophy in seminaries; those to be promoted to the order of diaconate;

7° in the presence of the grand chancellor or, in his absence, in the presence of the local ordinary, or in the presence of their delegates, the rector of an ecclesiastical or Catholic university at the beginning of the rector's term of office; in the presence of the rector, if the rector is a priest, or the local ordinary, or their delegates and at the beginning of their term of office, teachers in any universities whatsoever who teach disciplines which deal with faith or morals;

8° the superiors in clerical religious institutes and societies of apostolic life in accord with the norm of the constitutions.

LIBER IV
DE ECCLESIAE MUNERE SANCTIFICANDI

Can. 834 – § 1. Munus sancfificandi Ecclesia peculiari modo adimplet per sacram liturgiam, quae quidem habetur ut Iesu Christi muneris sacerdotalis exercitatio, in qua hominum sanctificatio per signa sensibilia significatur ac modo singulis proprio efficitur, atque a mystico Iesu Christi Corpore, Capite nempe et membris, integer cultus Dei publicus exercetur.

§ 2. Huiusmodi cultus tunc habetur, cum defertur nomine Ecclesiae a personis legitime deputatis et per actus ab Ecclesiae auctoritate probatos.

Can. 835 – § 1. Munus sanctificandi exercent imprimis Episcopi, qui sunt magni sacerdotes, mysteriorum Dei praecipui dispensatores, atque totius vitae liturgicae in Ecclesia sibi commissa moderatores, promotores atque custodes.

§ 2. Illud quoque exercent presbyteri, qui nempe, et ipsi Christi sacerdotii participes, ut eius ministri sub Episcopi auctoritate, ad cultum divinum celebrandum et populum sanctificandum consecrantur.

§ 3. Diaconi in divino cultu celebrando partem habent, ad normam iuris praescriptorum.

§ 4. In munere sanctificandi propriam sibi partem habent ceteri quoque christifideles actuose in liturgicis celebrationibus, in eucharistica praesertim, suo modo participando; peculiari modo idem munus participant parentes vitam coniugalem spiritu christiano ducendo et educationem christianam filiorum procurando.

Can. 836 – Cum cultus christianus, in quo sacerdotium commune christifidelium exercetur, opus sit quod a fide procedit et eadem innititur, ministri sacri eandem excitare et illustrare sedulo curent, ministerio praesertim verbi, quo fides nascitur et nutritur.

BOOK IV
THE OFFICE OF SANCTIFYING IN THE CHURCH

Can. 834 — §1. The Church fulfills its office of sanctifying in a special way in the sacred liturgy, which is indeed the exercise of the priestly office of Jesus Christ; in it through sensible signs the sanctification of humankind is signified and effected in a manner proper to each of the signs and the whole of the public worship of God is carried on by the mystical Body of Jesus Christ, that is, by the Head and the members.

§2. This worship takes place when it is carried out in the name of the Church by persons lawfully deputed and through acts approved by the authority of the Church.

Can. 835 — §1. First and foremost, the bishops exercise the office of sanctifying; they are high priests, principal dispensers of the mysteries of God and moderators, promoters and custodians of the whole liturgical life of the church committed to them.

§2. The presbyters also exercise this office; they are in fact sharers of the priesthood of Christ Himself so that they are consecrated as his ministers under the authority of the bishop to celebrate divine worship and sanctify the people.

§3. Deacons have a part in celebration of the divine worship in accord with the prescriptions of the law.

§4. The rest of the Christian faithful by active participation in celebrations of liturgy especially in the Eucharist in their own way also have their own part in the office of sanctification; parents share in the office of sanctification in a particular way by leading a conjugal life in the Christian spirit and by seeing to Christian education of their children.

Can. 836 — Since Christian worship, in which the common priesthood of the Christian faithful is exercised, is a work which proceeds from faith and is based on it, sacred ministers are to strive diligently to arouse and enlighten that faith, especially through the ministry of the word by which faith is born and nourished.

Can. 837 – § 1. Actiones liturgicae non sunt actiones privatae, sed celebrationes Ecclesiae ipsius, quae est « unitatis sacramentum », scilicet plebs sancta sub Episcopis adunata et ordinata ; quare ad universum corpus Ecclesiae pertinent illudque manifestant et afficiunt ; singula vero membra ipsius attingunt diverso modo, pro diversitate ordinum, munerum et actualis participationis.

§ 2. Actiones liturgicae, quatenus suapte natura celebrationem communem secumferant, ubi id fieri potest, cum frequentia et actuosa participatione christifidelium celebrentur.

Can. 838 – § 1. Sacrae liturgiae moderatio ab Ecclesiae auctoritate unice pendet : quae quidem est penes Apostolicam Sedem et, ad normam iuris, penes Episcopum dioecesanum.

§ 2. Apostolicae Sedis est sacram liturgiam Ecclesiae universae ordinare, libros liturgicos edere eorumque versiones in linguas vernaculas recognoscere, necnon advigilare ut ordinationes liturgicae ubique fideliter observentur.

§ 3. Ad Episcoporum conferentias spectat versiones librorum liturgicorum in linguas vernaculas, convenienter intra limites in ipsis libris liturgicis definitos aptatas, parare, easque edere, praevia recognitione Sanctae Sedis.

§ 4. Ad Episcopum dioecesanum in Ecclesia sibi commissa pertinet, intra limites suae competentiae, normas de re liturgica dare, quibus omnes tenentur.

Can. 839 – § 1. Aliis quoque mediis munus sanctificationis peragit Ecclesia, orationibus scilicet, quibus Deum deprecatur ut christifideles sanctificati sint in veritate, paenitentiae necnon caritatis operibus, quae quidem magnopere ad Regnum Christi in animis radicandum et roborandum adiuvant et ad mundi salutem conferunt.

§ 2. Curent locorum Ordinarii ut orationes necnon pia et sacra exercitia populi christiani normis Ecclesiae plene congruant.

PARS I
DE SACRAMENTIS

Can. 840 – Sacramenta Novi Testamenti, a Christo Domino instituta et Ecclesiae concredita, utpote actiones Christi et Ecclesiae, signa exstant ac media quibus fides exprimitur et roboratur, cultus Deo redditur et hominum sanctificatio efficitur, atque ideo ad communionem ecclesiasticam inducendam, firmandam et manifestandam summopere

Can. 837 — §1. Liturgical actions are not private actions but celebrations of the Church itself, which is "the sacrament of unity," namely, a holy people assembled and ordered under the bishops; therefore liturgical actions pertain to the whole body of the Church and manifest and affect it, but they affect the individual members of the Church in different ways according to the diversity of orders, functions and actual participation.

§2. Liturgical actions, to the extent that by their proper nature they involve a common celebration, are to be celebrated where possible with the presence and active participation of the Christian faithful.

Can. 838 — §1. The supervision of the sacred liturgy depends solely on the authority of the Church which resides in the Apostolic See and, in accord with the law, the diocesan bishop.

§2. It is for the Apostolic See to order the sacred liturgy of the universal Church, to publish the liturgical books, to review their translations into the vernacular languages and to see that liturgical ordinances are faithfully observed everywhere.

§3. It pertains to the conferences of bishops to prepare translations of the liturgical books into the vernacular languages, with the appropriate adaptations within the limits defined in the liturgical books themselves, and to publish them with the prior review by the Holy See.

§4. It pertains to the diocesan bishop in the church entrusted to him, within the limits of his competence, to issue liturgical norms by which all are bound.

Can. 839 — §1. The Church carries out the office of sanctification in other ways also, namely, in prayers by which God is asked that the Christian faithful be sanctified in truth, and by works of penance and charity which greatly help to root and strengthen the kingdom of Christ in souls and contribute to the salvation of the world.

§2. Local ordinaries are to see to it that the prayers and other pious and sacred exercises of the Christian people are fully in harmony with the norms of the Church.

PART I

THE SACRAMENTS

Can. 840 — The sacraments of the New Testament, instituted by Christ the Lord and entrusted to the Church, as they are the actions of Christ and the Church, stand out as the signs and means by which the faith is expressed and strengthened, worship is rendered to God and the sanctification of humankind is effected, and they thus contribute in the highest degree to the establishment, strengthening and manifestation of ecclesial communion; therefore

conferunt; quapropter in iis celebrandis summa veneratione debitaque diligentia uti debent tum sacri ministri tum ceteri christifideles.

Can. 841 – Cum sacramenta eadem sint pro universa Ecclesia et ad divinum depositum pertineant, unius supremae Ecclesiae auctoritatis est probare vel definire quae ad eorum validitatem sunt requisita, atque eiusdem aliusve auctoritatis competentis, ad normam can. 838, §§ 3 et 4, est decernere quae ad eorum celebrationem, administrationem et receptionem licitam necnon ad ordinem in eorum celebratione servandum spectant.

Can. 842 – § 1. Ad cetera sacramenta valide admitti nequit, qui baptismum non recepit.

§ 2. Sacramenta baptismi, confirmationis et sanctissimae Eucharistiae ita inter se coalescunt, ut ad plenam initiationem christianam requirantur.

Can. 843 – § 1. Ministri sacri denegare non possunt sacramenta iis qui opportune eadem petant, rite sint dispositi, nec iure ab iis recipiendis prohibeantur.

§ 2. Animarum pastores ceterique christifideles, pro suo quisque ecclesiastico munere, officium habent curandi ut qui sacramenta petunt debita evangelizatione necnon catechetica institutione ad eadem recipienda praeparentur, attentis normis a competenti auctoritate editis.

Can. 844 – § 1. Ministri catholici sacramenta licite administrant solis christifidelibus catholicis, qui pariter eadem a solis ministris catholicis licite recipiunt, salvis huius canonis §§ 2, 3 et 4, atque can. 861, § 2 praescriptis.

§ 2. Quoties necessitas id postulet aut vera spiritualis utilitas id suadeat, et dummodo periculum vitetur erroris vel indifferentismi, licet christifidelibus quibus physice aut moraliter impossibile sit accedere ad ministrum catholicum, sacramenta paenitentiae, Eucharistiae et unctionis infirmorum recipere a ministris non catholicis, in quorum Ecclesia valida exsistunt praedicta sacramenta.

§ 3. Ministri catholici licite sacramenta paenitentiae, Eucharistiae et unctionis infirmorum administrant membris Ecclesiarum orientalium quae plenam cum Ecclesia catholica communionem non habent, si sponte id petant et rite sint disposita; quod etiam valet quoad membra aliarum Ecclesiarum, quae iudicio Sedis Apostolicae, ad sacramenta quod attinet, in pari condicione ac praedictae Ecclesiae orientales versantur.

both the sacred ministers and the rest of the Christian faithful must employ the greatest reverence and the necessary diligence in their celebration.

Can. 841 — Since the sacraments are the same for the universal Church and pertain to the divine deposit, it is for the supreme authority of the Church alone to approve or define those things which are required for their validity; it is for the same supreme authority of the Church or other competent authority in accord with the norm of can. 838, §§3 and 4 to determine what pertains to their lawful celebration, administration and reception and also the order to be observed in their celebration.

Can. 842 — §1. One who has not received baptism cannot be validly admitted to the other sacraments.

§2. The sacraments of baptism, confirmation, and the Most Holy Eucharist are so interrelated that they are required for full Christian initiation.

Can. 843 — §1. The sacred ministers can not refuse the sacraments to those who ask for them at appropriate times, are properly disposed and are not prohibited by law from receiving them.

§2. Pastors of souls and the rest of the Christian faithful, according to their ecclesial function, have the duty to see that those who seek the sacraments are prepared to receive them by the necessary evangelization and catechetical formation, taking into account the norms published by the competent authority.

Can. 844 — §1. Catholic ministers may licitly administer the sacraments to Catholic members of the Christian faithful only and, likewise, the latter may licitly receive the sacraments only from Catholic ministers with due regard for §§2, 3, and 4 of this canon, and can. 861, §2.

§2. Whenever necessity requires or genuine spiritual advantage suggests, and provided that the danger of error or indifferentism is avoided, it is lawful for the faithful for whom it is physically or morally impossible to approach a Catholic minister, to receive the sacraments of penance, Eucharist, and anointing of the sick from non-Catholic ministers in whose churches these sacraments are valid.

§3. Catholic ministers may licitly administer the sacraments of penance, Eucharist and anointing of the sick to members of the oriental churches which do not have full communion with the Catholic Church, if they ask on their own for the sacraments and are properly disposed. This holds also for members of other churches, which in the judgment of the Apostolic See are in the same condition as the oriental churches as far as these sacraments are concerned.

§ 4. Si adsit periculum mortis aut, iudicio Episcopi dioecesani aut Episcoporum conferentiae, alia urgeat gravis necessitas, ministri catholici licite eadem sacramenta administrant ceteris quoque christianis plenam communionem cum Ecclesia catholica non habentibus, qui ad suae communitatis ministrum accedere nequeant atque sponte id petant, dummodo quoad eadem sacramenta fidem catholicam manifestent et rite sint dispositi.

§ 5. Pro casibus de quibus in §§ 2, 3 et 4, Episcopus dioecesanus aut Episcoporum conferentia generales normas ne ferant, nisi post consultationem cum auctoritate competenti saltem locali Ecclesiae vel communitatis non catholicae, cuius interest.

Can. 845 – § 1. Sacramenta baptismi, confirmationis et ordinis, quippe quae characterem imprimant, iterari nequeunt.

§ 2. Si, diligenti inquisitione peracta, prudens adhuc dubium supersit num sacramenta de quibus in § 1 revera aut valide collata fuerint, sub condicione conferantur.

Can. 846 – § 1. In sacramentis celebrandis fideliter serventur libri liturgici a competenti auctoritate probati; quapropter nemo in iisdem quidpiam proprio marte addat, demat aut mutet.

§ 2. Minister sacramenta celebret secundum proprium ritum.

Can. 847 – § 1. In administrandis sacramentis, in quibus sacra olea adhibenda sunt, minister uti debet oleis ex olivis aut aliis ex plantis expressis atque, salvo praescripto can. 999, n. 2, ab Episcopo consecratis vel benedictis, et quidem recenter; veteribus ne utatur, nisi adsit necessitas.

§ 2. Parochus olea sacra a proprio Episcopo impetret eaque decenti custodia diligenter asservet.

Can. 848 – Minister, praeter oblationes a competenti auctoritate definitas, pro sacramentorum administratione nihil petat, cauto semper ne egentes priventur auxilio sacramentorum ratione paupertatis.

TITULUS I
DE BAPTISMO

Can. 849 – Baptismus, ianua sacramentorum, in re vel saltem in voto ad salutem necessarius, quo homines a peccatis liberantur, in Dei filios regenerantur atque indelebili charactere Christo configurati Ecclesiae incorporantur, valide confertur tantummodo per lavacrum aquae verae cum debita verborum forma.

§4. If the danger of death is present or other grave necessity, in the judgment of the diocesan bishop or the conference of bishops, Catholic ministers may licitly administer these sacraments to other Christians who do not have full communion with the Catholic Church, who cannot approach a minister of their own community and on their own ask for it, provided they manifest Catholic faith in these sacraments and are properly disposed.

§5. For the cases in §§2, 3, and 4, neither the diocesan bishop nor the conference of bishops is to enact general norms except after consultation with at least the local competent authority of the interested non-Catholic church or community.

Can. 845 — §1. The sacraments of baptism, confirmation and orders cannot be repeated since they imprint a character.

§2. If, after diligent investigation, there is still a prudent doubt whether these sacraments mentioned in §1 have been truly or validly conferred, they are to be conditionally conferred.

Can. 846 — §1. The liturgical books approved by the competent authority are to be faithfully observed in the celebration of the sacraments; therefore no one on personal authority may add, remove or change anything in them.

§2. The ministers are to celebrate the sacraments according to their own rite.

Can. 847 — §1. In the administration of sacraments in which the sacred oils are to be used, the minister must use oils pressed from olives or from other plants that have been recently consecrated or blessed by the bishop, with due regard for the prescription of can. 999, n. 2; he is not to use old oils unless there is some necessity.

§2. The pastor is to obtain the sacred oils from his own bishop and keep them carefully in a fitting manner.

Can. 848 — The minister should ask nothing for the administration of the sacraments beyond the offerings defined by the competent authority, always being careful that the needy are not deprived of the help of the sacraments because of their poverty.

TITLE I
BAPTISM

Can. 849 — Baptism, the gate to the sacraments, necessary for salvation in fact or at least in intention, by which men and women are freed from their sins, are reborn as children of God and, configured to Christ by an indelible character, are incorporated in the Church, is validly conferred only by washing with true water together with the required form of words.

Caput I

DE BAPTISMI CELEBRATIONE

Can. 850 – Baptismus ministratur secundum ordinem in probatis liturgicis libris praescriptum, excepto casu necessitatis urgentis, in quo ea tantum observari debent, quae ad validitatem sacramenti requiruntur.

Can. 851 – Baptismi celebratio debite praeparetur oportet; itaque:

1° adultus, qui baptismum recipere intendit, ad catechumenatum admittatur et, quatenus fieri potest, per varios gradus ad initiationem sacramentalem perducatur, secundum ordinem initiationis ab Episcoporum conferentia aptatum et peculiares normas ab eadem editas;

2° infantis baptizandi parentes, itemque qui munus patrini sunt suscepturi, de significatione huius sacramenti deque obligationibus cum eo cohaerentibus rite edoceantur; parochus per se vel per alios curet ut ita pastoralibus monitionibus, immo et communi precatione, debite parentes instruantur, plures adunando familias atque, ubi fieri possit, eas visitando.

Can. 852 – § 1. Quae in canonibus de baptismo adulti habentur praescripta, applicantur omnibus qui, infantia egressi, rationis usum assecuti sunt.

§ 2. Infanti assimilatur, etiam ad baptismum quod attinet, qui non est sui compos.

Can. 853 – Aqua in baptismo conferendo adhibenda, extra casum necessitatis, benedicta sit oportet, secundum librorum liturgicorum praescripta.

Can. 854 – Baptismus conferatur sive per immersionem sive per infusionem, servatis Episcoporum conferentiae praescriptis.

Can. 855 – Curent parentes, patrini et parochus ne imponatur nomen a sensu christiano alienum.

Can. 856 – Licet baptismus quolibet die celebrari possit, commendatur tamen ut ordinarie die dominica aut, si fieri possit, in vigilia Paschatis, celebretur.

Can. 857 – § 1. Extra casum necessitatis, proprius baptismi locus est ecclesia aut oratorium.

§ 2. Pro regula habeatur ut adultus baptizetur in propria ecclesia paroeciali, infans vero in ecclesia paroeciali parentum propria, nisi iusta causa aliud suadeat.

CHAPTER I

THE CELEBRATION OF BAPTISM

Can. 850 — Baptism should be administered in accord with the order prescribed in the approved liturgical books, except for the case of urgent necessity when only what is required for the validity of the sacrament must be observed.

Can. 851 — It is necessary that the celebration of baptism be properly prepared. Thus:

1° an adult who intends to receive baptism is to be admitted to the catechumenate and, to the extent possible, be led through the several stages to sacramental initiation, in accord with the order of initiation adapted by the conference of bishops and the special norms published by it;

2° the parents of an infant who is to be baptized and likewise those who are to undertake the office of sponsor are to be properly instructed in the meaning of this sacrament and the obligations which are attached to it; personally or through others the pastor is to see to it that the parents are properly formed by pastoral directions and by common prayer, gathering several families together and where possible visiting them.

Can. 852 — §1. What is prescribed in the canons on the baptism of an adult is applicable to all who are no longer infants but have attained the use of reason.

§2. One who is not of sound mind (*non sui compos*) is equated with an infant so far as baptism is concerned.

Can. 853 — Outside a case of necessity the water to be used in the conferral of baptism should be blessed in accord with the prescriptions of the liturgical books.

Can. 854 — Baptism is to be conferred either by immersion or by pouring, the prescriptions of the conference of bishops being observed.

Can. 855 — Parents, sponsors and the pastor are to see that a name foreign to a Christian mentality is not given.

Can. 856 — Although baptism may be celebrated on any day, it is recommended that ordinarily it be celebrated on a Sunday or if possible at the Easter Vigil.

Can. 857 — §1. Outside a case of necessity, the proper place for baptism is a church or oratory.

§2. As a rule adults are to be baptized in their own parish church and infants in the parish church proper to their parents, unless a just cause suggests otherwise.

Can. 858 – § 1. Quaevis ecclesia paroecialis baptismalem fontem habeat, salvo iure cumulativo aliis ecclesiis iam quaesito.

§ 2. Loci Ordinarius, audito loci parocho, potest ad fidelium commoditatem permittere aut iubere, ut fons baptismalis habeatur etiam in alia ecclesia aut oratorio intra paroeciae fines.

Can. 859 – Si ad ecclesiam paroecialem aut ad aliam ecclesiam vel oratorium, de quo in can. 858, § 2, baptizandus, propter locorum distantiam aliave adiuncta, sine gravi incommodo accedere vel transferri nequeat, baptismus conferri potest et debet in alia propinquiore ecclesia vel oratorio, aut etiam alio in loco decenti.

Can. 860 – § 1. Praeter casum necessitatis, baptismus ne conferatur in domibus privatis, nisi loci Ordinarius gravi de causa id permiserit.

§ 2. In valetudinariis, nisi aliter Episcopus dioecesanus statuerit, baptismus ne celebretur, nisi in casu necessitatis vel alia ratione pastorali cogente.

Caput II
DE BAPTISMI MINISTRO

Can. 861 – § 1. Minister ordinarius baptismi est Episcopus, presbyter et diaconus, firmo praescripto can. 530, n. 1.

§ 2. Absente aut impedito ministro ordinario, licite baptismum confert catechista aliusve ad hoc munus ab Ordinario loci deputatus, immo, in casu necessitatis, quilibet homo debita intentione motus; solliciti sint animarum pastores, praesertim parochus, ut christifideles de recto baptizandi modo edoceantur.

Can. 862 – Excepto casu necessitatis, nemini licet, sine debita licentia, in alieno territorio baptismum conferre, ne suis quidem subditis.

Can. 863 – Baptismus adultorum, saltem eorum qui aetatem quattuordecim annorum expleverunt, ad Episcopum dioecesanum deferatur ut, si id expedire iudicaverit, ab ipso administretur.

Caput III
DE BAPTIZANDIS

Can. 864 – Baptismi capax est omnis et solus homo nondum baptizatus.

Can. 858 — §1. Every parish church is to have a baptismal font, with due regard for the cumulative right already acquired by other churches.

§2. The local ordinary, after hearing the pastor of the place, may permit or order for the convenience of the faithful that there be a baptismal font in another church or oratory within the boundaries of the parish.

Can. 859 — If due to grave inconvenience because of distance or other circumstances a person to be baptized cannot go or be taken to the parish church or to the other church or oratory mentioned in can. 858, §2, baptism may and must be conferred in some nearer church or oratory, or even in some other fitting place.

Can. 860 — §1. Outside the case of necessity, baptism is not to be conferred in private homes, unless the local ordinary has permitted this for a grave cause.

§2. Baptism is not to be celebrated in hospitals unless the diocesan bishop has decreed otherwise, except in case of necessity or some other compelling pastoral reason.

CHAPTER II
THE MINISTER OF BAPTISM

Can. 861 — §1. The ordinary minister of baptism is a bishop, presbyter or deacon, with due regard for the prescription of can. 530, n. 1.

§2. If the ordinary minister is absent or impeded, a catechist or other person deputed for this function by the local ordinary confers baptism licitly as does any person with the right intention in case of necessity; shepherds of souls, especially the pastor, are to be concerned that the faithful be instructed in the correct manner of baptizing.

Can. 862 — Outside the case of necessity, it is not lawful for anyone, without the required permission, to confer baptism in the territory of another, not even upon his own subjects.

Can. 863 — The baptism of adults, at least those who have completed fourteen years of age is to be referred to the bishop so that it may be conferred by him, if he judges it expedient.

CHAPTER III
THOSE TO BE BAPTIZED

Can. 864 — Every person not yet baptized and only such a person is able to be baptized.

Can. 865 – § 1. Ut adultus baptizari possit, eum oportet voluntatem baptismum recipiendi manifestaverit, de fidei veritatibus obligationibusque christianis sufficienter sit instructus atque in vita christiana per catechumenatum sit probatus; admoneatur etiam ut de peccatis suis doleat.

§ 2. Adultus, qui in periculo mortis versatur, baptizari potest si, aliquam de praecipuis fidei veritatibus cognitionem habens, quovis modo intentionem suam baptismum recipiendi manifestaverit et promittat se christianae religionis mandata esse servaturum.

Can. 866 – Adultus qui baptizatur, nisi gravis obstet ratio, statim post baptismum confirmetur atque celebrationem eucharisticam, communionem etiam recipiendo, participet.

Can. 867 – § 1. Parentes obligatione tenentur curandi ut infantes intra priores hebdomadas baptizentur; quam primum post nativitatem, immo iam ante eam, parochum adeant ut sacramentum pro filio petant et debite ad illud praeparentur.

§ 2. Si infans in periculo mortis versetur, sine ulla mora baptizetur.

Can. 868 – § 1. Ut infans licite baptizetur, oportet:

1° parentes, saltem eorum unus aut qui legitime eorundem locum tenet, consentiant;

2° spes habeatur fundata eum in religione catholica educatum iri; quae si prorsus deficiat, baptismus secundum praescripta iuris particularis differatur, monitis de ratione parentibus.

§ 2. Infans parentum catholicorum, immo et non catholicorum, in periculo mortis licite baptizatur, etiam invitis parentibus.

Can. 869 – § 1. Si dubitetur num quis baptizatus fuerit, aut baptismus valide collatus fuerit, dubio quidem post seriam investigationem permanente, baptismus eidem sub condicione conferatur.

§ 2. Baptizati in communitate ecclesiali non catholica non sunt sub condicione baptizandi, nisi, inspecta materia et verborum forma in baptismo collato adhibitis necnon attenta intentione baptizati adulti et ministri baptizantis, seria ratio adsit de baptismi validitate dubitandi.

§ 3. Quod si, in casibus de quibus in §§ 1 et 2, dubia remaneat baptismi collatio aut validitas, baptismus ne conferatur nisi postquam baptizando, si sit adultus, doctrina de baptismi sacramento exponatur, atque eidem aut, si de infante agitur, eius parentibus rationes dubiae validitatis baptismi celebrati declarentur.

Can. 865 — §1. To be baptized, it is required that an adult have manifested the will to receive baptism, be sufficiently instructed in the truths of faith and in Christian obligations and be tested in the Christian life by means of the catechumenate; the adult is also to be exhorted to have sorrow for personal sins.

§2. An adult in danger of death may be baptized if, having some knowledge of the principal truths of faith, the person has in any way manifested an intention of receiving baptism and promises to observe the commandments of the Christian religion.

Can. 866 — Unless a grave reason prevents it, an adult who is baptized is to be confirmed immediately after baptism and participate in the celebration of the Eucharist, also receiving Communion.

Can. 867 — §1. Parents are obliged to see to it that infants are baptized within the first weeks after birth; as soon as possible after the birth or even before it parents are to go to the pastor to request the sacrament for their child and to be properly prepared for it.

§2. An infant in danger of death, is to be baptized without any delay.

Can. 868 — §1. For the licit baptism of an infant it is necessary that:

1° the parents or at least one of them or the person who lawfully takes their place gives consent;

2° there be a founded hope that the infant will be brought up in the Catholic religion; if such a hope is altogether lacking, the baptism is to be put off according to the prescriptions of particular law and the parents are to be informed of the reason.

§2. The infant of Catholic parents, in fact of non-Catholic parents also, who is in danger of death is licitly baptized even against the will of the parents.

Can. 869 — §1. If there is a doubt whether one has been baptized or whether baptism was validly conferred and the doubt remains after serious investigation, baptism is to be conferred conditionally.

§2. Those baptized in a non-Catholic ecclesial community are not to be baptized conditionally unless, after an examination of the matter and the form of words used in the conferral of baptism and after a consideration of the intention of an adult baptized person and of the minister of the baptism, a serious reason for doubting the validity of the baptism is present.

§3. If the conferral or the validity of the baptism in the cases mentioned §§1 and 2 remains doubtful, baptism is not to be conferred until the doctrine of the sacrament of baptism is explained to the person, if an adult, and the reasons for the doubtful validity of the baptism have been explained to the adult recipient or, in the case of an infant, to the parents.

Can. 870 – Infans expositus aut inventus, nisi re diligenter investigata de eius baptismo constet, baptizetur.

Can. 871 – Fetus abortivi, si vivant, quatenus fieri potest, baptizentur.

Caput IV
DE PATRINIS

Can. 872 – Baptizando, quantum fieri potest, detur patrinus, cuius est baptizando adulto, in initiatione christiana adstare, et baptizandum infantem una cum parentibus ad baptismum praesentare itemque operam dare ut baptizatus vitam christianam baptismo congruam ducat obligationesque eidem inhaerentes fideliter adimpleat.

Can. 873 – Patrinus unus tantum vel matrina una vel etiam unus et una assumantur.

Can. 874 – § 1. Ut quis ad munus patrini suscipiendum admittatur, oportet:

1° ab ipso baptizando eiusve parentibus aut ab eo qui eorum locum tenet aut, his deficientibus, a parocho vel ministro sit designatus atque aptitudinem et intentionem habeat hoc munus gerendi;

2° decimum sextum aetatis annum expleverit, nisi alia aetas ab Episcopo dioecesano statuta fuerit vel exceptio iusta de causa parocho aut ministro admittenda videatur;

3° sit catholicus, confirmatus et sanctissimum Eucharistiae sacramentum iam receperit, idemque vitam ducat fidei et muneri suscipiendo congruam;

4° nulla poena canonica legitime irrogata vel declarata sit innodatus;

5° non sit pater aut mater baptizandi.

§ 2. Baptizatus ad communitatem ecclesialem non catholicam pertinens, nonnisi una cum patrino catholico, et quidem ut testis tantum baptismi, admittatur.

Caput V
DE COLLATI BAPTISMI PROBATIONE ET ADNOTATIONE

Can. 875 – Qui baptismum administrat curet ut, nisi adsit patrinus, habeatur saltem testis quo collatio baptismi probari possit.

Can. 870 — A foundling or abandoned child is to be baptized unless upon diligent investigation proof of baptism is established.

Can. 871 — If aborted fetuses are alive, they are to be baptized if this is possible.

CHAPTER IV
SPONSORS

Can. 872 — Insofar as possible one to be baptized is to be given a sponsor who is to assist an adult in Christian initiation, or, together with the parents, to present an infant at the baptism, and who will help the baptized to lead a Christian life in harmony with baptism, and to fulfill faithfully the obligations connected with it.

Can. 873 — Only one male or one female sponsor or one of each sex is to be employed.

Can. 874 — §1. To be admitted to the role of sponsor, a person must:

1° be designated by the one to be baptized, by the parents or the one who takes their place or, in their absence, by the pastor or minister and is to have the qualifications and intention of performing this role;

2° have completed the sixteenth year, unless a different age has been established by the diocesan bishop or it seems to the pastor or minister that an exception is to be made for a just cause;

3° be a Catholic who has been confirmed and has already received the sacrament of the Most Holy Eucharist and leads a life in harmony with the faith and the role to be undertaken;

4° not be bound by any canonical penalty legitimately imposed or declared;

5° not be the father or the mother of the one to be baptized.

§2. A baptized person who belongs to a non-Catholic ecclesial community may not be admitted except as a witness to baptism and together with a Catholic sponsor.

CHAPTER V
THE PROOF AND RECORD OF CONFERRED BAPTISM

Can. 875 — One who administers baptism is to see to it that, unless a sponsor is present, there be at least a witness by whom the conferral of baptism can be proved.

Can. 876 – Ad collatum baptismum comprobandum, si nemini fiat praeiudicium, sufficit declaratio unius testis omni exceptione maioris, aut ipsius baptizati iusiurandum, si ipse in aetate adulta baptismum receperit.

Can. 877 – § 1. Parochus loci, in quo baptismus celebratur, debet nomina baptizatorum, mentione facta de ministro, parentibus, patrinis necnon, si adsint, testibus, de loco ac die collati baptismi, in baptizatorum libro sedulo et sine ulla mora referre, simul indicatis die et loco nativitatis.

§ 2. Si de filio agatur e matre non nupta nato, matris nomen inserendum est, si publice de eius maternitate constet aut ipsa sponte sua, scripto vel coram duobus testibus, id petat; item nomen patris inscribendum est, si eius paternitas probatur aliquo publico documento aut ipsius declaratione coram parocho et duobus testibus facta; in ceteris casibus, inscribatur baptizatus, nulla facta de patris aut parentum nomine indicatione.

§ 3. Si de filio adoptivo agitur, inscribantur nomina adoptantium necnon, saltem si ita fiat in actu civili regionis, parentum naturalium ad normam §§ 1 et 2, attentis Episcoporum conferentiae praescriptis.

Can. 878 – Si baptismus neque a parocho neque eo praesente administratus fuerit, minister baptismi, quicumque est, de collato baptismo certiorem facere debet parochum paroeciae in qua baptismus administratus est, ut baptismum adnotet ad normam can. 877, § 1.

TITULUS II
DE SACRAMENTO CONFIRMATIONIS

Can. 879 – Sacramentum confirmationis, quod characterem imprimit et quo baptizati, iter initiationis christianae prosequentes, Spiritus Sancti dono ditantur atque perfectius Ecclesiae vinculantur, eosdem roborat arctiusque obligat ut verbo et opere testes sint Christi fidemque diffundant et defendant.

Caput I
DE CONFIRMATIONIS CELEBRATIONE

Can. 880 – § 1. Sacramentum confirmationis confertur per unctionem chrismatis in fronte, quae fit manus impositione atque per verba in probatis liturgicis libris praescripta.

Can. 876 — If it is not prejudicial to anyone, to prove the conferral of baptism, the declaration of a single witness who is above suspicion suffices or the oath of the baptized person, if the baptism was received at an adult age.

Can. 877 — §1. The pastor of the place where the baptism is celebrated must carefully and without delay record in the baptismal book the names of those baptized making mention of the minister, parents, sponsors, witnesses if any and the place and date of the conferred baptism, together with an indication of the date and place of birth.

§2. If it is a question of a child born of an unmarried mother, the name of the mother is to be inserted if there is public proof of her maternity or if she asks this willingly, either in writing or before two witnesses; likewise the name of the father is to be inserted if his paternity has been proved either by some public document or by his own declaration before the pastor and two witnesses; in other cases, the name of the one baptized is recorded without any indication of the name of the father or the parents.

§3. If it is a question of an adopted child, the names of the adopting parents are to be recorded, and also, at least if this is to be done in the civil records of the region, the names of the natural parents, in accord with §§1 and 2, with due regard for the prescriptions of the conference of bishops.

Can. 878 — If baptism was administered neither by the pastor nor in his presence, the minister of baptism, whoever it is, must inform the pastor of the parish in which the baptism was administered, so that he may record it in accord with can. 877, §1.

TITLE II
THE SACRAMENT OF CONFIRMATION

Can. 879 — The sacrament of confirmation impresses a character and by it the baptized, continuing on the path of Christian initiation, are enriched by the gift of the Holy Spirit and bound more perfectly to the Church; it strengthens them and obliges them more firmly to be witnesses to Christ by word and deed and to spread and defend the faith.

CHAPTER I
THE CELEBRATION OF CONFIRMATION

Can. 880 — §1. The sacrament of confirmation is conferred through anointing with chrism on the forehead, which is done by the imposition of the hand, and through the words prescribed in the approved liturgical books.

§ 2. Chrisma in sacramento confirmationis adhibendum debet esse ab Episcopo consecratum, etiamsi sacramentum a presbytero ministretur.

Can. 881 – Expedit ut confirmationis sacramentum in ecclesia, et quidem intra Missam celebretur; ex causa tamen iusta et rationabili, extra Missam et quolibet loco digno celebrari potest.

Caput II

DE CONFIRMATIONIS MINISTRO

Can. 882 – Confirmationis minister ordinàrius est Episcopus; valide hoc sacramentum confert presbyter quoque hac facultate vi iuris communis aut peculiaris concessionis competentis auctoritatis instructus.

Can. 883 – Ipso iure facultate confirmationem ministrandi gaudent:

1° intra fines suae dicionis, qui iure Episcopo dioecesano aequiparantur;

2° quoad personam de qua agitur, presbyter qui, vi officii vel mandati Episcopi dioecesani, infantia egressum baptizat aut iam baptizatum in plenam Ecclesiae catholicae communionem admittit;

3° quoad eos qui in periculo mortis versantur, parochus, immo quilibet presbyter.

Can. 884 – § 1. Episcopus dioecesanus confirmationem administret per se ipse aut curet ut per alium Episcopum administretur; quod si necessitas id requirat, facultatem concedere potest uni vel pluribus determinatis presbyteris, qui hoc sacramentum administrent.

§ 2. Gravi de causa, Episcopus itemque presbyter, vi iuris aut peculiaris concessionis competentis auctoritatis facultate confirmandi donatus, possunt in singulis casibus presbyteros, ut et ipsi sacramentum administrent, sibi sociare.

Can. 885 – § 1. Episcopus dioecesanus obligatione tenetur curandi ut sacramentum confirmationis subditis rite et rationabiliter petentibus conferatur.

§ 2. Presbyter, qui hac facultate gaudet, eadem uti debet erga eos in quorum favorem facultas concessa est.

Can. 886 – § 1. Episcopus in sua dioecesi sacramentum confirmationis legitime administrat etiam fidelibus non subditis, nisi obstet expressa proprii ipsorum Ordinarii prohibitio.

§2. The chrism to be used in the sacrament of confirmation must be consecrated by a bishop, even if the sacrament is administered by a presbyter.

Can. 881 — It is desirable that the sacrament of confirmation be celebrated in a church and during Mass, but for a just and reasonable cause it may be celebrated outside Mass and in any worthy place.

CHAPTER II

THE MINISTER OF CONFIRMATION

Can. 882 — The ordinary minister of confirmation is the bishop; a presbyter who has this faculty by virtue of either the common law or a special concession of competent authority also confers this sacrament validly.

Can. 883 — The following have the faculty of administering confirmation by the law itself:

1° within the limits of their territory, those who are equivalent in law to the diocesan bishop;

2° with regard to the person in question, the presbyter who by reason of office or mandate of the diocesan bishop baptizes one who is no longer an infant or one already baptized whom he admits into the full communion of the Catholic Church;

3° with regard to those in danger of death, the pastor or indeed any presbyter.

Can. 884 — §1. The diocesan bishop is to administer confirmation personally or see that it is administered by another bishop, but if necessity requires he may give the faculty to administer this sacrament to one or more specified presbyters.

§2. For a grave cause, a bishop and likewise a presbyter who has the faculty to confirm by virtue of law or special concession of competent authority may in individual cases associate presbyters with themselves so that they may administer the sacrament.

Can. 885 — §1. The diocesan bishop is obliged to see that the sacrament of confirmation is conferred on his subjects who properly and reasonably request it.

§2. A presbyter who has this faculty must use it for those in whose favor the faculty was granted.

Can. 886 — §1. In his own diocese the bishop legitimately administers the sacrament of confirmation even to the faithful who are not his subjects, unless there is an express prohibition by their own proper ordinary.

§ 2. Ut in aliena dioecesi confirmationem licite administret, Episcopus indiget, nisi agatur de suis subditis, licentia saltem rationabiliter praesumpta Episcopi dioecesani.

Can. 887 – Presbyter facultate confirmationem ministrandi gaudens, in territorio sibi designato hoc sacramentum extraneis quoque licite confert, nisi obstet proprii eorum Ordinarii vetitum; illud vero in alieno territorio nemini valide confert, salvo praescripto can. 883, n. 3.

Can. 888 – Intra territorium in quo confirmationem conferre valent, ministri in locis quoque exemptis eam ministrare possunt.

Caput III
DE CONFIRMANDIS

Can. 889 – § 1. Confirmationis recipiendae capax est omnis et solus baptizatus, nondum confirmatus.

§ 2. Extra periculum mortis, ut quis licite confirmationem recipiat, requiritur, si rationis usu polleat, ut sit apte institutus, rite dispositus et promissiones baptismales renovare valeat.

Can. 890 – Fideles tenentur obligatione hoc sacramentum tempestive recipiendi; curent parentes, animarum pastores, praesertim parochi, ut fideles ad illud recipiendum rite instruantur et opportuno tempore accedant.

Can. 891 – Sacramentum confirmationis conferatur fidelibus circa aetatem discretionis, nisi Episcoporum conferentia aliam aetatem determinaverit, aut adsit periculum mortis vel, de iudicio ministri, gravis causa aliud suadeat.

Caput IV
DE PATRINIS

Can. 892 – Confirmando, quantum id fieri potest, adsit patrinus, cuius est curare ut confirmatus tamquam verus Christi testis se gerat obligationesque eidem sacramento inhaerentes fideliter adimpleat.

Can. 893 – § 1. Ut quis patrini munere fungatur, condiciones adimpleat oportet, de quibus in can. 874.

§ 2. Expedit ut tamquam patrinus assumatur qui idem munus in baptismo suscepit.

§2. To administer confirmation licitly in another diocese, the bishop needs at least the reasonably presumed permission of the diocesan bishop, unless it is a question of his own subjects.

Can. 887 — A presbyter who has the faculty to administer confirmation licitly confers this sacrament even on externs in the territory designated for him, unless there is a prohibition of their own proper ordinary; but such a presbyter may not validly confer the sacrament on anyone in another territory with due regard for the prescription of can. 883, n.3.

Can. 888 — The ministers may administer confirmation even in exempt places within the territory where they are able to confer the sacrament.

Chapter III
THOSE TO BE CONFIRMED

Can. 889 — §1. All baptized persons who have not been confirmed and only they are capable of receiving confirmation.

§2. Outside the danger of death, to be licitly confirmed it is required, if the person has the use of reason, that one be suitably instructed, properly disposed and able to renew one's baptismal promises.

Can. 890 — The faithful are obliged to receive this sacrament at the appropriate time; their parents and shepherds of souls, especially pastors, are to see to it that the faithful are properly instructed to receive it and approach the sacrament at the appropriate time.

Can. 891 — The sacrament of confirmation is to be conferred on the faithful at about the age of discretion unless the conference of bishops determines another age or there is danger of death or in the judgment of the minister a grave cause urges otherwise.

Chapter IV
SPONSORS

Can. 892 — As far as possible a sponsor for the one to be confirmed should be present; it is for the sponsor to see that the confirmed person acts as a true witness to Christ and faithfully fulfills the obligations connected with this sacrament.

Can. 893 — §1. To perform the role of sponsor, it is necessary that a person fulfill the conditions mentioned in can. 874.

§2. It is desirable that the one who undertook the role of sponsor at baptism be sponsor for confirmation.

CAPUT V

DE COLLATAE CONFIRMATIONIS PROBATIONE
ET ADNOTATIONE

Can. 894 – Ad collatam confirmationem probandam serventur praescripta can. 876.

Can. 895 – Nomina confirmatorum, facta mentione ministri, parentum et patrinorum, loci et diei collatae confirmationis in librum confirmatorum Curiae dioecesanae adnotentur, vel, ubi id praescripserit Episcoporum conferentia aut Episcopus dioecesanus, in librum in archivo paroeciali conservandum; parochus debet de collata confirmatione monere parochum loci baptismi, ut adnotatio fiat in libro baptizatorum, ad normam can. 535, § 2.

Can. 896 – Si parochus loci praesens non fuerit, eundem de collata confirmatione minister per se vel per alium quam primum certiorem faciat.

TITULUS III
DE SANCTISSIMA EUCHARISTIA

Can. 897 – Augustissimum Sacramentum est sanctissima Eucharistia, in qua ipsemet Christus Dominus continetur, offertur ac sumitur, et qua continuo vivit et crescit Ecclesia. Sacrificium eucharisticum, memoriale mortis et resurrectionis Domini, in quo Sacrificium crucis in saecula perpetuatur, totius cultus et vitae christianae est culmen et fons, quo significatur et efficitur unitas populi Dei et corporis Christi aedificatio perficitur. Cetera enim sacramenta et omnia ecclesiastica apostolatus opera cum sanctissima Eucharistia cohaerent et ad eam ordinantur.

Can. 898 – Christifideles maximo in honore sanctissimam Eucharistiam habeant, actuosam in celebratione augustissimi Sacrificii partem habentes, devotissime et frequenter hoc sacramentum recipientes, atque summa cum adoratione idem colentes; animarum pastores doctrinam de hoc sacramento illustrantes, fideles hanc obligationem sedulo edoceant.

CAPUT I

DE EUCHARISTICA CELEBRATIONE

Can. 899 – § 1. Eucharistica celebratio actio est ipsius Christi et Ecclesiae, in qua Christus Dominus, ministerio sacerdotis, semetipsum,

Chapter V

THE PROOF AND RECORD OF CONFERRED CONFIRMATION

Can. 894 — The prescriptions of can. 876 are to be observed for the proof of the conferral of confirmation.

Can. 895 — The names of the confirmed with mention of the minister, the parents and the sponsors, the place and the date of the conferral of confirmation are to be noted in the confirmation register in the diocesan curia, or, where the conference of bishops or the diocesan bishop has prescribed it, in a book kept in the parish archive; the pastor must advise the pastor of the place of baptism about the conferral of confirmation so that notation be made in the baptismal register, in accord with the norm of can. 535, §2.

Can. 896 — If the pastor of the place were not present, the minister either personally or through another is to inform him of the confirmation as soon as possible.

TITLE III

THE MOST HOLY EUCHARIST

Can. 897 — The Most Holy Eucharist is the most august sacrament, in which Christ the Lord himself is contained, offered and received, and by which the Church constantly lives and grows. The Eucharistic Sacrifice, the memorial of the death and resurrection of the Lord, in which the sacrifice of the cross is perpetuated over the centuries, is the summit and the source of all Christian worship and life; it signifies and effects the unity of the people of God and achieves the building up of the Body of Christ. The other sacraments and all the ecclesiastical works of the apostolate are closely related to the Holy Eucharist and are directed to it.

Can. 898 — The faithful are to hold the Eucharist in highest honor, taking part in the celebration of the Most August Sacrifice, receiving the sacrament devoutly and frequently, and worshiping it with supreme adoration; pastors, clarifying the doctrine on this sacrament, are to instruct the faithful thoroughly about this obligation.

Chapter I

THE EUCHARISTIC CELEBRATION

Can. 899 — §1. The celebration of the Eucharist is the action of Christ Himself and the Church; in it Christ the Lord, by the ministry of a priest,

sub speciebus panis et vini substantialiter praesentem, Deo Patri offert atque fidelibus in sua oblatione sociatis se praebet ut cibum spiritualem.

§ 2. In eucharistica Synaxi populus Dei in unum convocatur, Episcopo aut, sub eius auctoritate, presbytero praeside, personam Christi gerente, atque omnes qui intersunt fideles, sive clerici sive laici, suo quisque modo pro ordinum et liturgicorum munerum diversitate, participando concurrunt.

§ 3. Celebratio eucharistica ita ordinetur, ut omnes participantes exinde plurimos capiant fructus, ad quos obtinendos Christus Dominus Sacrificium eucharisticum instituit.

Art. 1

DE SANCTISSIMAE EUCHARISTIAE MINISTRO

Can. 900 – § 1. Minister, qui in persona Christi sacramentum Eucharistiae conficere valet, est solus sacerdos valide ordinatus.

§ 2. Licite Eucharistiam celebrat sacerdos lege canonica non impeditus, servatis praescriptis canonum qui sequuntur.

Can. 901 – Integrum est sacerdoti Missam applicare pro quibusvis, tum vivis tum defunctis.

Can. 902 – Nisi utilitas christifidelium aliud requirat aut suadeat, sacerdotes Eucharistiam concelebrare possunt, integra tamen pro singulis libertate manente Eucharistiam individuali modo celebrandi, non vero eo tempore, quo in eadem ecclesia aut oratorio concelebratio habetur.

Can. 903 – Sacerdos ad celebrandum admittatur etiamsi rectori ecclesiae sit ignotus, dummodo aut litteras commendatitias sui Ordinarii vel sui Superioris, saltem intra annum datas, exhibeat, aut prudenter existimari possit eundem a celebratione non esse impeditum.

Can. 904 – Sacerdotes, memoria semper tenentes in mysterio Sacrificii eucharistici opus redemptionis continuo exerceri, frequenter celebrent; immo enixe commendatur celebratio cotidiana, quae quidem, etiam si praesentia fidelium haberi non possit, actus est Christi et Ecclesiae, in quo peragendo munus suum praecipuum sacerdotes adimplent.

Can. 905 – § 1. Exceptis casibus quibus ad normam iuris licitum est pluries eadem die Eucharistiam celebrare aut concelebrare, non licet sacerdoti plus semel in die celebrare.

offers Himself, substantially present under the forms of bread and wine, to God the Father and gives Himself as spiritual food to the faithful who are associated with His offering.

§2. In the Eucharistic banquet the people of God are called together, with the bishop or, under his authority, a presbyter presiding and acting in the person of Christ; and all the faithful present, whether clergy or laity, participate together, in their own way, according to the diversity of orders and liturgical roles.

§3. The celebration of the Eucharist is to be so arranged that all who take part receive from it the many fruits for which Christ the Lord instituted the Eucharistic Sacrifice.

Art. 1

The Minister of the Most Holy Eucharist

Can. 900 — §1. The minister, who in the person of Christ can confect the sacrament of the Eucharist, is solely a validly ordained priest.

§2. A priest who is not canonically impeded celebrates the Eucharist licitly observing the prescriptions of the following canons.

Can. 901 — A priest may apply the Mass for anyone, living or dead.

Can. 902 — Priests may concelebrate the Eucharist unless the welfare of the Christian faithful requires or urges otherwise but with due regard for the freedom of each priest to celebrate the Eucharist individually, though not during the time when there is a concelebration in the same church or oratory.

Can. 903 — A priest is to be permitted to celebrate even if he is unknown to the rector of the church provided he presents a letter of recommendation issued by his ordinary or superior within the year or provided it can be prudently judged that the priest is not prevented from celebrating.

Can. 904 — Remembering that the work of redemption is continually accomplished in the mystery of the Eucharistic Sacrifice, priests are to celebrate frequently; indeed daily celebration is strongly recommended, since even if the faithful cannot be present, it is the act of Christ and the Church in which priests fulfill their principal function.

Can. 905 — §1. It is not licit for a priest to celebrate the Eucharist more than once a day except for certain instances when the law permits such celebration or concelebration more than once.

§ 2. Si sacerdotum penuria habeatur, concedere potest loci Ordinarius ut sacerdotes, iusta de causa, bis in die, immo, necessitate pastorali
id postulant, etiam ter in diebus dominicis et festis de praecepto,
celebrent.

Can. 906 − Nisi iusta et rationabili de causa, sacerdos Sacrificium
eucharisticum ne celebret sine participatione alicuius saltem fidelis.

Can. 907 − In celebratione eucharistica diaconis et laicis non licet
orationes, speciatim precem eucharisticam, proferre vel actionibus fungi,
quae sacerdotis celebrantis sunt propriae.

Can. 908 − Sacerdotibus catholicis vetitum est una cum sacerdotibus vel ministris Ecclesiarum communitatumve ecclesialium plenam
communionem cum Ecclesia catholica non habentium, Eucharistiam
concelebrare.

Can. 909 − Sacerdos ne omittat ad eucharistici Sacrificii celebrationem oratione debite se praeparare, eoque expleto Deo gratias agere.

Can. 910 − § 1. Minister ordinarius sacrae communionis est Episcopus, presbyter et diaconus.

§ 2. Extraordinarius sacrae communionis minister est acolythus
necnon alius christifidelis ad normam can. 230, § 3 deputatus.

Can. 911 − § 1. Officium et ius sanctissimam Eucharistiam per modum Viatici ad infirmos deferendi habent parochus et vicarii paroeciales, cappellani, necnon Superior communitatis in clericalibus institutis
religiosis aut societatibus vitae apostolicae quoad omnes in domo versantes.

§ 2. In casu necessitatis aut de licentia saltem praesumpta parochi,
cappellani vel Superioris, cui postea notitiam dari oportet, hoc facere
debet quilibet sacerdos vel alius sacrae communionis minister.

Art. 2

DE SANCTISSIMA EUCHARISTIA PARTICIPANDA

Can. 912 − Quilibet baptizatus, qui iure non prohibetur, admitti
potest et debet ad sacram communionem.

Can. 913 − § 1. Ut sanctissima Eucharistia ministrari possit pueris,
requiritur ut ipsi sufficienti cognitione et accurata praeparatione gaudeant, ita ut mysterium Christi pro suo captu percipiant et Corpus
Domini cum fide et devotione sumere valeant.

§ 2. Pueris tamen in periculo mortis versantibus sanctissima Eucharistia ministrari potest, si Corpus Christi a communi cibo discernere et
communionem reverenter suscipere possint.

§2. If priests are lacking, the local ordinary may permit priests, for a just cause, to celebrate twice a day and even, if pastoral need requires it, three times on Sundays and holy days of obligation.

Can. 906 — A priest may not celebrate without the participation of at least some member of the faithful, except for a just and reasonable cause.

Can. 907 — In the celebration of the Eucharist it is not licit for deacons and lay persons to say prayers, in particular the Eucharistic prayer, or to perform actions which are proper to the celebrating priest.

Can. 908 — It is forbidden for Catholic priests to concelebrate the Eucharist with priests or ministers of churches or ecclesial communities which are not in full communion with the Catholic Church.

Can. 909 — The priest is not to fail to make the required prayerful preparation for the celebration of the Eucharistic Sacrifice or the thanksgiving to God upon its completion.

Can. 910 — §1. The ordinary minister of Holy Communion is a bishop, a presbyter or a deacon.

§2. The extraordinary minister of Holy Communion is an acolyte or other member of the Christian faithful deputed in accord with can. 230, §3.

Can. 911 — §1. The pastor and parochial vicars, chaplains and, for all who live in the house, the superior of the community in clerical religious institutes or societies of apostolic life have the right and the duty to bring the Most Holy Eucharist to the sick in the form of Viaticum.

§2. In case of necessity or with at least the presumed permission of the pastor, chaplain, or superior, who should later be notified, any priest or other minister of Holy Communion must do this.

Art. 2

PARTICIPATION IN THE MOST HOLY EUCHARIST

Can. 912 — Any baptized person who is not prohibited by law can and must be admitted to Holy Communion.

Can. 913 — §1. For the administration of the Most Holy Eucharist to children, it is required that they have sufficient knowledge and careful preparation so as to understand the mystery of Christ according to their capacity, and can receive the Body of the Lord with faith and devotion.

§2. The Most Holy Eucharist may be given to children who are in danger of death, however, if they are able to distinguish the Body of Christ from ordinary food and to receive Communion reverently.

Can. 914 – Parentum imprimis atque eorum qui parentum locum tenent necnon parochi officium est curandi ut pueri usum rationis assecuti debite praeparentur et quam primum, praemissa sacramentali confessione, hoc divino cibo reficiantur; parochi etiam est advigilare ne ad sacram Synaxim accedant pueri, qui rationis usum non sint adepti aut quos non sufficienter dispositos iudicaverit.

Can. 915 – Ad sacram communionem ne admittantur excommunicati et interdicti post irrogationem vel declarationem poenae aliique in manifesto gravi peccato obstinate perseverantes.

Can. 916 – Qui conscius est peccati gravis, sine praemissa sacramentali confessione Missam ne celebret neve Corpori Domini communicet, nisi adsit gravis ratio et deficiat opportunitas confitendi; quo in casu meminerit se obligatione teneri ad eliciendum actum perfectae contritionis, qui includit propositum quam primum confitendi.

Can. 917 – Qui sanctissimam Eucharistiam iam recepit, potest eam iterum eadem die suscipere solummodo intra eucharisticam celebrationem cui participat, salvo praescripto can. 921, § 2.

Can. 918 – Maxime commendatur ut fideles in ipsa eucharistica celebratione sacram communionem recipiant; ipsis tamen iusta de causa petentibus extra Missam ministretur, servatis liturgicis ritibus.

Can. 919 – § 1. Sanctissimam Eucharistiam recepturus per spatium saltem unius horae ante sacram communionem abstineat a quocumque cibo et potu, excepta tantummodo aqua atque medicina.

§ 2. Sacerdos, qui eadem die bis aut ter sanctissimam Eucharistiam celebrat, aliquid sumere potest ante secundam aut tertiam celebrationem, etiamsi non intercesserit spatium unius horae.

§ 3. Aetate provecti et infirmitate quadam laborantes necnon eorum curae addicti, sanctissimam Eucharistiam accipere possunt, etiamsi intra horam antecedentem aliquid sumpserint.

Can. 920 – § 1. Omnis fidelis, postquam ad sanctissimam Eucharistiam initiatus sit, obligatione tenetur semel saltem in anno, sacram communionem recipiendi.

§ 2. Hoc praeceptum impleri debet tempore paschali, nisi iusta de causa, alio tempore intra annum adimpleatur.

Can. 921 – § 1. Christifideles qui versantur in periculo mortis, quavis ex causa procedenti, sacra communione per modum Viatici reficiantur.

Can. 914 — It is the responsibility, in the first place, of parents and those who take the place of parents as well as of the pastor to see that children who have reached the use of reason are correctly prepared and are nourished by the divine food as early as possible, preceded by sacramental confession; it is also for the pastor to be vigilant lest any children come to the Holy Banquet who have not reached the use of reason or whom he judges are not sufficiently disposed.

Can. 915 — Those who are excommunicated or interdicted after the imposition or declaration of the penalty and others who obstinately persist in manifest grave sin are not to be admitted to Holy Communion.

Can. 916 — A person who is conscious of grave sin is not to celebrate Mass or to receive the Body of the Lord without prior sacramental confession unless a grave reason is present and there is no opportunity of confessing; in this case the person is to be mindful of the obligation to make an act of perfect contrition, including the intention of confessing as soon as possible.

Can. 917 — A person who has received the Most Holy Eucharist may receive it again on the same day only during the celebration of the Eucharist in which the person participates, with due regard for the prescription of can. 921, §2.

Can. 918 — It is highly recommended that the faithful receive Holy Communion during the celebration of the Eucharist itself, but it should be administered outside Mass to those who request it for a just cause, the liturgical rites being observed.

Can. 919 — §1. One who is to receive the Most Holy Eucharist is to abstain from any food or drink, with the exception only of water and medicine, for at least the period of one hour before Holy Communion.

§2. A priest who celebrates the Most Holy Eucharist two or three times on the same day may take something before the second or third celebration even if the period of one hour does not intervene.

§3. Those who are advanced in age or who suffer from any infirmity, as well as those who take care of them, can receive the Most Holy Eucharist even if they have taken something during the previous hour.

Can. 920 — §1. All the faithful, after they have been initiated into the Most Holy Eucharist, are bound by the obligation of receiving Communion at least once a year.

§2. This precept must be fulfilled during the Easter season unless it is fulfilled for a just cause at some other time during the year.

Can. 921 — §1. The Christian faithful who are in danger of death, arising from any cause, are to be nourished by Holy Communion in the form of Viaticum.

§ 2. Etiamsi eadem die sacra communione refecti fuerint, valde tamen suadetur ut qui in vitae discrimen adducti sint, denuo communicent.

§ 3. Perdurante mortis periculo, commendatur ut sacra communio pluries, distinctis diebus, administretur.

Can. 922 – Sanctum Viaticum infirmis ne nimium differatur; qui animarum curam gerunt sedulo advigilent, ut eodem infirmi plene sui compotes reficiantur.

Can. 923 – Christifideles Sacrificium eucharisticum participare et sacram communionem suscipere possunt quolibet ritu catholico, firmo praescripto can. 844.

Art. 3

DE RITIBUS

ET CAEREMONIIS EUCHARISTICAE CELEBRATIONIS

Can. 924 – § 1. Sacrosanctum eucharisticum Sacrificium celebrari debet ex pane et vino, cui modica aqua miscenda est.

§ 2. Panis debet esse mere triticeus et recenter confectus, ita ut nullum sit periculum corruptionis.

§ 3. Vinum debet esse naturale de genimine vitis et non corruptum.

Can. 925 – Sacra communio conferatur sub sola specie panis aut, ad normam legum liturgicarum, sub utraque specie; in casu autem necessitatis, etiam sub sola specie vini.

Can. 926 – In eucharistica celebratione secundum antiquam Ecclesiae latinae traditionem sacerdos adhibeat panem azymum ubicumque litat.

Can. 927 – Nefas est, urgente etiam extrema necessitate, alteram materiam sine altera, aut etiam utramque extra eucharisticam celebrationem, consecrare.

Can. 928 – Eucharistica celebratio peragatur lingua latina aut alia lingua, dummodo textus liturgici legitime approbati fuerint.

Can. 929 – Sacerdotes et diaconi in Eucharistia celebranda et ministranda sacra ornamenta rubricis praescripta deferant.

Can. 930 – § 1. Sacerdos infirmus aut aetate provectus, si stare nequeat, Sacrificium eucharisticum celebrare potest sedens, servatis quidem legibus liturgicis, non tamen coram populo, nisi de licentia loci Ordinarii.

§ 2. Sacerdos caecus aliave infirmitate laborans licite eucharisticum Sacrificium celebrat, adhibendo textum quemlibet Missae ex probatis, adstante, si casus ferat, alio sacerdote vel diacono, aut etiam laico rite instructo, qui eundem adiuvet.

§2. Even if they have received Communion in the same day, those who are in danger of death are strongly urged to receive again.

§3. While the danger of death lasts, it is recommended that Holy Communion be given repeatedly but on separate days.

Can. 922 — Holy Viaticum for the sick is not to be delayed too long; those who have the care of souls are to be zealous and vigilant that they are nourished by Viaticum while they are fully conscious.

Can. 923 — The Christian faithful may take part in the Eucharistic Sacrifice and receive Communion in any Catholic rite, with due regard for the prescription of can. 844.

Art. 3

RITES AND CEREMONIES OF EUCHARISTIC CELEBRATION

Can. 924 — §1. The Most Sacred Eucharistic Sacrifice must be celebrated with bread and wine, with which a small quantity of water is to be mixed.

§2. The bread must be made of wheat alone and recently made so that there is no danger of corruption.

§3. The wine must be natural wine of the grape and not corrupt.

Can. 925 — Holy Communion is to be given under the form of bread alone or under both kinds in accord with the norm of the liturgical laws or even under the form of wine alone in case of necessity.

Can. 926 — In accord with the ancient tradition of the Latin Church, the priest is to use unleavened bread in the celebration of the Eucharist whenever he offers it.

Can. 927 — It is sinful, even in extreme necessity, to consecrate one matter without the other or even both outside the celebration of the Eucharist.

Can. 928 — The Eucharist is to be celebrated in the Latin language or in another language provided the liturgical texts have been legitimately approved.

Can. 929 — In celebrating and administering the Eucharist, priests and deacons are to wear the liturgical vestments prescribed by the rubrics.

Can. 930 — §1. If a sick or aged priest is unable to stand, he may celebrate the Eucharistic Sacrifice while seated, observing the liturgical laws, but not with the people present unless by permission of the local ordinary.

§2. A blind priest or one with some other infirmity celebrates the Eucharistic Sacrifice licitly by using the text of any approved Mass, with another priest, deacon or even properly instructed lay person present to help him, if needed.

Art. 4

DE TEMPORE
ET LOCO CELEBRATIONIS EUCHARISTIAE

Can. 931 – Eucharistiae celebratio et distributio fieri potest qualibet die et hora, iis exceptis, quae secundum liturgicas normas excluduntur.

Can. 932 – § 1. Celebratio eucharistica peragatur in loco sacro, nisi in casu particulari necessitas aliud postulet; quo in casu, in loco honesto celebratio fieri debet.

§ 2. Sacrificium eucharisticum peragendum est super altare dedicatum vel benedictum; extra locum sacrum adhiberi potest mensa conveniens, retentis semper tobalea et corporali.

Can. 933 – Iusta de causa et de licentia expressa Ordinarii loci licet sacerdoti Eucharistiam celebrare in templo alicuius Ecclesiae aut communitatis ecclesialis plenam communionem cum Ecclesia catholica non habentium, remoto scandalo.

CAPUT II

DE SANCTISSIMA EUCHARISTIA ASSERVANDA
ET VENERANDA

Can. 934 – § 1. Sanctissima Eucharistia:

1° asservari debet in ecclesia cathedrali aut eidem aequiparata, in qualibet ecclesia paroeciali necnon in ecclesia vel oratorio domui instituti religiosi aut societatis vitae apostolicae adnexo;

2° asservari potest in sacello Episcopi et, de licentia Ordinarii loci, in aliis ecclesiis, oratoriis et sacellis.

§ 2. In locis sacris ubi sanctissima Eucharistia asservatur, adesse semper debet qui eius curam habeat et, quantum fieri potest, sacerdos saltem bis in mense Missam ibi celebret.

Can. 935 – Nemini licet sanctissimam Eucharistiam apud se retinere aut secum in itinere deferre, nisi necessitate pastorali urgente et servatis Episcopi dioecesani praescriptis.

Can. 936 – In domo instituti religiosi aliave pia domo, sanctissima Eucharistia asservetur tantummodo in ecclesia aut in oratorio principali domui adnexo; potest tamen iusta de causa Ordinarius permittere, ut etiam in alio oratorio eiusdem domus asservetur.

Can. 937 – Nisi gravis obstet ratio, ecclesia in qua sanctissima Eucharistia asservatur, per aliquot saltem horas cotidie fidelibus pateat, ut coram sanctissimo Sacramento orationi vacare possint.

Art. 4

THE TIME AND PLACE OF EUCHARISTIC CELEBRATION

Can. 931 — The celebration and distribution of the Eucharist may take place on any day and at any hour, except for those times excluded by the liturgical norms.

Can. 932 — §1. The celebration of the Eucharist is to be performed in a sacred place, unless in a particular case necessity demands otherwise; in such a case the celebration must be done in a respectable place.

§2. The Eucharistic Sacrifice is to be performed upon a dedicated or blessed altar; a suitable table can be used outside a sacred place, always retaining the use of a cloth and corporal.

Can. 933 — For a just cause and with the express permission of the local ordinary it is licit for a priest to celebrate the Eucharist in a sacred edifice of another church or ecclesial community that does not have full communion with the Catholic Church, scandal being avoided.

CHAPTER II

THE RESERVATION AND VENERATION OF THE MOST HOLY EUCHARIST

Can. 934 — §1. The Most Holy Eucharist:

1° must be reserved in the cathedral church or its equivalent, in every parish church and in the church or oratory attached to the house of a religious institute or society of apostolic life;

2° it can be reserved in the chapel of a bishop and, with the permission of the local ordinary, in other churches, oratories or chapels.

§2. In sacred places where the Most Holy Eucharist is reserved there must always be someone who has the care of it, and, insofar as possible, a priest is to celebrate Mass there at least twice a month.

Can. 935 — It is not licit to keep the Most Holy Eucharist on one's person or to carry it on a journey unless there is an urgent pastoral need and the precepts of the diocesan bishop are observed.

Can. 936 — In the house of a religious institute or in any other pious house the Most Holy Eucharist is to be reserved only in the church or principal oratory attached to the house, but, for a just cause the ordinary can permit that it be reserved in another oratory of the same house.

Can. 937 — Unless a grave reason prevents it, the church in which the Most Holy Eucharist is reserved should be open to the faithful for at least some hours each day so that they are able to spend time in prayer before the Most Blessed Sacrament.

Can. 938 – § 1. Sanctissima Eucharistia habitualiter in uno tantum ecclesiae vel oratorii tabernaculo asservetur.

§ 2. Tabernaculum, in quo sanctissima Eucharistia asservatur, situm sit in aliqua ecclesiae vel oratorii parte insigni, conspicua, decore ornata, ad orationem apta.

§ 3. Tabernaculum, in quo habitualiter sanctissima Eucharistia asservatur, sit inamovibile, materia solida non transparenti confectum, et ita clausum ut quam maxime periculum profanationis vitetur.

§ 4. Gravi de causa, licet sanctissimam Eucharistiam, nocturno praesertim tempore, alio in loco tutiore et decoro asservare.

§ 5. Qui ecclesiae vel oratorii curam habet, prospiciat ut clavis tabernaculi, in quo sanctissima Eucharistia asservatur, diligentissime custodiatur.

Can. 939 – Hostiae consecratae quantitate fidelium necessitatibus sufficienti in pyxide seu vasculo serventur, et frequenter, veteribus rite consumptis, renoventur.

Can. 940 – Coram tabernaculo, in quo sanctissima Eucharistia asservatur, peculiaris perenniter luceat lampas, qua indicetur et honoretur Christi praesentia.

Can. 941 – § 1. In ecclesiis aut oratoriis quibus datum est asservare sanctissimam Eucharistiam, fieri possunt expositiones sive cum pyxide sive cum ostensorio, servatis normis in libris liturgicis praescriptis.

§ 2. Celebratione Missae durante, ne habeatur in eadem ecclesiae vel oratorii aula sanctissimi Sacramenti expositio.

Can. 942 – Commendatur ut in iisdem ecclesiis et oratoriis quotannis fiat sollemnis sanctissimi Sacramenti expositio per congruum tempus, etsi non continuum, protracta, ut communitas localis eucharisticum mysterium impensius meditetur et adoret; huiusmodi tamen expositio fiat tantum si congruus praevideatur fidelium concursus et servatis normis statutis.

Can. 943 – Minister expositionis sanctissimi Sacramenti et benedictionis eucharisticae est sacerdos vel diaconus; in peculiaribus adiunctis, solius expositionis et repositionis, sine tamen benedictione, est acolythus, minister extraordinarius sacrae communionis aliusve ab Ordinario loci deputatus, servatis Episcopi dioecesani praescriptis.

Can. 944 – § 1. Ubi de iudicio Episcopi dioecesani fieri potest, in publicum erga sanctissimam Eucharistiam venerationis testimonium, habeatur, praesertim in sollemnitate Corporis et Sanguinis Christi, processio per vias publicas ducta.

Can. 938 — §1. The Most Holy Eucharist is to be reserved regularly in only one tabernacle of a church or oratory.

§2. The tablernacle in which the Most Holy Eucharist is reserved should be placed in a part of the church that is prominent, conspicuous, beautifully decorated, and suitable for prayer.

§3. The tabernacle in which the Eucharist is regularly reserved is to be immovable, made of solid and opaque material, and locked so that the danger of profanation may be entirely avoided.

§4. For a grave cause, it is licit to reserve the Most Holy Eucharist in another safer and becoming place especially during the night.

§5. The person who has charge of the church or oratory is to see to it that the key of the tabernacle in which the Most Holy Eucharist is reserved is safeguarded most diligently.

Can. 939 — Consecrated hosts are to be reserved in a ciborium or vessel in sufficient quantity for the needs of the faithful; they are to be frequently renewed and the old hosts properly consumed.

Can. 940 — A special lamp to indicate and honor the presence of Christ is to burn at all times before the tabernacle in which the Most Holy Eucharist is reserved.

Can. 941 — §1. In churches or oratories where it is permitted to reserve the Most Holy Eucharist, there can be expositions either with the ciborium or with a monstrance, observing the norms prescribed in the liturgical books.

§2. Exposition of the Most Holy Sacrament is not to be held in the same part of the church or oratory during the celebration of Mass.

Can. 942 — It is recommended that in these same churches and oratories an annual solemn exposition of the Most Holy Sacrament be held during a suitable period of time, even if not continuous, so that the local community may meditate and may adore the Eucharistic Mystery more profoundly; but this kind of exposition is to be held only if a suitable gathering of the faithful is foreseen and the established norms are observed.

Can. 943 — The minister of exposition of the Most Holy Sacrament and the Eucharistic benediction is a priest or deacon; in particular circumstances the minister of exposition and reposition only, without benediction, is an acolyte, an extraordinary minister of Holy Communion or another person deputed by the local ordinary observing the prescriptions of the diocesan bishop.

Can. 944 — §1. When it can be done in the judgment of the diocesan bishop, as a public witness of the veneration toward the Most Holy Eucharist, a procession is to be conducted through the public streets, especially on the solemnity of the Body and the Blood of Christ.

§ 2. Episcopi dioecesani est de processionibus statuere ordinationes, quibus earum participationi et dignitati prospiciatur.

Caput III
DE OBLATA AD MISSAE CELEBRATIONEM STIPE

Can. 945 – § 1. Secundum probatum Ecclesiae morem, sacerdoti cuilibet Missam celebranti aut concelebranti licet stipem oblatam recipere, ut iuxta certam intentionem Missam applicet.

§ 2. Enixe commendatur sacerdotibus ut, etiam nulla recepta stipe, Missam ad intentionem christifidelium praecipue egentium celebrent.

Can. 946 – Christifideles stipem offerentes ut ad suam intentionem Missa applicetur, ad bonum conferunt Ecclesiae atque eius curam in ministris operibusque sustinendis ea oblatione participant.

Can. 947 – A stipe Missarum quaelibet etiam species negotiationis vel mercaturae omnino arceatur.

Can. 948 – Distinctae applicandae sunt Missae ad eorum intentiones pro quibus singulis stips, licet exigua, oblata et acceptata est.

Can. 949 – Qui obligatione gravatur Missam celebrandi et applicandi ad intentionem eorum qui stipem obtulerunt, eadem obligatione tenetur, etiamsi sine ipsius culpa stipes perceptae perierint.

Can. 950 – Si pecuniae summa offertur pro Missarum applicatione, non indicato Missarum celebrandarum numero, hic supputetur attenta stipe statuta in loco in quo oblator commoratur, nisi aliam fuisse eius intentionem legitime praesumi debeat.

Can. 951 – § 1. Sacerdos plures eadem die Missas celebrans, singulas applicare potest ad intentionem pro qua stips oblata est, ea tamen lege ut, praeterquam in die Nativitatis Domini, stipem pro una tantum Missa faciat suam, ceteras vero in fines ab Ordinario praescriptos concredat, admissa quidem aliqua retributione ex titulo extrinseco.

§ 2. Sacerdos alteram Missam eadem die concelebrans, nullo titulo pro ea stipem recipere potest.

Can. 952 – § 1. Concilii provincialis aut conventus Episcoporum provinciae est pro universa provincia per decretum definire quaenam pro celebratione et applicatione Missae sit offerenda stips, nec licet sacerdoti summam maiorem expetere; ipsi tamen fas est stipem sponte

§2. It is for the diocesan bishop to enact regulations which concern the participation in and the dignity of the processions.

CHAPTER III
OFFERINGS GIVEN AT THE CELEBRATION OF THE MASS

Can. 945 — §1. In accord with the approved usage of the Church, it is lawful for any priest who celebrates or concelebrates Mass to receive an offering to apply the Mass according to a definite intention.

§2. It is strongly recommended that priests celebrate Mass for the intention of the Christian faithful, especially of the needy, even if no offering has been received.

Can. 946 — The Christian faithful who make an offering so that the Mass may be applied for their intention contribute to the good of the Church and by their offering take part in the concern of the Church for the support of its ministers and works.

Can. 947 — Any appearance of trafficking or commerce is to be entirely excluded from Mass offerings.

Can. 948 — Separate Masses are to be applied for the intentions for which an individual offering, even if small, has been made and accepted.

Can. 949 — One who has the obligation of celebrating Mass and applying it for the intention of those who made the offering is bound by the same obligation even if the offerings received have been lost, through no fault of his own.

Can. 950 — If the sum of money is offered for the application of Masses without an indication of the number of Masses to be celebrated, the number is to be computed in view of the offering established in the place where the donor resides unless the donor's intention must be lawfully presumed to have been different.

Can. 951 — §1. A priest who celebrates Mass more than once on the same day may apply the individual Mass for the intention for which the offering is made, but with the law that, except on Christmas, he may retain the offering for only one Mass, giving the other offerings to purposes prescribed by the ordinary, except for some recompense by reason of an extrinsic title.

§2. A priest who concelebrates a second Mass on the same day may not take an offering for it under any title.

Can. 952 — §1. It is for the provincial council or a meeting of the bishops of the province to determine by decree for the whole province what offering is to be made for the celebration and application of a Mass and it is not licit for a priest to ask for a larger sum; nevertheless it is lawful for a priest to

oblatam definita maiorem pro Missae applicatione accipere, et etiam minorem.

§ 2. Ubi desit tale decretum, servetur consuetudo in dioecesi vigens.

§ 3. Sodales quoque institutorum religiosorum quorumlibet stare debent eidem decreto aut consuetudini loci, de quibus in §§ 1 et 2.

Can. 953 – Nemini licet tot stipes Missarum per se applicandarum accipere, quibus intra annum satisfacere non potest.

Can. 954 – Si certis in ecclesiis aut oratoriis Missae petuntur celebrandae numero plures quam ut ibidem celebrari possint, earundem celebratio alibi fieri licet, nisi contrariam voluntatem oblatores expresse manifestaverint.

Can. 955 – § 1. Qui celebrationem Missarum applicandarum aliis committere intendat, earum celebrationem quam primum sacerdotibus sibi acceptis committat, dummodo ipsi constet eos esse omni exceptione maiores; integram stipem receptam transmittere debet, nisi certo constet excessum supra summam in dioecesi debitam datum esse intuitu personae; obligatione etiam tenetur Missarum celebrationem curandi, donec tum susceptae obligationis tum receptae stipis testimonium acceperit.

§ 2. Tempus intra quod Missae celebrandae sunt, initium habet a die quo sacerdos easdem celebraturus recepit, nisi aliud constet.

§ 3. Qui aliis Missas celebrandas committunt, sine mora in librum referant tum Missas quas acceperunt, tum eas, quas aliis tradiderunt, notatis etiam earundem stipibus.

§ 4. Quilibet sacerdos accurate notare debet Missas quas celebrandas acceperit, quibusque satisfecerit.

Can. 956 – Omnes et singuli administratores causarum piarum aut quoquo modo obligati ad Missarum celebrationem curandam, sive clerici sive laici, onera Missarum quibus intra annum non fuerit satisfactum suis Ordinariis tradant, secundum modum ab his definiendum.

Can. 957 – Officium et ius advigilandi ut Missarum onera adimpleantur, in ecclesiis cleri saecularis pertinet ad loci Ordinarium, in ecclesiis institutorum religiosorum aut societatum vitae apostolicae ad eorum Superiores.

Can. 958 – § 1. Parochus necnon rector ecclesiae aliusve pii loci, in quibus stipes Missarum recipi solent, peculiarem habeant librum, in quo accurate adnotent Missarum celebrandarum numerum, intentionem, stipem oblatam, necnon celebrationem peractam.

accept for the application of a Mass a voluntary offering that is larger or even smaller than the one determined.

§2. Where there is no such decree the custom in effect in the diocese is to be observed.

§3. Members of any religious institutes of any kind must also observe the decree or custom of the place mentioned in §§1 and 2.

Can. 953 — It is not lawful for anyone to accept more stipends for Masses to be applied by himself than he can satisfy within a year.

Can. 954 — If in certain churches or oratories Masses are requested for celebration in larger numbers than can be celebrated there, they may be celebrated elsewhere unless the donors have expressly indicated a contrary intention.

Can. 955 — §1. One who intends to entrust to others Masses to be applied, is to entrust their celebration as soon as possible to priests acceptable to him, provided it is clear to him that they are entirely above suspicion; he must transmit the entire stipend he received unless it is established with certainty that the excess over the appropriate amount in the diocese was given for personal reasons; he is also obliged to see to the celebration of the Masses until he has received notification that the obligation has been accepted and the stipend received.

§2. The time within which the Masses are to be celebrated begins on the day on which the priest who is to celebrate them receives them unless otherwise indicated.

§3. Those who entrusted to others Masses to be celebrated are to note in a book without delay both the Masses received and those sent to others, as well as their stipends.

§4. Every priest must accurately note Masses which he has accepted to celebrate and which have been satisfied.

Can. 956 — Each and every administrator of pious causes or those obliged in any way to see to the celebration of Masses, whether clergy or laity, are to give to their ordinaries, in a manner to be determined by the latter, Mass obligations which have not been satisfied within a year.

Can. 957 — The duty and right of seeing to it that Mass obligations are fulfilled belong to the local ordinary in the churches of secular clergy and to the superiors in the churches of religious institutes and societies of apostolic life.

Can. 958 — §1. The pastor and rector of a church or other pious place where Mass offerings are usually received are to have a special book in which they list accurately the number of Masses to be celebrated, the intention, the stipend given and their celebration.

§ 2. Ordinarius obligatione tenetur singulis annis huiusmodi libros per se aut per alios recognoscendi.

TITULUS IV
DE SACRAMENTO PAENITENTIAE

Can. 959 – In sacramento paenitentiae fideles peccata legitimo ministro confitentes, de iisdem contriti atque propositum sese emendandi habentes, per absolutionem ab eodem ministro impertitam, veniam peccatorum quae post baptismum commiserint a Deo obtinent simulque reconcilientur cum Ecclesia, quam peccando vulneraverunt.

Caput I
DE CELEBRATIONE SACRAMENTI

Can. 960 – Individualis et integra confessio atque absolutio unicum constituunt modum ordinarium, quo fidelis peccati gravis sibi conscius cum Deo et Ecclesia reconciliatur; solummodo impossibilitas physica vel moralis ab huiusmodi confessione excusat, quo in casu aliis quoque modis reconciliatio haberi potest.

Can. 961 – § 1. Absolutio pluribus insimul paenitentibus sine praevia individuali confessione, generali modo impertiri non potest, nisi:

1° immineat periculum mortis et tempus non suppetat sacerdoti vel sacerdotibus ad audiendas singulorum paenitentium confessiones;

2° adsit gravis necessitas, videlicet quando, attento paenitentium numero, confessariorum copia praesto non est ad rite audiendas singulorum confessiones intra congruum tempus, ita ut paenitentes, sine propria culpa, gratia sacramentali aut sacra communione diu carere cogantur; necessitas vero non censetur sufficiens, cum confessarii praesto esse non possunt, ratione solius magni concursus paenitentium, qualis haberi potest in magna aliqua festivitate aut peregrinatione.

§ 2. Iudicium ferre an dentur condiciones ad normam § 1, n. 2 requisitae, pertinet ad Episcopum dioecesanum, qui, attentis criteriis cum ceteris membris Episcoporum conferentiae concordatis, casus talis necessitatis determinare potest.

Can. 962 – § 1. Ut christifidelis sacramentali absolutione una simul pluribus data valide fruatur, requiritur non tantum ut sit apte dispositus, sed ut insimul sibi proponat singillatim debito tempore confiteri peccata gravia, quae in praesens ita confiteri nequit.

§ 2. Christifideles, quantum fieri potest etiam occasione absolutionis generalis recipiendae, de requisitis ad normam § 1 edoceantur et

§2. The ordinary is obliged to examine these books each year either personally or through others.

TITLE IV
THE SACRAMENT OF PENANCE

Can. 959 — In the sacrament of penance the faithful, confessing their sins to a legitimate minister, being sorry for them, and at the same time proposing to reform, obtain from God forgiveness of sins committed after baptism through the absolution imparted by the same minister; and they likewise are reconciled with the Church which they have wounded by sinning.

CHAPTER I
THE CELEBRATION OF THE SACRAMENT

Can. 960 — Individual and integral confession and absolution constitute the only ordinary way by which the faithful person who is aware of serious sin is reconciled with God and with the Church; only physical or moral impossibility excuses the person from confession of this type, in which case reconciliation can take place in other ways.

Can. 961 — §1. Absolution cannot be imparted in a general manner to a number of penitents at once without previous individual confession unless:

1° the danger of death is imminent and there is not time for the priest or priests to hear the confessions of the individual penitents;

2° a serious necessity exists, that is, when in light of the number of penitents a supply of confessors is not readily available rightly to hear the confessions of individuals within a suitable time so that the penitents are forced to be deprived of sacramental grace or holy communion for a long time through no fault of their own; it is not considered a sufficient necessity if confessors cannot be readily available only because of the great number of penitents as can occur on the occasion of some great feast or pilgrimage.

§2. It is for the diocesan bishop to judge whether the conditions required in §1, n. 2, are present; he can determine general cases of such necessity in the light of criteria agreed upon with other members of the conference of bishops.

Can. 962 — §1. For a member of the Christian faithful validly to enjoy sacramental absolution given to many at one time, it is required that this person not only be suitably disposed but also at the same time intend to confess individually the serious sins which at present cannot be so confessed.

§2. As much as can be done, the Christian faithful are to be instructed concerning the requirements specified in §1, also on the occasion of receiving

absolutioni generali, in· casu quoque periculi mortis, si tempus suppetat, praemittatur exhortatio ut actum contritionis quisque elicere
curet.

Can. 963 – Firma manente obligatione de qua in can. 989, is cui
generali absolutione gravia peccata remittuntur, ad confessionem individualem quam primum, occasione data, accedat, antequam aliam
recipiat absolutionem generalem, nisi iusta causa interveniat.

Can. 964 – § 1. Ad sacramentales confessiones excipiendas locus
proprius est ecclesia aut oratorium.

§ 2. Ad sedem confessionalem quod attinet, normae ab Episcoporum conferentia statuantur, cauto tamen ut semper habeantur in loco
patenti sedes confessionales crate fixa inter paenitentem et confessarium instructae, quibus libere uti possint fideles, qui id desiderent.

§ 3. Confessiones extra sedem confessionalem ne excipiantur, nisi
iusta de causa.

CAPUT II

DE SACRAMENTI PAENITENTIAE MINISTRO

Can. 965 – Minister sacramenti paenitentiae est solus sacerdos.

Can. 966 – § 1. Ad validam peccatorum absolutionem requiritur
ut minister, praeterquam potestate ordinis, facultate gaudeat eandem
in fideles, quibus absolutionem impertitur, exercendi.

§ 2. Hac facultate donari potest sacerdos, sive ipso iure sive concessione ab auctoritate competenti facta ad normam can. 969.

Can. 967 – § 1. Praeter Romanum Pontificem, facultate christifidelium ubique terrarum confessiones excipiendi ipso iure gaudent Cardinales; itemque Episcopi, qui eadem et licite ubique utuntur, nisi
Episcopus dioecesanus in casu particulari renuerit.

§ 2. Qui facultate confessiones habitualiter excipiendi gaudent sive
vi officii sive vi concessionis Ordinarii loci incardinationis aut loci in
quo domicilium habent, eandem facultatem ubique exercere possunt,
nisi loci Ordinarius in casu particulari renuerit, firmis praescriptis
can. 974, §§ 2 et 3.

§ 3. Ipso iure eadem facultate ubique potiuntur erga sodales aliosque
in domo instituti aut societatis diu noctuque degentes, qui vi officii aut
concessionis Superioris competentis ad normam cann. 968, § 2 et 969,
§ 2 facultate confessiones excipiendi sunt instructi; qui quidem eadem
et licite utuntur, nisi aliquis Superior maior quoad proprios subditos
in casu particulari renuerit.

general absolution; an exhortation that each person take care to make an act of contrition is to precede general absolution, even in danger of death if time is available.

Can. 963 — With due regard for the obligation mentioned in can. 989, a person who has had serious sins remitted by a general absolution is to approach individual confession as soon as there is an opportunity to do so before receiving another general absolution unless a just cause intervenes.

Can. 964 — §1. The proper place to hear sacramental confessions is a church or an oratory.

§2. The conference of bishops is to issue norms concerning the confessional, seeing to it that confessionals with a fixed grille between penitent and confessor are always located in an open area so that the faithful who wish to make use of them may do so freely.

§3. Confessions are not to be heard outside the confessional without a just cause.

Chapter II

THE MINISTER OF THE SACRAMENT OF PENANCE

Can. 965 — Only a priest is the minister of the sacrament of penance.

Can. 966 — §1. For the valid absolution of sins it is required that, besides the power received through sacred ordination, the minister possess the faculty to exercise that power over the faithful to whom he imparts absolution.

§2. A priest can be given this faculty either by the law itself or by a concession granted by competent authority in accord with the norm of can. 969.

Can. 967 — §1. Besides the Roman Pontiff, cardinals by the law itself possess the faculty to hear the confessions of the Christian faithful anywhere in the world; likewise, bishops possess this faculty and licitly use it anywhere unless the diocesan bishop denies it in a particular case.

§2. Those who enjoy the faculty of hearing confessions habitually whether in virtue of office or by grant from the ordinary of the place of incardination or the place in which they have a domicile can exercise the same faculty everywhere unless the local ordinary denies it in a particular case, with due regard for the prescriptions of can. 974, §§ 2 and 3.

§3. Those who have been granted the faculty to hear confessions in virtue of an office or by a grant from the competent superior in accord with the norms of cann. 968, §2 and 969, §2 can by the law itself use the faculty anywhere in respect to members and others who stay day and night in a house of the institute or society; such persons also exercise this faculty licitly unless some major superior has denied it concerning his own subjects in a particular case.

Can. 968 – § 1. Vi officii pro sua quisque dicione facultate ad confessiones excipiendas gaudent loci Ordinarius, canonicus paenitentiarius, itemque parochus aliique qui loco parochi sunt.

§ 2. Vi officii facultate gaudent confessiones excipiendi suorum subditorum aliorumque, in domo diu noctuque degentium, Superiores instituti religiosi aut societatis vitae apostolicae, si sint clericales iuris pontificii, ad normam constitutionum potestate regiminis exsecutiva fruentes, firmo tamen praescripto can. 630, § 4.

Can. 969 – § 1. Solus loci Ordinarius competens est qui facultatem ad confessiones quorumlibet fidelium excipiendas conferat presbyteris quibuslibet; presbyteri autem qui sodales sunt institutorum religiosorum, eadem ne utantur sine licentia saltem praesumpta sui Superioris.

§ 2. Superior instituti religiosi aut societatis vitae apostolicae, de quo in can. 968, § 2, competens est qui facultatem ad excipiendas confessiones suorum subditorum aliorumque in domo diu noctuque degentium presbyteris quibuslibet conferat.

Can. 970 – Facultas ad confessiones excipiendas ne concedatur nisi presbyteris qui idonei per examen reperti fuerint, aut de eorum idoneitate aliunde constet.

Can. 971 – Facultatem ad excipiendas habitualiter confessiones loci Ordinarius presbytero, etsi domicilium vel quasi-domicilium in sua dicione habenti, ne concedat, nisi prius, quantum fieri potest, audito eiusdem presbyteri Ordinario.

Can. 972 – Facultas ad confessiones excipiendas a competenti auctoritate, de qua in can. 969, concedi potest ad tempus sive indeterminatum sive determinatum.

Can. 973 – Facultas ad confessiones habitualiter excipiendas scripto concedatur.

Can. 974 – § 1. Loci Ordinarius, itemque Superior competens, facultatem ad confessiones excipiendas habitualiter concessam ne revocet nisi gravem ob causam.

§ 2. Revocata facultate ad confessiones excipiendas a loci Ordinario qui eam concessit, de quo in can. 967, § 2, presbyter eandem facultatem ubique amittit; revocata eadem facultate ab alio loci Ordinario, eandem amittit tantum in territorio revocantis.

§ 3. Quilibet loci Ordinarius qui alicui presbytero revocaverit facultatem ad confessiones excipiendas, certiorem reddat Ordinarium qui ratione incardinationis est presbyteri proprius, aut, si agatur de sodali instituti religiosi, eiusdem competentem Superiorem.

§ 4. Revocata facultate ad confessiones excipiendas a proprio Su-

Can. 968 — §1. In virtue of their office any local ordinary, canon penitentiary, as well as the pastor of a parish and those who take the place of the pastor of a parish possess the faculty to hear confessions within their jurisdiction.

§2. In virtue of their office superiors of a clerical religious institute or society of apostolic life of pontifical right who in accord with the norms of their constitutions possess executive power of governance enjoy the faculty to hear the confessions of their subjects and others staying in the religious house day and night, with due regard for the prescription of can. 630, §4.

Can. 969 — §1. The local ordinary alone is competent to confer upon any presbyters whatsoever the faculty to hear the confessions of any of the faithful; however, presbyters who are members of religious institutes should not use such a faculty without at least the presumed permission of their superior.

§2. The superior of a religious institute or of a society of apostolic life of pontifical right mentioned in can. 968, §2, is competent to confer on any presbyter whatsoever the faculty to hear the confessions of his subjects and others staying day and night in the house.

Can. 970 — The faculty to hear confessions is not to be granted to presbyters unless they are found to be qualified by means of an examination or their qualifications are evident from another source.

Can. 971 — The local ordinary is not to grant the faculty to hear confessions habitually to a presbyter, even one who has a domicile or quasi-domicile in his jurisdiction, without first consulting with his ordinary, if possible.

Can. 972 — The faculty to hear confessions can be granted by the competent authority mentioned in can. 969 for an indefinite or for a definite period of time.

Can. 973 — The faculty to hear confessions habitually is to be granted in writing.

Can. 974 — §1. The local ordinary as well as the competent superior is not to revoke the faculty to hear confessions habitually except for a serious cause.

§2. When the faculty to hear confessions is revoked by the local ordinary who granted it as mentioned in can. 967, §2, the presbyter loses that faculty everywhere; when this faculty is revoked by another local ordinary, the presbyter loses it only in the territory of the revoking ordinary.

§3. Any local ordinary who has revoked a presbyter's faculty to hear confessions is to inform the latter's own ordinary by reason of incardination or his competent superior in the case of a member of a religious institute.

§4. When the faculty to hear confessions is revoked by his own major

periore maiore, facultatem ad excipiendas confessiones ubique erga sodales instituti amittit presbyter; revocata autem eadem facultate ab alio Superiore competenti, eandem amittit erga solos in eiusdem dicione subditos.

Can. 975 – Praeterquam revocatione, facultas de qua in can. 967, § 2 cessat amissione officii vel excardinatione aut amissione domicilii.

Can. 976 – Quilibet sacerdos, licet ad confessiones excipiendas facultate careat, quoslibet paenitentes in periculo mortis versantes valide et licite absolvit a quibusvis censuris et peccatis, etiamsi praesens sit sacerdos approbatus.

Can. 977 – Absolutio complicis in peccato contra sextum Decalogi praeceptum invalida est, praeterquam in periculo mortis.

Can. 978 – § 1. Meminerit sacerdos in audiendis confessionibus se iudicis pariter et medici personam sustinere ac divinae iustitiae simul et misericordiae ministrum a Deo constitutum esse, ut honori divino et animarum saluti consulat.

§ 2. Confessarius, utpote minister Ecclesiae, in administrando sacramento, doctrinae Magisterii et normis a competenti auctoritate latis fideliter adhaereat.

Can. 979 – Sacerdos in quaestionibus ponendis cum prudentia et discretione procedat, attenta quidem condicione et aetate paenitentis, abstineatque a nomine complicis inquirendo.

Can. 980 – Si confessario dubium non est de paenitentis dispositione et hic absolutionem petat, absolutio ne denegetur nec differatur.

Can. 981 – Pro qualitate et numero peccatorum, habita tamen ratione paenitentis condicionis, salutares et convenientes satisfactiones confessarius iniungat; quas paenitens per se ipse implendi obligatione tenetur.

Can. 982 – Qui confitetur se falso confessarium innocentem apud auctoritatem ecclesiasticam denuntiasse de crimine sollicitationis ad peccatum contra sextum Decalogi praeceptum, ne absolvatur nisi prius falsam denuntiationem formaliter retractaverit et paratus sit ad damna, si quae habeantur, reparanda.

Can. 983 – § 1. Sacramentale sigillum inviolabile est; quare nefas est confessario verbis vel alio quovis modo et quavis de causa aliquatenus prodere paenitentem.

§ 2. Obligatione secretum servandi tenentur quoque interpres, si detur, necnon omnes alii ad quos ex confessione notitia peccatorum quoquo modo pervenerit.

superior, the presbyter loses the faculty to hear the confessions of the members of the institute everywhere; when the faculty is revoked by another competent superior, the presbyter loses it only as regards the subjects of the superior's jurisdiction.

Can. 975 — Besides by revocation, the faculty referred to in can. 976, §2 ceases by loss of office, excardination or loss of domicile.

Can. 976 — Even though he lacks the faculty to hear confessions, any priest validly and licitly absolves from any kind of censures and sins any penitent who is in danger of death, even if an approved priest is present.

Can. 977 — The absolution of an accomplice in a sin against the sixth commandment of the Decalogue is invalid, except in danger of death.

Can. 978 — §1. In hearing confessions the priest is to remember that he acts as a judge as well as a healer and is placed by God as the minister of divine justice as well as of mercy, concerned with the divine honor and the salvation of souls.

§2. In the administration of the sacrament, the confessor, as a minister of the Church, is to adhere faithfully to the doctrine of the magisterium and the norms enacted by competent authority.

Can. 979 — The priest in posing questions is to proceed with prudence and discretion, with attention to the condition and age of the penitent, and he is to refrain from asking the name of an accomplice.

Can. 980 — If the confessor has no doubt about the disposition of a penitent who asks for absolution, absolution is not to be refused or delayed.

Can. 981 — The confessor is to enjoin salutary and suitable penances in keeping with the quality and number of the sins but with attention to the condition of the penitent; the penitent is obliged to perform the penances personally.

Can. 982 — One who confesses the false denunciation of an innocent confessor to ecclesiastical authority concerning the crime of solicitation to sin against the sixth commandment of the Decalogue is not to be absolved unless that person has first formally retracted the false denunciation and is prepared to repair damages, if they have occurred.

Can. 983 — §1. The sacramental seal is inviolable; therefore, it is a crime for a confessor in any way to betray a penitent by word or in any other manner or for any reason.

§2. An interpreter, if there is one present, is also obliged to preserve the secret, and also all others to whom knowledge of sins from confession shall come in any way.

Can. 984 – § 1. Omnino confessario prohibetur scientiae ex confessione acquisitae usus cum paenitentis gravamine, etiam quovis revelationis periculo excluso.

§ 2. Qui in auctoritate est constitutus, notitia quam de peccatis in confessione quovis tempore excepta habuerit, ad exteriorem gubernationem nullo modo uti potest.

Can. 985 – Magister novitiorum eiusque socius, rector seminarii aliusve instituti educationis sacramentales confessiones suorum alumnorum in eadem domo commorantium ne audiant, nisi alumni in casibus particularibus sponte id petant.

Can. 986 – § 1. Omnis cui animarum cura vi muneris est demandata, obligatione tenetur providendi ut audiantur confessiones fidelium sibi commissorum, qui rationabiliter audiri petant, utque iisdem opportunitas praebeatur ad confessionem individualem, diebus ac horis in eorum commodum statutis, accedendi.

§ 2. Urgente necessitate, quilibet confessarius obligatione tenetur confessiones christifidelium excipiendi, et in periculo mortis quilibet sacerdos.

Caput III
DE IPSO PAENITENTE

Can. 987 – Christifidelis, ut sacramenti paenitentiae remedium percipiat salutiferum, ita dispositus sit oportet ut, peccata quae commiserit repudians et propositum sese emendandi habens, ad Deum convertatur.

Can. 988 – § 1. Christifidelis obligatione tenetur in specie et numero confitendi omnia peccata gravia post baptismum perpetrata et nondum per claves Ecclesiae directe remissa neque in confessione individuali accusata, quorum post diligentem sui discussionem conscientiam habeat.

§ 2. Commendatur christifidelibus ut etiam peccata venialia confiteantur.

Can. 989 – Omnis fidelis, postquam ad annos discretionis pervenerit, obligatione tenetur peccata sua gravia, saltem semel in anno, fideliter confitendi.

Can. 990 – Nemo prohibetur quominus per interpretem confiteatur, vitatis quidem abusibus et scandalis atque firmo praescripto can. 983, § 2.

Can. 991 – Cuivis christifideli integrum est confessario legitime approbato etiam alius ritus, cui maluerit, peccata confiteri.

Can. 984 — §1. Even if every danger of revelation is excluded, a confessor is absolutely forbidden to use knowledge acquired from confession when it might harm the penitent.

§2. One who is placed in authority can in no way use for external governance knowledge about sins which he has received in confession at any time.

Can. 985 — A director of novices and his associate, the rector of a seminary or other institution of education are not to hear the sacramental confessions of their students living in the same house unless the students in particular cases spontaneously request it.

Can. 986 — §1. All to whom the care of souls is committted by reason of an office are obliged to provide that the confessions of the faithful entrusted to their care be heard when they reasonably ask to be heard and that the opportunity be given to them to come to individual confession on days and hours set for their convenience.

§2. In urgent necessity any confessor is obliged to hear the confessions of the Christian faithful, and in danger of death any priest is so obliged.

Chapter III

THE PENITENT

Can. 987 — In order to receive the salvific remedy of the sacrament of penance, the Christian faithful ought to be so disposed that, having repudiated the sins committed and having a purpose of amendment, they are converted to God.

Can. 988 — §1. A member of the Christian faithful is obliged to confess in kind and in number all serious sins committed after baptism and not yet directly remitted through the keys of the Church nor acknowledged in individual confession, of which one is conscious after diligent examination of conscience.

§2. It is to be recommended to the Christian faithful that venial sins also be confessed.

Can. 989 — After having attained the age of discretion, each of the faithful is bound by an obligation faithfully to confess serious sins at least once a year.

Can. 990 — No one is prohibited from confessing through an interpreter, avoiding abuses and scandals; the prescription of can. 983, §2 is to be observed.

Can. 991 — The Christian faithful are free to confess to a legitimately approved confessor of their choice, even one of another rite.

Caput IV

DE INDULGENTIIS

Can. 992 – Indulgentia est remissio coram Deo poenae temporalis pro peccatis, ad culpam quod attinet iam deletis, quam christifidelis, apte dispositus et certis ac definitis condicionibus, consequitur ope Ecclesiae quae, ut ministra redemptionis, thesaurum satisfactionum Christi et Sanctorum auctoritative dispensat et applicat.

Can. 993 – Indulgentia est partialis aut plenaria, prout a poena temporali pro peccatis debita liberat ex parte aut ex toto.

Can. 994 – Quivis fidelis potest indulgentias sive partiales sive plenarias, aut sibi ipsi lucrari, aut defunctis applicare ad modum suffragii.

Can. 995 – § 1. Praeter supremam Ecclesiae auctoritatem ii tantum possunt indulgentias elargiri, quibus haec potestas iure agnoscitur aut a Romano Pontifice conceditur.

§ 2. Nulla auctoritas infra Romanum Pontificem potest potestatem concedendi indulgentias aliis committere, nisi id ei a Sede Apostolica expresse fuerit indultum.

Can. 996 – § 1. Ut quis capax sit lucrandi indulgentias debet esse baptizatus, non excommunicatus, in statu gratiae saltem in fine operum praescriptorum.

§ 2. Ut vero subiectum capax eas lucretur, habere debet intentionem saltem eas acquirendi et opera iniuncta implere statuto tempore ac debito modo, secundum concessionis tenorem.

Can. 997 – Ad indulgentiarum concessionem et usum quod attinet, servanda sunt insuper cetera praescripta quae in peculiaribus Ecclesiae legibus continentur.

TITULUS V

DE SACRAMENTO UNCTIONIS INFIRMORUM

Can. 998 – Unctio infirmorum, qua Ecclesia fideles periculose aegrotantes Domino patienti et glorificato, ut eos allevet et salvet, commendat, confertur eos liniendo oleo atque verba proferendo in liturgicis libris praescripta.

CHAPTER IV

INDULGENCES

Can. 992 — An indulgence is a remission before God of the temporal punishment for sin the guilt of which is already forgiven, which a properly disposed member of the Christian faithful obtains under certain and definite conditions with the help of the Church which, as the minister of redemption, dispenses and applies authoritatively the treasury of the satisfactions of Christ and the saints.

Can. 993 — An indulgence is partial or plenary in as far as it frees from the temporal punishment due to sin either partly or totally.

Can. 994 — The faithful can gain partial or plenary indulgences for themselves or apply them for the dead by way of suffrage.

Can. 995 — §1. Besides the supreme authority of the Church, only those can grant indulgences to whom this power has been given by the law or granted by the Roman Pontiff.

§2. No authority beneath the Roman Pontiff can commit to others the power to grant indulgences unless it was expressly given to him by the Apostolic See.

Can. 996 — §1. In order that one be capable of gaining indulgences one must be baptized and not excommunicated and in the state of grace at least at the completion of the prescribed works.

§2. In order that one be a capable subject for gaining indulgences one must have at least the intention of receiving them and fulfill the enjoined works at the stated time in due fashion, according to the tenor of the grant.

Can. 997 — In regard to the granting and use of indulgences other prescriptions contained in the particular laws of the Church must be also observed.

TITLE V

THE SACRAMENT OF THE ANOINTING OF THE SICK

Can. 998 — The anointing of the sick by which the Church commends to the suffering and glorified Lord the faithful who are dangerously sick so that He relieve and save them, is conferred by anointing them with oil and using the words prescribed in the liturgical books.

Caput I
DE SACRAMENTI CELEBRATIONE

Can. 999 – Praeter Episcopum, oleum in unctione infirmorum adhibendum benedicere possunt :

1° qui iure Episcopo dioecesano aequiparantur ;

2° in casu necessitatis, quilibet presbyter in ipsa tamen celebratione sacramenti.

Can. 1000 – § 1. Unctiones verbis, ordine et modo praescriptis in liturgicis libris, accurate peragantur ; in casu tamen necessitatis, sufficit unctio unica in fronte vel etiam in alia corporis parte, integra formula prolata.

§ 2. Unctiones peragat minister propria manu, nisi gravis ratio usum instrumenti suadeat.

Can. 1001 – Curent animarum pastores et infirmorum propinqui, ut tempore opportuno infirmi hoc sacramento subleventur.

Can. 1002 – Celebratio communis unctionis infirmorum, pro pluribus infirmis simul, qui apte sint praeparati et rite dispositi, iuxta Episcopi dioecesani praescripta peragi potest.

Caput II
DE MINISTRO UNCTIONIS INFIRMORUM

Can. 1003 – § 1. Unctionem infirmorum valide administrat omnis et solus sacerdos.

§ 2. Officium et ius unctionis infirmorum ministrandi habent omnes sacerdotes, quibus demandata est cura animarum, erga fideles suo pastorali officio commissos ; ex rationabili causa, quilibet alius sacerdos hoc sacramentum ministrare potest de consensu saltem praesumpto sacerdotis de quo supra.

§ 3. Cuilibet sacerdoti licet oleum benedictum secumferre ut, in casu necessitatis, sacramentum unctionis infirmorum ministrare valeat.

CHAPTER I

THE CELEBRATION OF THE SACRAMENT

Can. 999 — Besides a bishop those can bless the oil to be used in the anointing of the sick:

1° who are equivalent in law to a diocesan bishop;

2° in case of necessity, any priest but only in the celebration of the sacrament.

Can. 1000 — §1. The anointings are to be carefully performed while observing the words, the order and the manner prescribed in the liturgical books; but in case of necessity it is sufficient that one anointing be made on the forehead, or even on another part of the body, while saying the entire formula.

§2. The minister is to perform the anointing with his own hand unless a serious reason persuades him to use an instrument.

Can. 1001 — Pastors of souls and persons who are close to the sick are to see to it that they are supported by this sacrament at an appropriate time.

Can. 1002 — The communal celebration of the anointing of the sick for many of the sick at the same time who are duly prepared and rightly disposed can be performed according to the prescriptions of the diocesan bishop.

CHAPTER II

THE MINISTER OF THE ANOINTING OF THE SICK

Can. 1003 — §1. Every priest, and only a priest, validly administers the anointing of the sick.

§2. All priests to whom the care of souls has been committed have the duty and the right to administer the anointing of the sick to all the faithful committed to their pastoral office; for a reasonable cause any other priest can administer this sacrament with at least the presumed consent of the aforementioned priest.

§3. Every priest is allowed to carry blessed oil with him so that he can administer the sacrament of the anointing of the sick in case of necessity.

CAPUT III

DE IIS QUIBUS UNCTIO INFIRMORUM CONFERENDA SIT

Can. 1004 – § 1. Unctio infirmorum ministrari potest fideli qui, adepto rationis usu, ob infirmitatem vel senium in periculo incipit versari.

§ 2. Hoc sacramentum iterari potest, si infirmus, postquam convaluerit, denuo in gravem infirmitatem inciderit aut si, eadem infirmitate perdurante, discrimen factum gravius sit.

Can. 1005 – In dubio utrum infirmus rationis usum attigerit, an periculose aegrotet vel mortuus sit, hoc sacramentum ministretur.

Can. 1006 – Infirmis qui, cum suae mentis compotes essent, hoc sacramentum implicite saltem petierint, conferatur.

Can. 1007 – Unctio infirmorum ne conferatur illis, qui in manifesto gravi peccato obstinate perseverent.

TITULUS VI

DE ORDINE

Can. 1008 – Sacramento ordinis ex divina institutione inter christifideles quidam, charactere indelebili quo signantur, constituuntur sacri ministri, qui nempe consecrantur et deputantur ut, pro suo quisque gradu, in persona Christi Capitis munera docendi, sanctificandi et regendi adimplentes, Dei populum pascant.

Can. 1009 – § 1. Ordines sunt episcopatus, presbyteratus et diaconatus.

§ 2. Conferuntur manuum impositione et precatione consecratoria, quam pro singulis gradibus libri liturgici praescribunt.

CAPUT I

DE ORDINATIONIS CELEBRATIONE ET MINISTRO

Can. 1010 – Ordinatio intra Missarum sollemnia celebretur, die dominico vel festo de praecepto, sed ob rationes pastorales aliis etiam diebus, ferialibus non exceptis, fieri potest.

CHAPTER III

THOSE ON WHOM THE ANOINTING
OF THE SICK IS CONFERRED

Can. 1004 — §1. The anointing of the sick can be administered to a member of the faithful who, after having reached the use of reason, begins to be in danger due to sickness or old age.

§2. This sacrament can be repeated whenever the sick person again falls into a serious sickness after convalescence or whenever a more serious crisis develops during the same sickness.

Can. 1005 — This sacrament is to be administered when there is a doubt whether the sick person has attained the use of reason, whether the person is dangerously ill, or whether the person is dead.

Can. 1006 — This sacrament is to be conferred upon sick persons who requested it at least implicitly when they were in control of their faculties.

Can. 1007 — The anointing of the sick is not to be conferred upon those who obstinately persist in manifest serious sin.

TITLE VI

ORDERS

Can. 1008 — By divine institution some among the Christian faithful are constituted sacred ministers through the sacrament of orders by means of the indelible character with which they are marked; accordingly they are consecrated and deputed to shepherd the people of God, each in accord with his own grade of orders, by fulfilling in the person of Christ the Head the functions of teaching, sanctifying and governing.

Can. 1009 — §1. The orders are the episcopacy, the presbyterate, and the diaconate.

§2. They are conferred by an imposition of hands and by the consecratory prayer which the liturgical books prescribe for the individual grades.

CHAPTER I

THE CELEBRATION AND MINISTER OF ORDINATION

Can. 1010 — Ordination is to be celebrated within the solemnities of Mass on a Sunday or on a holy day of obligation; for pastoral reasons, however, it can take place on other days, even on ordinary weekdays.

Can. 1011 – § 1. Ordinatio generaliter in cathedrali ecclesia celebretur; ob rationes tamen pastorales in alia ecclesia aut oratorio celebrari potest.

§ 2. Ad ordinationem invitandi sunt clerici aliique christifideles, ut quam maxima frequentia celebrationi intersint.

Can. 1012 – Sacrae ordinationis minister est Episcopus consecratus.

Can. 1013 – Nulli Episcopo licet quemquam consecrare in Episcopum, nisi prius constet de pontificio mandato.

Can. 1014 – Nisi Sedis Apostolicae dispensatio intercesserit, Episcopus consecrator principalis in consecratione episcopali duos saltem Episcopos consecrantes sibi adiungat; valde convenit autem, ut una cum iisdem omnes Episcopi praesentes electum consecrent.

Can. 1015 – § 1. Unusquisque ad presbyteratum et ad diaconatum a proprio Episcopo ordinetur aut cum legitimis eiusdem litteris dimissoriis.

§ 2. Episcopus proprius, iusta de causa non impeditus, per se ipse suos subditos ordinet; sed subditum orientalis ritus, sine apostolico indulto, licite ordinare non potest.

§ 3. Qui potest litteras dimissorias ad ordines recipiendos dare, potest quoque eosdem ordines per se ipse conferre, si charactere episcopali polleat.

Can. 1016 – Episcopus proprius, quod attinet ad ordinationem diaconalem eorum qui clero saeculari se adscribi intendant, est Episcopus dioecesis, in qua promovendus habet domicilium, aut dioecesis cui promovendus sese devovere statuit; quod attinet ad ordinationem presbyteralem clericorum saecularium, est Episcopus dioecesis, cui promovendus per diaconatum est incardinatus.

Can. 1017 – Episcopus extra propriam dicionem nonnisi cum licentia Episcopi dioecesani ordines conferre potest.

Can. 1018 – § 1. Litteras dimissorias pro saecularibus dare possunt:

1° Episcopus proprius, de quo in can. 1016;

2° Administrator apostolicus atque, de consensu collegii consultorum, Administrator dioecesanus; de consensu consilii, de quo in can. 495, § 2, Pro-vicarius et Pro-praefectus apostolicus.

§ 2. Administrator dioecesanus, Pro-vicarius et Pro-praefectus apostolicus litteras dimissorias ne iis concedant, quibus ab Episcopo dioecesano aut a Vicario vel Praefecto apostolico accessus ad ordines denegatus fuerit.

Can. 1011 — §1. As a rule ordination is to be celebrated in the cathedral church; for pastoral reasons, however, it can be celebrated in another church or oratory.

§2. The clergy and other members of the Christian faithful are to be invited to the ordination so that a large congregation may be present for the celebration.

Can. 1012 — The minister of sacred ordination is a consecrated bishop.

Can. 1013 — No bishop is permitted to consecrate anyone a bishop unless it is first evident that there is a pontifical mandate.

Can. 1014 — Unless a dispensation has been granted by the Apostolic See, the principal consecrating bishop in an episcopal consecration is to associate to himself at least two other consecrating bishops; but it is especially appropriate that all the bishops who are present should consecrate the bishop-elect along with the bishops mentioned.

Can. 1015 — §1. Each candidate is to be ordained to the presbyterate or the diaconate by his own bishop or with legitimate dimissorial letters from him.

§2. The candidates' own bishop is to ordain his own subjects personally unless he is impeded from doing so by a just cause; he cannot, however, licitly ordain a subject of an oriental rite without an apostolic indult.

§3. The person who can grant dimissorial letters to receive orders can also confer these same orders personally provided he possesses the episcopal character.

Can. 1016 — As regards the diaconal ordination of those who intend to become members of the secular clergy, the proper bishop is the bishop of the diocese in which the candidate has a domicile or the diocese to which he intends to devote himself; as regards the presbyteral ordination of secular clerics, the proper bishop is the bishop of the diocese into which the candidate has been incardinated through the diaconate.

Can. 1017 — A bishop can confer orders outside his own jurisdiction only with the permission of the diocesan bishop.

Can. 1018 — §1. The following can grant dimissorial letters for the secular clergy:

1° the proper bishop mentioned in can. 1016;

2° an apostolic administrator and, with the consent of the college of consultors, the diocesan administrator; and with the consent of the council mentioned in can. 495, §2, an apostolic pro-vicar and pro-prefect.

§2. A diocesan administrator, a pro-vicar apostolic, and a pro-prefect apostolic are not to grant dimissorial letters to those who have been denied access to orders by their diocesan bishop, vicar apostolic, or prefect apostolic.

Can. 1019 – § 1. Superiori maiori instituti religiosi clericalis iuris pontificii aut societatis clericalis vitae apostolicae iuris pontificii competit ut suis subditis, iuxta constitutiones perpetuo vel definitive instituto aut societati adscriptis, concedat litteras dimissorias ad diaconatum et ad presbyteratum.

§ 2. Ordinatio ceterorum omnium alumnorum cuiusvis instituti aut societatis regitur iure clericorum saecularium, revocato quolibet indulto Superioribus concesso.

Can. 1020 – Litterae dimissoriae ne concedantur, nisi habitis antea omnibus testimoniis et documentis, quae iure exiguntur ad normam cann. 1050 et 1051.

Can. 1021 – Litterae dimissoriae mitti possunt ad quemlibet Episcopum communionem cum Sede Apostolica habentem, excepto tantum, citra apostolicum indultum, Episcopo ritus diversi a ritu promovendi.

Can. 1022 – Episcopus ordinans, acceptis legitimis litteris dimissoriis, ad ordinationem ne procedat, nisi de germana litterarum fide plane constet.

Can. 1023 – Litterae dimissoriae possunt ab ipso concedente aut ab eius successore limitibus circumscribi aut revocari, sed semel concessae non extinguuntur resoluto iure concedentis.

Caput II

DE ORDINANDIS

Can. 1024 – Sacram ordinationem valide recipit solus vir baptizatus.

Can. 1025 – § 1. Ad licite ordines presbyteratus vel diaconatus conferendos requiritur ut candidatus, probatione ad normam iuris peracta, debitis qualitatibus, iudicio proprii Episcopi aut Superioris maioris competentis, praeditus sit, nulla detineatur irregularitate nulloque impedimento, atque praerequisita, ad normam cann. 1033-1039 adimpleverit; praeterea documenta habeantur, de quibus in can. 1050, atque scrutinium peractum sit, de quo in can. 1051.

§ 2. Insuper requiritur ut, iudicio eiusdem legitimi Superioris, ad Ecclesiae ministerium utilis habeatur.

§ 3. Episcopo ordinanti proprium subditum, qui servitio alius dioecesis destinetur, constare debet ordinandum huic dioecesi addictum iri.

Can. 1019 — §1. The major superior of a clerical religious institute of pontifical right or the major superior of a clerical society of apostolic life of pontifical right is competent to grant dimissorial letters for the diaconate and for the presbyterate on behalf of the subjects who have become perpetually or definitively members of the institute or society in accord with their constitutions.

§2. The ordination of all other members of any institute or society is governed by the law for seculars; any other indult whatsoever which has been granted to superiors is revoked.

Can. 1020 — Dimissorial letters are not to be granted unless all the testimonials and documents which are demanded by law in accord with cann. 1050 and 1051 have been obtained beforehand.

Can. 1021 — Dimissorial letters can be sent to any bishop who is in communion with the Apostolic See with the exception of a bishop who is of a rite different from the rite of the candidate, which requires an apostolic indult.

Can. 1022 — After he has received legitimate dimissorial letters, the ordaining bishop is not to proceed to the ordination unless there is clear proof that they are genuine.

Can. 1023 — Dimissorial letters can be circumscribed with restrictions or revoked by the one who granted them or his successor; but once they have been granted, they do not cease to be operative when the authority of the one granting them ceases.

Chapter II

CANDIDATES FOR ORDINATION

Can. 1024 — Only a baptized male validly receives sacred ordination.

Can. 1025 — §1. In order for one to be ordained licitly to the presbyterate or to the diaconate, it is required: that the candidate having completed a period of probation according to the norm of law is endowed with the required qualities in the judgment of the proper bishop or competent major superior; that he is not restrained by any irregularity or by any impediment; that he has fulfilled the prerequisites according to the norms of cann. 1033-1039; in addition the documents mentioned in can. 1050 have been obtained, and the investigation mentioned in can. 1051 has been conducted.

§2. Furthermore, it is required that in the judgment of the same legitimate superior he is considered to be useful for the ministry of the Church.

§3. The bishop who ordains his own subject who is destined for the service of another diocese must be sure that the person to be ordained is going to be assigned to the other diocese.

Art. 1

DE REQUISITIS IN ORDINANDIS

Can. 1026 – Ut quis ordinetur debita libertate gaudeat oportet; nefas est quemquam, quovis modo, ob quamlibet causam ad ordines recipiendos cogere, vel canonice idoneum ab iisdem recipiendis avertere.

Can. 1027 – Aspirantes ad diaconatum et presbyteratum accurata praeparatione efformentur, ad normam iuris.

Can. 1028 – Curet Episcopus dioecesanus aut Superior competens ut candidati, antequam ad ordinem aliquem promoveantur, rite edoceantur de iis, quae ad ordinem eiusque obligationes pertinent.

Can. 1029 – Ad ordines ii soli promoveantur qui, prudenti iudicio Episcopi proprii aut Superioris maioris competentis, omnibus perpensis, integram habent fidem, recta moventur intentione, debita pollent scientia, bona gaudent existimatione, integris moribus probatisque virtutibus atque aliis qualitatibus physicis et psychicis ordini recipiendo congruentibus sunt praediti.

Can. 1030 – Nonnisi ex causa canonica, licet occulta, proprius Episcopus vel Superior maior competens diaconis ad presbyteratum destinatis, sibi subditis, ascensum ad presbyteratum interdicere potest, salvo recursu ad normam iuris.

Can. 1031 – § 1. Presbyteratus ne conferatur nisi iis qui aetatis annum vigesimum quintum expleverint et sufficienti gaudeant maturitate, servato insuper intervallo sex saltem mensium inter diaconatum et presbyteratum; qui ad presbyteratum destinantur, ad diaconatus ordinem tantummodo post expletum aetatis annum vigesimum tertium admittantur.

§ 2. Candidatus ad diaconatum permanentem qui non sit uxoratus ad eundem diaconatum ne admittatur, nisi post expletum vigesimum quintum saltem aetatis annum; qui matrimonio coniunctus est, nonnisi post expletum trigesimum quintum saltem aetatis annum, atque de uxoris consensu.

§ 3. Integrum est Episcoporum conferentiis normam statuere, qua provectior ad presbyteratum et ad diaconatum permanentem requiratur aetas.

§ 4. Dispensatio ultra annum super aetate requisita ad normam §§ 1 et 2, Apostolicae Sedi reservatur.

Can. 1032 – § 1. Aspirantes ad presbyteratum promoveri possunt ad diaconatum solummodo post expletum quintum curriculi studiorum philosophico-theologicorum annum.

Art. 1

REQUIREMENTS IN THE CANDIDATES

Can. 1026 — In order for one to be ordained he ought to possess the required freedom; it is unlawful to force someone to receive orders or to deter one who is canonically suitable from receiving them by whatever means and for whatever reason.

Can. 1027 — Those who aspire to the diaconate or the presbyterate are to receive an accurate formation in accord with the norm of law.

Can. 1028 — The diocesan bishop or the competent superior is to see to it that candidates are duly instructed concerning those matters which pertain to the order to be received and its obligations before they are promoted to that order.

Can. 1029 — After all circumstances have been taken into account in the prudent judgment of the proper bishop or the competent major superior, only those should be promoted to orders who have an integral faith, are motivated by a right intention, possess the required knowledge, and enjoy a good reputation, good morals, and proven virtues, and other physical and psychological qualities which are appropriate to the order to be received.

Can. 1030 — Only for a canonical reason, even if it be occult, can the proper bishop or the competent major superior forbid access to the presbyterate to deacons destined for the presbyterate subject to them and with due regard for recourse in accord with the norm of law.

Can. 1031 — §1. The presbyterate is not to be conferred upon those who have not yet completed the age of twenty-five and who do not possess sufficient maturity; an interval of at least six months is to be observed between the diaconate and the presbyterate; men destined for the presbyterate are to be admitted to the order of diaconate only after they have completed the age of twenty-three.

§2. A candidate for the permanent diaconate who is not married is not to be admitted to the diaconate unless he has completed at least twenty-five years of age; if the candidate is married, he is not to be admitted to the permanent diaconate unless he has completed at least thirty-five years of age and has the consent of his wife.

§3. The conference of bishops may determine a norm by which an older age is required for the presbyterate and the permanent diaconate.

§4. The Apostolic See reserves to itself the dispensation from the age required in §§1 and 2 when it is a question of more than one year.

Can. 1032 — §1. Candidates for the presbyterate can be promoted to the diaconate only after they have completed a five-year curriculum of philosophical and theological studies.

§ 2. Post expletum studiorum curriculum, diaconus per tempus congruum, ab Episcopo vel a Superiore maiore competenti definiendum, in cura pastorali partem habeat, diaconalem exercens ordinem, antequam ad presbyteratum promoveatur.

§ 3. Aspirans ad diaconatum permanentem, ad hunc ordinem ne promoveatur nisi post expletum formationis tempus.

Art. 2

DE PRAEREQUISITIS AD ORDINATIONEM

Can. 1033 – Licite ad ordines promovetur tantum qui recepit sacrae confirmationis sacramentum.

Can. 1034 – § 1. Ad diaconatum vel presbyteratum aspirans ne ordinetur, nisi prius per liturgicum admissionis ritum ab auctoritate, de qua in cann. 1016 et 1019, adscriptionem inter candidatos obtinuerit post praeviam suam petitionem propria manu exaratam et subscriptam, atque ab eadem auctoritate in scriptis acceptatam.

§ 2. Ad eandem admissionem obtinendam non tenetur, qui per vota in clericale institutum cooptatus est.

Can. 1035 – § 1. Antequam quis ad diaconatum sive permanentem sive transeuntem promoveatur, requiritur ut ministeria lectoris et acolythi receperit et per congruum tempus exercuerit.

§ 2. Inter acolythatus et diaconatus collationem intervallum intercedat sex saltem mensium.

Can. 1036 – Candidatus, ut ad ordinem diaconatus aut presbyteratus promoveri possit, Episcopo proprio aut Superiori maiori competenti declarationem tradat propria manu exaratam et subscriptam, qua testificetur se sponte ac libere sacrum ordinem suscepturum atque se ministerio ecclesiastico perpetuo mancipaturum esse, insimul petens ut ad ordinem recipiendum admittatur.

Can. 1037 – Promovendus ad diaconatum permanentem qui non sit uxoratus, itemque promovendus ad presbyteratum, ad ordinem diaconatus ne admittantur, nisi ritu praescripto publice coram Deo et Ecclesia obligationem caelibatus assumpserint, aut vota perpetua in instituto religioso emiserint.

Can. 1038 – Diaconus, qui ad presbyteratum promoveri renuat, ab ordinis recepti exercitio prohiberi non potest, nisi impedimento detineatur canonico aliave gravi causa, de iudicio Episcopi dioecesani aut Superioris maioris competentis aestimanda.

§2. After he has completed the curriculum of studies and before he is promoted to the presbyterate, a deacon is to participate in pastoral care, exercising his diaconal order for a suitable period of time, to be determined by the bishop or by the competent major superior.

§3. An aspirant to the permanent diaconate is not to be promoted to that order unless he has completed the time of formation.

Art. 2
PREREQUISITES FOR ORDINATION

Can. 1033 — One is licitly promoted to orders only if he has received the sacrament of confirmation.

Can. 1034 — §1. An aspirant to the diaconate or to the presbyterate is not to be ordained unless he has first been inscribed as a candidate by the authority mentioned in cann. 1016 and 1019 in a liturgical rite of admission; this is done after he has submitted a signed petition written in his own hand and accepted in writing by the aforementioned authority.

§2. A man who has been admitted through vows to a clerical institute is not bound to obtain this type of admission.

Can. 1035 — §1. Before anyone is promoted to either the permanent or the transitional diaconate he is required to have received the ministries of lector and acolyte and to have exercised them for a suitable period of time.

§2. Between the conferral of acolyte and diaconate, there is to be an interval of at least six months.

Can. 1036 — In order to be promoted to the order of diaconate or of presbyterate the candidate is to give to his own bishop or to the competent major superior a signed declaration written in his own hand, testifying that he is about to receive sacred orders of his own accord and freely and that he will devote himself perpetually to the ecclesiastical ministry; this declaration is also to contain his petition for admission to the reception of orders.

Can. 1037 — An unmarried candidate for the permanent diaconate and a candidate for the presbyterate is not to be admitted to the order of diaconate unless in a prescribed rite he has assumed publicly before God and the Church the obligation of celibacy or professed perpetual vows in a religious institute.

Can. 1038 — A deacon who refuses to be promoted to the presbyterate cannot be forbidden the exercise of the order he has received unless he is prevented from exercising it by a canonical impediment or some other serious cause to be evaluated in the judgment of the diocesan bishop or competent major superior.

Can. 1039 – Omnes qui ad aliquem ordinem promovendi sunt, exercitiis spiritualibus vacent per quinque saltem dies, loco et modo ab Ordinario determinatis; Episcopus, antequam ad ordinationem procedat, certior factus sit oportet candidatos rite iisdem exercitiis vacasse.

Art. 3
De irregularitatibus aliisque impedimentis

Can. 1040 – A recipiendis ordinibus arcentur qui quovis impedimento afficiuntur sive perpetuo, quod venit nomine irregularitatis, sive simplici; nullum autem impedimentum contrahitur, quod in canonibus qui sequuntur non contineatur.

Can. 1041 – Ad recipiendos ordines sunt irregulares:

1° qui aliqua forma laborat amentiae aliusve psychicae infirmitatis, qua, consultis peritis, inhabilis iudicatur ad ministerium rite implendum;

2° qui delictum apostasiae, haeresis aut schismatis commiserit;

3° qui matrimonium etiam civile tantum attentaverit, vel ipsemet vinculo matrimoniali aut ordine sacro aut voto publico perpetuo castitatis a matrimonio ineundo impeditus, vel cum muliere matrimonio valido coniuncta aut eodem voto adstricta;

4° qui voluntarium homicidium perpetraverit aut abortum procuraverit, effectu secuto, omnesque positive cooperantes;

5° qui seipsum vel alium graviter et dolose mutilaverit vel sibi vitam adimere tentaverit;

6° qui actum ordinis posuerit constitutis in ordine episcopatus vel presbyteratus reservatum, vel eodem carens, vel ab eius exercitio poena aliqua canonica declarata vel irrogata prohibitus.

Can. 1042 – Sunt a recipiendis ordinibus simpliciter impediti:

1° vir uxorem habens, nisi ad diaconatum permanentem legitime destinetur;

2° qui officium vel administrationem gerit clericis ad normam cann. 285 et 286 vetitam cuius rationem reddere debet, donec, depositis officio et administratione atque rationibus redditis, liber factus sit;

3° neophytus, nisi, iudicio Ordinarii, sufficienter probatus fuerit.

Can. 1039 — All those who are to be promoted to some order are to make a retreat for at least five days in a place and in a manner determined by the ordinary; before he proceeds to the ordination, the bishop must be certain that the candidates have duly made this retreat.

Art. 3

Irregularities and Other Impediments

Can. 1040 — Persons who are affected by a perpetual impediment, which is called an irregularity, or a simple impediment are prevented from receiving orders; the only impediments which can be contracted are contained in the following canons.

Can. 1041 — The following are irregular as regards the reception of orders:

1° a person who labors under some form of insanity or other psychic defect due to which, after consultation with experts, he is judged incapable of rightly carrying out the ministry;

2° a person who has committed the delict of apostasy, heresy or schism;

3° a person who has attempted marriage, even a civil one only, either while he was impeded from entering marriage due to an existing matrimonial bond, sacred orders or a public perpetual vow of chastity, or with a woman bound by a valid marriage or by the same type of vow;

4° a person who has committed voluntary homicide or who has procured an effective abortion and all persons who positively cooperated in either;

5° a person who has seriously and maliciously mutilated himself or another person or a person who has attempted suicide;

6° a person who has performed an act of orders which has been reserved to those who are in the order of episcopacy or presbyterate while the person either lacked that order or had been forbidden its exercise by some declared or inflicted canonical penalty.

Can. 1042 — The following are simply impeded from receiving orders:

1° a man who has a wife, unless he is legitimately destined for the permanent diaconate;

2° a person who holds an office or position of administration which is forbidden to clerics by cann. 285 and 286 and for which he must render an account until he becomes free by relinquishing the office and position of administration and has rendered an account of it;

3° a neophyte, unless he has been sufficiently proven in the judgment of the ordinary.

Can. 1043 – Christifideles obligatione tenentur impedimenta ad sacros ordines, si qua norint, Ordinario vel parocho ante ordinationem revelandi.

Can. 1044 – § 1. Ad exercendos ordines receptos sunt irregulares :

1° qui irregularitate ad ordines recipiendos dum afficiebatur, illegitime ordines recepit ;

2° qui delictum commisit, de quo in can. 1041, n. 2, si delictum est publicum ;

3° qui delictum commisit, de quibus in can. 1041, nn. 3, 4, 5, 6.

§ 2. Ab ordinibus exercendis impediuntur :

1° qui impedimento ad ordines recipiendos detentus, illegitime ordines recepit ;

2° qui amentia aliave infirmitate psychica de qua in can. 1041, n. 1 afficitur, donec Ordinarius, consulto perito, eiusdem ordinis exercitium permiserit.

Can. 1045 – Ignorantia irregularitatum atque impedimentorum ab eisdem non eximit.

Can. 1046 – Irregularitates et impedimenta multiplicantur ex diversis eorundem causis, non autem ex repetita eadem causa, nisi agatur de irregularitate ex homicidio voluntario aut ex procurato abortu, effectu secuto.

Can. 1047 – § 1. Uni Apostolicae Sedi reservatur dispensatio ab omnibus irregularitatibus, si factum quo innituntur ad forum iudiciale deductum fuerit.

§ 2. Eidem etiam reservatur dispensatio ab irregularitatibus et impedimentis ad ordines recipiendos, quae sequuntur :

1° ab irregularitatibus ex delictis publicis, de quibus in can. 1041, nn. 2 et 3 ;

2° ab irregularitate ex delicto sive publico sive occulto, de quo in can. 1041, n. 4 :

3° ab impedimento, de quo in can. 1042, n. 1.

§ 3. Apostolicae Sedi etiam reservatur dispensatio ab irregularitatibus ad exercitium ordinis suscepti, de quibus in can. 1041, n. 3, in casibus publicis tantum, atque in eodem canone, n. 4, etiam in casibus occultis.

§ 4. Ab irregularitatibus et impedimentis Sanctae Sedi non reservatis dispensare valet Ordinarius.

Can. 1043 — The Christian faithful are obliged to reveal impediments to sacred orders, if they know of any, to the ordinary or to the pastor before ordination.

Can. 1044 — §1. The following are irregular as regards the exercise of orders already received:

1° a person who has illegitimately received orders while he had an irregularity precluding his receiving orders;

2° a person who has committed a delict mentioned in can. 1041, n. 2 , if the delict is public;

3° a person who has committed a delict mentioned in can. 1041, nn. 3, 4, 5, 6.

§2. The following are impeded from exercising orders:

1° a person who has illegitimately received orders while he was bound by an impediment precluding his receiving orders;

2° a person who is afflicted with insanity or some other psychic defect mentioned in can. 1041, n. 1, until the time when the ordinary, after consultation with an expert, permits him the exercise of that order.

Can. 1045 — Ignorance of the irregularities and impediments does not exempt from them.

Can. 1046 — Irregularities and impediments are multiplied when they arise from different causes. They are not multiplied by the repetition of the same cause except in the case of the irregularity arising from voluntary homicide or the effective procuring of an abortion.

Can. 1047 — §1. A dispensation from all irregularities is reserved to the Apostolic See if the fact upon which they are based has been brought to the judicial forum.

§2. A dispensation from the following irregularities and impediments to receiving orders is also reserved to the Holy See:

1° from the irregularity arising from the public delict mentioned in can. 1041, nn. 2 and 3;

2° from the irregularity arising from the public or occult delict mentioned in can. 1041, n. 4;

3° from the impediment mentioned in can. 1042, n. 1.

§3. Also reserved to the Apostolic See is a dispensation from the irregularities precluding the exercise of an order already received which are mentioned in can. 1041, n. 3, but only in public cases, and in can. 1041, n. 4, even in occult cases.

§4. The ordinary can dispense from irregularities and impediments not reserved to the Holy See.

Can. 1048 – In casibus occultis urgentioribus, si adiri nequeat Ordinarius aut cum de irregularitatibus agatur de quibus in can. 1041, nn. 3 et 4, Paenitentiaria, et si periculum immineat gravis damni aut infamiae, potest qui irregularitate ab ordine exercendo impeditur eundem exercere, firmo tamen manente onere quam primum recurrendi ad Ordinarium aut Paenitentiariam, reticito nomine et per confessarium.

Can. 1049 – § 1. In precibus ad obtinendam irregularitatum et impedimentorum dispensationem, omnes irregularitates et impedimenta indicanda sunt; attamen, dispensatio generalis valet etiam pro reticitis bona fide, exceptis irregularitatibus de quibus in can. 1041, n. 4, aliisve ad forum iudiciale deductis, non autem pro reticitis mala fide.

§ 2. Si agatur de irregularitate ex voluntario homicidio aut ex procurato abortu, etiam numerus delictorum ad validitatem dispensationis exprimendus est.

§ 3. Dispensatio generalis ab irregularitatibus et impedimentis ad ordines recipiendos valet pro omnibus ordinibus.

Art. IV

DE DOCUMENTIS REQUISITIS ET DE SCRUTINIO

Can. 1050 – Ut quis ad sacros ordines promoveri possit, sequentia requiruntur documenta :

1° testimonium de studiis rite peractis ad normam can. 1032;

2° si agatur de ordinandis ad presbyteratum, testimonium recepti diaconatus;

3° si agatur de promovendis ad diaconatum, testimonium recepti baptismi et confirmationis, atque receptorum ministeriorum de quibus in can. 1035; item testimonium factae declarationis de qua in can. 1036, necnon, si ordinandus qui promovendus est ad diaconatum permanentem sit uxoratus, testimonia celebrati matrimonii et consensus uxoris.

Can. 1051 – Ad scrutinium de qualitatibus in ordinando requisitis quod attinet, serventur praescripta quae sequuntur :

Can. 1048 — If, in more urgent occult cases access to the ordinary cannot be had or when it is a question of the irregularities mentioned in can. 1041, nn. 3 and 4, access to the Sacred Penitentiary cannot be had and if there is a danger of serious harm or infamy, the person who is impeded by an irregularity from exercising an order can exercise it, with due regard, however, for the responsibility of making recourse as soon as possible to the ordinary or Sacred Pentitentiary through a confessor and without mentioning the name of the person who has the irregularity.

Can. 1049 — §1. In the petition to obtain a dispensation from irregularities and impediments, all the irregularities and impediments are to be indicated; nevertheless, general dispensation is valid even for those which have been omitted in good faith with the exception of the irregularities mentioned in can. 1041, n. 4, or others which have been brought to the judicial forum; however, a general dispensation is not valid for those which have been omitted in bad faith.

§2. If it is a question of the irregularity arising from voluntary homicide or from procuring an abortion the number of the delicts is also to be mentioned for the dispensation to be valid.

§3. A general dispensation from the irregularities and impediments to receive orders is valid for all the orders.

Art. 4

Required Documents and Examination

Can. 1050 — For one to be promoted to sacred orders the following documents are required:

1° certification that the studies prescribed by can. 1032, have been duly completed;

2° certification that the diaconate has been received if it is a question of those to be ordained to the presbyterate;

3° certification that baptism and confirmation have been received and that the ministries mentioned in can. 1035 have been received if it is a question of those to be promoted to the diaconate; also, certification that the declaration mentioned in can. 1036 has been made; and, if the ordinand who is to be promoted to the permanent diaconate is married, certification of the marriage that was celebrated and of the wife's consent.

Can. 1051 — As regards the inquiry concerning the qualities required of an ordinand the following prescriptions are to be observed:

1° habeatur testimonium rectoris seminarii vel domus formationis de qualitatibus ad ordinem recipiendum requisitis, scilicet de candidati recta doctrina, genuina pietate, bonis moribus, aptitudine ad ministerium exercendum; itemque, rite peracta inquisitione, de eius statu valetudinis physicae et psychicae;

2° Episcopus dioecesanus aut Superior maior, ut scrutinium rite peragatur, potest alia adhibere media quae sibi, pro temporis et loci adiunctis, utilia videantur, uti sunt litterae testimoniales, publicationes vel aliae informationes.

Can. 1052 – § 1. Ut Episcopus ordinationem iure proprio conferens ad eam procedere possit, ipsi constare debet documenta, de quibus in can. 1050, praesto esse atque, scrutinio ad normam iuris peracto, idoneitatem candidati positivis argumentis esse probatam.

§ 2. Ut Episcopus ad ordinationem procedat alieni subditi, sufficit ut litterae dimissoriae referant eadem documenta praesto esse, scrutinium ad normam iuris esse peractum atque de idoneitate candidati constare; quod si promovendus sit sodalis instituti religiosi aut societatis vitae apostolicae, eaedem litterae insuper testari debent ipsum in institutum vel societatem definitive cooptatum fuisse et esse subditum Superioris qui dat litteras.

§ 3. Si, his omnibus non obstantibus, ob certas rationes Episcopus dubitat num candidatus sit idoneus ad ordines recipiendos, eundem ne promoveat.

CAPUT III

DE ADNOTATIONE
AC TESTIMONIO PERACTAE ORDINATIONIS

Can. 1053 – § 1. Expleta ordinatione, nomina singulorum ordinatorum ac ministri ordinantis, locus et dies ordinationis notentur in peculiari libro apud curiam loci ordinationis diligenter custodiendo, et omnia singularum ordinationum documenta accurate serventur.

§ 2. Singulis ordinatis det Episcopus ordinans authenticum ordinationis receptae testimonium; qui, si ab Episcopo extraneo cum litteris dimissoriis promoti fuerint, illud proprio Ordinario exhibeant pro ordinationis adnotatione in speciali libro in archivo servando.

1° a testimonial is to be furnished by the rector of the seminary or the house of formation concerning the qualities required for the reception of orders; that is, the candidate's correct doctrine, genuine piety, good morals and his suitability for exercising the ministry; and, after a duly executed inquiry, the state of his physical and psychological health;

2° in order that the inquiry may be properly conducted, the diocesan bishop or the major superior can employ other means which seem useful in accord with the circumstances of time and place, for example testimonial letters, public announcements or other means for gaining information.

Can. 1052 — §1. In order for a bishop conferring an ordination in virtue of his own proper right to proceed to the ordination, he must be certain that the documents mentioned in can. 1050 have been furnished and that the suitability of the candidate has been proved through positive arguments after the inquiry has been conducted in accord with the norm of law.

§2. In order for a bishop to proceed to the ordination of one who is not his own subject, it is sufficient that the dimissorial letters refer to the fact that such documents have been furnished, that the inquiry has been conducted in accord with the norm of law and that the suitability of the candidate has been proved; but if the candidate is a member of a religious institute or a society of apostolic life, the dimissorial letters must also certify that he has definitively become a member and that he is a subject of the superior who grants the letters.

§3. If despite all the above considerations the bishop has certain reasons for doubting the suitability of the candidate for ordination, he is not to ordain him.

Chapter III

REGISTRATION AND CERTIFICATION OF ORDINATION CONFERRED

Can. 1053 — §1. After the ordination has been conferred, the names of those ordained and the ordaining minister, along with the place and date of the ordination, are to be noted in a special register which is to be carefully kept in the curia of the place of ordination; all the documents for each ordination are also to be carefully preserved.

§2. The ordaining bishop is to give each of the ordained an authentic certificate of the ordination which was received; those who have been promoted through dimissorial letters by a bishop other than their own are to show this certificate to their own ordinary so that the registration of the ordination is recorded in the special register to be kept in the archives.

Can. 1054 – Loci Ordinarius, si agatur de saecularibus, aut Superior maior competens, si agatur de ipsius subditis, notitiam uniuscuiusque celebratae ordinationis transmittat ad parochum loci baptismi, qui id adnotet in suo baptizatorum libro, ad normam can. 535, § 2.

TITULUS VII
DE MATRIMONIO

Can. 1055 – § 1. Matrimoniale foedus, quo vir et mulier inter se totius vitae consortium constituunt, indole sua naturali ad bonum coniugum atque ad prolis generationem et educationem ordinatum, a Christo Domino ad sacramenti dignitatem inter baptizatos evectum est.

§ 2. Quare inter baptizatos nequit matrimonialis contractus validus consistere, quin sit eo ipso sacramentum.

Can. 1056 – Essentiales matrimonii proprietates sunt unitas et indissolubilitas, quae in matrimonio christiano ratione sacramenti peculiarem obtinent firmitatem.

Can. 1057 – § 1. Matrimonium facit partium consensus inter personas iure habiles legitime manifestatus, qui nulla humana potestate suppleri valet.

§ 2. Consensus matrimonialis est actus voluntatis, quo vir et mulier foedere irrevocabili sese mutuo tradunt et accipiunt ad constituendum matrimonium.

Can. 1058 – Omnes possunt matrimonium contrahere, qui iure non prohibentur.

catholica **Can. 1059** – Matrimonium catholicorum, etsi una tantum pars sit ~~baptizata,~~ regitur iure non solum divino, sed etiam canonico, salva competentia civilis potestatis circa mere civiles eiusdem matrimonii effectus.

Can. 1060 – Matrimonium gaudet favore iuris; quare in dubio standum est pro valore matrimonii, donec contrarium probetur.

Can. 1061 – § 1. Matrimonium inter baptizatos validum dicitur ratum tantum, si non est consummatum; ratum et consummatum, si coniuges inter se humano modo posuerunt coniugalem actum per se aptum ad prolis generationem, ad quem natura sua ordinatur matrimonium, et quo coniuges fiunt una caro.

Can. 1054 — In the case of seculars the local ordinary and in the case of those who are subject to him the competent major superior, are to send notification of every ordination celebrated to the pastor of the place where the ordained person has been baptized so that a notation may be made in the baptismal register according to the norm of can. 535, §2.

TITLE VII
MARRIAGE

Can. 1055 — §1. The matrimonial covenant, by which a man and a woman establish between themselves a partnership of the whole of life, is by its nature ordered toward the good of the spouses and the procreation and education of offspring; this covenant between baptized persons has been raised by Christ the Lord to the dignity of a sacrament.

§2. For this reason a matrimonial contract cannot validly exist between baptized persons unless it is also a sacrament by that fact.

Can. 1056 — The essential properties of marriage are unity and indissolubility, which in Christian marriage obtain a special firmness in virtue of the sacrament.

Can. 1057 — §1. Marriage is brought about through the consent of the parties, legitimately manifested between persons who are capable according to law of giving consent; no human power can replace this consent.

§2. Matrimonial consent is an act of the will by which a man and a woman, through an irrevocable covenant, mutually give and accept each other in order to establish marriage.

Can. 1058 — All persons who are not prohibited by law can contract marriage.

Can. 1059 — Even if only one party is ~~baptized~~ catholic, the marriage of Catholics is regulated not only by divine law but also by canon law, with due regard for the competence of civil authority concerning the merely civil effects of such a marriage.

Can. 1060 — Marriage enjoys the favor of the law; consequently, when a doubt exists the validity of a marriage is to be upheld until the contrary is proven.

Can. 1061 — §1. A valid marriage between baptized persons is called ratified only if it has not been consummated; it is called ratified and consummated if the parties have performed between themselves in a human manner the conjugal act which is per se suitable for the generation of children, to which marriage is ordered by its very nature and by which the spouses become one flesh.

§ 2. Celebrato matrimonio, si coniuges cohabitaverint, praesumitur consummatio, donec contrarium probetur.

§ 3. Matrimonium invalidum dicitur putativum, si bona fide ab una saltem parte celebratum fuerit, donec utraque pars de eiusdem nullitate certa evadat.

Can. 1062 – § 1. Matrimonii promissio sive unilateralis sive bilateralis, quam sponsalia vocant, regitur iure particulari, quod ab Episcoporum conferentia, habita ratione consuetudinum et legum civilium, si quae sint, statutum fuit.

§ 2. Ex matrimonii promissione non datur actio ad petendam matrimonii celebrationem; datur tamen ad reparationem damnorum, si qua debeatur.

CAPUT I

DE CURA PASTORALI ET DE IIS
QUAE MATRIMONII CELEBRATIONI PRAEMITTI DEBENT

Can. 1063 – Pastores animarum obligatione tenentur curandi ut propria ecclesiastica communitas christifidelibus assistentiam praebeat, qua status matrimonialis in spiritu christiano servetur et in perfectione progrediatur. Haec assistentia imprimis praebenda est:

1° praedicatione, catechesi minoribus, iuvenibus et adultis aptata, immo usu instrumentorum communicationis socialis, quibus christifideles de significatione matrimonii christiani deque munere coniugum ac parentum christianorum instituantur;

2° praeparatione personali ad matrimonium ineundum, qua sponsi ad novi sui status sanctitatem et officia disponantur;

3° fructuosa liturgica matrimonii celebratione, qua eluceat coniuges mysterium unitatis et fecundi amoris inter Christum et Ecclesiam significare atque participare;

4° auxilio coniugatis praestito, ut ipsi foedus coniugale fideliter servantes atque tuentes, ad sanctiorem in dies plenioremque in familia vitam ducendam perveniant.

Can. 1064 – Ordinarii loci est curare ut debite ordinetur eadem assistentia, auditis etiam, si opportunum videatur, viris et mulieribus experientia et peritia probatis.

Can. 1065 – § 1. Catholici qui sacramentum confirmationis nondum receperint, illud, antequam ad matrimonium admittantur, recipiant, si id fieri possit sine gravi incommodo.

§2. After marriage has been celebrated, if the spouses have cohabited consummation is presumed until the contrary is proven.

§3. An invalid marriage is called putative if it has been celebrated in good faith by at least one of the parties, until both parties become certain of its nullity.

Can. 1062 — §1. A promise of marriage, be it unilateral or bilateral, called an engagement, is regulated by particular law which has been established by the conference of bishops after it has taken into consideration any existing customs and civil laws.

§2. A promise to marry does not give rise to an action to seek the celebration of marriage; an action for reparation of damages, however, does arise if it is warranted.

CHAPTER I

PASTORAL CARE AND WHAT MUST PRECEDE CELEBRATION OF MARRIAGE

Can. 1063 — Pastors of souls are obliged to see to it that their own ecclesial community furnishes the Christian faithful assistance so that the matrimonial state is maintained in a Christian spirit and makes progress toward perfection. This assistance is especially to be furnished through:

1° preaching, catechesis adapted to minors, youths and adults, and even the use of the media of social communications so that through these means the Christian faithful may be instructed concerning the meaning of Christian marriage and the duty of Christian spouses and parents;

2° personal preparation for entering marriage so that through such preparation the parties may be predisposed toward the holiness and duties of their new state;

3° a fruitful liturgical celebration of marriage clarifying that the spouses signify and share in that mystery of unity and of fruitful love that exists between Christ and the Church;

4° assistance furnished to those already married so that, while faithfully maintaining and protecting the conjugal covenant, they may day by day come to lead holier and fuller lives in their families.

Can. 1064 — It is up to the local ordinary to make provisions that such assistance is duly organized, even after consulting men and women of proven experience and skill, if it seems appropriate.

Can. 1065 — §1. If they can do so without serious inconvenience, Catholics who have not yet received the sacrament of confirmation are to receive it before being admitted to marriage.

§ 2. Ut fructuose sacramentum matrimonii recipiatur, enixe sponsis commendatur, ut ad sacramenta paenitentiae et sanctissimae Eucharistiae accedant.

Can. 1066 – Antequam matrimonium celebretur, constare debet nihil eius validae ac licitae celebrationi obsistere.

Can. 1067 – Episcoporum conferentia statuat normas de examine sponsorum, necnon de publicationibus matrimonialibus aliisve opportunis mediis ad investigationes peragendas, quae ante matrimonium necessaria sunt, quibus diligenter observatis, parochus procedere possit ad matrimonio assistendum.

Can. 1068 – In periculo mortis, si aliae probationes haberi nequeant, sufficit, nisi contraria adsint indicia, affirmatio contrahentium, si casus ferat etiam iurata, se baptizatos esse et nullo detineri impedimento.

Can. 1069 – Omnes fideles obligatione tenentur impedimenta, si quae norint, parocho aut loci Ordinario, ante matrimonii celebrationem, revelandi.

Can. 1070 – Si alius quam parochus, cuius est assistere matrimonio, investigationes peregerit, de harum exitu quam primum per authenticum documentum eundem parochum certiorem reddat.

Can. 1071 – § 1. Excepto casu necessitatis, sine licentia Ordinarii loci ne quis assistat :

1° matrimonio vagorum ;

2° matrimonio quod ad normam legis civilis agnosci vel celebrari nequeat ;

3° matrimonio eius qui obligationibus teneatur naturalibus erga aliam partem filiosve ex praecedenti unione ortis ;

4° matrimonio eius qui notorie catholicam fidem abiecerit ;

5° matrimonio eius qui censura innodatus sit ;

6° matrimonio filii familias minoris, insciis aut rationabiliter invitis parentibus ;

7° matrimonio per procuratorem ineundo, de quo in can. 1105.

§ 2. Ordinarius loci licentiam assistendi matrimonio eius qui notorie catholicam fidem abiecerit ne concedat, nisi servatis normis de quibus in can. 1125, congrua congruis referendo.

Can. 1072 – Curent animarum pastores a matrimonii celebratione avertere iuvenes ante aetatem, qua secundum regionis receptos mores matrimonium iniri solet.

§2. It is strongly recommended that those to be married approach the sacraments of penance and the Most Holy Eucharist so that they may fruitfully receive the sacrament of marriage.

Can. 1066 — Before marriage is celebrated, it must be evident that nothing stands in the way of its valid and licit celebration.

Can. 1067 — The conference of bishops is to issue norms concerning the examination of the parties, and the marriage banns or other appropriate means for carrying out the necessary inquiries which are to precede marriage. The pastor can proceed to assist at a marriage after such norms have been diligently observed.

Can. 1068 — Unless contrary indications are present, in danger of death, if other means of proof cannot be obtained, it is sufficient that the parties affirm—even under oath, if the case warrants it—that they have been baptized and that they are not held back by any impediment.

Can. 1069 — All the faithful are obliged to reveal any impediments they are aware of to the pastor or to the local ordinary before the celebration of marriage.

Can. 1070 — If someone other than the pastor who is to assist at the marriage has conducted the investigations, that person is to notify the pastor of the results as soon as possible through an authentic document.

Can. 1071 — §1. Except in case of necessity, no one is to assist at the following marriages without the permission of the local ordinary:

1° the marriage of transients;

2° a marriage which cannot be recognized or celebrated in accord with the norm of civil law;

3° a marriage of a person who is bound by natural obligations toward another party or toward children, arising from a prior union;

4° a marriage of a person who has notoriously rejected the Catholic faith;

5° a marriage of a person who is bound by a censure;

6° a marriage of a minor child when the parents are unaware of it or are reasonably opposed to it;

7° a marriage to be entered by means of a proxy, mentioned in can. 1105.

§2. The local ordinary is not to grant permission for assisting at the marriage of a person who has notoriously rejected the Catholic faith unless the norms of can. 1125 have been observed, making any necessary adaptations.

Can. 1072 — Pastors of souls are to take care to prevent youths from celebrating marriage before the age at which marriage is usually contracted in accord with the accepted practice of the region.

Caput II

DE IMPEDIMENTIS DIRIMENTIBUS IN GENERE

Can. 1073 – Impedimentum dirimens personam inhabilem reddit ad matrimonium valide contrahendum.

Can. 1074 – Publicum censetur impedimentum, quod probari in foro externo potest; secus est occultum.

Can. 1075 – § 1. Supremae tantum Ecclesiae auctoritatis est authentice declarare quandonam ius divinum matrimonium prohibeat vel dirimat.

§ 2. Uni quoque supremae auctoritati ius est alia impedimenta pro baptizatis constituere.

Can. 1076 – Consuetudo novum impedimentum inducens aut impedimentis exsistentibus contraria reprobatur.

Can. 1077 – § 1. Ordinarius loci propriis subditis ubique commorantibus et omnibus in proprio territorio actu degentibus vetare potest matrimonium in casu peculiari, sed ad tempus tantum, gravi de causa eaque perdurante.

§ 2. Vetito clausulam dirimentem una suprema Ecclesiae auctoritas addere potest.

Can. 1078 – § 1. Ordinarius loci proprios subditos ubique commorantes et omnes in proprio territorio actu degentes ab omnibus impedimentis iuris ecclesiastici dispensare potest, exceptis iis, quorum dispensatio Sedi Apostolicae reservatur.

§ 2. Impedimenta quorum dispensatio Sedi Apostolicae reservatur sunt:

1° impedimentum ortum ex sacris ordinibus aut ex voto publico perpetuo castitatis in instituto religioso iuris pontificii;

2° impedimentum criminis de quo in can. 1090.

§ 3. Numquam datur dispensatio ab impedimento consanguinitatis in linea recta aut in secundo gradu lineae collateralis.

Can. 1079 – § 1. Urgente mortis periculo, loci Ordinarius potest tum super forma in matrimonii celebratione servanda, tum super omnibus et singulis impedimentis iuris ecclesiastici sive publicis sive occultis, dispensare proprios subditos ubique commorantes et omnes in proprio territorio actu degentes, excepto impedimento orto ex sacro ordine presbyteratus.

CHAPTER II

DIRIMENT IMPEDIMENTS IN GENERAL

Can. 1073 — A diriment impediment renders a person incapable of contracting marriage validly.

Can. 1074 — An impediment which can be proven in the external forum is considered to be a public impediment; otherwise, it is an occult impediment.

Can. 1075 — §1. The supreme authority of the Church alone has the competency to declare authentically when divine law prohibits or voids a marriage.

§2. Only the supreme authority has the right to establish other impediments for the baptized.

Can. 1076 — A custom which introduces a new impediment or which is contrary to existing impediments is reprobated.

Can. 1077 — §1. In a particular case the local ordinary can prohibit the marriage of his own subjects wherever they are staying and of all persons actually present in his own territory, but only for a time, for a serious cause and as long as that cause exists.

§2. Only the supreme authority of the Church can add an invalidating clause to a prohibition.

Can. 1078 — §1. The local ordinary can dispense his own subjects wherever they are staying as well as all persons actually present in his own territory from all the impediments of ecclesiastical law with the exception of those impediments whose dispensation is reserved to the Apostolic See.

§2. A dispensation from the following impediments is reserved to the Apostolic See:

1° the impediment arising from sacred orders or from a public perpetual vow of chastity in a religious institute of pontifical right;

2° the impediment of crime mentioned in can. 1090.

§3. A dispensation is never given from the impediment of consanguinity in the direct line or in the second degree of the collateral line.

Can. 1079 — §1. In danger of death, the local ordinary can dispense his own subjects wherever they are staying as well as all persons who are actually present in his territory both from the form prescribed for the celebration of matrimony and from each and every impediment of ecclesiastical law, whether it be public or occult, except the impediment arising from sacred order of the presbyterate.

§ 2. In eisdem rerum adiunctis, de quibus in § 1, sed solum pro casibus in quibus ne loci quidem Ordinarius adiri possit, eadem dispensandi potestate pollet tum parochus, tum minister sacer rite delegatus, tum sacerdos vel diaconus qui matrimonio, ad normam can. 1116, § 2, assistit.

§ 3. In periculo mortis confessarius gaudet potestate dispensandi ab impedimentis occultis pro foro interno sive intra sive extra actum sacramentalis confessionis.

§ 4. In casu de quo in § 2, loci Ordinarius censetur adiri non posse. si tantum per telegraphum vel telephonum id fieri possit.

Can. 1080 – § 1. Quoties impedimentum detegatur cum iam omnia sunt parata ad nuptias, nec matrimonium sine probabili gravis mali periculo differri possit usquedum a competenti auctoritate dispensatio obtineatur, potestate gaudent dispensandi ab omnibus impedimentis, iis exceptis de quibus in can. 1078, § 2, n. 1, loci Ordinarius et, dummodo casus sit occultus, omnes de quibus in can. 1079, §§ 2-3, servatis condicionibus ibidem praescriptis.

§ 2. Haec potestas valet etiam ad matrimonium convalidandum, si idem periculum sit in mora nec tempus suppetat recurrendi ad Sedem Apostolicam, vel ad loci Ordinarium, quod attinet ad impedimenta a quibus dispensare valet.

Can. 1081 – Parochus aut sacerdos vel diaconus, de quibus in can. 1079, § 2, de concessa dispensatione pro foro externo Ordinarium loci statim certiorem faciat; eaque adnotetur in libro matrimoniorum.

Can. 1082 – Nisi aliud ferat Paenitentiariae rescriptum, dispensatio in foro interno non sacramentali concessa super impedimento occulto, adnotetur in libro, qui in secreto curiae archivo asservandus est, nec alia dispensatio pro foro externo est necessaria, si postea occultum impedimentum publicum evaserit.

Caput III

DE IMPEDIMENTIS DIRIMENTIBUS IN SPECIE

Can. 1083 – § 1. Vir ante decimum sextum aetatis annum completum, mulier ante decimum quartum item completum, matrimonium validum inire non possunt.

§ 2. Integrum est Episcoporum conferentiae aetatem superiorem ad licitam matrimonii celebrationem statuere.

§2. In the same situation mentioned in §1 and only for cases in which the local ordinary cannot be reached, the pastor, the properly delegated sacred minister and the priest or deacon who assists at matrimony in accord with the norm of can. 1116, §2, also possess the faculty to dispense from the same impediments.

§3. In danger of death a confessor enjoys the faculty to dispense from occult impediments for the internal forum, whether within or outside the act of sacramental confession.

§4. In the case mentioned in §2, the local ordinary is not considered to be accessible if he can be contacted only by means of telegraph or telephone.

Can. 1080 — §1. Whenever an impediment is discovered after all the wedding preparations are made and the marriage cannot be deferred without probable danger of serious harm until a dispensation can be obtained from competent authority, the following persons enjoy the faculty to dispense from all the impediments with the exception of the ones mentioned in can. 1078, §2, n. 1: the local ordinary and, as long as the case is an occult one, all persons mentioned in can. 1079, §§2 and 3, observing the conditions prescribed in that canon.

§2. This power is also operative for the convalidation of a marriage if the same danger exists in delay and there is insufficient time to have recourse to the Apostolic See, or to the local ordinary concerning impediments from which he is able to dispense.

Can. 1081 — The pastor or the priest or deacon mentioned in can. 1079, §2, is immediately to inform the local ordinary of a dispensation granted for the external forum; it is also to be recorded in the marriage register.

Can. 1082 — Unless a rescript from the Penitentiary states otherwise, a dispensation from an occult impediment granted in the internal non-sacramental forum is to be recorded in a book which is to be kept in the secret archive of the curia; if the occult impediment becomes public later on, no other dispensation is necessary for the external forum.

CHAPTER III

DIRIMENT IMPEDIMENTS SPECIFICALLY

Can. 1083 — §1. A man before he has completed his sixteenth year of age, and likewise a woman before she has completed her fourteenth year of age, cannot enter a valid marriage.

§2. It is within the power of the conference of bishops to establish an older age for the licit celebration of marriage.

Can. 1084 – § 1. Impotentia coeundi antecedens et perpetua, sive ex parte viri sive ex parte mulieris, sive absoluta sive relativa, matrimonium ex ipsa eius natura dirimit.

§ 2. Si impedimentum impotentiae dubium sit, sive dubio iuris sive dubio facti, matrimonium non est impediendum, nec stante dubio, nullum declarandum.

§ 3. Sterilitas matrimonium nec prohibet nec dirimit, firmo praescripto can. 1098.

Can. 1085 – § 1. Invalide matrimonium attentat qui vinculo tenetur prioris matrimonii, quamquam non consummati.

§ 2. Quamvis prius matrimonium sit irritum aut solutum qualibet ex causa, non ideo licet aliud contrahere, antequam de prioris nullitate aut solutione legitime et certo constiterit.

Can. 1086 – § 1. Matrimonium inter duas personas, quarum altera sit baptizata in Ecclesia catholica vel in eandem recepta nec actu formali ab ea defecerit, et altera non baptizata, invalidum est.

§ 2. Ab hoc impedimento ne dispensetur, nisi impletis condicionibus de quibus in cann. 1125 et 1126.

§ 3. Si pars tempore contracti matrimonii tamquam baptizata communiter habebatur aut eius baptismus erat dubius, praesumenda est, ad normam can. 1060, validitas matrimonii, donec certo probetur alteram partem baptizatam esse, alteram vero non baptizatam.

Can. 1087 – Invalide matrimonium attentant qui in sacris ordinibus sunt constituti.

Can. 1088 – Invalide matrimonium attentant, qui voto publico perpetuo castitatis in instituto religioso adstricti sunt.

Can. 1089 – Inter virum et mulierem abductam vel saltem retentam intuitu matrimonii cum ea contrahendi, nullum matrimonium consistere potest, nisi postea mulier a raptore separata et in loco tuto ac libero constituta, matrimonium sponte eligat.

Can. 1090 – § 1. Qui intuitu matrimonii cum certa persona ineundi, huius coniugi vel proprio coniugi mortem intulerit, invalide hoc matrimonium attentat.

§ 2. Invalide quoque matrimonium inter se attentant qui mutua opera physica vel morali mortem coniugi intulerunt.

Can. 1084 — §1. Antecedent and perpetual impotence to have intercourse, whether on the part of the man or of the woman, which is either absolute or relative, of its very nature invalidates marriage.

§2. If the impediment of impotence is doubtful, either by reason of a doubt of law or a doubt of fact, a marriage is neither to be impeded nor is it to be declared null as long as the doubt exists.

§3. Sterility neither prohibits nor invalidates marriage, with due regard for the prescription of can. 1098.

Can. 1085 — §1. A person who is held to the bond of a prior marriage, even if it has not been consummated, invalidly attempts marriage.

§2. Even if the prior marriage is invalid or dissolved for any reason whatsoever, it is not on that account permitted to contract another before the nullity or the dissolution of the prior marriage has been legitimately and certainly established.

Can. 1086 — §1. Marriage between two persons, one of whom is baptized in the Catholic Church or has been received into it and has not left it by means of a formal act, and the other of whom is non-baptized, is invalid.

§2. This impediment is not to be dispensed unless the conditions mentioned in cann. 1125 and 1126 are fulfilled.

§3. If at the time the marriage was contracted one party was commonly considered to be baptized or the person's baptism was doubted, the validity of the marriage is to be presumed in accord with the norm of can. 1060 until it is proven with certainty that one party was baptized and the other was not.

Can. 1087 — Persons who are in holy orders invalidly attempt marriage.

Can. 1088 — Persons who are bound by a public perpetual vow of chastity in a religious institute invalidly attempt marriage.

Can. 1089 — No marriage can exist between a man and a woman abducted or at least detained for the purpose of contracting marriage with her, unless the woman of her own accord chooses marriage after she has been separated from her abductor and established in a place where she is safe and free.

Can. 1090 — §1. A person who for the purpose of entering marriage with a certain person has brought about the death of that person's spouse or one's own spouse, invalidly attempts such a marriage.

§2. They also invalidly attempt marriage between themselves who have brought about the death of the spouse of one of them through mutual physical or moral cooperation.

Can. 1091 – § 1. In linea recta consanguinitatis matrimonium irritum est inter omnes ascendentes et descendentes tum legitimos tum naturales.

§ 2. In linea collaterali irritum est usque ad quartum gradum inclusive.

§ 3. Impedimentum consanguinitatis non multiplicatur.

§ 4. Numquam matrimonium permittatur, si quod subest dubium num partes sint consanguineae in aliquo gradu lineae rectae aut in secundo gradu lineae collateralis.

Can. 1092 – Affinitas in linea recta dirimit matrimonium in quolibet gradu.

Can. 1093 – Impedimentum publicae honestatis oritur ex matrimonio invalido post instauratam vitam communem aut ex notorio vel publico concubinatu; et nuptias dirimit in primo gradu lineae rectae inter virum et consanguineas mulieris, ac vice versa.

Can. 1094 – Matrimonium inter se valide contrahere nequeunt qui cognatione legali ex adoptione orta, in linea recta aut in secundo gradu lineae collateralis, coniuncti sunt.

CAPUT IV

DE CONSENSU MATRIMONIALI

Can. 1095 – Sunt incapaces matrimonii contrahendi:

1° qui sufficienti rationis usu carent;

2° qui laborant gravi defectu discretionis iudicii circa iura et officia matrimonialia essentialia mutuo tradenda et acceptanda;

3° qui ob causas naturae psychicae obligationes matrimonii essentiales assumere non valent.

Can. 1096 – § 1. Ut consensus matrimonialis haberi possit, necesse est ut contrahentes saltem non ignorent matrimonium esse consortium permanens inter virum et mulierem ordinatum ad prolem, cooperatione aliqua sexuali, procreandam.

§ 2. Haec ignorantia post pubertatem non praesumitur.

Can. 1097 – § 1. Error in persona invalidum reddit matrimonium.

§ 2. Error in qualitate personae, etsi det causam contractui, matrimonium irritum non reddit, nisi haec qualitas directe et principaliter intendatur.

Can. 1091 — §1. In the direct line of consanguinity, marriage is invalid between all ancestors and descendants, whether they be related legitimately or naturally.

§2. In the collateral line of consanguinity, marriage is invalid up to and including the fourth degree.

§3. The impediment of consanguinity is not multiplied.

§4. If there exists any doubt whether the parties are related through consanguinity in any degree of the direct line or in the second degree of the collateral line, marriage is never permitted.

Can. 1092 — Affinity in the direct line in any degree whatsoever invalidates matrimony.

Can. 1093 — The impediment of public propriety arises from an invalid marriage after common life has been established or from notorious and public concubinage; it invalidates marriage in the first degree of the direct line between the man and the blood relatives of the woman, and vice-versa.

Can. 1094 — They cannot validly contract marriage between themselves who are related in the direct line or in the second degree of the collateral line through a legal relationship arising from adoption.

CHAPTER IV

MATRIMONIAL CONSENT

Can. 1095 — They are incapable of contracting marriage:

1° who lack the sufficient use of reason;

2° who suffer from grave lack of discretion of judgment concerning essential matrimonial rights and duties which are to be mutually given and accepted;

3° who are not capable of assuming the essential obligations of matrimony due to causes of a psychic nature.

Can. 1096 — §1. For matrimonial consent to be valid it is necessary that the contracting parties at least not be ignorant that marriage is a permanent consortium between a man and a woman which is ordered toward the procreation of offspring by means of some sexual cooperation.

§2. Such ignorance is not presumed after puberty.

Can. 1097 — §1. Error concerning the person renders marriage invalid.

§2. Error concerning a quality of a person, even if such error is the cause of the contract, does not invalidate matrimony unless this quality was directly and principally intended.

Can. 1098 – Qui matrimonium init deceptus dolo, ad obtinendum consensum patrato, circa aliquam alterius partis qualitatem, quae suapte natura consortium vitae coniugalis graviter perturbare potest, invalide contrahit.

Can. 1099 – Error circa matrimonii unitatem vel indissolubilitatem aut sacramentalem dignitatem, dummodo non determinet voluntatem, non vitiat consensum matrimonialem.

Can. 1100 – Scientia aut opinio nullitatis matrimonii consensum matrimonialem non necessario excludit.

Can. 1101 – § 1. Internus animi consensus praesumitur conformis verbis vel signis in celebrando matrimonio adhibitis.

§ 2. At si alterutra vel utraque pars positivo voluntatis actu excludat matrimonium ipsum vel matrimonii essentiale aliquod elementum, vel essentialem aliquam proprietatem, invalide contrahit.

Can. 1102 – § 1. Matrimonium sub condicione de futuro valide contrahi nequit.

§ 2. Matrimonium sub condicione de praeterito vel de praesenti initum est validum vel non, prout id quod condicioni subest, exsistit vel non.

§ 3. Condicio autem, de qua in § 2, licite apponi nequit, nisi cum licentia Ordinarii loci scripto data.

Can. 1103 – Invalidum est matrimonium initum ob vim vel metum gravem ab extrinseco, etiam haud consulto incussum, a quo ut quis se liberet, eligere cogatur matrimonium.

Can. 1104 – § 1. Ad matrimonium valide contrahendum necesse est ut contrahentes sint praesentes una simul sive per se ipsi, sive per procuratorem.

§ 2. Sponsi consensum matrimonialem verbis exprimant; si vero loqui non possunt, signis aequipollentibus.

Can. 1105 – § 1. Ad matrimonium per procuratorem valide ineundum requiritur:

1° ut adsit mandatum speciale ad contrahendum cum certa persona;

2° ut procurator ab ipso mandante designetur, et munere suo per se ipse fungatur.

§ 2. Mandatum, ut valeat, subscribendum est a mandante et praeterea a parocho vel Ordinario loci in quo mandatum datur, aut a

Can. 1098 — A person contracts invalidly who enters marriage deceived by fraud, perpetrated to obtain consent, concerning some quality of the other party which of its very nature can seriously disturb the partnership of conjugal life.

Can. 1099 — Error concerning the unity, indissolubility or sacramental dignity of matrimony does not vitiate matrimonial consent so long as it does not determine the will.

Can. 1100 — The knowledge or opinion of the nullity of a marriage does not necessarily exclude matrimonial consent.

Can. 1101 — §1. The internal consent of the mind is presumed to be in agreement with the words or signs employed in celebrating matrimony.

§2. But if either or both parties through a positive act of the will should exclude marriage itself, some essential element or an essential property of marriage, it is invalidly contracted.

Can 1102 — §1. Marriage based on a condition concerning the future cannot be contracted validly.

§2. Marriage based on a condition concerning the past or the present is valid or invalid, insofar as the subject matter of the condition exists or not.

§3. The condition mentioned in §2 cannot be placed licitly without the written permission of the local ordinary.

Can. 1103 — A marriage is invalid if it is entered into due to force or grave fear inflicted from outside the person, even when inflicted unintentionally, which is of such a type that the person is compelled to choose matrimony in order to be freed from it.

Can. 1104 — §1. In order for marriage to be contracted validly, it is necessary that the contracting parties be present together, either in person or by proxy.

§2. Those to be married are to express their matrimonial consent in words; however, if they cannot speak, they are to express it by equivalent signs.

Can. 1105 — §1. In order for marriage to be entered validly by proxy, it is required that:

1° there be a special mandate to contract marriage with a certain person;

2° the proxy be appointed by the person who gave the mandate and that the proxy fulfill this function in person.

§2. To be valid a mandate must be signed by the person who gave it as well as by the pastor or the local ordinary where the mandate was issued, or by a

sacerdote ab alterutro delegato, aut a duobus saltem testibus, aut confici debet per documentum ad normam iuris civilis authenticum.

§ 3. Si mandans scribere nequeat, id in ipso mandato adnotetur et alius testis addatur qui scripturam ipse quoque subsignet; secus mandatum irritum est.

§ 4. Si mandans, antequam procurator eius nomine contrahat, mandatum revocaverit aut in amentiam inciderit, invalidum est matrimonium, licet sive procurator sive altera pars contrahens haec ignoraverit.

Can. 1106 – Matrimonium per interpretem contrahi potest; cui tamen parochus ne assistat, nisi de interpretis fide sibi constet.

Can. 1107 – Etsi matrimonium invalide ratione impedimenti vel defectus formae initum fuerit, consensus praestitus praesumitur perseverare, donec de eius revocatione constiterit.

Caput V
DE FORMA CELEBRATIONIS MATRIMONII

Can. 1108 – § 1. Ea tantum matrimonia valida sunt, quae contrahuntur coram loci Ordinario aut parocho aut sacerdote vel diacono ab alterutro delegato qui assistant, necnon coram duobus testibus, secundum tamen regulas expressas in canonibus qui sequuntur, et salvis exceptionibus de quibus in cann. 144, 1112, § 1, 1116 et 1127, §§ 2-3.

§ 2. Assistens matrimonio intellegitur tantum qui praesens exquirit manifestationem contrahentium consensus eamque nomine Ecclesiae recipit.

Can. 1109 – Loci Ordinarius et parochus, nisi per sententiam vel per decretum fuerint excommunicati vel interdicti vel suspensi ab officio aut tales declarati, vi officii, intra fines sui territorii, valide matrimoniis assistunt non tantum subditorum, sed etiam non subditorum, dummodo eorum alteruter sit ritus latini.

Can. 1110 – Ordinarius et parochus personalis vi officii matrimonio solummodo eorum valide assistunt, quorum saltem alteruter subditus sit intra fines suae dicionis.

Can. 1111 – § 1. Loci Ordinarius et parochus, quamdiu valide officio funguntur, possunt facultatem intra fines sui territorii matrimoniis assistendi, etiam generalem, sacerdotibus et diaconis delegare.

priest delegated by either of these, or at least by two witnesses, or it must be arranged by means of a document which is authentic according to civil law.

§3. If the person giving the mandate cannot write, this is to be noted in the mandate itself and another witness is to be added who also must sign the document; otherwise, the mandate is invalid.

§4. If the person who gave the mandate revokes it or becomes insane before the proxy has contracted the marriage in that person's name, the marriage is invalid even though either the proxy or the other contracting party was unaware of these developments.

Can. 1106 — Marriage can be contracted through an interpreter; however, the pastor is not to assist at such a marriage unless he is convinced of the interpreter's trustworthiness.

Can. 1107 — Even if a marriage was entered invalidly by reason of an impediment or lack of form, the consent which was furnished is presumed to continue until its revocation has been proved.

CHAPTER V

THE FORM OF THE CELEBRATION OF MARRIAGE

Can. 1108 — §1. Only those marriages are valid which are contracted in the presence of the local ordinary or the pastor or a priest or deacon delegated by either of them, who assist, and in the presence of two witnesses, according to the rules expressed in the following canons, with due regard for the exceptions mentioned in cann. 144, 1112, §1, 1116 and 1127, §§2 and 3.

§2. The one assisting at a marriage is understood to be only that person who, present at the ceremony, asks for the contractants' manifestation of consent and receives it in the name of the Church.

Can. 1109 — Unless they have been excommunicated, interdicted or suspended from office or declared such, whether by sentence or decree, within the confines of their territory, the local ordinary and the pastor in virtue of their office, validly assist at the marriages of their subjects as well as of non-subjects provided one of the contractants is of the Latin rite.

Can. 1110 — In virtue of their office and within the limits of their jurisdiction an ordinary and a personal pastor validly assist only at marriages involving at least one of their subjects.

Can. 1111 — §1. As long as they validly hold office, the local ordinary and the pastor can delegate to priests and deacons the faculty, even a general one, to assist at marriages within the limits of their territory.

§ 2. Ut valida sit delegatio facultatis assistendi matrimoniis, determinatis personis expresse dari debet; si agitur de delegatione speciali, ad determinatum matrimonium danda est; si vero agitur de delegatione generali, scripto est concedenda.

Can. 1112 – § 1. Ubi desunt sacerdotes et diaconi, potest Episcopus dioecesanus, praevio voto favorabili Episcoporum conferentiae et obtenta licentia Sanctae Sedis, delegare laicos, qui matrimoniis assistant.

§ 2. Laicus seligatur idoneus, ad institutionem nupturientibus tradendam capax et qui liturgiae matrimoniali rite peragendae aptus sit.

Can. 1113 – Antequam delegatio concedatur specialis, omnia provideantur, quae ius statuit ad libertatem status comprobandam.

Can. 1114 – Assistens matrimonio illicite agit, nisi ipsi constiterit de libero statu contrahentium ad normam iuris atque, si fieri potest, de licentia parochi, quoties vi delegationis generalis assistit.

Can. 1115 – Matrimonia celebrentur in paroecia ubi alterutra pars contrahentium habet domicilium vel quasi-domicilium vel menstruam commorationem, aut, si de vagis agitur, in paroecia ubi actu commorantur; cum licentia proprii Ordinarii aut parochi proprii, alibi celebrari potest.

Can. 1116 – § 1. Si haberi vel adiri nequeat sine gravi incommodo assistens ad normam iuris competens, qui intendunt verum matrimonium inire, illud valide ac licite coram solis testibus contrahere possunt:

1° in mortis periculo;

2° extra mortis periculum, dummodo prudenter praevideatur earum rerum condicionem esse per mensem duraturam.

§ 2. In utroque casu, si praesto sit alius sacerdos vel diaconus qui adesse possit, vocari et, una cum testibus, matrimonii celebrationi adesse debet, salva coniugii validitate coram solis testibus.

Can. 1117 – Statuta superius forma servanda est, si saltem alterutra pars matrimonium contrahentium in Ecclesia catholica baptizata vel in eandem recepta sit neque actu formali ab ea defecerit, salvis praescriptis can. 1127, § 2.

Can. 1118 – § 1. Matrimonium inter catholicos vel inter partem catholicam et partem non catholicam baptizatam celebretur in ecclesia paroeciali; in alia ecclesia aut oratorio celebrari poterit de licentia Ordinarii loci vel parochi.

§2. To be valid the delegation of the faculty to assist at marriages must be given expressly to specified persons; if it is a question of a special delegation, it is to be granted for a specific marriage; however, if it is a question of a general delegation, it is to be granted in writing.

Can. 1112 — §1. With the prior favorable opinion of the conference of bishops and after the permission of the Holy See has been obtained, the diocesan bishop can delegate lay persons to assist at marriages where priests or deacons are lacking.

§2. A suitable lay person is to be chosen who is capable of giving instructions to those to be wed and qualified to perform the marriage liturgy correctly.

Can. 1113 — Before special delegation is granted, all the legal requirements for establishing freedom to marry are to have been fulfilled.

Can. 1114 — The person who assists at the celebration of a marriage acts illicitly unless the freedom of the contracting parties has been established in accord with the norm of law and the permission of the pastor has been obtained, if possible, when one is functioning in virtue of general delegation.

Can. 1115 — Marriages are to be celebrated in the parish where either of the contractants has a domicile, quasi-domicile or month-long residence; the marriages of transients are to be celebrated in the parish where they actually reside; marriage can be celebrated elsewhere with the permission of the proper ordinary or pastor.

Can. 1116 — §1. If the presence of or access to a person who is competent to assist at marriage in accord with the norm of law is impossible without serious inconvenience, persons intending to enter a true marriage can validly and licitly contract it before witnesses alone:

1° in danger of death;

2° outside the danger of death, as long as it is prudently foreseen that such circumstances will continue for a month.

§2. In either case and with due regard for the validity of a marriage celebrated before witnesses alone, if another priest or deacon who can be present is readily available, he must be called upon and must be present at the celebration of the marriage, along with the witnesses.

Can. 1117 — With due regard for the prescriptions of can. 1127, §2, the form stated above is to be observed whenever at least one of the contractants was baptized in the Catholic Church or was received into it and has not left it by a formal act.

Can. 1118 — §1. Marriage between Catholics or between a Catholic and a baptized non-Catholic party is to be celebrated in a parish church; with the permission of the local ordinary or the pastor, it can be celebrated in another church or oratory.

§ 2. Matrimonium in alio convenienti loco celebrari Ordinarius loci permittere potest.

§ 3. Matrimonium inter partem catholicam et partem non baptizatam in ecclesia vel in alio convenienti loco celebrari poterit.

Can. 1119 – Extra casum necessitatis, in matrimonii celebratione serventur ritus in libris liturgicis, ab Ecclesia probatis, praescripti aut legitimis consuetudinibus recepti.

Can. 1120 – Episcoporum conferentia exarare potest ritum proprium matrimonii, a Sancta Sede recognoscendum, congruentem locorum et populorum usibus ad spiritum christianum aptatis, firma tamen lege ut assistens matrimonio praesens requirat manifestationem consensus contrahentium eamque recipiat.

Can. 1121 – § 1. Celebrato matrimonio, parochus loci celebrationis vel qui eius vices gerit, etsi neuter eidem astiterit, quam primum adnotet in matrimoniorum regestis nomina coniugum, assistentis ac testium, locum et diem celebrationis matrimonii, iuxta modum ab Episcoporum conferentia aut ab Episcopo dioecesano praescriptum.

§ 2. Quoties matrimonium ad normam can. 1116 contrahitur, sacerdos vel diaconus, si celebrationi adfuerit, secus testes tenentur in solidum cum contrahentibus parochum aut Ordinarium loci de inito coniugio quam primum certiorem reddere.

§ 3. Ad matrimonium quod attinet cum dispensatione a forma canonica contractum, loci Ordinarius, qui dispensationem concessit, curet ut inscribatur dispensatio et celebratio in libro matrimoniorum tum curiae tum paroeciae propriae partis catholicae, cuius parochus inquisitiones de statu libero peregit; de celebrato matrimonio eundem Ordinarium et parochum quam primum certiorem reddere tenetur coniux catholicus, indicans etiam locum celebrationis necnon formam publicam servatam.

Can. 1122 – § 1. Matrimonium contractum adnotetur etiam in regestis baptizatorum, in quibus baptismus coniugum inscriptus est.

§ 2. Si coniux matrimonium contraxerit non in paroecia in qua baptizatus est, parochus loci celebrationis notitiam initi coniugii ad parochum loci collati baptismi quam primum transmittat.

Can. 1123 – Quoties matrimonium vel convalidatur pro foro externo, vel nullum declaratur, vel legitime praeterquam morte solvitur, parochus loci celebrationis matrimonii certior fieri debet, ut adnotatio in regestis matrimoniorum et baptizatorum rite fiat.

§2. The local ordinary can permit marriage to be celebrated in some other suitable place.

§3. Marriage between a Catholic party and a non-baptized party can be celebrated in a church or in some other suitable place.

Can. 1119 — Outside of a case of necessity, the rites prescribed in the liturgical books approved by the Church or received through legitimate customs are to be observed in the celebration of marriage.

Can. 1120 — The conference of bishops can draw up its own marriage ritual, to be reviewed by the Holy See; such a ritual, in harmony with the usages of the area and its people adapted to the Christian spirit, must provide that the person assisting at the marriage be present, ask for the manifestation of the contractants' consent and receive it.

Can. 1121 — §1. After a marriage has been celebrated, the pastor of the place of celebration or the person who takes his place, even if neither has assisted at the marriage, should as soon as possible note the following in the marriage register: the names of the spouses, the person who assisted and the witnesses, the place and date of the marriage celebration; these notations are to be made in accord with the method prescribed by the conference of bishops or the diocesan bishop.

§2. Whenever a marriage is contracted in accord with can. 1116, if a priest or deacon was present at the celebration he is bound to inform the pastor or the local ordinary concerning the marriage entered as soon as possible; otherwise, the witnesses jointly with the contractants are bound to do so.

§3. If the marriage has been contracted with a dispensation from canonical form, the local ordinary who granted the dispensation is to see that the dispensation and the celebration are inscribed in the marriage register at the curia and at the parish of the Catholic party whose pastor made the investigation concerning their free state; the Catholic spouse is bound to inform the same ordinary and pastor as soon as possible of the celebration of the marriage, the place of celebration and the public form that was observed.

Can. 1122 — §1. The contracted marriage is also to be noted in the baptismal register in which the baptism of the spouses has been inscribed.

§2. If the marriage was contracted in a parish where a spouse was not baptized, the pastor of the place where it was celebrated is to send a notice of the contracted marriage as soon as possible to the pastor where the baptism was conferred.

Can. 1123 — Whenever a marriage is convalidated in the external forum, is declared null or is legitimately dissolved other than by death, the pastor of the place where it was celebrated must be informed so that a notation may be duly made in the marriage and baptismal registers.

Caput VI

DE MATRIMONIIS MIXTIS

Can. 1124 – Matrimonium inter duas personas baptizatas, quarum altera sit in Ecclesia catholica baptizata vel in eandem post baptismum recepta, quaeque nec ab ea actu formali defecerit, altera vero Ecclesiae vel communitati ecclesiali plenam communionem cum Ecclesia catholica non habenti adscripta, sine expressa auctoritatis competentis licentia prohibitum est.

Can. 1125 – Huiusmodi licentiam concedere potest Ordinarius loci, si iusta et rationabilis causa habeatur; eam ne concedat, nisi impletis condicionibus quae sequuntur :

1° pars catholica declaret se paratam esse pericula a fide deficiendi removere atque sinceram promissionem praestet se omnia pro viribus facturam esse, ut universa proles in Ecclesia catholica baptizetur et educetur;

2° de his promissionibus a parte catholica faciendis altera pars tempestive certior fiat, adeo ut constet ipsam vere consciam esse promissionis et obligationis partis catholicae;

3° ambae partes edoceantur de finibus et proprietatibus essentialibus matrimonii, a neutro contrahente excludendis.

Can. 1126 – Episcoporum conferentiae est tum modum statuere, quo hae declarationes et promissiones, quae semper requiruntur, faciendae sint, tum rationem definire, qua de ipsis et in foro externo constet et pars non catholica certior reddatur.

Can. 1127 – § 1. Ad formam quod attinet in matrimonio mixto adhibendam, serventur praescripta can. 1108; si tamen pars catholica matrimonium contrahit cum parte non catholica ritus orientalis, forma canonica celebrationis servanda est ad liceitatem tantum; ad validitatem autem requiritur interventus ministri sacri, servatis aliis de iure servandis.

§ 2. Si graves difficultates formae canonicae servandae obstent, Ordinario loci partis catholicae ius est ab eadem in singulis casibus dispensandi, consulto tamen Ordinario loci in quo matrimonium celebratur, et salva ad validitatem aliqua publica forma celebrationis; Episcoporum conferentiae est normas statuere, quibus praedicta dispensatio concordi ratione concedatur.

§ 3. Vetatur, ne ante vel post canonicam celebrationem ad normam § 1, alia habeatur eiusdem matrimonii celebratio religiosa ad matrimonialem consensum praestandum vel renovandum; item ne fiat celebra-

CHAPTER VI
MIXED MARRIAGES

Can. 1124 — Without the express permission of the competent authority, marriage is forbidden between two baptized persons, one of whom was baptized in the Catholic Church or received into it after baptism and has not left it by a formal act, and the other of whom is a member of a church or ecclesial community which is not in full communion with the Catholic Church.

Can. 1125 — The local ordinary can grant this permission if there is a just and reasonable cause; he is not to grant it unless the following conditions have been fulfilled:

1° the Catholic party declares that he or she is prepared to remove dangers of falling away from the faith and makes a sincere promise to do all in his or her power to have all the children baptized and brought up in the Catholic Church;

2° the other party is to be informed at an appropriate time of these promises which the Catholic party has to make, so that it is clear that the other party is truly aware of the promise and obligation of the Catholic party;

3° both parties are to be instructed on the essential ends and properties of marriage, which are not to be excluded by either party.

Can. 1126 — The conference of bishops is to establish the way in which these declarations and promises, which are always required, are to be made, what proof of them there should be in the external forum and how they are to be brought to the attention of the non-Catholic party.

Can. 1127 — §1. The prescriptions of can. 1108 are to be observed concerning the form to be employed in a mixed marriage; if a Catholic party contracts marriage with a non-Catholic of an oriental rite, the canonical form of celebration is to be observed only for liceity; for validity, however, the presence of a sacred minister is required along with the observance of the other requirements of law.

§2. If serious difficulties pose an obstacle to the observance of the canonical form, the local ordinary of the Catholic party has the right to dispense from the form in individual cases, but after consulting the ordinary of the place where the marriage is to be celebrated and with due regard, for validity, for some public form of celebration; the conference of bishops is to issue norms by which such a dispensation may be granted in an orderly manner.

§3. Before or after the canonical celebration held in accord with the norm of §1, it is forbidden to have another religious celebration of the same marriage to express or renew matrimonial consent; it is likewise forbidden to

tio religiosa, in qua assistens catholicus et minister non catholicus insimul, suum quisque ritum peragens, partium consensum exquirant.

Can. 1128 – Locorum Ordinarii aliique animarum pastores curent, ne coniugi catholico et filiis e matrimonio mixto natis auxilium spirituale desit ad eorum obligationes adimplendas atque coniuges adiuvent ad vitae coniugalis et familiaris fovendam unitatem.

Can. 1129 – Praescripta cann. 1127 et 1128 applicanda sunt quoque matrimoniis, quibus obstat impedimentum disparitatis cultus, de quo in can. 1086, § 1.

CAPUT VII

DE MATRIMONIO SECRETO CELEBRANDO

Can. 1130 – Ex gravi et urgenti causa loci Ordinarius permittere potest, ut matrimonium secreto celebretur.

Can. 1131 – Permissio matrimonium secreto celebrandi secumfert :

1° ut secreto fiant investigationes quae ante matrimonium peragendae sunt ;

2° ut secretum de matrimonio celebrato servetur ab Ordinario loci, assistente, testibus, coniugibus.

Can. 1132 – Obligatio secretum servandi, de qua in can. 1131, n. 2, ex parte Ordinarii loci cessat si grave scandalum aut gravis erga matrimonii sanctitatem iniuria ex secreti observantia immineat, idque notum fiat partibus ante matrimonii celebrationem.

Can. 1133 – Matrimonium secreto celebratum in peculiari tantummodo regesto, servando in secreto curiae archivo, adnotetur.

CAPUT VIII

DE MATRIMONII EFFECTIBUS

Can. 1134 – Ex valido matrimonio enascitur inter coniuges vinculum natura sua perpetuum et exclusivum; in matrimonio praeterea christiano coniuges ad sui status officia et dignitatem peculiari sacramento roborantur et veluti consecrantur.

Can. 1135 – Utrique coniugi aequum officium et ius est ad ea quae pertinent ad consortium vitae coniugalis.

Can. 1136 – Parentes officium gravissimum et ius primarium habent prolis educationem tum physicam, socialem et culturalem, tum moralem et religiosam pro viribus curandi.

have a religious celebration in which a Catholic and a non-Catholic minister, assisting together but following their respective rituals, ask for the consent of the parties.

Can. 1128 — Local ordinaries and other pastors of souls are to see to it that the Catholic spouse and the children born of a mixed marriage do not lack spiritual assistance in fulfilling their obligations and are to aid the spouses in fostering the unity of conjugal and family life.

Can. 1129 — The prescriptions of cann. 1127 and 1128 are also to be applied to marriages involving the impediment of disparity of cult mentioned in can. 1086, §1.

Chapter VII
MARRIAGES SECRETLY CELEBRATED

Can. 1130 — For a serious and urgent reason the local ordinary can permit a marriage to be celebrated secretly.

Can. 1131 — The permission to celebrate a marriage secretly also includes:

1° permission that the pre-matrimonial investigation be made secretly;

2° the obligation that secrecy concerning the marriage be observed by the local ordinary, the assisting minister, the witnesses and the spouses.

Can. 1132 — The obligation to observe secrecy mentioned in can. 1131, n.2, ceases on the part of the local ordinary if serious scandal or serious harm to the sanctity of marriage is threatened by observing the secret and this is to be made known to the parties before the celebration of the marriage.

Can. 1133 — A marriage celebrated secretly is to be noted only in the special register which is to be kept in the secret archive of the curia.

Chapter VIII
THE EFFECTS OF MARRIAGE

Can. 1134 — From a valid marriage arises a bond between the spouses which by its very nature is perpetual and exclusive; furthermore, in a Christian marriage the spouses are strengthened and, as it were, consecrated for the duties and the dignity of their state by a special sacrament.

Can. 1135 — Each of the spouses has equal obligations and rights to those things which pertain to the partnership of conjugal life.

Can 1136 — Parents have the most serious duty and the primary right to do all in their power to see to the physical, social, cultural, moral and religious upbringing of their children.

Can. 1137 – Legitimi sunt filii concepti aut nati ex matrimonio valido vel putativo.

Can. 1138 – § 1. Pater is est, quem iustae nuptiae demonstrant, nisi evidentibus argumentis contrarium probetur.

§ 2. Legitimi praesumuntur filii, qui nati sunt saltem post dies 180 a die celebrati matrimonii, vel infra dies 300 a die dissolutae vitae coniugalis.

Can. 1139 – Filii illegitimi legitimantur per subsequens matrimo-nium parentum sive validum sive putativum, vel per rescriptum Sanc-tae Sedis.

Can. 1140 – Filii legitimati, ad effectus canonicos quod attinet, in omnibus aequiparantur legitimis, nisi aliud expresse iure cautum fuerit.

Caput IX

DE SEPARATIONE CONIUGUM

Art. 1

De dissolutione vinculi

Can. 1141 – Matrimonium ratum et consummatum nulla humana potestate nullaque causa, praeterquam morte, dissolvi potest.

Can. 1142 – Matrimonium non consummatum inter baptizatos vel inter partem baptizatam et partem non baptizatam a Romano Pon-tifice dissolvi potest iusta de causa, utraque parte rogante vel alterutra, etsi altera pars sit invita.

Can. 1143 – § 1. Matrimonium initum a duobus non baptizatis sol-vitur ex privilegio paulino in favorem fidei partis quae baptismum re-cepit, ipso facto quo novum matrimonium ab eadem parte contrahitur, dummodo pars non baptizata discedat.

§ 2. Discedere censetur pars non baptizata, si nolit cum parte bap-tizata cohabitare vel cohabitare pacifice sine contumelia Creatoris, nisi haec post baptismum receptum iustam illi dederit discedendi causam.

Can. 1144 – § 1. Ut pars baptizata novum matrimonium valide contrahat, pars non baptizata semper interpellari debet an :

1° velit et ipsa baptismum recipere ;

2° saltem velit cum parte baptizata pacifice cohabitare, sine con-tumelia Creatoris.

Can. 1137 — Children conceived or born of a valid or putative marriage are legitimate.

Can 1138 — §1. The father is he whom a lawful marriage indicates unless evident arguments prove otherwise.

§2. Children are presumed to be legitimate if they are born at least 180 days after the celebration of the marriage or within 300 days from the date when conjugal life was terminated.

Can. 1139 — Illegitimate children are rendered legitimate through the subsequent valid or putative marriage of their parents, or through a rescript of the Holy See.

Can. 1140 — Insofar as canonical effects are concerned, legitimized children are equivalent in everything to legitimate children unless the law expressly states otherwise.

CHAPTER IX

THE SEPARATION OF THE SPOUSES

Art. 1
DISSOLUTION OF THE BOND

Can 1141 — A ratified and consummated marriage cannot be dissolved by any human power or for any reason other than death.

Can. 1142 — A non-consummated marriage between baptized persons or between a baptized party and non-baptized party can be dissolved by the Roman Pontiff for a just cause, at the request of both parties or of one of the parties, even if the other party is unwilling.

Can. 1143 — §1. A marriage entered by two non-baptized persons is dissolved by means of the pauline privilege in favor of the faith of a party who has received baptism by the very fact that a new marriage is contracted by the party who has been baptized, provided the non-baptized party departs.

§2. The non-baptized party is considered to have departed if he or she does not wish to cohabit with the baptized party or does not wish to cohabit in peace without insult to the Creator unless, after receiving baptism, the baptized party gave the other party a just cause for departure.

Can. 1144 — §1. In order for the baptized party to contract a new marriage validly, the non-baptized party must always be interrogated on the following points:

1° whether he or she also wishes to receive baptism;

2° whether he or she at least wishes to cohabit in peace with the baptized party without insult to the Creator.

§ 2. Haec interpellatio post baptismum fieri debet; at loci Ordinarius, gravi de causa, permittere potest ut interpellatio ante baptismum fiat, immo et ab interpellatione dispensare, sive ante sive post baptismum, dummodo constet modo procedendi saltem summario et extraiudiciali eam fieri non posse aut fore inutilem.

Can. 1145 – § 1. Interpellatio fiat regulariter de auctoritate loci Ordinarii partis conversae; a quo Ordinario concedendae sunt alteri coniugi, si quidem eas petierit, induciae ad respondendum, eodem tamen monito ut, si induciae inutiliter praeterlabantur, eius silentium pro responsione negativa habeatur.

§ 2. Interpellatio etiam privatim facta ab ipsa parte conversa valet, immo est licita, si forma superius praescripta servari nequeat.

§ 3. In utroque casu de interpellatione facta deque eiusdem exitu in foro externo legitime constare debet.

Can. 1146 – Pars baptizata ius habet novas nuptias contrahendi cum parte catholica:

1° si altera pars negative interpellationi responderit, aut si interpellatio legitime omissa fuerit;

2° si pars non baptizata, sive iam interpellata sive non, prius perseverans in pacifica cohabitatione sine contumelia Creatoris, postea sine iusta causa discesserit, firmis praescriptis cann. 1144 et 1145.

Can. 1147 – Ordinarius loci tamen, gravi de causa, concedere potest ut pars baptizata, utens privilegio paulino, contrahat matrimonium cum parte non catholica sive baptizata sive non baptizata, servatis etiam praescriptis canonum de matrimoniis mixtis.

Can. 1148 – § 1. Non baptizatus, qui plures uxores non baptizatas simul habeat, recepto in Ecclesia catholica baptismo, si durum ei sit cum earum prima permanere, unam ex illis, ceteris dimissis, retinere potest. Idem valet de muliere non baptizata, quae plures maritos non baptizatos simul habeat.

§ 2. In casibus de quibus in § 1, matrimonium, recepto baptismo, forma legitima contrahendum est, servatis etiam, si opus sit, praescriptis de matrimoniis mixtis et aliis de iure servandis.

§ 3. Ordinarius loci, prae oculis habita condicione morali, sociali, oeconomica locorum et personarum, curet ut primae uxoris ceterarumque dimissarum necessitatibus satis provisum sit, iuxta normas iustitiae, christianae caritatis et naturalis aequitatis.

Can. 1149 – Non baptizatus qui, recepto in Ecclesia catholica baptismo, cum coniuge non baptizato ratione captivitatis vel persecutionis

§2. This interrogation must take place after baptism; for a serious reason, however, the local ordinary can permit this interrogation to take place before the baptism, or even dispense from this interrogation either before or after the baptism, provided it is evident in light of at least a summary and extra-judicial process, that it cannot take place or that it would be useless.

Can. 1145 — §1. As a rule, the interrogation is to take place on the authority of the local ordinary of the converted party; if the other spouse asks for a period of time during which to answer, the same ordinary is to grant it while warning the party that after this period has elapsed without any answer, the person's silence will be considered to be a negative answer.

§2. An interrogation carried out privately by the converted party is also valid and is indeed licit if the form prescribed above cannot be observed.

§3. In either case the fact that the interrogation took place and its outcome must legitimately be evident in the external forum.

Can. 1146 — The baptized party has the right to contract a new marriage with a Catholic party:

1° if the other party answered negatively to the interrogation or if the interrogation has been legitimately omitted;

2° if the non-baptized party, interrogated or not, at first peacefully cohabited without insult to the Creator but afterwards departed without a just cause, with due regard for the prescriptions of cann. 1144 and 1145.

Can. 1147 — For a serious cause the local ordinary can permit the baptized party who employs the pauline privilege to contract marriage with a non-Catholic party, whether baptized or not, while observing the prescriptions of the canons on mixed marriages.

Can. 1148 — §1. After he has received baptism in the Catholic Church, a previously non-baptized man who simultaneously has several non-baptized wives can keep one of them as his wife while dismissing the others if it is difficult for him to remain with the first. The same is true for a non-baptized woman who simultaneously has several non-baptized husbands.

§2. In the situations mentioned in §1, marriage is to be contracted according to the the legitimate form after the reception of baptism, while observing the prescriptions on mixed marriages if necessary, as well as the other requirements of law.

§3. After considering the moral, social and economic situation of the area and of the persons, the local ordinary is to take care that sufficient provision is made in accord with the norms of justice, Christian charity and natural equity for the needs of the first wife and of the other wives who are dismissed.

Can. 1149 — A non-baptized person who, once having received baptism in the Catholic Church, cannot restore cohabitation with a non-baptized

cohabitationem restaurare nequeat, aliud matrimonium contrahere potest, etiamsi altera pars baptismum interea receperit, firmo praescripto can. 1141.

Can. 1150 – In re dubia privilegium fidei gaudet favore iuris.

Art. 2

DE SEPARATIONE MANENTE VINCULO

Can. 1151 – Coniuges habent officium et ius servandi convictum coniugalem, nisi legitima causa eos excuset.

Can. 1152 – § 1. Licet enixe commendetur ut coniux, caritate christiana motus et boni familiae sollicitus, veniam non abnuat comparti adulterae atque vitam coniugalem non disrumpat, si tamen eiusdem culpam expresse aut tacite non condonaverit, ius ipsi est solvendi coniugalem convictum, nisi in adulterium consenserit aut eidem causam dederit aut ipse quoque adulterium commiserit.

§ 2. Tacita condonatio habetur si coniux innocens, postquam de adulterio certior factus est, sponte cum altero coniuge maritali affectu conversatus fuerit; praesumitur vero, si per sex menses coniugalem convictum servaverit, neque recursum apud auctoritatem ecclesiasticam vel civilem fecerit.

§ 3. Si coniux innocens sponte convictum coniugalem solverit, intra sex menses causam separationis deferat ad competentem auctoritatem ecclesiasticam, quae, omnibus inspectis adiunctis, perpendat si coniux innocens adduci possit ad culpam condonandam et ad separationem in perpetuum non protrahendam.

Can. 1153 – § 1. Si alteruter coniugum grave seu animi seu corporis periculum alteri aut proli facessat, vel aliter vitam communem nimis duram reddat, alteri legitimam praebet causam discedendi, decreto Ordinarii loci et, si periculum sit in mora, etiam propria auctoritate.

§ 2. In omnibus casibus, causa separationis cessante, coniugalis convictus restaurandus est, nisi ab auctoritate ecclesiastica aliter statuatur.

Can. 1154 – Instituta separatione coniugum, opportune semper cavendum est debitae filiorum sustentationi et educationi.

Can. 1155 – Coniux innocens laudabiliter alterum coniugem ad vitam coniugalem rursus admittere potest, quo in casu iuri separationis renuntiat.

spouse due to captivity or persecution can contract another marriage even if the other party received baptism in the meantime, with due regard for the prescription of can. 1141.

Can. 1150 — In a doubtful matter the privilege of the faith enjoys the favor of the law.

Art. 2

SEPARATION WHILE THE BOND ENDURES

Can. 1151 — Spouses have the duty and the right to preserve conjugal living unless a legitimate cause excuses them.

Can. 1152 — §1. Although it is earnestly recommended that a spouse, moved by Christian charity and a concern for the good of the family, not refuse pardon to an adulterous partner and not break up conjugal life, nevertheless, if the spouse has not expressly or tacitly condoned the misdeed of the other spouse, the former does have the right to sever conjugal living, unless he or she consented to the adultery, gave cause for it, or likewise committed adultery.

§2. Tacit condonation exists if the innocent spouse, after having become aware of the adultery, continued voluntarily to live with the other spouse in marital affection. Tacit condonation is presumed if the innocent spouse continued conjugal living for a period of six months and has not had recourse to ecclesiastical or civil authority.

§3. If the innocent spouse spontaneously severed conjugal living, that spouse within six months is to bring a suit for separation before the competent ecclesiastical authority; this authority, after having investigated all the circumstances, is to decide whether the innocent spouse can be induced to forgive the misdeed and not to prolong the separation permanently.

Can. 1153 — §1. If either of the spouses causes serious danger of spirit or body to the other spouse or to the children, or otherwise renders common life too hard, that spouse gives the other a legitimate cause for separating in virtue of a decree of the local ordinary, or even on his or her own authority if there is danger in delay.

§2. In all cases, when the reason for the separation ceases to exist, conjugal living is to be restored unless ecclesiastical authority decides otherwise.

Can. 1154 — After the separation of the spouses, suitable provision is to be made for the adequate support and education of the children.

Can. 1155 — The innocent spouse can laudably readmit the other spouse to conjugal life, in which case the former renounces the right to separate.

Caput X ,

DE MATRIMONII CONVALIDATIONE

Art. 1

De convalidatione simplici

Can. 1156 - § 1. Ad convalidandum matrimonium irritum ob impedimentum dirimens, requiritur ut cesset impedimentum vel ab eodem dispensetur, et consensum renovet saltem pars impedimenti conscia.

§ 2. Haec renovatio iure ecclesiastico requiritur ad validitatem convalidationis, etiamsi initio utraque pars consensum praestiterit nec postea revocaverit.

Can. 1157 – Renovatio consensus debet esse novus voluntatis actus in matrimonium, quod pars renovans scit aut opinatur ab initio nullum fuisse.

Can. 1158 – § 1. Si impedimentum sit publicum, consensus ab utraque parte renovandus est forma canonica, salvo praescripto can. 1127, § 3.

§ 2. Si impedimentum probari nequeat, satis est ut consensus renovetur privatim et secreto, et quidem a parte impedimenti conscia, dummodo altera in consensu praestito perseveret, aut ab utraque parte, si impedimentum sit utrique parti notum.

Can. 1159 – § 1. Matrimonium irritum ob defectum consensus convalidatur, si pars quae non consenserat, iam consentiat, dummodo consensus ab altera parte praestitus perseveret.

§ 2. Si defectus consensus probari nequeat, satis est ut pars, quae non consenserat, privatim et secreto consensum praestet.

§ 3. Si defectus consensus probari potest, necesse est ut consensus forma canonica praestetur.

Can. 1160 – Matrimonium nullum ob defectum formae, ut validum fiat, contrahi denuo debet forma canonica, salvo praescripto can. 1127, § 3.

2

CHAPTER X
CONVALIDATION OF MARRIAGE

Art. 1
SIMPLE CONVALIDATION

Can 1156 — §1. To convalidate a marriage which is invalid due to a diriment impediment, it is required that the impediment cease or that it be dispensed and that at least the party who is aware of the impediment renew consent.

§2. This renewal of consent is required by ecclesiastical law for the validity of the convalidation even if both parties furnished consent at the beginning and have not revoked it later.

Can. 1157 — The renewal of consent must be a new act of the will concerning a marriage which the person who is renewing consent knows or thinks was null from the beginning.

Can. 1158 — §1. If the impediment is a public one, the consent is to be renewed by both parties according to the canonical form, with due regard for the prescription of can. 1127, §3.

§2. If the impediment cannot be proven to exist, it is sufficient that the consent be renewed privately and in secret by the party who is aware of the impediment, provided the other party perseveres in the consent already given, or by both parties when each of them knows about the impediment.

Can. 1159 — §1. A marriage which is invalid due to a defect of consent is convalidated when the party who had not consented now gives consent, provided the consent given by the other party still exists.

§2. If the defect of consent cannot be proven it is sufficient that the party who did not consent gives consent privately and in secret.

§3. If the defect of consent can be proven it is necessary that the consent be given according to the canonical form.

Can. 1160 — With due regard for the prescription of can. 1127, §3,* marriage which is invalid due to a defect of form must be contracted anew according to canonical form in order to become valid.

---

*Apparently should read 1127, §2.—Trans.

Art. 2

DE SANATIONE IN RADICE

Can. 1161 – § 1. Matrimonii irriti sanatio in radice est eiusdem, sine renovatione consensus, convalidatio, a competenti auctoritate concessa, secumferens dispensationem ab impedimento, si adsit, atque a forma canonica, si servata non fuerit, necnon retrotractionem effectuum canonicorum ad praeteritum.

§ 2. Convalidatio fit a momento concessionis gratiae; retrotractio vero intellegitur facta ad momentum celebrationis matrimonii, nisi aliud expresse caveatur.

§ 3. Sanatio in radice ne concedatur, nisi probabile sit partes in vita coniugali perseverare velle.

Can. 1162 – § 1. Si in utraque vel alterutra parte deficiat consensus, matrimonium nequit sanari in radice, sive consensus ab initio defuerit, sive ab initio praestitus, postea fuerit revocatus.

§ 2. Quod si consensus ab initio quidem defuerat, sed postea praestitus est, sanatio concedi potest a momento praestiti consensus.

Can. 1163 – § 1. Matrimonium irritum ob impedimentum vel ob defectum legitimae formae sanari potest, dummodo consensus utriusque partis perseveret.

§ 2. Matrimonium irritum ob impedimentum iuris naturalis aut divini positivi sanari potest solummodo postquam impedimentum cessavit.

Can. 1164 – Sanatio valide concedi potest etiam alterutra vel utraque parte inscia; ne autem concedatur nisi ob gravem causam.

Can. 1165 – § 1. Sanatio in radice concedi potest ab Apostolica Sede.

§ 2. Concedi potest ab Episcopo dioecesano in singulis casibus, etiam si plures nullitatis rationes in eodem matrimonio concurrant, impletis condicionibus, de quibus in can. 1125, pro sanatione matrimonii mixti; concedi autem ab eodem nequit, si adsit impedimentum cuius dispensatio Sedi Apostolicae reservatur ad normam can. 1078, § 2, aut agatur de impedimento iuris naturalis aut divini positivi quod iam cessavit.

Art. 2

RADICAL SANATION

Can. 1161 — §1. The radical sanation of an invalid marriage is its convalidation without the renewal of consent, granted by competent authority and including a dispensation from an impediment, if there was one, and from the canonical form, if it was not observed, and the retroactivity into the past of canonical effects.

§2. The convalidation occurs at the moment the favor is granted; it is understood to be retroactive, however, to the moment the marriage was celebrated unless something else is expressly stated.

§3. A radical sanation is not to be granted unless it is probable that the parties intend to persevere in conjugal life.

Can. 1162 — §1. A marriage cannot be radically sanated if consent is lacking in either or both of the parties, whether the consent was lacking from the beginning or was given in the beginning but afterwards revoked.

§2. If, however, consent was indeed lacking in the beginning but afterwards was given, a sanation can be granted from the moment the consent was given.

Can. 1163 — §1. A marriage which is invalid due to an impediment or due to defect of legitimate form can be sanated provided the consent of each party continues to exist.

§2. A marriage which is invalid due to an impediment of the natural law or of divine positive law can be sanated only after the impediment has ceased to exist.

Can. 1164 — A sanation can be granted validly even when one or both of the parties are unaware of it, but it is not to be granted except for serious reason.

Can. 1165 — §1. Radical sanation can be granted by the Apostolic See.

§2. In individual cases radical sanation can be granted by the diocesan bishop, even if several reasons for nullity exist in the same marriage, provided the conditions mentioned in can. 1125 concerning the sanation of a mixed marriage are fulfilled. The diocesan bishop cannot grant radical sanation, however, if there is present an impediment whose dispensation is reserved to the Apostolic See in accord with can. 1078, §2, or if it is a question of an impediment of the natural law or of the divine positive law which has ceased to exist.

PARS II
DE CETERIS ACTIBUS CULTUS DIVINI

TITULUS I
DE SACRAMENTALIBUS

Can. 1166 – Sacramentalia sunt signa sacra, quibus, ad aliquam sacramentorum imitationem, effectus praesertim spirituales significantur et ex Ecclesiae impetratione obtinentur.

Can. 1167 – § 1. Nova sacramentalia constituere aut recepta authentice interpretari, ex eis aliqua abolere aut mutare, sola potest Sedes Apostolica.

§ 2. In sacramentalibus conficiendis seu administrandis accurate serventur ritus et formulae ab Ecclesiae auctoritate probata.

Can. 1168 – Sacramentalium minister est clericus debita potestate instructus ; quaedam sacramentalia, ad normam librorum liturgicorum, de iudicio loci Ordinarii, a laicis quoque, congruis qualitatibus praeditis, administrari possunt.

Can. 1169 – § 1. Consecrationes et dedicationes valide peragere possunt qui charactere episcopali insigniti sunt, necnon presbyteri quibus iure vel legitima concessione id permittitur.

§ 2. Benedictiones, exceptis iis quae Romano Pontifici aut Episcopis reservantur, impertire potest quilibet presbyter.

§ 3. Diaconus illas tantum benedictiones impertire potest, quae ipsi expresse iure permittuntur.

Can. 1170 – Benedictiones, imprimis impertiendae catholicis, dari possunt catechumenis quoque, immo, nisi obstet Ecclesiae prohibitio, etiam non catholicis.

Can. 1171 – Res sacrae, quae dedicatione vel benedictione ad divinum cultum destinatae sunt, reverenter tractentur nec ad usum profanum vel non proprium adhibeantur, etiamsi in dominio sint privatorum.

Can. 1172 – § 1. Nemo exorcismos in obsessos proferre legitime potest, nisi ab Ordinario loci peculiarem et expressam licentiam obtinuerit.

§ 2. Haec licentia ab Ordinario loci concedatur tantummodo presbytero pietate, scientia, prudentia ac vitae integritate praedito.

PART II

OTHER ACTS OF DIVINE WORSHIP

TITLE I

THE SACRAMENTALS

Can. 1166 — Somewhat in imitation of the sacraments, sacramentals are sacred signs by which spiritual effects especially are signified and are obtained by the intercession of the Church.

Can. 1167 — §1. The Apostolic See alone can establish new sacramentals, authentically interpret those already accepted, abolish or change any of them.

§2. The rites and formulae approved by church authority are to be carefully observed in confecting or administering the sacramentals.

Can. 1168 — The minister of the sacramentals is a cleric who has been given the necessary power; in accord with the norm of the liturgical books and according to the judgment of the local ordinary, some sacramentals can also be administered by lay persons who are endowed with the appropriate qualities.

Can. 1169 — §1. Persons who possess the episcopal character as well as presbyters to whom it is permitted by law or by legitimate concession can validly perform consecrations and dedications.

§2. Any presbyter can impart blessings, except those which are reserved to the Roman Pontiff or to bishops.

§3. A deacon can impart only those blessings which are expressly permitted to him by law.

Can. 1170 — Blessings, to be imparted especially to Catholics, can also be given to catechumens and even to non-Catholics unless a church prohibition precludes this.

Can. 1171 — Sacred things which are destined for divine worship through dedication or a blessing are to be treated with reverence and not be employed for improper or profane use even if they are under the control of private individuals.

Can 1172 — §1. No one can legitimately perform exorcisms over the possessed unless he has obtained special and express permission from the local ordinary.

§2. Such permission from the local ordinary is to be granted only to a presbyter endowed with piety, knowledge, prudence and integrity of life.

TITULUS II
DE LITURGIA HORARUM

Can. 1173 – Ecclesia, sacerdotale munus Christi adimplens, liturgiam horarum celebrat, qua Deum ad populum suum loquentem audiens et memoriam mysterii salutis agens, Ipsum sine intermissione, cantu et oratione, laudat atque interpellat pro totius mundi salute.

Can. 1174 – § 1. Obligatione liturgiae horarum persolvendae adstringuntur clerici, ad normam can. 276, § 2, n. 3; sodales vero institutorum vitae consecratae necnon societatum vitae apostolicae, ad normam suarum constitutionum.

§ 2. Ad participandam liturgiam horarum, utpote actionem Ecclesiae, etiam ceteri christifideles, pro adiunctis, enixe invitantur.

Can. 1175 – In liturgia horarum persolvenda, quantum fieri potest, verum tempus servetur uniuscuiusque horae.

TITULUS III
DE EXEQUIIS ECCLESIASTICIS

Can. 1176 – § 1. Christifideles defuncti exequiis ecclesiasticis ad normam iuris donandi sunt.

§ 2. Exequiae ecclesiasticae, quibus Ecclesia defunctis spiritualem opem impetrat eorumque corpora honorat ac simul vivis spei solacium affert, celebrandae sunt ad normam legum liturgicarum.

§ 3. Enixe commendat Ecclesia, ut pia consuetudo defunctorum corpora sepeliendi servetur; non tamen prohibet cremationem, nisi ob rationes christianae doctrinae contrarias electa fuerit.

CAPUT I
DE EXEQUIARUM CELEBRATIONE

Can. 1177 – § 1. Exequiae pro quolibet fideli defuncto generatim in propriae paroeciae ecclesia celebrari debent.

§ 2. Fas est autem cuilibet fideli, vel iis quibus fidelis defuncti exequias curare competit, aliam ecclesiam funeris eligere de consensu eius,

TITLE II

THE LITURGY OF THE HOURS

Can. 1173 — The Church, fulfilling the priestly function of Christ, celebrates the liturgy of the hours, whereby hearing God speaking to His people and memorializing the mystery of salvation, the Church praises Him in song and prayer without interruption and intercedes for the salvation of the whole world.

Can. 1174 — §1. Clerics are obliged to perform the liturgy of the hours according to the norm of can. 276, §2, n. 3; members of institutes of consecrated life and societies of apostolic life are bound according to the norm of their constitutions.

§2. Other members of the Christian faithful according to circumstances are also earnestly invited to participate in the liturgy of the hours inasmuch as it is the action of the Church.

Can. 1175 — In performing the liturgy of the hours the true time of each hour is to be observed as much as possible.

TITLE III

ECCLESIASTICAL FUNERAL RITES

Can. 1176 — §1. The Christian faithful departed are to be given ecclesiastical funeral rites according to the norm of law.

§2. Through ecclesiastical funeral rites the Church asks spiritual assistance for the departed, honors their bodies, and at the same time brings the solace of hope to the living; such rites are to be celebrated according to the norm of liturgical laws.

§3. The Church earnestly recommends that the pious custom of burying the bodies of the dead be observed; it does not, however, forbid cremation unless it has been chosen for reasons which are contrary to Christian teaching.

CHAPTER I

THE CELEBRATION OF FUNERAL RITES

Can. 1177 — §1. As a rule the funeral rites for any of the faithful departed must be celebrated in his or her own parish church.

§2. However, any member of the Christian faithful or those commissioned to arrange for his or her funeral may choose another church for the funeral

qui eam regit, et monito defuncti parocho proprio.

§ 3. Si extra propriam paroeciam mors acciderit, neque cadaver ad eam translatum fuerit, neque aliqua ecclesia funeris legitime electa, exequiae celebrentur in ecclesia paroeciae ubi mors accidit, nisi alia iure particulari designata sit.

Can. 1178 − Exequiae Episcopi dioecesani in propria ecclesia ca-thedrali celebrentur, nisi ipse aliam ecclesiam elegerit.

Can. 1179 − Exequiae religiosorum aut sodalium societatis vitae apostolicae generatim celebrentur in propria ecclesia aut oratorio a Superiore, si institutum aut societas sint clericalia, secus a cappellano.

Can. 1180 − § 1. Si paroecia proprium habeat coemeterium, in eo tumulandi sunt fideles defuncti, nisi aliud coemeterium legitime elec-tum fuerit ab ipso defuncto vel ab iis quibus defuncti sepulturam curare competit.

§ 2. Omnibus autem licet, nisi iure prohibeantur, eligere coemete-rium sepulturae.

Can. 1181 − Ad oblationes occasione funerum quod attinet, ser-ventur praescripta can. 1264, cauto tamen ne ulla fiat in exequiis perso-narum acceptio neve pauperes debitis exequiis priventur.

Can. 1182 − Expleta tumulatione, inscriptio in librum defunctorum fiat ad normam iuris particularis.

CAPUT II

DE IIS QUIBUS EXEQUIAE ECCLESIASTICAE CONCEDENDAE SUNT AUT DENEGANDAE

Can. 1183 − § 1. Ad exequias quod attinet, christifidelibus cate-chumeni accensendi sunt.

§ 2. Ordinarius loci permittere potest ut parvuli, quos parentes baptizare intendebant quique autem ante baptismum mortui sunt, exe-quiis ecclesiasticis donentur.

§ 3. Baptizatis alicui Ecclesiae aut communitati ecclesiali non catho-licae adscriptis, exequiae ecclesiasticae concedi possunt de prudenti Ordinarii loci iudicio, nisi constet de contraria eorum voluntate et dummodo minister proprius haberi nequeat.

rites with the consent of its rector and after informing the departed person's pastor.

§3. If death has occurred outside the person's own parish, and the corpse has not been transferred to that parish and another church has not been legitimately chosen for the funeral, the funeral rites are to be celebrated in the church of the parish where the death occurred unless another church has been designated by particular law.

Can. 1178 — The funeral rites of a diocesan bishop are to be celebrated in his own cathedral church unless he has chosen another church.

Can. 1179 — As a rule the funeral rites of religious or members of societies of apostolic life are to be celebrated in their own church or oratory by their superior if it is a clerical institute or society, otherwise by the chaplain.

Can. 1180 — §1. If a parish has its own cemetery, the faithful departed are to be interred in it unless another cemetery has been legitimately chosen either by the departed person or by those who are responsible to arrange for his or her interment.

§2. However, everyone, unless prohibited by law, is permitted to choose a cemetery for burial.

Can. 1181 — The prescriptions of can. 1264 are to be observed in regard to the offerings given on the occasion of funerals; precautions are nevertheless to be taken in funeral rites against any favoritism toward persons and against depriving the poor of the funeral rites which are their due.

Can. 1182 — After the interment an entry is to be made in the death register in accord with the norm of particular law.

CHAPTER II

THOSE TO WHOM ECCLESIASTICAL FUNERAL RITES ARE TO BE GRANTED OR TO BE DENIED

Can. 1183 — §1. As regards funeral rites catechumens are to be considered members of the Christian faithful.

§2. The local ordinary can permit children to be given ecclesiastical funeral rites if their parents intended to baptize them but they died before their baptism.

§3. In the prudent judgment of the local ordinary, ecclesiastical funeral rites can be granted to baptized members of some non-Catholic church or ecclesial community unless it is evidently contrary to their will and provided their own minister is unavailable.

Can. 1184 – § 1. Exequiis ecclesiasticis privandi sunt, nisi ante mortem aliqua dederint paenitentiae signa :

1° notorii apostatae, haeretici et schismatici ;

2° qui proprii corporis cremationem elegerint ob rationes fidei christianae adversas ;

3° alii peccatores manifesti, quibus exequiae ecclesiasticae non sine publico fidelium scandalo concedi possunt.

§ 2. Occurrente aliquo dubio, consulatur loci Ordinarius, cuius iudicio standum est.

Can. 1185 – Excluso ab ecclesiasticis exequiis deneganda quoque est quaelibet Missa exequialis.

TITULUS IV
DE CULTU SANCTORUM, SACRARUM IMAGINUM ET RELIQUIARUM

Can. 1186 – Ad sanctificationem populi Dei fovendam, Ecclesia peculiari et filiali christifidelium venerationi commendat Beatam Mariam semper Virginem, Dei Matrem, quam Christus hominum omnium Matrem constituit, atque verum et authenticum promovet cultum aliorum Sanctorum, quorum quidem exemplo christifideles aedificantur et intercessione sustentantur.

Can. 1187 – Cultu publico eos tantum Dei servos venerari licet, qui auctoritate Ecclesiae in album Sanctorum vel Beatorum relati sint.

Can. 1188 – Firma maneat praxis in ecclesiis sacras imagines fidelium venerationi proponendi ; attamen moderato numero et congruo ordine exponantur, ne populi christiani admiratio excitetur, neve devotioni minus rectae ansa praebeatur.

Can. 1189 – Imagines pretiosae, idest vetustate, arte, aut cultu praestantes, in ecclesiis vel oratoriis fidelium venerationi expositae, si quando reparatione indigeant, numquam restaurentur sine data scripto licentia ab Ordinario ; qui, antequam eam concedat, peritos consulat.

Can. 1190 – § 1. Sacras reliquias vendere nefas est.

§ 2. Insignes reliquiae itemque aliae, quae magna populi veneratione honorantur, nequeunt quoquo modo valide alienari neque perpetuo transferri sine Apostolicae Sedis licentia.

§ 3. Praescriptum § 2 valet etiam pro imaginibus, quae in aliqua ecclesia magna populi veneratione honorantur.

Can. 1184 — §1. Unless they have given some signs of repentance before their death, the following are to be deprived of ecclesiastical funeral rites:

1° notorious apostates, heretics and schismatics;

2° persons who had chosen the cremation of their own bodies for reasons opposed to the Christian faith;

3° other manifest sinners for whom ecclesiastical funeral rites cannot be granted without public scandal to the faithful.

§2. If some doubt should arise, the local ordinary is to be consulted; and his judgment is to be followed.

Can. 1185 — Any funeral Mass whatsoever is also to be denied a person excluded from ecclesiastical funeral rites.

TITLE IV
THE VENERATION OF THE SAINTS, SACRED IMAGES AND RELICS

Can. 1186 — To foster the sanctification of the people of God the Church recommends to the particular and filial veneration of the Christian faithful the Blessed Mary ever Virgin, the Mother of God, whom Christ established as the Mother of the human race; it also promotes true and authentic devotion to the other saints by whose example the Christian faithful are edified and through whose intercession they are sustained.

Can. 1187 — Veneration through public cult is permitted only to those servants of God who are listed in the catalog of the saints or of the blessed by the authority of the Church.

Can. 1188 — The practice of displaying sacred images in the churches for the veneration of the faithful is to remain in force; nevertheless they are to be exhibited in moderate number and in suitable order lest they bewilder the Christian people and give opportunity for questionable devotion.

Can. 1189 — Whenever valuable images, that is, those which are outstanding due to age, art or cult, which are exhibited in churches or oratories for the veneration of the faithful need repair, they are never to be restored without the written permission of the ordinary who is to consult experts before he grants permission.

Can. 1190 — §1. It is absolutely forbidden to sell sacred relics.

§2. Significant relics or other ones which are honored with great veneration by the people cannot in any manner be validly alienated or perpetually transferred without the permission of the Apostolic See.

§3. The prescription of §2 is also applicable to images in any church which are honored with great veneration by the people.

TITULUS V
DE VOTO ET IUREIURANDO

CAPUT I
DE VOTO

Can. 1191 – § 1. Votum, idest promissio deliberata ac libera Deo facta de bono possibili et meliore, ex virtute religionis impleri debet.

§ 2. Nisi iure prohibeantur, omnes congruenti rationis usu pollentes, sunt voti capaces.

§ 3. Votum metu gravi et iniusto vel dolo emissum ipso iure nullum est.

Can. 1192 – § 1. Votum est *publicum,* si nomine Ecclesiae a legitimo Superiore accepetur; secus *privatum.*

§ 2. *Sollemne,* si ab Ecclesia uti tale fuerit agnitum; secus *simplex.*

§ 3. *Personale,* quo actio voventis promittitur; *reale,* quo promittitur res aliqua; *mixtum,* quod personalis et realis naturam participat.

Can. 1193 – Votum non obligat, ratione sui, nisi emittentem.

Can. 1194 – Cessat votum lapsu temporis ad finiendam obligationem appositi, mutatione substantiali materiae promissae, deficiente condicione a qua votum pendet aut eiusdem causa finali, dispensatione, commutatione.

Can. 1195 – Qui potestatem in voti materiam habet, potest voti obligationem tamdiu suspendere, quamdiu voti adimpletio sibi praeiudicium afferat.

Can. 1196 – Praeter Romanum Pontificem, vota privata possunt iusta de causa dispensare, dummodo dispensatio ne laedat ius aliis quaesitum :

1° loci Ordinarius et parochus, quod attinet ad omnes ipsorum subditos atque etiam peregrinos ;

2° Superior instituti religiosi aut societatis vitae apostolicae, si sint clericalia iuris pontificii, quod attinet ad sodales, novitios atque personas, quae diu noctuque in domo instituti aut societatis degunt;

3° ii quibus ab Apostolica Sede vel ab Ordinario loci delegata fuerit dispensandi potestas.

TITLE V
A VOW AND AN OATH

CHAPTER I
A VOW

Can. 1191 — §1. A vow is a deliberate and free promise made to God concerning a possible and better good which must be fulfilled by reason of the virtue of religion.

§2. Unless they are forbidden by law, all who have the suitable use of reason are capable of making a vow.

§3. A vow made through grave and unjust fear or fraud is null by the law itself.

Can. 1192 — §1. A vow is *public* if it is accepted in the name of the Church by a legitimate superior; otherwise, it is *private*.

§2. A vow is *solemn* if it is acknowledged as such by the Church; otherwise, it is *simple*.

§3. A vow is *personal* if an act of the vowing person is promised; it is *real* if some thing is promised; it is *mixed* if it shares the nature of a personal and real vow.

Can. 1193 — By its nature a vow obligates only the person who makes it.

Can. 1194 — A vow ceases when the time appointed for the fulfillment of its obligation has passed, when there is a substantial change in the matter promised or when the condition on which the vow depends or the purpose for which it was made no longer exists; it also ceases through dispensation or commutation.

Can. 1195 — A person who has power over the matter of the vow can suspend its obligation for as long as its fulfillment would prejudice such a person.

Can. 1196 — Besides the Roman Pontiff, the following persons can dispense from private vows for a just reason provided a dispensation does not injure a right acquired by others:

1° the local ordinary and the pastor as regards all their own subjects as well as travelers;

2° the superior of a religious institute or society of apostolic life if they are clerical of pontifical right as regards members, novices, and persons who stay day and night in a house of the institute or society;

3° persons to whom the power of dispensation has been delegated by the Apostolic See or by the local ordinary.

Can. 1197 – Opus voto privato promissum potest in maius vel in aequale bonum ab ipso vovente commutari ; in minus vero bonum, ab illo cui potestas est dispensandi ad normam can. 1196.

Can. 1198 – Vota ante professionem religiosam emissa suspenduntur, donec vovens in instituto religioso permanserit.

CAPUT II

DE IUREIURANDO

Can. 1199 – § 1. Iusiurandum, idest invocatio Nominis divini in testem veritatis, praestari nequit, nisi in veritate, in iudicio et in iustitia.

§ 2. Iusiurandum quod canones exigunt vel admittunt, per procuratorem praestari valide nequit.

Can. 1200 – § 1. Qui libere iurat se aliquid facturum, peculiari religionis obligatione tenetur implendi, quod iureiurando firmaverit.

§ 2. Iusiurandum dolo, vi aut metu gravi extortum, ipso iure nullum est.

Can. 1201 – § 1. Iusiurandum promissorium sequitur naturam et condiciones actus cui adicitur.

§ 2. Si actui directe vergenti in damnum aliorum aut in praeiudicium boni publici vel salutis aeternae iusiurandum adiciatur, nullam exinde actus consequitur firmitatem.

Can. 1202 – Obligatio iureiurando promissorio inducta desinit :

1° si remittatur ab eo in cuius commodum iusiurandum emissum fuerat ;

2° si res iurata substantialiter mutetur, aut, mutatis adiunctis, fiat vel mala vel omnino indifferens, vel denique maius bonum impediat :

3° deficiente causa finali aut condicione sub qua forte iusiurandum datum est ;

4° dispensatione, commutatione, ad normam can. 1203.

Can. 1203 – Qui suspendere, dispensare, commutare possunt votum, eandem potestatem eademque ratione habent circa iusiurandum promissorium ; sed si iurisiurandi dispensatio vergat in praeiudicium aliorum qui obligationem remittere recusent, una Apostolica Sedes potest iusiurandum dispensare.

Can. 1197 — The work promised in a private vow can be commuted to a greater or an equal good by the person who makes the vow; however, a person who has the power of dispensation according to the norm of can. 1196 can commute it to a lesser good.

Can. 1198 — Vows made before religious profession are suspended as long as the person who makes the vow remains in a religious institute.

Chapter II
AN OATH

Can. 1199 — §1. An oath, that is the invocation of the divine name as a witness to truth, cannot be taken unless in truth, in judgment and in justice.

§2. An oath which the canons demand or admit cannot be taken validly through a proxy.

Can. 1200 — §1. A person who freely swears to do something in the future is bound by a special obligation of religion to fulfill what has been affirmed by oath.

§2. An oath extorted through fraud, force, or grave fear is null by the law itself.

Can. 1201 — §1. A promissory oath follows the nature and the condition of the act to which it is attached.

§2. If an oath is attached to an act which directly tends towards the injury of others or towards the prejudice of the public good or of eternal salvation, the act is not reinforced by the oath.

Can. 1202 — The obligation arising from a promissory oath ceases:

1° if it is remitted by the person for whose advantage the oath has been taken;

2° if the thing sworn to is substantially changed or if, due to changed circumstances, it becomes either evil or entirely indifferent or, finally, if it would impede a greater good;

3° if the final purpose for or condition under which the oath may have been taken no longer exists;

4° through its dispensation or commutation in accord with the norm of can. 1203.

Can. 1203 — The persons who can suspend, dispense or commute a vow have the same power over a promissory oath for the same reasons; but if the dispensation from the oath tends to prejudice others who refuse to remit its obligation, only the Apostolic See can dispense the oath.

Can. 1204 – Iusiurandum stricte est interpretandum secundum ius et secundum intentionem iurantis aut, si hic dolo agat, secundum intentionem illius cui iusiurandum praestatur.

PARS III
DE LOCIS ET TEMPORIBUS SACRIS

TITULUS I
DE LOCIS SACRIS

Can. 1205 – Loca sacra ea sunt quae divino cultui fideliumve sepulturae deputantur dedicatione vel benedictione, quam liturgici libri ad hoc praescribunt.

Can. 1206 – Dedicatio alicuius loci spectat ad Episcopum dioecesanum et ad eos qui ipsi iure aequiparantur; iidem possunt cuilibet Episcopo vel, in casibus exceptionalibus, presbytero munus committere dedicationem peragendi in suo territorio.

Can. 1207 – Loca sacra benedicuntur ab Ordinario; benedictio tamen ecclesiarum reservatur Episcopo dioecesano; uterque vero potest alium sacerdotem ad hoc delegare.

Can. 1208 – De peracta dedicatione vel benedictione ecclesiae, itemque de benedictione coemeterii redigatur documentum, cuius alterum exemplar in curia dioecesana, alterum in ecclesiae archivo servetur.

Can. 1209 – Dedicatio vel benedictio alicuius loci, modo nemini damnum fiat, satis probatur etiam per unum testem omni exceptione maiorem.

Can. 1210 – In loco sacro ea tantum admittantur quae cultui, pietati, religioni exercendis vel promovendis inserviunt, ac vetatur quidquid a loci sanctitate absonum sit. Ordinarius vero per modum actus alios usus, sanctitati tamen loci non contrarios, permittere potest.

Can. 1211 – Loca sacra violantur per actiones graviter iniuriosas cum scandalo fidelium ibi positas, quae, de iudicio Ordinarii loci, ita graves et sanctitati loci contrariae sunt ut non liceat in eis cultum exercere, donec ritu paenitentiali ad normam librorum liturgicorum iniuria reparetur.

Can. 1204 — An oath is to be strictly interpreted according to the law and the intention of the person taking the oath, or if that person acts out of fraud, according to the intention of the person to whom the oath is made.

PART III

SACRED PLACES AND TIMES

TITLE I

SACRED PLACES

Can. 1205 — Sacred places are those which have been designated for divine worship or for the burial of the faithful through a dedication or blessing which the liturgical books prescribe for this purpose.

Can. 1206 — The dedication of any place is within the competency of the diocesan bishop and those who are equivalent to him in law; they can commission any bishop or, in exceptional cases, a presbyter to perform a dedication within their own territory.

Can. 1207 — Sacred places are blessed by an ordinary; the blessing of churches, however, is reserved to the diocesan bishop; but either one of these can delegate another priest for this purpose.

Can. 1208 — A document is to be drawn up attesting that the dedication or blessing of a church or the blessing of a cemetery has been performed; one copy is to be kept in the diocesan curia and another copy in the church's archive.

Can. 1209 — Provided no one suffers damage from it, the dedication or blessing of any place is sufficiently proven even through one witness who is above all suspicion.

Can. 1210 — Only those things which serve the exercise or promotion of worship, piety and religion are to be admitted into a sacred place; anything which is not in accord with the holiness of the place is forbidden. The ordinary, however, can permit other uses which are not contrary to the holiness of the place, in individual instances.

Can. 1211 — Sacred places are violated through seriously harmful actions posited in them which scandalize the faithful and are so serious and contrary to the holiness of the place, in the judgment of the local ordinary, that it is not licit to perform acts of worship in them until the harm is repaired through a penitential rite in accord with the norm of the liturgical books.

Can. 1212 – Dedicationem vel benedictionem amittunt loca sacra, si magna ex parte destructa fuerint, vel ad usus profanos permanenter decreto competentis Ordinarii vel de facto reducta.

Can. 1213 – Potestates suas et munera auctoritas ecclesiastica in locis sacris libere exercet.

Caput I

DE ECCLESIIS

Can. 1214 – Ecclesiae nomine intellegitur aedes sacra divino cultui destinata, ad quam fidelibus ius est adeundi ad divinum cultum praesertim publice exercendum.

Can. 1215 – § 1. Nulla ecclesia aedificetur sine expresso Episcopi dioecesani consensu scriptis dato.

§ 2. Episcopus dioecesanus consensum ne praebeat nisi, audito consilio presbyterali et vicinarum ecclesiarum rectoribus, censeat novam ecclesiam bono animarum inservire posse, et media ad ecclesiae aedificationem et ad cultum divinum necessaria non esse defutura.

§ 3. Etiam instituta religiosa, licet consensum constituendae novae domus in dioecesi vel civitate ab Episcopo dioecesano rettulerint, antequam tamen ecclesiam in certo ac determinato loco aedificent, eiusdem licentiam obtinere debent.

Can. 1216 – In ecclesiarum aedificatione et refectione, adhibito peritorum consilio, serventur principia et normae liturgiae et artis sacrae.

Can. 1217 – § 1. Aedificatione rite peracta, nova ecclesia quam primum dedicetur aut saltem benedicatur, sacrae liturgiae legibus servatis.

§ 2. Sollemni ritu dedicentur ecclesiae, praesertim cathedrales et paroeciales.

Can. 1218 – Unaquaeque ecclesia suum habeat titulum qui, peracta ecclesiae dedicatione, mutari nequit.

Can. 1219 – In ecclesia legitime dedicata vel benedicta omnes actus cultus divini perfici possunt, salvis iuribus paroecialibus.

Can. 1220 – § 1. Curent omnes ad quos res pertinet, ut in ecclesiis illa munditia ac decor serventur, quae domum Dei addeceant, et ab iisdem arceatur quidquid a sanctitate loci absonum sit.

Can. 1212 — Sacred places lose their dedication or blessing if they suffer major destruction or if they have been permanently given over to profane uses, de facto or through a decree of the competent ordinary.

Can. 1213 — Ecclesiastical authority freely exercises its powers and functions in sacred places.

CHAPTER I

CHURCHES

Can. 1214 — The term church signifies a sacred building destined for divine worship to which the faithful have a right of access for divine worship, especially its public exercise.

Can. 1215 — §1. No church is to be built without the expressed written consent of the diocesan bishop.

§2. The diocesan bishop is not to furnish this consent unless he judges that a new church could serve the good of souls and that the means necessary for building the church and for divine worship would not be lacking in the future; he is to make this judgment after listening to the presbyteral council and the rectors of neighboring churches.

§3. Even religious institutes must obtain the permission of the diocesan bishop before they build a church in a certain and determined place even if they have received the consent of the diocesan bishop to establish a new house in the diocese or city.

Can. 1216 — The principles and norms of the liturgy and of sacred art are to be observed in the building and repair of churches; the advice of experts is also to be employed.

Can. 1217 — §1. As soon as its construction is properly completed, a new church is to be dedicated or at least blessed as soon as possible, observing the laws of the sacred liturgy.

§2. Churches, especially cathedral and parochial churches, are to be dedicated with a solemn rite.

Can. 1218 — Each church is to have its title which cannot be changed after its dedication.

Can. 1219 — All acts of divine worship can be performed in a church legitimately dedicated or blessed, with due regard for parochial rights.

Can. 1220 — §1. All whose concern it is are to take care that such cleanliness and propriety is preserved in churches as befits the house of God and that anything which is out of keeping with the sanctity of the place is precluded.

§ 2. Ad bona sacra et pretiosa tuenda ordinaria conservationis cura et opportuna securitatis media adhibeantur.

Can. 1221 – Ingressus in ecclesiam tempore sacrarum celebrationum sit liber et gratuitus.

Can. 1222 – § 1. Si qua ecclesia nullo modo ad cultum divinum adhiberi queat et possibilitas non detur eam reficiendi, in usum profanum non sordidum ab Episcopo dioecesano redigi potest.

§ 2. Ubi aliae graves causae suadeant ut aliqua ecclesia ad divinum cultum amplius non adhibeatur, eam Episcopus dioecesanus, audito consilio presbyterali, in usum profanum non sordidum redigere potest, de consensu eorum qui iura in eadem sibi legitime vindicent, et dum modo animarum bonum nullum inde detrimentum capiat.

CAPUT II

DE ORATORIIS ET DE SACELLIS PRIVATIS

Can. 1223 – Oratorii nomine intellegitur locus divino cultui, in commodum alicuius communitatis vel coetus fidelium eo convenientium, de licentia Ordinarii destinatus, ad quem etiam alii fideles de consensu Superioris competentis accedere possunt.

Can. 1224 – § 1. Ordinarius licentiam ad constituendum oratorium requisitam ne concedat, nisi prius per se vel per alium locum ad oratorium destinatum visitaverit et decenter instructum reppererit.

§ 2. Data autem licentia, oratorium ad usus profanos converti nequit sine eiusdem Ordinarii auctoritate.

Can. 1225 – In oratoriis legitime constitutis omnes celebrationes sacrae peragi possunt, nisi quae iure aut Ordinarii loci praescripto excipiantur, aut obstent normae liturgicae.

Can. 1226 – Nomine sacelli privati intellegitur locus divino cultui, in commodum unius vel plurium personarum physicarum, de licentia Ordinarii loci destinatus.

Can. 1227 – Episcopi sacellum privatum sibi constituere possunt, quod iisdem iuribus ac oratorium gaudet.

Can. 1228 – Firmo praescripto can. 1227, ad Missam aliasve sacras celebrationes in aliquo sacello privato peragendas requiritur Ordinarii loci licentia.

Can. 1229 – Oratoria et sacella privata benedici convenit secundum ritum in libris liturgicis praescriptum; debent autem esse divino tantum cultui reservata et ab omnibus domesticis usibus libera.

§2. Ordinary concern for preservation and appropriate security measures are to be used to protect sacred and precious goods.

Can. 1221 — Entrance to a church during the time of sacred celebrations is to be free and gratuitous.

Can. 1222 — §1. If a church can in no way be employed for divine worship and it is impossible to repair it, it can be relegated to profane but not sordid use by the diocesan bishop.

§2. Where other serious reasons suggest that a church no longer be used for divine worship the diocesan bishop, after hearing the presbyteral council, can relegate it to profane but not sordid use with the consent of those who legitimately claim rights regarding the church and as long as the good of souls is not thereby impaired.

CHAPTER II

ORATORIES AND PRIVATE CHAPELS

Can. 1223 — The term oratory signifies a place designated by permission of the ordinary for divine worship for the benefit of some community or assembly of the faithful who gather there; other members of the faithful may also have access to it with the consent of the competent superior.

Can. 1224 — §1. The ordinary is not to grant the permission required to establish an oratory unless he first visits the place destined for the oratory himself or through another and finds it suitably constructed.

§2. Once this permission is granted, however, the oratory cannot be converted to profane uses without the authority of the same ordinary.

Can. 1225 — All sacred celebrations can be carried out in oratories legitimately established unless liturgical norms prevent this or the law or a prescription of the local ordinary has made certain exceptions.

Can. 1226 — The term private chapel signifies a place designated for divine worship for the advantage of one or several physical persons with the permission of the local ordinary.

Can. 1227 — Bishops can establish for themselves a private chapel which enjoys the same rights as an oratory.

Can. 1228 — With due regard for the prescription of can. 1227, the permission of the local ordinary is required for Mass and other sacred celebrations to take place in a private chapel.

Can. 1229 — It is fitting that oratories and private chapels be blessed according to the rite prescribed in the liturgical books; they must, however, be reserved only for divine worship and be free from all domestic uses.

Caput III

DE SANCTUARIIS

Can. 1230 – Sanctuarii nomine intelleguntur ecclesia vel alius locus sacer ad quos, ob peculiarem pietatis causam, fideles frequentes, approbante Ordinario loci, peregrinantur.

Can. 1231 – Ut sanctuarium dici possit nationale, accedere debet approbatio Episcoporum conferentiae; ut dici possit internationale, requiritur approbatio Sanctae Sedis.

Can. 1232 – § 1. Ad approbanda statuta sanctuarii dioecesani, competens est Ordinarius loci; ad statuta sanctuarii nationalis, Episcoporum conferentia; ad statuta sanctuarii internationalis, sola Sancta Sedes.

§ 2. In statutis determinentur praesertim finis, auctoritas rectoris, dominium et administratio bonorum.

Can. 1233 – Sanctuariis quaedam privilegia concedi poterunt, quoties locorum circumstantiae, peregrinantium frequentia et praesertim fidelium bonum id suadere videantur.

Can. 1234 – § 1. In sanctuariis abundantius fidelibus suppeditentur media salutis, verbum Dei sedulo annuntiando, vitam liturgicam praesertim per Eucharistiae et paenitentiae celebrationem apte fovendo, necnon probatas pietatis popularis formas colendo.

§ 2. Votiva artis popularis et pietatis documenta in sanctuariis aut locis adiacentibus spectabilia serventur atque secure custodiantur.

Caput IV

DE ALTARIBUS

Can. 1235 – § 1. Altare, seu mensa super quam Sacrificium eucharisticum celebratur, *fixum* dicitur, si ita exstruatur ut cum pavimento cohaereat ideoque amoveri nequeat; *mobile* vero, si transferri possit.

§ 2. Expedit in omni ecclesia altare fixum inesse; ceteris vero in locis, sacris celebrationibus destinatis, altare fixum vel mobile.

Can. 1236 – § 1. Iuxta traditum Ecclesiae morem mensa altaris fixi sit lapidea, et quidem ex unico lapide naturali; attamen etiam alia materia digna et solida, de iudicio Episcoporum conferentiae, adhiberi potest. Stipites vero seu basis ex qualibet materia confici possunt.

§ 2. Altare mobile ex qualibet materia solida, usui liturgico congruenti, extrui potest.

Chapter III
SHRINES

Can. 1230 — The term shrine signifies a church or other sacred place to which the faithful make pilgrimages for a particular pious reason with the approval of the local ordinary.

Can. 1231 — For a shrine to be called a national one, the conference of bishops must approve; for it to be called an international one, the Holy See must approve.

Can. 1232 — §1. The local ordinary is competent to approve the statutes of a diocesan shrine; the conference of bishops for a national shrine; the Holy See alone for an international shrine.

§2. These statutes are to determine especially the purpose of the shrine, the authority of its rector and the ownership and administration of goods.

Can. 1233 — Certain privileges can be granted to shrines as often as local circumstances, the large number of pilgrims and especially the good of the faithful seem to suggest it.

Can. 1234 — §1. At shrines more abundant means of salvation are to be provided the faithful; the word of God is to be carefully proclaimed; liturgical life is to be appropriately fostered especially through the celebration of the Eucharist and penance; and approved forms of popular piety are to be cultivated.

§2. Votive gifts of popular art and piety are to be displayed in shrines or adjacent places and kept secure.

Chapter IV
ALTARS

Can. 1235 — §1. An altar or a table on which the Eucharistic Sacrifice is celebrated is said to be *fixed* if it is so constructed that it is joined to the floor and therefore cannot be moved; it is *movable* if it can be transferred.

§2. It is fitting that there be a fixed altar in every church; in other places designated for sacred celebration, a fixed altar or a movable altar.

Can. 1236 — §1. According to church custom the table of a fixed altar is to be of stone, in fact of a single natural stone; nevertheless, even another material, worthy and solid, in the judgment of the conference of bishops also can be used. The supports or the foundation can be made of any material.

§2. A movable altar can be constructed from any solid material appropriate for liturgical use.

Can. 1237 – § 1. Altaria fixa dedicanda sunt, mobilia vero dedicanda aut benedicenda, iuxta ritus in liturgicis libris praescriptos.

§ 2. Antiqua traditio Martyrum aliorumve Sanctorum reliquias sub altari fixo condendi servetur, iuxta normas in libris liturgicis traditas.

Can. 1238 – § 1. Altare dedicationem vel benedictionem amittit ad normam can. 1212.

§ 2. Per reductionem ecclesiae vel alius loci sacri ad usus profanos, altaria sive fixa sive mobilia non amittunt dedicationem vel benedictionem.

Can. 1239 – § 1. Altare tum fixum tum mobile divino dumtaxat cultui reservandum est, quolibet profano usu prorsus excluso.

§ 2. Subtus altare nullum sit reconditum cadaver; secus Missam super illud celebrare non licet.

Caput V

DE COEMETERIIS

Can. 1240 – § 1. Coemeteria Ecclesiae propria, ubi fieri potest, habeantur, vel saltem spatia in coemeteriis civilibus fidelibus defunctis destinata, rite benedicenda.

§ 2. Si vero hoc obtineri nequeat, toties quoties singuli tumuli rite benedicantur.

Can. 1241 – § 1. Paroeciae et instituta religiosa coemeterium proprium habere possunt.

§ 2. Etiam aliae personae iuridicae vel familiae habere possunt peculiare coemeterium seu sepulcrum, de iudicio Ordinarii loci benedicendum.

Can. 1242 – In ecclesiis cadavera ne sepeliantur, nisi agatur de Romano Pontifice aut Cardinalibus vel Episcopis dioecesanis etiam emeritis in propria ecclesia sepeliendis.

Can. 1243 – Opportunae normae de disciplina in coemeteriis servanda, praesertim ad eorum indolem sacram tuendam et fovendam quod attinet, iure particulari statuantur.

Can. 1237 — §1. Fixed altars are to be dedicated; movable altars, however, are to be dedicated or blessed according to the rites prescribed in the liturgical books.

§2. The ancient tradition of keeping the relics of martyrs and other saints under a fixed altar is to be preserved according to the norms given in the liturgical books.

Can. 1238 — §1. An altar loses its dedication or blessing according to the norm of can. 1212.

§2. Altars, be they fixed or movable, do not lose their dedication or blessing through the reduction of a church or other sacred place to profane uses.

Can. 1239 — §1. Both a fixed and a movable altar are to be reserved exclusively for divine worship and entirely exempt from profane use.

§2. No corpse may be buried beneath the altar; otherwise Mass may not be celebrated on it.

CHAPTER V
CEMETERIES

Can. 1240 — §1. The Church is to have its own cemeteries wherever this can be done, or at least spaces in civil cemeteries destined for the faithful departed and properly blessed.

§2. If however, this cannot be achieved, individual graves are to be properly blessed as often as needed.

Can. 1241 — §1. Parishes and religious institutes can have their own cemetery.

§2. Other juridic persons or families can also have their own particular cemetery or burial place to be blessed according to the judgment of the local ordinary.

Can. 1242 — Corpses are not to be buried in churches unless it is a question of interring in their proper church the Roman Pontiff, cardinals or diocesan bishops, even those who are retired.

Can. 1243 — Particular law is to determine appropriate norms on the discipline to be observed in cemeteries, especially regarding the protecting and fostering of their sacred character.

TITULUS II
DE TEMPORIBUS SACRIS

Can. 1244 – § 1. Dies festos itemque dies paenitentiae, universae Ecclesiae communes, constituere, transferre, abolere, unius est supremae ecclesiasticae auctoritatis, firmo praescripto can. 1246, § 2.

§ 2. Episcopi dioecesani peculiares suis dioecesibus seu locis dies festos aut dies paenitentiae possunt, per modum tantum actus, indicere.

Can. 1245 – Firmo iure Episcoporum dioecesanorum de quo in can. 87, parochus, iusta de causa et secundum Episcopi dioecesani praescripta, singulis in casibus concedere potest dispensationem ab obligatione servandi diem festum vel diem paenitentiae aut commutationem eiusdem in alia pia opera; idque potest etiam Superior instituti religiosi aut societatis vitae apostolicae, si sint clericalia iuris pontificii, quoad proprios subditos aliosque in domo diu noctuque degentes.

CAPUT I
DE DIEBUS FESTIS

Can. 1246 – § 1. Dies dominica in qua mysterium paschale celebratur, ex apostolica traditione, in universa Ecclesia uti primordialis dies festus de praecepto servanda est. Itemque servari debent dies Nativitatis Domini Nostri Iesu Christi, Epiphaniae, Ascensionis et sanctissimi Corporis et Sanguinis Christi, Sanctae Dei Genetricis Mariae, eiusdem Immaculatae Conceptionis et Assumptionis, sancti Ioseph, sanctorum Petri et Pauli Apostolorum, omnium denique Sanctorum.

§ 2. Episcoporum conferentia tamen potest, praevia Apostolicae Sedis approbatione, quosdam ex diebus festis de praecepto abolere vel ad diem dominicam transferre.

Can. 1247 – Die dominica aliisque diebus festis de praecepto fideles obligatione tenentur Missam participandi; abstineant insuper ab illis operibus et negotiis quae cultum Deo reddendum, laetitiam diei Domini propriam, aut debitam mentis ac corporis relaxationem impediant.

Can. 1248 – § 1. Praecepto de Missa participanda satisfacit qui Missae assistit ubicumque celebratur ritu catholico vel ipso die festo vel vespere diei praecedentis.

§ 2. Si deficiente ministro sacro aliave gravi de causa participatio eucharisticae celebrationis impossibilis evadat, valde commendatur ut

TITLE II
SACRED TIMES

Can. 1244 — §1. It is within the competence of the supreme ecclesiastical authority alone to establish, transfer or abolish feast days or days of penance which are common to the universal Church, with due regard for the prescription of can. 1246, §2.

§2. Diocesan bishops can determine special feast days or days of penance for their dioceses or places but only *per modum actus*.

Can. 1245 — With due regard for the right of diocesan bishops which is mentioned in can. 87, for a just reason and in accord with the prescriptions of the diocesan bishop, the pastor in individual cases can dispense from the obligation to observe a feast day or a day of penance; or he can commute it to other pious works; the superior of a religious institute or a society of apostolic life of pontifical right if they are clerical can also do the same for his own subjects and others staying in his house day and night.

CHAPTER I
FEAST DAYS

Can. 1246 — §1. Sunday is the day on which the paschal mystery is celebrated in light of the apostolic tradition and is to be observed as the foremost holy day of obligation in the universal Church. Also to be observed are the day of the Nativity of Our Lord Jesus Christ, the Epiphany, the Ascension and the Most Holy Body and Blood of Christ, Holy Mary Mother of God and her Immaculate Conception and Assumption, Saint Joseph, the Apostles Saints Peter and Paul, and finally, All Saints.

§2. However, the conference of bishops can abolish certain holy days of obligation or transfer them to a Sunday with prior approval of the Apostolic See.

Can. 1247 — On Sundays and other holy days of obligation the faithful are bound to participate in the Mass; they are also to abstain from those labors and business concerns which impede the worship to be rendered to God, the joy which is proper to the Lord's Day, or the proper relaxation of mind and body.

Can. 1248 — §1. The precept of participating in the Mass is satisfied by assistance at a Mass which is celebrated anywhere in a Catholic rite either on the holy day or on the evening of the preceding day.

§2. If because of lack of a sacred minister or for other grave cause participation in the celebration of the Eucharist is impossible, it is specially recom-

fideles in liturgia Verbi, si quae sit in ecclesia paroeciali aliove sacro loco, iuxta Episcopi dioecesani praescripta celebrata, partem habeant, aut orationi per debitum tempus personaliter aut in familia vel pro opportunitate in familiarum coetibus vacent.

Caput II

DE DIEBUS PAENITENTIAE

Can. 1249 – Omnes christifideles, suo quisque modo, paenitentiam agere ex lege divina tenentur; ut vero cuncti communi quadam paeni- tentiae observatione inter se coniungantur, dies paenitentiales prae- scribuntur, in quibus christifideles speciali modo orationi vacent, opera pietatis et caritatis exerceant, se ipsos abnegent, proprias obligationes fidelius adimplendo et praesertim ieiunium et abstinentiam, ad normam canonum qui sequuntur, observando.

Can. 1250 – Dies et tempora paenitentialia in universa Ecclesia sunt singulae feriae sextae totius anni et tempus quadragesimae.

Can. 1251 – Abstinentia a carnis comestione vel ab alio cibo iuxta conferentiae Episcoporum praescripta, servetur singulis anni sextis feriis, nisi cum aliquo die inter sollemnitates recensito occurrant; ab- stinentia vero et ieiunium, feria quarta Cinerum et feria sexta in Pas- sione et Morte Domini 'Nostri Iesu Christi.

Can. 1252 – Lege abstinentiae tenentur qui decimum quartum aeta- tis annum expleverint; lege vero ieiunii adstringuntur omnes aetate maiores usque ad annum inceptum sexagesimum. Curent tamen ani- marum pastores et parentes ut etiam ii qui, ratione minoris aetatis ad legem ieiunii et abstinentiae non tenentur, ad genuinum paenitentiae sensum informentur.

Can. 1253 – Episcoporum conferentia potest pressius determinare observantiam ieiunii et abstinentiae, necnon alias formas paenitentiae, praesertim opera caritatis et exercitationes pietatis, ex toto vel ex parte pro abstinentia et ieiunio substituere.

mended that the faithful take part in the liturgy of the word if it is celebrated in the parish church or in another sacred place according to the prescriptions of the diocesan bishop, or engage in prayer for an appropriate amount of time personally or in a family or, as occasion offers, in groups of families.

CHAPTER II
DAYS OF PENANCE

Can. 1249 — All members of the Christian faithful in their own way are bound to do penance in virtue of divine law; in order that all may be joined in a common observance of penance, penitential days are prescribed in which the Christian faithful in a special way pray, exercise works of piety and charity, and deny themselves by fulfilling their responsibilities more faithfully and especially by observing fast and abstinence according to the norm of the following canons.

Can. 1250 — All Fridays through the year and the time of Lent are penitential days and times throughout the universal Church.

Can. 1251 — Abstinence from eating meat or another food according to the prescriptions of the conference of bishops is to be observed on Fridays throughout the year unless they are solemnities; abstinence and fast are to be observed on Ash Wednesday and on the Friday of the Passion and Death of Our Lord Jesus Christ.

Can. 1252 — All persons who have completed their fourteenth year are bound by the law of abstinence; all adults are bound by the law of fast up to the beginning of their sixtieth year. Nevertheless, pastors and parents are to see to it that minors who are not bound by the law of fast and abstinence are educated in an authentic sense of penance.

Can. 1253 — It is for the conference of bishops to determine more precisely the observance of fast and abstinence and to substitute in whole or in part for fast and abstinence other forms of penance, especially works of charity and exercises of piety.

LIBER V
DE BONIS ECCLESIAE TEMPORALIBUS

Can. 1254 – § 1. Ecclesia catholica bona temporalia iure nativo, independenter a civili potestate, acquirere, retinere, administrare et alienare valet ad fines sibi proprios prosequendos.

§ 2. Fines vero proprii praecipue sunt: cultus divinus ordinandus, honesta cleri aliorumque ministrorum sustentatio procuranda, opera sacri apostolatus et caritatis, praesertim erga egenos, exercenda.

Can. 1255 – Ecclesia universa atque Apostolica Sedes, Ecclesiae particulares necnon alia quaevis persona iuridica, sive publica sive privata, subiecta sunt capacia bona temporalia acquirendi, retinendi, administrandi et alienandi ad normam iuris.

Can. 1256 – Dominium bonorum, sub suprema auctoritate Romani Pontificis, ad eam pertinet iuridicam personam, quae eadem bona legitime acquisiverit.

Can. 1257 – § 1. Bona temporalia omnia quae ad Ecclesiam universam, Apostolicam Sedem aliasve in Ecclesia personas iuridicas publicas pertinent, sunt bona ecclesiastica et reguntur canonibus qui sequuntur, necnon propriis statutis.

§ 2. Bona temporalia personae iuridicae privatae reguntur propriis statutis, non autem hisce canonibus, nisi expresse aliud caveatur.

Can. 1258 – In canonibus qui sequuntur nomine Ecclesiae significatur non solum Ecclesia universa aut Sedes Apostolica, sed etiam quaelibet persona iuridica publica in Ecclesia, nisi ex contextu sermonis vel ex natura rei aliud appareat.

BOOK V

THE TEMPORAL GOODS OF THE CHURCH

Can. 1254 — §1. The Catholic Church has an innate right to acquire, retain, administer and alienate temporal goods in pursuit of its proper ends independently of civil power.

§2. The following ends are especially proper to the Church: to order divine worship; to provide decent support for the clergy and other ministers; to perform the works of the sacred apostolate and of charity, especially towards the needy.

Can. 1255 — The universal Church and the Apostolic See, the particular churches as well as any other juridic person, whether public or private, are capable of acquiring, retaining, administering and alienating temporal goods in accord with the norm of law.

Can. 1256 — The right of ownership over goods under the supreme authority of the Roman Pontiff belongs to that juridic person which has lawfully acquired them.

Can. 1257 — §1. All temporal goods which belong to the universal Church, the Apostolic See, or other public juridic persons within the Church are ecclesiastical goods and are regulated by the following canons as well as by their own statutes.

§2. The temporal goods of a private juridic person are regulated by their own statutes, but not by the following canons unless express provision is made to the contrary.

Can. 1258 — In the following canons the term Church signifies not only the universal Church or the Apostolic See, but also any public juridic person within the Church unless it is otherwise apparent from the context of what is written or from the nature of the matter.

TITULUS I
DE ACQUISITIONE BONORUM

Can. 1259 – Ecclesia acquirere bona temporalia potest omnibus iustis modis iuris sive naturalis sive positivi, quibus aliis licet.

Can. 1260 – Ecclesiae nativum ius est exigendi a christifidelibus, quae ad fines sibi proprios sint necessaria.

Can. 1261 – § 1. Integrum est christifidelibus bona temporalia in favorem Ecclesiae conferre.

§ 2. Episcopus dioecesanus fideles de obligatione, de qua in can. 222, § 1, monere tenetur et opportuno modo eam urgere.

Can. 1262 – Fideles subsidia Ecclesiae conferant per subventiones rogatas et iuxta normas ab Episcoporum conferentia latas.

Can. 1263 – Ius est Episcopo dioecesano, auditis consilio a rebus oeconomicis et consilio presbyterali, pro dioecesis necessitatibus, personis iuridicis publicis suo regimini subiectis, moderatum tributum, earum redditibus proportionatum, imponendi; ceteris personis physicis et iuridicis ipsi licet tantum, in casu gravis necessitatis et sub iisdem condicionibus, extraordinariam et moderatam exactionem imponere, salvis legibus et consuetudinibus particularibus quae eidem potiora iura tribuant.

Can. 1264 – Nisi aliud iure cautum sit, conventus Episcoporum provinciae est :

1° praefinire taxas pro actibus potestatis exsecutivae gratiosae vel pro exsecutione rescriptorum Sedis Apostolicae, ab ipsa Sede Apostolica approbandas ;

2° definire oblationes occasione ministrationis sacramentorum et sacramentalium.

Can. 1265 – § 1. Salvo iure religiosorum mendicantium, vetatur persona quaevis privata, sive physica sive iuridica, sine proprii Ordinarii et Ordinarii loci licentia, in scriptis data, stipem cogere pro quolibet pio aut ecclesiastico instituto vel fine.

§ 2. Episcoporum conferentia potest normas de stipe quaeritanda statuere, quae ab omnibus servari debent, iis non exclusis, qui ex institutione mendicantes vocantur et sunt.

Can. 1266 – In omnibus ecclesiis et oratoriis, etiam ad instituta religiosa pertinentibus, quae de facto habitualiter christifidelibus pateant, Ordinarius loci praecipere potest ut specialis stips colligatur

TITLE I

THE ACQUISITION OF GOODS

Can. 1259 — The Church can acquire temporal goods by every just means of natural or positive law permitted to others.

Can. 1260 — The Church has an innate right to require from the Christian faithful whatever is necessary for the ends proper to it.

Can. 1261 — §1. The Christian faithful may freely give temporal goods to the Church.

§2. The diocesan bishop is bound to admonish the faithful concerning the obligation mentioned in can. 222, §1 and to urge its observance in an appropriate manner.

Can. 1262 — The faithful are to contribute to the support of the Church by collections and according to the norms laid down by the conference of bishops.

Can. 1263 — The diocesan bishop has the right to impose a moderate tax on public juridic persons subject to his authority; this tax, which should be proportionate to their income, is for diocesan needs and may be imposed only after hearing the diocesan finance council and the presbyteral council; he can impose an extraordinary and moderate tax on other physical and juridic persons only in cases of grave necessity and under the same conditions with due regard for particular laws and customs attributing even more significant rights to him.

Can. 1264 — Unless the law has provided otherwise, it is the responsibility of a meeting of the bishops of a province:

1° to fix the amounts of the tax for acts of discretionary executive power or for the execution of rescripts of the Apostolic See, to be approved by the Apostolic See;

2° to set a limit on the offerings given on the occasion of administering the sacraments and sacramentals.

Can. 1265 — §1. With due regard for the right of religious mendicants private persons whether physical or juridic are forbidden to raise funds for any pious or ecclesiastical institution or purpose without the written permission of their own ordinary and that of the local ordinary.

§2. The conference of bishops can determine norms on fund-raising, which must be observed by everyone including those who are called and really are mendicants by their foundation.

Can. 1266 — The local ordinary may prescribe the taking up of a special collection for specific parochial, diocesan, national or universal projects in all the churches and oratories which are, in fact, habitually open to the

pro determinatis inceptis paroecialibus, dioecesanis, nationalibus vel universalibus, ad curiam dioecesanam postea sedulo mittenda.

Can. 1267 – § 1. Nisi contrarium constet, oblationes quae fiunt Superioribus vel administratoribus cuiusvis personae iuridicae ecclesiasticae, etiam privatae, praesumuntur ipsi personae iuridicae factae.

§ 2. Oblationes, de quibus in § 1, repudiari nequeunt, nisi iusta de causa et, in rebus maioris momenti, de licentia Ordinarii, si agitur de persona iuridica publica; eiusdem Ordinarii licentia requiritur ut acceptentur quae onere modali vel condicione gravantur, firmo praescripto can. 1295.

§ 3. Oblationes a fidelibus ad certum finem factae, nonnisi ad eundem finem destinari possunt.

Can. 1268 – Praescriptionem, tamquam acquirendi et se liberandi modum, Ecclesia pro bonis temporalibus recipit, ad normam cann. 197-199.

Can. 1269 – Res sacrae, si in dominio privatorum sunt, praescriptione acquiri a privatis personis possunt, sed eas adhibere ad usus profanos non licet, nisi dedicationem vel benedictionem amiserint; si vero ad personam iuridicam ecclesiasticam publicam pertinent, tantum ab alia persona iuridica ecclesiastica publica acquiri possunt.

Can. 1270 – Res immobiles, mobiles pretiosae, iura et actiones sive personales sive reales, quae pertinent ad Sedem Apostolicam, spatio centum annorum praescribuntur; quae ad aliam personam iuridicam publicam ecclesiasticam, spatio triginta annorum.

Can. 1271 – Episcopi, ratione vinculi unitatis et caritatis, pro suae dioecesis facultatibus, conferant ad media procuranda, quibus Sedes Apostolica secundum temporum condiciones indiget, ut servitium erga Ecclesiam universam rite praestare valeat.

Can. 1272 – In regionibus ubi beneficia proprie dicta adhuc exsistunt, Episcoporum conferentiae est, opportunis normis cum Apostolica Sede concordatis et ab ea approbatis, huiusmodi beneficiorum regimen moderari, ita ut reditus, immo quatenus possibile sit ipsa dos beneficiorum ad institutum, de quo in can. 1274, § 1, paulatim deferatur.

TITULUS II
DE ADMINISTRATIONE BONORUM

Can. 1273 – Romanus Pontifex, vi primatus regiminis, est omnium bonorum ecclesiasticorum supremus administrator et dispensator.

Christian faithful, including those belonging to religious institutes; this collection is to be diligently transmitted afterwards to the diocesan curia.

Can. 1267 — §1. Unless the contrary is established, the offerings given to the superiors or administrators of any ecclesiastical juridic person, even to a private one, are presumed to be given to that juridic person.

§2. The offerings mentioned in §1 may not be refused without a just cause and, in matters of greater importance, without the permission of the ordinary if it is a question of a public juridic person; with due regard for the prescription of can. 1295, the permission of the same ordinary is required to accept those gifts to which are attached a condition or a modal obligation.

§3. The offerings given by the faithful for a definite purpose can be applied only for that same purpose.

Can. 1268 — Prescription as a means of acquiring property and freeing oneself from an obligation is admitted by the Church in regard to temporal goods according to the norm of cann. 197-199.

Can. 1269 — If sacred objects are privately owned, they may be acquired even by private persons by means of prescription; but it is not lawful to employ them for profane uses unless they have lost their dedication or blessing; if, however, they belong to a public ecclesiastical juridic person, they can be acquired only by another public ecclesiastical juridic person.

Can. 1270 — Immovable properties, precious movable objects, and the personal or real rights and claims which belong to the Apostolic See are subject to a prescription period of one hundred years; those which belong to another public ecclesiastical juridic person are subject to a prescription period of thirty years.

Can. 1271 — In view of their bond of unity and charity and in accord with the resources of their dioceses, bishops are to assist in procuring those means whereby the Apostolic See can properly provide for its service of the universal Church according to the conditions of the times.

Can. 1272 — In regions where benefices in the strict sense still exist, it is the responsibility of the conference of bishops to supervise the management of such benefices through appropriate norms which are agreeable to and approved by the Apostolic See; this is to be accomplished in such a way that the income from and to the extent that it is possible even the original endowment of these benefices are gradually bestowed upon the institute mentioned in can. 1274, §1.

TITLE II

THE ADMINISTRATION OF GOODS

Can. 1273 — By virtue of his primacy in governance the Roman Pontiff is the supreme administrator and steward of all ecclesiastical goods.

Can. 1274 – § 1. Habeatur in singulis dioecesibus speciale institutum, quod bona vel oblationes colligat eum in finem ut sustentationi clericorum, qui in favorem dioecesis servitium praestant, ad normam can. 281 provideatur, nisi aliter eisdem provisum sit.

§ 2. Ubi praevidentia socialis in favorem cleri nondum apte ordinata est, curet Episcoporum conferentia ut habeatur institutum, quo securitati sociali clericorum satis provideatur.

§ 3. In singulis dioecesibus constituatur, quatenus opus sit, massa communis qua valeant Episcopi obligationibus erga alias personas Ecclesiae deservientes satisfacere variisque dioecesis necessitatibus occurrere, quaque etiam dioeceses divitiores possint pauperioribus subvenire.

§ 4. Pro diversis locorum adiunctis, fines de quibus in §§ 2 et 3 aptius obtineri possunt per instituta dioecesana inter se foederata, vel per cooperationem aut etiam per convenientem consociationem pro variis dioecesibus, immo et pro toto territorio ipsius Episcoporum conferentiae constitutam.

§ 5. Haec instituta, si fieri possit, ita constituenda sunt, ut efficaciam quoque in iure civili obtineant.

Can. 1275 – Massa bonorum ex diversis dioecesibus provenientium administratur secundum normas ab Episcopis, quorum interest, opportune concordatas.

Can. 1276 – § 1. Ordinarii est sedulo advigilare administrationi omnium bonorum, quae ad personas iuridicas publicas sibi subiectas pertinent, salvis legitimis titulis quibus eidem Ordinario potiora iura tribuantur.

§ 2. Habita ratione iurium, legitimarum consuetudinum et circumstantiarum, Ordinarii, editis peculiaribus instructionibus intra fines iuris universalis et particularis, universum administrationis bonorum ecclesiasticorum negotium ordinandum curent.

Can. 1277 – Episcopus dioecesanus quod attinet ad actus administrationis ponendos, qui, attento statu oeconomico dioecesis, sunt maioris momenti, consilium a rebus oeconomicis et collegium consultorum audire debet; eiusdem tamen consilii atque etiam collegii consultorum consensu eget, praeterquam in casibus iure universali vel tabulis fundationis specialiter expressis, ad ponendos actus extraordinariae administrationis. Conferentiae autem Episcoporum est definire quinam actus habendi sint extraordinariae administrationis.

Can. 1278 – Praeter munera de quibus in can. 494, §§ 3 et 4, oeconomo committi possunt ab Episcopo dioecesano munera de quibus in cann. 1276, § 1 et 1279, § 2.

Can. 1274 — §1. Unless other provisions have been made for the support of the clergy, each diocese is to have a special institute which collects goods and offerings and whose purpose is to provide, according to the norm of can. 281, for the support of the clergy who offer their services for the benefit of the diocese.

§2. The conference of bishops is to see to it that an institute exists which sufficiently provides for the social security of the clergy wherever social insurance has not yet been suitably arranged for the benefit of the clergy.

§3. Insofar as it is necessary, each diocese is to establish a common fund through which the bishops can satisfy obligations toward other persons who serve the Church and meet the various needs of the diocese and through which the richer dioceses can also aid poorer ones.

§4. In accord with different local circumstances, the purposes mentioned in §§2 and 3 may be more appropriately obtained through a federation of such diocesan institutes, through some cooperative venture or even through some suitable association established for various dioceses or even for the entire territory of a conference of bishops.

§5. If it is possible, these institutes are to be so established that they are also recognized as effective under the civil law.

Can. 1275 — An aggregate of goods which come from different dioceses is administered according to the norms appropriately agreed upon by the bishops concerned.

Can. 1276 — §1. It is the responsibility of the ordinary to supervise carefully the administration of all the goods which belong to the public juridic persons subject to him with due regard for legitimate titles attributing even more significant rights to the same ordinary.

§2. Ordinaries are to see to the organization of the entire administration of ecclesiastical goods by issuing special instructions within the limits of universal and particular law with due regard for rights, legitimate customs and circumstances.

Can. 1277 — The diocesan bishop must hear the finance council and the college of consultors in order to perform the more important acts of administration in light of the economic situation of the diocese; he needs the consent of this council and that of the college of consultors in order to perform acts of extraordinary administration besides cases specifically mentioned in universal law or in the charter of a foundation. It is for the conference of bishops to define what is meant by acts of extraordinary administration.

Can. 1278 — In addition to the functions mentioned in can. 494, §§3 and 4, the diocesan bishop can assign to the finance officer the duties mentioned in cann. 1276, §1 and 1279, §2.

Can. 1279 – § 1. Administratio bonorum ecclesiasticorum ei competit, qui immediate regit personam ad quam eadem bona pertinent, nisi aliud ferant ius particulare, statuta aut legitima consuetudo, et salvo iure Ordinarii interveniendi in casu neglegentiae administratoris.

§ 2. In administratione bonorum personae iuridicae publicae, quae ex iure vel tabulis fundationis aut propriis statutis suos non habeat administratores, Ordinarius, cui eadem subiecta est, personas idoneas ad triennium assumat; eaedem ab Ordinario iterum nominari possunt.

Can. 1280 – Quaevis persona iuridica suum habeat consilium a rebus oeconomicis vel saltem duos consiliarios, qui administratorem, ad normam statutorum, in munere adimplendo adiuvent.

Can. 1281 – § 1. Firmis statutorum praescriptis, administratores invalide ponunt actus qui fines modumque ordinariae administrationis excedunt, nisi prius ab Ordinario facultatem scripto datam obtinuerint.

§ 2. In statutis definiantur actus qui finem et modum ordinariae administrationis excedunt; si vero de hac re sileant statuta, competit Episcopo dioecesano, audito consilio a rebus oeconomicis, huiusmodi actus pro personis sibi subiectis determinare.

§ 3. Nisi quando et quatenus in rem suam versum sit, persona iuridica non tenetur respondere de actibus ab administratoribus invalide positis; de actibus autem ab administratoribus illegitime sed valide positis respondebit ipsa persona iuridica, salva eius actione seu recursu adversus administratores qui damna eidem intulerint.

Can. 1282 – Omnes, sive clerici sive laici, qui legitimo titulo partes habent in administratione bonorum ecclesiasticorum, munera sua adimplere tenentur nomine Ecclesiae, ad normam iuris.

Can. 1283 – Antequam administratores suum munus ineant:

1° debent se bene et fideliter administraturos coram Ordinario vel eius delegato iureiurando spondere;

2° accuratum ac distinctum inventarium, ab ipsis subscribendum, rerum immobilium, rerum mobilium sive pretiosarum sive utcumque ad bona culturalia pertinentium aliarumve cum descriptione atque aestimatione earundem redigatur, redactumque recognoscatur;

3° huius inventarii alterum exemplar conservetur in tabulario administrationis, alterum in archivo curiae; et in utroque quaelibet immutatio adnotetur, quam patrimonium subire contingat.

Can. 1284 – § 1. Omnes administratores diligentia boni patrisfamilias suum munus implere tenentur.

§ 2. Exinde debent:

Can. 1279 — §1. The administration of ecclesiastical goods is the responsibility of the individual who immediately governs the person to whom the goods belong unless particular law, statutes or lawful custom provide otherwise and with due regard for the right of the ordinary to intervene in case of negligence by an adminstrator.

§2. As regards the administration of the goods of a public juridic person which does not have its own administrators in virtue of law or the charter of the foundation or its own statutes, the ordinary to whom such a person is subject is to appoint suitable persons as administrators for three year terms, and they may be reappointed by the ordinary.

Can. 1280 — Each juridic person is to have its own finance council or at least two advisors, who according to the norm of its statutes assist the administrator in carrying out his or her function.

Can. 1281 — §1. With due regard for the prescriptions of their statutes, administrators invalidily posit acts which go beyond the limits and procedures of ordinary administration unless they first obtain written authority from the ordinary.

§2. The acts which go beyond the limits and procedures of ordinary administration are to be defined in the statutes; if, however, the statutes do not mention such acts, it is within the competence of the diocesan bishop to determine such acts for persons subject to him after he has heard the finance council.

§3. Unless and to the extent that it is to its own advantage, a juridic person is not held to answer for acts invalidly posited by its administrators. A juridic person, however, is responsible for acts illegitimately but validly posited by its administrators with due regard for the right to sue or to have recourse against administrators who have damaged it.

Can. 1282 — All clerics or lay persons who through a legitimate title take part in the administration of ecclesiastical goods are bound to fulfill their duties in the name of the Church and in accord with the norm of law.

Can. 1283 — Before administrators take office:

1° they must take an oath before the ordinary or his delegate that they will be efficient and faithful administrators;

2° they are to prepare, sign and subsequently renew an accurate and detailed inventory of immovable goods, movable goods, either precious or of significant cultural value, or other goods along with a description and appraisal of them;

3° one copy of this inventory is to be kept in the archives of the administration; the other, in the curial archives; any change whatever which the patrimony may undergo is to be noted on each copy.

Can. 1284 — §1. All administrators are bound to fulfill their office with the diligence of a good householder.

§2. For this reason they must:

1° vigilare ne bona suae curae concredita quoquo modo pereant aut detrimentum capiant, initis in hunc finem, quatenus opus sit, contractibus assecurationis;

2° curare ut proprietas bonorum ecclesiasticorum modis civiliter validis in tuto ponatur;

3° praescripta servare iuris tam canonici quam civilis, aut quae a fundatore vel donatore vel legitima auctoritate imposita sint, ac praesertim cavere ne ex legum civilium inobservantia damnum Ecclesiae obveniat;

4° reditus bonorum ac proventus accurate et iusto tempore exigere exactosque tuto servare et secundum fundatoris mentem aut legitimas normas impendere;

5° foenus vel mutui vel hypothecae causa solvendum, statuto tempore solvere, ipsamque debiti summam capitalem opportune reddendam curare;

6° pecuniam, quae de expensis supersit et utiliter collocari possit, de consensu Ordinarii in fines personae iuridicae occupare;

7° accepti et expensi libros bene ordinatos habere;

8° rationem administrationis singulis exeuntibus annis componere;

9° documenta et instrumenta, quibus Ecclesiae aut instituti iura in bona nituntur, rite ordinare et in archivo convenienti et apto custodire; authentica vero eorum exemplaria, ubi commode fieri potest, in archivo curiae deponere.

§ 3. Provisiones accepti et expensi, ut ab administratoribus quotannis componantur enixe commendatur; iuri autem particulari relinquitur eas praecipere et pressius determinare modos quibus exhibendae sint.

Can. 1285 – Intra limites dumtaxat ordinariae administrationis fas est administratoribus de bonis mobilibus, quae ad patrimonium stabile non pertinent, donationes ad fines pietatis aut christianae caritatis facere.

Can. 1286 – Administratores bonorum:

1° in operarum locatione leges etiam civiles, quae ad laborem et vitam socialem attinent, adamussim servent, iuxta principia ab Ecclesia tradita;

2° iis, qui operam ex condicto praestant, iustam et honestam mercedem tribuant, ita ut iidem suis et suorum necessitatibus convenienter providere valeant.

Can. 1287 – § 1. Reprobata contraria consuetudine, administratores tam clerici quam laici quorumvis bonorum ecclesiasticorum. quae ab Episcopi dioecesani potestate regiminis non sint legitime subducta,

1° take care that none of the goods entrusted to their care is in any way lost or damaged and take out insurance policies for this purpose, insofar as such is necessary;

2° take care that the ownership of ecclesiastical goods is safeguarded through civilly valid methods;

3° observe the prescriptions of both canon and civil law or those imposed by the founder, donor or legitimate authority; they must especially be on guard lest the Church be harmed through the non-observance of civil laws;

4° accurately collect the revenues and income of goods when they are legally due, safeguard them once collected and apply them according to the intention of the founder or according to legitimate norms;

5° pay the interest on a loan or mortgage when it is due and take care that the capital debt itself is repaid in due time;

6° with the consent of the ordinary invest the money which is left over after expenses and which can be profitably allocated for the goals of the juridic person;

7° keep well ordered books of receipts and expenditures;

8° draw up a report on their administration at the end of each year;

9° duly arrange and keep in a suitable and safe archive the documents and deeds upon which are based the rights of the Church or the institution to its goods; deposit authentic copies of them in the archive of the curia when it can be done conveniently.

§3. It is strongly recommended that administrators prepare annual budgets of receipts and expenditures; however, it is left to particular law to issue regulations concerning such budgets and to determine more precisely how they are to be presented.

Can. 1285 — Within the limits of ordinary administration only, it is permissible for administrators to make donations for purposes of piety or Christian charity from movable goods which do not pertain to the stable patrimony.

Can. 1286 — Administrators of goods:

1° are to observe meticulously the civil laws pertaining to labor and social policy according to Church principles in the employment of workers;

2° are to pay employees a just and decent wage so that they may provide appropriately for their needs and those of their family.

Can. 1287 — §1. Both clerical and lay administrators of any ecclesiastical goods whatsoever which have not been legitimately exempted from the governing power of the diocesan bishop are bound by their office to present the

singulis annis officio tenentur rationes Ordinario loci exhibendi, qui eas consilio a rebus oeconomicis examinandas committat.

§ 2. De bonis, quae a fidelibus Ecclesiae offeruntur, administratores rationes fidelibus reddant iuxta normas iure particulari statuendas.

Can. 1288 – Administratores litem nomine personae iuridicae publicae ne inchoent neve contestentur in foro civili, nisi licentiam scripto datam Ordinarii proprii obtinuerint.

Can. 1289 – Quamvis ad administrationem non teneantur titulo officii ecclesiastici, administratores munus susceptum arbitratu suo dimittere nequeunt; quod si ex arbitraria dimissione damnum Ecclesiae obveniat, ad restitutionem tenentur.

TITULUS III
DE CONTRACTIBUS AC PRAESERTIM DE ALIENATIONE

Can. 1290 – Quae ius civile in territorio statuit de contractibus tam in genere, quam in specie et de solutionibus, eadem iure canonico quoad res potestati regiminis Ecclesiae subiectas iisdem cum effectibus serventur, nisi iuri divino contraria sint aut aliud iure canonico caveatur, et firmo praescripto can. 1547.

Can. 1291 – Ad valide alienanda bona, quae personae iuridicae publicae ex legitima assignatione patrimonium stabile constituunt et quorum valor summam iure definitam excedit, requiritur licentia auctoritatis ad normam iuris competentis.

Can. 1292 – § 1. Salvo praescripto can. 638, § 3, cum valor bonorum, quorum alienatio proponitur, continetur intra summam minimam et summam maximam ab Episcoporum conferentia pro sua cuiusque regione definiendas, auctoritas competens, si agatur de personis iuridicis Episcopo dioecesano non subiectis, propriis determinatur statutis; secus, auctoritas competens est Episcopus dioecesanus cum consensu consilii a rebus oeconomicis et collegii consultorum necnon eorum quorum interest. Eorundem quoque consensu eget ipse Episcopus dioecesanus ad bona dioecesis alienanda.

§ 2. Si tamen agatur de rebus quarum valor summam maximam excedit, vel de rebus ex voto Ecclesiae donatis, vel de rebus pretiosis artis vel historiae causa, ad validitatem alienationis requiritur insuper licentia Sanctae Sedis.

local ordinary with an annual report, which in turn he is to present to the finance council for its consideration; any contrary custom is reprobated.

§2. Administrators are to render an account to the faithful concerning the goods offered by the faithful to the Church, according to norms to be determined by particular law.

Can. 1288 — Administrators are neither to initiate nor to contest a law suit on behalf of a public juridic person in civil court unless they obtain the written permission of their own ordinary.

Can. 1289 — Even if they are not bound to administration by the title of an ecclesiastical office, administrators cannot relinquish their responsibilities on their own initiative; if, however, the Church is harmed by such an arbitrary abandonment of duty they are bound to restitution.

TITLE III
CONTRACTS AND ALIENATION IN PARTICULAR

Can. 1290 — Whatever general and specific regulations on contracts and payments are determined in civil law for a given territory are to be observed in canon law with the same effects in a matter which is subject to the governing power of the Church, unless the civil regulations are contrary to divine law or canon law makes some other provision, with due regard for the prescription of can. 1547.

Can. 1291 — The permission of the competent authority according to the norm of law is required in order validly to alienate the goods which through lawful designation constitute the stable patrimony of a public juridic person and whose value exceeds the sum determined in law.

Can. 1292 — §1. With due regard for the prescription of can. 638, §3, when the value of the goods whose alienation is proposed is within the range of the minimum and maximum amounts which are to be determined by the conference of bishops for its region, the competent authority is determined in the group's own statutes when it is a question of juridic persons who are not subject to the diocesan bishop; otherwise, the competent authority is the diocesan bishop with the consent of the finance council, the college of consultors and the parties concerned. The diocesan bishop also needs their consent to alienate the goods of the diocese.

§2. The permission of the Holy See is also required for valid alienation when it is a case of goods whose value exceeds the maximum amount, goods donated to the Church through a vow or goods which are especially valuable due to their artistic or historical value.

§ 3. Si res alienanda sit divisibilis, in petenda licentia pro alienatione exprimi debent partes antea alienatae; secus licentia irrita est.

§ 4. Ii, qui in alienandis bonis consilio vel consensu partem habere debent, ne praebeant consilium vel consensum nisi prius exacte fuerint edocti tam de statu oeconomico personae iuridicae cuius bona alienanda proponuntur, quam de alienationibus iam peractis.

Can. 1293 – § 1. Ad alienanda bona, quorum valor summam minimam definitam excedit, requiritur insuper :

1° iusta causa, veluti urgens necessitas, evidens utilitas, pietas, caritas vel gravis alia ratio pastoralis;

2° aestimatio rei alienandae a peritis scripto facta.

§ 2. Aliae quoque cautelae a legitima auctoritate praescriptae serventur, ut Ecclesiae damnum vitetur.

Can. 1294 – § 1. Res alienari minore pretio ordinarie non debet, quam quod in aestimatione indicatur.

§ 2. Pecunia ex alienatione percepta vel in commodum Ecclesiae caute collocetur vel, iuxta alienationis fines, prudenter erogetur.

Can. 1295 – Requisita ad normam cann. 1291-1294, quibus etiam statuta personarum iuridicarum conformanda sunt, servari debent non solum in alienatione, sed etiam in quolibet negotio, quo condicio patrimonialis personae iuridicae peior fieri possit.

Can. 1296 – Si quando bona ecclesiastica sine debitis quidem sollemnitatibus canonicis alienata fuerint, sed alienatio sit civiliter valida, auctoritatis competentis est decernere, omnibus mature perpensis, an et qualis actio, personalis scilicet vel realis, a quonam et contra quemnam instituenda sit ad Ecclesiae iura vindicanda.

Can. 1297 – Conferentiae Episcoporum est, attentis locorum adiunctis, normas statuere de bonis Ecclesiae locandis, praesertim de licentia a competenti auctoritate ecclesiastica obtinenda.

Can. 1298 – Nisi res sit minimi momenti, bona ecclesiastica propriis administratoribus eorumve propinquis usque ad quartum consanguinitatis vel affinitatis gradum non sunt vendenda aut locanda sine speciali competentis auctoritatis licentia scripto data.

§3. If the object to be alienated is divisible, the parts which have previously been alienated must be mentioned in seeking the permission for alienation; otherwise the permission is invalid.

§4. The persons who must take part in alienating goods through their advice or consent are not to give their advice or consent unless they have first been thoroughly informed concerning the economic situation of the juridic person whose goods are proposed for alienation and concerning previous alienations.

Can. 1293 — §1. To alienate goods whose value exceeds the minimum amount which has been determined, also required are:

1° a just cause such as urgent necessity, evident usefulness, piety, charity or some other serious pastoral reason;

2° a written estimate from experts concerning the value of the object to be alienated.

§2. Other safeguards prescribed by legitimate authority are also to be observed to prevent harm to the Church.

Can. 1294 — §1. Ordinarily an object must not be alienated for a price which is less than that indicated in the estimate.

§2. The money realized from the alienation is either to be invested carefully for the advantage of the Church or wisely expended in accord with the purposes of the alienation.

Can. 1295 — The requirements mentioned in cann. 1291–1294, with which the statutes of juridic persons are to be in conformity, must be observed not only in an alienation but also in any transaction through which the patrimonial condition of a juridic person can be worsened.

Can. 1296 — Whenever ecclesiastical goods have been alienated without the required canonical formalities but the alienation is civilly valid, it is the responsibility of the competent authority, after a thorough consideration of the situation, to decide whether and what type of action, that is, a personal or real action, is to be initiated to vindicate the rights of the Church as well as by whom and against whom such an action is to be initiated.

Can. 1297 — After considering local circumstances, it is the responsibility of the conference of bishops to establish norms concerning the leasing of church goods, especially the permission to be obtained from competent ecclesiastical authority.

Can. 1298 — Unless it is an object of little importance, ecclesiastical goods are not to be sold or leased out to their own administrators or to their relatives up to the fourth degree of consanguinity or affinity without the special written permission of the competent authority.

TITULUS IV
DE PIIS VOLUNTATIBUS IN GENERE
ET DE PIIS FUNDATIONIBUS

Can. 1299 – § 1. Qui ex iure naturae et canonico libere valet de suis bonis statuere, potest ad causas pias, sive per actum inter vivos sive per actum mortis causa, bona relinquere.

§ 2. In dispositionibus mortis causa in bonum Ecclesiae serventur, si fieri possit, sollemnitates iuris civilis; quae si omissae fuerint, heredes moneri debent de obligatione, qua tenentur, adimplendi testatoris voluntatem.

Can. 1300 – Voluntates fidelium facultates suas in pias causas donantium vel relinquentium, sive per actum inter vivos sive per actum mortis causa, legitime acceptatae, diligentissime impleantur etiam circa modum administrationis et erogationis bonorum, firmo praescripto can. 1301, § 3.

Can. 1301 – § 1. Ordinarius omnium piarum voluntatum tam mortis causa quam inter vivos exsecutor est.

§ 2. Hoc ex iure Ordinarius vigilare potest ac debet, etiam per visitationem, ut piae voluntates impleantur, eique ceteri exsecutores, perfuncti munere, reddere rationem tenentur.

§ 3. Clausulae huic Ordinarii iuri contrariae, ultimis voluntatibus adiectae, tamquam non appositae habeantur.

Can. 1302 – § 1. Qui bona ad pias causas sive per actum inter vivos sive ex testamento fiduciarie accepit, debet de sua fiducia Ordinarium certiorem reddere, eique omnia istiusmodi bona mobilia vel immobilia cum oneribus adiunctis indicare; quod si donator id expresse et omnino prohibuerit, fiduciam ne acceptet.

§ 2. Ordinarius debet exigere ut bona fiduciaria in tuto collocentur, itemque vigilare pro exsecutione piae voluntatis ad normam can. 1301.

§ 3. Bonis fiduciariis alicui sodali instituti religiosi aut societatis vitae apostolicae commissis, si quidem bona sint attributa loco seu dioecesi eorumve incolis aut piis causis iuvandis, Ordinarius, de quo in §§ 1 et 2, est loci Ordinarius; secus est Superior maior in instituto clericali iuris pontificii et in clericalibus societatibus vitae apostolicae iuris pontificii, aut Ordinarius eiusdem sodalis proprius in aliis institutis religiosis.

TITLE IV
PIOUS WILLS IN GENERAL AND PIOUS FOUNDATIONS

Can. 1299 — §1. Those who in virtue of natural and canon law are free to dispose of their own goods can leave goods for pious causes through an act which becomes effective during life or at death.

§2. If it is possible, the formalities of civil law are to be observed in the dispositions made for the good of the Church on the occasion of death; if such formalities have been neglected, the heirs must be advised of the obligation by which they are bound to fulfill the will of the testator.

Can. 1300 — The legitimately accepted wills of the faithful who give or leave their resources to pious causes, whether through an act which becomes effective during life or at death, are to be fulfilled with the greatest diligence even as regards the manner of the administration and distribution of the goods, with due regard for the prescription of can. 1301, §3.

Can. 1301 — §1. The ordinary is the executor of all pious wills whether they be made during life or on the occasion of death.

§2. In virtue of this right the ordinary can and must exercise vigilance, even through visitation, so that pious wills are fulfilled; other executors must render him an account concerning the performance of their duty.

§3. Stipulations added to last wills and contrary to this right of the ordinary are to be considered non-existent.

Can. 1302 — §1. A person who accepts the role of trustee for goods bequeathed for pious causes either through an act made during life or through a last will and testament must inform the ordinary of this trust and also indicate all such goods, whether immovable or movable, along with the obligations attached to them; if, however, the donor expressly and completely prohibits this, the person is not to accept the trust.

§2. The ordinary must demand that the goods held in trust be safeguarded and must exercise vigilance on behalf of the execution of the pious will in accord with the norm of can. 1301.

§3. When goods committed in trust to some member of a religious institute or a society of apostolic life have been designated for the assistance of a place or diocese or their inhabitants or pious causes, the ordinary mentioned in §§1 and 2 is the local ordinary; otherwise, it is the major superior in a clerical institute of pontifical right and in a clerical society of apostolic life of pontifical right or the proper ordinary of a member in other religious institutes.

Can. 1303 – § 1. Nomine piarum fundationum in iure veniunt :

1° *piae fundationes autonomae,* scilicet universitates rerum ad fines de quibus in can. 114, § 2 destinatae et a competenti auctoritate ecclesiastica in personam iuridicam erectae;

2° *piae fundationes non autonomae,* scilicet bona temporalia alicui personae iuridicae publicae quoquo modo data cum onere in diuturnum tempus, iure particulari determinandum, ex reditibus annuis Missas celebrandi aliasque praefinitas functiones ecclesiasticas peragendi, aut fines de quibus in can. 114, § 2 aliter persequendi.

§ 2. Bona piae fundationis non autonomae, si concredita fuerint personae iuridicae Episcopo dioecesano subiectae, expleto tempore, ad institutum de quo in can. 1274, § 1 destinari debent, nisi alia fuerit fundatoris voluntas expresse manifestata; secus ipsi personae iuridicae cedunt.

Can. 1304 – § 1. Ut fundatio a persona iuridica valide acceptari possit, requiritur licentia Ordinarii in scriptis data; qui eam ne praebeat, antequam legitime compererit personam iuridicam tum novo oneri suscipiendo, tum iam susceptis satisfacere posse; maximeque caveat ut reditus omnino respondeant oneribus adiunctis, secundum cuiusque loci vel regionis morem.

§ 2. Ulteriores condiciones ad constitutionem et acceptationem fundationum quod attinet, iure particulari definiantur.

Can. 1305 – Pecunia et bona mobilia, dotationis nomine assignata, statim in loco tuto ab Ordinario approbando deponantur eum in finem, ut eadem pecunia vel bonorum mobilium pretium custodiantur et quam primum caute et utiliter secundum prudens eiusdem Ordinarii iudicium, auditis et iis quorum interest et proprio a rebus oeconomicis consilio, collocentur in commodum eiusdem fundationis cum expressa et individua mentione oneris.

Can. 1306 – § 1. Fundationes, etiam viva voce factae, scripto consignentur.

§ 2. Alterum tabularum exemplar in curiae archivo, alterum in archivo personae iuridicae ad quam fundatio spectat, tuto asserventur.

Can. 1307 – § 1. Servatis praescriptis cann. 1300-1302, et 1287, onerum ex piis fundationibus incumbentium tabella conficiatur, quae in loco patenti exponatur, ne obligationes adimplendae in oblivionem cadant.

Can. 1303 — §1. In the law under the title of pious foundations are included:

1° *autonomous pious foundations*, that is, aggregates of things destined for all the purposes mentioned in can. 114, §2 and erected as a juridic person by competent ecclesiastical authority;

2° *non-autonomous pious foundations*, that is, temporal goods given in some manner to a public juridic person with the obligation for a long time, to be determined by particular law, to arrange from the annual income for the celebration of Masses or other specified ecclesiastical functions or otherwise to pursue the purposes mentioned in can. 114, §2.

§2. If the goods of a non-autonomous pious foundation are entrusted to a juridic person subject to a diocesan bishop, they are to be remanded to the institute mentioned in can. 1274, §1 when the specified period of time is completed unless another intention of the founder was expressly manifest; otherwise they belong to the juridic person itself.

Can. 1304 — §1. In order for a foundation to be validly accepted by a juridic person the written permission of the ordinary is required; and he is not to grant that permission until he legitimately determines that the juridic person can fulfill the new obligation as well as those already accepted; he should most specially take care that the income entirely corresponds to the attached obligations in accord with the customs of the place or region.

§2. Further conditions for constituting and accepting foundations are to be defined in particular law.

Can. 1305 — Money and movable goods assigned to an endowment are immediately to be deposited in a safe place to be approved by the ordinary so that the money or the value of the movable goods will be safeguarded; as soon as possible, these goods are to be invested cautiously and profitably for the benefit of the foundation with express and specific mention made of the burdens attached to the endowment; this investment is to be made in accord with the prudent judgment of the ordinary who is to consult the interested parties as well as his finance council on this matter.

Can. 1306 — §1. Foundations, even if made orally, are to be put into writing.

§2. A copy of the terms of the foundation is to be securely filed in the curial archive and another copy is to be securely filed in the archive of the juridic person to whom the foundation pertains.

Can. 1307 — §1. With due regard for the prescriptions of cann. 1300–1302 and can. 1287, a list of obligations arising from pious foundations is to be drawn up and retained in an obvious place lest the obligations to be fulfilled be neglected.

§ 2. Praeter librum de quo in can. 958, § 1, alter liber retineatur et apud parochum vel rectorem servetur, in quo singula onera eorumque adimpletio et eleemosynae adnotentur.

Can. 1308 – § 1. Reductio onerum Missarum, ex iusta tantum et necessaria causa facienda, reservatur Sedi Apostolicae, salvis praescriptis quae sequuntur.

§ 2. Si in tabulis fundationum id expresse caveatur, Ordinarius ob imminutos reditus onera Missarum reducere valet.

§ 3. Episcopo dioecesano competit potestas reducendi ob deminutionem reditum, quamdiu causa perduret, ad rationem eleemosynae in dioecesi legitime vigentis, Missas legatorum vel quoquo modo fundatas, quae sint per se stantia, dummodo nemo sit qui obligatione teneatur et utiliter cogi possit ad eleemosynae augmentum faciendum.

§ 4. Eidem competit potestas reducendi onera seu legata Missarum gravantia institutum ecclesiasticum, si reditus insufficientes evaserint ad finem proprium eiusdem instituti congruenter consequendum.

§ 5. Iisdem potestatibus, de quibus in §§ 3 et 4, gaudet supremus Moderator instituti religiosi clericalis iuris pontificii.

Can. 1309 – Iisdem auctoritatibus, de quibus in can. 1308, potestas insuper competit transferendi, congrua de causa, onera Missarum in dies, ecclesias vel altaria diversa ab illis, quae in fundationibus sunt statuta.

Can. 1310 – § 1. Fidelium voluntatum pro piis causis reductio, moderatio, commutatio, si fundator potestatem hanc Ordinario expresse concesserit, potest ab eodem fieri ex iusta tantum et necessaria causa.

§ 2. Si exsecutio onerum impositorum, ob imminutos reditus aliamve causam, nulla administratorum culpa, impossibilis evaserit, Ordinarius, auditis iis quorum interest et proprio consilio a rebus oeconomicis atque servata, meliore quo fieri potest modo, fundatoris voluntate, poterit eadem onera aeque imminuere, excepta Missarum reductione, quae praescriptis can. 1308 regitur.

§ 3. In ceteris casibus recurrendum est ad Sedem Apostolicam.

§2. Besides the book referred to in can. 958, §1, another book is to be kept by the pastor or rector in which the individual obligations, their fulfillment and the offerings are noted.

Can. 1308 — §1. The reduction of Mass obligations, to be done only for a just and necessary reason, is reserved to the Apostolic See with due regard for the following prescriptions.

§2. If it is expressly provided for in the articles of the foundation, the ordinary is empowered to reduce Mass obligations because of diminished income.

§3. The diocesan bishop has the power, when income diminishes, of reducing Masses from independent legacies or foundations of any kind to conform to the level of the offering legitimately established in the diocese for as long as the reason for this reduction continues, provided that there is no one who is bound by the obligation of increasing the offering and can be successfully induced to do so.

§4. The same authority has the power of reducing the obligations or legacies for Masses which bind ecclesiastical institutes if the income proves insufficient to pursue successfully the proper goal of the ecclesiastical institute.

§5. These same powers mentioned in §§3 and 4 are also enjoyed by the supreme moderator of clerical institutes of pontifical right.

Can. 1309 — The same authorities mentioned in can. 1308 also enjoy the power of transferring for a suitable reason Mass obligations to days, churches or altars different from those determined in the foundation.

Can. 1310 — §1. The ordinary, only for a just and necessary reason, may reduce, moderate or commute the wills of the faithful for pious causes provided such power has been expressly granted him by the founder.

§2. If, through no fault of the administrator, the fulfillment of the obligations becomes impossible due to diminished income or some other reason, the ordinary can diminish them equitably after consulting the interested parties and his finance council, with due regard for the will of the founder as much as possible; this is not true for Mass obligations, whose reduction is governed by the prescriptions of can. 1308.

§3. In other cases recourse is to be made to the Apostolic See.

LIBER VI
DE SANCTIONIBUS IN ECCLESIA

PARS I
DE DELICTIS ET POENIS IN GENERE

TITULUS I
DE DELICTORUM PUNITIONE GENERATIM

Can. 1311 – Nativum et proprium Ecclesiae ius est christifideles delinquentes poenalibus sanctionibus coercere.

Can. 1312 – § 1. Sanctiones poenales in Ecclesia sunt:

1° poenae medicinales seu censurae, quae in cann. 1331-1333 recensentur;

2° poenae expiatoriae, de quibus in can. 1336.

§ 2. Lex alias poenas expiatorias constituere potest, quae christifidelem aliquo bono spirituali vel temporali privent et supernaturali Ecclesiae fini sint consentaneae.

§ 3. Praeterea remedia poenalia et paenitentiae adhibentur, illa quidem praesertim ad delicta praecavenda, hae potius ad poenam substituendam vel augendam.

TITULUS II
DE LEGE POENALI AC DE PRAECEPTO POENALI

Can. 1313 – § 1. Si post delictum commissum lex mutetur, applicanda est lex reo favorabilior.

§ 2. Quod si lex posterior tollat legem vel saltem poenam, haec statim cessat.

BOOK VI
SANCTIONS IN THE CHURCH

PART I
OFFENSES AND PENALTIES IN GENERAL

TITLE I
THE PUNISHMENT OF OFFENSES IN GENERAL

Can. 1311 — The Church has an innate and proper right to coerce offending members of the Christian faithful by means of penal sanctions.

Can. 1312 — §1. The following penal sanctions exist in the Church:

1° medicinal penalties or censures enumerated in cann. 1331–1333;

2° expiatory penalties enumerated in can. 1336.

§2. The law can establish other expiatory penalties which deprive a believer of some spiritual or temporal good and are consistent with the supernatural end of the Church.

§3. Penal remedies and penances are likewise employed; the former especially in order to prevent offenses, the latter rather to substitute for or to increase a penalty.

TITLE II
PENAL LAW AND PENAL PRECEPTS

Can. 1313 — §1. If a law is changed after an offense has been committed the law which is more favorable to the accused is to be applied.

§2. But if the second law abolishes the first law or at least its penalty, the penalty immediately ceases.

471

Can. 1314 – Poena plerumque est ferendae sententiae, ita ut reum non teneat, nisi postquam irrogata sit; est autem latae sententiae, ita ut in eam incurratur ipso facto commissi delicti, si lex vel praeceptum id expresse statuat.

Can. 1315 – § 1. Qui legislativam habet potestatem, potest etiam poenales leges ferre; potest autem suis legibus etiam legem divinam vel legem ecclesiasticam, a superiore auctoritate latam, congrua poena munire, servatis suae competentiae limitibus ratione territorii vel personarum.

§ 2. Lex ipsa potest poenam determinare vel prudenti iudicis aestimatione determinandam relinquere.

§ 3. Lex particularis potest etiam poenis universali lege constitutis in aliquod delictum alias addere; id autem ne faciat, nisi ex gravissima necessitate. Quod si lex universalis indeterminatam vel facultativam poenam comminetur, lex particularis potest etiam in illius locum poenam determinatam vel obligatoriam constituere.

Can. 1316 – Curent Episcopi dioecesani ut, quatenus fieri potest, in eadem civitate vel regione uniformes ferantur, si quae ferendae sint, poenales leges.

Can. 1317 – Poenae eatenus constituantur, quatenus vere necessariae sint ad aptius providendum ecclesiasticae disciplinae. Dimissio autem e statu clericali lege particulari constitui nequit.

Can. 1318 – Latae sententiae poenas ne comminetur legislator, nisi forte in singularia quaedam delicta dolosa, quae vel graviori esse possint scandalo vel efficaciter puniri poenis ferendae sententiae non possint; censuras autem, praesertim excommunicationem, ne constituat, nisi maxima cum moderatione et in sola delicta graviora.

Can. 1319 – § 1. Quatenus quis potest vi potestatis regiminis in foro externo praecepta imponere, eatenus potest etiam poenas determinatas, exceptis expiatoriis perpetuis, per praeceptum comminari.

§ 2. Praeceptum poenale ne feratur, nisi re mature perpensa, et iis servatis, quae in cann. 1317 et 1318 de legibus particularibus statuuntur.

Can. 1320 – In omnibus in quibus religiosi subsunt Ordinario loci, possunt ab eodem poenis coerceri.

Can. 1314 — Ordinarily a penalty is to be inflicted by a sentence (*ferendae sententiae*) so that it does not bind the guilty party until after it has been imposed; however, a penalty is incurred automatically by the very commission of the offense (*latae sententiae*) if the law or precept expressly determines this.

Can. 1315 — §1. Those who have legislative power can also issue penal laws; within the existing limits of their competence by reason of territory or persons, they can by means of their own laws safeguard with an appropriate penalty any divine law or an ecclesiastical law made by a higher authority.

§2. The law itself can determine a penalty or its determination can be left to the prudent assessment of a judge.

§3. Particular law can also add other penalties to the penalties established in universal law for some offense, but this is not to be done except for the most serious necessity. If the universal law threatens a penalty which is indeterminate or facultative, however, particular law can establish in its place a determinate or obligatory penalty.

Can. 1316 — Diocesan bishops are to see to it that penal laws if they are to be enacted are uniform in the same city or region to the extent that this is possible.

Can. 1317 — Penalties should be established to the extent to which they are truly necessary to provide more suitably for ecclesiastical discipline. Dismissal from the clerical state, however, cannot be established by particular law.

Can. 1318 — A legislator is not to threaten automatic penalties (*latae sententiae*) unless perhaps against certain particularly treacherous offenses which either can result in more serious scandal or cannot be effectively punished by means of inflicted penalties (*ferendae sententiae*); a legislator is not to establish censures, especially excommunication, except with the greatest moderation and only for more serious offenses.

Can. 1319 — §1. To the extent that one can impose precepts in the external forum by virtue of the power of governance, to that same extent one can also threaten determinate penalties through a precept with the exception of perpetual expiatory penalties.

§2. A penal precept is not to be issued without a mature consideration of the matter and without observing what is stated in cann. 1317 and 1318 concerning particular laws.

Can. 1320 — Religious can be coerced by penalties by the local ordinary in all matters in which they are subject to him.

TITULUS III
DE SUBIECTO POENALIBUS SANCTIONIBUS OBNOXIO

Can. 1321 – § 1. Nemo punitur, nisi externa legis vel praecepti violatio, ab eo commissa, sit graviter imputabilis ex dolo vel ex culpa.

§ 2. Poena lege vel praecepto statuta is tenetur, qui legem vel praeceptum deliberate violavit; qui vero id egit ex omissione debitae dili-
gentiae, non punitur, nisi lex vel praeceptum aliter caveat.

§ 3. Posita externa violatione, imputabilitas praesumitur, nisi aliud
appareat.

Can. 1322 – Qui habitualiter rationis usu carent, etsi legem vel
praeceptum violaverint dum sani videbantur, delicti incapaces habentur.

Can. 1323 – Nulli poenae est obnoxius qui, cum legem vel praeceptum violavit:

1° sextum decimum aetatis annum nondum explevit;

2° sine culpa ignoravit se legem vel praeceptum violare; ignoran-
tiae autem inadvertentia et error aequiparantur;

3° egit ex vi physica vel ex casu fortuito, quem praevidere vel cui
praeviso occurrere non potuit;

4° metu gravi, quamvis relative tantum, coactus egit, aut ex necessitate vel gravi incommodo, nisi tamen actus sit intrinsece malus aut
vergat in animarum damnum;

5° legitimae tutelae causa contra iniustum sui vel alterius aggressorem egit, debitum servans moderamen;

6° rationis usu carebat, firmis praescriptis cann. 1324, § 1, n. 2
et 1325;

7° sine culpa putavit aliquam adesse ex circumstantiis, de quibus
in nn. 4 vel 5.

Can. 1324 – § 1. Violationis auctor non eximitur a poena, sed poena
lege vel praecepto statuta temperari debet vel in eius locum paenitentia
adhiberi, si delictum patratum sit:

1° ab eo, qui rationis usum imperfectum tantum habuerit;

2° ab eo qui rationis usu carebat propter ebrietatem aliamve simi-
lem mentis perturbationem, quae culpabilis fuerit;

3° ex gravi passionis aestu, qui non omnem tamen mentis delibera-
tionem et voluntatis consensum praecesserit et impedierit, et dummodo
passio ipsa ne fuerit voluntarie excitata vel nutrita;

TITLE III

THOSE SUBJECT TO PENAL SANCTIONS

Can. 1321 — §1. No one is punished unless the external violation of a law or a precept committed by the person is seriously imputable to that person by reason of malice or culpability.

§2. A person who has deliberately violated a law or a precept is bound by the penalty stated in that law or that precept; unless a law or a precept provides otherwise, a person who has violated that law or that precept through a lack of necessary diligence is not punished.

§3. Unless it is otherwise evident, imputability is presumed whenever an external violation has occurred.

Can. 1322 — Persons who habitually lack the use of reason are considered incapable of an offense even if they have violated a law or a precept while appearing to be sane.

Can. 1323 — The following are not subject to penalties when they have violated a law or precept:

1° a person who has not yet completed the sixteenth year of age;

2° a person who without any fault was unaware of violating a law or precept; however, inadvertence and error are equivalent to ignorance;

3° a person who acted out of physical force or in virtue of a mere accident which could neither be foreseen nor prevented when foreseen;

4° a person who acted out of grave fear, even if only relatively grave, or out of necessity or out of serious inconvenience unless the act is intrinsically evil or verges on harm to souls;

5° a person who for the sake of legitimate self-defense or defense of another acted against an unjust aggressor with due moderation;

6° a person who lacked the use of reason with due regard for the prescriptions of cann. 1324, §1, n. 2 and 1325;

7° a person who without any fault felt that the circumstances in nn. 4 or 5 were verified.

Can. 1324 — §1. One who violates a law or precept is not exempt from a penalty but the penalty set by law or precept must be tempered or a penance substituted in its place if the offense was committed:

1° by a person with only the imperfect use of reason;

2° by a person who lacked the use of reason due to drunkenness or another similar mental disturbance which was culpable;

3° in the serious heat of passion which did not precede and impede all deliberation of mind and consent of will as long as the passion itself had not been voluntarily stirred up or fostered;

4° a minore, qui aetatem sedecim annorum explevit;

5° ab eo, qui metu gravi, quamvis relative tantum, coactus est, aut ex necessitate vel gravi incommodo, si delictum sit intrinsece malum vel in animarum damnum vergat;

6° ab eo, qui legitimae tutelae causa contra iniustum sui vel alterius aggressorem egit, nec tamen debitum servavit moderamen;

7° adversus aliquem graviter et iniuste provocantem;

8° ab eo, qui per errorem, ex sua tamen culpa, putavit aliquam adesse ex circumstantiis, de quibus in can. 1323, nn. 4 vel 5;

9° ab eo, qui sine culpa ignoravit poenam legi vel praecepto esse adnexam;

10° ab eo, qui egit sine plena imputabilitate, dummodo haec gravis permanserit.

§ 2. Idem potest iudex facere, si qua alia adsit circumstantia, quae delicti gravitatem deminuat.

§ 3. In circumstantiis, de quibus in § 1, reus poena latae sententiae non tenetur.

Can. 1325 – Ignorantia crassa vel supina vel affectata numquam considerari potest in applicandis praescriptis cann. 1323 et 1324; item ebrietas aliaeve mentis perturbationes, si sint de industria ad delictum patrandum vel excusandum quaesitae, et passio, quae voluntarie excitata vel nutrita sit.

Can. 1326 – § 1. Iudex gravius punire potest quam lex vel praeceptum statuit:

1° eum, qui post condemnationem vel poenae declarationem ita delinquere pergit, ut ex adiunctis prudenter eius pertinacia in mala voluntate conici possit;

2° eum, qui in dignitate aliqua constitutus est, vel qui auctoritate aut officio abusus est ad delictum patrandum;

3° reum, qui, cum poena in delictum culposum constituta sit, eventum praevidit et nihilominus cautiones ad eum vitandum omisit, quas diligens quilibet adhibuisset.

§ 2. In casibus, de quibus in § 1, si poena constituta sit latae sententiae, alia poena addi potest vel paenitentia.

Can. 1327 – Lex particularis potest alias circumstantias eximentes, attenuantes vel aggravantes, praeter casus in cann. 1323-1326, statuere, sive generali norma, sive pro singulis delictis. Item in praecepto possunt circumstantiae statui, quae a poena praecepto constituta eximant, vel eam attenuent vel aggravent.

4° by a minor who has completed the age of sixteen years;

5° by a person who was forced through grave fear, even if only relatively grave, or through necessity or serious inconvenience, if the offense was intrinsically evil or verged on harm to souls;

6° by a person who for the sake of legitimate self-defense or defense of another acted against an unjust aggressor but without due moderation;

7° against one gravely and unjustly provoking it;

8° by one who erroneously yet culpably thought one of the circumstances in can. 1323, nn. 4 and 5 was verified;

9° by one who without any fault was unaware that a penalty was attached to the law or precept;

10° by one who acted without full imputability provided there was grave imputability.

§2. A judge can act in the same manner if any other circumstance exists which would lessen the seriousness of the offense.

§3. An accused is not bound by an automatic penalty (*latae sententiae*) in the presence of any of the circumstances enumerated in §1.

Can. 1325 — Crass, supine or affected ingnorance can never be considered in applying the prescriptions of cann. 1323 and 1324; the same is true for drunkenness and other mental disturbances if they are deliberately induced to commit or excuse the offense; this is also true for passion which is deliberately aroused or fostered.

Can. 1326 — §1. A judge can punish more severely than a law or a precept has stated:

1° a person who after condemnation or after a declaration of a penalty still commits an offense so as to be prudently presumed to be in continuing bad will in light of the circumstances;

2° a person who has been given some dignified position or who has abused authority or office in order to commit the offense;

3° an accused who although a penalty has been established against a culpable offense, foresaw what was to happen yet nonetheless did not take the precautions which any diligent person would have employed to avoid it.

§2. If the penalty established is an automatic one (*latae sententiae*), another penalty or a penance can be added in those cases mentioned in §1.

Can. 1327 — Particular law can determine other exempting, mitigating or aggravating circumstances besides the cases in cann. 1323–1326 either by general norm or for individual offenses. Furthermore, circumstances can be determined in a precept which exempt or mitigate or increase the penalty determined in a precept.

Can. 1328 – § 1. Qui aliquid ad delictum patrandum egit vel omisit, nec tamen, praeter suam voluntatem, delictum consummavit, non tenetur poena in delictum consummatum statuta, nisi lex vel praeceptum aliter caveat.

§ 2. Quod si actus vel omissiones natura sua ad delicti exsecutionem conducant, auctor potest paenitentiae vel remedio poenali subici, nisi sponte ab incepta delicti exsecutione destiterit. Si autem scandalum aliudve grave damnum vel periculum evenerit, auctor, etsi sponte destiterit, iusta potest poena puniri, leviore tamen quam quae in delictum consummatum constituta est.

Can. 1329 – § 1. Qui communi delinquendi consilio in delictum concurrunt, neque in lege vel praecepto expresse nominantur, si poenae ferendae sententiae in auctorem principalem constitutae sint, iisdem poenis subiciuntur vel aliis eiusdem vel minoris gravitatis.

§ 2. In poenam latae sententiae delicto adnexam incurrunt complices, qui in lege vel praecepto non nominantur, si sine eorum opera delictum patratum non esset, et poena sit talis naturae, ut ipsos afficere possit; secus poenis ferendae sententiae puniri possunt.

Can. 1330 – Delictum quod in declaratione consistat vel in alia voluntatis vel doctrinae vel scientiae manifestatione, tamquam non consummatum censendum est, si nemo eam declarationem vel manifestationem percipiat.

TITULUS IV
DE POENIS ALIISQUE PUNITIONIBUS

CAPUT I
DE CENSURIS

Can. 1331 – § 1. Excommunicatus vetatur:

1° ullam habere participationem ministerialem in celebrandis Eucharistiae Sacrificio vel quibuslibet aliis cultus caerimoniis;

2° sacramenta vel sacramentalia celebrare et sacramenta recipere;

3° ecclesiasticis officiis vel ministeriis vel muneribus quibuslibet fungi vel actus regiminis ponere.

Can. 1328 — §1. A person who has done or omitted something in order to commit an offense but, unwittingly, has not completed it, is not bound by the penalty stated for a completed delict unless the law or precept provides otherwise.

§2. But if such acts or omissions are of their nature conducive to the execution of an offense, their author can be subjected to a penance or a penal remedy unless the author spontaneously ceased from the execution of the offense which had been begun. If, however, scandal or some serious injury or danger has occurred, the author can be punished with a just penalty even if he or she had ceased spontaneously; but it is to be lighter than that which is established for a completed offense.

Can. 1329 — §1. If the penalties established against the principal author are inflicted ones (*ferendae sententiae*), then those who collaborate to commit an offense through a common conspiracy but who are not expressly named in a law or a precept are subject to the same penalties or to other penalties of the same or lesser severity.

§2. Accomplices who are not named in a law or in a precept incur an automatic penalty (*latae sententiae*) attached to an offense if it would not have been committed without their efforts and the penalty is of such a nature that it can punish them; otherwise, they can be punished by inflicted penalties (*ferendae sententiae*).

Can. 1330 — An offense which consists of some declaration or of some other manifestation of will, doctrine or knowledge is not to be considered completed if no one perceives such a declaration or manifestation.

TITLE IV
PENALTIES AND OTHER PUNISHMENTS

CHAPTER I
CENSURES

Can. 1331 — §1. An excommunicated person is forbidden:

1° to have any ministerial participation in celebrating the Eucharistic Sacrifice or in any other ceremonies whatsoever of public worship;

2° to celebrate the sacraments and sacramentals and to receive the sacraments;

3° to discharge any ecclesiastical offices, ministries or functions whatsoever, or to place acts of governance.

§ 2. Quod si excommunicatio irrogata vel declarata sit, reus :

1° si agere velit contra praescriptum § 1, n. 1, est arcendus aut a liturgica actione est cessandum, nisi gravis obstet causa ;

2° invalide ponit actus regiminis, qui ad normam § 1, n. 3, sunt illiciti ;

3° vetatur frui privilegiis antea concessis :

4° nequit valide consequi dignitatem, officium aliudve munus in Ecclesia ;

5° fructus dignitatis, officii, muneris cuiuslibet, pensionis, quam quidem habeat in Ecclesia, non facit suos.

Can. 1332 – Interdictus tenetur vetitis, de quibus in can. 1331, § 1, nn. 1 et 2 ; quod si interdictum irrogatum vel declaratum sit, praescriptum can. 1331, § 2, n. 1 servandum est.

Can. 1333 – § 1. Suspensio, quae clericos tantum afficere potest, vetat :

1° vel omnes vel aliquos actus potestatis ordinis ;

2° vel omnes vel aliquos actus potestatis regiminis ;

3° exercitium vel omnium vel aliquorum iurium vel munerum officio inhaerentium.

§ 2. In lege vel praecepto statui potest, ut post sententiam condemnatoriam vel declaratoriam actus regiminis suspensus valide ponere nequeat.

§ 3. Vetitum numquam afficit :

1° officia vel regiminis potestatem, quae non sint sub potestate Superioris poenam constituentis ;

2° ius habitandi, si quod reus ratione officii habeat ;

3° ius administrandi bona, quae ad ipsius suspensi officium forte pertineant, si poena sit latae sententiae.

§ 4. Suspensio vetans fructus, stipendium, pensiones aliave eiusmodi percipere, obligationem secumfert restituendi quidquid illegitime, quamvis bona fide, perceptum sit.

Can. 1334 – § 1. Suspensionis ambitus, intra limites canone praecedenti statutos, aut ipsa lege vel praecepto definitur, aut sententia vel decreto quo poena irrogatur.

§ 2. Lex, non autem praeceptum, potest latae sententiae suspensionem, nulla addita determinatione vel limitatione, constituere ; eiusmodi autem poena omnes effectus habet, qui in can. 1333, § 1 recensentur.

§2. If the excommunication has been imposed or declared, the guilty party:

1° wishing to act against the prescriptions of §1, n. 1, is to be prevented from doing so or the liturgical action is to stop unless a serious cause intervenes;

2° invalidly places acts of governance which are only illicit in accord with the norms of §1, n. 3;

3° is forbidden to enjoy privileges formerly granted;

4° cannot validly acquire a dignity, office or other function in the Church;

5° cannot appropriate the revenues from any dignity, office, function or pension in the Church.

Can. 1332 — An interdicted person is bound by the prohibitions of can. 1331, §1, nn. 1 and 2; if, however, the interdict has been imposed or declared, the prescription of can. 1331, §2, n. 1, is to be observed.

Can. 1333 — §1. A suspension, which can affect clerics alone, forbids:

1° either all or some acts of the power of orders;

2° either all or some acts of the power of governance;

3° the exercise of either all or some rights or functions which are attached to an office.

§2. It can be stated in a law or a precept that a suspended cleric cannot validly place acts of governance after a condemnatory or declaratory sentence.

§3. A prohibition never affects:

1° the offices or the power of governance which are not subject to the power of the superior who establishes the penalty;

2° the right to a dwelling place which the accused may have by reason of his office;

3° the right to administer goods which may pertain to the office of the suspended cleric himself if the penalty is an automatic one (*latae sententiae*).

§4. A suspension forbidding one to collect revenues, stipends, pensions or any other such thing carries with it an obligation to make restitution for anything illegitimately collected even in good faith.

Can. 1334 — §1. Within the limits stated in the preceding canon, the extent of the suspension is defined by the law or precept itself or by the sentence or decree by which it is imposed.

§2. A law but not a precept can establish an automatic suspension (*latae sententiae*) without any further determination or limitation; such a penalty has all the effects enumerated in can. 1333, §1.

Can. 1335 – Si censura vetet celebrare sacramenta vel sacramentalia vel ponere actum regiminis, vetitum suspenditur, quoties id necessarium sit ad consulendum fidelibus in mortis periculo constitutis; quod si censura latae sententiae non sit declarata, vetitum praeterea suspenditur, quoties fidelis petit sacramentum vel sacramentale vel actum regiminis; id autem petere ex qualibet iusta causa licet.

Caput II

DE POENIS EXPIATORIIS

Can. 1336 – § 1. Poenae expiatoriae, quae delinquentem afficere possunt aut in perpetuum aut in tempus praefinitum aut in tempus indeterminatum, praeter alias, quas forte lex constituerit, hae sunt:

1° prohibitio vel praescriptio commorandi in certo loco vel territorio;

2° privatio potestatis, officii, muneris, iuris, privilegii, facultatis, gratiae, tituli, insignis, etiam mere honorifici;

3° prohibitio ea exercendi, quae sub n. 2 recensentur, vel prohibitio ea in certo loco vel extra certum locum exercendi; quae prohibitiones numquam sunt sub poena nullitatis;

4° translatio poenalis ad aliud officium;

5° dimissio e statu clericali.

§ 2. Latae sententiae eae tantum poenae expiatoriae esse possunt, quae in § 1, n. 3 recensentur.

Can. 1337 – § 1. Prohibitio commorandi in certo loco vel territorio sive clericos sive religiosos afficere potest; praescriptio autem commorandi, clericos saeculares et, intra limites constitutionum, religiosos.

§ 2. Ut praescriptio commorandi in certo loco vel territorio irrogetur, accedat oportet consensus Ordinarii illius loci, nisi agatur de domo extradioecesanis quoque clericis paenitentibus vel emendandis destinata.

Can. 1338 – § 1. Privationes et prohibitiones, quae in can. 1336, § 1, nn. 2 et 3 recensentur, numquam afficiunt potestates, officia, munera, iura, privilegia, facultates, gratias, titulos, insignia, quae non sint sub potestate Superioris poenam constituentis.

§ 2. Potestatis ordinis privatio dari nequit, sed tantum prohibitio eam vel aliquos eius actus exercendi; item dari nequit privatio graduum academicorum.

§ 3. De prohibitionibus, quae in can. 1336, § 1, n. 3 indicantur, norma servanda est, quae de censuris datur in can. 1335.

Can. 1335 — If a censure prohibits the celebration of the sacraments or sacramentals or the placing of an act of governance, the prohibition is suspended whenever it is necessary to take care of the faithful who are in danger of death; and if an automatic censure (*latae sententiae*) is not a declared one, the prohibition is also suspended whenever a member of the faithful requests a sacrament, a sacramental or act of governance; this request can be made for any just cause whatsoever.

Chapter II
EXPIATORY PENALTIES

Can. 1336 — §1. Besides other penalties which the law may establish, the following are expiatory penalties which can punish an offender in perpetuity, for a prescribed time or for an indeterminate time:

1° a prohibition or an order concerning living in a certain place or territory;

2° deprivation of power, office, function, right, privilege, faculty, favor, title or insignia, even merely honorary;

3° a prohibition against exercising those things mentioned in n. 2 or a prohibition against exercising them in a certain place or outside a certain place; which prohibitions are never under pain of nullity;

4° a penal transfer to another office;

5° dismissal from the clerical state.

§2. The only expiatory penalties which can be automatic (*latae sententiae*) are those enumerated in §1, n. 3.

Can. 1337 — §1. A prohibition against living in a certain place or territory can affect either clerics or religious; an order to live in a certain place or territory, however, can affect secular clerics and religious within the limits of their constitutions.

§2. An order to live in a certain place or territory requires the consent of the ordinary of that place unless it is a question of a house of penance or correction set aside also for clerics from outside that diocese.

Can. 1338 — §1. The deprivations and prohibitions enumerated in can. 1336, §1, nn. 2 and 3, never affect the powers, offices, functions, rights, privileges, faculties, favors, titles or insignia which are not subject to the power of the superior who establishes the penalty.

§2. There is no such penalty as deprivation of the power of orders, but only the prohibition against exercising it or some acts of orders; there is likewise no such penalty as a deprivation of academic degrees.

§3. The prohibitions listed in can. 1336, §1, n. 3, are to be regulated by the norm given in can. 1335 concerning censures.

Caput III

DE REMEDIIS POENALIBUS ET PAENITENTIIS

Can. 1339 – § 1. Eum, qui versatur in proxima delinquendi occasione, vel in quem, ex investigatione peracta, gravis cadit suspicio delicti commissi, Ordinarius per se vel per alium monere potest.

§ 2. Eum vero, ex cuius conversatione scandalum vel gravis ordinis perturbatio oriatur, etiam corripere potest, modo peculiaribus personae et facti condicionibus accommodato.

§ 3. De monitione et correptione constare semper debet saltem ex aliquo documento, quod in secreto curiae archivo servetur.

Can. 1340 – § 1. Paenitentia, quae imponi potest in foro externo, est aliquod religionis vel pietatis vel caritatis opus peragendum.

§ 2. Ob transgressionem occultam numquam publica imponatur paenitentia.

§ 3. Paenitentias Ordinarius pro sua prudentia addere potest poenali remedio monitionis vel correptionis.

TITULUS V

DE POENIS APPLICANDIS

Can. 1341 – Ordinarius procuderam iudicialem vel administrativam ad poenas irrogandas vel declarandas tunc tantum promovendam curet, cum perspexerit neque fraterna correctione neque correptione neque aliis pastoralis sollicitudinis viis satis posse scandalum reparari, iustitiam restitui, reum emendari.

Can. 1342 – § 1. Quoties iustae obstent causae ne iudicialis processus fiat, poena irrogari vel declarari potest per decretum extra iudicium; remedia poenalia autem et paenitentiae applicari possunt per decretum in quolibet casu.

§ 2. Per decretum irrogari vel declarari non possunt poenae perpetuae, neque poenae quas lex vel praeceptum eas constituens vetet per decretum applicare.

§ 3. Quae in lege vel praecepto dicuntur de iudice, quod attinet ad poenam irrogandam vel declarandam in iudicio, applicanda sunt ad Superiorem, qui per decretum extra iudicium poenam irroget vel declaret, nisi aliter constet neque agatur de praescriptis quae ad procedendi tantum rationem attineant.

Chapter III
PENAL REMEDIES AND PENANCES

Can. 1339 — §1. An ordinary can admonish personally or through another person one who is in the proximate occasion of committing an offense or upon whom, after an investigation has been made, there has fallen a serious suspicion of having committed an offense.

§2. An ordinary can likewise rebuke a person from whose behavior there arises scandal or serious disturbance of order in a manner accommodated to the special conditions of the person and the deed.

§3. Proof of admonishment and of rebuke must always be retained, at least by some document which is preserved in the secret archive of the curia.

Can. 1340 — §1. A penance, which can be imposed in the external forum, is some work of religion, piety or charity to be performed.

§2. A public penance is never to be imposed for an occult transgression.

§3. An ordinary can prudently attach penances to the penal remedy of admonishment or of rebuke.

TITLE V
THE APPLICATION OF PENALTIES

Can. 1341 — Only after he has ascertained that scandal cannot sufficiently be repaired, that justice cannot sufficiently be restored and that the accused cannot sufficiently be reformed by fraternal correction, rebuke and other ways of pastoral care is the ordinary then to provide for a judicial or administrative procedure to impose or to declare penalties.

Can. 1342 — §1. As often as just causes preclude a judicial process a penalty can be imposed or declared by an extra-judicial decree; penal remedies and penances, however, can be applied by a decree in any case whatsoever.

§2. Perpetual penalties cannot be imposed or declared by a decree; neither can penalties be so applied when the law or the precept which established them forbids their application by a decree.

§3. What is said in a law or a precept concerning a judge's imposing or declaring a penalty in a trial is to be applied to a superior who would impose or declare a penalty by means of an extra-judicial decree, unless the contrary is evident or unless it is a question of prescriptions which deal only with procedural matters.

Can. 1343 – Si lex vel praeceptum iudici det potestatem applicandi vel non applicandi poenam, iudex potest etiam, pro sua conscientia et prudentia, poenam temperare vel in eius locum paenitentiam
imponere.

Can. 1344 – Etiamsi lex utatur verbis praeceptivis, iudex pro sua
conscientia et prudentia potest :

1° poenae irrogationem in tempus magis opportunum differre,
si ex praepropera rei punitione maiora mala eventura praevideantur ;

2° a poena irroganda abstinere vel poenam mitiorem irrogare
aut paenitentiam adhibere, si reus emendatus sit et scandalum repa-
raverit, aut si ipse satis a civili auctoritate punitus sit vel punitum
iri praevideatur ;

3° si reus primum post vitam laudabiliter peractam deliquerit
neque necessitas urgeat reparandi scandalum, obligationem servandi
poenam expiatoriam suspendere, ita tamen ut, si reus intra tempus
ab ipso iudice determinatum rursus deliquerit, poenam utrique delicto debitam luat, nisi interim tempus decurrerit ad actionis poenalis
pro priore delicto praescriptionem.

Can. 1345 – Quoties delinquens vel usum rationis imperfectum tantum habuerit, vel delictum ex metu vel necessitate vel passionis aestu
vel in ebrietate aliave simili mentis perturbatione patraverit, iudex
potest etiam a qualibet punitione irroganda abstinere, si censeat aliter
posse melius consuli eius emendationi.

Can. 1346 – Quoties reus plura delicta patraverit, si nimius videatur
poenarum ferendae sententiae cumulus, prudenti iudicis arbitrio relinquitur poenas intra aequos terminos moderari.

Can. 1347 – § 1. Censura irrogari valide nequit, nisi antea reus
semel saltem monitus sit ut a contumacia recedat, dato congruo ad
resipiscentiam tempore.

§ 2. A contumacia recessisse dicendus est reus, quem delicti vere
paenituerit, quique praeterea congruam damnorum et scandali reparationem dederit vel saltem serio promiserit.

Can. 1348 – Cum reus ab accusatione absolvitur vel nulla poena ei
irrogatur, Ordinarius potest opportunis monitis aliisque pastoralis sollicitudinis viis, vel etiam, si res ferat, poenalibus remediis eius utilitati
et publico bono consulere.

Can. 1343 — If a law or a precept gives the judge the power to apply or not to apply a penalty, the judge can also temper the penalty or impose a penance in its place in accord with his own conscience and prudence.

Can. 1344 — Although a law may employ preceptive words, the judge in accord with his own conscience and prudence can:

1° postpone to a more opportune time the infliction of a penalty if it is foreseen that greater evils will occur from an overly prompt punishment of the accused;

2° refrain from imposing a penalty, or impose a lighter penalty, or employ a penance if the accused has reformed and scandal has been repaired, or if the accused has been or, it is foreseen, will be sufficiently punished by civil authority;

3° suspend the obligation to observe an expiatory penalty if it was the person's first offense after having led a praiseworthy life and if the need to repair scandal is not pressing; in such a situation, however, if the accused should again commit an offense within the time period set by the judge, the person is to pay the penalty required for both offenses unless, in the interim, time had run out for initiating a penal action for the first offense. *3 yrs*

Can. 1345 — As often as the offender had only an imperfect use of reason or committed the offense from fear or necessity or in the heat of passion or in drunkenness or another similar mental disturbance, the judge can also abstain from inflicting any penalty if he judges that reform can be better provided for otherwise.

Can. 1346 — Whenever the accused has committed several offenses, it is *does not apply to f.s* left to the prudent determination of the judge to moderate the penalties *apply to f.s.* within equitable limits if the cumulative burden of the inflicted (*ferendae sententiae*) penalties appears excessive. *— apply to censures f.s. from general precept or law*

Can. 1347 — §1. A censure cannot be imposed validly unless the accused *does not apply to exp. penalt.* has been warned at least once in advance that he or she should withdraw from contumacy and be given a suitable time for repentance.

§2. The guilty party is to be said to have withdrawn from contumacy when he or she has truly repented the offense and furthermore has made suitable reparation for damages and scandal or at least has seriously promised to do so.

Can. 1348 — When the accused is acquitted of the charge or when no *not judge* penalty is otherwise imposed on the accused, the ordinary can provide for the public good and for the person's own good by means of appropriate admonitions and other ways of pastoral care or even through penal remedies, if circumstances warrant it.

Can. 1349 – Si poena sit indeterminata neque aliud lex caveat, iudex poenas graviores, praesertim censuras, ne irroget, nisi casus gravitas id omnino postulet; perpetuas autem poenas irrogare non potest.

Can. 1350 – § 1. In poenis clerico irrogandis semper cavendum est, ne iis quae ad honestam sustentationem sunt necessaria ipse careat, nisi agatur de dimissione e statu clericali.

§ 2. Dimisso autem e statu clericali, qui propter poenam vere indigeat, Ordinarius meliore quo fieri potest modo providere curet.

Can. 1351 – Poena reum ubique tenet, etiam resoluto iure eius qui poenam constituit vel irrogavit, nisi aliud expresse caveatur.

Can. 1352 – § 1. Si poena vetet recipere sacramenta vel sacramentalia, vetitum suspenditur, quamdiu reus in mortis periculo versatur.

§ 2. Obligatio servandi poenam latae sententiae, quae neque declarata sit neque sit notoria in loco ubi delinquens versatur, eatenus ex toto vel ex parte suspenditur, quatenus reus eam servare nequeat sine periculo gravis scandali vel infamiae.

Can. 1353 – Appellatio vel recursus a sententiis iudicialibus vel a decretis, quae poenam quamlibet irrogent vel declarent, habent effectum suspensivum.

TITULUS VI
DE POENARUM CESSATIONE

Can. 1354 – § 1. Praeter eos, qui in cann. 1355-1356 recensentur, omnes, qui a lege, quae poena munita est, dispensare possunt vel a praecepto poenam comminanti eximere, possunt etiam eam poenam remittere.

§ 2. Potest praeterea lex vel praeceptum, poenam constituens, aliis quoque potestatem facere remittendi.

§ 3. Si Apostolica Sedes poenae remissionem sibi vel aliis reservaverit, reservatio stricte est interpretanda.

Can. 1355 – § 1. Poenam lege constitutam si sit irrogata vel declarata remittere possunt, dummodo non sit Apostolicae Sedi reservata:

1° Ordinarius, qui iudicium ad poenam irrogandam vel declarandam promovit vel decreto eam per se vel per alium irrogavit vel declaravit;

Can. 1349 — If the penalty is indeterminate and the law does not provide otherwise, the judge is not to impose heavier penalties, especially censures, unless the seriousness of the case clearly demands it; he cannot, however, impose perpetual penalties. *only censures, temp exp penalties, penal remedies, penances*

Can. 1350 — §1. Unless it is a question of dismissal from the clerical state, when penalties are imposed upon a cleric provision must always be made that he does not lack those things which are necessary for his decent support. *semper sed non pro semper*

§2. In the best manner possible the ordinary is to see to the care of a person dismissed from the clerical state who is truly in need due to the penalty.

Can. 1351 — Unless express provision is made otherwise, a penalty binds the guilty party everywhere, even when the authority of the one who established or imposed the penalty has lapsed.

Can. 1352 — §1. If a penalty prohibits the reception of the sacraments or sacramentals, the prohibition is suspended as long as the guilty party is in danger of death. *CC 1357, 1335*

§2. The obligation to observe an automatic penalty (*latae sententiae*) which has not been declared and which is not notorious in the place where the offender is living is totally or partially suspended to the extent that the person cannot observe it without danger of serious scandal or infamy. *does not apply to declared l.s. and to f.s.*

Can. 1353 — An appeal or recourse from judicial sentences or from decrees which impose or declare any penalty whatsoever has a suspensive effect. *apply to f.s., l.s. decl.*

TITLE VI

THE CESSATION OF PENALTIES

Can. 1354 — §1. Besides the persons enumerated in cann. 1355–1356, all who can dispense from a law which includes a penalty and all who can exempt one from a precept which threatens a penalty can also remit that penalty.

§2. Furthermore, a law or a precept which establishes a penalty can also give the power of remission to other persons.

§3. If the Apostolic See reserves to itself or to another the remission of a penalty, such a reservation is to be interpreted strictly.

Can. 1355 — §1. Unless it is reserved to the Apostolic See, the following can remit an imposed or declared penalty established by law:

1° the ordinary who set in motion the trial in order to impose or declare the penalty or who imposed or declared it by decree personally or through another;

2° Ordinarius loci in quo delinquens versatur, consulto tamen, nisi propter extraordinarias circumstantias impossibile sit, Ordinario, de quo sub n. 1.

§ 2. Poenam latae sententiae nondum declaratam lege constitutam, si Sedi Apostolicae non sit reservata, potest Ordinarius remittere suis subditis et iis qui in ipsius territorio versantur vel ibi deliquerint, et etiam quilibet Episcopus in actu tamen sacramentalis confessionis.

Can. 1356 – § 1. Poenam ferendae vel latae sententiae constitutam praecepto quod non sit ab Apostolica Sede latum, remittere possunt:

1° Ordinarius loci, in quo delinquens versatur;

2° si poena sit irrogata vel declarata, etiam Ordinarius qui iudicium ad poenam irrogandam vel declarandam promovit vel decreto eam per se vel per alium irrogavit vel declaravit.

§ 2. Antequam remissio fiat, consulendus est, nisi propter extraordinarias circumstantias impossibile sit, praecepti auctor.

Can. 1357 – § 1. Firmis praescriptis cann. 508 et 976, censuram latae sententiae excommunicationis vel interdicti non declaratam confessarius remittere potest in foro interno sacramentali, si paenitenti durum sit in statu gravis peccati permanere per tempus necessarium ut Superior competens provideat.

§ 2. In remissione concedenda confessarius paenitenti onus iniungat recurrendi intra mensem sub poena reincidentiae ad Superiorem competentem vel ad sacerdotem facultate praeditum, et standi huius mandatis; interim imponat congruam paenitentiam et, quatenus urgeat, scandali et damni reparationem; recursus autem fieri potest etiam per confessarium, sine nominis mentione.

§ 3. Eodem onere recurrendi tenentur, postquam convaluerint, ii quibus ad normam can. 976 remissa est censura irrogata vel declarata vel Sedi Apostolicae reservata.

Can. 1358 – § 1. Remissio censurae dari non potest nisi delinquenti qui a contumacia, ad normam can. 1347, § 2, recesserit; recedenti autem denegari nequit.

§ 2. Qui censuram remittit, potest ad normam can. 1348 providere vel etiam paenitentiam imponere.

Can. 1359 – Si quis pluribus poenis detineatur, remissio valet tantummodo pro poenis in ipsa expressis; generalis autem remissio omnes aufert poenas, iis exceptis quas in petitione reus mala fide reticuerit.

2° the ordinary of the place where the offender lives, after consulting with the ordinary mentioned in n. 1, unless this is impossible due to extraordinary circumstances.

§2. Unless it is reserved to the Apostolic See an ordinary can remit an automatic (*latae sententiae*) penalty established by law but not declared for his own subjects and those who are living in his territory or who committed an offense there; any bishop, however, can also do this in the act of sacramental confession.

Can. 1356 — §1. The following can remit an inflicted (*ferendae sententiae*) or automatic (*latae sententiae*) penalty established by a precept not issued by the Holy See:

1° the ordinary of the place where the offender lives;

2° if the penalty has been imposed or declared, the ordinary who set in motion the trial in order to impose or declare the penalty or who imposed or declared it by decree personally or through another.

§2. Before such a remission occurs, the author of the precept is to be consulted unless this is impossible due to extraordinary circumstances.

Can. 1357 — §1. With due regard for the prescriptions of cann. 508 and 976, any confessor can remit in the internal sacramental forum an automatic (*latae sententiae*) censure of excommunication or interdict which has not been declared if it would be hard on the penitent to remain in a state of serious sin during the time necessary for the competent superior to provide.

§2. In granting a remission, the confessor is to impose on the penitent the burden of having recourse within a month to a superior or a priest endowed with faculties and obeying his mandates under pain of reincidence of the penalty; in the meantime he should impose an appropriate penance and the reparation of any scandal or damage to the extent that it is imperative; recourse can also be made by the confessor without mentioning any names.

§3. After they have recovered, those absolved in accord with can. 976 from an imposed or declared censure or one reserved to the Holy See are bound by the same obligation of recourse.

Can. 1358 — §1. A remission of a censure cannot be granted unless an offender has withdrawn from contumacy in accord with the norm of can. 1347, §2; remission cannot be denied, however, to a person who withdraws from contumacy.

§2. A person who remits a censure can act in accord with the norm of can. 1348 or even impose a penance.

Can. 1359 — If a person is bound by many penalties, the remission has force only for those penalties expressly mentioned in the remission; a general remission, however, takes away all penalties with the exception of those about which the guilty party kept silent in the petition in bad faith.

Can. 1360 – Poenae remissio metu gravi extorta irrita est.

Can. 1361 – § 1. Remissio dari potest etiam absenti vel sub con-dicione.

§ 2. Remissio in foro externo detur scripto, nisi gravis causa aliud suadeat.

§ 3. Caveatur ne remissionis petitio vel ipsa remissio divulgetur, nisi quatenus id vel utile sit ad rei famam tuendam vel necessarium ad scandalum reparandum.

Can. 1362 – § 1. Actio criminalis praescriptione extinguitur trien-nio, nisi agatur:

1° de delictis Congregationi pro Doctrina Fidei reservatis;

2° de actione ob delicta de quibus in cann. 1394, 1395, 1397, 1398, quae quinquennio praescribitur;

3° de delictis quae non sunt iure communi punita, si lex parti-cularis alium praescriptionis terminum statuerit.

§ 2. Praescriptio decurrit ex die quo delictum patratum est, vel, si delictum sit permanens vel habituale, ex die quo cessavit.

Can. 1363 – § 1. Si intra terminos de quibus in can. 1362, ex die quo sententia condemnatoria in rem iudicatam transierit computan-dos, non sit reo notificatum exsecutorium iudicis decretum de quo in can. 1651, actio ad poenam exsequendam praescriptione extinguitur.

§ 2. Idem valet, servatis servandis, si poena per decretum extra iudicium irrogata sit.

PARS II
DE POENIS IN SINGULA DELICTA

TITULUS I
DE DELICTIS CONTRA RELIGIONEM
ET ECCLESIAE UNITATEM

Can. 1364 – § 1. Apostata a fide, haereticus vel schismaticus in excommunicationem latae sententiae incurrit, firmo praescripto can. 194, § 1, n. 2; clericus praeterea potest poenis, de quibus in can. 1336, § 1, nn. 1, 2 et 3, puniri.

Can. 1360 — If the remission of a penalty was extorted through grave fear, it is invalid.

Can. 1361 — §1. A remission can be granted even to a person who is not present or even under a condition.

§2. A remission in the external forum is to be given in writing unless a serious cause persuades otherwise.

§3. Care should be taken that a petition for remission or the remission itself not be made public, except to the extent that it would be advantageous to protect the reputation of the guilty party or necessary to repair scandal.

Can. 1362 — §1. A criminal action is extinguished by prescription in three years unless it is a question of:

1° offenses reserved to the Sacred Congregation for the Doctrine of the Faith;

2° an action due to offenses mentioned in cann. 1394, 1395, 1397 and 1398, which have a prescription of five years;

3° offenses which are not punished in common law if particular law has stated another term of prescription.

§2. Prescription starts on the day the offense was committed or on the day when it ceased if the offense is continuous or habitual.

Can. 1363 — §1. An action to execute a penalty is extinguished by prescription if the guilty party has not been notified of the judge's executive decree mentioned in can. 1651 within the time limits indicated in can. 1362 which are to be computed from the day on which the condemnatory sentence became a finally judged matter (*res iudicata*).

§2. All other things being observed that are to be observed, the same holds true if the penalty was imposed through an extra-judicial decree.

PART II

PENALTIES FOR SPECIFIC OFFENSES

TITLE I

OFFENSES AGAINST RELIGION AND THE UNITY OF THE CHURCH

Can. 1364 — §1. With due regard for can. 194, §1, n. 2, an apostate from the faith, a heretic or a schismatic incurs automatic (*latae sententiae*) excommunication and if a cleric, he can also be punished by the penalties mentioned in can. 1336, §1, nn. 1, 2 and 3.

§ 2. Si diuturna contumacia vel scandali gravitas postulet, aliae poenae addi possunt, non excepta dimissione e statu clericali.

Can. 1365 – Reus vetitae communicationis in sacris iusta poena puniatur.

Can. 1366 – Parentes vel parentum locum tenentes, qui liberos in religione acatholica baptizandos vel educandos tradunt, censura aliave iusta poena puniantur.

Can. 1367 – Qui species consecratas abicit aut in sacrilegum finem abducit vel retinet, in excommunicationem latae sententiae Sedi Apostolicae reservatam incurrit; clericus praeterea alia poena, non exclusa dimissione e statu clericali, puniri potest.

Can. 1368 – Si quis, asserens vel promittens aliquid coram ecclesiastica auctoritate, periurium committit, iusta poena puniatur.

Can. 1369 – Qui in publico spectaculo vel concione, vel in scripto publice evulgato, vel aliter instrumentis communicationis socialis utens, blasphemiam profert, aut bonos mores graviter laedit, aut in religionem vel Ecclesiam iniurias exprimit vel odium contemptumve excitat, iusta poena puniatur.

TITULUS II

DE DELICTIS CONTRA ECCLESIASTICAS AUCTORITATES ET ECCLESIAE LIBERTATEM

Can. 1370 – § 1. Qui vim physicam in Romanum Pontificem adhibet, in excommunicationem latae sententiae Sedi Apostolicae reservatam incurrit, cui, si clericus sit, alia poena, non exclusa dimissione e statu clericali, pro delicti gravitate addi potest.

§ 2. Qui id agit in eum qui episcopali charactere pollet, in interdictum latae sententiae et, si sit clericus, etiam in suspensionem latae sententiae incurrit.

§ 3. Qui vim physicam in clericum vel religiosum adhibet in fidei vel Ecclesiae vel ecclesiasticae potestatis vel ministerii contemptum, iusta poena puniatur.

Can. 1371 – Iusta poena puniatur:

1° qui, praeter casum de quo in can. 1364, § 1, doctrinam a Romano Pontifice vel a Concilio Oecumenico damnatam docet vel doctrinam, de qua in can. 752, pertinaciter respuit, et ab Apostolica Sede vel ab Ordinario admonitus non retractat;

§2. If long lasting contumacy or the seriousness of scandal warrants it, other penalties can be added including dismissal from the clerical state.

Can. 1365 — A person guilty of prohibited participation in sacred rites (*communicatio in sacris*) is to be punished with a just penalty.

Can. 1366 — Parents or those who substitute for parents are to be punished with a censure or another just penalty if they hand their children over to be baptized or educated in a non-Catholic religion.

Can. 1367 — A person who throws away the consecrated species or who takes them or retains them for a sacrilegious purpose incurs an automatic (*latae sententiae*) excommunication reserved to the Apostolic See; if a cleric, he can be punished with another penalty including dismissal from the clerical state.

Can. 1368 — A person who commits perjury while asserting something or promising something before an ecclesiastical authority is to be punished with a just penalty.

Can. 1369 — A person who uses a public show or speech, published writings, or other media of social communication to blaspheme, seriously damage good morals, express wrongs against religion or against the Church or stir up hatred or contempt against religion or the Church is to be punished with a just penalty.

TITLE II

OFFENSES AGAINST ECCLESIASTICAL AUTHORITIES AND THE FREEDOM OF THE CHURCH

Can. 1370 — §1. One who uses physical force against the Roman Pontiff incurs an automatic (*latae sententiae*) excommunication reserved to the Apostolic See; if he is a cleric, another penalty including dismissal from the clerical state can be added in accord with the seriousness of the offense.

§2. One who does this against a person possessing the episcopal character incurs an automatic (*latae sententiae*) interdict; and, if a cleric, he also incurs an automatic (*latae sententiae*) suspension.

§3. One who uses physical force against a cleric or religious out of contempt for the faith, or the Church, or ecclesiastical power, or ministry is to be punished with a just penalty.

Can. 1371 — The following are to be punished with a just penalty:

1° besides the situation mentioned in can. 1364, §1, a person who teaches a doctrine condemned by the Roman Pontiff or by an ecumenical council or who pertinaciously rejects the doctrine mentioned in can. 752 and who does not make a retraction after having been admonished by the Apostolic See or by the ordinary;

2° qui aliter Sedi Apostolicae, Ordinario, vel Superiori legitime praecipienti vel prohibenti non obtemperat, et post monitum in inoboedientia persistit.

Can. 1372 – Qui contra Romani Pontificis actum ad Concilium Oecumenicum vel ad Episcoporum collegium recurrit censura puniatur.

Can. 1373 – Qui publice aut subditorum simultates vel odia adversus Sedem Apostolicam vel Ordinarium excitat propter aliquem potestatis vel ministerii ecclesiastici actum, aut subditos ad inoboedientiam in eos provocat, interdicto vel aliis iustis poenis puniatur.

Can. 1374 – Qui nomen dat consociationi, quae contra Ecclesiam machinatur, iusta poena puniatur; qui autem eiusmodi consociationem promovet vel moderatur, interdicto puniatur.

Can. 1375 – Qui impediunt libertatem ministerii vel electionis vel potestatis ecclesiasticae aut legitimum bonorum sacrorum aliorumve ecclesiasticorum bonorum usum, aut perterrent electorem vel electum vel eum qui potestatem vel ministerium ecclesiasticum exercuit, iusta poena puniri possunt.

Can. 1376 – Qui rem sacram, mobilem vel immobilem, profanat iusta poena puniatur.

Can. 1377 – Qui sine praescripta licentia bona ecclesiastica alienat, iusta poena puniatur.

TITULUS III
DE MUNERUM ECCLESIASTICORUM USURPATIONE DEQUE DELICTIS IN IIS EXERCENDIS

Can. 1378 – § 1. Sacerdos qui contra praescriptum can. 977 agit, in excommunicationem latae sententiae Sedi Apostolicae reservatam incurrit.

§ 2. In poenam latae sententiae interdicti vel, si sit clericus, suspensionis incurrit:

1° qui ad ordinem sacerdotalem non promotus liturgicam eucharistici Sacrificii actionem attentat;

2° qui, praeter casum de quo in § 1, cum sacramentalem absolutionem dare valide nequeat, eam impertire attentat, vel sacramentalem confessionem audit.

§ 3. In casibus de quibus in § 2, pro delicti gravitate, aliae poenae, non exclusa excommunicatione, addi possunt.

Can. 1379 – Qui, praeter casus de quibus in can. 1378, sacramentum se administrare simulat, iusta poena puniatur.

2° a person who wrongly does not otherwise comply with the legitimate precepts or prohibitions of the Apostolic See, the ordinary or the superior and who persists in disobedience, after a warning.

Can. 1372 — One who takes recourse against an act of a Roman Pontiff to an ecumenical council or to the college of bishops is to be punished with a censure.

Can. 1373 — One who publicly either stirs up hostilities or hatred among subjects against the Apostolic See or against an ordinary on account of some act of ecclesiastical power or ministry or incites subjects to disobey them is to be punished by an interdict or by other just penalties.

Can. 1374 — One who joins an association which plots against the Church is to be punished with a just penalty; one who promotes or moderates such an association, however, is to be punished with an interdict.

Can. 1375 — Those who impede the freedom of ecclesiastical ministry or election or power, or the legitimate use of sacred goods or other ecclesiastical goods, or who grossly intimidate an elector, or the elected, or the one who exercises ecclesiastical ministry or power, can be punished with a just penalty.

Can. 1376 — One who profanes a movable or immovable sacred thing is to be punished with a just penalty.

Can. 1377 — One who alienates ecclesiastical goods without the prescribed permission is to be punished with a just penalty.

TITLE III

USURPATION OF ECCLESIASTICAL FUNCTIONS AND OFFENSES IN THEIR EXERCISE

Can. 1378 — §1. A priest who acts against the prescription of can. 977 incurs an automatic (*latae sententiae*) excommunication reserved to the Apostolic See.

§2. The following incur an automatic (*latae sententiae*) penalty of interdict or if a cleric, an automatic (*latae sententiae*) suspension:

1° one who has not been promoted to the priestly order and who attempts to enact the liturgical action of the Eucharistic Sacrifice;

2° outside the case mentioned in §1, a person who attempts to impart sacramental absolution or a person who hears a sacramental confession when one cannot validly give sacramental absolution.

§3. In the case mentioned in §2 other penalties including excommunication can be added in accord with the seriousness of the offense.

Can. 1379 — Outside the cases mentioned in can. 1378, one who simulates the administration of a sacrament is to be punished with a just penalty.

Can. 1380 – Qui per simoniam sacramentum celebrat vel recipit, interdicto vel suspensione puniatur.

Can. 1381 – § 1. Quicumque officium ecclesiasticum usurpat, iusta poena puniatur.

§ 2. Usurpationi aequiparatur illegitima, post privationem vel cessationem a munere, eiusdem retentio.

Can. 1382 – Episcopus qui sine pontificio mandato aliquem consecrat in Episcopum, itemque qui ab eo consecrationem recipit, in excommunicationem latae sententiae Sedi Apostolicae reservatam incurrunt.

Can. 1383 – Episcopus qui, contra praescriptum can. 1015, alienum subditum sine legitimis litteris dimissoriis ordinavit, prohibetur per annum ordinem conferre. Qui vero ordinationem recepit, est ipso facto a recepto ordine suspensus.

Can. 1384 – Qui, praeter casus, de quibus in cann. 1378-1383, sacerdotale munus vel aliud sacrum ministerium illegitime exsequitur, iusta poena puniri potest.

Can. 1385 – Qui quaestum illegitime facit ex Missae stipe, censura vel alia iusta poena puniatur.

Can. 1386 – Qui quidvis donat vel pollicetur ut quis, munus in Ecclesia exercens, illegitime quid agat vel omittat, iusta poena puniatur; item qui ea dona vel pollicitationes acceptat.

Can. 1387 – Sacerdos, qui in actu vel occasione vel praetextu confessionis paenitentem ad peccatum contra sextum Decalogi praeceptum sollicitat, pro delicti gravitate, suspensione, prohibitionibus, privationibus puniatur, et in casibus gravioribus dimittatur e statu clericali.

Can. 1388 – § 1. Confessarius, qui sacramentale sigillum directe violat, in excommunicationem latae sententiae Sedi Apostolicae reservatam incurrit; qui vero indirecte tantum, pro delicti gravitate puniatur.

§ 2. Interpres aliique, de quibus in can. 983, § 2, qui secretum violant, iusta poena puniantur, non exclusa excommunicatione.

Can. 1389 – § 1. Ecclesiastica potestate vel munere abutens pro actus vel omissionis gravitate puniatur, non exclusa officii privatione, nisi in eum abusum iam poena sit lege vel praecepto constituta.

Can. 1380 — One who celebrates or receives a sacrament through simony is to be punished with an interdict or a suspension.

Can. 1381 — §1. Whoever usurps an ecclesiastical office is to be punished with a just penalty.

§2. Illegitimate retention after deprivation or cessation of office is equivalent to usurpation.

Can. 1382 — A bishop who consecrates someone a bishop and the person who receives such a consecration from a bishop without a pontifical mandate incur an automatic (*latae sententiae*) excommunication reserved to the Apostolic See.

Can. 1383 — A bishop who violates the prescription of can. 1015 and ordains a person who is not his subject without legitimate dimissorial letters is prohibited for a year from conferring the order; a person who has received ordination in such circumstances is automatically (*ipso facto*) suspended from the order received.

Can. 1384 — Outside the cases mentioned in cann. 1378–1383, one who illegitimately carries out a priestly function or another sacred ministry can be punished with a just penalty.

Can. 1385 — One who illegitimately makes a profit from a Mass stipend is to be punished with a censure or another just penalty.

Can. 1386 — One who gives or promises something so that someone who exercises a function in the Church would illegitimately do or omit something is to be punished with a just penalty; likewise, the person who accepts such gifts or promises.

Can. 1387 — Whether in the act or on the occasion or under the pretext of confession, a priest who solicits a penitent to sin against the sixth commandment of the Decalogue is to be punished with suspension, prohibitions and deprivations in accord with the seriousness of the offense; and in more serious cases, he is to be dismissed from the clerical state.

Can. 1388 — §1. A confessor who directly violates the seal of confession incurs an automatic (*latae sententiae*) excommunication reserved to the Apostolic See; if he does so only indirectly, he is to be punished in accord with the seriousness of the offense.

§2. An interpreter and other persons mentioned in can. 983, §2, who violate this secrecy are to be punished with a just penalty, not excluding excommunication.

Can. 1389 — §1. One who abuses ecclesiastical power or function is to be punished in accord with the seriousness of the act or omission not excluding deprivation from office unless a penalty for such abuse has already been established by a law or a precept.

§ 2. Qui vero, ex culpabili neglegentia, ecclesiasticae potestatis vel ministerii vel muneris actum illegitime cum damno alieno ponit vel omittit, iusta poena puniatur.

TITULUS IV
DE CRIMINE FALSI

Can. 1390 – § 1. Qui confessarium de delicto, de quo in can. 1387, apud ecclesiasticum Superiorem falso denuntiat, in interdictum latae sententiae incurrit et, si sit clericus, etiam in suspensionem.

§ 2. Qui aliam ecclesiastico Superiori calumniosam praebet delicti denuntiationem, vel aliter alterius bonam famam laedit, iusta poena, non exclusa censura, puniri potest.

§ 3. Calumniator potest cogi etiam ad congruam satisfactionem praestandam.

Can. 1391 – Iusta poena pro delicti gravitate puniri potest :

1° qui ecclesiasticum documentum publicum falsum conficit, vel verum mutat, destruit, occultat, vel falso vel mutato utitur ;

2° qui alio falso vel mutato documento utitur in re ecclesiastica ;

3° qui in publico ecclesiastico documento falsum asserit.

TITULUS V
DE DELICTIS CONTRA SPECIALES OBLIGATIONES

Can. 1392 – Clerici vel religiosi mercaturam vel negotiationem contra canonum praescripta exercentes pro delicti gravitate puniantur.

Can. 1393 – Qui obligationes sibi ex poena impositas violat, iusta poena puniri potest.

Can. 1394 – § 1. Firmo praescripto can. 194, § 1, n. 3, clericus matrimonium, etiam civiliter tantum, attentans, in suspensionem latae sententiae incurrit ; quod si monitus non resipuerit et scandalum dare perrexerit, gradatim privationibus ac vel etiam dimissione e statu clericali puniri potest.

§2. One who through culpable negligence illegitimately places or omits an act of ecclesiastical power, ministry or function which damages another person is to be punished with a just penalty.

TITLE IV

THE CRIME OF FALSEHOOD

Can. 1390 — §1. One who falsely accuses a confessor before an ecclesiastical superior of the offense mentioned in can. 1387 incurs an automatic (*latae sententiae*) interdict; and if a cleric, also a suspension.

§2. One who furnishes an ecclesiastical superior with any other calumnious denunciation of an offense or who otherwise injures the good reputation of another person can be punished with a just penalty, even including a censure.

§3. A calumniator can be coerced also to make suitable reparation.

Can. 1391 — The following can be punished with a just penalty in accord with the seriousness of the offense:

1° one who fabricates a false public ecclesiastical document, or changes, destroys or conceals an authentic document, or uses a false or changed document;

2° one who uses another false or changed document in an ecclesiastical matter;

3° one who states a falsehood in a public ecclesiastical document.

TITLE V

OFFENSES AGAINST PARTICULAR OBLIGATIONS

Can. 1392 — Clerics or religious who practice trade or business against the prescriptions of the canons are to be punished in accord with the seriousness of the offense.

Can. 1393 — One who violates the obligations imposed by a penalty can be punished by a just penalty.

Can. 1394 — §1. With due regard for the prescription of can. 194, §1, n. 3, a cleric who attempts even a civil marriage incurs an automatic (*latae sententiae*) suspension; but if he is given a warning and he does not have a change of heart and continues to give scandal, he can be punished gradually with various deprivations, even to the point of dismissal from the clerical state.

§ 2. Religiosus a votis perpetuis, qui non sit clericus, matrimonium etiam civiliter tantum attentans in interdictum latae sententiae incurrit, firmo praescripto can. 694.

Can. 1395 – § 1. Clericus concubinarius, praeter casum de quo in can. 1394, et clericus in alio peccato externo contra sextum Decalogi praeceptum cum scandalo permanens, suspensione puniantur, cui, persistente post monitionem delicto, aliae poenae gradatim addi possunt usque ad dimissionem e statu clericali.

§ 2. Clericus qui aliter contra sextum Decalogi praeceptum deliquerit, si quidem delictum vi vel minis vel publice vel cum minore infra aetatem sedecim annorum patratum sit, iustis poenis puniatur, non exclusa, si casus ferat, dimissione e statu clericali.

Can. 1396 – Qui graviter violat residentiae obligationem cui ratione ecclesiastici officii tenetur, iusta poena puniatur, non exclusa, post monitionem, officii privatione.

TITULUS VI
DE DELICTIS CONTRA HOMINIS VITAM ET LIBERTATEM

Can. 1397 – Qui homicidium patrat, vel hominem vi aut fraude rapit vel detinet vel mutilat vel graviter vulnerat, privationibus et prohibitionibus, de quibus in can. 1336, pro delicti gravitate puniatur; homicidium autem in personas de quibus in can. 1370, poenis ibi statutis punitur.

Can. 1398 – Qui abortum procurat, effectu secuto, in excommunicationem latae sententiae incurrit.

TITULUS VII
NORMA GENERALIS

Can. 1399 – Praeter casus hac vel aliis legibus statutos, divinae vel canonicae legis externa violatio tunc tantum potest iusta quidem poena puniri, cum specialis violationis gravitas punitionem postulat, et necessitas urget scandala praeveniendi vel reparandi.

§2. A religious in perpetual vows who is not a cleric and who attempts even a civil marriage incurs an automatic (*latae sententiae*) interdict, with due regard for the prescription of can. 694.

Can. 1395 — §1. Outside the case mentioned in can. 1394, a cleric who lives in concubinage or a cleric who remains in another external sin against the sixth commandment of the Decalogue which produces scandal is to be punished with a suspension; and if such a cleric persists in such an offense after having been admonished, other penalties can be added gradually including dismissal from the clerical state.

§2. If a cleric has otherwise committed an offense against the sixth commandment of the Decalogue with force or threats or publicly or with a minor below the age of sixteen, the cleric is to be punished with just penalties, including dismissal from the clerical state if the case warrants it.

Can. 1396 — One who seriously violates the obligation of residence to which he is bound by reason of an ecclesiastical office is to be punished with a just penalty including even deprivation of office after a warning.

TITLE VI
OFFENSES AGAINST HUMAN LIFE AND FREEDOM

Can. 1397 — One who commits homicide or who fraudulently or forcibly kidnaps, detains, mutilates or seriously wounds a person is to be punished with the deprivations and prohibitions mentioned in can. 1336 in accord with the seriousness of the offense; however, homicide against the persons mentioned in can. 1370 is punished by the penalties specified there.

Can. 1398 — A person who procures a successful abortion incurs an automatic (*latae sententiae*) excommunication.

TITLE VII
GENERAL NORM

Can. 1399 — Besides the cases stated here or in other laws, an external violation of a divine or an ecclesiastical law can be punished by a just penalty only when the particular seriousness of the violation demands punishment and there is an urgent need to preclude or repair scandal.

LIBER VII
DE PROCESSIBUS

PARS I
DE IUDICIIS IN GENERE

Can. 1400 – § 1. Obiectum iudicii sunt :

1° personarum physicarum vel iuridicarum iura persequenda aut vindicanda, vel facta iuridica declaranda;

2° delicta, quod spectat ad poenam irrogandam vel declarandam.

§ 2. Attamen controversiae ortae ex actu potestatis administrativae deferri possunt solummodo ad Superiorem vel ad tribunal administrativum.

Can. 1401 – Ecclesia iure proprio et exclusivo cognoscit :

1° de causis quae respiciunt res spirituales et spiritualibus adnexas;

2° de violatione legum ecclesiasticarum deque omnibus in quibus inest ratio peccati, quod attinet ad culpae definitionem et poenarum ecclesiasticarum irrogationem.

Can. 1402 – Omnia Ecclesiae tribunalia reguntur canonibus qui sequuntur, salvis normis tribunalium Apostolicae Sedis.

Can. 1403 – § 1. Causae canonizationis Servorum Dei reguntur peculiari lege pontificia.

§ 2. Iisdem causis applicantur praeterea praescripta huius Codicis, quoties in eadem lege ad ius universale remissio fit vel de normis agitur quae, ex ipsa rei natura, easdem quoque causas afficiunt.

BOOK VII
PROCESSES

PART I
TRIALS IN GENERAL

Can. 1400 — §1. The object of a trial is:

1° to prosecute or to vindicate the rights of physical or juridic persons, or to declare juridic facts;

2° to impose or declare the penalty for offenses.

§2. However, controversies which have arisen from an act of administrative power can be brought only before the superior or an administrative tribunal.

Can. 1401 — By proper and exclusive right the Church adjudicates:

1° cases concerning spiritual matters or connected with the spiritual;

2° the violation of ecclesiastical laws and all those cases in which there is a question of sin in respect to the determination of culpability and the imposition of ecclesiastical penalties.

Can. 1402 — With due regard for the norms established for the tribunals of the Apostolic See, all the tribunals of the Church are regulated by the following canons.

Can. 1403 — §1. The causes of the canonization of the servants of God are regulated by special pontifical law.

§2. The prescriptions of this Code, however, are applicable to the aforementioned causes whenever the pontifical law refers to the universal law or when it is a question of norms which affect those causes from the very nature of the matter.

TITULUS I
DE FORO COMPETENTI

Can. 1404 – Prima Sedes a nemine iudicatur.

Can. 1405 – § 1. Ipsius Romani Pontificis dumtaxat ius est iudicandi in causis de quibus in can. 1401 :

1° eos qui supremum tenent civitatis magistratum ;

2° Patres Cardinales ;

3° Legatos Sedis Apostolicae, et in causis poenalibus Episcopos ;

4° alias causas quas ipse ad suum advocaverit iudicium.

§ 2. Iudex de actu vel instrumento a Romano Pontifice in forma specifica confirmato videre non potest, nisi ipsius praecesserit mandatum.

§ 3. Rotae Romanae reservatur iudicare :

1° Episcopos in contentiosis, firmo praescripto can. 1419, § 2 ;

2° Abbatem primatem, vel Abbatem superiorem congregationis monasticae, et supremum Moderatorem institutorum religiosorum iuris pontificii ;

3° dioeceses aliasve personas ecclesiasticas, sive physicas sive iuridicas, quae Superiorem infra Romanum Pontificem · non habent.

Can. 1406 – § 1. Violato praescripto can. 1404, acta et decisiones pro infectis habentur.

§ 2. In causis, de quibus in can. 1405, aliorum iudicum incompetentia est absoluta.

Can. 1407 – § 1. Nemo in prima instantia conveniri potest, nisi coram iudice ecclesiastico qui competens sit ob unum ex titulis qui in cann. 1408-1414 determinantur.

§ 2. Incompetentia iudicis, cui nullus ex his titulis suffragatur, dicitur relativa.

§ 3. Actor sequitur forum partis conventae ; quod si pars conventa multiplex forum habet, optio fori actori conceditur.

Can. 1408 – Quilibet conveniri potest coram tribunali domicilii vel quasi-domicilii.

Can. 1409 – § 1. Vagus forum habet in loco ubi actu commoratur.

§ 2. Is, cuius neque domicilium aut quasi-domicilium neque locus commorationis nota sint, conveniri potest in foro actoris, dummodo aliud forum legitimum non suppetat.

TITLE I
THE COMPETENT FORUM

Can. 1404 — The First See is judged by no one.

Can. 1405 — §1. It is the right of the Roman Pontiff himself alone to judge in cases mentioned in can. 1401:

1° those who hold the highest civil office in a state;

2° cardinals;

3° legates of the Apostolic See and, in penal cases, bishops;

4° other cases which he has called to his own judgment.

§2. A judge cannot review an act or instrument explicitly (*in forma specifica*) confirmed by the Roman Pontiff without his prior mandate.

§3. Judgment of the following is reserved to the Roman Rota:

1° bishops in contentious cases, with due regard for the prescription of can. 1419, §2;

2° an abbot primate or an abbot superior of a monastic congregation and the supreme moderator of religious institutes of pontifical right;

3° dioceses or other ecclesiastical persons, whether physical or juridic, which do not have a superior below the Roman Pontiff.

Can. 1406 — §1. Acts and decisions made in violation of the prescription of can. 1404 are considered invalid.

§2. The incompetence of other judges is absolute in the cases mentioned in can. 1405.

Can. 1407 — §1. No one can be brought into a court of first instance unless before an ecclesiastical judge who is competent in virtue of one of the titles determined in cann. 1408–1414.

§2. The incompetence of a judge who posseses none of these titles is termed relative.

§3. The petitioner follows the forum of the respondent; but if the respondent has a number of fora, the choice of one among them is granted to the petitioner.

Can. 1408 — Anyone can be brought into court before the tribunal of one's own domicile or quasi-domicile.

Can. 1409 — §1. A transient has the forum of the place of actual residence.

§2. A person whose domicile, quasi-domicile or place of residence is not known can be brought into court in the forum of the petitioner provided no other legitimate forum is available.

Can. 1410 – Ratione rei sitae, pars conveniri potest coram tribunali loci, ubi res litigiosa sita est, quoties actio in rem directa sit, aut de spolio agatur.

Can. 1411 – § 1. Ratione contractus pars conveniri potest coram tribunali loci in quo contractus initus est vel adimpleri debet, nisi partes concorditer aliud tribunal elegerint.

§ 2. Si causa versetur circa obligationes quae ex alio titulo proveniant, pars conveniri potest coram tribunali loci, in quo obligatio vel orta est vel est adimplenda.

Can. 1412 – In causis poenalibus accusatus, licet absens, conveniri potest coram tribunali loci, in quo delictum patratum est.

Can. 1413 – Pars conveniri potest :

1° in causis quae circa administrationem versantur, coram tribunali loci ubi administratio gesta est;

2° in causis quae respiciunt hereditates vel legata pia, coram tribunali ultimi domicilii vel quasi-domicilii vel commorationis, ad normam cann. 1408-1409, illius de cuius hereditate vel legato pio agitur, nisi agatur de mera exsecutione legati, quae videnda est secundum ordinarias competentiae normas.

Can. 1414 – Ratione conexionis, ab uno eodemque tribunali et in eodem processu cognoscendae sunt causae inter se conexae, nisi legis praescriptum obstet.

Can. 1415 – Ratione praeventionis, si duo vel plura tribunalia aeque competentia sunt, ei ius est causam cognoscendi, quod prius partem conventam legitime citaverit.

Can. 1416 – Conflictus competentiae inter tribunalia eidem tribunali appellationis subiecta, ab hoc tribunali solvuntur; a Signatura Apostolica, si eidem tribunali appellationis non subsunt.

TITULUS II
DE VARIIS TRIBUNALIUM GRADIBUS ET SPECIEBUS

Can. 1417 – § 1. Ob primatum Romani Pontificis integrum est cuilibet fideli causam suam sive contentiosam sive poenalem, in quovis iudicii gradu et in quovis litis statu, cognoscendam ad Sanctam Sedem deferre vel apud eandem introducere.

§ 2. Provocatio tamen ad Sedem Apostolicam interposita non suspendit, praeter casum appellationis, exercitium iurisdictionis in iudice

Can. 1410 — By reason of the location of a disputed item, a party can be brought into court before the tribunal of the place where the litigated thing is located whenever the action is directed against the thing or whenever it is a question of ~~damages.~~ privation of possession.

Can. 1411 — §1. By reason of contract a party can be brought into court before the tribunal of the place in which the contract was entered or must be fulfilled, unless the parties agree to choose another tribunal.

§2. If the case revolves around obligations which arise from another title, the party can be brought into court before the tribunal of the place in which the obligation either originated or is to be fulfilled.

Can. 1412 — In penal cases the accused, even if absent, can be cited before the tribunal of the place where the offense was perpetrated.

Can. 1413 — A party can be brought into court:

1° in cases which concern administration before the tribunal of the place where the administration was conducted;

2° in cases which concern inheritances or pious legacies before the tribunal of the last domicile, quasi-domicile or place of residence of the person whose inheritance or pious legacy is the object of the action, in accord with the norm of cann. 1408–1409 unless it is a question of the mere execution of a legacy, which is to be examined according to the ordinary norms of competence.

Can. 1414 — Unless a prescription of the law blocks this, by reason of connection cases which are interrelated are to be tried by one and the same tribunal and in the same procedure.

Can. 1415 — By reason of prevention, if two or several tribunals are equally competent, the tribunal which has first legitimately cited the respondent has the right to judge the case.

Can. 1416 — Conflicts of competence between tribunals subject to the same appellate tribunal are resolved by that tribunal; if the tribunals are not subject to the same appellate tribunal, conflicts of competence are resolved by the Apostolic Signatura.

TITLE II
VARIOUS GRADES AND KINDS OF TRIBUNALS

Can. 1417 — §1. In virtue of the primacy of the Roman Pontiff, anyone of the faithful is free to bring to or introduce before the Holy See a case either contentious or penal in any grade of judgment and at any stage of litigation.

§2. A recourse made to the Apostolic See, however, does not suspend the exercise of jurisdiction by a judge who has already begun to adjudicate the

qui causam iam cognoscere coepit; quique idcirco poterit iudicium prosequi usque ad definitivam sententiam, nisi Sedes Apostolica iudici
significaverit se causam advocasse.

Can. 1418 – Quodlibet tribunal ius habet in auxilium vocandi aliud
tribunal ad causam instruendam vel ad actus intimandos.

Caput I
DE TRIBUNALI PRIMAE INSTANTIAE

Art. 1
De iudice

Can. 1419 – § 1. In unaquaque dioecesi et pro omnibus causis iure
expresse non exceptis, iudex primae instantiae est Episcopus dioecesanus, qui iudicialem potestatem exercere potest per se ipse vel per
alios, secundum canones qui sequuntur.

§ 2. Si vero agatur de iuribus aut bonis temporalibus personae iuridicae ab Episcopo repraesentatae, iudicat in primo gradu tribunal
appellationis.

Can. 1420 – § 1. Quilibet Episcopus dioecesanus tenetur Vicarium
iudicialem seu Officialem constituere cum potestate ordinaria iudicandi,
a Vicario generali distinctum, nisi parvitas dioecesis aut paucitas causarum aliud suadeat.

§ 2. Vicarius iudicialis unum constituit tribunal cum Episcopo,
sed nequit iudicare causas quas Episcopus sibi reservat.

§ 3. Vicario iudiciali dari possunt adiutores, quibus nomen est
Vicariorum iudicialium adiunctorum seu Vice-officialium.

§ 4. Tum Vicarius iudicialis tum Vicarii iudiciales adiuncti esse
debent sacerdotes, integrae famae, in iure canonico doctores vel saltem
licentiati, annos nati non minus triginta.

§ 5. Ipsi, sede vacante, a munere non cessant nec ab Administratore dioecesano amoveri possunt; adveniente autem novo Episcopo, indigent confirmatione.

Can. 1421 – § 1. In dioecesi constituantur ab Episcopo iudices
dioecesani, qui sint clerici.

§ 2. Episcoporum conferentia permittere potest ut etiam laici iudices constituantur, e quibus, suadente necessitate, unus assumi potest
ad collegium efformandum.

case except in the case of an appeal; for this reason, the judge can pursue judgment up to the definitive sentence unless the Apostolic See has informed the judge that it has called the case to itself.

Can. 1418 — Every tribunal has the right to call upon the assistance of another tribunal to instruct a case or to communicate acts.

CHAPTER I
THE TRIBUNAL OF FIRST INSTANCE

Art. 1
THE JUDGE

Can. 1419 — §1. The diocesan bishop is the judge of first instance in each diocese and for all cases not expressly excepted by law; he can exercise his judicial power personally or through others in accord with the following canons.

§2. But if the action concerns the rights or the temporal goods of a juridic person represented by the bishop, the appellate tribunal judges in first instance.

Can. 1420 — §1. Each diocesan bishop is bound to appoint a judicial vicar or officialis with ordinary power to judge, distinct from the vicar general unless the smallness of the diocese or the small number of cases suggests otherwise.

§2. The judicial vicar constitutes one tribunal with the bishop but he cannot judge cases which the bishop reserves to himself.

§3. The judicial vicar can be given assistants whose title is adjutant judicial vicars or vice-officiales.

§4. Both the judicial vicar and the adjutant judicial vicars must be priests of unimpaired reputations, holding doctorates or at least licentiates in canon law and not less than thirty years of age.

§5. When the see is vacant, they do not cease from their office and they cannot be removed by the diocesan administrator; when the new bishop arrives, however, they need confirmation.

Can. 1421 — §1. The bishop is to appoint diocesan judges in the diocese who are clerics.

§2. The conference of bishops can permit lay persons to be appointed judges; when it is necessary, one of them can be employed to form a collegiate tribunal.

§ 3. Iudices sint integrae famae et in iure canonico doctores vel saltem licentiati.

Can. 1422 – Vicarius iudicialis, Vicarii iudiciales adiuncti et ceteri iudices nominantur ad definitum tempus, firmo praescripto can. 1420, § 5, nec removeri possunt nisi ex legitima gravique causa.

Can. 1423 – § 1. Plures dioecesani Episcopi, probante Sede Apostolica, possunt concordes, in locum tribunalium dioecesanorum de quibus in cann. 1419-1421, unicum constituere in suis dioecesibus tribunal primae instantiae; quo in casu ipsorum Episcoporum coetui vel Episcopo ab eisdem designato omnes competunt potestates, quas Episcopus dioecesanus habet circa suum tribunal.

§ 2. Tribunalia, de quibus in § 1, constitui possunt vel ad causas quaslibet vel ad aliqua tantum causarum genera.

Can. 1424 – Unicus iudex in quolibet iudicio duos assessores, clericos vel laicos probatae vitae, sibi consulentes asciscere potest.

Can. 1425 – § 1. Reprobata contraria consuetudine, tribunali collegiali trium iudicum reservantur :

1° causae contentiosae : *a*) de vinculo sacrae ordinationis ; *b*) de vinculo matrimonii, firmis praescriptis cann. 1686 et 1688 ;

2° causae poenales : *a*) de delictis quae poenam dimissionis e statu clericali secumferre possunt ; *b*) de irroganda vel declaranda excommunicatione.

§ 2. Episcopus causas difficiliores vel maioris momenti committere potest iudicio trium vel quinque iudicum.

§ 3. Vicarius iudicialis ad singulas causas cognoscendas iudices ex ordine per turnum advocet, nisi Episcopus in singulis casibus aliter statuerit.

§ 4. In primo iudicii gradu, si forte collegium constitui nequeat, Episcoporum conferentia, quamdiu huiusmodi impossibilitas perduret, permittere potest ut Episcopus causas unico iudici clerico committat, qui, ubi fieri possit, assessorem et auditorem sibi asciscat.

§ 5. Iudices semel designatos ne subroget Vicarius iudicialis, nisi ex gravissima causa in decreto exprimenda.

Can. 1426 – § 1. Tribunal collegiale collegialiter procedere debet, et per maiorem suffragiorum partem sententias ferre.

§ 2. Eidem praeesse debet, quatenus fieri potest, Vicarius iudicialis vel Vicarius iudicialis adiunctus.

§3. The judges are to be of unimpaired reputation and possess doctorates, or at least licentiates, in canon law.

Can. 1422 — The judicial vicar, the adjutant judicial vicars and the other judges are to be appointed for a definite period of time with due regard for the prescription of can. 1420, §5; they cannot be removed except for legitimate and serious cause.

Can. 1423 — §1. With the approval of the Apostolic See, several diocesan bishops may agree to establish for their dioceses a single tribunal of first instance in place of the diocesan tribunals mentioned in cann. 1419–1421; in this case the group of bishops or a bishop designated by them has all the powers which a diocesan bishop has over his own tribunal.

§2. The tribunals mentioned in §1 can be established either for any case whatsoever or only for some types of cases.

Can. 1424 — In any trial a single judge can make use of two assessors, who are clerics or lay persons of upright life, to serve as his consultors.

Can. 1425 — §1. Every contrary custom being reprobated, the following cases are reserved to a collegiate tribunal of three judges:

1° contentious cases: a) concerning the bond of sacred ordination; b) concerning the bond of marriage with due regard for the prescriptions of cann. 1686 and 1688;

2° penal cases: a) concerning offenses which can entail the penalty of dismissal from the clerical state; b) concerning the imposition or declaration of excommunication.

§2. The bishop can entrust more difficult cases or cases of greater importance to the judgment of three or five judges.

§3. Unless the bishop has determined otherwise for individual cases, the judicial vicar is to assign the judges in order by turn to adjudicate the individual cases.

§4. If it happens that a collegiate tribunal cannot be established for a trial of first instance, the conference of bishops can permit the bishop to entrust cases to a single clerical judge as long as the impossibility of establishing a college perdures; he is to be a cleric and is to employ an assessor and an auditor where possible.

§5. The judicial vicar is not to appoint substitutes for judges once they are assigned unless for a most serious reason, expressed in a decree.

Can. 1426 — §1. A collegiate tribunal must proceed as a collegial body and pass its sentences by majority vote.

§2. The judicial vicar or the adjutant judicial vicar must preside over a collegiate tribunal insofar as this is possible.

Can. 1427 – § 1. Si controversia sit inter religiosos vel domos eius-dem instituti religiosi clericalis iuris pontificii, iudex primae instan-tiae, nisi aliud in constitutionibus caveatur, est Superior provincialis, aut, si monasterium sit sui iuris, Abbas localis.

§ 2. Salvo diverso constitutionum praescripto, si res contentiosa agatur inter duas provincias, in prima instantia iudicabit per se ipse vel per delegatum supremus Moderator; si inter duo monasteria, Abbas superior congregationis monasticae.

§ 3. Si demum controversia enascatur inter religiosas personas phy-sicas vel iuridicas diversorum institutorum religiosorum, aut etiam eiusdem instituti clericalis iuris dioecesani vel laicalis, aut inter per-sonam religiosam et clericum saecularem vel laicum vel personam iuri-dicam non religiosam, iudicat in prima instantia tribunal dioecesanum.

Art. 2

De auditoribus et relatoribus

Can. 1428 – § 1. Iudex vel tribunalis collegialis praeses possunt auditorem designare ad causae instructionem peragendam, eum seligen-tes aut ex tribunalis iudicibus aut ex personis ab Episcopo ad hoc munus approbatis.

§ 2. Episcopus potest ad auditoris munus approbare clericos vel laicos, qui bonis moribus, prudentia et doctrina fulgeant.

§ 3. Auditoris est, secundum iudicis mandatum, probationes tan-tum colligere easque collectas iudici tradere; potest autem, nisi iudicis mandatum obstet, interim decidere quae et quomodo probationes col-ligendae sint, si forte de hac re quaestio oriatur, dum ipse munus suum exercet.

Can. 1429 – Tribunalis collegialis praeses debet unum ex iudicibus collegii ponentem seu relatorem designare, qui in coetu iudicum de causa referat et sententias in scriptis redigat; in ipsius locum idem praeses alium ex iusta causa substituere potest.

Can. 1427 — §1. If there is a controversy between religious or houses of the same clerical religious institute of pontifical right, the judge of first instance is the provincial superior unless the constitutions provide otherwise; if it is an autonomous monastery, it is the local abbot.

§2. With due regard for the different prescriptions of the constitutions, if it is a contentious case between two provinces, the supreme moderator himself personally or through a delegate shall be the judge in first instance; if the contention is between two monasteries, it shall be the abbot superior of the monastic congregation.

§3. If the controversy arises between religious persons, physical or juridic, of different religious institutes or even of the same clerical or lay institute of diocesan right, or between a religious person and a secular cleric, or a lay person, or a non-religious juridic person, the diocesan tribunal judges in first instance.

Art. 2

Auditors and Relators

Can. 1428 — §1. A judge or the president of a collegiate tribunal can designate an auditor to carry out the instruction of a case, selecting one either from among the judges of the tribunal or from among the persons approved for this function by the bishop.

§2. The bishop can approve for the function of auditor clerics or lay persons who are outstanding for their good character, prudence and learning.

§3. The only task of the auditor is to collect the proofs according to the mandate of the judge and to present them to the judge; unless the mandate of the judge states otherwise, the auditor can in the meantime decide which proofs are to be collected and how they are to be collected if such a question perhaps arises while the auditor is exercising his or her function.

Can. 1429 — The president of a collegiate tribunal must assign one of the collegiate judges as *ponens* or *relator* who reports on the case at the meeting of the judges and puts the sentence into writing; for a just cause the president may substitute another in place of the original *relator*.

Art. 3

DE PROMOTORE IUSTITIAE, VINCULI DEFENSORE ET NOTARIO

Can. 1430 – Ad causas contentiosas, in quibus bonum publicum in discrimen vocari potest, et ad causas poenales constituatur in dioecesi promotor iustitiae, qui officio tenetur providendi bono publico.

Can. 1431 – § 1. In causis contentiosis, Episcopi dioecesani est iudicare utrum bonum publicum in discrimen vocari possit necne, nisi interventus promotoris iustitiae a lege praecipiatur vel ex natura rei evidenter necessarius sit.

§ 2. Si in praecedenti instantia intervenerit promotor iustitiae, in ulteriore gradu huius interventus praesumitur necessarius.

Can. 1432 – Ad causas, in quibus agitur de nullitate sacrae ordinationis aut de nullitate vel solutione matrimonii, constituatur in dioecesi defensor vinculi, qui officio tenetur proponendi et exponendi omnia quae rationabiliter adduci possint adversus nullitatem vel solutionem.

Can. 1433 – In causis in quibus promotoris iustitiae aut defensoris vinculi praesentia requiritur, iis non citatis, acta irrita sunt, nisi ipsi, etsi non citati, revera interfuerint, aut saltem ante sententiam, actis inspectis, munere suo fungi potuerint.

Can. 1434 – Nisi aliud expresse caveatur :
1° quoties lex praecipit ut iudex partes earumve alteram audiat, etiam promotor iustitiae et vinculi defensor, si iudicio intersint, audiendi sunt;
2° quoties instantia partis requiritur ut iudex aliquid decernere possit, instantia promotoris iustitiae vel vinculi defensoris, qui iudicio intersint, eandem vim habet.

Can. 1435 – Episcopi est promotorem iustitiae et vinculi defensorem nominare, qui sint clerici vel laici, integrae famae, in iure canonico doctores vel licentiati, ac prudentia et iustitiae zelo probati.

Can. 1436 – § 1. Eadem persona, non autem in eadem causa, officium promotoris iustitiae et defensoris vinculi gerere potest.

§ 2. Promotor et defensor constitui possunt tum ad universitatem causarum tum ad singulas causas; possunt autem ab Episcopo, iusta de causa, removeri.

Art. 3

THE PROMOTER OF JUSTICE, THE DEFENDER OF THE BOND AND THE NOTARY

Can. 1430 — A promoter of justice is to be appointed in a diocese for contentious cases in which the public good could be at stake and for penal cases; the promoter of justice is bound by office to provide for the public good.

Can. 1431 — §1. In contentious cases it is the task of the diocesan bishop to judge whether or not the public good could be at stake unless the intervention of the promoter of justice is prescribed by law or it is clearly necessary from the nature of the matter.

§2. If the promoter of justice has intervened in a preceding instance, such intervention is presumed to be necessary in a further instance.

Can. 1432 — A defender of the bond is to be appointed in a diocese for cases concerning the nullity of sacred ordination or the nullity or dissolution of marriage; the defender of the bond is bound by office to propose and clarify everything which can be reasonably adduced against nullity or dissolution.

Can. 1433 — In cases which require the presence of the promoter of justice or the defender of the bond, the acts are invalid if they were not cited, unless, although not cited, they were actually present, or, at least before the sentence, could have fulfilled their office by inspecting the acts.

Can. 1434 — Unless express provision is made to the contrary:

1° as often as the law requires the judge to hear the parties or one or other of them, the promoter of justice and the defender of the bond are also to be heard if they are present in court;

2° as often as the judge is required to decide something at the request of a party, the request of the promoter of justice or the defender of the bond has the same force when they are present in the court.

Can. 1435 — It is the task of the bishop to name the promoter of justice and the defender of the bond who are to be clerics or lay persons of unimpaired reputation who hold doctorates or licentiates in canon law and are proven in prudence and in zeal for justice.

Can. 1436 — §1. The same person can hold the office of promoter of justice and of defender of the bond but not in the same case.

§2. The promoter and defender can be appointed for all cases or for particular cases; they can, however, be removed by the bishop for a just cause.

Can. 1437 – § 1. Cuilibet processui intersit notarius, adeo ut nulla habeantur acta, si non fuerint ab eo subscripta.

§ 2. Acta, quae notarii conficiunt, publicam fidem faciunt.

Caput II
DE TRIBUNALI SECUNDAE INSTANTIAE

Can. 1438 – Firmo praescripto can. 1444, § 1, n. 1:

1° a tribunali Episcopi suffraganei appellatur ad tribunal Metropolitae, salvo praescripto can. 1439;

2° in causis in prima instantia pertractatis coram Metropolita fit appellatio ad tribunal quod ipse, probante Sede Apostolica, stabiliter designaverit;

3° pro causis coram Superiore provinciali actis tribunal secundae instantiae est penes supremum Moderatorem; pro causis actis coram Abbate locali, penes Abbatem superiorem congregationis monasticae.

Can. 1439 – § 1. Si quod tribunal primae instantiae unicum pro pluribus dioecesibus, ad normam can. 1423, constitutum sit, Episcoporum conferentia debet tribunal secundae instantiae, probante Sede Apostolica, constituere, nisi dioeceses sint omnes eiusdem archidioecesis suffraganeae.

§ 2. Episcoporum conferentia potest, probante Sede Apostolica, unum vel plura tribunalia secundae instantiae constituere, etiam praeter casus de quibus in § 1.

§ 3. Quod attinet ad tribunalia secundae instantiae, de quibus in §§ 1-2, Episcoporum conferentia vel Episcopus ab ea designatus omnes habent potestates, quae Episcopo dioecesano competunt circa suum tribunal.

Can. 1440 – Si competentia ratione gradus, ad normam cann. 1438 et 1439 non servetur, incompetentia iudicis est absoluta.

Can. 1441 – Tribunal secundae instantiae eodem modo quo tribunal primae instantiae constitui debet. Si tamen in primo iudicii gradu, secundum can. 1425, § 4, iudex unicus sententiam tulit, tribunal secundae instantiae collegialiter procedat.

Can. 1437 — §1. A notary is to be present during each procedure so that the acts are considered null if they have not been signed by the notary.

§2. Acts which notaries draw up warrant public trust.

CHAPTER II

THE TRIBUNAL OF SECOND INSTANCE

Can. 1438 — With due regard for the prescription of can. 1444, §1, n. 1:

1° from the tribunal of a suffragan bishop appeal is made to the metropolitan tribunal but the prescription of can. 1439 is to be observed;

2° in cases in first instance tried before the metropolitan, appeal is made to the tribunal which he has permanently designated with the approval of the Apostolic See;

3° for cases tried before a provincial superior, the tribunal of second instance is before the supreme moderator; for cases tried before the local abbot, the tribunal of second instance is before the abbot superior of the monastic congregation.

Can. 1439 — §1. If a single tribunal of first instance has been established for several dioceses in accord with the norm of can. 1423, the conference of bishops must establish a tribunal of second instance with the approval of the Apostolic See unless these dioceses are all suffragans of the same archdiocese.

§2. The conference of bishops can establish one or several tribunals of second instance with the approval of the Apostolic See even beyond the cases mentioned in §1.

§3. The conference of bishops or a bishop designated by it has all the powers over the tribunals of second instance mentioned in §§1 and 2 which the diocesan bishop has over his own tribunal.

Can. 1440 — If competence by reason of grade in accord with cann. 1438 and 1439 is not observed, the incompetence of the judge is absolute.

Can. 1441 — A tribunal of second instance must be constituted in the same way as a tribunal of first instance; nevertheless if a single judge passed sentence in a first instance court in accord with can. 1425, §4, the tribunal of second instance is to proceed in a collegial manner.

Caput III

DE APOSTOLICAE SEDIS TRIBUNALIBUS

Can. 1442 – Romanus Pontifex pro toto orbe catholico iudex est supremus, qui vel per se ipse ius dicit, vel per ordinaria Sedis Apostolicae tribunalia, vel per iudices a se delegatos.

Can. 1443 – Tribunal ordinarium a Romano Pontifice constitutum appellationibus recipiendis est Rota Romana.

Can. 1444 – § 1. Rota Romana iudicat:

1° in secunda instantia, causas quae ab ordinariis tribunalibus primae instantiae diiudicatae fuerint et ad Sanctam Sedem per appellationem legitimam deferantur;

2° in tertia vel ulteriori instantia, causas ab ipsa Rota Romana et ab aliis quibusvis tribunalibus iam cognitas, nisi res iudicata habeatur.

§ 2. Hoc tribunal iudicat etiam in prima instantia causas de quibus in can. 1405, § 3, aliasve quas Romanus Pontifex sive motu proprio, sive ad instantiam partium ad suum tribunal advocaverit et Rotae Romanae commiserit; easque, nisi aliud cautum sit in commissi muneris rescripto, ipsa Rota iudicat etiam in secunda et ulteriore instantia.

Can. 1445 – § 1. Supremum Signaturae Apostolicae Tribunal cognoscit:

1° querelas nullitatis et petitiones restitutionis in integrum et alios recursus contra sententias rotales;

2° recursus in causis de statu personarum, quas ad novum examen Rota Romana admittere renuit;

3° exceptiones suspicionis aliasque causas contra Auditores Rotae Romanae propter acta in exercitio ipsorum muneris;

4° conflictus competentiae de quibus in can. 1416.

§ 2. Ipsum Tribunal videt de contentionibus ortis ex actu potestatis administrativae ecclesiasticae ad eam legitime delatis, de aliis controversiis administrativis quae a Romano Pontifice vel a Romanae Curiae dicasteriis ipsi deferantur, et de conflictu competentiae inter eadem dicasteria.

§ 3. Supremi huius Tribunalis praeterea est:

1° rectae administrationi iustitiae invigilare et in advocatos vel procuratores, si opus sit, animadvertere;

2° tribunalium competentiam prorogare;

3° promovere et approbare erectionem tribunalium, de quibus in cann. 1423 et 1439.

CHAPTER III

THE TRIBUNALS OF THE APOSTOLIC SEE

Can. 1442 — The Roman Pontiff is the supreme judge for the entire Catholic world; he tries cases either personally or through the ordinary tribunals of the Apostolic See or through judges delegated by himself.

Can. 1443 — The ordinary tribunal established by the Roman Pontiff to receive appeals is the Roman Rota.

Can. 1444 — §1. The Roman Rota tries:

1° in second instance, cases which have been adjudicated by the ordinary tribunals of first instance and brought before the Holy See by means of legitimate appeal;

2° in third and further instance, cases already tried by the Roman Rota itself or by any other tribunals whatsoever, unless the case is considered *res iudicata*.

§2. This tribunal also tries in first instance the cases mentioned in can. 1405, §3 and other cases which the Roman Pontiff has summoned to his own tribunal and has entrusted to the Roman Rota of his own accord or at the request of the parties; unless other provisions are made in the rescript of commission, the Rota tries these cases in second and further instance as well.

Can. 1445 — §1. The Supreme Tribunal of the Apostolic Signatura adjudicates:

1° complaints of nullity, petitions for *restitutio in integrum*, and other recourses against rotal sentences;

2° recourses in cases involving the status of persons which the Roman Rota refuses to admit to a new examination;

3° exceptions of suspicion and other cases against the auditors of the Roman Rota because of acts in the exercise of their function;

4° conflicts of competence mentioned in can. 1416.

§2. This same tribunal deals with contentions legitimately referred to it which arise from an act of ecclesiastical administrative power, with other administrative controversies which are referred to it by the Roman Pontiff or by the dicasteries of the Roman Curia, and with a conflict of competence among these dicasteries.

§3. Furthermore it is the task of this Supreme Tribunal:

1° to exercise its vigilance over the correct administration of justice and to discipline advocates or procurators, if necessary;

2° to extend the competence of tribunals;

3° to promote and approve the erection of the tribunals mentioned in cann. 1423 and 1439.

TITULUS III
DE DISCIPLINA IN TRIBUNALIBUS SERVANDA

CAPUT I
DE OFFICIO IUDICUM ET TRIBUNALIS MINISTRORUM

Can. 1446 – § 1. Christifideles omnes, in primis autem Episcopi, sedulo annitantur ut, salva iustitia, lites in populo Dei, quantum fieri possit, vitentur et pacifice quam primum componantur.

§ 2. Iudex in limine litis, et etiam quolibet alio momento, quotiescumque spem aliquam boni exitus perspicit, partes hortari et adiuvare ne omittat, ut de aequa controversiae solutione quaerenda communi consilio curent, viasque ad hoc propositum idoneas ipsis indicet, gravibus quoque hominibus ad mediationem adhibitis.

§ 3. Quod si circa privatum partium bonum lis versetur, dispiciat iudex num transactione vel arbitrorum iudicio, ad normam cann. 1717- 1720, controversia finem habere utiliter possit.

1713-1716

Can. 1447 – Qui causae interfuit tamquam iudex, promotor iustitiae, defensor vinculi, procurator, advocatus, testis aut peritus, nequit postea valide eandem causam in alia instantia tamquam iudex definire aut in eadem munus assessoris sustinere.

Can. 1448 – § 1. Iudex cognoscendam ne suscipiat causam, in qua ratione consanguinitatis vel affinitatis in quolibet gradu lineae rectae et usque ad quartum gradum lineae collateralis, vel ratione tutelae et curatelae, intimae vitae consuetudinis, magnae simultatis, vel lucri faciendi aut damni vitandi, aliquid ipsius intersit.

§ 2. In iisdem adiunctis ab officio suo abstinere debent iustitiae promotor, defensor vinculi, assessor et auditor.

Can. 1449 – § 1. In casibus, de quibus in can. 1448, nisi iudex ipse abstineat, pars potest eum recusare.

§ 2. De recusatione videt Vicarius iudicialis; si ipse recusetur, videt Episcopus qui tribunali praeest.

§ 3. Si Episcopus sit iudex et contra eum recusatio opponatur, ipse abstineat a iudicando.

TITLE III

THE DISCIPLINE TO BE OBSERVED IN TRIBUNALS

CHAPTER I

THE OFFICE OF JUDGES AND OFFICERS OF THE TRIBUNAL

Can. 1446 — §1. With due regard for justice, all the Christian faithful especially bishops are to strive earnestly to avoid lawsuits among the people of God as much as possible and to resolve them peacefully as soon as possible.

§2. At the very start or even at any point during the litigation, whenever some hope of a happy outcome is perceived, the judge is not to neglect to encourage and assist the parties to collaborate in working out an equitable solution to the controversy as well as indicating suitable ways of reaching such a solution, perhaps even employing the services of reputable persons for mediation.

§3. If the litigation concerns the private good of the parties, the judge should find out whether it can profitably be resolved through a negotiated settlement or through arbitration in accord with the norms of cann. 1717–1720*.

Can. 1447 — A person who has taken part in a case as a judge, promoter of justice, defender of the bond, procurator, advocate, witness or expert cannot afterwards in another instance validly resolve the same case as a judge or act as an assessor in another instance.

Can. 1448 — §1. A judge is not to undertake the adjudication of a case in which the judge may have some interest due to consanguinity or affinity in any degree of the direct line and up to the fourth degree of the collateral line, due to functioning as a guardian or trustee, due to close friendship, due to great animosity, or due to a desire to make some profit or avoid some loss.

§2. In the same circumstances the promoter of justice, the defender of the bond, the assessor, and the auditor must disqualify themselves from their office.

Can. 1449 — §1. If, in the cases mentioned in can. 1448, the judge does not withdraw, the party can lodge an objection against the judge.

§2. The judicial vicar deals with the issue of such an objection; if the judicial vicar is the one objected against, the bishop who is in charge of the tribunal deals with the issue.

§3. If the bishop himself is the judge and an objection is lodged against him, he is to disqualify himself from judging.

---

*Apparently should read 1713–1716.—Trans.

§ 4. Si recusatio opponatur contra promotorem iustitiae, defensorem vinculi aut alios tribunalis administros, de hac exceptione videt praeses in tribunali collegiali vel ipse iudex, si unicus sit.

Can. 1450 – Recusatione admissa, personae mutari debent, non vero iudicii gradus.

Can. 1451 – § 1. Quaestio de recusatione expeditissime definienda est, auditis partibus, promotore iustitiae vel vinculi defensore, si inter sint, neque ipsi recusati sint.

§ 2. Actus positi a iudice antequam recusetur, validi sunt; qui autem positi sunt post propositam recusationem, rescindi debent, si pars petat intra decem dies ab admissa recusatione.

Can. 1452 – § 1. In negotio quod privatorum solummodo interest, iudex procedere potest dumtaxat ad instantiam partis. Causa autem legitime introducta, iudex procedere potest et debet etiam ex officio in causis poenalibus aliisque, quae publicum Ecclesiae bonum aut animarum salutem respiciunt.

§ 2. Potest autem praeterea iudex partium neglegentiam in probationibus afferendis vel in exceptionibus opponendis supplere, quoties id necessarium censeat ad vitandam graviter iniustam sententiam, firmis praescriptis can. 1600.

Can. 1453 – Iudices et tribunalia curent ut quam primum, salva iustitia, causae omnes terminentur, utque in tribunali primae instantiae ultra annum ne protrahantur, in tribunali vero secundae instantiae, ultra sex menses.

Can. 1454 – Omnes qui tribunal constituunt aut eidem opem ferunt, iusiurandum de munere rite et fideliter implendo praestare debent.

Can. 1455 – § 1. In iudicio poenali semper, in contentioso autem si ex revelatione alicuius actus processualis praeiudicium partibus obvenire possit, iudices et tribunalis adiutores tenentur ad secretum officii servandum.

§ 2. Tenentur etiam semper ad secretum servandum de discussione quae inter iudices in tribunali collegiali ante ferendam sententiam habetur, tum etiam de variis suffragiis et opinionibus ibidem prolatis, firmo praescripto can. 1609, § 4.

§ 3. Immo, quoties natura causae vel probationum talis sit ut ex actorum vel probationum evulgatione aliorum fama periclitetur, vel praebeatur ansa dissidiis, aut scandalum aliudve id genus incommodum oriatur, iudex poterit testes, peritos, partes earumque advocatos vel procuratores iureiurando astringere ad secretum servandum.

§4. If the objection is lodged against the promoter of justice, the defender of the bond or other officers of the tribunal, the president of the collegiate tribunal or the single judge deals with this exception.

Can. 1450 — If the objection is accepted, the persons must be changed, but the grade of the court does not change.

Can. 1451 — §1. The issue of an objection is to be solved without delay after having heard the parties, the promoter of justice or defender of the bond if they are present and an objection has not been lodged against them.

§2. The acts posited by a judge prior to an objection are valid; but those acts posited after the objection has been moved must be rescinded if the party petitions within ten days from the acceptance of the objection.

Can. 1452 — §1. In a matter which concerns private individuals only, a judge can proceed only at the request of a party; once a case has been legitimately introduced, however, a judge can and must proceed, even ex officio, in penal cases and in other cases which involve the public good of the Church or the salvation of souls.

§2. Furthermore, a judge can supply for the negligence of parties in furnishing proofs or in placing exceptions as often as it is judged necessary in order to avoid a seriously unjust sentence, with due regard for the prescriptions of can. 1600.

Can. 1453 — Judges and tribunals are to see to it that, with due regard for justice, all cases are concluded as soon as possible so that in a tribunal of first instance they are not prolonged beyond a year and in a tribunal of second instance beyond six months.

Can. 1454 — All persons who constitute a tribunal or assist it must take an oath that they will fulfill their function properly and faithfully.

Can. 1455 — §1. Judges and tribunal personnel are always bound to secrecy of office in a penal case; they are also thus bound in a contentious case if the parties may be harmed by the revelation of some procedural act.

§2. They are also always bound to observe secrecy concerning the discussion among the judges in a collegiate tribunal before passing the sentence and concerning the various votes and opinions offered during the discussion with due regard for the prescription of can. 1609, §4.

§3. Moreover, as often as the nature of a case or the proofs is such that the reputation of others is endangered by divulging the acts or proofs, or an opportunity for discord is provided or scandal or some other similar disadvantage might arise, the judge can bind the witnesses, the experts, the parties and their advocates or proxies by oath to observe secrecy.

Can. 1456 – Iudex et omnes tribunalis administri, occasione agendi iudicii, dona quaevis acceptare prohibentur.

Can. 1457 – § 1. Iudices qui, cum certe et evidenter competentes sint, ius reddere recusent, vel nullo suffragante iuris praescripto se competentes declarent atque causas cognoscant ac definiant, vel secreti legem violent, vel ex dolo aut gravi neglegentia aliud litigantibus damnum inferant, congruis poenis a competenti auctoritate puniri possunt, non exclusa officii privatione.

§ 2. Iisdem sanctionibus subsunt tribunalis ministri et adiutores, si officio suo, ut supra, defuerint; quos omnes etiam iudex punire potest.

Caput II
DE ORDINE COGNITIONUM

Can. 1458 – Causae cognoscendae sunt eo ordine quo fuerunt propositae et in albo inscriptae, nisi ex iis aliqua celerem prae ceteris expeditionem exigat, quod quidem peculiari decreto, rationibus suffulto, statuendum est.

Can. 1459 – § 1. Vitia, quibus sententiae nullitas haberi potest, in quolibet iudicii statu vel gradu excipi possunt itemque a iudice ex officio declarari.

§ 2. Praeter casus de quibus in § 1, exceptiones dilatoriae, eae praesertim quae respiciunt personas et modum iudicii, proponendae sunt ante contestationem litis, nisi contestata iam lite emerserint, et quam primum definiendae.

Can. 1460 – § 1. Si exceptio proponatur contra iudicis competentiam, hac de re ipse iudex videre debet.

§ 2. In casu exceptionis de incompetentia relativa, si iudex se competentem pronuntiet, eius decisio non admittit appellationem, at non prohibentur querela nullitatis et restitutio in integrum.

§ 3. Quod si iudex se incompetentem declaret, pars quae se gravatam reputat, potest intra quindecim dies utiles provocare ad tribunal appellationis.

Can. 1461 – Iudex in quovis stadio causae se absolute incompetentem agnoscens, suam incompetentiam declarare debet.

Can. 1462 – § 1. Exceptiones rei iudicatae, transactionis et aliae peremptoriae quae dicuntur *litis finitae,* proponi et cognosci debent ante contestationem litis; qui serius eas opposuerit, non est reiciendus, sed condemnetur ad expensas, nisi probet se oppositionem malitiose non distulisse.

Can. 1456 — The judge and all tribunal offcers are forbidden to accept any gifts whatsoever on the occasion of their functioning in a trial.

Can. 1457 — §1. Judges who refuse to try a case when they are certainly and obviously competent, who declare themselves competent without any legal basis and hear and decide cases, who violate the law of secrecy or who inflict some damage on litigants out of malice or serious negligence can be punished by the competent authority with fitting penalties, including deprivation of office.

§2. Officers and personnel of the tribunal are subject to the same sanctions if they do not fulfill their function as above; the judge can also punish all of them.

CHAPTER II
THE ORDER OF ADJUDICATION

Can. 1458 — Cases are to be tried in the order in which they are presented and put on the docket unless some of them demand speedier treatment than others, which fact is to be determined in a special decree which states the reasons.

Can. 1459 — §1. Defects which can render a sentence invalid can be introduced as an exception during any stage or grade of a trial; a judge can likewise declare them ex officio.

§2. Besides the cases mentioned in §1, dilatory exceptions, especially those which concern the persons and the manner of the trial, are to be proposed before the joinder of issues (*contestatio litis*), unless they first emerged only after it; and they are to be settled as soon as possible.

Can. 1460 — §1. If an exception is proposed against the competence of the judge, the same judge must deal with the matter.

§2. In the case of an exception of relative incompetence, if the judge finds for competence, the decision does not admit of appeal; however, a complaint of nullity and *restitutio in integrum* are not forbidden.

§3. But if the judge finds for incompetence, the person who feels injured can appeal to the appellate tribunal within fifteen available days (*dies utiles*).

Can. 1461 — Judges who become aware of their absolute incompetence during any stage of a case must declare that incompetence.

Can. 1462 — §1. The exceptions that the matter has become *res iudicata* and that an agreement had been already reached (*transactio*), as well as other peremptory exceptions which are called *litis finitae* must be proposed and adjudicated before the joinder of issues (*contestatio litis*); a person who proposes them later is not to be rejected but is liable for the court costs unless there is proof that presentation was not maliciously delayed.

§ 2. Aliae exceptiones peremptoriae proponantur in contestatione litis, et suo tempore tractandae sunt secundum regulas circa quaestiones incidentes.

Can. 1463 – § 1. Actiones reconventionales proponi valide nequeunt, nisi intra triginta dies a lite contestata.

§ 2. Eaedem autem cognoscantur simul cum conventionali actione, hoc est pari gradu cum ea, nisi eas separatim cognoscere necessarium sit aut iudex id opportunius existimaverit.

Can. 1464 – Quaestiones de cautione pro expensis iudicialibus praestanda aut de concessione gratuiti patrocinii, quod statim ab initio postulatum fuerit, et aliae huiusmodi regulariter videndae sunt ante litis contestationem.

Caput III
DE TERMINIS ET DILATIONIBUS

Can. 1465 – § 1. Fatalia legis quae dicuntur, id est termini perimendis iuribus lege constituti, prorogari non possunt, neque valide, nisi petentibus partibus, coarctari.

§ 2. Termini autem iudiciales et conventionales, ante eorum lapsum, poterunt, iusta intercedente causa, a iudice, auditis vel petentibus partibus, prorogari, numquam autem, nisi partibus consentientibus, valide coarctari.

§ 3. Caveat tamen iudex ne nimis diuturna lis fiat ex prorogatione.

Can. 1466 – Ubi lex terminos haud statuat ad actus processuales peragendos, iudex illos praefinire debet, habita ratione naturae uniuscuiusque actus.

Can. 1467 – Si die ad actum iudicialem indicto vacaverit tribunal, terminus intellegitur prorogatus ad primum sequentem diem non feriatum.

Caput IV
DE LOCO IUDICII

Can. 1468 – Uniuscuiusque tribunalis sedes sit, quantum fieri potest, stabilis, quae statutis horis pateat.

Can. 1469 – § 1. Iudex e territorio suo vi expulsus vel a iurisdictione ibi exercenda impeditus, potest extra territorium iurisdictionem

§2. Other peremptory exceptions are to be lodged during the joinder of issues (*contestatio litis*) and are to be treated at their proper time in accord with the regulations which deal with incidental questions.

Can. 1463 — §1. Counter-claim actions cannot be lodged validly except within thirty days from the joinder of issues (*contestatio litis*).

§2. However, they are to be adjudicated at the same time as the original action, that is, on the same grade with it unless it is necessary to try them separately or the judge deems it more appropriate to try them separately.

Can. 1464 — Questions concerning a deposit for judicial expenses or the granting of gratuitous legal assistance which has been requested from the beginning and other such questions are to be dealt with before the joinder of issues (*contestatio litis*) as a general rule.

CHAPTER III

TIME LIMITS AND DELAYS

Can. 1465 — §1. *Fatalia legis* or the time limits set by law for extinguishing the right to act cannot be extended nor validly shortened unless the parties request it.

§2. Before they have lapsed, however, judicial time limits and agreed upon time limits can be extended by the judge for a just cause after hearing the parties or if they request it; such time limits, however, may never validly be shortened unless the parties agree.

§3. But the judge is to see to it that the litigation is not overly prolonged by such extensions.

Can. 1466 — When the law does not establish time limits for positing of procedural acts, the judge must define them taking into consideration the nature of each act.

Can. 1467 — If the tribunal is closed on the day scheduled for a judicial act the time limit is extended to the first day following which is not a holiday.

CHAPTER IV

THE PLACE OF THE TRIAL

Can. 1468 — To the extent that it is possible, each tribunal is to be in a permanent place which is open during specified hours.

Can. 1469 — §1. Judges who have been forcibly expelled from their own territory or have been impeded in the exercise of jurisdiction there can

suam exercere et sententiam ferre, certiore tamen hac de re facto Episcopo dioecesano.

§ 2. Praeter casum de quo in § 1, iudex, ex iusta causa et auditis partibus, potest ad probationes acquirendas etiam extra proprium territorium se conferre, de licentia tamen Episcopi dioecesani loci adeundi et in sede ab eodem designata.

Caput V

DE PERSONIS IN AULAM ADMITTENDIS ET DE MODO CONFICIENDI ET CONSERVANDI ACTA

Can. 1470 – § 1. Nisi aliter lex particularis caveat, dum causae coram tribunali aguntur, ii tantummodo adsint in aula quos lex aut iudex ad processum expediendum necessarios esse statuerit.

§ 2. Omnes iudicio assistentes, qui reverentiae et oboedientiae tribunali debitae graviter defuerint, iudex potest congruis poenis ad officium reducere, advocatos praeterea et procuratores etiam a munere apud tribunalia ecclesiastica exercendo suspendere.

Can. 1471 – Si qua persona interroganda utatur lingua iudici vel partibus ignota, adhibeatur interpres iuratus a iudice designatus. Declarationes tamen scripto redigantur lingua originaria et translatio addatur. Interpres etiam adhibeatur si surdus vel mutus interrogari debet, nisi forte malit iudex quaestionibus a se datis scripto respondeatur.

Can. 1472 – § 1. Acta iudicialia, tum quae meritum quaestionis respiciunt, seu acta causae, tum quae ad formam procedendi pertinent, seu acta processus, scripto redacta esse debent.

§ 2. Singula folia actorum numerentur et authenticitatis signo muniantur.

Can. 1473 – Quoties in actis iudicialibus partium aut testium subscriptio requiritur, si pars aut testis subscribere nequeat vel nolit, id in ipsis actis adnotetur, simulque iudex et notarius fidem faciant actum ipsum de verbo ad verbum parti aut testi perlectum fuisse, et partem aut testem vel non potuisse vel noluisse subscribere.

Can. 1474 – § 1. In casu appellationis, actorum exemplar, fide facta a notario de eius authenticitate, ad tribunal superius mittatur.

§ 2. Si acta exarata fuerint lingua tribunali superiori ignota, transferantur in aliam eidem tribunali cognitam, cautelis adhibitis, ut de fideli translatione constet.

exercise jurisdiction and render a sentence outside that territory; however, the diocesan bishop should be informed of this fact by the judge.

§2. Besides the case mentioned in §1, for a just cause and after hearing the parties, judges can travel outside their own territory in order to acquire proofs with the permission of the diocesan bishop of the place they enter and at a site designated by the bishop.

CHAPTER V

PERSONS TO BE ADMITTED TO THE TRIAL AND THE MANNER OF ASSEMBLING AND PRESERVING THE ACTS

Can. 1470 — §1. Unless particular law provides otherwise, while cases are being tried before a tribunal only those persons are to be present in court whom the law or the judge decides are necessary to expedite the process.

§2. With appropriate penalties a judge can demand compliance on the part of all who assist at the trial and who are seriously lacking in the respect and obedience owed the tribunal; the judge can also suspend advocates and procurators from exercising their function before ecclesiastical tribunals.

Can. 1471 — If a person to be interrogated speaks a language which is not known by the judge or the parties, a sworn interpreter designated by the judge is to be employed. Their statements, however, are to be put into writing in the original language and a translation is to be added. An interpreter is also to be employed if a deaf or mute person must be interrogated unless the judge perhaps prefers that the person respond to questions in writing.

Can. 1472 — §1. Judicial acts, both the acts of the case, that is, those acts which concern the merits of the question, and the acts of the process, that is, those which pertain to the formal procedure, must be put into writing.

§2. The individual pages of the acts are to be numbered and authenticated with a seal.

Can. 1473 — Whenever the signature of the parties or witnesses is required for judicial acts and a party or a witness cannot or will not sign, this is to be noted in the acts; both the judge and the notary are to attest that the act has been read to the party or witness verbatim and that the party or witness either could not or would not sign.

Can. 1474 — §1. In case of appeal, a copy of the acts authenticated by the attestation of a notary is to be sent to a higher tribunal.

§2. If the acts as drawn up are in a language unknown to the higher tribunal, they are to be translated into a language known to that tribunal, with due precautions being taken that it be a faithful translation.

Can. 1475 – § 1. Iudicio expleto, documenta quae in privatorum dominio sunt, restitui debent, retento tamen eorum exemplari.

§ 2. Notarii et cancellarius sine iudicis mandato tradere prohibentur exemplar actorum iudicialium et documentorum, quae sunt processui acquisita.

TITULUS IV

DE PARTIBus IN CAUSA

Caput I

DE ACTORE ET DE PARTE CONVENTA

Can. 1476 – Quilibet, sive baptizatus sive non baptizatus, potest in iudicio agere; pars autem legitime conventa respondere debet.

Can. 1477 – Licet actor vel pars conventa procuratorem vel advocatum constituerit, semper tamen tenetur in iudicio ipsemet adesse ad praescriptum iuris vel iudicis.

Can. 1478 – § 1. Minores et ii, qui rationis usu destituti sunt, stare in iudicio tantummodo possunt per eorum parentes aut tutores vel curatores, salvo praescripto § 3.

§ 2. Si iudex existimet minorum iura esse in conflictu cum iuribus parentum vel tutorum vel curatorum, aut hos non satis tueri posse ipsorum iura, tunc stent in iudicio per tutorem vel curatorem a iudice datum.

§ 3. Sed in causis spiritualibus et cum spiritualibus conexis, si minores usum rationis assecuti sint, agere et respondere queunt sine parentum vel tutoris consensu, et quidem per se ipsi, si aetatem quattuordecim annorum expleverint; secus per curatorem a iudice constitutum.

§ 4. Bonis interdicti, et ii qui minus firmae mentis sunt, stare in iudicio per se ipsi possunt tantummodo ut de propriis delictis respondeant, aut ad praescriptum iudicis; in ceteris agere et respondere debent per suos curatores.

Can. 1479 – Quoties adest tutor aut curator ab auctoritate civili constitutus, idem potest a iudice ecclesiastico admitti, audito, si fieri potest, Episcopo dioecesano eius cui datus est; quod si non adsit aut non videatur admittendus, ipse iudex tutorem aut curatorem pro causa designabit.

Can. 1475 — §1. At the completion of the trial documents which belong to private individuals must be returned but a copy of them is to be retained.

§2. Notaries and the chancellor are forbidden to furnish a copy of judicial acts and of documents which have been acquired for the process without a mandate from the judge.

TITLE IV
THE PARTIES IN A CASE

CHAPTER I
THE PETITIONER AND THE RESPONDENT

Can. 1476 — Anyone, whether baptized or not, can act in a trial; however, the respondent who has been legitimately cited must answer.

Can. 1477 — Although a petitioner or respondent has appointed a procurator or an advocate, they themselves are nevertheless bound to be present in person at the trial when the law or the judge prescribes it.

Can. 1478 — §1. Minors and those who lack the use of reason can stand trial only through their parents or guardians or curators, with due regard for the prescription of §3.

§2. If the judge decides that the rights of minors are in conflict with the rights of the parents, guardians or curators, or that the latter cannot satisfactorily safeguard the rights of the former, then they are to be represented in the trial by a guardian or curator appointed by the judge.

§3. But in spiritual cases and in cases connected with spiritual matters, if minors have attained the use of reason, they can act and respond without the consent of parents or guardian; if they have completed their fourteenth year of age, they can do so on their own; if not, through a curator appointed by the judge.

§4. Those deprived of the administration of their goods and those who are of diminished mental capacity can stand trial personally only to answer for their own offenses or at the prescription of the judge; in all other cases they must act and respond through their curators.

Can. 1479 — Whenever a guardian or curator appointed by civil authority is present, this person can be admitted by an ecclesiastical judge after having heard the diocesan bishop of the person to whom the guardian or curator has been given, if this can be done; but if a guardian or curator is not present or does not appear admissible, the judge shall designate a guardian or curator for the case.

Can. 1480 – § 1. Personae iuridicae in iudicio stant per suos legitimos repraesentantes.

§ 2. In casu vero defectus vel neglegentiae repraesentantis, potest ipse Ordinarius per se vel per alium stare in iudicio nomine personarum iuridicarum, quae sub eius potestate sunt.

CAPUT II

DE PROCURATORIBUS AD LITES ET ADVOCATIS

Can. 1481 – § 1. Pars libere potest advocatum et procuratorem sibi constituere; sed praeter casus in §§ 2 et 3 statutos, potest etiam per se ipsa agere et respondere, nisi iudex procuratoris vel advocati ministerium necessarium existimaverit.

§ 2. In iudicio poenali accusatus aut a se constitutum aut a iudice datum semper habere debet advocatum.

§ 3. In iudicio contentioso, si agatur de minoribus aut de iudicio in quo bonum publicum vertitur, exceptis causis matrimonialibus, iudex parti carenti defensorem ex officio constituat.

Can. 1482 – § 1. Unicum sibi quisque potest constituere procuratorem, qui nequit alium sibimet substituere, nisi expressa facultas eidem facta fuerit.

§ 2. Quod si tamen, iusta causa suadente, plures ab eodem constituantur, hi ita designentur, ut detur inter ipsos locus praeventioni.

§ 3. Advocati autem plures simul constitui queunt.

Can. 1483 – Procurator et advocatus esse debent aetate maiores et bonae famae; advocatus debet praeterea esse catholicus, nisi Episcopus dioecesanus aliter permittat, et doctor in iure canonico, vel alioquin vere peritus et ab eodem Episcopo approbatus.

Can. 1484 – § 1. Procurator et advocatus antequam munus suscipiant, mandatum authenticum apud tribunal deponere debent.

§ 2. Ad iuris tamen extinctionem impediendam iudex potest procuratorem admittere etiam non exhibito mandato, praestita, si res ferat, idonea cautione; actus autem qualibet vi caret, si intra terminum peremptorium a iudice statuendum, procurator mandatum rite non exhibeat.

Can. 1480 — §1. Juridic persons stand trial through their legitimate representatives.

§2. In a case where the representative is lacking or is negligent, the ordinary himself can stand trial personally or through another in the name of juridic persons which are subject to his power.

CHAPTER II

PROCURATORS FOR THE TRIAL AND ADVOCATES

Can. 1481 — §1. A party can freely appoint a personal advocate and procurator; however, except for the cases stated in §§2 and 3, the party can petition and respond personally unless the judge has decided that the services of a procurator or an advocate are necessary.

§2. The accused in a penal trial must always have an advocate either appointed by the accused or given by the judge.

§3. In a contentious trial which involves minors or the public good except for marriage cases, the judge is to appoint ex officio a defender for a party who lacks one.

Can. 1482 — §1. A person can appoint only a single procurator who cannot substitute another unless an expressed faculty has been granted the procurator to do this.

§2. But if several procurators are appointed by the same party for some just cause, they are to be so designated that prevention is operative among them.

§3. However, several advocates can be appointed to act together.

Can. 1483 — The procurator and the advocate must have at least attained majority and be of good reputation; furthermore, the advocate must be a Catholic unless the diocesan bishop permits otherwise, must have a doctorate in canon law or be otherwise truly expert and must be approved by the same bishop.

Can. 1484 — §1. Before a procurator and advocate undertake their function, they must present an authentic mandate to the tribunal.

§2. To prevent the extinction of a right, however, the judge can admit a procurator without the presentation of the mandate provided that some suitable security is furnished if necessary; the procurator's acts, however, lack all force unless the mandate is correctly presented within the peremptory time limits set by the judge.

Can. 1485 – Nisi speciale mandatum habuerit, procurator non potest valide renuntiare actioni, instantiae vel actis iudicialibus, nec transigere, pacisci, compromittere in arbitros et generatim ea agere pro quibus ius requirit mandatum speciale.

Can. 1486 – § 1. Ut procuratoris vel advocati remotio effectum sortiatur, necesse est ipsis intimetur, et, si lis iam contestata fuerit, iudex et adversa pars certiores facti sint de remotione.

§ 2. Lata definitiva sententia, ius et officium appellandi, si mandans non renuat, procuratori manet.

Can. 1487 – Tum procurator tum advocatus possunt a iudice, dato decreto, repelli sive ex officio sive ad instantiam partis, gravi tamen de causa.

Can. 1488 – § 1. Vetatur uterque emere litem, aut sibi de immodico emolumento vel rei litigiosae parte vindicata pacisci. Quae si fecerint, nulla est pactio, et a iudice poterunt poena pecuniaria mulctari. Advocatus praeterea tum ab officio suspendi, tum etiam, si recidivus sit, ab Episcopo, qui tribunali praeest, ex albo advocatorum expungi potest.

§ 2. Eodem modo puniri possunt advocati et procuratores qui a competentibus tribunalibus causas, in fraudem legis, subtrahunt ut ab aliis favorabilius definiantur.

Can. 1489 – Advocati ac procuratores qui ob dona aut pollicitationes aut quamlibet aliam rationem suum officium prodiderint, a patrocinio exercendo suspendantur, et mulcta pecuniaria aliisve congruis poenis plectantur.

Can. 1490 – In unoquoque tribunali, quatenus fieri possit, stabiles patroni constituantur, ab ipso tribunali stipendium recipientes, qui munus advocati vel procuratoris in causis praesertim matrimonialibus pro partibus quae eos seligere malint, exerceant.

TITULUS V
DE ACTIONIBUS ET EXCEPTIONIBUS

CAPUT I
DE ACTIONIBUS ET EXCEPTIONIBUS IN GENERE

Can. 1491 – Quodlibet ius non solum actione munitur, nisi aliud expresse cautum sit, sed etiam exceptione.

Can. 1485 — Without a special mandate the procurator cannot validly renounce an action, instance or judicial acts, make a settlement, strike a bargain, enter into arbitration and in general do those things for which the law requires a special mandate.

Can. 1486 — §1. For the removal of a procurator or advocate to take effect, it is necessary that they be informed and that the judge and the opposing party be notified of the removal if the joinder of issues (*contestatio litis*) has already taken place.

§2. After a definitive sentence has been issued, the procurator retains the right and duty to appeal unless the mandating party has renounced this.

Can. 1487 — For serious cause both the procurator and the advocate can be expelled from the trial by the judge by means of a decree either ex officio or at the request of a party.

Can. 1488 — §1. Both the procurator and the advocate are forbidden to win the suit through bribery or to strike a bargain for excessive profit or for a claim upon a share of the litigated thing. If they do such things, the agreement is null and the judge can fine them. Furthermore, an advocate can be suspended from office and also stricken from the list of advocates by the bishop in charge of the tribunal if it happens again and again.

§2. Advocates and procurators are liable to the same penalties if they withdraw cases from competent tribunals and submit them to other more favorable tribunals for adjudication in deceit of the law.

Can. 1489 — Advocates and procurators who have betrayed their office for the sake of gifts, promises or any other reason are to be suspended from the exercise of office and fined or punished with other suitable penalties.

Can. 1490 — Insofar as it is possible, permanent advocates are to be appointed in every tribunal and paid a stipend by that tribunal to exercise the function of advocate or procurator on behalf of parties who wish to choose them especially for marriage cases.

TITLE V
ACTIONS AND EXCEPTIONS

CHAPTER I
ACTIONS AND EXCEPTIONS IN GENERAL

Can. 1491 — Every right whatsoever is safeguarded not only by an action but also by an exception unless something to the contrary is expressly stated.

Can. 1492 – § 1. Quaevis actio extinguitur praescriptione ad normam iuris aliove legitimo modo, exceptis actionibus de statu personarum, quae numquam extinguuntur.

§ 2. Exceptio, salvo praescripto can. 1462, semper competit et est suapte natura perpetua.

Can. 1493 – Actor pluribus simul actionibus, quae tamen inter se non confligant, sive de eadem re sive de diversis, aliquem convenire potest, si aditi tribunalis competentiam non egrediantur.

Can. 1494 – § 1. Pars conventa potest coram eodem iudice in eodem iudicio contra actorem vel propter causae nexum cum actione principali vel ad submovendam vel ad minuendam actoris petitionem, actionem reconventionalem instituere.

§ 2. Reconventio reconventionis non admittitur.

Can. 1495 – Actio reconventionalis proponenda est iudici coram quo actio prior instituta est, licet ad unam causam dumtaxat delegato vel alioquin relative incompetenti.

Caput II
DE ACTIONIBUS ET EXCEPTIONIBUS IN SPECIE

Can. 1496 – § 1. Qui probabilibus saltem argumentis ostenderit super aliqua re ab alio detenta ius se habere, sibique damnum imminere nisi res ipsa custodienda tradatur, ius habet obtinendi a iudice eiusdem rei sequestrationem.

§ 2. In similibus rerum adiunctis obtinere potest, ut iuris exercitium alicui inhibeatur.

Can. 1497 – § 1. Ad crediti quoque securitatem sequestratio rei admittitur, dummodo de creditoris iure satis constet.

§ 2. Sequestratio extendi potest etiam ad res debitoris quae quolibet titulo apud alias personas reperiantur, et ad debitoris credita.

Can. 1498 – Sequestratio rei et inhibitio exercitii iuris decerni nullatenus possunt, si damnum quod timetur possit aliter reparari et idonea cautio de eo reparando offeratur.

Can. 1499 – Iudex potest ei, cui sequestrationem rei vel inhibitionem exercitii iuris concedit, praeviam imponere cautionem de damnis, si ius suum non probaverit, resarciendis.

Can. 1492 — §1. Every action is terminated through prescription in accord with the norm of law or by another legitimate method except actions concerning the status of persons which are never terminated.

§2. An exception is always available and is of its very nature perpetual, with due regard for the prescription of can. 1462.

Can. 1493 — A petitioner can bring a respondent to court by several actions at the same time provided they do not conflict among themselves, whether on the same or different matters, and if they do not exceed the competence of the tribunal approached.

Can. 1494 — §1. A respondent can file a counter-claim action against the petitioner before the same judge in the same trial either due to a connection of a case with the principal action or to remove or to lessen the charge of the petitioner.

§2. A counter-claim to the counter-claim is not admissible.

Can. 1495 — The counter-claim action is to be presented to the judge before whom the first action was filed even if he were delegated for only one case or were otherwise relatively incompetent.

Chapter II

ACTIONS AND EXCEPTIONS SPECIFICALLY

Can. 1496 — §1. A person who through at least probable arguments, has demonstrated a right to something retained by another and the threat of damage if that thing is not placed in safe keeping, has the right to obtain its sequestration from the judge.

§2. In similar circumstances a person can obtain an order restraining another from exercising a right.

Can. 1497 — §1. Sequestration of the object is also admitted as security for credit provided the right of the creditor is sufficiently evident.

§2. Sequestration can also be extended to the goods of the debtor which are discovered in the possession of others under any title and to the credit of the debtor.

Can. 1498 — Sequestration of a thing and an order to restrain the exercise of a right can in no way be decreed if the harm that is feared can otherwise be repaired and suitable security for its repair can be furnished.

Can. 1499 — The judge, in granting sequestration of a thing or an order restraining the exercise of a right, can impose on the person a prior obligation to compensate for damages if the right is not proven.

Can. 1500 – Ad naturam et vim actionis possessoriae quod atti-net, serventur praescripta iuris civilis loci ubi sita est res de cuius possessione agitur.

PARS II
DE IUDICIO CONTENTIOSO

SECTIO I
DE IUDICIO CONTENTIOSO ORDINARIO

TITULUS I
DE CAUSAE INTRODUCTIONE

CAPUT I
DE LIBELLO LITIS INTRODUCTORIO

Can. 1501 – Iudex nullam causam cognoscere potest, nisi petitio, ad normam canonum, proposita sit ab eo cuius interest, vel a promotore iustitiae.

Can. 1502 – Qui aliquem convenire vult, debet libellum compe-tenti iudici exhibere, in quo controversiae obiectum proponatur, et mi-nisterium iudicis expostuletur.

Can. 1503 – § 1. Petitionem oralem iudex admittere potest, quoties vel actor libellum exhibere impediatur vel causa sit facilis investigationis et minoris momenti.

§ 2. In utroque tamen casu iudex notarium iubeat scriptis actum redigere qui actori legendus est et ab eo probandus, quique locum tenet libelli ab actore scripti ad omnes iuris effectus.

Can. 1504 – Libellus, quo lis introducitur, debet:

1° exprimere coram quo iudice causa introducatur, quid petatur et a quo petatur;

2° indicare quo iure innitatur actor et generatim saltem quibus factis et probationibus ad evincenda ea quae asseruntur;

Can. 1500 — In regard to the nature and force of a possessory action the prescriptions of the civil law of the place where the thing, the possession of which is in question, is located, are to be observed.

PART II
THE CONTENTIOUS TRIAL

SECTION I
THE ORDINARY CONTENTIOUS TRIAL

TITLE I
THE INTRODUCTION OF THE CASE

CHAPTER I
THE INTRODUCTORY PETITION OF THE SUIT

Can. 1501 — A judge cannot adjudicate any case unless the party concerned or the promoter of justice has presented a petition in accord with the norm of the canons.

Can. 1502 — A person who wishes to bring another to court must present a *libellus* to a competent judge, which explains the object of the controversy and requests the services of the judge.

Can. 1503 — §1. The judge may accept an oral petition if either the petitioner is impeded from presenting a *libellus* or the case can be easily investigated and is of lesser importance.

§2. But in either situation the judge is to require the notary to put the act into writing, which is to be read to and approved by the petitioner; this then takes the place of and has all the legal effects of a *libellus* written by the petitioner.

Can. 1504 — A *libellus* which introduces a suit must:

1° express before which judge the case is being introduced, what is being petitioned and by whom the petition is being made;

2° indicate the basis for the petitioner's right and at least in general the facts and proofs which will be used to prove what has been alleged;

3° subscribi ab actore vel eius procuratore, appositis die, mense et anno, necnon loco in quo actor vel eius procurator habitant, aut residere se dixerint actorum recipiendorum gratia ;

4° indicare domicilium vel quasi-domicilium partis conventae.

Can. 1505 - § 1. Iudex unicus vel tribunalis collegialis praeses, postquam viderint et rem esse suae competentiae et actori legitimam personam standi in iudicio non deesse, debent suo decreto quam primum libellum aut admittere aut reicere.

§ 2. Libellus reici potest tantum :

1° si iudex vel tribunal incompetens sit ;

2° si sine dubio constet actori legitimam deesse personam standi in iudicio ;

3° si non servata sint praescripta can. 1504, nn. 1-3 ;

4° si certo pateat ex ipso libello petitionem quolibet carere fundamento, neque fieri posse, ut aliquod ex processu fundamentum appareat.

§ 3. Si libellus reiectus fuerit ob vitia quae emendari possunt, actor novum libellum rite confectum potest eidem iudici denuo exhibere.

§ 4. Adversus libelli reiectionem integrum semper est parti intra tempus utile decem dierum recursum rationibus suffultum interponere vel ad tribunal appellationis vel ad collegium, si libellus reiectus fuerit a praeside ; quaestio autem reiectionis expeditissime definienda est.

Can. 1506 - Si iudex intra mensem ab exhibito libello decretum non ediderit, quo libellum admittit vel reicit ad normam can. 1505, pars, cuius interest, instare potest ut iudex suo munere fungatur ; quod si nihilominus iudex sileat, inutiliter lapsis decem diebus a facta instantia, libellus pro admisso habeatur.

Caput II

DE CITATIONE ET DENUNTIATIONE ACTORUM IUDICIALIUM

Can. 1507 - § 1. In decreto, quo actoris libellus admittitur, debet iudex vel praeses ceteras partes in iudicium vocare seu citare ad litem contestandam, statuens utrum eae scripto respondere debeant an coram ipso se sistere ad dubia concordanda. Quod si ex scriptis responsionibus perspiciat necessitatem partes convocandi, id potest novo decreto statuere.

3° be signed by the petitioner or procurator, adding the day, month and year, as well as the address of the petitioner or procurator or the place where they say they reside for the purpose of receiving the acts;

4° indicate the domicile or quasi-domicile of the respondent.

Can. 1505 — §1. After the single judge or the president of a collegiate tribunal has recognized both that the matter is within his competence and that the petitioner does not lack legitimate personal standing in court, he must accept or reject the *libellus* as soon as possible through a decree.

§2. A *libellus* can be rejected only:

1° if the judge or the tribunal is incompetent;

2° if it is undoubtedly clear that the petitioner lacks legitimate personal standing in court;

3° if the prescriptions of can. 1504, nn. 1-3 have not been observed;

4° if from the *libellus* itself it is certainly obvious that it lacks any basis whatsoever and that it is impossible that any such basis would appear through a process.

§3. If the *libellus* has been rejected due to defects which can be corrected, the petitioner can properly draw up a new *libellus* and again present it to the same judge.

§4. A party is always free within ten available days (*tempus utile*) to lodge a reasoned recourse against the rejection of the *libellus* before the appellate tribunal or the college if it had been rejected by its president; the question of the rejection is to be resolved as quickly as possible.

Can. 1506 — If within a month from the presentation of the *libellus* the judge has not issued a decree by which he accepts or rejects the *libellus* in accord with the norm of can. 1505, the interested party can insist that the judge fulfill his duty; but if the judge, nevertheless, remains silent for ten days after the petitioner's insistence, the petition is considered as having been accepted.

CHAPTER II

THE CITATION AND NOTIFICATION OF JUDICIAL ACTS

Can. 1507 — §1. In the decree which accepts the *libellus* of the petitioner the judge or president must either call into court or cite the other parties for the joinder of issues (*contestatio litis*), determining whether they must respond in writing or present themselves personally before the judge in order to join the issues. But if from the written responses the judge perceives that it is necessary to call the parties together for a session, that can be determined in a new decree.

§ 2. Si libellus pro admisso habetur ad normam can. 1506, decretum citationis in iudicium fieri debet intra viginti dies a facta instantia, de qua in eo canone.

§ 3. Quod si partes litigantes de facto coram iudice se sistant ad causam agendam, opus non est citatione, sed actuarius significet in actis partes iudicio adfuisse.

Can. 1508 – § 1. Decretum citationis in iudicium debet statim parti conventae notificari, et simul ceteris, qui comparere debent, notum fieri.

§ 2. Citationi libellus litis introductorius adiungatur, nisi iudex propter graves causas censeat libellum significandum non esse parti, antequam haec deposuerit in iudicium.

§ 3. Si lis moveatur adversus eum qui non habet liberum exercitium suorum iurium, vel liberam administrationem rerum de quibus disceptatur, citatio denuntianda est, prout casus ferat, tutori, curatori, procuratori speciali, seu ei qui ipsius nomine iudicium suscipere tenetur ad normam iuris.

Can. 1509 – § 1. Citationum, decretorum, sententiarum aliorumque iudicialium actorum notificatio facienda est per publicos tabellarios vel alio modo qui tutissimus sit, servatis normis lege particulari statutis.

§ 2. De facto notificationis et de eius modo constare debet in actis.

Can. 1510 – Conventus, qui citatoriam schedam recipere recuset, vel qui impedit quominus citatio ad se perveniat, legitime citatus habeatur.

Can. 1511 – Si citatio non fuerit legitime notificata, nulla sunt acta processus, salvo praescripto can. 1507, § 3.

Can. 1512 – Cum citatio legitime notificata fuerit aut partes coram iudice steterint ad causam agendam :

1° res desinit esse integra ;

2° causa fit propria illius iudicis aut tribunalis ceteroquin competentis, coram quo actio instituta est ;

3° in iudice delegato firma redditur iurisdictio, ita ut non expiret resoluto iure delegantis ;

4° interrumpitur praescriptio, nisi aliud cautum sit ;

5° lis pendere incipit ; et ideo statim locum habet principium « *lite pendente, nihil innovetur* ».

§2. If the *libellus* is considered as having been accepted in virtue of the norm of can. 1506, the decree of citation must be made in court within twenty days from the party's insistence on action as mentioned in that canon.

§3. But if the litigating parties de facto present themselves before the judge in order to proceed with the case, there is no need for a citation; the notary, however, is to note in the acts that the parties were present for the trial.

Can. 1508 — §1. The decree of citation to the trial must be forwarded immediately to the respondent and at the same time to others who are to appear.

§2. The introductory *libellus* is to be joined to the citation unless for serious reasons the judge determines that the *libellus* is not to be made known to the respondent before the latter makes a deposition during the trial.

§3. If the suit is filed against a person who does not have the free exercise of personal rights or the free administration of the controverted items, the citation is to be made known to the guardian, curator or special procurator, as the case may be, or to the person who is bound to enter the trial in the respondent's name according to the norm of law.

Can. 1509 — §1. Notification of citations, decrees, sentences and other judicial acts are to be made in accordance with the norms determined in particular law through the public postal services or through another method which is the safest.

§2. The fact and method of notification must be clear in the acts.

Can. 1510 — A respondent who refuses to accept the document of citation or who prevents its arrival is considered as having been legitimately cited.

Can. 1511 — If the citation has not been legitimately communicated, the acts of the process are null, with due regard for the prescription of can. 1507, §3.

Can. 1512 — Once the citation has been legitimately communicated or the parties have appeared before the judge to pursue the case:

1° the issue ceases to be *res integra*;

2° the case becomes proper to that judge or tribunal before whom the action was begun and is competent in other respects;

3° the jurisdiction of a delegated judge is firmly established so that it does not expire when the right of the one delegating ceases;

4° prescription is interrupted unless otherwise provided;

5° the litigation begins to be pending and therefore the principle becomes operative: *while a suit is pending, nothing new is to be introduced.*

TITULUS II
DE LITIS CONTESTATIONE

Can. 1513 – § 1. Contestatio litis habetur cum per iudicis decretum controversiae termini, ex partium petitionibus et responsionibus desumpti, definiuntur.

§ 2. Partium petitiones responsionesque, praeterquam in libello litis introductorio, possunt vel in responsione ad citationem exprimi vel in declarationibus ore coram iudice factis; in causis autem difficilioribus partes convocandae sunt a iudice ad dubium vel dubia concordanda, quibus in sententia respondendum sit.

§ 3. Decretum iudicis partibus notificandum est; quae nisi iam consenserint, possunt intra decem dies ad ipsum iudicem recurrere, ut mutetur; quaestio autem expeditissime ipsius iudicis decreto dirimenda est.

Can. 1514 – Controversiae termini semel statuti mutari valide nequeunt, nisi novo decreto, ex gravi causa, ad instantiam partis et auditis reliquis partibus earumque rationibus perpensis.

Can. 1515 – Lite contestata, possessor rei alienae desinit esse bonae fidei; ideoque, si damnatur ut rem restituat, fructus quoque a contestationis die reddere debet et damna sarcire.

Can. 1516 – Lite contestata, iudex congruum tempus partibus praestituat probationibus proponendis et explendis.

TITULUS III
DE LITIS INSTANTIA

Can. 1517 – Instantiae initium fit citatione; finis autem non solum pronuntiatione sententiae definitivae, sed etiam aliis modis iure praefinitis.

Can. 1518 – Si pars litigans moriatur aut statum mutet aut cesset ab officio cuius ratione agit:

1° causa nondum conclusa, instantia suspenditur donec heres defuncti aut successor aut is, cuius intersit, litem resumat;

2° causa conclusa, iudex procedere debet ad ulteriora, citato procuratore, si adsit, secus defuncti herede vel successore.

TITLE II

THE JOINDER OF ISSUES (*CONTESTATIO LITIS*)

Can. 1513 — §1. The joinder of issues (*contestatio litis*) occurs when the terms of the controversy based on the petitions and responses of the parties are specified by the decree of the judge.

§2. The petitions and responses of the parties, besides those in the *libellus* introducing the suit, can be expressed either in response to the citation or in a declaration made orally before the judge; in more difficult cases, however, the parties are to be called together by the judge to specify the question or questions to be answered in the sentence.

§3. The decree of the judge is to be made known to the parties; unless they have already reached an agreement, they can within ten days make recourse to that judge that it be changed; however, the issue is to be resolved as quickly as possible by a decree of that judge.

Can. 1514 — Once the terms of the controversy have been determined, they cannot validly be changed except for a serious reason through a new decree at the request of one party and after hearing the other parties and considering their reasons.

Can. 1515 — Once the joinder of issues (*contestatio litis*) has occurred, the possessor of another's property ceases to be in good faith; if therefore, the possessor is sentenced to make restitution, the profits made from the day of the joinder of issues (*contestatio litis*) must also be returned and any damages compensated.

Can. 1516 — Once the joinder of issues (*contestatio litis*) has occurred, the judge is to furnish the parties suitable time to present and complete proofs.

TITLE III

THE PROSECUTION OF THE SUIT

Can. 1517 — The prosecution of a suit begins with the citation; it ends not only with the pronouncement of a definitive sentence but also through the other methods defined by law.

Can. 1518 — If the litigating party dies, or changes status, or ceases from the office on behalf of which the suit was initiated:

1° if the case is not concluded, its prosecution is suspended until the heir of the deceased, the successor or an interested party resumes the suit;

2° if the case is concluded, the judge must proceed to the final acts after having cited the procurator if present or otherwise the heir or the successor of the deceased.

Can. 1519 – § 1. Si a munere cesset tutor vel curator vel procurator, qui sit ad normam can. 1481, §§ 1 et 3 necessarius, instantia interim suspenditur.

§ 2. Alium autem tutorem vel curatorem iudex quam primum constituat; procuratorem vero ad litem constituere potest, si pars neglexerit intra brevem terminum ab ipso iudice statutum.

Can. 1520 – Si nullus actus processualis, nullo obstante impedimento, ponatur a partibus per sex menses, instantia perimitur. Lex particularis alios peremptionis terminos statuere potest.

Can. 1521 – Peremptio obtinet ipso iure et adversus omnes, minores quoque aliosve minoribus aequiparatos, atque etiam ex officio declarari debet, salvo iure petendi indemnitatem adversus tutores, curatores, administratores, procuratores, qui culpa se caruisse non probaverint.

Can. 1522 – Peremptio exstinguit acta processus, non vero acta causae; immo haec vim habere possunt etiam in alia instantia, dummodo causa inter easdem personas et super eadem re intercedat; sed ad extraneos quod attinet, non aliam vim obtinent nisi documentorum.

Can. 1523 – Perempti iudicii expensas, quas quisque ex litigantibus fecerit, ipse ferat.

Can. 1524 – § 1. In quolibet statu et gradu iudicii potest actor instantiae renuntiare; item tum actor tum pars conventa possunt processus actis renuntiare sive omnibus sive nonnullis tantum.

§ 2. Tutores et administratores personarum iuridicarum, ut renuntiare possint instantiae, egent consilio vel consensu eorum, quorum concursus requiritur ad ponendos actus, qui ordinariae administrationis fines excedunt.

§ 3. Renuntiatio, ut valeat, peragenda est scripto, eademque a parte vel ab eius procuratore, speciali tamen mandato munito, debet subscribi, cum altera parte communicari, ab eaque acceptari vel saltem non impugnari, et a iudice admitti.

Can. 1525 – Renuntiatio a iudice admissa, pro actis quibus renuntiatum est, eosdem parit effectus ac peremptio instantiae, itemque obligat renuntiantem ad solvendas expensas actorum, quibus renuntiatum fuit.

TITULUS IV
DE PROBATIONIBUS

Can. 1526 – § 1. Onus probandi incumbit ei qui asserit.

§ 2. Non indigent probatione :

1° quae ab ipsa lege praesumuntur ;

Can. 1519 — §1. If a guardian, curator or procurator who is necessary in accord with the norms of can. 1481, §§1 and 3, ceases from office, the prosecution of the suit is suspended in the interim.

§2. However, the judge is to appoint another guardian or curator as soon as possible; the judge can appoint a procurator for the suit if the party has neglected to do so within the brief time period stated by the judge.

Can. 1520 — Barring some impediment, if no procedural act is proposed by the parties for six months, the prosecution of the suit is abated. Particular law can state other time limits for abatement.

Can. 1521 — Abatement takes effect by the law itself against all persons, including minors and those equivalent to minors, and it must also be declared ex officio with due regard for the right of petitioning for indemnity against tutors, guardians, administrators or procurators who have not proved that they were not at fault.

Can. 1522 — Abatement extinguishes the acts of the process, but not the acts of the case, which in fact may be operative in another instance provided that the case involves the same persons and the same issue; as regards outsiders the acts of the case have no other value than that of documents.

Can. 1523 — When a trial is abated, each of the litigants is to bear the expenses which he or she has incurred.

Can. 1524 — §1. A petitioner can renounce the instance at any stage or grade of trial; both petitioner and respondent can likewise renounce either all or some of the acts of the process.

§2. In order for them to renounce an instance, the guardians and administrators of juridic persons need to consult with or obtain the consent of those whose involvement is required to place acts which go beyond the limits of ordinary administration.

§3. In order for a renunciation to be valid it is to be made in writing and also signed by the party or by the party's procurator with a special mandate to do so; it must be communicated to the other party, accepted, or at least not attacked, by that party, and admitted by the judge.

Can. 1525 — A renunciation admitted by the judge has the same effects concerning the renounced acts as an abatement of an instance and it obliges the renouncing party to pay the expenses for the renounced acts.

TITLE IV
PROOFS

Can. 1526 — §1. The burden of proof rests upon the person who makes the allegations.

§2. The following do not need proof:

1° matters which are presumed by the law itself;

2° facta ab uno ex contendentibus asserta et ab altero admissa, nisi iure vel a iudice probatio nihilominus exigatur.

Can. 1527 – § 1. Probationes cuiuslibet generis, quae ad causam cognoscendam utiles videantur et sint licitae, adduci possunt.

§ 2. Si pars instet ut probatio a iudice reiecta admittatur, ipse iudex rem expeditissime definiat.

Can. 1528 – Si pars vel testis se sistere ad respondendum coram iudice renuant, licet eos audire etiam per laicum a iudice designatum aut requirere eorum declarationem coram publico notario vel quovis alio legitimo modo.

Can. 1529 – Iudex ad probationes colligendas ne procedat ante litis contestationem nisi ob gravem causam.

Caput I
DE PARTIUM DECLARATIONIBUS

Can. 1530 – Iudex ad veritatem aptius eruendam partes interrogare semper potest, immo debet, ad instantiam partis vel ad probandum factum quod publice interest extra dubium poni.

Can. 1531 – § 1. Pars legitime interrogata respondere debet et veritatem integre fateri.

§ 2. Quod si respondere recusaverit, iudicis est aestimare quid ad factorum probationem exinde erui possit.

Can. 1532 – In casibus, in quibus bonum publicum in causa est, iudex partibus iusiurandum de veritate dicenda aut saltem de veritate dictorum deferat, nisi gravis causa aliud suadeat; in aliis casibus, potest pro sua prudentia.

Can. 1533 – Partes, promotor iustitiae et defensor vinculi possunt iudici exhibere articulos, super quibus pars interrogetur.

Can. 1534 – Circa partium interrogationem cum proportione serventur, quae in cann. 1548, § 2, n. 1, 1552 et 1558-1565 de testibus statuuntur.

Can. 1535 – Assertio de aliquo facto, scripto vel ore, coram iudice competenti, ab aliqua parte circa ipsam iudicii materiam, sive sponte sive iudice interrogante, contra se peracta, est confessio iudicialis.

Can. 1536 – § 1. Confessio iudicialis unius partis, si agatur de negotio aliquo privato et in causa non sit bonum publicum, ceteras relevat ab onere probandi.

2° facts alleged by one of the contending parties and admitted by the other unless proof is nonetheless demanded by the law or by the judge.

Can. 1527 — §1. Proofs of any type whatever which seem useful for deciding the case and which are licit can be adduced.

§2. If a party insists that a proof rejected by the judge be admitted, the judge is to determine the matter most expeditiously.

Can. 1528 — If a party or a witness refuses to appear before the judge to testify, it is permitted to hear the person through a lay person assigned by the judge or to seek the person's declaration before a notary public or in any other legitimate manner.

Can. 1529 — Except for a serious cause, the judge is not to proceed to gather proofs before the joinder of issues (*contestatio litis*).

CHAPTER I

THE DECLARATION OF THE PARTIES

Can. 1530 — The judge can always interrogate the parties so as to reveal the truth more effectively; in fact the judge must do so at the request of a party or to prove a fact which is to be established beyond doubt for the sake of the public interest.

Can. 1531 — §1. A party legitimately interrogated must answer and tell the whole truth.

§2. But if a party has refused to answer, it is for the judge to evaluate what can be drawn from that refusal concerning the proof of the facts.

Can. 1532 — Unless a serious cause persuades otherwise, the judge is to administer an oath to the parties to tell the truth or at least to confirm the truth of their testimony in cases where the public good is at stake; the judge, in accord with prudential judgment, can do the same in other cases.

Can. 1533 — The parties, the promoter of justice and the defender of the bond can present to the judge items on which a party is to be interrogated.

Can. 1534 — To the extent it is possible the regulations of cann. 1548, §2, n.1, 1552 and 1558–1565 on witnesses are to be observed in the interrogation of the parties.

Can. 1535 — A judicial confession is a written or oral assertion against oneself made by any party regarding the matter under trial and made before a competent judge, whether spontaneously or upon interrogation by the judge.

Can. 1536 — §1. If it is a question of some private matter and the public good is not at stake the judicial confession of one party relieves the other parties from the burden of proof.

§ 2. In causis autem quae respiciunt bonum publicum, confessio iudicialis et partium declarationes, quae non sint confessiones, vim probandi habere possunt, a iudice aestimandam una cum ceteris causae adiunctis, at vis plenae probationis ipsis tribui nequit, nisi alia accedant elementa quae eas omnino corroborent.

Can. 1537 – Quoad extraiudicialem confessionem in iudicium deductam, iudicis est, perpensis omnibus adiunctis, aestimare quanti ea sit facienda.

Can. 1538 – Confessio vel alia quaevis partis declaratio qualibet vi caret, si constet eam ex errore facti esse prolatam, aut vi vel metu gravi extortam.

Caput II
DE PROBATIONE PER DOCUMENTA

Can. 1539 – In quolibet iudicii genere admittitur probatio per documenta tum publica tum privata.

Art. 1
De natura et fide documentorum

Can. 1540 – § 1. Documenta publica ecclesiastica ea sunt, quae persona publica in exercitio sui muneris in Ecclesia confecit, servatis sollemnitatibus iure praescriptis.

§ 2. Documenta publica civilia ea sunt, quae secundum uniuscuiusque loci leges talia iure censentur.

§ 3. Cetera documenta sunt privata.

Can. 1541 – Nisi contrariis et evidentibus argumentis aliud evincatur, documenta publica fidem faciunt de omnibus quae directe et principaliter in iis affirmantur.

Can. 1542 – Documentum privatum, sive agnitum a parte sive recognitum a iudice, eandem probandi vim habet adversus auctorem vel subscriptorem et causam ab iis habentes, ac confessio extra iudicium facta; adversus extraneos eandem vim habet ac partium declarationes quae non sint confessiones, ad normam can. 1536, § 2.

Can. 1543 – Si abrasa, correcta, interpolata aliove vitio documenta infecta demonstrentur, iudicis est aestimare an et quanti huiusmodi documenta sint facienda.

§2. In cases which concern the public good, however, a judicial confession and the declarations of the parties which are not confessions can have a probative force to be evaluated by the judge along with the other circumstances of the case; but complete probative force cannot be attributed to them unless other elements are present which thoroughly corroborate them.

Can. 1537 — Having weighed all the circumstances, it is for the judge to evaluate the worth of an extra-judicial confession which has been introduced into the trial.

Can. 1538 — A confession or any other declaration of a party lacks all probative force if it is proved that it was made through an error of fact or it was extorted by force or grave fear.

CHAPTER II

PROOF BY DOCUMENTS

Can. 1539 — In every type of trial, proof by means of both public and private documents is admitted.

Art. 1

THE NATURE AND TRUSTWORTHINESS OF DOCUMENTS

Can. 1540 — §1. Public ecclesiastical documents are those which official persons have drawn up in the exercise of their function in the Church, after having observed the formalities prescribed by law.

§2. Public civil documents are those which are considered to be such in law in accord with the laws of the individual place.

§3. Other documents are private ones.

Can. 1541 — Unless contrary and evident arguments show otherwise, public documents are to be trusted concerning everything which is directly and principally affirmed in them.

Can. 1542 — A private document whether acknowledged by a party or recognized by the judge has the same probative force against its author or signer and those deriving a case from them as does an extra-judicial confession; against outsiders it has the same force as the declarations of the parties which are not confessions, in accord with the norm of can. 1536, §2.

Can. 1543 — If the documents are shown to have been erased, corrected, interpolated, or affected by another such defect, it is for the judge to assess whether such documents have value and how much.

Art. 2

DE PRODUCTIONE DOCUMENTORUM

Can. 1544 – Documenta vim probandi in iudicio non habent, nisi originalia sint aut in exemplari authentico exhibita et penes tribunalis cancellariam deposita, ut a iudice et ab adversario examinari possint.

Can. 1545 – Iudex praecipere potest ut documentum utrique parti commune exhibeatur in processu.

Can. 1546 – § 1. Nemo exhibere tenetur documenta, etsi communia, quae communicari nequeunt sine periculo damni ad normam can. 1548, § 2, n. 2 aut sine periculo violationis secreti servandi.

§ 2. Attamen si qua saltem documenti particula describi possit et in exemplari exhiberi sine memoratis incommodis, iudex decernere potest ut eadem producatur.

Caput III

DE TESTIBUS ET ATTESTATIONIBUS

Can. 1547 – Probatio per testes in quibuslibet causis admittitur, sub iudicis moderatione.

Can. 1548 – § 1. Testes iudici legitime interroganti veritatem fateri debent.

§ 2. Salvo praescripto can. 1550, § 2, n. 2, ab obligatione respondendi eximuntur:

1° clerici, quod attinet ad ea quae ipsis manifestata sunt ratione sacri ministerii; civitatum magistratus, medici, obstetrices, advocati, notarii aliique qui ad secretum officii etiam ratione praestiti consilii tenentur, quod attinet ad negotia huic secreto obnoxia;

2° qui ex testificatione sua sibi aut coniugi aut proximis consanguineis vel affinibus infamiam, periculosas vexationes, aliave mala gravia obventura timent.

Art. 1

QUI TESTES ESSE POSSINT

Can. 1549 – Omnes possunt esse testes, nisi expresse iure repellantur vel in totum vel ex parte.

Art. 2

THE PRESENTATION OF DOCUMENTS

Can. 1544 — Documents do not have probative force in a trial unless they are originals or presented in authentic copy and are deposited with the chancery of the tribunal so that they may be examined by the judge and the opposing party.

Can. 1545 — The judge can order that a document which is common to both parties be exhibited in the process.

Can. 1546 — §1. Even if documents are common, no one is obliged to exhibit those which cannot be communicated without risk of harm in accordance with the norm of can. 1548, §2, n. 2, or without risk of violating the obligation to observe secrecy.

§2. Nonetheless, if some excerpt, at least, of a document can be transcribed and can be presented in copy form without the above-mentioned hazards the judge can decree that it be produced.

CHAPTER III

WITNESSES AND TESTIMONIES

Can. 1547 — Proof by means of witnesses is admitted in every kind of case under the supervision of the judge.

Can. 1548 — §1. When the judge legitimately interrogates witnesses they must tell the truth.

§2. With due regard for the prescription of can. 1550, §2, n.2, the following are exempted from the obligation to answer:

1° clerics in regard to whatever was made known to them in connection with their sacred ministry; civil officials, doctors, obstetricians, advocates, notaries and others who are bound to professional secrecy, even by reason of advice rendered, as regards matters subject to this secrecy;

2° persons who fear that infamy, dangerous vexations or other serious evils will happen to themselves, or their spouse, or persons related to them by consanguinity or affinity, as a result of their testimony.

Art. 1

THOSE WHO CAN BE WITNESSES

Can. 1549 — All persons can be witnesses unless they are expressly excluded by law, either completely or partially.

Can. 1550 – § 1. Ne admittantur ad testimonium ferendum minores infra decimum quartum aetatis annum et mente debiles; audiri tamen poterunt ex decreto iudicis, quo id expedire declaretur.

§ 2. Incapaces habentur:

1° qui partes sunt in causa, aut partium nomine in iudicio consistunt, iudex eiusve assistentes, advocatus aliique qui partibus in eadem causa assistunt vel astiterunt;

2° sacerdotes, quod attinet ad ea omnia quae ipsis ex confessione sacramentali innotuerunt, etsi poenitens eorum manifestationem petierit; immo audita a quovis et quoquo modo occasione confessionis, ne ut indicium quidem veritatis recipi possunt.

Art. 2

DE INDUCENDIS ET EXCLUDENDIS TESTIBUS

Can. 1551 – Pars, quae testem induxit, potest eius examini renuntiare; sed adversa pars postulare potest ut nihilominus testis examinetur.

Can. 1552 – § 1. Cum probatio per testes postulatur, eorum nomina et domicilium tribunali indicentur.

§ 2. Exhibeantur, intra terminum a iudice praestitutum, articuli argumentorum super quibus petitur testium interrogatio; alioquin petitio censeatur deserta.

Can. 1553 – Iudicis est nimiam multitudinem testium refrenare.

Can. 1554 – Antequam testes examinentur, eorum nomina cum partibus communicentur; quod si id, prudenti iudicis existimatione, fieri sine gravi difficultate nequeat, saltem ante testimoniorum publicationem fiat.

Can. 1555 – Firmo praescripto can. 1550, pars petere potest ut testis excludatur, si iusta exclusionis causa demonstretur ante testis excussionem.

Can. 1556 – Citatio testis fit decreto iudicis testi legitime notificato.

Can. 1557 – Testis rite citatus pareat aut causam suae absentiae iudici notam faciat.

Can. 1550 — §1. Minors below the fourteenth year of age and those who are feebleminded are not allowed to give testimony; however, they may be heard by reason of a decree of the judge which declares such a hearing expedient.

§2. The following are considered incapable:

1° those who are parties in the case, or who represent the parties in the trial; the judge and assistants, the advocate and others who are assisting or have assisted the parties in the same case;

2° priests as regards everything which has become known to them by reason of sacramental confession, even if the penitent requests their manifestatation; moreover, whatever has been heard by anyone or in any way on the occasion of confession cannot be accepted as even an indication of the truth.

Art. 2

The Introduction and Exclusion of Witnesses

Can. 1551 — The party who has introduced a witness can forego the examination of the witness; but the opposing party can demand that the witness be examined notwithstanding that action.

Can. 1552 — §1. When proof by means of witnesses is demanded, their names and domicile are to be made known to the tribunal.

§2. The items of discussion upon which interrogation of the witnesses is sought are to be presented within the time limit set by the judge; otherwise the petition is to be considered as abandoned.

Can. 1553 — It is the judge's responsibility to curb an excessive number of witnesses.

Can. 1554 — Before witnesses are examined, their names are to be made known to the parties; however, if in the prudent assessment of the judge, that cannot be done without serious difficulty, it is to be done at least before the publication of the testimony.

Can. 1555 — With due regard for the prescription of can. 1550, a party can request that a witness be excluded if a just cause for exclusion is demonstrated before the interrogation of the witness.

Can. 1556 — The citation of a witness is done by a decree of the judge made known to the witness according to law.

Can. 1557 — A witness who has been duly cited is to appear or inform the judge of the reason for the absence.

Art. 3

DE TESTIUM EXAMINE

Can. 1558 – § 1. Testes sunt examini subiciendi in ipsa tribunalis sede, nisi aliud iudici videatur.

§ 2. Cardinales, Patriarchae, Episcopi et ii qui, suae civitatis iure, simili favore gaudent, audiantur in loco ab ipsis selecto.

§ 3. Iudex decernat ubi audiendi sint ii, quibus propter distantiam, morbum aliudve impedimentum impossibile vel difficile sit tribunalis sedem adire, firmis praescriptis cann. 1418 et 1469, § 2.

Can. 1559 – Examini testium partes assistere nequeunt, nisi iudex, praesertim cum res est de bono privato, eas admittendas censuerit. Assistere tamen possunt earum advocati vel procuratores, nisi iudex propter rerum et personarum adiuncta censuerit secreto esse procedendum.

Can. 1560 – § 1. Testes seorsim singuli examinandi sunt.

§ 2. Si testes inter se aut cum parte in re gravi dissentiant, iudex discrepantes inter se conferre seu comparare potest, remotis, quantum fieri poterit, dissidiis et scandalo.

Can. 1561 – Examen testis fit a iudice, vel ab eius delegato aut auditore, cui assistat oportet notarius; quapropter partes, vel promotor iustitiae, vel defensor vinculi, vel advocati qui examini intersint, si alias interrogationes testi faciendas habeant, has non testi, sed iudici vel eius locum tenenti proponant, ut eas ipse deferat, nisi aliter lex particularis caveat.

Can. 1562 – § 1. Iudex testi in mentem revocet gravem obligationem dicendi totam et solam veritatem.

§ 2. Iudex testi deferat iuramentum iuxta can. 1532; quod si testis renuat illud emittere, iniuratus audiatur.

Can. 1563 – Iudex imprimis testis identitatem comprobet; exquirat quaenam sit ipsi cum partibus necessitudo et, cum ipsi interrogationes specificas circa causam defert, sciscitetur quoque fontes eius scientiae et quo definito tempore ea, quae asserit, cognoverit.

Can. 1564 – Interrogationes breves sunto, interrogandi captui accommodatae, non plura simul complectentes, non captiosae, non subdolae, non suggerentes responsionem, remotae a cuiusvis offensione et pertinentes ad causam quae agitur.

Art. 3

THE EXAMINATION OF WITNESSES

Can. 1558 — §1. Witnesses must be examined at the tribunal unless it appears otherwise appropriate to the judge.

§2. Cardinals, patriarchs, bishops and those who, by the law of their state, enjoy a similar right, are to be heard in a place which they themselves select.

§3. The judge is to decide where those are to be heard for whom it is impossible or difficult to come to the tribunal because of distance, illness or other impediment with due regard for the prescriptions of cann. 1418 and 1469, §2.

Can. 1559 — The parties may not assist at the examination of witnesses unless the judge believes that they must be admitted, especially when the matter concerns the private good. On the other hand, their advocates or their procurators may assist unless the judge believes that the process must be carried on in secret because of the circumstances of things or persons.

Can. 1560 — §1. Each of the witnesses must be examined individually.

§2. If the witnesses disagree among themselves or with a party in a serious matter the judge can bring them together or have them come to an agreement with one another, precluding disputes and scandal insofar as it is possible.

Can. 1561 — The examination of a witness is conducted by the judge, a delegate or an auditor, who is to be assisted by a notary; as a result, if the parties, or the promoter of justice, or the defender of the bond, or the advocates who are present at the examination have further questions to be put to the witness, they are to propose these questions not to the witness but to the judge or the person taking the judge's place who is to ask them, unless particular law provides otherwise.

Can. 1562 — §1. The judge is to call to the attention of the witness the serious obligation to tell the whole truth and only the truth.

§2. The judge is to administer the oath to the witness in accord with can. 1532; but the witness who refuses to take it is to be heard without the oath.

Can. 1563 — The judge, first of all, is to establish the identity of the witness; the judge should seek out what is the relationship of the witness with the parties, and, when addressing specific questions to the witness regarding the case, the judge is also to inquire about the sources of the witness' knowledge and the precise time the witness learned what is asserted.

Can. 1564 — The questions are to be brief, accommodated to the intelligence of the person being interrogated, not comprising several points at the same time, not captious, nor crafty, nor suggestive of the answer, free from every kind of offense and pertinent to the case being tried.

Can. 1565 – § 1. Interrogationes non sunt cum testibus antea communicandae.

§ 2. Attamen si ea quae testificanda sunt ita a memoria sint remota, ut nisi prius recolantur certo affirmari nequeant, poterit iudex nonnulla testem praemonere, si id sine periculo fieri posse censeat.

Can. 1566 – Testes ore testimonium dicant, et scriptum ne legant, nisi de calculo et rationibus agatur; hoc enim in casu, adnotationes, quas secum attulerint, consulere poterunt.

Can. 1567 – § 1. Responsio statim redigenda est scripto a notario et referre debet ipsa editi testimonii verba, saltem quod attinet ad ea quae iudicii materiam directe attingunt.

§ 2. Admitti potest usus machinae magnetophonicae, dummodo dein responsiones scripto consignentur et subscribantur, si fieri potest, a deponentibus.

Can. 1568 – Notarius in actis mentionem faciat de praestito, remisso aut recusato iureiurando, de partium aliorumque praesentia, de interrogationibus ex officio additis et generatim de omnibus memoria dignis quae forte acciderint, cum testes excutiebantur.

Can. 1569 – § 1. In fine examinis, testi legi debent quae notarius de eius depositione scripto redegit, vel ipsi audita facere quae ope magnetophonii de eius depositione incisa sunt, data eidem testi facultate addendi, supprimendi, corrigendi, variandi.

§ 2. Denique actui subscribere debent testis, iudex et notarius.

Can. 1570 – Testes, quamvis iam excussi, poterunt parte postulante aut ex officio, antequam acta seu testificationes publici iuris fiant, denuo ad examen vocari, si iudex id necessarium vel utile ducat, dummodo collusionis vel corruptelae quodvis absit periculum.

Can. 1571 – Testibus, iuxta aequam iudicis taxationem, refundi debent tum expensae, quas fecerint, tum lucrum, quod amiserint, testificationis reddendae causa.

Art. 4

DE TESTIMONIORUM FIDE

Can. 1572 – In aestimandis testimoniis iudex, requisitis, si opus sit, testimonialibus litteris, consideret:

Can. 1565 — §1. The questions must not be communicated to the witnesses ahead of time.

§2. However, if the matters which are to be testified to are so removed from memory that unless they are recalled earlier they cannot be affirmed with certainty, the judge may advise the witness of some matters if it is thought that this can be done without danger.

Can. 1566 — Witnesses are to give testimony orally; they are not to read from written memoranda, unless there is question of calculation and accounts; in such a case they may consult the notes which they brought with them.

Can. 1567 — §1. The answer is to be put in writing at once by the notary who must report the exact words of the testimony given, at least as regards those points which touch directly upon the matter of the trial.

§2. Use of a tape recorder is allowed provided that, afterwards, the answers are transcribed and are signed by those making the depositions, if possible.

Can. 1568 — The notary is to make mention in the acts whether the oath was taken, omitted, or refused, also of the presence of the parties and of other persons, the questions added ex officio and, in general, everything noteworthy which may have occurred while the witnesses were being examined.

Can. 1569 — §1. At the conclusion of the examination what the notary has put in writing from the deposition must be read to the witness or the witness must be given an opportunity to listen to the tape recording of the deposition with the option of adding to, suppressing, correcting or changing it.

§2. Finally the acts must be signed by the witness, the judge and the notary.

Can. 1570 — Although witnesses have already been examined, they can be recalled for another examination at the request of a party or ex officio but before the acts or the testimony have been published; this is true if the judge believes such a reexamination necessary or useful, provided, however, that there is no danger of collusion or corruption.

Can. 1571 — In accord with an equitable assessment of the judge, witnesses must be compensated both for the expenses they have incurred and for the income they have lost by rendering testimony.

Art. 4

The Trustworthiness of Testimonies

Can. 1572 — In evaluating testimony, after having obtained testimonial letters if need be, the judge should consider:

1° quae condicio sit personae, quaeve honestas;

2° utrum de scientia propria, praesertim de visu et auditu proprio testificetur, an de sua opinione, de fama, aut de auditu ab aliis;

3° utrum testis constans sit et firmiter sibi cohaereat, an varius,
incertus vel vacillans;

4° utrum testimonii contestes habeat, aliisve probationis elementis confirmetur necne.

Can. 1573 – Unius testis depositio plenam fidem facere non potest, nisi agatur de teste qualificato qui deponat de rebus ex officio
gestis, aut rerum et personarum adiuncta aliud suadeant.

Caput IV
DE PERITIS

Can. 1574 – Peritorum opera utendum est quoties ex iuris vel
iudicis praescripto eorum examen et votum, praeceptis artis vel scientiae
innixum, requiruntur ad factum aliquod comprobandum vel ad veram
alicuius rei naturam dignosc ndam.

Can. 1575 – Iudicis est peritos nominare, auditis vel proponen-
tibus partibus, aut, si casus ferat, relationes ab aliis peritis iam factas
assumere.

Can. 1576 – Easdem ob causas quibus testis, etiam periti excluduntur aut recusari possunt.

Can. 1577 – § 1. Iudex, attentis iis quae a litigantibus forte dedu-
cantur, singula capita decreto suo definiat circa quae periti opera versari debeat.

§ 2. Perito remittenda sunt acta causae aliaque documenta et subsidia quibus egere potest ad suum munus rite et fideliter exsequendum.

§ 3. Iudex, ipso perito audito, tempus praefiniat intra quod examen
perficiendum est et relatio proferenda.

Can. 1578 – § 1. Periti suam quisque relationem a ceteris distinc-
tam conficiant, nisi iudex unam a singulis subscribendam fieri iubeat:
quod si fiat, sententiarum discrimina, si qua fuerint, diligenter adnotentur.

§ 2. Periti debent indicare perspicue quibus documentis vel aliis
idoneis modis certiores facti sint de personarum vel rerum vel locorum

1° the condition and good reputation of the person;

2° whether the witness testifies in virtue of personal knowledge, especially what has been seen and heard personally, or whether the testimony is the witness' opinion, or a rumor or hearsay from others;

3° whether the witness is reliable and firmly consistent or rather inconsistent, uncertain or vacillating;

4° whether the witness has supporting witnesses or whether there is support from other sources of proof.

Can. 1573 — The deposition of a single witness cannot constitute full proof unless a witness acting in an official capacity makes a deposition regarding duties performed ex officio or unless circumstances of things and persons suggest otherwise.

CHAPTER IV
EXPERTS

Can. 1574 — The services of experts must be used whenever their examination and opinion, based on the laws of art or science, are required in order to establish some fact or to clarify the true nature of some thing by reason of a prescription of the law or a judge.

Can. 1575 — It is the responsibility of the judge either to name experts after listening to the parties and the names they propose, or to make use of reports, if warranted, already drawn up by other experts.

Can. 1576 — Experts can be excluded or rejected for the same reasons that witnesses can be.

Can. 1577 — §1. After paying attention to those points which may have been brought forward by the litigants, the judge is to specify by a decree the individual points on which the expert's services must focus.

§2. The acts of the case and other documents and aids which the expert may need in order to function properly and faithfully must be turned over to the expert.

§3. After listening to the expert, the judge should fix the time within which the examination is to be carried out and the report presented.

Can. 1578 — §1. Each of the experts should draw up a report distinct from the others unless the judge orders that one report be made and signed by the experts individually; if this latter is done, differences of opinion, if any, are to be carefully noted.

§2. The experts must indicate clearly by what documents or other apt means they have been informed about the identity of persons, things or

identitate, qua via et ratione processerint in explendo munere sibi demandato et quibus potissimum argumentis suae conclusiones nitantur.

§ 3. Peritus accersiri potest a iudice ut explicationes, quae ulterius necessariae videantur, suppeditet.

Can. 1579 – § 1. Iudex non peritorum tantum conclusiones, etsi
concordes, sed cetera quoque causae adiuncta attente perpendat.

§ 2. Cum reddit rationes decidendi, exprimere debet quibus motus
argumentis peritorum conclusiones aut admiserit aut reiecerit.

Can. 1580 – Peritis solvenda sunt expensae et honoraria a iudice
ex bono et aequo determinanda, servato iure particulari.

Can. 1581 – § 1. Partes possunt peritos privatos, a iudice proban-
dos, designare.

§ 2. Hi, si iudex admittat, possunt acta causae, quatenus opus
sit, inspicere, peritiae exsecutioni interesse; semper autem possunt
suam relationem exhibere.

Caput V
DE ACCESSU ET DE RECOGNITIONE IUDICIALI

Can. 1582 – Si ad definitionem causae iudex opportunum duxerit
ad aliquem locum accedere vel aliquam rem inspicere, decreto id praestituat, quo ea quae in accessu praestanda sint, auditis partibus,
summatim describat.

Can. 1583 – Peractae recognitionis instrumentum conficiatur.

Caput VI
DE PRAESUMPTIONIBUS

Can. 1584 – Praesumptio est rei incertae probabilis coniectura;
eaque alia est iuris, quae ab ipsa lege statuitur; alia hominis, quae a
iudice conicitur.

Can. 1585 – Qui habet pro se iuris praesumptionem, liberatur ab
onere probandi, quod recidit in partem adversam.

places, by what path and method they proceeded in discharging the function given to them and on what grounds, for the most part, their conclusions are based.

§3. An expert can be summoned by the judge to supply further explanations which may seem necessary.

Can. 1579 — §1. The judge is to weigh attentively not only the conclusions of the experts, even when they are concordant, but also the other circumstances of the case.

§2. In giving the reasons for the decision, the judge must express what considerations prompted him or her to admit or reject the conclusions of the experts.

Can. 1580 — Both the expenses and the stipends which must be paid to the experts are to be determined justly and equitably by the judge with due regard for particular law.

Can. 1581 — §1. The parties may designate private experts who must be approved by the judge.

§2. If the judge admits them, they may inspect the acts of the case if necessary and be present at the discharging of the court experts' function; moreover they can always present their own report.

CHAPTER V

ACCESS AND JUDICIAL RECOGNIZANCE

Can. 1582 — If in order to settle a case the judge considers it opportune to have access to a given place or to inspect something, this should be specified in a decree which describes in summary fashion those elements which must be exhibited at the access, after hearing the parties.

Can. 1583 — When the recognizance has been completed, a report of it is to be drawn up.

CHAPTER VI

PRESUMPTIONS

Can. 1584 — A presumption is a probable conjecture about an uncertain matter; one is a presumption of law, which is established by the law itself; another is human, which is formulated by a judge.

Can. 1585 — A person who has a favorable legal presumption is freed from the burden of proof which then devolves upon the other party.

Can. 1586 – Praesumptiones, quae non statuuntur a iure, iudex ne coniciat, nisi ex facto certo et determinato, quod cum eo, de quo controversia est, directe cohaereat.

TITULUS V
DE CAUSIS INCIDENTIBUS

Can. 1587 – Causa incidens habetur, quoties, incepto per citatio-nem iudicio, quaestio proponitur quae, tametsi libello, quo lis introdu-citur, non contineatur expresse, nihilominus ita ad causam pertinet ut resolvi plerumque debeat ante quaestionem principalem.

Can. 1588 – Causa incidens proponitur scripto vel ore, indicato nexu qui intercedit inter ipsam et causam principalem, coram iudice competenti ad causam principalem definiendam.

Can. 1589 – § 1. Iudex, recepta petitione et auditis partibus, expe-ditissime decernat utrum proposita incidens quaestio fundamentum habere videatur et nexum cum principali iudicio, an vero sit in limine reicienda; et, si eam admittat, utrum talis sit gravitatis, ut solvi debeat per sententiam interlocutoriam vel per decretum.

§ 2. Si vero iudicet quaestionem incidentem non esse resolvendam ante sententiam definitivam, decernat ut eiusdem ratio habeatur, cum causa principalis definietur.

Can. 1590 – § 1. Si quaestio incidens solvi debeat per sententiam, serventur normae de processu contentioso orali, nisi, attenta rei gra-vitate, aliud iudici videatur.

§ 2. Si vero solvi debeat per decretum, tribunal potest rem com-mittere auditori vel praesidi.

Can. 1591 – Antequam finiatur causa principalis, iudex vel tribunal potest decretum vel sententiam interlocutoriam, iusta intercedente ra-tione, revocare aut reformare, sive ad partis instantiam, sive ex officio, auditis partibus.

CAPUT I
DE PARTIBUS NON COMPARENTIBUS

Can. 1592 – § 1. Si pars conventa citata non comparuerit nec ido-neam absentiae excusationem attulerit aut non responderit ad normam can. 1507, § 1, iudex eam a iudicio absentem declaret et decernat ut

Can. 1586 — The judge is not to formulate presumptions which are not determined by law unless they arise from a certain and determined fact which is directly connected with the subject matter of the controversy.

TITLE V
INCIDENTAL CASES

Can. 1587 — An incidental case is had whenever, after the trial has begun by the citation, a question is proposed which is so pertinent to the case that it very often must be resolved before the principal question, although it is not expressly contained in the *libellus* introducing the suit.

Can. 1588 — An incidental case is proposed in writing or orally before the judge who is competent to settle the principal case with an indication of the connection between it and the principal case.

Can. 1589 — §1. The judge, having received the petition and heard the parties, is to decide very promptly whether the proposed incidental question seems to have a basis and a connection with the principal issue, or whether it must be rejected from the outset; and, if it is admitted, whether it is of such seriousness that it must be resolved by an interlocutory sentence or by a decree.

§2. On the other hand, if the judge decides that the incidental question is not to be resolved before the definitive sentence, the judge is to decree that it will be considered when the principal case is settled.

Can. 1590 — §1. If the incidental question must be resolved by sentence, the norms of the oral contentious process are to be observed, unless the judge decides otherwise given the seriousness of the matter.

§2. But if it must be resolved by decree, the tribunal may turn the matter over to the auditor or to the presiding officer.

Can. 1591 — Before the principal case is closed, if there is just cause, the judge or the tribunal can revoke or reform the decree or the interlocutory sentence either at the request of a party or ex officio after hearing the parties.

CHAPTER I
PARTIES WHO DO NOT APPEAR IN COURT

Can. 1592 — §1. If the respondent, after having been cited, has neither appeared nor offered a suitable excuse for being absent, nor responded in accord with can. 1507, §1, the judge is to declare the respondent absent from

causa, servatis servandis, usque ad sententiam definitivam eiusque exsecutionem procedat.

§ 2. Antequam decretum, de quo in § 1, feratur, debet, etiam per
novam citationem si opus fuerit, constare citationem, legitime factam,
ad partem conventam tempore utili pervenisse.

Can. 1593 – § 1. Si pars conventa dein in iudicio se sistat aut responsum dederit ante causae definitionem, conclusiones probationesque
afferre potest, firmo praescripto can. 1600; caveat autem iudex, ne de
industria in longiores et non necessarias moras iudicium protrahatur.

§ 2. Etsi non comparuerit aut responsum non dederit ante causae
definitionem, impugnationibus uti potest adversus sententiam; quod si
probet se legitimo impedimento fuisse detentam, quod sine sua culpa
antea demonstrare non potuerit, querela nullitatis uti potest.

Can. 1594 – Si die et hora ad litis contestationem praestitutis actor
neque comparuerit neque idoneam excusationem attulerit:

1° iudex eum citet iterum;

2° si actor novae citationi non paruerit, praesumitur instantiae
renuntiasse ad normam cann. 1524-1525;

3° quod si postea in processu intervenire velit, servetur can. 1593.

Can. 1595 – § 1. Pars absens a iudicio, sive actor sive pars conventa, quae iustum impedimentum non comprobaverit, tenetur obligatione tum solvendi litis expensas, quae ob ipsius absentiam factae sunt,
tum etiam, si opus sit, indemnitatem alteri parti praestandi.

§ 2. Si tum actor tum pars conventa fuerint absentes a iudicio,
ipsi obligatione expensas litis solvendi tenentur in solidum.

CAPUT II

DE INTERVENTU TERTII IN CAUSA

Can. 1596 – § 1. Is cuius interest admitti potest ad interveniendum
in causa, in qualibet litis instantia, sive ut pars quae proprium ius
defendit, sive accessorie ad aliquem litigantem adiuvandum.

the trial and is to decree that the case should proceed to the definitive sentence and its execution, while observing all the formalities which are to be observed.

§2. Before issuing the decree mentioned in §1, the judge must have proof that the citation drawn up by law reached the respondent within available time even by issuing a new citation if necessary.

Can. 1593 — §1. If the respondent is present in court later or responds before the settlement of the case, the respondent can adduce conclusions and proofs, with due regard for the prescription of can. 1600; however the judge is to take care that the trial is not intentionally prolonged through rather long and unnecessary delays.

§2. Even if the respondent has not appeared or responded before the settlement of the case, the respondent can use challenges against the sentence; if the respondent proves that there was a legitimate impediment for being detained which without personal fault was unable to be made known earlier, the respondent can use a complaint of nullity.

Can. 1594 — If the petitioner has not appeared on the day and at the hour set for the joinder of issues (*contestatio litis*) and has not offered a suitable excuse:

1° the judge is to cite the petitioner again;

2° a petitioner who does not obey the new citation, is presumed to have renounced the suit in accord with cann. 1524–1525;

3° but if the petitioner later wishes to intervene in the process, can. 1593 is to be observed.

Can. 1595 — §1. A party who is absent from the trial, whether the petitioner or the respondent, and who has not given proof of a just impediment, is obliged both to pay the expenses of the lawsuit which were incurred because of the absence and also to provide indemnity to the other party, if necessary.

§2. If both the petitioner and the respondent were absent from the trial, they are jointly obliged to pay the expenses of the lawsuit.

Chapter II

INTERVENTION OF A THIRD PARTY IN A CASE

Can. 1596 — §1. An interested party can be admitted to intervene in a case at any stage of the suit, either as a party defending one's own right or as an accessory to help a given litigant.

§ 2. Sed ut admittatur, debet ante conclusionem in causa libellum iudici exhibere, in quo breviter suum ius interveniendi demonstret.

§ 3. Qui intervenit in causa, admittendus est in eo statu in quo causa reperitur, assignato eidem brevi ac peremptorio termino ad probationes suas exhibendas, si causa ad periodum probatoriam pervenerit.

Can. 1597 – Tertium, cuius interventus videatur necessarius, iudex, auditis partibus, debet in iudicium vocare.

TITULUS VI
DE ACTORUM PUBLICATIONE, DE CONCLUSIONE IN CAUSA ET DE CAUSAE DISCUSSIONE

Can. 1598 – § 1. Acquisitis probationibus, iudex decreto partibus et earum advocatis permittere debet, sub poena nullitatis, ut acta nondum eis nota apud tribunalis cancellariam inspiciant; quin etiam advocatis id petentibus dari potest actorum exemplar; in causis vero ad bonum publicum spectantibus iudex ad gravissima pericula evitanda aliquod actum nemini manifestandum esse decernere potest, cauto tamen ut ius defensionis semper integrum maneat.

§ 2. Ad probationes complendas partes possunt alias iudici proponere; quibus acquisitis, si iudex necessarium duxerit, iterum est locus decreto de quo in § 1.

Can. 1599 – § 1. Expletis omnibus quae ad probationes producendas pertinent, ad conclusionem in causa devenitur.

§ 2. Haec conclusio habetur quoties aut partes declarent se nihil aliud adducendum habere, aut utile proponendis probationibus tempus a iudice praestitutum elapsum sit, aut iudex declaret se satis instructam causam habere.

§ 3. De peracta conclusione in causa, quocumque modo ea acciderit, iudex decretum ferat.

Can. 1600 – § 1. Post conclusionem in causa iudex potest adhuc eosdem testes vel alios vocare aut alias probationes, quae antea non fuerint petitae, disponere tantummodo:

1° in causis, in quibus agitur de solo privato partium bono, si omnes partes consentiant;

2° in ceteris causis, auditis partibus et dummodo gravis exstet ratio itemque quodlibet fraudis vel subornationis periculum removeatur;

§2. However, in order to be admitted, such an interested party before the conclusion of the case must present to the judge a *libellus* briefly demonstrating the right to intervene.

§3. The person who intervenes in a case must be admitted at that stage which the case has reached with a brief and peremptory period of time assigned to present proofs if the case has reached the probatory stage.

Can. 1597 — After hearing the parties, the judge must summon to the trial a third party whose intervention seems necessary.

TITLE VI
PUBLICATION OF THE ACTS, CONCLUSION OF THE CASE AND DISCUSSION OF THE CASE

Can. 1598 — §1. After the proofs have been collected the judge by a decree must, under pain of nullity, permit the parties and their advocates to inspect at the tribunal chancery the acts which are not yet known to them; a copy of the acts can also be given to advocates upon request; however, in cases concerned with the public good, in order to avoid very serious dangers, the judge can decree that a given act is not to be shown to anyone, with due concern, however, that the right of defense always remains intact.

§2. In order to complete the proofs the parties may propose additional proofs to the judge; when these have been collected there is an occasion for repeating the decree mentioned in §1 if the judge thinks it necessary.

Can. 1599 — §1. When everything pertinent to the production of proofs has been completed, it is time for the conclusion of the case.

§2. The conclusion takes place whenever the parties declare that they have nothing more to add, or the time set by the judge for proposing proofs has expired, or the judge declares that the case is sufficiently instructed.

§3. The judge is to issue a decree that the conclusion of the case has been completed, in whatever manner it took place.

Can. 1600 — §1. After the conclusion of the case, the judge can still call the same or other witnesses, or arrange for other proofs which had not been previously asked for, only:

1° in cases in which it is a question solely of the private good of the parties and if all the parties give consent;

2° in other cases, after hearing the parties and provided that there exists a serious reason and all danger of fraud or subornation is removed;

3° in omnibus causis, quoties verisimile est, nisi probatio nova admittatur, sententiam iniustam futuram esse propter rationes, de quibus in can. 1645, § 2, nn. 1-3.

§ 2. Potest autem iudex iubere vel admittere ut exhibeatur documentum, quod forte antea sine culpa eius cuius interest, exhiberi non potuit.

§ 3. Novae probationes publicentur, servato can. 1598, § 1.

Can. 1601 – Facta conclusione in causa, iudex congruum temporis spatium praestituat ad defensiones vel animadversiones exhibendas.

Can. 1602 – § 1. Defensiones et animadversiones scriptae sint, nisi disputationem pro tribunali sedente iudex, consentientibus partibus, satis esse censeat.

§ 2. Si defensiones cum praecipuis documentis typis imprimantur, praevia iudicis licentia requiritur, salva secreti obligatione, si qua sit.

§ 3. Quoad extensionem defensionum, numerum exemplarium, aliaque huiusmodi adiuncta, servetur ordinatio tribunalis.

Can. 1603 – § 1. Communicatis vicissim defensionibus atque animadversionibus, utrique parti responsiones exhibere licet, intra breve tempus a iudice praestitutum.

§ 2. Hoc ius partibus semel tantum esto, nisi iudici gravi ex causa iterum videatur concedendum; tunc autem concessio, uni parti facta, alteri quoque data censeatur.

§ 3. Promotor iustitiae et defensor vinculi ius habent iterum replicandi partium responsionibus.

Can. 1604 – § 1. Omnino prohibentur partium vel advocatorum vel etiam aliorum informationes iudici datae, quae maneant extra acta causae.

§ 2. Si causae discussio scripto facta sit, iudex potest statuere ut moderata disputatio fiat ore pro tribunali sedente, ad quaestiones nonnullas illustrandas.

Can. 1605 – Disputationi orali, de qua in cann. 1602, § 1 et 1604, § 2, assistat notarius ad hoc ut, si iudex praecipiat aut pars postulet et iudex consentiat, de disceptatis et conclusis scripto statim referre possit.

3° in all cases, whenever it is likely that the future sentence may turn out to be unjust because of the reasons listed in can. 1645, §2, nn. 1–3, if new proof is not admitted.

§2. However, the judge can order or allow that a document be exhibited which, perhaps, could not have been exhibited earlier, through no fault of the interested party.

§3. The new proofs are to be published with due regard for can. 1598, §1.

Can. 1601 — After the conclusion of the case, the judge is to determine an appropriate period of time for the presentation of defense briefs or observations.

Can. 1602 — §1. The defense briefs and observations are to be in writing unless the judge with the consent of the parties decides that an oral debate before the tribunal is sufficient.

§2. If the defense briefs together with the principal documents are to be printed, the prior authorization of the judge is required but with the obligation of secrecy if it exists.

§3. The regulations of the tribunal are to be observed as regards the length of the defense briefs, the number of copies and other additional matters of this kind.

Can. 1603 — §1. After the defense briefs and observations have been communicated to each one, both parties are permitted to present rejoinders within a short period of time set by the judge.

§2. This right is granted to the parties only once unless it seems to the judge that it must be granted a second time for a serious reason; however, in that case, the grant made to one party is considered made also to the other party.

§3. The promoter of justice and the defender of the bond have the right to reply again to the rejoinders of the parties.

Can. 1604 — §1. It is absolutely forbidden that information given to the judge by the parties or the advocates or other persons remain outside the acts of the case.

§2. If the discussion of the case has been done in writing, the judge can determine that moderate oral debate take place before the tribunal to elucidate certain questions.

Can. 1605 — A notary is to be present at the oral debate mentioned in cann. 1602, §1 and 1604, §2, so that, if the judge orders it or if a party requests it and the judge consents, the notary can immediately record in writing the points discussed and the conclusions.

Can. 1606 – Si partes parare sibi tempore utili defensionem neglexerint, aut se remittant iudicis scientiae et conscientiae, iudex, si ex actis et probatis rem habeat plane perspectam, poterit statim sententiam pronuntiare, requisitis tamen animadversionibus promotoris iustitiae et defensoris vinculi, si iudicio intersint.

TITULUS VII
DE IUDICIS PRONUNTIATIONIBUS

Can. 1607 – Causa iudiciali modo pertractata, si sit principalis, definitur a iudice per sententiam definitivam; si sit incidens, per sententiam interlocutoriam, firmo praescripto can. 1589, § 1.

Can. 1608 – § 1. Ad pronuntiationem cuiuslibet sententiae requiritur in iudicis animo moralis certitudo circa rem sententia definiendam.

§ 2. Hanc certitudinem iudex haurire debet ex actis et probatis.

§ 3. Probationes autem aestimare iudex debet ex sua conscientia, firmis praescriptis legis de quarundam probationum efficacia.

§ 4. Iudex qui eam certitudinem adipisci non potuit, pronuntiet non constare de iure actoris et conventum absolutum dimittat, nisi agatur de causa iuris favore fruente, quo in casu pro ipsa pronuntiandum est.

Can. 1609 – § 1. In tribunali collegiali, qua die et hora iudices ad deliberandum conveniant, collegii praeses statuat, et nisi peculiaris causa aliud suadeat, in ipsa tribunalis sede conventus habeatur.

§ 2. Assignata conventui die, singuli iudices scriptas afferant conclusiones suas in merito causae, et rationes tam in iure quam in facto, quibus ad conclusionem suam venerint; quae conclusiones actis causae adiungantur, secreto servandae.

§ 3. Post divini Nominis invocationem, prolatis ex ordine singulorum conclusionibus secundum praecedentiam, ita tamen ut semper a causae ponente seu relatore initium fiat, habeatur discussio sub tribunalis praesidis ductu, praesertim ut constabiliatur quid statuendum sit in parte dispositiva sententiae.

Can. 1606 — If the parties neglect to prepare a defense brief within the time available to them, or if they entrust themselves to the knowledge and the conscience of the judge, the judge can pronounce sentence at once after requesting the observations of the promoter of justice and of the defender of the bond when they are involved in the trial, if the issue is plainly and fully known from the acts and proofs.

TITLE VII
THE PRONOUNCEMENTS OF THE JUDGE

Can. 1607 — After the case has been tried in a judicial manner, if it is the principal case, it is settled by the judge by a definitive sentence; if it is an incidental case, it is settled by an interlocutory sentence, with due regard for the prescription of can. 1589, §1.

Can. 1608 — §1. For the pronouncement of any kind of sentence, there must be in the mind of the judge moral certitude regarding the matter to be settled by the sentence.

§2. The judge must derive this certitude from the acts and the proofs.

§3. However, the judge must evaluate the proofs conscientiously with due regard for the prescriptions of the law concerning the efficacy of certain proofs.

§4. A judge who cannot arrive at this certitude, is to pronounce that the right of the petitioner is not established, and is to dismiss the respondent as absolved, unless there is question of a case which enjoys the favor of the law, in which case the decision must be in favor of it.

Can. 1609 — §1. If the tribunal is collegiate, the presiding judge of the college is to determine on what day and at what hour the judges are to convene for their deliberation; and the meeting is to be held at the tribunal unless a special reason suggests otherwise.

§2. On the day assigned for the meeting, the judges shall individually submit in writing their conclusions on the merits of the case and the reasons, both in law and in fact, for arriving at these conclusions, which are to be appended to the acts of the case and are to be kept secret.

§3. After the invocation of the Divine Name, the conclusions of the individual judge are to be made known in the order of precedence, but beginning always with the *ponens* or the *relator* of the case, and there is to be a discussion under the leadership of the the presiding judge, especially in order to decide what is to be determined in the dispositive part of the sentence.

§ 4. In discussione autem fas unicuique est a pristina sua conclusione recedere. Iudex vero qui ad decisionem aliorum accedere noluit, exigere potest ut, si fiat appellatio, suae conclusiones ad tribunal superius transmittantur.

§ 5. Quod si iudices in prima discussione ad sententiam devenire aut nolint aut nequeant, differri poterit decisio ad novum conventum, non tamen ultra hebdomadam, nisi ad normam can. 1600 complenda sit causae instructio.

Can. 1610 – § 1. Si iudex sit unicus, ipse sententiam exarabit.

§ 2. In tribunali collegiali, ponentis seu relatoris est exarare sententiam, desumendo motiva ex iis quae singuli iudices in discussione attulerunt, nisi a maiore numero iudicum praefinita fuerint motiva praeferenda; sententia dein singulorum iudicum subicienda est approbationi.

§ 3. Sententia edenda est non ultra mensem a die quo causa definita est, nisi, in tribunali collegiali, iudices gravi ex ratione longius tempus praestituerint.

Can. 1611 – Sententia debet:
1° definire controversiam coram tribunali agitatam, data singulis dubiis congrua responsione;
2° determinare quae sint partium obligationes ex iudicio ortae et quomodo implendae sint;
3° exponere rationes seu motiva, tam in iure quam in facto, quibus dispositiva sententiae pars innititur;
4° statuere de litis expensis.

Can. 1612 – § 1. Sententia, post divini Nominis invocationem, exprimat oportet ex ordine qui sit iudex aut tribunal; qui sit actor, pars conventa, procurator, nominibus et domiciliis rite designatis, promotor iustitiae, defensor vinculi, si partem in iudicio habuerint.

§ 2. Referre postea debet breviter facti speciem cum partium conclusionibus et formula dubiorum.

§ 3. Hisce subsequatur pars dispositiva sententiae, praemissis rationibus quibus innititur.

§ 4. Claudatur cum indicatione diei et loci in quibus prolata est et cum subscriptione iudicis vel, si de tribunali collegiali agatur, omnium iudicum et notarii.

Can. 1613 – Regulae superius positae de sententia definitiva, sententiae quoque interlocutoriae aptandae sunt.

§4. In the discussion, however, each judge has the right to retract his or her original conclusions; on the other hand, a judge who does not wish to accede to the decision of the others, can demand that his or her conclusions be transmitted to the higher tribunal if there is an appeal.

§5. But if the judges are unwilling or unable to arrive at a sentence in the first discussion, the decision can be deferred to another meeting but not beyond one week unless the instruction of the case must be completed in accord with the norm of can. 1600.

Can. 1610 — §1. If there is only one judge, he himself will write the sentence.

§2. In a collegiate tribunal it is the duty of the *ponens* or *relator* to write the sentence, drawing the reasons from those which the individual judges brought out in the discussion, unless it has been previously decided by the majority of the judges which reasons are to be preferred; then the sentence is to be submitted for the approval of the individual judges.

§3. The sentence must be issued not beyond one month from the day on which the case was settled, unless, in a collegiate tribunal, the judges set a longer period of time for a serious reason.

Can. 1611 — A sentence must:

1° settle the controversy discussed before the tribunal with an appropriate response given to each one of the questions;

2° determine what obligations of the parties arise from the trial and how they must be fulfilled;

3° set forth the reasons, that is, the motives both in law and in fact on which the dispositive section of the sentence is based;

4° make a determination about the expenses of the suit.

Can. 1612 — §1. After the invocation of the Divine Name, the sentence must express in sequence who is the judge or the tribunal; who is the petitioner, the respondent, the procurator, with the names and domiciles correctly indicated; the promoter of justice and the defender of the bond, if they took part in the trial.

§2. Next, it must briefly report the facts together with the conclusions of the parties and the formulation of the doubts.

§3. Following these points is the dispositive section of the sentence preceded by the reasons on which it is based.

§4. It is to close with an indication of the day and place where it was rendered and with the signature of the judge or, if it is a collegiate tribunal, with the signatures of all the judges and the notary.

Can. 1613 — The regulations mentioned above concerning a definitive sentence are to be adapted to an interlocutory sentence.

Can. 1614 – Sententia quam primum publicetur, indicatis modis quibus impugnari potest; neque ante publicationem vim ullam habet, etiamsi dispositiva pars, iudice permittente, partibus significata sit.

Can. 1615 – Publicatio seu intimatio sententiae fieri potest vel tradendo exemplar sententiae partibus aut earum procuratoribus, vel eisdem transmittendo idem exemplar ad normam can. 1509.

Can. 1616 – § 1. Si in sententiae textu vel error irrepserit in calculis, vel error materialis acciderit in transcribenda parte dispositiva aut in factis vel partium petitionibus referendis, vel omissa sint quae can. 1612, § 4 requirit, sententia ab ipso tribunali, quod eam tulit, corrigi vel compleri debet sive ad partis instantiam sive ex officio, semper tamen auditis partibus et decreto ad calcem sententiae apposito.

§ 2. Si qua pars refragetur, quaestio incidens decreto definiatur.

Can. 1617 – Ceterae iudicis pronuntiationes, praeter sententiam, sunt decreta, quae si mere ordinatoria non sint, vim non habent, nisi saltem summarie motiva exprimant, vel ad motiva in alio actu expressa remittant.

Can. 1618 – Sententia interlocutoria vel decretum vim sententiae definitivae habent, si iudicium impediunt vel ipsi iudicio aut alicui ipsius gradui finem ponunt, quod attinet ad aliquam saltem partem in causa.

TITULUS VIII
DE IMPUGNATIONE SENTENTIAE

Caput I
DE QUERELA NULLITATIS CONTRA SENTENTIAM

Can. 1619 – Firmis cann. 1622 et 1623, nullitates actuum, positivo iure statutae, quae, cum essent notae parti querelam proponenti, non sint ante sententiam iudici denuntiatae, per ipsam sententiam sanantur, quoties agitur de causa ad privatorum bonum attinenti.

Can. 1620 – Sententia vitio insanabilis nullitatis laborat, si :

1° lata est a iudice absolute incompetenti ;

2° lata est ab eo, qui careat potestate iudicandi in tribunali in quo causa definita est ;

3° iudex vi vel metu gravi coactus sententiam tulit ;

Can. 1614 — The sentence is to be published as soon as possible with an indication of the ways in which it can be challenged; it has no force before publication even if the dispositive section has been made known to the parties with the permission of the judge.

Can. 1615 — The publication or announcement of the sentence can be made either by giving a copy of the sentence to the parties or their procurators or by sending a copy to them in accord with the norm of can. 1509.

Can. 1616 — §1. If in the text of the sentence either an error in calculations has crept in, or a material error has occurred in transcribing the dispositive section, or reporting the facts or the petitions of the parties, or if the points required by can. 612, §4 were omitted, the sentence must be corrected or completed at the request of the parties or ex officio by the tribunal which issued the sentence; the parties, moreover, must always be heard and a decree appended at the bottom of the sentence.

§2. If any party objects, the incidental question is to be settled by decree.

Can. 1617 — The other pronouncements of a judge, over and above the sentence, are decrees which, if they are not merely procedural, have no force unless they express the reasons at least in a summary fashion, or refer to reasons expressed in some other act.

Can. 1618 — An interlocutory sentence or a decree has the force of a definitive sentence if it stops the trial, or if it puts an end to the trial or to some grade of the trial as regards at least some party in the case.

TITLE VIII
CHALLENGE OF THE SENTENCE

CHAPTER I
COMPLAINT OF NULLITY AGAINST THE SENTENCE

Can. 1619 — With due regard for cann. 1622 and 1623, nullities of acts which are established by positive law and which, although they were known to the party proposing the complaint, have not been denounced to the judge before the sentence, are sanated by the sentence itself if it is a case involving the private good.

Can. 1620 — A sentence is vitiated by irremediable nullity if:

1° it was rendered by a judge who is absolutely incompetent;

2° it was rendered by a person who lacks the power of judging in the tribunal in which the case was settled;

3° the judge passed the sentence under duress from force or grave fear;

4° iudicium factum est sine iudiciali petitione, de qua in can. 1501, vel non institutum fuit adversus aliquam partem conventam;

5° lata est inter partes, quarum altera saltem non habeat personam standi in iudicio;

6° nomine alterius quis egit sine legitimo mandato;

7° ius defensionis alterutri parti denegatum fuit;

8° controversia ne ex parte quidem definita est.

Can. 1621 – Querela nullitatis, de qua in can. 1620, proponi potest per modum exceptionis in perpetuum, per modum vero actionis coram iudice qui sententiam tulit intra decem annos a die publicationis sententiae.

Can. 1622 – Sententia vitio sanabilis nullitatis dumtaxat laborat, si:

1° lata est a non legitimo numero iudicum, contra praescriptum can. 1425, § 1;

2° motiva seu rationes decidendi non continet;

3° subscriptionibus caret iure praescriptis;

4° non refert indicationem anni, mensis, diei et loci in quo prolata fuit;

5° actu iudiciali nullo innititur, cuius nullitas non sit ad normam can. 1619 sanata;

6° lata est contra partem legitime absentem, iuxta can. 1593, § 2.

Can. 1623 – Querela nullitatis in casibus, de quibus in can. 1622, proponi potest intra tres menses a notitia publicationis sententiae.

Can. 1624 – De querela nullitatis videt ipse iudex qui sententiam tulit; quod si pars vereatur ne iudex, qui sententiam querela nullitatis impugnatam tulit, praeoccupatum animum habeat ideoque eum suspectum existimet, exigere potest ut alius iudex in eius locum subrogetur ad normam can. 1450.

Can. 1625 – Querela nullitatis proponi potest una cum appellatione, intra terminum ad appellationem statutum.

Can. 1626 – § 1. Querelam nullitatis interponere possunt non solum partes, quae se gravatas putant, sed etiam promotor iustitiae aut defensor vinculi, quoties ipsis ius est interveniendi.

§ 2. Ipse iudex potest ex officio sententiam nullam a se latam retractare vel emendare intra terminum ad agendum can. 1623 statutum, nisi

4° the trial was instituted without the judicial petition mentioned in can. 1501, or was not instituted against some respondent;

5° it was rendered between parties one of whom at least did not have standing in court;

6° one person acted in the name of another without a legitimate mandate;

7° the right of defense was denied to one or other party;

8° it did not settle the controversy even partially.

Can. 1621 — The complaint of nullity mentioned in can. 1620 can always be proposed by way of exception in perpetuity and by way of action before the judge who pronounced the sentence within ten years from the date of publication of the sentence.

Can. 1622 — A sentence is vitiated by remediable nullity only, if:

1° it was rendered by an illegitimate number of judges contrary to the prescription of can. 1425, §1;

2° it does not contain the motives, that is, the reasons for the decision;

3° it lacks the signatures prescribed by law;

4° it does not contain reference to the year, month, day and place in which it was pronounced;

5° it is based on a judicial act which is null and whose nullity was not sanated according to the norm of can. 1619;

6° it was rendered against a party who was legitimately absent as provided for in can. 1593, §2.

Can. 1623 — The complaint of nullity in the cases mentioned in can. 1622 can be proposed within three months from the notification of publication of the sentence.

Can. 1624 — The judge who pronounced the sentence examines the complaint of nullity; but if the party fears that the judge who pronounced the sentence which is being challenged by the complaint of nullity, may be prejudiced and, as a result, regards him or her as suspect, the party can demand that another judge be substituted according to the norm of can. 1450.

Can. 1625 — A complaint of nullity can be proposed together with an appeal within the time determined for an appeal.

Can. 1626 — §1. Not only the parties who feel themselves aggrieved can file a complaint of nullity but also the promoter of justice or the defender of the bond whenever they have the right to intervene.

§2. A judge himself can ex officio retract or amend an invalid sentence which he has pronounced, within the time period for acting set by can. 1623

interea appellatio una cum querela nullitatis interposita fuerit, aut nullitas sanata sit per decursum termini de quo in can. 1623.

Can. 1627 – Causae de querela nullitatis secundum normas de pro cessu contentioso orali tractari possunt.

Caput II
DE APPELLATIONE

Can. 1628 – Pars quae aliqua sententia se gravatam putat, itemque promotor iustitiae et defensor vinculi in causis in quibus eorum prae sentia requiritur, ius habent a sententia appellandi ad iudicem superio rem, salvo praescripto can. 1629.

Can. 1629 – Non est locus appellationi :

1° a sententia ipsius Summi Pontificis vel Signaturae Apostolicae :

2° a sententia vitio nullitatis infecta, nisi cumuletur cum querela nullitatis ad normam can. 1625 ;

3° a sententia quae in rem iudicatam transiit ;

4° a iudicis decreto vel a sententia interlocutoria, quae non ha beant vim sententiae definitivae, nisi cumuletur cum appellatione a sententia definitiva ;

5° a sententia vel a decreto in causa de qua ius cavet expeditissime rem esse definiendam.

Can. 1630 – § 1. Appellatio interponi debet coram iudice a quo sententia prolata sit, intra peremptorium terminum quindecim dierum utilium a notitia publicationis sententiae.

§ 2. Si ore fiat, notarius eam scripto coram ipso appellante redigat.

Can. 1631 – Si quaestio oriatur de iure appellandi, de ea videat expeditissime tribunal appellationis iuxta normas processus contentiosi oralis.

Can. 1632 – § 1. Si in appellatione non indicetur ad quod tribunal ipsa dirigatur, praesumitur facta tribunali de quo in cann. 1438 et 1439.

§ 2. Si alia pars ad aliud tribunal appellationis provocaverit, de causa videt tribunal quod superioris est gradus, salvo can. 1415.

Can. 1633 – Appellatio prosequenda est coram iudice *ad quem* di rigitur intra mensem ab eius interpositione, nisi iudex *a quo* longius tempus ad eam prosequendam parti praestituerit.

unless meanwhile an appeal together with a complaint of nullity has been filed, or unless the nullity has been sanated during the course of the time mentioned in can. 1623.

Can. 1627 — Cases involving a complaint of nullity can be treated according to the norms for the oral contentious process.

CHAPTER II
THE APPEAL

Can. 1628 — The party who feels aggrieved by a given sentence and likewise the promoter of justice and the defender of the bond in cases in which their presence is required, have the right to appeal from a sentence to a higher judge, with due regard for the prescription of can. 1629.

Can. 1629 — There is no room for appeal:

1° from a sentence of the Supreme Pontiff himself or of the Apostolic Signatura;

2° from a sentence vitiated by nullity unless it is joined with a complaint of nullity according to the norm of can. 1625;

3° from a sentence which has become *res iudicata*;

4° from the decree of a judge or an interlocutory sentence which does not have the force of a definitive sentence, unless it is joined with an appeal from a definitive sentence;

5° from a sentence or from a decree in a case in which the law provides for a settlement of the matter as quickly as possible.

Can. 1630 — §1. An appeal must be filed before the judge who pronounced the sentence within the peremptory time limit of fifteen available days (*tempus utile*) from notification of the publication of the sentence.

§2. If it is made orally, the notary is to put it in writing in the presence of the appellant.

Can. 1631 — If a question arises regarding the right of appeal, the appellate tribunal should examine it as quickly as possible according to the norms of the oral contentious process.

Can. 1632 — §1. If in the appeal there is no indication of the tribunal to which it is directed, it is presumed to be made to the tribunal mentioned in cann. 1438 and 1439.

§2. If the other party has recourse to another appellate tribunal, the tribunal of higher grade examines the case, with due regard for can. 1415.

Can. 1633 — An appeal must be prosecuted within a month of its being filed before the judge to whom it is directed, unless the judge from whom appeal is made has set a longer period of time for the party to prosecute it.

Can. 1634 – § 1. Ad prosequendam appellationem requiritur et sufficit ut pars ministerium invocet iudicis superioris ad impugnatae sententiae emendationem, adiuncto exemplari huius sententiae et indicatis appellationis rationibus.

§ 2. Quod si pars exemplar impugnatae sententiae intra utile tempus a tribunali *a quo* obtinere nequeat, interim termini non decurrunt, et impedimentum significandum est iudici appellationis, qui iudicem *a quo* praecepto obstringat officio suo quam primum satisfaciendi.

§ 3. Interea iudex *a quo* debet acta ad normam can. 1474 iudici appellationis transmittere.

Can. 1635 – Inutiliter elapsis fatalibus appellatoriis sive coram iudice *a quo* sive coram iudice *ad quem,* deserta censetur appellatio.

Can. 1636 – § 1. Appellans potest appellationi renuntiare cum effectibus, de quibus in can. 1525.

§ 2. Si appellatio proposita sit a vinculi defensore vel a promotore iustitiae, renuntiatio fieri potest, nisi lex aliter caveat, a vinculi defensore vel promotore iustitiae tribunalis appellationis.

Can. 1637 – § 1. Appellatio facta ab actore prodest etiam convento, et vicissim.

§ 2. Si plures sunt conventi vel actores et ab uno vel contra unum tantum ex ipsis sententia impugnetur, impugnatio censetur ab omnibus et contra omnes facta, quoties res petita est individua aut obligatio solidalis.

§ 3. Si interponatur ab una parte super aliquo sententiae capite, pars adversa, etsi fatalia appellationis fuerint transacta, potest super aliis capitibus incidenter appellare intra terminum peremptorium quindecim dierum a die, quo ipsi appellatio principalis notificata est.

§ 4. Nisi aliud constet, appellatio praesumitur facta contra omnia sententiae capita.

Can. 1638 – Appellatio exsecutionem sententiae suspendit.

Can. 1639 – § 1. Salvo praescripto can. 1683, in gradu appellationis non potest admitti nova petendi causa, ne per modum quidem utilis cumulationis; ideoque litis contestatio in eo tantum versari potest, ut prior sententia vel confirmetur vel reformetur sive ex toto sive ex parte.

§ 2. Novae autem probationes admittuntur tantum ad normam can. 1600.

Can. 1640 – In gradu appellationis eodem modo, quo in prima instantia, congrua congruis referendo, procedendum est; sed, nisi forte

Can. 1634 — §1. In order to prosecute an appeal, it is required and suffices that the party call upon the services of the higher judge for the emendation of the challenged sentence, append a copy of this sentence, and indicate the reasons for the appeal.

§2. If the party is unable to obtain a copy of the challenged sentence from the tribunal from which the appeal is being made within the available time, the time limits do not run out in the interval; and the impediment must be indicated to the appellate judge who is to bind the judge from whom the appeal is made with a precept to perform his duty as soon as possible.

§3. Meanwhile the judge from whom the appeal is being made must transmit the acts to the appellate judge according to the norm of can. 1474.

Can. 1635 — If the deadline for appeal either before the judge from whom the appeal is being made or before the judge to whom the appeal is directed has passed without result, the appeal is considered abandoned.

Can. 1636 — §1. The appellant can renounce the appeal with the effects mentioned in can. 1525.

§2. If the appeal was proposed by the defender of the bond or the promoter of justice, it can be renounced by the defender of the bond or the promoter of justice of the appellate tribunal unless the law provides otherwise.

Can. 1637 — §1. An appeal lodged by the petitioner also benefits the respondent and vice versa.

§2. If there are several respondents or petitioners, and if the sentence is challenged by only one or against only one of them, the challenge is considered made by all of them and against all of them whenever the matter sought is indivisible or it is a joint obligation.

§3. If an appeal is filed by one party regarding one part of the sentence, the other party can place an incidental appeal regarding the other parts within a peremptory time period of fifteen days from the date of being notified of the principal appeal even though the deadline for an appeal has expired.

§4. Unless there is evidence to the contrary, it is presumed that an appeal is made against all parts of a sentence.

Can. 1638 — An appeal suspends the execution of a sentence.

Can. 1639 — §1. With due regard for the prescription of can. 1683, a new basis for petitioning may not be admitted at the appellate level not even by way of helpful cumulation; consequently, the joinder of issues (*contestatio litis*) can focus only on whether the prior sentence is to be confirmed or revised, either totally or partially.

§2. Moreover, new proofs are admitted only in accord with the norm of can. 1600.

Can. 1640 — At the appellate level the procedure is the same as in first instance insofar as it is applicable; however, immediately after the joinder of

complendae sint probationes, statim post litem ad normam can. 1513, § 1
et can. 1639, § 1 contestatam, ad causae discussionem deveniatur et ad
sententiam.

TITULUS IX
DE RE IUDICATA
ET DE RESTITUTIONE IN INTEGRUM

CAPUT I
DE RE IUDICATA

Can. 1641 – Firmo praescripto can. 1643, res iudicata habetur :

1° si duplex intercesserit inter easdem partes sententia conformis
de eodem petito et ex eadem causa petendi ;

2° si appellatio adversus sententiam non fuerit intra tempus utile
proposita ;

3° si, in gradu appellationis, instantia perempta sit vel eidem renuntiatum fuerit ;

4° si lata sit sententia definitiva, a qua non datur appellatio ad
normam can. 1629.

Can. 1642 – § 1. Res iudicata firmitate iuris gaudet nec impugnari
potest directe, nisi ad normam can. 1645, § 1.

§ 2. Eadem facit ius inter partes et dat actionem iudicati atque exceptionem rei iudicatae, quam iudex ex officio quoque declarare potest ad
impediendam novam eiusdem causae introductionem.

Can. 1643 – Numquam transeunt in rem iudicatam causae de statu
personarum, haud exceptis causis de coniugum separatione.

Can. 1644 – § 1. Si duplex sententia conformis in causa de statu
personarum prolata sit, potest quovis tempore ad tribunal appellationis
provocari, novis iisque gravibus probationibus vel argumentis intra peremptorium terminum triginta dierum a proposita impugnatione allatis.
Tribunal autem appellationis intra mensem ab exhibitis novis probationibus et argumentis debet decreto statuere utrum nova causae propositio admitti debeat necne.

§ 2. Provocatio ad superius tribunal ut nova causae propositio obtineatur, exsecutionem sententiae non suspendit, nisi aut lex aliter caveat
aut tribunal appellationis ad normam can. 1650, § 3 suspensionem iubeat.

issues has taken place in accord with the norm of cann. 1513, §1 and 1639, §1, the case is to be discussed and the sentence rendered unless perhaps the proofs must be completed.

TITLE IX
RES JUDICATA AND *RESTITUTIO IN INTEGRUM*

CHAPTER I
RES JUDICATA

Can. 1641 — With due regard for the prescription of can. 1643, a *res judicata* results:

1° if two concordant sentences have been issued between the same persons regarding the same petition and arising out of the same basis for petitioning;

2° if an appeal against the sentence has not been filed within the available time;

3° if, at the appellate level, the prosecution of the suit has been estopped or renounced;

4° if a definitive sentence has been rendered from which no appeal is granted according to the norm of can. 1629.

Can. 1642 — §1. A *res judicata* enjoys the stability of law and cannot be directly challenged except in accord with the norm of can. 1645, §1.

§2. It settles an issue between the parties and gives rise to an action for execution and an exception of *res judicata* which the judge can declare ex officio to prevent a new introduction of the same case.

Can. 1643 — Cases concerning the status of persons, especially those concerning the separation of spouses, never become a *res judicata*.

Can. 1644 — §1. If two concordant sentences have been pronounced in a case concerning the status of persons, it can be appealed at any time to an appellate tribunal if new and serious proofs or arguments are brought forward within the peremptory time period of thirty days from the proposed challenge. However, within a month from the presentation of the new proofs and arguments, the appellate tribunal must settle by decree whether a new presentation of the case must be admitted or not.

§2. An appeal to a higher tribunal to obtain a new presentation of the case does not suspend the execution of the sentence, unless either the law provides otherwise or the appellate tribunal orders its suspension, in accord with the norm of can. 1650, §3.

Caput II

DE RESTITUTIONE IN INTEGRUM

Can. 1645 – § 1. Adversus sententiam quae transierit in rem iudicatam, dummodo de eius iniustitia manifesto constet, datur restitutio in integrum.

§ 2. De iniustitia autem manifesto constare non censetur, nisi :

1° sententia ita probationibus innitatur, quae postea falsae deprehensae sint, ut sine illis probationibus pars sententiae dispositiva non sustineatur ;

2° postea detecta fuerint documenta, quae facta nova et contrariam decisionem exigentia indubitanter probent ;

3° sententia ex dolo partis prolata fuerit in damnum alterius ;

4° legis non mere processualis praescriptum evidenter neglectum fuerit ;

5° sententia adversetur praecedenti decisioni, quae in rem iudicatam transierit.

Can. 1646 – § 1. Restitutio in integrum propter motiva, de quibus in can. 1645, § 2, nn. 1-3, petenda est a iudice qui sententiam tulit intra tres menses a die cognitionis eorundem motivorum computandos.

§ 2. Restitutio in integrum propter motiva, de quibus in can. 1645, § 2, nn. 4 et 5, petenda est a tribunali appellationis, intra tres menses a notitia publicationis sententiae ; quod si in casu, de quo in can. 1645, § 2, n. 5, notitia praecedentis decisionis serius habeatur, terminus ab hac notitia decurrit.

§ 3. Termini de quibus supra non decurrunt, quamdiu laesus minoris sit aetatis.

Can. 1647 – § 1. Petitio restitutionis in integrum sententiae exsecutionem nondum inceptam suspendit.

§ 2. Si tamen ex probabilibus indiciis suspicio sit petitionem factam esse ad moras exsecutioni nectendas, iudex decernere potest ut sententia exsecutioni demandetur, assignata tamen restitutionem petenti idonea cautione ut, si restituatur in integrum, indemnis fiat.

Can. 1648 – Concessa restitutione in integrum, iudex pronuntiare debet de merito causae.

CHAPTER II

RESTITUTIO IN INTEGRUM

Can. 1645 — §1. *Restitutio in integrum* is granted against a sentence which has become a *res judicata* provided that there is clear proof of its injustice.

§2. However, clear proof of injustice is verified only if:

1° the sentence is so based on proofs which are later discovered to be false so that without those proofs the dispositive section of the sentence would not be sustained;

2° afterwards documents have been found which undoubtedly prove new facts which demand a contrary decision;

3° the sentence was pronounced because of the fraud of one party which harmed the other;

4° a prescription of the law which is not merely procedural has been evidently neglected;

5° the sentence is contrary to a preceding sentence which has become a *res iudicata*.

Can. 1646 — §1. *Restitutio in integrum* for the reasons mentioned in can. 1645, §2, nn. 1–3 must be sought from the judge who issued the sentence, within three months to be computed from the date of one's becoming aware of the reasons.

§2. *Restitutio in integrum* for the reasons mentioned in can. 1645, §2, nn. 4 and 5 must be sought from the appellate tribunal within three months from notification of the publication of the sentence; but if, in the case mentioned in can. 1645, §2, n. 5, notification of the preceding decision is had later, the time limit runs from this notification.

§3. The time limits mentioned above do not expire as long as the injured person is a minor.

Can. 1647 — §1. A petition of *restitutio in integrum* suspends the execution of a sentence if the execution has not yet begun.

§2. If, however, from probable indications there is a suspicion that the petition has been made in order to delay the execution of the sentence, the judge can decree that the sentence be executed but with due caution being taken to indemnify the person seeking *restitutio in integrum* if it is granted.

Can. 1648 — If *restitutio in integrum* is granted, the judge must pronounce on the merits of the case.

TITULUS X
DE EXPENSIS IUDICIALIBUS
ET DE GRATUITO PATROCINIO

Can. 1649 - § 1. Episcopus, cuius est tribunal moderari, statuat normas :

1° de partibus damnandis ad expensas iudiciales solvendas vel compensandas ;

2° de procuratorum, advocatorum, peritorum et interpretum honorariis deque testium indemnitate ;

3° de gratuito patrocinio vel expensarum deminutione concedendis ;

4° de damnorum refectione quae debetur ab eo qui non solum in iudicio succubuit, sed temere litigavit ;

5° de pecuniae deposito vel cautione praestanda circa expensas solvendas et damna reficienda.

§ 2. A pronuntiatione circa expensas, honoraria et damna reficienda non datur distincta appellatio, sed pars recurrere potest intra quindecim dies ad eundem iudicem, qui poterit taxationem emendare.

TITULUS XI
DE EXSECUTIONE SENTENTIAE

Can. 1650 - § 1. Sententia quae transiit in rem iudicatam, exsecutioni mandari potest, salvo praescripto can. 1647.

§ 2. Iudex qui sententiam tulit et, si appellatio proposita sit, etiam iudex appellationis, sententiae, quae nondum transierit in rem iudicatam, provisoriam exsecutionem iubere possunt ex officio vel ad instantiam partis, idoneis, si casus ferat, praestitis cautionibus, si agatur de provisionibus seu praestationibus ad necessariam sustentationem ordinatis, vel alia iusta causa urgeat.

§ 3. Quod si sententia, de qua in § 2, impugnetur, iudex qui de impugnatione cognoscere debet, si videt hanc probabiliter fundatam esse et irreparabile damnum ex exsecutione oriri posse, potest vel exsecutionem ipsam suspendere vel eam cautioni subicere.

Can. 1651 - Non antea exsecutioni locus esse poterit, quam exsecutorium iudicis decretum habeatur, quo edicatur sententiam ipsam exsecutioni mandari debere ; quod decretum pro diversa causarum natura vel in ipso sententiae tenore includatur vel separatim edatur.

TITLE X
COURT COSTS AND GRATUITOUS LEGAL ASSISTANCE

Can. 1649 — §1. The bishop whose responsibility it is to supervise the tribunal, is to determine norms regarding:

1° the parties to be liable for paying or compensating for judicial expenses;

2° the honoraria for procurators, advocates, experts and interpreters and the indemnification of witnesses.

3° the granting of gratuitous legal assistance or a diminution of expenses;

4° the recovery of damages which are owed by the one who not only lost the case but also engaged in litigation rashly;

5° the depositing of money or the guarantees to be made concerning the expenses to be paid and the damages to be recovered.

§2. From a pronouncement relating to expenses, honoraria and recovery of damages, there is no separate appeal; but the party can have recourse within fifteen days to the same judge who can adjust the assessment.

TITLE XI
EXECUTION OF THE SENTENCE

Can. 1650 — §1. A sentence which has become a *res judicata* can be executed with due regard for the prescription of can. 1647.

§2. The judge who rendered the sentence and also the appellate judge if an appeal has been filed, can ex officio or at the request of a party order a provisional execution of a sentence which has not yet become a *res judicata* after having arranged, if the case warrants, for the rendering of appropriate guarantees if there is question of provisions or payments for necessary sustenance or if some other just cause is pressing.

§3. On the other hand if the sentence mentioned in §2 is challenged and if the judge who must take cognizance of the challenge sees that it is probably well-founded and irreparable harm could arise from the execution of the sentence, the judge can suspend its execution or subject it to a safeguard.

Can. 1651 — There can be no execution of a sentence prior to an executory decree of the judge in which it is stated that the sentence must be executed; this decree is to be included in the text of the sentence or issued separately, according to the different types of cases.

Can. 1652 – Si sententiae exsecutio praeviam rationum redditionem exigat, quaestio incidens habetur, ab illo ipso iudice decidenda, qui tulit sententiam exsecutioni mandandam.

Can. 1653 – § 1. Nisi lex particularis aliud statuat, sententiam exsecutioni mandare debet per se vel per alium Episcopus dioecesis, in qua sententia primi gradus lata est.

§ 2. Quod si hic renuat vel neglegat, parte cuius interest instante vel etiam ex officio, exsecutio spectat ad auctoritatem cui tribunal appellationis ad normam can. 1439, § 3 subicitur.

§ 3. Inter religiosos exsecutio sententiae spectat ad Superiorem qui sententiam exsecutioni mandandam tulit aut iudicem delegavit.

Can. 1654 – § 1. Exsecutor, nisi quid eius arbitrio in ipso sententiae tenore fuerit permissum, debet sententiam ipsam, secundum obvium verborum sensum, exsecutioni mandare.

§ 2. Licet ei videre de exceptionibus circa modum et vim exsecutionis, non autem de merito causae; quod si habeat aliunde compertum sententiam esse nullam vel manifeste iniustam ad normam cann. 1620, 1622, 1645, abstineat ab exsecutione, et rem ad tribunal a quo lata est sententia remittat, partibus certioribus factis.

Can. 1655 – § 1. Quod attinet ad reales actiones, quoties adiudicata actori res aliqua est, haec actori tradenda est statim ac res iudicata habetur.

§ 2. Quod vero attinet ad actiones personales, cum reus damnatus est ad rem mobilem praestandam, vel ad solvendam pecuniam, vel ad aliud dandum aut faciendum, iudex in ipso tenore sententiae vel exsecutor pro suo arbitrio et prudentia terminum statuat ad implendam obligationem, qui tamen neque infra quindecim dies coarctetur neque sex menses excedat.

SECTIO II
DE PROCESSU CONTENTIOSO ORALI

Can. 1656 – § 1. Processu contentioso orali, de quo in hac sectione, tractari possunt omnes causae a iure non exclusae, nisi pars processum contentiosum ordinarium petat.

§ 2. Si processus oralis adhibeatur extra casus iure permissos, actus iudiciales sunt nulli.

Can. 1657 – Processus contentiosus oralis fit in primo gradu coram iudice unico, ad normam can. 1424.

Can. 1652 — If the execution of the sentence demands a prior rendering of accounts, it is an incidental question which must be decided by the judge who passed the sentence ordering the execution.

Can. 1653 — §1. Unless particular law determines otherwise, the bishop of the diocese in which the first instance sentence was rendered, must execute the sentence personally or through another.

§2. If he refuses or neglects to do so, the execution belongs to the authority to which the appellate tribunal is subject in accord with the provision of can. 1439, §3, at the request of an interested party or ex officio.

§3. Among religious the execution of a sentence belongs to the superior who passed the sentence to be executed or who delegated the judge.

Can. 1654 — §1. Unless something is left to the discretion of the executor in the text of the sentence, the executor must execute the sentence according to the obvious meaning of the words.

§2. The executor may consider exceptions regarding the manner and force of the execution but not regarding the merits of the case; but if it has been discovered from other sources that the sentence is invalid or manifestly unjust according to the norm of cann. 1620, 1622 and 1645 the executor is to refrain from executing it, refer the matter to the tribunal which issued the sentence, and inform the parties.

Can. 1655 — §1. As regards real actions, wherever a given thing has been adjudicated as belonging to the petitioner, it must be handed over to the petitioner as soon as there is a *res iudicata*.

§2. However, as regards personal actions, when the respondent is condemned to furnish something mobile, to pay money, or to give or to do something else, the judge in the text of the sentence, or the executor with personal discretion and prudence is to set a time limit for fulfilling the obligation, which, however, is not to be less than fifteen days nor more than six months.

SECTION II

THE ORAL CONTENTIOUS PROCESS

Can. 1656 — §1. All cases which are not excluded by law can be tried in the oral contentious process dealt with in this section, unless a party requests the ordinary contentious process.

§2. If the oral process is used outside of cases permitted by law, the judicial acts are null.

Can. 1657 — The oral contentious process takes place in first instance before a single judge according to the norm of can. 1424.

Can. 1658 – § 1. Libellus quo lis introducitur, praeter ea quae in can. 1504 recensentur, debet:

1° facta quibus actoris petitiones innitantur, breviter, integre et perspicue exponere;

2° probationes quibus actor facta demonstrare intendit, quasque simul afferre nequit, ita indicare ut statim colligi a iudice possint.

§ 2. Libello adnecti debent, saltem in exemplari authentico, documenta quibus petitio innititur.

Can. 1659 – § 1. Si conamen conciliationis ad normam can. 1446, § 2 inutile cesserit, iudex, si aestimet libellum aliquo fundamento niti, intra tres dies, decreto ad calcem ipsius libelli apposito, praecipiat ut exemplar petitionis notificetur parti conventae, facta huic facultate mittendi, intra quindecim dies, ad cancellariam tribunalis scriptam responsionem.

§ 2. Haec notificatio effectus habet citationis iudicialis, de quibus in can. 1512.

Can. 1660 – Si exceptiones partis conventae id exigant, iudex parti actrici praefiniat terminum ad respondendum, ita ut ex allatis utriusque partis elementis ipse controversiae obiectum perspectum habeat.

Can. 1661 – § 1. Elapsis terminis, de quibus in cann. 1659 et 1660, iudex, perspectis actis, formulam dubii determinet; dein ad audientiam, non ultra triginta dies celebrandam, omnes citet qui in ea interesse debent, addita pro partibus dubii formula.

§ 2. In citatione partes certiores fiant se posse, tres saltem ante audientiam dies, aliquod breve scriptum tribunali exhibere ad sua asserta comprobanda.

Can. 1662 – In audientia primum tractantur quaestiones de quibus in cann. 1459-1464.

Can. 1663 – § 1. Probationes colliguntur in audientia, salvo praescripto can. 1418.

§ 2. Pars eiusque advocatus assistere possunt excussioni ceterarum partium, testium et peritorum.

Can. 1664 – Responsiones partium, testium, peritorum, petitiones et exceptiones advocatorum, redigendae sunt scripto a notario, sed summatim et in iis tantummodo quae pertinent ad substantiam rei controversae, et a deponentibus subsignandae.

Can. 1665 – Probationes, quae non sint in petitione vel responsione allatae aut petitae, potest iudex admittere tantum ad normam

Can. 1658 — §1. In addition to the points mentioned in can. 1504, the *libellus* by which the suit is introduced must:

1° set forth briefly, completely and clearly the facts on which the requests of the petitioner are based;

2° so indicate the proofs by which the petitioner intends to demonstrate the facts, but which cannot be produced at once, so that they can be gathered at once by the judge.

§2. The documents on which the petition is based must be attached to the *libellus*, at least in an authentic copy.

Can. 1659 — §1. If an attempt at reconciliation according to the norm of can. 1446, §2, has been fruitless, the judge, if he believes that the *libellus* has some foundation, is to order within three days by a decree appended to the bottom of the *libellus* that a copy of the petition be communicated to the respondent, granting the latter the right to send a written response to the chancery of the tribunal within fifteen days.

§2. This notification has the effects of the judicial citation mentioned in can. 1512.

Can. 1660 — If the exceptions of the respondent demand it, the judge is to set a time limit for the petitioner to respond so as to clarify the object of the controversy from the points raised by each of them.

Can. 1661 — §1. When the time limits mentioned in cann. 1659 and 1660 have expired, the judge, after having examined the acts, is to determine the formulation of the doubt; next, the judge is to cite to a hearing, to be held within thirty days, all who must be present at it; the judge is to attach the formula of the doubt to the citation for the parties.

§2. In the citation the parties are to be informed that they can present to the tribunal a brief written statement in support of their allegations at least three days prior to the hearing.

Can. 1662 — At the hearing the questions mentioned in cann. 1459–1464 are to be treated first.

Can. 1663 — §1. The proofs are collected at the hearing with due regard for the prescription of can. 1418.

§2. The party and his or her advocate can be present at the examination of the other parties, of the witnesses, and the experts.

Can. 1664 — The responses of the parties, witnesses, and the experts, and the petitions and exceptions of the advocates must be put in writing by the notary but in a summary fashion and only as regards those matters which pertain to the substance of the controverted matter, and they must be signed by those making depositions.

Can. 1665 — Only in accord with the norm of can. 1452 can the judge admit proofs which have not been presented or asked for in the petition or

can. 1452; postquam autem vel unus testis auditus est, iudex potest tantummodo ad normam can. 1600 novas probationes decernere.

Can. 1666 – Si in audientia probationes omnes colligi non potuerint, altera statuatur audientia.

Can. 1667 – Probationibus collectis, fit in eadem audientia discussio oralis.

Can. 1668 – § 1. Nisi ex discussione aliquid supplendum in causae instructione comperiatur, vel aliud exsistat quod impediat sententiam rite proferri, iudex illico, expleta audientia, causam seorsum decidat; dispositiva sententiae pars statim coram partibus praesentibus legatur.

§ 2. Potest autem tribunal propter rei difficultatem vel aliam iustam causam usque ad quintum utilem diem decisionem differre.

§ 3. Integer sententiae textus, motivis expressis, quam primum, ordinarie non ultra quindecim dies, partibus notificetur.

Can. 1669 – Si tribunal appellationis perspiciat in inferiore iudicii gradu processum contentiosum oralem esse adhibitum in casibus a iure exclusis, nullitatem sententiae declaret et causam remittat tribunali quod sententiam tulit.

Can. 1670 – In ceteris quae ad rationem procedendi attinent, serventur praescripta canonum de iudicio contentioso ordinario. Tribunal autem potest suo decreto, motivis praedito, normis processualibus, quae non sint ad validitatem statutae, derogare, ut celeritati, salva iustitia, consulat.

the response; however, after even a single witness has been heard, the judge can decree new proofs only in accord with the norm of can. 1600.

Can. 1666 — If all the proofs cannot be collected at the hearing, a second hearing is to be scheduled.

Can. 1667 — When the proofs have been collected, the oral discussion takes place at the same hearing.

Can. 1668 — §1. Unless from the discussion it is discovered that something must be supplied in the instruction of the case or something else turns up which prevents the due pronouncement of the sentence, the judge immediately decides the case privately when the hearing has been completed; the dispositive part of the sentence is to be read at once in the presence of the parties.

§2. However, the tribunal can defer the decision until the fifth available day because of the difficulty of the matter or for another just cause.

§3. The complete text of the sentence with the reasons expressed is to be made known to the parties as soon as possible, ordinarily not beyond fifteen days.

Can. 1669 — If the appellate tribunal should discover that in a lower grade of the trial the oral contentious process was used in cases excluded by the law, it is to declare the nullity of the sentence and remand the case to the tribunal which passed it.

Can. 1670 — In other matters which pertain to the mode of procedure, the prescriptions of the canons concerning the ordinary contentious trial are to be observed. However, the tribunal by a decree giving the reasons, can derogate from procedural norms which have not been determined for validity, in order to expedite matters with due regard for justice.

PARS III
DE QUIBUSDAM PROCESSIBUS SPECIALIBUS

TITULUS I
DE PROCESSIBUS MATRIMONIALIBUS

CAPUT I
DE CAUSIS AD MATRIMONII NULLITATEM DECLARANDAM

Art. 1
DE FORO COMPETENTI

Can. 1671 – Causae matrimoniales baptizatorum iure proprio ad iudicem ecclesiasticum spectant.

Can. 1672 – Causae de effectibus matrimonii mere civilibus pertinent ad civilem magistratum, nisi ius particulare statuat easdem causas, si incidenter et accessorie agantur, posse a iudice ecclesiastico cognosci ac definiri.

Can. 1673 – In causis de matrimonii nullitate, quae non sint Sedi Apostolicae reservatae, competentes sunt:

1° tribunal loci in quo matrimonium celebratum est;

2° tribunal loci in quo pars conventa domicilium vel quasi-domicilium habet;

3° tribunal loci in quo pars actrix domicilium habet, dummodo utraque pars in territorio eiusdem Episcoporum conferentiae degat et Vicarius iudicialis domicilii partis conventae, ipsa audita, consentiat;

4° tribunal loci in quo de facto colligendae sunt pleraeque probationes, dummodo accedat consensus Vicarii iudicialis domicilii partis conventae, qui prius ipsam interroget, num quid excipiendum habeat.

PART III
CERTAIN SPECIAL PROCEDURES

TITLE I
MATRIMONIAL PROCEDURES

CHAPTER I
CASES DECLARING NULLITY OF MARRIAGE

Art. 1
THE COMPETENT FORUM

Can. 1671 — Marriage cases of the baptized belong to the ecclesiastical judge by proper right.

Can. 1672 — Cases involving the merely civil effects of marriage belong to the civil magistrate unless particular law determines that these cases can be tried and decided by the ecclesiastical judge when they arise as incidental and accessory.

Can. 1673 — In cases regarding the nullity of marriage which are not reserved to the Apostolic See the following are competent:

1° the tribunal of the place in which the marriage was celebrated;

2° the tribunal of the place in which the respondent has a domicile or quasi-domicile;

3° the tribunal of the place in which the petitioner has a domicile, provided that both parties live in the territory of the same conference of bishops and the judicial vicar of the domicile of the respondent agrees, after hearing the respondent;

4° the tribunal of the place in which de facto most of the proofs are to be collected provided that the judicial vicar of the domicile of the respondent gives consent who, before he does so, is to ask if the respondent has any exceptions.

Art. 2

DE IURE IMPUGNANDI MATRIMONIUM

Can. 1674 – Habiles sunt ad matrimonium impugnandum :

1° coniuges ;

2° promotor iustitiae, cum nullitas iam divulgata est, si matrimonium convalidari nequeat aut non expediat.

Can. 1675 – § 1. Matrimonium quod, utroque coniuge vivente, non fuit accusatum, post mortem alterutrius vel utriusque coniugis accusari non potest, nisi quaestio de validitate sit praeiudicialis ad aliam solvendam controversiam sive in foro canonico sive in foro civili.

§ 2. Si autem coniux moriatur pendente causa, servetur can. 1518.

Art. 3

DE OFFICIO IUDICUM

Can. 1676 – Iudex, antequam causam acceptet et quotiescumque spem boni exitus perspicit, pastoralia media adhibeat, ut coniuges, si fieri potest, ad matrimonium forte convalidandum et ad coniugalem convictum restaurandum inducantur.

Can. 1677 – § 1. Libello acceptato, praeses vel ponens procedat ad notificationem decreti citationis ad normam can. 1508.

§ 2. Transacto termino quindecim dierum a notificatione, praeses vel ponens, nisi alterutra pars sessionem ad litem contestandam petierit, intra decem dies formulam dubii vel dubiorum decreto suo statuat ex officio et partibus notificet.

§ 3. Formula dubii non tantum quaerat an constet de nullitate matrimonii in casu, sed determinare etiam debet quo capite vel quibus capitibus nuptiarum validitas impugnetur.

§ 4. Post decem dies a notificatione decreti, si partes nihil opposuerint, praeses vel ponens novo decreto causae instructionem disponat.

Art. 2

The Right to Challenge a Marriage

Can. 1674 — The following are capable of challenging a marriage:

1° the spouses;

2° the promoter of justice when the nullity has become public, if the marriage cannot be convalidated or this is not expedient.

Can. 1675 — §1. A marriage which has not been impugned during the lifetime of both spouses cannot be impugned after the death of either one or both spouses unless the question of validity is prejudicial to the resolution of another controversy either in the canonical forum or in the civil forum.

§2. However, if a spouse dies while a case is pending, can. 1518 is to be observed.

Art. 3

The Office of the Judges

Can. 1676 — Before accepting a case and whenever there seems to be hope of a successful outcome, the judge is to use pastoral means to induce the spouses, if at all possible, to convalidate the marriage and to restore conjugal living.

Can. 1677 — §1. When the *libellus* has been accepted, the presiding judge or the *ponens* is to proceed to the communication of the decree of citation according to the norms of can. 1508.

§2. Unless either party has petitioned for a session on the joinder of the issues (*contestatio litis*), when fifteen days have passed after such a communication, the presiding judge or the *ponens* is to determine the formulation of the doubt or doubts within ten days by a decree ex officio and notify the parties.

§3. The formulation of the doubt not only is to ask whether there is proof of nullity of marriage in the case, but it also must determine on what ground or grounds the validity of the marriage is to be challenged.

§4. Ten days after the the communication of the decree, the presiding judge or the *ponens* is to arrange for the instruction of the case by a new decree if the parties were not opposed.

Art. 4

DE PROBATIONIBUS

Can. 1678 – § 1. Defensori vinculi, partium patronis et, si in iudicio sit, etiam promotori iustitiae ius est:

1° examini partium, testium et peritorum adesse, salvo praescripto can. 1559;

2° acta iudicialia, etsi nondum publicata, invisere et documenta a partibus producta recognoscere.

§ 2. Examini, de quo in § 1, n. 1, partes assistere nequeunt.

Can. 1679 – Nisi probationes aliunde plenae habeantur, iudex, ad partium depositiones ad normam can. 1536 aestimandas, testes de ipsarum partium credibilitate, si fieri potest, adhibeat, praeter alia indicia et adminicula.

Can. 1680 – In causis de impotentia vel de consensus defectu propter mentis morbum iudex unius periti vel plurium opera utatur, nisi ex adiunctis inutilis evidenter appareat; in ceteris causis servetur praescriptum can. 1574.

Art. 5

DE SENTENTIA ET APPELLATIONE

Can. 1681 – Quoties in instructione causae dubium valde probabile emerserit de non secuta matrimonii consummatione, tribunal potest, suspensa de consensu partium causa nullitatis, instructionem complere pro dispensatione super rato, ac tandem acta transmittere ad Sedem Apostolicam una cum petitione dispensationis ab alterutro vel utroque coniuge et cum voto tribunalis et Episcopi.

Can. 1682 – § 1. Sententia, quae matrimonii nullitatem primum declaraverit, una cum appellationibus, si quae sint, et ceteris iudicii actis, intra viginti dies a sententiae publicatione ad tribunal appellationis ex officio transmittatur.

§ 2. Si sententia pro matrimonii nullitate prolata sit in primo iudicii gradu, tribunal appellationis, perpensis animadversionibus defensoris vinculi et, si quae sint, etiam partium, suo decreto vel decisionem continenter confirmet vel ad ordinarium examen novi gradus causam admittat.

Art. 4
PROOFS

Can. 1678 — §1. The defender of the bond, the advocates of the parties and the promoter of justice, if intervening in the suit, have the right:

1° to be present at the examination of the parties, the witnesses and the experts, with due regard for the prescription of can. 1559;

2° to inspect the judicial acts even though not published and to review the documents produced by the parties.

§2. The parties cannot assist at the examination mentioned in §1, n. 1.

Can. 1679 — Unless full proofs are present from other sources, in evaluating the depositions of the parties in accord with can. 1536, the judge is to use witnesses regarding the credibility of the parties, if possible, as well as other indications and aids.

Can. 1680 — In cases of impotence or defect of consent due to mental illness, the judge is to use the services of one or more experts unless it is obvious from the circumstances that this would be useless; in other cases the prescription of can. 1574 is to be observed.

Art. 5
THE SENTENCE AND THE APPEAL

Can. 1681 — During the instruction of a case, whenever a very probable doubt emerges that the marriage was not consummated, after suspending the nullity case with the consent of the parties, the tribunal can complete the instruction of the case for a dispensation *super rato* and then submit the acts to the Apostolic See together with a petition from either one or from both spouses for a dispensation and with the opinion of the tribunal and the bishop.

Can. 1682 — §1. The sentence which first declared the nullity of the marriage together with the appeals if there are any and the other acts of the trial, are to be sent ex officio to the appellate tribunal within twenty days from the publication of the sentence.

§2. If the sentence rendered in favor of the nullity of marriage was in the first grade of trial, the appellate tribunal by its own decree is to confirm the decision without delay or admit the case to an ordinary examination of a new grade of trial, after considering the observations of the defender of the bond and those of the parties if there are any.

Can. 1683 – Si in gradu appellationis novum nullitatis matrimonii caput afferatur, tribunal potest, tamquam in prima instantia, illud admittere et de eo iudicare.

Can. 1684 – § 1. Postquam sententia, quae matrimonii nullitatem primum declaravit, in gradu appellationis confirmata est vel decreto vel altera sententia, ii, quorum matrimonium declaratum est nullum, possunt novas nuptias contrahere statim ac decretum vel altera sententia ipsis notificata est, nisi vetito ipsi sententiae aut decreto apposito vel ab Ordinario loci statuto id prohibeatur.

§ 2. Praescripta can. 1644 servanda sunt, etiam si sententia, quae matrimonii nullitatem declaraverit, non altera sententia sed decreto confirmata sit.

Can. 1685 – Statim ac sententia facta est exsecutiva, Vicarius iudicialis debet eandem notificare Ordinario loci in quo matrimonium celebratum est. Is autem curare debet ut quam primum de decreta nullitate matrimonii et de vetitis forte statutis in matrimoniorum et baptizatorum libris mentio fiat.

Art. 6

DE PROCESSU DOCUMENTALI

Can. 1686 – Recepta petitione ad normam can. 1677 proposita, Vicarius iudicialis vel iudex ab ipso designatus potest, praetermissis sollemnitatibus ordinarii processus sed citatis partibus et cum interventu defensoris vinculi, matrimonii nullitatem sententia declarare, si ex documento, quod nulli contradictioni vel exceptioni sit obnoxium, certo constet de exsistentia impedimenti dirimentis vel de defectu legitimae formae, dummodo pari certitudine pateat dispensationem datam non esse, aut de defectu validi mandati procuratoris.

Can. 1687 – § 1. Adversus hanc declarationem defensor vinculi, si prudenter existimaverit vel vitia de quibus in can. 1686 vel dispensationis defectum non esse certa, appellare debet ad iudicem secundae instantiae, ad quem acta sunt transmittenda quique scripto monendus est agi de processu documentali.

§ 2. Integrum manet parti, quae se gravatam putet, ius appellandi.

Can. 1688 – Iudex alterius instantiae, cum interventu defensoris vinculi et auditis partibus, decernet eodem modo, de quo in can. 1686, utrum sententia sit confirmanda, an potius procedendum in causa sit iuxta ordinarium tramitem iuris; quo in casu eam remittit ad tribunal primae instantiae.

Can. 1683 — If at the appellate level a new ground of nullity of the marriage is offered, the tribunal can admit it and judge it as if in first instance.

Can. 1684 — §1. After the sentence which first declared the nullity of marriage has been confirmed at the appellate level either by decree or by another sentence, those persons whose marriage was declared null can contract new marriages immediately after the decree or the second sentence has been made known to them unless a prohibition is attached to this sentence or decree, or it is prohibited by a determination of the local ordinary.

§2. The prescriptions of can. 1644 must be observed, even if the sentence which declared the nullity of marriage was not confirmed by another sentence but by a decree.

Can. 1685 — Immediately after the sentence has been executed, the judicial vicar must notify the ordinary of the place in which the marriage was celebrated about this. He must take care that notation be made quickly in the matrimonial and baptismal registers concerning the nullity of the marriage and any prohibitions which may have been determined.

Art. 6

THE DOCUMENTARY PROCESS

Can. 1686 — When a petition has been received in accord with can. 1677, the judicial vicar or a judge designated by him, omitting the formalities of the ordinary process but having cited the parties and with the intervention of the defender of the bond, can declare the nullity of a marriage by a sentence, if from a document which is subject to no contradiction or exception there is certain proof of the existence of a diriment impediment or a defect of legitimate form, provided that it is clear with equal certitude that a dispensation was not granted; this can also be done if there is certain proof of the defect of a valid mandate of procurator.

Can. 1687 — §1. If the defender of the bond prudently thinks that either the flaws mentioned in can. 1686 or the lack of a dispensation are not certain, the defender of the bond must appeal against this declaration to the judge of second instance, to whom the acts must be sent and who must be advised in writing that it is a question of a documentary process.

§2. The party who feels aggrieved retains the right to appeal.

Can. 1688 — The judge in second instance with the intervention of the defender of the bond, having heard the parties, shall decree in the same way as in can. 1686 whether the sentence is to be confirmed or whether the case must rather be handled according to the ordinary process of law; and in that case the judge remands it to the tribunal of first instance.

Art. 7

Normae generales

Can. 1689 – In sententia partes moneantur de obligationibus moralibus vel etiam civilibus, quibus forte teneantur, altera erga alteram et erga prolem, ad sustentationem et educationem praestandam.

Can. 1690 – Causae ad matrimonii nullitatem declarandam nequeunt processu contentioso orali tractari.

Can. 1691 – In ceteris quae ad rationem procedendi attinent, applicandi sunt, nisi rei natura obstet, canones de iudiciis in genere et de iudicio contentioso ordinario, servatis specialibus normis circa causas de statu personarum et causas ad bonum publicum spectantes.

Caput II

DE CAUSIS SEPARATIONIS CONIUGUM

Can. 1692 – § 1. Separatio personalis coniugum baptizatorum, nisi aliter pro locis particularibus legitime provisum sit, decerni potest Episcopi dioecesani decreto, vel iudicis sententia ad normam canonum qui sequuntur.

§ 2. Ubi decisio ecclesiastica effectus civiles non sortitur, vel si sententia civilis praevidetur non contraria iuri divino, Episcopus dioecesis commorationis coniugum poterit, perpensis peculiaribus adiunctis, licentiam concedere adeundi forum civile.

§ 3. Si causa versetur etiam circa effectus mere civiles matrimonii, satagat iudex ut, servato praescripto § 2, causa inde ab initio ad forum civile deferatur.

Can. 1693 – § 1. Nisi qua pars vel promotor iustitiae processum contentiosum ordinarium petant, processus contentiosus oralis adhibeatur.

§ 2. Si processus contentiosus ordinarius adhibitus sit et appellatio proponatur, tribunal secundi gradus ad normam can. 1682, § 2 procedat, servatis servandis.

Can. 1694 – Quod attinet ad tribunalis competentiam, serventur praescripta can. 1673.

Can. 1695 – Iudex, antequam causam acceptet et quotiescumque spem boni exitus perspicit, pastoralia media adhibeat, ut coniuges concilientur et ad coniugalem convictum restaurandum inducantur.

Can. 1696 – Causae de coniugum separatione ad publicum quoque bonum spectant; ideoque iis interesse semper debet promotor iustitiae, ad normam can. 1433.

Art. 7
GENERAL NORMS

Can. 1689 — In the sentence the parties are to be advised of the moral and even civil obligations which they may have to each other and to their children as regards the support and education of the latter.

Can. 1690 — Cases declaring the nullity of marriage cannot be treated in an oral contentious process.

Can. 1691 — In other procedural matters, the canons on trials in general and on the ordinary contentious trial are to be applied unless the nature of the matter precludes it; however, the special norms on cases involving the status of persons and affecting the public good are to be observed.

CHAPTER II
CASES OF SEPARATION OF SPOUSES

Can. 1692 — §1. Personal separation of baptized spouses, unless otherwise legally provided for in particular places, can be decided by a decree of a diocesan bishop, or by a sentence of a judge in accord with the following canons.

§2. Where an ecclesiastical decision has no civil effects, or if it is foreseen that a civil sentence is not contrary to divine law, the bishop of the diocese of residence of the spouses can give them permission to approach the civil forum, having considered the particular circumstances.

§3. Also, if a case is concerned only with the merely civil effects of marriage, the judge can determine it is sufficient that the case be deferred to the civil forum from the start, with due regard for the prescription of §2.

Can. 1693 — §1. Unless one party or the promoter of justice seeks an ordinary contentious process, an oral contentious process is to be used.

§2. If the ordinary contentious process has been used and an appeal is proposed, the appellate tribunal is to proceed in accord with the norm of can. 1682, §2 while observing everything that is to be observed.

Can. 1694 — The prescriptions of can. 1673 are to be observed in regard to the competence of the tribunal.

Can. 1695 — Before accepting the case and whenever it is perceived that there is hope of a successful outcome, the judge is to use pastoral means to reconcile the spouses and induce them to restore conjugal living.

Can. 1696 — Cases involving the separation of spouses also pertain to the public good; therefore, the promoter of justice must always intervene at them in accord with the norm of can. 1433.

CAPUT III

DE PROCESSU AD DISPENSATIONEM SUPER MATRIMONIO
RATO ET NON CONSUMMATO

Can. 1697 – Soli coniuges, vel alteruter, quamvis altero invito, ius habent petendi gratiam dispensationis super matrimonio rato et non consummato.

Can. 1698 – § 1. Una Sedes Apostolica cognoscit de facto inconsummationis matrimonii et de exsistentia iustae causae ad dispensationem concedendam.

§ 2. Dispensatio vero ab uno Romano Pontifice conceditur.

Can. 1699 – § 1. Competens ad accipiendum libellum, quo petitur dispensatio, est Episcopus dioecesanus domicilii vel quasi-domicilii oratoris, qui, si constiterit de fundamento precum, processus instructionem disponere debet.

§ 2. Si tamen casus propositus speciales habeat difficultates ordinis iuridici vel moralis, Episcopus dioecesanus consulat Sedem Apostolicam.

§ 3. Adversus decretum quo Episcopus libellum reicit, patet recursus ad Sedem Apostolicam.

Can. 1700 – § 1. Firmo praescripto can. 1681, horum processuum instructionem committat Episcopus, stabiliter vel in singulis casibus, tribunali suae vel alienae dioecesis aut idoneo sacerdoti.

§ 2. Quod si introducta sit petitio iudicialis ad declarandam nullitatem eiusdem matrimonii, instructio ad idem tribunal committatur.

Can. 1701 – § 1. In his processibus semper intervenire debet vinculi defensor.

§ 2. Patronus non admittitur, sed, propter casus difficultatem, Episcopus permittere potest ut iurisperiti opera orator vel pars conventa iuvetur.

Can. 1702 – In instructione uterque coniux audiatur et serventur, quatenus fieri possit, canones de probationibus colligendis in iudicio contentioso ordinario et in causis de matrimonii nullitate, dummodo cum horum processuum indole componi queant.

Can. 1703 – § 1. Non fit publicatio actorum; iudex tamen, si conspiciat petitioni partis oratricis vel exceptioni partis conventae grave obstaculum obvenire ob adductas probationes, id parti cuius interest prudenter patefaciat.

§ 2. Parti instanti documentum allatum vel testimonium receptum iudex ostendere poterit et tempus praefinire ad deductiones exhibendas.

CHAPTER III

PROCEDURE FOR DISPENSATION OF
RATIFIED AND NON-CONSUMMATED MARRIAGE

Can. 1697 — Only the spouses or either one, even if the other is not willing, have the right to petition for the favor of a dispensation from a ratified and not consummated marriage.

Can. 1698 — §1. The Apostolic See alone adjudicates the fact of the non-consummation of marriage and of the existence of a just cause for granting the dispensation.

§2. The dispensation, however, is granted by the Roman Pontiff alone.

Can. 1699 — §1. The person competent to accept the *libellus* seeking a dispensation is the diocesan bishop of the domicile or quasi-domicile of the petitioner, who must arrange for the instruction of the process if he is sure of the basis of the pleas.

§2. But if the proposed case has special difficulties of the juridical or moral order the diocesan bishop is to consult the Apostolic See.

§3. Recourse is open to the Apostolic See against a decree by which a bishop rejects a *libellus*.

Can. 1700 — §1. With due regard for the prescription of can. 1681, the bishop is to commit the instruction of these processes, either permanently or in individual cases, to his own tribunal, the tribunal of another diocese, or a suitable priest.

§2. But if a judicial petition has been introduced to declare the nullity of this same marriage the instruction is to be committed to the same tribunal.

Can. 1701 — §1. The defender of the bond must always intervene in these procedures.

§2. An advocate is not admitted but, because of the difficulties of a case, the bishop can permit that the petitioner or the respondent have the aid of a legal expert.

Can. 1702 — Insofar as it is possible, each spouse is to be heard during the instruction of the case; and the canons on the collection of proofs in ordinary contentious trials and in cases of marital nullity are to be observed provided they can be reconciled with the distinctive character of these processes.

Can. 1703 — §1. There is no publication of the acts; however, when the judge sees that from the proofs introduced a grave obstacle has arisen to the petition of the plaintiff or an exception of the respondent, he is to reveal this prudently to the interested party.

§2. The judge can show to the interested party seeking it a document introduced or testimony received and set a time within which to offer observations.

Can. 1704 – § 1. Instructor, peracta instructione, omnia acta cum apta relatione deferat ad Episcopum, qui votum pro rei veritate promat tum super facto inconsummationis tum super iusta causa ad dispensandum et gratiae opportunitate.

§ 2. Si instructio processus commissa sit alieno tribunali ad normam can. 1700, animadversiones pro vinculo in eodem foro conficiantur, sed votum de quo in § 1 spectat ad Episcopum committentem, cui instructor simul cum actis aptam relationem tradat.

Can. 1705 – § 1. Acta omnia Episcopus una cum suo voto et animadversionibus defensoris vinculi transmittat ad Sedem Apostolicam.

§ 2. Si, iudicio Apostolicae Sedis, requiratur supplementum instructionis, id Episcopo significabitur, indicatis elementis circa quae instructio complenda est.

§ 3. Quod si Apostolica Sedes rescripserit ex deductis non constare de inconsummatione, tunc iurisperitus de quo in can. 1701, § 2 potest acta processus, non vero votum Episcopi, invisere in sede tribunalis ad perpendendum num quid grave adduci possit ad petitionem denuo proponendam.

Can. 1706 – Rescriptum dispensationis a Sede Apostolica transmittitur ad Episcopum; is vero rescriptum partibus notificabit et praeterea parocho tum loci contracti matrimonii tum suscepti baptismi quam primum mandabit, ut in libris matrimoniorum et baptizatorum de concessa dispensatione mentio fiat.

CAPUT IV

DE PROCESSU PRAESUMPTAE MORTIS CONIUGIS

Can. 1707 – § 1. Quoties coniugis mors authentico documento ecclesiastico vel civili comprobari nequit, alter coniux a vinculo matrimonii solutus non habeatur, nisi post declarationem de morte praesumpta ab Episcopo dioecesano prolatam.

§ 2. Declarationem, de qua in § 1, Episcopus dioecesanus tantummodo proferre valet si, peractis opportunis investigationibus, ex testium depositionibus, ex fama aut ex indiciis moralem certitudinem de coniugis obitu obtinuerit. Sola coniugis absentia, quamvis diuturna, non sufficit.

§ 3. In casibus incertis et implexis Episcopus Sedem Apostolicam consulat.

Can. 1704 — §1. Having finished the instruction, the judge instructor is to hand over all the acts with an appropriate report to the bishop, who is to prepare his opinion on the truth of the matter both concerning the fact of non-consummation, and the just cause for a dispensation and the opportuneness of the favor.

§2. If the instruction of the process has been committed to another tribunal in accord with can. 1700, the observations in favor of the bond are to be made in the same forum, but the opinion mentioned in §1 pertains to the bishop committing it, to whom the instructor is to forward the acts with an appropriate report.

Can. 1705 — §1. The bishop is to send to the Apostolic See all the acts with his opinion and the observations of the defender of the bond.

§2. If, in the judgment of the Apostolic See, a supplement to the instruction is required, the bishop will be informed about the points on which the instruction must be completed.

§3. But, if the Apostolic See responds that non-consummation has not been established from the proofs, then the legal expert mentioned in can. 1701, §2 can review the acts of the process but not the opinion of the bishop, at the tribunal, to see whether any serious reasons warrant resubmitting the petition.

Can. 1706 — The rescript of dispensation is sent to the bishop by the Apostolic See; he shall notify the parties about the rescript and also as soon as possible order the pastor of the place where the marriage was contracted and the pastor of the place of baptism to note the granted dispensation in the registers of marriage and of baptism.

Chapter IV

PROCEDURE IN PRESUMED DEATH OF A SPOUSE

Can. 1707 — §1. Whenever the death of a spouse cannot be proven by an authentic ecclesiastical or civil document, the other spouse is not considered free from the bond of marriage until after a declaration of presumed death is made by the diocesan bishop.

§2. The diocesan bishop can make the declaration mentioned in §1 only after appropriate investigations have enabled him to attain moral certitude of the death of a spouse from the depositions of witnesses, from rumor, or from indications. The mere absence of a spouse, even for a long time, is insufficient.

§3. The bishop is to consult the Apostolic See about uncertain and complex cases.

TITULUS II
DE CAUSIS AD SACRAE ORDINATIONIS NULLITATEM DECLARANDAM

Can. 1708 – Validitatem sacrae ordinationis ius habent accusandi sive ipse clericus sive Ordinarius, cui clericus subest vel in cuius dioecesi ordinatus est.

Can. 1709 – § 1. Libellus mitti debet ad competentem Congregationem, quae decernet utrum causa ab ipsa Curiae Romanae Congregatione an a tribunali ab ea designato sit agenda.

§ 2. Misso libello, clericus ordines exercere ipso iure vetatur.

Can. 1710 – Si Congregatio causam ad tribunal remiserit, serventur, nisi rei natura obstet, canones de iudiciis in genere et de iudicio contentioso ordinario, salvis praescriptis huius tituli.

Can. 1711 – In his causis defensor vinculi iisdem gaudet iuribus iisdemque tenetur officiis, quibus defensor vinculi matrimonialis.

Can. 1712 – Post secundam sententiam, quae nullitatem sacrae ordinationis confirmavit, clericus omnia iura statui clericali propria amittit et ab omnibus obligationibus liberatur.

TITULUS III
DE MODIS EVITANDI IUDICIA

Can. 1713 – Ad evitandas iudiciales contentiones transactio seu reconciliatio utiliter adhibetur, aut controversia iudicio unius vel plurium arbitrorum committi potest.

Can. 1714 – De transactione, de compromisso, deque iudicio arbitrali serventur normae a partibus selectae vel, si partes nullas selegerint, lex ab Episcoporum conferentia lata, si qua sit, vel lex civilis vigens in loco ubi conventio initur.

Can. 1715 – § 1. Nequit transactio aut compromissum valide fieri circa ea quae ad bonum publicum pertinent, aliaque de quibus libere disponere partes non possunt.

§ 2. Si agitur de bonis ecclesiasticis temporalibus, serventur, quoties materia id postulat, sollemnitates iure statutae pro rerum ecclesiasticarum alienatione.

TITLE II

CASES FOR DECLARING NULLITY OF SACRED ORDINATION

Can. 1708 — The cleric himself, the ordinary to whom he is subject, or the ordinary in whose diocese he was ordained have the right to impugn the validity of sacred ordination.

Can. 1709 — §1. The *libellus* must be sent to the competent congregation, which shall decide whether the case is to be handled by the congregation of the Roman Curia or by a tribunal designated by it.

§2. Once the *libellus* is sent, the cleric is forbidden to exercise orders by the law itself.

Can. 1710 — If the congregation remands the case to a tribunal, the canons on trials in general and on the ordinary contentious trial are to be observed unless the nature of the matter precludes this, with due regard for the prescriptions of this title.

Can. 1711 — In these cases the defender of the bond enjoys the same rights and is bound by the same duties as the defender of the marriage bond.

Can. 1712 — After the second sentence which has confirmed the nullity of sacred ordination the cleric loses all rights proper to the clerical state and is free of all obligations.

TITLE III

METHODS OF AVOIDING A TRIAL

Can. 1713 — To avoid judicial contentions a settlement or reconciliation is usefully employed or the controversy can be entrusted to the judgment of one or more arbiters.

Can. 1714 — The norms chosen by the parties are to be observed in a settlement, a compromise or a trial by arbiters; or, if the parties choose no norms, the law enacted by the conference of bishops is to be observed if there is such, or the civil law in force in the place where the agreement is entered into.

Can. 1715 — §1. A settlement or compromise cannot be made validly concerning matters which pertain to the public good and other matters about which the parties cannot freely dispose.

§2. If it is a question of temporal ecclesiastical goods, whenever the matter requires this, the formalities specified by law for the alienation of ecclesiastical goods are to be observed.

Can. 1716 – § 1. Si lex civilis arbitrali sententiae vim non agnoscat, nisi a iudice confirmetur, sententia arbitralis de controversia ecclesiastica, ut vim habeat in foro canonico, confirmatione indiget iudicis
ecclesiastici loci, in quo lata est.

§ 2. Si autem lex civilis admittat sententiae arbitralis coram civili
iudice impugnationem, in foro canonico eadem impugnatio proponi potest coram iudice ecclesiastico, qui in primo gradu competens est ad controversiam iudicandam.

PARS IV
DE PROCESSU POENALI

Caput I
DE PRAEVIA INVESTIGATIONE

Can. 1717 – § 1. Quoties Ordinarius notitiam, saltem veri simi-
lem, habet de delicto, caute inquirat, per se vel per aliam idoneam
personam, circa facta et circumstantias et circa imputabilitatem, nisi
haec inquisitio omnino superflua videatur.

§ 2. Cavendum est ne ex hac investigatione bonum cuiusquam nomen
in discrimen vocetur.

§ 3. Qui investigationem agit, easdem habet, quas auditor in processu, potestates et obligationes; idemque nequit, si postea iudicialis
processus promoveatur, in eo iudicem agere.

Can. 1718 – § 1. Cum satis collecta videantur elementa, decernat
Ordinarius:

1° num processus ad poenam irrogandam vel declarandam promoveri possit;

2° num id, attento can. 1341, expediat;

3° utrum processus iudicialis sit adhibendus an, nisi lex vetet, sit
procedendum per decretum extra iudicium.

§ 2. Ordinarius decretum, de quo in § 1, revocet vel mutet, quoties
ex novis elementis aliud sibi decernendum videtur.

§ 3. In ferendis decretis, de quibus in §§ 1 et 2, audiat Ordinarius, si
prudenter censeat, duos iudices aliosve iuris peritos.

Can. 1716 — §1. If the civil law does not recognize the force of a sentence by arbiters unless it is confirmed by a judge, a sentence by arbiters in an ecclesiastical controversy needs confirmation by an ecclesiastical judge of the place where the sentence was rendered in order to have force in the canonical forum.

§2. However, if the civil law admits the challenging of a sentence by arbiters before a civil judge, the same challenge can be proposed before an ecclesiastical judge who is competent to judge the controversy in the first instance.

PART IV

PENAL PROCEDURE

CHAPTER I

THE PRIOR INVESTIGATION

Can. 1717 — §1. Whenever the ordinary receives information which at least seems to be true of an offense, he shall cautiously inquire personally or through another suitable person about the facts and circumstances and about imputability unless this investigation appears to be entirely superfluous.

§2. Care must be taken lest anyone's good name be endangered by this investigation.

§3. The one who conducts the investigation has the same powers and obligations as an auditor in the process; this person cannot act as a judge in the matter, if a judicial process is set in motion later.

Can. 1718 — §1. When sufficient evidence appears to have been collected, the ordinary shall decide:

1° whether the process for inflicting or declaring a penalty can be set in motion;

2° whether this is expedient in light of can. 1341;

3° whether a judicial process must be used or unless the law forbids it whether he must proceed by a decree without a trial.

§2. The ordinary is to revoke or change the decree mentioned in §1 whenever it appears to him from new evidence that a different decision is called for.

§3. In issuing the decrees mentioned in §§1 and 2, the ordinary is to hear two or more judges or other experts in the law, if he prudently sees fit to do so.

§ 4. Antequam ad normam § 1 decernat, consideret Ordinarius num, ad vitanda inutilia iudicia, expediat ut, partibus consentientibus, vel ipse vel investigator quaestionem de damnis ex bono et aequo dirimat.

Can. 1719 – Investigationis acta et Ordinarii decreta, quibus investigatio initur vel clauditur, eaque omnia quae investigationem praecedunt, si necessaria non sint ad poenalem processum, in secreto curiae archivo custodiantur.

Caput II

DE PROCESSUS EVOLUTIONE

Can. 1720 – Si Ordinarius censuerit per decretum extra iudicium esse procedendum :
1° reo accusationem atque probationes, data facultate sese defendendi, significet, nisi reus, rite vocatus, comparere neglexerit ;
2° probationes et argumenta omnia cum duobus assessoribus accurate perpendat ;
3° si de delicto certo constet neque actio criminalis sit extincta, decretum ferat ad normam cann. 1342-1350, expositis, breviter saltem, rationibus in iure et in facto.

Can. 1721 – § 1. Si Ordinarius decreverit processum poenalem iudicialem esse ineundum, acta investigationis promotori iustitiae tradat, qui accusationis libellum iudici ad normam cann. 1502 et 1504 exhibeat.

§ 2. Coram tribunali superiore partes actoris gerit promotor iustitiae apud illud tribunal constitutus.

Can. 1722 – Ad scandala praevenienda, ad testium libertatem protegendam et ad iustitiae cursum tutandum, potest Ordinarius, audito promotore iustitiae et citato ipso accusato, in quolibet processus stadio accusatum a sacro ministerio vel ab aliquo officio et munere ecclesiastico arcere, ei imponere vel interdicere commorationem in aliquo loco vel territorio, vel etiam publicam sanctissimae Eucharistiae participationem prohibere ; quae omnia, causa cessante, sunt revocanda, eaque ipso iure finem habent, cessante processu poenali.

Can. 1723 – § 1. Iudex reum citans debet eum invitare ad advocatum, ad normam can. 1481, § 1, intra terminum ab ipso iudice praefinitum, sibi constituendum.

§4. In order to avoid useless trials, before he makes a decision in accord with §1, the ordinary is to consider whether it is expedient that either he or the investigator equitably solve the question of damages with the consent of the parties.

Can. 1719 — The acts of the investigation, the decrees of the ordinary by which the investigation was opened and closed, and all that preceded it are to be kept in the secret archive of the curia if they are not necessary for the penal process.

CHAPTER II

THE DEVELOPMENT OF THE PROCESS

Can. 1720 — If the ordinary decides that he is to proceed by a decree without a trial:

1° he is to inform the accused about the accusation and the proofs, giving the person the opportunity of self-defense unless the accused neglects to be in court after having been duly summoned;

2° he is to consider carefully the proofs and arguments with two assessors;

3° if the offense is certainly proved and the criminal action has not been terminated, he is to issue the decree in accord with cann. 1342–1350, explaining the reasons in law and in fact, at least briefly.

Can. 1721 — §1. If the ordinary decrees that a judicial penal process is to be begun, he is to give the acts of the investigation to the promoter of justice who is to present a *libellus* of accusation to the judge in accord with the norms of cann. 1502 and 1504.

§2. The promoter of justice constituted as such by the higher court acts as the petitioner before that tribunal.

Can. 1722 — To preclude scandals, to protect the freedom of witnesses and to safeguard the course of justice, having heard the promoter of justice and having cited the accused, the ordinary at any stage of the process can remove the accused from the sacred ministry or from any ecclesiastical office or function, can impose or prohibit residence in a given place or territory, or even prohibit public participation in the Most Holy Eucharist; all these measures must be revoked once the reason for them ceases; they also end by the law itself when the penal process ceases.

Can. 1723 — §1. When citing the accused, the judge must invite the accused to appoint an advocate in accord with the norm of can. 1481, §1, within a period of time set by the judge.

§ 2. Quod si reus non providerit, iudex ante litis contestationem advocatum ipse nominet, tamdiu in munere mansurum quamdiu reus sibi advocatum non constituerit.

Can. 1724 – § 1. In quolibet iudicii gradu renuntiatio instantiae fieri potest a promotore iustitiae, mandante vel consentiente Ordinario, ex cuius deliberatione processus promotus est.

§ 2. Renuntiatio, ut valeat, debet a reo acceptari, nisi ipse sit a iudicio absens declaratus.

Can. 1725 – In causae discussione, sive scripto haec fit sive ore, accusatus semper ius habeat ut ipse vel eius advocatus vel procurator postremus scribat vel loquatur.

Can. 1726 – In quolibet poenalis iudicii gradu et stadio, si evidenter constet delictum non esse a reo patratum, iudex debet id sententia declarare et reum absolvere, etiamsi simul constet actionem criminalem esse extinctam.

Can. 1727 – § 1. Appellationem proponere potest reus, etiam si sententia ipsum ideo tantum dimiserit, quia poena erat facultativa, vel quia iudex potestate usus est, de qua in cann. 1344 et 1345.

§ 2. Promotor iustitiae appellare potest quoties censet scandali reparationi vel iustitiae restitutioni satis provisum non esse.

Can. 1728 – § 1. Salvis praescriptis canonum huius tituli, in iudicio poenali applicandi sunt, nisi rei natura obstet, canones de iudiciis in genere et de iudicio contentioso ordinario, servatis specialibus normis de causis quae ad bonum publicum spectant.

§ 2. Accusatus ad confitendum delictum non tenetur, nec ipsi iusiurandum deferri potest.

Caput III
DE ACTIONE AD DAMNA REPARANDA

Can. 1729 – § 1. Pars laesa potest actionem contentiosam ad damna reparanda ex delicto sibi illata in ipso poenali iudicio exercere, ad normam can. 1596.

§ 2. Interventus partis laesae, de quo in § 1, non amplius admittitur, si factus non sit in primo iudicii poenalis gradu.

§ 3. Appellatio in causa de damnis fit ad normam cann. 1628-1640, etiamsi appellatio in poenali iudicio fieri non possit; quod si utraque

§2. But if the accused does not provide for this the judge is to name an advocate before the joinder of issues (*contestatio litis*) who will remain in this function as long as the accused has not personally appointed an advocate.

Can. 1724 — §1. In any grade of the trial, renunciation of the instance can be made by the promoter of justice either at the order of or with the consent of the ordinary in light of whose deliberation the process was set in motion.

§2. For validity, the renunciation must be accepted by the accused unless such a one is declared to be absent from the trial.

Can. 1725 — In the discussion of the case, whether it be done in writing or orally, the accused always has the right to write or speak last either personally or through an advocate or procurator.

Can. 1726 — In any grade or stage of the penal trial, if it becomes clearly proven that the offense was not perpetrated by the accused, the judge must declare this in a sentence and absolve the accused, even if it is also proven that the criminal action is terminated.

Can. 1727 — §1. The accused can propose an appeal even though dismissed in a sentence solely because the penalty was facultative or because the judge used the power mentioned in cann. 1344 and 1345.

§2. The promoter of justice can appeal whenever it appears that the reparation of scandal or the restitution of justice has not been provided sufficiently.

Can. 1728 — §1. With due regard for the prescriptions of the canons of this title, unless the nature of the matter is opposed, the canons on trials in general and on ordinary contentious trials must be applied in the penal trial, observing the special norms for cases which refer to the public good.

§2. The accused is not bound to confess the offense and cannot be constrained to take an oath.

CHAPTER III

ACTION FOR REPARATION OF DAMAGES

Can. 1729 — §1. In accord with the norm of can. 1596, an injured party can exercise in the penal trial itself a contentious action for the repairing of damages sustained due to the offense.

§2. The intervention of an injured party, mentioned in §1, is not admitted afterwards if it was not made in the first grade of the penal trial.

§3. The appeal in a case for damages is made in accord with cann. 1628–1640 even if an appeal in the penal trial cannot be made; but if both appeals

appellatio, licet a diversis partibus, proponatur, unicum fiat iudicium appellationis, salvo praescripto can. ~~1731~~. 1730

Can. 1730 – § 1. Ad nimias poenalis iudicii moras vitandas potest iudex iudicium de damnis differre usque dum sententiam definitivam in iudicio poenali protulerit.

§ 2. Iudex, qui ita egerit, debet, postquam sententiam tulerit in poenali iudicio, de damnis cognoscere, etiamsi iudicium poenale propter propositam impugnationem adhuc pendeat, vel reus absolutus sit propter causam quae non auferat obligationem reparandi damna.

Can. 1731 – Sententia lata in poenali iudicio, etiamsi in rem iudicatam transierit, nullo modo ius facit erga partem laesam, nisi haec intervenerit ad normam can. ~~1733~~. 1729

PARS V

DE RATIONE PROCEDENDI IN RECURSIBUS ADMINISTRATIVIS ATQUE IN PAROCHIS AMOVENDIS VEL TRANSFERENDIS

SECTIO I

DE RECURSU ADVERSUS DECRETA ADMINISTRATIVA

Can. 1732 – Quae in canonibus huius sectionis de decretis statuuntur, eadem applicanda sunt ad omnes administrativos actus singulares, qui in foro externo extra iudicium dantur, iis exceptis, qui ab ipso Romano Pontifice vel ab ipso Concilio Oecumenico ferantur.

Can. 1733 – § 1. Valde optandum est ut, quoties quis gravatum se decreto putet, vitetur inter ipsum et decreti auctorem contentio atque inter eos de aequa solutione quaerenda communi consilio curetur, gravibus quoque personis ad mediationem et studium forte adhibitis, ita ut per idoneam viam controversia praecaveatur vel dirimatur.

§ 2. Episcoporum conferentia statuere potest ut in unaquaque dioecesi officium quoddam vel consilium stabiliter constituatur, cui, secundum normas ab ipsa conferentia statuendas, munus sit aequas solutiones quaerere et suggerere; quod si conferentia id non iusserit, potest Episcopus eiusmodi consilium vel officium constituere.

are proposed, though by different parties, there is to be a single appellate trial with due regard for the prescription of can. 1734.* *1730*

Can. 1730 — §1. To avoid excessive delays in a penal trial, the judge can postpone a trial for damages until he has rendered a definitive sentence in the penal trial.

§2. The judge who does this must take cognizance of damages after rendering the sentence in a penal trial even if the penal trial is still pending due to a proposed challenge or if the accused has been acquitted for a reason which does not take away the obligaton of repairing damage.

Can. 1731 — Even if the sentence rendered in the penal trial has become a *res judicata*, in no way does it establish the right of the injured party unless this party has intervened in accord with can. 1733.** *1729*

PART V

ON THE MANNER OF PROCEDURE IN ADMINISTRATIVE RECOURSE AND THE REMOVAL AND TRANSFER OF PASTORS

SECTION I

RECOURSE AGAINST ADMINISTRATIVE DECREES

Can. 1732 — What is determined concerning decrees in the canons of this section is also to be applied to all particular administrative acts which are posited in the external forum outside a trial with the exception of those issued by the Roman Pontiff or an ecumenical council.

Can. 1733 — §1. It is very desirable that whenever someone feels injured by a decree, there not be a contention between this person and the author of the decree but that care be taken by common counsel to find an equitable solution between them, perhaps through the use of wise persons in mediation and study so that the controversy may be avoided or solved by some suitable means.

§2. The conference of bishops can determine that in every diocese some office or council be permanently established whose function is to find and suggest equitable solutions in accord with norms determined by the same conference; but if the conference has not done this, a bishop can establish a council or office of this kind.

---

*Apparently should read 1730.—Trans.   **Apparently should read 1729.—Trans.

§ 3. Officium vel consilium, de quo in § 2, tunc praecipue operam navet, cum revocatio decreti petita est ad normam can. 1734, neque termini ad recurrendum sunt elapsi; quod si adversus decretum recursus propositus sit, ipse Superior, qui de recursu videt, recurrentem et decreti auctorem hortetur, quotiescumque spem boni exitus perspicit, ad eiusmodi solutiones quaerendas.

Can. 1734 – § 1. Antequam quis recursum proponat, debet decreti revocationem vel emendationem scripto ab ipsius auctore petere; qua petitione proposita, etiam suspensio exsecutionis eo ipso petita intellegitur.

§ 2. Petitio fieri debet intra peremptorium terminum decem dierum utilium a decreto legitime intimato.

§ 3. Normae §§ 1 et 2 non valent:

1° de recursu proponendo ad Episcopum adversus decreta lata ab auctoritatibus, quae ei subsunt;

2° de recursu proponendo adversus decretum, quo recursus hierarchicus deciditur, nisi decisio data sit ab Episcopo;

3° de recursibus proponendis ad normam cann. 57 et 1735.

Can. 1735 – Si intra triginta dies, ex quo petitio, de qua in can. 1734, ad auctorem decreti pervenit, is novum decretum intimet, quo vel prius emendet vel petitionem reiciendam esse decernat, termini ad recurrendum decurrunt ex novi decreti intimatione; si autem intra triginta dies nihil decernat, termini decurrunt ex tricesimo die.

Can. 1736 – § 1. In iis materiis, in quibus recursus hierarchicus suspendit decreti exsecutionem, idem efficit etiam petitio, de qua in can. 1734.

§ 2. In ceteris casibus, nisi intra decem dies, ex quo petitio de qua in can. 1734 ad ipsum auctorem decreti pervenit, is exsecutionem suspendendam decreverit, potest suspensio interim peti ab eius Superiore hierarchico, qui eam decernere potest gravibus tantum de causis et cauto semper ne quid salus animarum detrimenti capiat.

§ 3. Suspensa decreti exsecutione ad normam § 2, si postea recursus proponatur, is qui de recursu videre debet, ad normam can. 1737, § 3 decernat utrum suspensio sit confirmanda an revocanda.

§ 4. Si nullus recursus intra statutum terminum adversus decretum proponatur, suspensio exsecutionis, ad normam § 1 vel § 2 interim effecta, eo ipso cessat.

§3. The office or council mentioned in §2 is to be of assistance especially at the time when revocation of a decree has been petitioned in accord with the norm of can. 1734 and the time for recourse has not elapsed; but if recourse has been taken against the decree, the superior who examines the recourse is to urge the one making the recourse and the author of the decree to seek a solution of this type whenever the superior sees hope of a successful outcome.

Can. 1734 — §1. Before proposing recourse, a person must seek the revocation or emendation of the decree in writing from its author; when such a petition is proposed it is understood that the suspension of the execution of the decree is also being petitioned.

§2. The petition must be made within a peremptory period of ten available days (*tempus utile*) from legal notice of the decree.

§3. The norms of §§1 and 2 are not valid:

1° concerning recourse proposed to the bishop against decrees issued by authorities subject to him;

2° concerning recourse proposed against a decree by which hierarchic recourse is decided unless the decision has been made by the bishop;

3° concerning recourses to be proposed in accord with cann. 57 and 1735.

Can. 1735 — If, within thirty days from the time when the petition mentioned in can. 1734 has come to him, the author of the decree communicates a new decree by which he corrects the prior one or decrees that the petition must be rejected, the period for recourse runs from the notice of the new decree; but if within the thirty days he decrees nothing the period runs from the thirtieth day.

Can. 1736 — §1. In those matters in which hierarchic recourse suspends the execution of the decree, the petition also has the same effect as that mentioned in can. 1734.

§2. In other cases, unless within ten days from the time when the petition mentioned in can. 1734 has come to him, the author of the decree decrees that its execution is to be suspended, a suspension can meanwhile be petitioned from his hierarchic superior who can decree it only for grave reasons and always cautiously lest the salvation of souls be injured in some way.

§3. When the execution of the decree has been suspended in accord with §2, if recourse is proposed later, the one who must deal with the recourse in accord with can. 1737, §3 is to determine whether the suspension is to be confirmed or revoked.

§4. If no recourse is proposed against the decree within the stated period, the suspension of the execution effected in the interim in accord with §§1 or 2 ceases by that very fact.

Can. 1737 – § 1. Qui se decreto gravatum esse contendit, potest ad Superiorem hierarchicum eius, qui decretum tulit, propter quodlibet iustum motivum recurrere; recursus proponi potest coram ipso decreti auctore, qui eum statim ad competentem Superiorem hierarchicum transmittere debet.

§ 2. Recursus proponendus est intra peremptorium terminum quindecim dierum utilium, qui in casibus de quibus in can. 1734, § 3 decurrunt ex die quo decretum intimatum est, in ceteris autem casibus decurrunt ad normam can. 1735.

§ 3. Etiam in casibus, in quibus recursus non suspendit ipso iure decreti exsecutionem neque suspensio ad normam can. 1736, § 2 decreta est, potest tamen gravi de causa Superior iubere ut exsecutio suspendatur, cauto tamen ne quid salus animarum detrimenti capiat.

Can. 1738 – Recurrens semper ius habet advocatum vel procuratorem adhibendi, vitatis inutilibus moris; immo vero patronus ex officio constituatur, si recurrens patrono careat et Superior id necessarium censeat; semper tamen potest Superior iubere ut recurrens ipse compareat ut interrogetur.

Can. 1739 – Superiori, qui de recursu videt, licet, prout casus ferat, non solum decretum confirmare vel irritum declarare, sed etiam rescindere, revocare, vel, si id Superiori magis expedire videatur, emendare, subrogare, ei obrogare.

SECTIO II

DE PROCEDURA IN PAROCHIS AMOVENDIS VEL TRANSFERENDIS

CAPUT I

DE MODO PROCEDENDI IN AMOTIONE PAROCHORUM

Can. 1740 – Cum alicuius parochi ministerium ob aliquam causam, etiam citra gravem ipsius culpam, noxium aut saltem inefficax evadat, potest ipse ab Episcopo dioecesano a paroecia amoveri.

Can. 1741 – Causae, ob quas parochus a sua paroecia legitime amoveri potest, hae praesertim sunt:

1° modus agendi qui ecclesiasticae communioni grave detrimentum vel perturbationem afferat;

2° imperitia aut permanens mentis vel corporis infirmitas, quae parochum suis muneribus utiliter obeundis imparem reddunt;

Can. 1737 — §1. One who claims to have been injured by a decree can make recourse for any just reason to the hierarchic superior of the one who issued the decree; the recourse can be proposed before the author of the decree, who must immediately transmit it to the competent hierarchic superior.

§2. Recourse must be proposed within a peremptory period of fifteen available days which run from the day on which the decree was published in cases mentioned in can. 1734, §3, but in other cases they run in accord with the norm of can. 1735.

§3. Also in cases in which recourse does not suspend execution of the decree by the law itself, and the suspension was not decreed in accord with can. 1736, §2, nevertheless, the superior can order that the execution be suspended for a grave cause yet cautiously lest the salvation of souls suffer any harm.

Can. 1738 — The one taking recourse always has a right to use an advocate or a procurator, avoiding useless delays; and indeed an advocate ex officio is to be constituted, if the one taking recourse lacks an advocate and the superior thinks one necessary; but the superior can always command that the one taking recourse be present to be questioned.

Can. 1739 — The superior who examines the recourse has the power, as the case requires, not only to confirm the decree or to declare it null but also to rescind, to revoke, or, if it appears to the superior to be more expedient, to amend, subrogate or obrogate the decree.

SECTION II

PROCEDURE IN REMOVAL AND TRANSFER OF PASTORS

CHAPTER I

THE MANNER OF PROCEDURE IN REMOVING PASTORS

Can. 1740 — When the ministry of any pastor has become detrimental or at least ineffective for any reason, even through no grave fault of his own, he can be removed from the parish by the diocesan bishop.

Can. 1741 — The reasons for which a pastor can be legitimately removed from his parish are especially the following:

1° a way of acting which is gravely detrimental or disturbing to the ecclesial community;

2° incompetence or a permanent infirmity of mind or body which renders a pastor incapable of performing his duties in a useful way;

3° bonae existimationis amissio penes probos et graves paroecianos vel aversio in parochum, quae praevideantur non brevi cessaturae;

4° gravis neglectus vel violatio officiorum paroecialium quae post monitionem persistat;

5° mala rerum temporalium administratio cum gravi Ecclesiae damno, quoties huic malo aliud remedium afferri nequeat.

Can. 1742 – § 1. Si ex instructione peracta constiterit adesse causam de qua in can. 1740, Episcopus rem discutiat cum duobus parochis e coetu ad hoc stabiliter a consilio presbyterali, Episcopo proponente, selectis; quod si exinde censeat ad amotionem esse deveniendum, causa et argumentis ad validitatem indicatis, parocho paterne suadeat ut intra tempus quindecim dierum renuntiet.

§ 2. De parochis qui sunt sodales instituti religiosi aut societatis vitae apostolicae, servetur praescriptum can. 682, § 2.

Can. 1743 – Renuntiatio a parocho fieri potest non solum pure et simpliciter, sed etiam sub condicione, dummodo haec ab Episcopo legitime acceptari possit et reapse acceptetur.

Can. 1744 – § 1. Si parochus intra praestitutos dies non responderit, Episcopus iteret invitationem prorogando tempus utile ad respondendum.

§ 2. Si Episcopo constiterit parochum alteram invitationem recepisse, non autem respondisse etsi nullo impedimento detentum, aut si parochus renuntiationem nullis adductis motivis recuset, Episcopus decretum amotionis ferat.

Can. 1745 – Si vero parochus causam adductam eiusque rationes oppugnet, motiva allegans quae insufficientia Episcopo videantur, hic ut valide agat:

1° invitet illum ut, inspectis actis, suas impugnationes in relatione scripta colligat, immo probationes in contrarium, si quas habeat, afferat;

2° deinde, completa, si opus sit, instructione, una cum iisdem parochis de quibus in can. 1742, § 1, nisi alii propter illorum impossibilitatem sint designandi, rem perpendat;

3° tandem statuat utrum parochus sit amovendus necne, et mox decretum de re ferat.

Can. 1746 – Amoto parocho, Episcopus consulat sive assignatione alius officii, si ad hoc idoneus sit, sive pensione, prout casus ferat et adiuncta permittant.

3° loss of good reputation among upright and good parishoners or aversion to the pastor which are foreseen as not ceasing in a short time;

4° grave neglect or violation of parochial duties which persist after a warning;

5° poor administration of temporal affairs with grave damage to the Church whenever this problem cannot be remedied in any other way.

Can. 1742 — §1. If after an inquiry has been conducted, it is proven that a cause mentioned in can. 1740 is present, the bishop is to discuss the matter with two pastors from the group permanently selected for this by the presbyteral council after their being proposed by the bishop; but if subsequently he decides that the removal must take place, he is paternally to persuade the pastor to resign the pastorate within a period of fifteen days, after he has explained, for validity, the reason and the arguments for removal.

§2. The prescription of can. 682, §2 is to be observed concerning pastors who are members of a religious institute or a society of apostolic life.

Can. 1743 — A resignation by a pastor can be submitted not only purely and simply but also conditionally provided that this can be legitimately accepted by the bishop and is actually accepted.

Can. 1744 — §1. If the pastor has not answered within the aforementioned time period the bishop is to repeat the invitation extending the available time for response.

§2. If the bishop has the proof that the pastor has received the second invitation but has not responded although not hindered by any impediment or if the pastor refuses to resign giving no reasons, the bishop is to issue the decree of removal.

Can. 1745 — But if the pastor opposes the cause alleged for removal and its reasons, alleging reasons which appear insufficient to the bishop, in order for the latter to act validly, he is to:

1° invite the pastor to organize his challenges to removal in a written report, having inspected the acts, and also to offer proofs to the contrary, if he has any;

2° consider the matter with the same pastors mentioned in can. 1742, §1 unless others must be designated due to their inability, after he has completed the instruction if necessary;

3° finally determine whether or not the pastor must be removed and promptly issue a decree on the matter.

Can. 1746 — When the pastor has been removed, the bishop is to provide for him through an assignment to another office, if he is suitable for this, or through a pension, as the case requires and circumstances permit.

Can. 1747 – § 1. Parochus amotus debet a parochi munere exercendo abstinere, quam primum liberam relinquere paroecialem domum, et omnia quae ad paroeciam pertinent ei tradere, cui Episcopus paroeciam commiserit.

§ 2. Si autem de infirmo agatur, qui e paroeciali domo sine incommodo nequeat alio transferri, Episcopus eidem relinquat eius usum etiam exclusivum, eadem necessitate durante.

§ 3. Pendente recursu adversus amotionis decretum, Episcopus non potest novum parochum nominare, sed per administratorem paroecialem interim provideat.

Caput II

DE MODO PROCEDENDI IN TRANSLATIONE PAROCHORUM

Can. 1748 – Si bonum animarum vel Ecclesiae necessitas aut utilitas postulet, ut parochus a sua, quam utiliter regit, ad aliam paroeciam aut ad aliud officium transferatur, Episcopus eidem translationem scripto proponat ac suadeat ut pro Dei atque animarum amore consentiat.

Can. 1749 – Si parochus consilio ac suasionibus Episcopi obsequi non intendat, rationes in scriptis exponat.

Can. 1750 – Episcopus, si, non obstantibus allatis rationibus, iudicet a proposito non esse recedendum, cum duobus parochis ad normam can. 1742, § 1 selectis, rationes perpendat quae translationi faveant vel obstent; quod si exinde translationem peragendam censeat, paternas exhortationes parocho iteret.

Can. 1751 – § 1. His peractis, si adhuc et parochus renuat et Episcopus putet translationem esse faciendam, hic decretum translationis ferat, statuens paroeciam, elapso praefinito tempore, esse vacaturam.

§ 2. Hoc tempore inutiliter transacto, paroeciam vacantem declaret.

Can. 1752 – In causis translationis applicentur praescripta canonis 1747, servata aequitate canonica et prae oculis habita salute animarum, quae in Ecclesia suprema semper lex esse debet.

Can. 1747 — §1. The removed pastor must abstain from exercising the office of pastor, vacate the rectory immediately, and hand over all that pertains to the parish to the one to whom the bishop shall entrust the parish.

§2. If there is question of a sick pastor who cannot be transferred elsewhere from the rectory without inconvenience, the bishop is to leave the rectory even to his exclusive use while this need lasts.

§3. While recourse is pending against the decree of removal, the bishop cannot name a new pastor but meanwhile is to provide a parish administrator.

Chapter II

THE MANNER OF PROCEDURE IN TRANSFERRING PASTORS

Can. 1748 — If the good of souls or the need or advantage of the Church requires that a pastor be transferred from his parish which he is governing usefully to another parish or to another office, the bishop is to propose the transfer to him in writing and persuade him to consent to it for the love of God and of souls.

Can. 1749 — If the pastor does not intend to yield to the counsel and persuasion of the bishop, he is to explain his reasons in writing.

Can. 1750 — Notwithstanding the reasons alleged, if the bishop judges that he is not going to change his plans, he is to discuss the reasons which favor or oppose the transfer with the two pastors chosen in accord with can. 1742, §1; if he then decides to implement the transfer, he is to repeat the paternal exhortations to the pastor.

Can. 1751 — §1. When this has been done, if the pastor still refuses and the bishop thinks the transfer must be made, he is to issue a decree of transfer stating that the parish shall be vacant after the lapse of a predetermined time.

§2. If this period of time has passed in vain, he is to declare the parish vacant.

Can. 1752 — In cases of transfer, the prescriptions of can. 1747 are to be applied, with due regard for canonical equity and having before one's eyes the salvation of souls, which is always the supreme law of the Church.

A GLOSSARY OF SOME LATIN TERMS

The following expressions, because they are technical terms in canon law, have been retained in their Latin form in the translation. This glossary attempts to provide: (1) a reference to one or two of the canons where the term is employed; (2) a rough translation of the expression; (3) a descriptive definition of the term.

ad beneplacitum nostrum (c.81) at our good pleasure; a clause added to a rescript or privilege which makes it clear that the favor or privilege granted expires with the expiration of the authority of the one granting it.

ad limina (c.395, §2) to the threshold (of the tombs of the apostles Peter and Paul); refers to the special visit made by diocesan bishops to Rome at the time of their five-year report.

communicatio in sacris (cc.844; 1365) participation in sacred rites; sharing sacraments or other liturgical worship with those of other faith communities.

contestatio litis (c.1513, §1) the joinder of issues; that step in the judicial process wherein the limits of the controversy are defined; the hearing in which the court determines the precise issue to be settled in a case.

ex integro (c.6, §1, n.4) in entirety; areas or institutes of the law which have been wholly or entirely reorganized.

fatalia legis (c.1465, §1) legal deadline; the fixed time limit beyond which the law denies the right to bring action; time at which rights are extinguished.

ferendae sententiae (c.1314) imposed by a sentence; the infliction of a penalty by the court or by the action of a legitimate superior (as over against the automatic imposition of a penalty by the law itself, *latae sententiae*).

in pectore (c.351, §3) in one's heart; used to denote that the pope has named someone to an office or honor but has not made the name public at the time of the appointment, reserving it to himself for announcement later.

in solidum (cc.140; 517, §1) as a body; several persons delegated to act in the same matter, or designated to act as a single group or team.

latae sententiae (c.1314)   sentence already passed; a penalty inflicted by the law itself immediately upon the commission of the offense; the automatic imposition of a penalty (as over against one imposed by the action of a judge or superior, *ferendae sententiae*).

legatus a latere (c.358)   legate from one's side; one sent specifically to represent the pope personally at some event or for some purpose.

libellus (c.1502)   bill of complaint; the formal petition which introduces a case into court, identifies the object of the controversy and requests the services of the judge.

litis finitae (c. 1462)   controversy terminated; a type of exception in court cases which, when raised, could put an end to the litigation.

missus specialis (c.358)   special envoy; someone sent to fulfill a specific mission.

motu proprio (c.38)   on one's own initiative; an act or instruction given on one's own initiative rather than in response to a request.

non sui compos (c.97)   incompetent; one who is not legally in control of oneself or responsible for one's actions.

ordines (c.95)   rules of order; the norms or rules of order to be followed in an assembly or gathering of people or in a celebration.

per modum actus (c. 1244, §2)   by means of an act; a juridic act placed in a particular situation with its juridic effects limited to that situation.

ponens (or *relator*) (c.1429)   reporting judge; the collegiate judge who studies the case and reports on it at the meeting of the panel of judges and who commits the sentence to writing.

praeter ius (cc.5, §2; 26)   apart from the law; customs outside or beyond the stated law.

res integra (c.1512, §1)   a matter still whole; a matter not yet before the court; a matter which has not been brought to the judicial forum.

res iudicata (c.1641)   a matter finally judged; a case irrevocably adjudged so that it cannot be opened again by any court in ordinary procedure.

restitutio in integrum (c.1645)   reinstatement in one's former position; all things are restored to the way they were before sentence was pronounced.

sui iuris (c.111, §1)   of its own right; an acknowledged autonomy with regard to government and discipline.

super rato (c.1681)   on a ratified (and non-consummated marriage); an abbreviated reference to the process of dispensing from a marriage which was never sexually consummated.

ternus (cc.377, §3)   slate of three names; a list of names of possible candidates to be appointed to an office or task.

transactio (c.1462; 1713)   a settlement; an agreement by which a controversial matter is settled without a formal trial.

INDEX

Abbot
  cc. 370; 620
  cases against: c. 1405, §3, 2°
  as judge: cc. 1427, §§1, 2; 1438, 3°

Abortion
  effect on irregularity for orders/exercise of orders: cc. 1041, 4°; 1044, §1,
      3°; 1046; 1047, §2, 2°, §3; 1048; 1049, §§1, 2
  penalty for: c. 1398

Absolution
  attempted: c. 1378, §2, 2°
  of accomplice: c. 977
  sacramental: cc. 959-963; 966; 980

Abstinence
  from food before Communion: c. 919
  from meat: c. 1251

Acolyte
  cc. 230, §1; 1035
  as minister of communion: c. 910, §2
  as minister of exposition: c. 943

Ad limina visit
  c. 395, §2

Administrative act
  cc. 35-47

Administrative recourse
  cc. 1732-1739

Advocate
  cc. 1447; 1481; 1482, §3; 1438; 1484, §1; 1486; 1487-1490; 1548, §2, 1°;
      1550, §2, 1°; 1559; 1561; 1598, §1; 1649, §1, 2°; 1663, §2; 1664; 1678;
      1723; 1738

633

Affinity
  c. 109
  and conflict of interest: cc. 1448; 1548, §2, 2°
  as matrimonial impediment: c. 1092
Age
  cc. 11; 97; 112, §1, 3°; 185; 354
  dispensation for ordination: c. 1031, §4
  effect on penalties: cc. 1323, 1°; 1324, §1, 4°; 1395, §2
  effect on witness: c. 1550, §1
  for acting in a case: c. 1478, §3
      anointing of the sick: c. 1004, §1
      baptismal sponsor: c. 874, §1, 2°
      conferral of baptism by a bishop: c. 863
      diocesan administrator: c. 425, §1
      entry to novitiate: c. 643, §1, 1°
      entry to probation in secular institute: c. 721, §1, 1°
      episcopacy: c. 378, §1, 3°
      episcopal vicar/vicar general: c. 478, §1
      Eucharistic fast: c. 919, §3
      judicial vicar: c. 1420, §4
      marriage: cc. 1072; 1083
      perpetual profession: c. 658, 1°
      reception of confirmation: c. 891
      reception of diaconal orders: c. 1031, §§1-3
      reception of presbyteral orders: c. 1031, §§1, 3
      sacrament of penance: c. 989
      temporary profession: c. 656, 1°
  to submit resignation as bishop: c. 401, §1
  to submit resignation as pastor: c. 538, §3
Alienation
  cc. 1254, §1; 1291; 1296; 1715, §2
  of property by religious institute: c. 638, §3
Altar
  cc. 1235-1239
  as place for celebration of the Eucharist: c. 932, §2
Apostasy
  c. 751
  effect on irregularity for orders: c. 1041, 2°
Apostolate
  diocesan bishop and: c. 394
  exemption of religious institute and: c. 591
  of associations of the faithful: cc. 311; 317, §4; 323, §2; 329

Cremation
cc. 1176, §3; 1184, §1, 2°

Crime
as marriage impediment: cc. 1078, §2, 2°; 1090

Culpability
cc. 1321; 1324, §1, 2°, 7°; 1389, §2
and responsibility for damages: c. 129, §1

Custom
cc. 5; 23-28; 38
and ritual for marriage: c. 1119
in introducing marriage impediments: c. 1076
regarding collegiate tribunal: c. 1425, §1

Deacon
admission to clerical state: c. 266;
age required for ordination as: c. 1031
as minister of baptism: c. 861, §1
            of Communion: c. 910, §1
            of exposition: c. 943
assistance at marriage: cc. 1108; 1111; 1116, §2; 1121, §2
blessings: c. 1169, §3
cardinal deacon: cc. 350, §§1, 2, 5, 6; 355, §2
dimissorial letters for: c. 1019, §1
dispensations from marriage impediments: cc. 1079, §2; 1081
formation program: c. 236
liturgical garb: c. 929
order of: c. 1009, §1
ordination as: cc. 1015, §1; 1016
pastoral care of parish: c. 517, §2
preaching: c. 767, §1
requirements for ordination as: cc. 1024-1029; 1032-1037; 1039
rights and obligations: cc. 276, §2, 2°, 3°; 281, §3; 288

Dean (Vicar Forane)
cc. 553-555

Dean, Cardinal
cc. 350, §4; 352; 355, §1

Death
as dissolution of marriage bond: c. 1141
baptism in danger of: cc. 865, §2; 867, §2; 869, §2
care for those in danger of: cc. 529, §1; 530, 2°; 566, §1
confirmation in danger of: cc. 883, 3°; 891
effect on marriage nullity case: c. 1675
Eucharist in danger of: cc. 913, §2; 921

Donor
  cc. 1284, §2, 3°; 1302, §1
Doubt
  c. 21;
  heresy as: c. 751
  of fact: cc. 14; 144, §1;
  of law: cc. 14; 16, §1; 17; 144, §1
  regarding impediment: cc. 1084, §2; 1091, §4
  regarding previous reception of sacraments: cc. 845, §2; 869
Ecumenical council
  cc. 337, §1; 338-341
  teaching authority of: c. 749, §2
Ecumenism
  bishop's role in fostering: c. 383, §3
Education
  Catholic: cc. 793-805
  obligation of parents: c. 1689
  of children as matrimonial duty: cc. 1055, §1; 1154
  of clerics: cc. 232-264
  parents' right and obligation to provide: c. 226, §2
  pastor's role in: c. 528, §1
  right to a Christian: c. 217
  role of parents in: c. 853, §4
Election
  cc. 147; 164-179
  of dean of college of cardinals: c. 352, §2
  of diocesan administrator: cc. 421-424; 427, §2; 430, §2
  of Pontiff: cc. 332, §1; 349
  of presbyteral council: cc. 497, 1°; 498; 499
  of religious superior: cc. 625; 626
  penalty for impeding: c. 1375
  to synod of bishops: cc. 344, 2°; 346; 348, §1
Episcopal vicar
  cc. 476-478; 479, §§2, 3; 480; 481
  as ordinary: cc. 134, §§1, 3
  diocesan synod: cc. 462, §2; 463, §1, 2°; 473, §§2, 4
  diocesan visitation: c. 396, §1
  granting of rescripts: c. 65
  impeded see: c. 413, §1
  vacant see: cc. 417; 418, 1°
Error
  concerning law: c. 15

Error (*Continued*)
    effect on judicial confession: c. 1538
        on marriage: cc. 1097; 1099
        on penalty: c. 1323, 2°
    in judicial sentence: c. 1616, §1
    in rescript: c. 66
    juridic act: c. 126
    resignation from office: c. 188
    (See also: common error)

Eucharist
    cc. 897-958
    as sacrament of initiation: c. 842, §2
    bishop and: c. 389
    children's reception of: c. 777, 2°
    communicatio in sacris: c. 844, §§2, 3
    pastor and: cc. 528, §2; 530, 7°
    religious institute and: cc. 608; 719, §2
    society of apostolic life and: c. 733, §2
    vicar forane and: c. 555, §1, 3°

Excardination
    cc. 267-270; 271, §1; 272

Exception
    judicial: cc. 1449, §4; 1452, §2; 1459; 1460, §§1, 2; 1462; 1491; 1492; 1496-
        1500; 1621; 1642; 1660; 1664; 1673, 4°; 1703, §1

Exclaustration
    cc. 686; 687

Excommunication
    cc. 1318; 1331; 1357; 1364, §1; 1367; 1370, §1; 1378, §§1, 3; 1382; 1388;
        1398
    and membership in association of the faithful: c. 316
    judgment regarding: c. 1425, §1, 2°

Expert
    cc. 1447; 1455, §3
    evaluation by: cc. 1041, 1°; 1044, §2, 2°
    in the judicial process: cc. 1574-1581

Expiatory penalty
    c. 1344, 3°

Exposition
    of Eucharist: cc. 941-943

Faculties
    and power of governance: cc. 132; 144

Marriage (*Continued*)
   as grounds for dismissal from religious institute: c. 694, §1
   attempted by cleric: cc. 194, §1, 3°; 1394, §1
                  by religious: c. 1394, §2
   cases involving: cc. 1425, §1, 1°; 1432; 1490; 1671-1690
   effect on one's rite: c. 112, §1, 2°, 3°
   impediment to entry to novitiate: c. 643, §1, 2°
   record of: c. 535, §§1, 2
   rights and duties of: c. 226

Metropolitan
   cc. 435-438
   and selection of bishop: c. 377, §3
   in judicial matters: c. 1438
   role and responsibilities: cc. 395, §4; 413, §1; 415; 421, §2; 425, §1; 432;
      442; 501, §3

Minor
   cc. 97; 98, §2
   canonical penalty: c. 1324, §1, 4°
   domicile of: c. 105, §1
   marriage of: c. 1071, §1, 6°

Mixed marriage
   cc. 1124-1128; 1147; 1148, §2
   and rite of children: c. 112, §1, 3°

Moderator of the curia
   cc. 473, §2, 3; 474; 487; 488

Non-consummation
   of marriage: cc. 1697-1706
Notary
   cc. 474; 482, §3; 483-485; 1437; 1473; 1474, §1; 1503, §2; 1507, §3; 1561;
      1567, §1; 1568; 1569; 1605; 1612, §4; 1630; §2; 1664
   in dismissal procedure: c. 695, §2
   witness of decree: c. 55
Novice
   status of: c. 653
Novitiate
   cc. 641-653; 690
Nuns
   monastery of: cc. 609, §2; 614; 616, §4; 630, §3
   cloister of: c. 667, §§3, 4
   exclaustration of: c. 686, §2

Particular church
  cc. 368; 369; 372
  incardination/excardination of cleric in: cc. 265; 266, §§1, 3; 267-269; 271; 272
  missionary endeavors: c. 782, §2
  ordinary of: c. 134, §1

Pastor
  cc. 510, §§2, 3; 515, §1; 519; 520, §1; 521-523; 526-530; 532-539; 541, §1; 543, §1; 547
  acquired through domicle or quasi-domicile: c. 107
  catechetics: cc. 773; 776; 777
  celebration of marriage: cc. 1063; 1067; 1069, 1°; 1070; 1072; 1079, §2; 1081; 1105, §2; 1106; 1108; 1109; 1111, §1; 1114; 1115; 1118; 1121; 1122, §2; 1123; 1128
  dispensation from private vows: c. 1196, 1°
  dispensation from observation of feast days, days of penance: c. 1245
  education: c. 794, §2
  funeral rites: c. 1177, §2
  ministry of the word: cc. 757; 767, §4; 770; 771
  pope as supreme: cc. 331; 333, §2
  power to dispense: c. 89
  recording of Mass obligations: c. 1307, §2
  rector as: c. 262
  removal of: cc. 1740-1747
  sacramental role of: cc. 852, 2°; 855; 8611, §2; 877, §1; 878; 883, 3°; 890; 895; 898; 911, §1; 914; 958; 968, §1
  transfer of: cc. 1748-1752

Pastoral council
  cc. 443, §5; 463, §1, 5°
  diocesan: cc. 511-514
  parish: c. 536

Pauline privilege
  cc. 1143-1147

Penalty
  cc. 1312; 1314; 1315; 1317-1320; 1321, §2; 1324; 1326; 1327-1329; 1399
  application of: cc. 1341-1353
  cessation of: cc. 1354-1363
  dismissal from clerical state as: c. 290
  effect on reception of Communion: c. 915
        role as sponsor: c. 874, §1, 4°
  for specific offenses: cc. 1364-1398
  interpretation of laws establishing: c. 18

Publication of the acts
  c. 1598

Quasi-domicile
  cc. 12, §3; 100; 101, §1; 102, §§2, 3; 103-106; 107, §§1, 3
  effect on competence of tribunal: cc. 1408; 1409, §2; 1413, 2°; 1673, 2°;
      1699, §1
  effect on place of marriage: c. 1115

Quasi-parish
  c. 516

Rector
  cc. 238, §2; 239, §1; 260-262; 556-563
  recording of Mass obligations: c. 1307, §2
  testimonials from: c. 645, §2

Register
  baptism, marriage, etc. c. 535, §§1, 2
  baptismal: cc. 876-878; 1122; 1123
  confirmation: c. 895
  death: c. 1182
  marriage: cc. 1081; 1121, §§1, 3;
  ordination: cc. 1053; 1054
  secret: c. 1133

Relator
  c. 1429

Relics
  cc. 1190; 1237, §2

Religious institute
  cc. 607-709
  apostolate of: cc. 673-683
  association of the faithful and: cc. 312, §2; 318, §2; 320, §2
  chaplain for: c. 567, §1
  formation in: cc. 641-658
  governance in: cc. 617-640
  houses of: cc. 608-616
  inscription of cleric in: c. 265
  judicial process involving: c. 1427
  parish and: cc. 520, 538, §2
  property of: cc. 534-640
  rights and obligations in: cc. 662-672
  separation from: cc. 684-704

Religious profession
  cc. 654-658

Schism
  c. 751
  effect on irregularity for ordination: c. 1041, 2°

School
  cc. 796-806

Secrecy
  in giving consent/counsel: c. 127, §3
  in judicial procedures: cc. 1546, §1; 1548, §2, 1°; 1602, §2
  in penal procedures: c. 1455
  marriage: cc. 1130-1133
  of confessional seal: c. 1388
  of election: c. 172, §1, 2°
  of testimonials: c. 269, 2°

Secular institute
  cc. 710-730
  incardination and: c. 266, §3
  transfer to/from: c. 684, §5

Seminary
  cc. 234-364; 295

Sentence
  cc. 1517; 1592; 1593, §2; 1606-1608; 1610-1612; 1614-1617;
  execution of: cc. 1650-1655
  interlocutory: cc. 1589-1591; 1607; 1613; 1618
  judicial: cc. 1426, §1; 1429
  nullity of: cc. 1619-1627
  penal: cc. 1314; 1333, §2; 1334, §1; 1363, §1

Separation of the spouses
  cc. 1151-1155; 1643; 1692-1696
  by dissolution of marriage: cc. 1141-1150

Signatura
  cc. 1416; 1445

Society of apostolic life
  cc. 731-746
  care of parish: cc. 520; 528, §2
  incardination/excardination: cc. 266, §2; 268, §2
  presbyteral council: c. 498, §1, 2°
  transfer to/from: cc. 684, §5; 721, §1

Sponsor
  baptismal: cc. 851, 2°; 855; 872-874; 877, §1
  confirmation: cc. 892; 893; 895

Composition by Cambridge Typesetters, Ltd., Bethesda, MD
Printing and Binding by Braun-Brumfield, Inc., Ann Arbor, MI
Made in U.S.A.